Novels
for Students

National Advisory Board

Novels
for Students

Presenting Analysis, Context, and Criticism on Commonly Studied Novels

Volume 16

David Galens, Project Editor

Foreword by Anne Devereaux Jordan

GALE®

THOMSON
★ ™
GALE

Detroit • New York • San Diego • San Francisco • Cleveland • New Haven, Conn. • Waterville, Maine • London • Munich

THOMSON
GALE

Novels for Students, Volume 16

Project Editor
David Galens

Editorial
Anne Marie Hacht, Sara Constantakis, Ira Mark Milne, Pam Revitzer, Kathy Sauer, Timothy J. Sisler, Jennifer Smith, Daniel Toronto, Carol Ullmann

Research
Sarah Genik

Permissions
Debra Freitas, Shalice Shah-Caldwell

Manufacturing
Stacy Melson

Imaging and Multimedia
Lezlie Light, Kelly A. Quin, Luke Rademacher

Product Design
Pamela A. E. Galbreath, Michael Logusz

ISBN 0-7876-4899-X
ISSN 1094-3552

Printed in the United States of America
10 9 8 7 6 5 4 3 2 1

Table of Contents

The Informed Dialogue: Interacting with Literature

When we pick up a book, we usually do so with the anticipation of pleasure. We hope that by entering the time and place of the novel and sharing the thoughts and actions of the characters, we will find enjoyment. Unfortunately, this is often not the case; we are disappointed. But we should ask, has the author failed us, or have we failed the author?

We establish a dialogue with the author, the book, and with ourselves when we read. Consciously and unconsciously, we ask questions: "Why did the author write this book?" "Why did the author choose that time, place, or character?" "How did the author achieve that effect?" "Why did the character act that way?" "Would I act in the same way?" The answers we receive depend upon how much information about literature in general and about that book specifically we ourselves bring to our reading.

Young children have limited life and literary experiences. Being young, children frequently do not know how to go about exploring a book, nor sometimes, even know the questions to ask of a book. The books they read help them answer questions, the author often coming right out and *telling* young readers the things they are learning or are expected to learn. The perennial classic, *The Little Engine That Could, tells* its readers that, among other things, it is good to help others and brings happiness:

"Hurray, hurray," cried the funny little clown and all the dolls and toys. "The good little boys and girls in the city will be happy because you helped us, kind, Little Blue Engine."

In picture books, messages are often blatant and simple, the dialogue between the author and reader one-sided. Young children are concerned with the end result of a book—the enjoyment gained, the lesson learned—rather than with how that result was obtained. As we grow older and read further, however, we question more. We come to expect that the world within the book will closely mirror the concerns of our world, and that the author will *show* these through the events, descriptions, and conversations within the story, rather than *telling* of them. We are now expected to do the interpreting, carry on our share of the dialogue with the book and author, and glean not only the author's message, but comprehend how that message and the overall affect of the book were achieved. Sometimes, however, we need help to do these things. *Novels for Students* provides that help.

A novel is made up of many parts interacting to create a coherent whole. In reading a novel, the more obvious features can be easily spotted—theme, characters, plot—but we may overlook the more subtle elements that greatly influence how the novel is perceived by the reader: viewpoint, mood and tone, symbolism, or the use of humor. By focusing on both the obvious and more subtle literary elements within a novel, *Novels for Students* aids readers in both analyzing for message and in determining how and why that message is communicated. In the discussion on Harper Lee's *To*

Kill a Mockingbird (Vol. 2), for example, the mockingbird as a symbol of innocence is dealt with, among other things, as is the importance of Lee's use of humor which "enlivens a serious plot, adds depth to the characterization, and creates a sense of familiarity and universality." The reader comes to understand the internal elements of each novel discussed—as well as the external influences that help shape it.

"The desire to write greatly," Harold Bloom of Yale University says, "is the desire to be elsewhere, in a time and place of one's own, in an originality that must compound with inheritance, with an anxiety of influence." A writer seeks to create a unique world within a story, but although it is unique, it is not disconnected from our own world. It speaks to us *because* of what the writer brings to the writing from our world: how he or she was raised and educated; his or her likes and dislikes; the events occurring in the real world at the time of the writing, and while the author was growing up. When we know what an author has brought to his or her work, we gain a greater insight into both the "originality" (the world of the book), and the things that "compound" it. This insight enables us to question that created world and find answers more readily. By informing ourselves, we are able to establish a more effective dialogue with both book and author.

Novels for Students, in addition to providing a plot summary and descriptive list of characters—to remind readers of what they have read—also explores the external influences that shaped each book. Each entry includes a discussion of the author's background, and the historical context in which the novel was written. It is vital to know, for instance, that when Ray Bradbury was writing *Fahrenheit 451* (Vol. 1), the threat of Nazi domination had recently ended in Europe, and the McCarthy hearings were taking place in Washington, D.C. This information goes far in answering the question, "Why did he write a story of oppressive government control and book burning?" Similarly, it is important to know that Harper Lee, author of *To Kill a Mockingbird,* was born and raised in Monroeville, Alabama, and that her father was a lawyer.

Readers can now see why she chose the south as a setting for her novel—it is the place with which she was most familiar—and start to comprehend her characters and their actions.

Novels for Students helps readers find the answers they seek when they establish a dialogue with a particular novel. It also aids in the posing of questions by providing the opinions and interpretations of various critics and reviewers, broadening that dialogue. Some reviewers of *To Kill A Mockingbird,* for example, "faulted the novel's climax as melodramatic." This statement leads readers to ask, "Is it, indeed, melodramatic?" "If not, why did some reviewers see it as such?" "If it is, why did Lee choose to make it melodramatic?" "Is melodrama ever justified?" By being spurred to ask these questions, readers not only learn more about the book and its writer, but about the nature of writing itself.

The literature included for discussion in *Novels for Students* has been chosen because it has something vital to say to us. *Of Mice and Men, Catch-22, The Joy Luck Club, My Antonia, A Separate Peace* and the other novels here speak of life and modern sensibility. In addition to their individual, specific messages of prejudice, power, love or hate, living and dying, however, they and all great literature also share a common intent. They force us to *think*—about life, literature, and about others, not just about ourselves. They pry us from the narrow confines of our minds and thrust us outward to confront the world of books and the larger, real world we all share. *Novels for Students* helps us in this confrontation by providing the means of enriching our conversation with literature and the world, by creating an *informed* dialogue, one that brings true pleasure to the personal act of reading.

Sources

Harold Bloom, *The Western Canon, The Books and School of the Ages,* Riverhead Books, 1994.

Watty Piper, *The Little Engine That Could,* Platt & Munk, 1930.

Anne Devereaux Jordan
Senior Editor, TALL
(Teaching and Learning Literature)

Introduction

Purpose of the Book

The purpose of *Novels for Students (NfS)* is to provide readers with a guide to understanding, enjoying, and studying novels by giving them easy access to information about the work. Part of Gale's "For Students" Literature line, *NfS* is specifically designed to meet the curricular needs of high school and undergraduate college students and their teachers, as well as the interests of general readers and researchers considering specific novels. While each volume contains entries on "classic" novels frequently studied in classrooms, there are also entries containing hard-to-find information on contemporary novels, including works by multicultural, international, and women novelists.

The information covered in each entry includes an introduction to the novel and the novel's author; a plot summary, to help readers unravel and understand the events in a novel; descriptions of important characters, including explanation of a given character's role in the novel as well as discussion about that character's relationship to other characters in the novel; analysis of important themes in the novel; and an explanation of important literary techniques and movements as they are demonstrated in the novel.

In addition to this material, which helps the readers analyze the novel itself, students are also provided with important information on the literary and historical background informing each work. This includes a historical context essay, a box comparing the time or place the novel was written to modern Western culture, a critical essay, and excerpts from critical essays on the novel. A unique feature of *NfS* is a specially commissioned critical essay on each novel, targeted toward the student reader.

To further aid the student in studying and enjoying each novel, information on media adaptations is provided, as well as reading suggestions for works of fiction and nonfiction on similar themes and topics. Classroom aids include ideas for research papers and lists of critical sources that provide additional material on the novel.

Selection Criteria

The titles for each volume of *NfS* were selected by surveying numerous sources on teaching literature and analyzing course curricula for various school districts. Some of the sources surveyed included: literature anthologies; *Reading Lists for College-Bound Students: The Books Most Recommended by America's Top Colleges;* textbooks on teaching the novel; a College Board survey of novels commonly studied in high schools; a National Council of Teachers of English (NCTE) survey of novels commonly studied in high schools; the NCTE's *Teaching Literature in High School: The Novel;* and the Young Adult Library Services Association (YALSA) list of best books for young adults of the past twenty-five years.

Input was also solicited from our advisory board, as well as educators from various areas. From these discussions, it was determined that each volume should have a mix of "classic" novels (those works commonly taught in literature classes) and contemporary novels for which information is often hard to find. Because of the interest in expanding the canon of literature, an emphasis was also placed on including works by international, multicultural, and women authors. Our advisory board members—educational professionals—helped pare down the list for each volume. If a work was not selected for the present volume, it was often noted as a possibility for a future volume. As always, the editor welcomes suggestions for titles to be included in future volumes.

How Each Entry Is Organized

Each entry, or chapter, in *NfS* focuses on one novel. Each entry heading lists the full name of the novel, the author's name, and the date of the novel's publication. The following elements are contained in each entry:

- **Introduction:** a brief overview of the novel which provides information about its first appearance, its literary standing, any controversies surrounding the work, and major conflicts or themes within the work.

- **Author Biography:** this section includes basic facts about the author's life, and focuses on events and times in the author's life that inspired the novel in question.

- **Plot Summary:** a factual description of the major events in the novel. Lengthy summaries are broken down with subheads.

- **Characters:** an alphabetical listing of major characters in the novel. Each character name is followed by a brief to an extensive description of the character's role in the novel, as well as discussion of the character's actions, relationships, and possible motivation.

  Characters are listed alphabetically by last name. If a character is unnamed—for instance, the narrator in *Invisible Man*–the character is listed as "The Narrator" and alphabetized as "Narrator." If a character's first name is the only one given, the name will appear alphabetically by that name.

  Variant names are also included for each character. Thus, the full name "Jean Louise Finch" would head the listing for the narrator of *To Kill a Mockingbird,* but listed in a separate cross-reference would be the nickname "Scout Finch."

- **Themes:** a thorough overview of how the major topics, themes, and issues are addressed within the novel. Each theme discussed appears in a separate subhead, and is easily accessed through the boldface entries in the Subject/Theme Index.

- **Style:** this section addresses important style elements of the novel, such as setting, point of view, and narration; important literary devices used, such as imagery, foreshadowing, symbolism; and, if applicable, genres to which the work might have belonged, such as Gothicism or Romanticism. Literary terms are explained within the entry, but can also be found in the Glossary.

- **Historical Context:** This section outlines the social, political, and cultural climate *in which the author lived and the novel was created.* This section may include descriptions of related historical events, pertinent aspects of daily life in the culture, and the artistic and literary sensibilities of the time in which the work was written. If the novel is a historical work, information regarding the time in which the novel is set is also included. Each section is broken down with helpful subheads.

- **Critical Overview:** this section provides background on the critical reputation of the novel, including bannings or any other public controversies surrounding the work. For older works, this section includes a history of how the novel was first received and how perceptions of it may have changed over the years; for more recent novels, direct quotes from early reviews may also be included.

- **Criticism:** an essay commissioned by *NfS* which specifically deals with the novel and is written specifically for the student audience, as well as excerpts from previously published criticism on the work (if available).

- **Sources:** an alphabetical list of critical material used in compiling the entry, with full bibliographical information.

- **Further Reading:** an alphabetical list of other critical sources which may prove useful for the student. It includes full bibliographical information and a brief annotation.

In addition, each entry contains the following highlighted sections, set apart from the main text as sidebars:

- **Media Adaptations:** a list of important film and television adaptations of the novel, including source information. The list also includes stage adaptations, audio recordings, musical adaptations, etc.

- **Topics for Further Study:** a list of potential study questions or research topics dealing with the novel. This section includes questions related to other disciplines the student may be studying, such as American history, world history, science, math, government, business, geography, economics, psychology, etc.

- **Compare and Contrast Box:** an "at-a-glance" comparison of the cultural and historical differences between the author's time and culture and late twentieth century/early twenty-first century Western culture. This box includes pertinent parallels between the major scientific, political, and cultural movements of the time or place the novel was written, the time or place the novel was set (if a historical work), and modern Western culture. Works written after 1990 may not have this box.

- **What Do I Read Next?:** a list of works that might complement the featured novel or serve as a contrast to it. This includes works by the same author and others, works of fiction and nonfiction, and works from various genres, cultures, and eras.

Other Features

NfS includes "The Informed Dialogue: Interacting with Literature," a foreword by Anne Devereaux Jordan, Senior Editor for *Teaching and Learning Literature* (*TALL*), and a founder of the Children's Literature Association. This essay provides an enlightening look at how readers interact with literature and how *Novels for Students* can help teachers show students how to enrich their own reading experiences.

A Cumulative Author/Title Index lists the authors and titles covered in each volume of the *NfS* series.

A Cumulative Nationality/Ethnicity Index breaks down the authors and titles covered in each volume of the *NfS* series by nationality and ethnicity.

A Subject/Theme Index, specific to each volume, provides easy reference for users who may be studying a particular subject or theme rather than a single work. Significant subjects from events to broad themes are included, and the entries pointing to the specific theme discussions in each entry are indicated in **boldface.**

Each entry may have several illustrations, including photos of the author, stills from film adaptations, maps, and/or photos of key historical events, if available.

Citing Novels for Students

When writing papers, students who quote directly from any volume of *Novels for Students* may use the following general forms. These examples are based on MLA style; teachers may request that students adhere to a different style, so the following examples may be adapted as needed.

When citing text from *NfS* that is not attributed to a particular author (i.e., the Themes, Style, Historical Context sections, etc.), the following format should be used in the bibliography section:

"Night." *Novels for Students.* Ed. Marie Rose Napierkowski. Vol. 4. Detroit: Gale, 1998. 234–35.

When quoting the specially commissioned essay from *NfS* (usually the first piece under the "Criticism" subhead), the following format should be used:

Miller, Tyrus. Critical Essay on "Winesburg, Ohio." *Novels for Students.* Ed. Marie Rose Napierkowski. Vol. 4. Detroit: Gale, 1998. 335–39.

When quoting a journal or newspaper essay that is reprinted in a volume of *NfS,* the following form may be used:

Malak, Amin. "Margaret Atwood's *The Handmaid's Tale* and the Dystopian Tradition," *Canadian Literature* No. 112 (Spring, 1987), 9–16; excerpted and reprinted in *Novels for Students,* Vol. 4, ed. Marie Rose Napierkowski (Detroit: Gale, 1998), pp. 133–36.

When quoting material reprinted from a book that appears in a volume of *NfS,* the following form may be used:

Adams, Timothy Dow. "Richard Wright: Wearing the Mask," in *Telling Lies in Modern American Autobiography* (University of North Carolina Press, 1990), 69–83; excerpted and reprinted in *Novels for Students,* Vol. 1, ed. Diane Telgen (Detroit: Gale, 1997), pp. 59–61.

We Welcome Your Suggestions

The editor of *Novels for Students* welcomes your comments and ideas. Readers who wish to suggest novels to appear in future volumes, or who have other suggestions, are cordially invited to contact the editor. You may contact the editor via e-mail at: **ForStudentsEditors@gale.com.** Or write to the editor at:

Editor, *Novels for Students*
Gale Group
27500 Drake Road
Farmington Hills, MI 48331–3535

Literary Chronology

1752: Fanny Burney is born on June 13 in King's Lyn, Norfolk, England.

1778: Fanny Burney's *Evelina; or, The History of a Young Lady's Entrance into the World* is published.

1818: Ivan Turgenev is born on October 28 in Orel, a provincial town in Russia.

1840: Fanny Burney dies.

1843: Henry James is born on April 15 on the edge of Greenwich Village in New York City.

1857: Joseph Conrad (born Teodor Józef Konrad Nalecz Korzeniowski) is born on December 3 in the Polish Ukraine.

1862: Ivan Turgenev's *Fathers and Sons* is published.

1883: Ivan Turgenev dies on August 22 in his chalet at Bougival.

1898: Henry James's *The Turn of the Screw* is published.

1900: Joseph Conrad's *Lord Jim* is published.

1903: Nathanael West (born Nathan Weinstein) is born on October 17 in New York City.

1904: Graham Greene is born on October 2 in Hertfordshire, England.

1905: Ayn Rand (born Alisa Rosenbaum) is born on February 2 in St. Petersburg, Russia.

1913: Albert Camus is born on November 7 in Mondavi, Algeria.

1916: Henry James dies of edema on February 28 in London.

1920: Mario Puzo is born to a family of Italian immigrants.

1924: Joseph Conrad dies of a heart attack on August 3 in Kent, England.

1933: Ernest J. Gaines is born on January 15 on the River Lake Plantation near New Roads, Pointe Coupee Parish, Louisiana.

1939: Nathanael West's *The Day of the Locust* is published.

1940: Nathanael West dies in an automobile accident with his wife of only nine months, Eileen McKenney, on December 22, when he drives through a stop sign near El Centro, California.

1943: Ayn Rand's *The Fountainhead* is published.

1948: Albert Camus's *The Plague* is published.

1950: Susan Eloise (S. E.) Hinton is born in Tulsa, Oklahoma.

1951: Graham Greene's *The End of the Affair* is published.

1957: Albert Camus recieves the Nobel Prize for literature.

1960: Albert Camus dies in an automobile accident in France on January 4 at the age of forty-six.

1969: Mario Puzo's *The Godfather* is published.

1971: S. E. Hinton's *That Was Then, This Is Now* is published.

1982: Ayn Rand dies on March 6 in New York City.

1983: Ernest J. Gaines's *A Gathering of Old Men* is published.

1991: Graham Greene dies of blood disease on April 3 in Vevey, Switzerland.

1999: Mario Puzo dies of heart failure on July 2 at the age of seventy-nine.

Acknowledgments

The editors wish to thank the copyright holders of the excerpted criticism included in this volume and the permissions managers of many book and magazine publishing companies for assisting us in securing reproduction rights. We are also grateful to the staffs of the Detroit Public Library, the Library of Congress, the University of Detroit Mercy Library, Wayne State University Purdy/Kresge Library Complex, and the University of Michigan Libraries for making their resources available to us. Following is a list of the copyright holders who have granted us permission to reproduce material in this volume of *Novels for Students (NfS)*. Every effort has been made to trace copyright, but if omissions have been made, please let us know.

COPYRIGHTED MATERIALS IN *NfS,* VOLUME 16, WERE REPRODUCED FROM THE FOLLOWING PERIODICALS:

CLA Journal, v. xxxi, March, 1988. Copyright, 1988 by The College Language Association. Used by permission of The College Language Association.—*College English,* v. 26, 1965 for "The Verbal Failure of *Lord Jim*" by Eben Bass. Copyright © 1965 by the National Council of Teachers of English. Reproduced by permission of the publisher and the author.—*College Literature,* v. 24, February, 1997. Copyright © 1997 by West Chester University. Reproduced by permission.—*Delta,* v. 15, November, 1982 for "*Turn of the Screw* and the *recherche de l'absolu*" by Millicent Bell. Reproduced by permission of the author.—*Extrapolation,* v. 27, 1986. Copyright © 1986 by The Kent State University Press. Reproduced by permission.—*The Nation* (New York), v. 238, January 14, 1984; v. 242, March 8, 1986; v. 266, May 4, 1998. © 1984, 1986, 1998 The Nation magazine/ The Nation Company, Inc. All reproduced by permission.—*New Orleans Review,* v. 14, Winter, 1987. Copyright © 1987 by Loyola University. Reproduced by permission.—*Revue des langues vivantes,* v. xxxiv, 1968 for "Tragedy and Self-Deception in Turgenev's *Fathers and Sons,*" by Charles R. Bachman./ v. xxxvi, 1970 for "Ayn Rand's Neurotic Personalities of Our Times" by Paul Deane. Both reproduced by permission of the authors.—*Texas Studies in Language and Literature,* v. 26, Summer, 1984. Reproduced by permission of the publisher.

COPYRIGHTED MATERIALS IN *NfS,* VOLUME 16, WERE REPRODUCED FROM THE FOLLOWING BOOKS:

Bloom, Edward A. From *Evelina; or, the History of a Young Lady's Entrance into the World.* By Frances Burney. Edited by Edward A. Bloom. Oxford University Press (London), 1968. © Oxford University Press 1968. Reprinted by permission of the publisher.—Cutting-Gray, Joanne. From *Woman as "Nobody" and the Novels of Fanny Burney.* University Press of Florida, 1992. Copyright 1992 by the Board of Regents of the State of Florida. Reproduced with the permission of the University Press of Florida.—Ferraro, Thomas J. From *Ethnic Passages: Literary Immigrants in Twentieth-Century America.* University of

Chicago Press, 1993. Copyright © 1993 by The University of Chicago. Reproduced by permission.—GardaphJ, Fred L. From *Italian Signs, American Streets: The Evolution of Italian American Narrative*. Duke University Press, 1996. © 1996 by Duke University Press, Durham, NC. Reproduced by permission.—Lowe, David. From *Turgenev's Fathers and Sons*. Ardis, 1983. © 1983 by Ardis Publishers. Reproduced by permission.—Nadel, I. B. From *Reference Guide to American Literature, 4th edition*. Edited by Jim Kamp. St. James Press, 2000. Copyright © 2000 St. James Press. All rights reserved. Reproduced by permission of the Gale Group.—Widner, Kingsley. From *Nathanael West*. Twayne Publishers, 1982. Copyright © 1982 by G.K. Hall & Company. All rights reserved.

PHOTOGRAPHS AND ILLUSTRATIONS APPEARING IN *NfS*, VOLUME 16, WERE RECEIVED FROM THE FOLLOWING SOURCES:

An area near St. Pancras Station in London showing the damage caused by a German air raid during the London blitz in WW II, photograph. Hulton Archive/Getty Images. Reproduced by permission.—Book photograph by Liaison Agency, Inc. From "High School Hazing: When Rites Become Wrongs," Hank Nuwer. Franklin Watts, 2000. Reproduced by permission of GettyImages.—Brando, Marlon, in the film "The Godfather (Part I)," by Mario Puzo, photograph. The Kobal Collection. Reproduced by permission.—Burney, Edward Francesco. Scene from *Evelina*, by Fanny Burney, illustration. National Portrait Gallery. Reproduced by permission.—Burney, Fanny, engraving. Archive Photos, Inc. Reproduced by permission.—Camus, Albert, photograph. Associated Press (London). Reproduced by permission.—Conrad, Joseph (facing right), 1904, photograph. Archive Photos, Inc. Reproduced by permission.—Cooper, Gary, in the film "The Fountainhead," by Ayn Rand, photograph. The Kobal Collection. Reproduced by permission.—Crowd gathering at the movie premier of "Gone with the Wind," photograph. A/P Wide World. Reproduced by permission.—The Dreadful Plague in London, engraving. Hulton Archive/Getty Images. Reproduced by permission.—Estevez, Emilio, in the film "That Was Then, This Is Now," by S.E. Hinton. The Kobal Collection. Reproduced by permission.—Gaines, Ernest, photograph. AP/Wide World Photos. Reproduced with permission.—Gossett, Louis, Jr, Woody Strode, from a scene in the film "A Gathering of Old Men," based on the novel by Ernest J. Gaines. The Kobal Collection. Reproduced by permission.—Greene, Graham, 1969, photograph. AP/Wide World Photos. Reproduced by permission.—Hinton, S.E., photograph by Thomas Victor. Reproduced by permission of the Estate of Thomas Victor.—James, Henry, photograph. AP/Wide World Photos. Reproduced by permission.—Liberation of the Russian serfs after their emancipation by Czar Alexander, engraving. (c) Bettmann/Corbis. Reproduced by permission.—Lynching victim, photograph. The Library of Congress.—Moore, Julianne, Ralph Fiennes, from a scene of "The End of the Affair," based on the novel by Graham Greene, photograph. The Kobal Collection. Reproduced by permission.—O'Toole, Peter, as Lord Jim in the film version of *Lord Jim*, by Joseph Conrad. The Kobal Collection. Reproduced by permission.—Pacino, Al, Marlon Brando, James Caan, and John Cazale, in the film "The Godfather," 1972, photograph. The Kobal Collection. Reproduced by permission.—Pears, Tenor Peter, in a production of Britten's "The Turn of the Screw," based on the book by Henry James, photograph. Hulton Archive/Getty Images. Reproduced by permission.—Puzo, Mario, photograph by Jerry Bauer. Reproduced by permission.—Rand, Ayn, photograph. AP/Wide World Photos. Reproduced by permission.—Still from the film version of "The Day of the Locust," based on the book by Nathanael West, photograph. The Kobal Collection. Reproduced by permission—Turgenev, Ivan, photograph. The Library of Congress.

Contributors

Bryan Aubrey: Aubrey holds a Ph.D. in English and has published many articles on twentieth-century literature. Entries on *A Gathering of Old Men* and *The Plague*. Original essays on *A Gathering of Old Men* and *The Plague*.

Jennifer Bussey: Bussey holds a master's degree in interdisciplinary studies and a bachelor's degree in English literature. She is an independent writer specializing in literature. Entry on *The End of the Affair*. Original essay on *The End of the Affair*.

Erik France: France is a librarian, college counselor, and teacher at University Liggett School, and he teaches writing at Macomb Community College near Detroit, Michigan. Original essay on *That Was Then, This Is Now*.

Joyce Hart: Hart holds degrees in English literature and creative writing and focuses her writing on literary themes. Entry on *Evelina; or, The History of a Young Lady's Entrance into the World*. Original essay on *Evelina; or, The History of a Young Lady's Entrance into the World*.

David Kelly: Kelly is an instructor of creative writing and composition at Oakton Community College in Illinois. Entry on *The Godfather*. Original essay on *The Godfather*.

Laura Kryhoski: Kryhoski is currently working as a freelance writer. She has also taught English literature in addition to English as a Second Language overseas. Original essay on *The End of the Affair*.

Wendy Perkins: Perkins teaches American literature and film and has published several essays on American and British authors. Entry on *The Fountainhead*. Original essay on *The Fountainhead*.

Ryan D. Poquette: Poquette holds a bachelor's degree in English and specializes in writing about literature. Entries on *Fathers and Sons*, *Lord Jim*, *That Was Then, This Is Now*, and *The Turn of the Screw*. Original essays on *Fathers and Sons*, *Lord Jim*, *That Was Then, This Is Now*, and *The Turn of the Screw*.

Tamara Sakuda: Sakuda holds a bachelor of arts degree in communications and is an independent writer. Original essay on *The Fountainhead*.

Susan Sanderson: Sanderson holds a master of fine arts degree in fiction writing and is an independent writer. Entry on *The Day of the Locust*. Original essay on *The Day of the Locust*.

The Day of the Locust

Nathanael West
1939

The Day of the Locust, by Nathanael West, is set in 1930s Hollywood and follows the lives of a handful of people peripherally associated with the movie industry. Today, many critics consider it the best novel about Hollywood ever written, but it received little notice from the general public when it was released in 1939. According to Richard B. Gehman in his introduction to the 1976 reprint of the novel, many critics at the time considered the novel to be in "bad taste."

The novel combines realistic features, such as characters who are flawed, with the artificial and surreal atmosphere of the movie industry. Tod Hackett, recently graduated from Yale University, is an illustrator and set designer for a film company. He lives in the same apartment building as Faye Greener, an aspiring and ambitious actress who will not date Tod because he is neither rich nor handsome. Through Faye, Tod meets a cast of seedy and sad characters whom he intends to include in his large painting, "The Burning of Los Angeles." Tod's life is spent unsuccessfully pursuing Faye and imagining the violent scenes that will make up his painting.

Author Biography

Nathanael West was born Nathan Weinstein in New York City on October 17, 1903. (He legally changed his name in 1926.) West was the son of

Jewish immigrants Max Weinstein, a prosperous building contractor, and Anna Wallenstein Weinstein. Mr. Weinstein wanted his son to go into the family business and gave Nathan copies of the Horatio Alger books, a series of novels in which honest young men do well for themselves in business. West, whose friends gave him the nickname Pep because he was so lazy, was uninterested in the typical trappings of upper middle-class success and dropped out of high school. He lied his way into Tufts University, which expelled him for poor grades, and then got himself admitted to Brown University by using someone else's transcripts. West graduated from Brown in 1924, where he was better known for his sense of humor and interest in parties than any scholarly abilities.

After finishing college, West spent two years in Paris, courtesy of his father. He was called back to the United States in 1927, as the family's contracting business was experiencing the first economic shudders that would become more widespread in 1929. West's family found him a series of jobs managing residential hotels so that he could earn a living. Through these jobs, West was able to provide many impoverished writers with rent-free places to stay in New York City and to meet many writers who would soon become famous, including Dashiell Hammett, Erskine Caldwell, Lillian Hellman, and S. J. Perelman, West's brother-in-law. West found the desperate lives of some of his tenants fascinating, and he was known to steam open and read their letters. During this period, he finished his first book, *The Dream Life of Balso Snell*, and published it to almost no critical or commercial notice in 1931.

West published his second book, *Miss Lonelyhearts*, in 1933 to great admiration from the critics and others within his literary circle, but it received very little attention from the book-buying public. Concerned about his apparent inability to earn money from his books, West moved to California in 1933 to take a job as a screenwriter for Columbia Pictures. This job only lasted about a year, so West moved back to New York City to write his third book, *A Cool Million: The Dismantling of Lemuel Pitkin*. In 1935, a major movie studio bought the rights to the novel, so West went to California to try his hand at screenwriting again. Upon his return, West lived in cheap hotels much like the ones he had lived in and managed in New York City. West enjoyed learning about the lives of the people he met at these hotels, and soon his circle of friends included prostitutes, petty criminals, and stuntmen. West's struggle for screen-writing work lasted about a year, during which he was supported by money from his brother-in-law, Perelman, before he found a job with a minor studio that produced low-budget films.

Through his newfound income from screen-writing, West was able to afford a more comfortable lifestyle, one that allowed him to focus more artistically on his novels and plays. He published *The Day of the Locust* in 1939. Like *Miss Lonelyhearts*, it received some acclaim but little notice from the general public. Over the course of his lifetime, West earned only about $1,300 from his novels. He died in an automobile accident with his wife of only nine months, Eileen McKenney, on December 22, 1940, when he drove through a stop sign near El Centro, California.

Plot Summary

Chapters 1–7

The Day of the Locust begins after Tod Hackett has recently graduated from Yale University, and has been living in Hollywood for about three months. While preparing to go to a party, he thinks about Faye Greener, the very attractive aspiring actress who lives just below him with her father, Harry. He is also reminded of his friend Abe Kusich, because he has found Abe's card stuck in his door, a note on it offering a tip on a horse race. He also thinks about his planned painting, "The Burning of Los Angeles," and the people who "come to California to die" that he will depict in it. When Tod sees these people on the streets, he notices that they are poorly dressed and "their eyes are filled with hatred."

At the party, hosted by Claude Estee, a successful screenwriter, Tod sees the fake dead horse the Estees have bought to shock and surprise their guests. He tries to leave the party, but Claude grabs him and forces him to come with the rest of the partyers to Audrey Jenning's whorehouse to watch a dirty movie. The movie projector, playing *Le Predicament de Marie*, breaks just as the exciting part is about to start, and the guests hoot and clap in displeasure.

Tod begins to spend more time at Faye's apartment, helping out with Faye's sick father. Tod enjoys hearing the stories Harry tells of his life as a clown in vaudeville shows. He meets Homer Simpson, one of Faye's suitors. Homer is shy and naive and has just moved to Hollywood from the Midwest.

Chapters 8–12

The novel begins to focus on Homer and how he came to live in Hollywood. He moved to California at the suggestion of his doctor after he became quite ill with pneumonia. While he was absent from work, he lost his bookkeeping job of twenty years. When Homer thinks about his life in Iowa, he also thinks about Romola Martin, who was a drunken resident of the hotel where he worked. When Homer first met Romola, she disturbed him with her drunken and flirtatious behavior, and he "hurriedly labeled his excitement disgust." Later, when his boss asked that he evict her from her room, Homer realized, "through his growing excitement," that he was sexually attracted to her. While evicting Romola, Homer offered her money to pay her back rent, which she happily interpreted as money for sex. Just as they begin holding each other on her bed, the phone rang; it was one of Homer's colleagues checking to make sure he did not need the police to help with the eviction. This interruption completely ruined the moment for Homer. Now in California, Homer feels that he missed his chance to be with Romola, and he still cries about that missed opportunity.

Homer's house is in the style of an Irish cottage, complete with a thatched roof. He gets settled in very quickly because he has very few possessions. About a month after he has moved into the Irish cottage, Harry Greener shows up at his front door, selling his homemade silver polish. Harry gets inside the house by asking for some water, and when he becomes ill, he asks for Faye to be brought inside. This is a con that Harry and Faye do with regularity, but this time Harry is really sick. Homer gives Faye some lunch while Harry is resting on the couch, and Homer begins to fall in love with her. Days pass and Homer continues to think about Faye. He decides to visit Faye and Harry at their apartment. This is the day when Tod first meets Homer.

Chapters 13–17

Harry is still sick, and Tod is continuing to spend a lot of time with him. One night, when Faye thinks Harry is about to die, she runs up to Tod's apartment and asks him to come and help. By the time Tod gets there, Harry is breathing better. Faye spends the rest of the evening telling Tod about her ideas for movies, which she suggests that he could write, so that they could both become rich and famous. Tod thinks her ideas are awful, but he still tries to sneak a kiss. She lets him kiss her at the door to her apartment, but when he tries to embrace

her, she stops him. Back at his apartment, Tod thinks of his painting, "The Burning of Los Angeles," and how Faye will be a naked girl running in the left foreground, being chased by an angry mob.

As he has done a few times before, Tod accompanies Faye on a date with Earle Shoop, a former cowboy from Arizona. Earle and his friends live in a sort of permanent camp outside the city, where Earle traps small game to survive. Earle is broke again, but Faye does not let Tod pay for their meals as he usually does. Instead, the three of them drive to Earle's camp. There, Earle has some pheasants trapped that they can cook and eat for dinner. They meet Miguel, who shows Tod the fighting roosters he raises. After dinner and tequila, Miguel and Faye dance in a very provocative and drunken manner. Earle tries to join them, but his "crude hoedown" dance steps do not fit in. When Faye's back is turned, Earle strikes Miguel with a club. Tod tries to stop Faye from running away, but he just misses grabbing her. He thinks about what it would be like to run after Faye, bringing her down to the ground and raping her. He also thinks about his painting.

Harry dies. Faye keeps saying that she killed him because she was in the apartment when he died but was so busy looking at herself in the mirror that she did not notice him until it was too late. Mrs. Johnson, the janitor, offers to help Faye with the funeral arrangements, but Faye has no money. Faye gets the idea to work at Mrs. Jenning's whorehouse to earn some money, but Tod is horrified and tries to talk her out of it. She and Mary, Faye's prostitute friend, laugh at him.

Tod attends Harry's funeral after he has been drinking heavily. He finds Faye and tries to talk her out of working at Mrs. Jenning's, but he is too drunk.

Chapters 18–20

The day after the funeral, Faye moves out of the San Bernardino Arms. The next time Tod sees her it is through the window of his office, but she only waves when he tries to flag her down. From her costume, he guesses that she is an extra in a picture being filmed on a nearby lot. He leaves his office to chase her but finds himself wandering through set after set of various pieces of scenery.

After a short while, Faye leaves Mrs. Jenning's whorehouse and moves in with Homer. They have a "business arrangement" in which Homer serves as Faye's patron, buying her nice clothes, because he believes that Faye will soon be a big movie star. Tod has dinner at their house, where he and Homer

Media Adaptations

- *The Day of the Locust*, starring William Atherton as Tod Hackett, Donald Sutherland as Homer Simpson, and Karen Valentine as Faye Greener, was adapted to film by Waldo Salt and directed by John Schlesinger. Paramount produced the film in 1975.

meet Maybelle Loomis and her eight-year-old son, Adore. Maybelle has brought Adore to Hollywood to become a star and has trained Adore to act as if he is a man with perfect manners, not a child. She has also trained him to sing a sexually suggestive song, which he does for Homer and Tod, complete with erotic moves.

Tod spends the next few months trying to get over Faye. He spends time at some local churches, hunting for more models for his painting. Tod believes he will "paint their fury with respect, appreciating its awful, anarchic power and aware that they had it in them to destroy civilization." The people Tod plans to portray in his painting have moved to California after working at miserable jobs all their lives and having to save for the day when they can live in the sunshine and eat oranges all day. Tod believes that they have become bored with this easy life and crave excitement in any form: a Hollywood sex scandal, a plane crash, or some other disaster. He believes that because the easy life is so disappointing, these sun-seekers will feel cheated and their subsequent anger will lead them to turn on the city. Some of the dissatisfied thousands seek answers at the many churches in Los Angeles that preach such odd doctrines as the "Crusade Against Salt" and "Brain-Breathing, the Secret of the Aztecs."

Homer and Faye's relationship is beginning to sour. Faye finds him boring and has taken to taunting him. Homer and Tod go to a nightclub with Faye so she will not be bored. Tod learns that Miguel and Earle have moved into Homer's garage with the fighting roosters, at Faye's insistence. Tod urges Homer to remove Miguel from his garage,

but Homer says that Faye has threatened to leave if he does and, besides, he believes that they are "nice enough fellows, just down on their luck." Faye later asks Tod if he will come to watch a cock fight the next night at their house.

Chapters 21–27

Tod brings Claude Estee to the cockfight in Homer's garage, but when they get there they discover that the original fight is off. Miguel sells Claude a rooster so that Claude can see a fight, but the bird is old and has a cracked beak. The fight takes place with Abe handling Claude's red rooster, but the rooster is badly beaten by Miguel's bird and dies.

Homer and Faye invite everyone into their house for a party after the fight, but the party is mostly Faye walking around in sexy green pajamas and dancing with Claude, Earle, and Miguel. Because Tod is drunk and frustrated that Homer is so unaware of Faye's increasingly reckless behavior, he tells Homer that she is a "whore." A fight breaks out between Earle and Abe, with Miguel helping his friend by picking up Abe and throwing him against the wall. Tod and Claude leave the party with Abe.

Tod wakes up the next morning with a hangover and calls in sick to his office. He later walks over to Homer's house to apologize for calling Faye a whore. Homer is there, sitting in the middle of the wrecked living room with his head in his hands and the curtains drawn. Tod tries to talk to him, but he starts crying loudly and tells Tod that Faye has left him and that he is going back to Iowa.

Homer tells Tod what happened earlier that morning. Thinking that Faye was sick, Homer took her some aspirin and water. When he opened the door, he saw Miguel naked in bed with Faye. Moments later, Earle showed up, and he and Miguel started fighting so violently that Homer ran to his room, too afraid to watch. He fell asleep and when he awoke, everything in Faye's room was gone and so was Faye.

Tod leaves Homer sleeping, but on his way back home, he stops at Kahn's Persian Palace Theatre to watch the crowd gathering for a movie premiere. There are spotlights sweeping the sky and thousands of people behind a roped-off area, straining and pushing to get a closer look at their favorite stars.

Tod sees Homer walking through the crowd as if he is an automaton, dressed in his nightshirt and a pair of slacks and carrying a suitcase. He says he is going back to Iowa. Tod tries to get him a cab, thinking he must take Homer to a hospital, but he is unsuccessful in getting Homer to walk with him. He leaves Homer sitting on a bench, away from the crowd, thinking of what to do next while watching Homer from across the street. He spies Adore behind a tree, trying to get Homer's attention by pulling a purse attached to a string along the ground. Homer is completely oblivious. This angers Adore, and he throws a rock that hits Homer. Homer violently erupts and begins stomping Adore. Tod tries to intervene, but the crowd sees what is going on and surrounds and absorbs Homer and the boy, pushing Tod further and further away. The crowd shifts and turns, and Tod is carried around with it, crushed and barely able to breath. Tod begins thinking about his painting and what he can add to it. In addition to the flames consuming the city and the mob holding torches, he has Faye, Harry, Claude, Homer, and himself running in front of the mob.

A policeman is able to lift Tod from the crowd and helps him walk to an ambulance. In the ambulance the sirens sound, and Tod thinks he is making the noise until he realizes that his lips are shut. He laughs and imitates the sound of the siren.

Characters

Calvin

Calvin is one of Earle's cowboy friends who hangs out with him in front of Tuttle's Trading Post, a Western-wear store and souvenir shop. He appears in rodeos to earn money and enjoys making jokes about people.

Mary Dove

Mary Dove is Faye's best friend and works at Mrs. Jenning's whorehouse as a prostitute. She encourages Faye to come work at Mrs. Jenning's place after Harry dies and Faye needs money for his funeral expenses. Mary acts tough when Tod is upset at the thought of Faye becoming a whore.

Claude Estee

Claude Estee is a well-known screenwriter with "a reputation for worldliness and wit." He lives in a mansion built to look exactly like a famous plantation home in Mississippi. While in his house, he struts around and drawls, pretending to be a southern gentleman in his plantation home even though he is a small, "dried-up little man."

Claude seems desperate for excitement. He places a rubber horse in his pool to amuse his guests during a party and, when he goes to a cock fight only to find that the event has been canceled, he hastily buys a rooster—an injured one, no less—so that he can witness a cock fight after all.

Faye Greener

Faye Greener is a seventeen-year-old aspiring actress who lives one floor below Tod at the San Bernardino Arms with her father, Harry. She admits that, even though Tod is nice, she will not go out with him because he is neither rich nor good-looking. Faye is tall with "platinum" hair. She drives Harry around in her Model-T car and participates in his "act" during his sales calls. Faye occasionally takes a job as an extra in movies, but she is convinced that she is just moments away from becoming a huge star. She works as a whore for a brief period to pay off her father's funeral expenses.

Faye, like her father, usually acts as if she is on stage. She has an affected manner that would normally repel Tod, but on Faye it seems only charming to him. He also finds her attractive because she has "some critical ability, almost enough to recognize the ridiculous" and even makes fun of herself sometimes. However, he does not consider her terribly smart.

She is very ambitious and will do just about anything to get ahead in the movie industry. Men flock to her, even though she primarily teases them with her flirtatious behavior. After her father dies, she moves in with Homer. They have a "business arrangement" in which Homer pays for everything in the expectation that Faye will soon become a star and be able to pay him back. He also lets her stay because he is desperately lonely and in love with her. Faye has a mean streak and taunts Homer for his naiveté. Eventually, Faye becomes bored with Homer and leaves him.

Harry Greener

Harry is Faye's father. He is old and ill and lives with Faye. In the past, Harry worked as a clown in vaudeville shows but was never very successful. He moved to Hollywood to see if he could get a few small parts in the movies but ended up having to make money selling his homemade silver polish door-to-door. Tod likes Harry and enjoys sitting with him for long hours, listening to his stories. Harry has a maniacal laugh that Faye hates; it often starts arguments between the two of them.

When Harry goes on his sales calls, he tries to execute a con in which he becomes sick and must call in Faye from the car to help him. They proceed to have a fight, prompting the customer to feel sorry for Harry and buy more of his polish. Harry, even when he is not acting or working as a salesman, always behaves as if he is on stage, telling jokes or pretending to trip over something on the floor that is not there. Harry's face, like those of all actors, according to Tod, is a mask.

Harry dies one evening while Faye is looking at herself in the mirror, not paying attention to him. She feels guilty and wants Harry to have an expensive funeral, which requires her to work as a prostitute for a brief period.

Tod Hackett

Tod Hackett is a young man, an art school grad just a few months out of Yale University, who works at a Hollywood studio as an illustrator. He is not particularly handsome and has a "doltish" air, but he believes that he has a "complicated" interior. Tod is in love with Faye Greener, who lives one floor below him at the San Bernardino Arms apartments, but she will have nothing to do with him primarily because he is neither handsome nor rich. An autographed movie still of Faye is tucked into the frame of a mirror in his apartment.

Tod is planning a painting entitled, "The Burning of Los Angeles." It features a mob of the sad and angry people he sees on the streets of Hollywood, intent on destroying the city. He seems to have trouble making any true, heartfelt connections with other people, and the only dates he goes on are Faye's dates with other men. She sometimes invites Tod along, at least partly because he often pays.

Tod's fascinations with violence and with Faye cause him to have very vivid dreams about raping her. He has incorporated images of her running away from him into his concept of the painting.

Mrs. Audrey Jenning

Audrey Jenning was once a famous silent film actress, but the new films with sound have "made it impossible for her to get work." She decides, instead, to open up a whorehouse, or "callhouse." Everyone agrees that her callhouse is run well and in good taste. Mrs. Jenning interviews all of her prospective clients to make sure they are men of "wealth and distinction" and "taste and discretion," and she conducts intellectual discussions while the men are waiting for their girls. Faye briefly goes to work for Mrs. Jenning to earn money to pay her father's funeral expenses.

Mrs. Johnson

Mrs. Johnson is the janitor at the San Bernardino Arms apartments. Tod does not like her because she is "an officious, bustling woman with a face like a baked apple, soft and blotched." Her hobby is funerals; she is interested in the clothes the mourners wear, the flower arrangements, and other details. She offers to help Faye with Harry's funeral arrangements.

Chief Kiss-My-Towkus

Chief Kiss-My-Towkus is an American Indian who has been hired to walk around town wearing a sandwich board that advertises Tuttle's Trading Post. He is one of Calvin's friends. His name is a joke and not his own idea, but he laughs and says, "You gotta live."

Abe Kusich

Abe Kusich is a dwarf with horse-racing and betting connections. He and Tod first meet when Abe is sleeping in the hallway of Tod's apartment. Abe's girlfriend kicked him out of her apartment without any of his clothes, and he went into Tod's apartment to get dressed. Abe refers to himself as "Honest Abe Kusich" on his business cards.

Abe has a hot temper and is easily angered. During the cockfight, he demands to inspect the rooster Miguel sold Claude and discovers that it has a crack in its beak. This enrages Abe, who believes that Miguel is trying to cheat Claude and the others who are interested in betting on the fight, but he still helps Claude handle the rooster during the fight. Later that evening, Abe gets into a fight with Earle over Faye.

Adore Loomis

Adore Loomis is Maybelle Loomis's eight-year-old son. She has trained him to behave as a young man with extremely formal manners. When Maybelle introduces him to Homer and Tod, Adore behaves "like a soldier at the command of a drill sergeant," shaking their hands and bowing and clicking his heels. When his mother's back is turned, he makes horrible faces at her, but he will sing a sexually suggestive song and shake his body when she demands it. Homer beats up Adore when the boy teases him one too many times, sparking the riot near the movie theater at the book's end.

Maybelle Loomis

Maybelle Loomis is one of Homer's neighbors and Adore's mother. She moved to Hollywood to get her son in the movies and is convinced that he is not as big a success as Shirley Temple because of "favoritism" and "pull." Her husband, Mr. Loomis, died six years earlier. Tod has seen many such women around the studios, spending every dime they have to send their children to "one of the innumerable talent schools." Maybelle is a follower of Dr. Pierce, the leader of a raw food cult. "Death comes from eating dead things," Maybelle believes.

Miss Romola Martin

When Homer worked at an Iowa residential hotel as a bookkeeper, Romola Martin rented a room in his hotel. She was a drunk and always behind in her rent, but Homer soon discovered that he was attracted to her because of her flirtatious and bold behavior. One day, the hotel management asked Homer to get the back rent from Romola and kick her out. When Romola started crying, Homer threw his wallet down on her bed, indicating that she should take his money and use it to pay her rent. She interpreted his gesture as a request for sex. They began touching each other, but an ill-timed phone call from one of Homer's colleagues ruined the moment for Homer. Even in Hollywood, Homer still cries about his lost chance to be with her.

Mig

See Miguel

Miguel

Miguel lives in a camp two canyons away from the city and raises fighting chickens. He is very poor and wears ragged clothes. Tod refers to Miguel's eyes as "Armenian," but he is Mexican. Miguel eventually moves into Homer's garage with his fighting chickens, at Faye's insistence. Homer discovers Miguel and Faye in bed together after a party.

Earle Shoop

Earle Shoop is another one of Faye's suitors, but he is much more successful than Tod. He is "criminally handsome," according to Faye, a quiet and skinny former cowboy from a small town in Arizona. Faye often invites Tod along on their dates, and Tod usually ends up paying for dinner because Earle is always broke. Earle has a violent temper and becomes jealous when another man gets too close to Faye.

Homer Simpson

Homer Simpson is one of Faye's suitors, a shy, lumbering, and naive middle-aged man. He is a large man, like "Picasso's great sterile athletes, who brood hopelessly on pink sand, staring at veined marble waves," according to Tod. His hands seem to have a life of their own and are often moving when Homer is trying to remain still.

Homer moved to California from Iowa on his doctor's advice after he became sick with pneumonia and lost his twenty-year bookkeeping job at a residential hotel.

Homer falls in love with Faye when she and her father show up on his doorstep to sell their silver polish. She is polite to him at first but does not seem romantically interested in him. After her father dies and she has no money, she moves in with Homer as part of a "business arrangement": Homer gives her all the money she needs to dress and act like a movie star, and she will pay him back when she becomes a star. Homer has allowed her to move in, though, primarily because he is lonely and enjoys having her around.

The riot at the end of the book is prompted when Homer, depressed and on the verge of returning to Iowa because Faye has left him, bludgeons Adore for taunting him one too many times. The movie theater mob, bored with waiting for their favorite stars, turns on Homer and he disappears.

Themes

Illusions

The theme of illusions forms the basis for much of what happens in the novel. West includes unreal and illusory images throughout the novel to indicate that what keeps Hollywood functioning are fantasies and dreams. Like the movie sets Tod designs and often has to walk through when he is at the studio, life in Hollywood in the 1930s is one-dimensional and flimsy.

Nothing seems to be indigenous in Hollywood; like most of the people living in Hollywood and the architecture of the buildings they inhabit, almost everything has been borrowed or brought from another place. The houses have been designed to look like Irish cottages, Spanish villas, or southern plantations. The characters often imagine themselves as someone different than they are really; for example, Claude Estee walks and talks as if he is a potbellied Confederate general, even though he

Much of Tod's thinking is devoted to whom he will put in the painting and what he will have them doing. The painting itself is an illusion, as it depicts what Tod secretly hopes will happen to the city when the residents who came from other parts of the country to experience the good life in California become disillusioned and destroy the city in a violent, fiery riot.

Topics for Further Study

- West's death after running a stop sign recalls the implied and explicit violence in his novel. Learn more about West's life and death and compare and contrast him with Tod Hackett.

- Watch a few of the most popular films released between 1929 and 1939 or research their content in books about film history. Many historians have argued that the content of these films helped reinforce popular American values such as individuality and hard work. From what you learn about these films, do you agree with this statement? How does the content of the films compare with West's description of the industry that made the films?

- After finishing West's last novel, read one of his earlier novels. Do you think that he was improving as a writer? What in the two novels supports your opinion? If he had lived to write for another thirty years, what topics do you think he would have covered in his later novels?

- Using what you know about the characters in the novel, write an epilogue in which you tell what becomes of them. Does Faye become a movie star? If not, what does she do? Does Tod finish his painting? Does Homer survive the riot and return to Iowa?

- Choose a scene in the novel, change its outcome, and write about how this would influence the rest of the novel. For example, imagine what might have happened in the rest of the book if Earle had killed Miguel when he hit him with a club after the pheasant dinner in the canyon.

is a "dried up little man with the rubbed features and stooped shoulders of a postal clerk." Harry Greener, a washed-up vaudeville clown, acts as if he has had a long and distinguished career on the stage.

A continuing motif in the book is Tod's planned painting, "The Burning of Los Angeles."

Emotional and Physical Disconnection

West has created characters in his novel who have few, if any, solid attachments to other people or to places. Most have come to Hollywood from somewhere else, leaving other lives behind them. Their disconnection mimics the lack of substance that they see around them in the movie industry and in the architecture and atmosphere of the city. Many of the characters appear cold and callous, such as Faye when she tells Tod that she can never love him because he is neither rich nor handsome. He still desires her, yet admits that "her beauty was structural like a tree's, not a quality of her mind or heart." Tod does not require or expect an emotional connection to Faye; he only wants her body and even considers paying her for sex.

Power

To replace the lack of solid human relationships in the novel, West has given his characters relationships that are based solely on power. Everything of value in the book involves the use of power over a person or group of people. Faye has power over Homer, for example, and it defines their relationship: in exchange for a place to live and plenty of money for nice clothes, Homer receives flirtatious attention from Faye, the fantasy that he has a normal life with a beautiful live-in companion, and the possibility, however remote, of sexual fulfillment. Faye and Homer even refer to their relationship as "a business arrangement."

In the novel, California and Hollywood exert a power over those who have given up their lives elsewhere and arrive expecting to become beautiful or handsome, rich, famous, and tanned. In this relationship, though, the newcomers to the city very often receive nothing in return for their travels. According to Tod, "they discovered that sunshine isn't enough.... Nothing happens. They don't know what to do with their time.... If only a plane would crash once in a while" to relieve their boredom.

Violence

Much of the power in the book is exhibited through violence, and often violence is the primary way in which people relate to one another. One of the first in a series of violent images in the book involves a horse's body floating in Claude Estee's swimming pool. It is a fake horse and has been placed in the pool for the amusement of Claude's party guests. Another guest becomes angry with Tod, in fact, when the horse does not amuse him. She calls him "an old meanie," and explains, "Think of how happy the Estees must feel, showing it to people and listening to their merriment."

Most of the characters are attracted to violence, as it makes them feel alive in a city where, according to Tod, many have come to die. Their lives are dull and empty, and only the prospect of death and destruction interests them. When Earle slams a club into Miguel's head, for example, Tod's response is not one of horror but of dreamy reverie. He begins to imagine a rape scene involving Faye, then plots out more of his painting depicting the violent overthrow and ruin of Los Angeles. Claude so desperately wants to see a cock fight that he buys a rooster to fight Miguel's, even though it is barely alive and has a cracked beak. Bloodshed raises the possibility that something real, something with consequences, will happen, however horrible.

Failure and Impotence

None of the characters in West's novel is a success or creates anything with substance. West's repeated use of failure and impotence reiterates the inadequate nature of the relationships in the novel. While Tod plans his painting, he is never seen actually working on it. Homer finds himself attracted to Faye and to another woman, but he does not know what to do with those feelings. And the only way that Tod can satisfy his misplaced and unrequited desire for Faye is to imagine raping her.

Style

Omniscient Point of View

West's book is written in the third person with an omniscient narrator, a voice that not only is able to report what events are taking place but also what thoughts and feelings are going on inside each character.

West's omniscient narrator shifts the focus a number of times during the course of the novel. The novel begins with Tod; his background, thoughts, and actions are the primary focus of the story. Then, in chapter eight, the focus shifts to Homer. While Homer settles into his new house in Hollywood, he

remembers his old life in Iowa and thinks about his hopes for a new life in California. The focus is on Homer until chapter thirteen, when it shifts back to Tod. The narrator's focus also shifts between characters within some of the chapters.

Short Chapters

Chapters form the structure of this novel, and their brevity gives the book a particularly fast pace, much like episodic scenes in a movie. Many of the twenty-seven chapters are only one or two pages long, occur in one place, and cover only a few minutes or an hour. The longer chapters cover events that move from place to place and may last throughout an afternoon or evening, such as chapter fifteen, in which Tod tags along with Earle and Faye on their date. The final, climactic chapter, in which Tod is trapped by the mob at the movie premiere, is also one of the longer ones.

Use of Slang

West wrote his novel during the 1930s, using the popular slang of that period. His use of such language lets the reader know that the characters are involved in popular or youth culture or are not necessarily well-educated—with the exception of Tod. Though Tod has a degree from a very prestigious university, he uses slang words on occasion, mostly to fit in with the seedy residents of his apartment building. When he tries to convince Faye not to become a prostitute to pay for her father's funeral, he says, "Listen kid, . . . Why go on the turf? I can get the dough."

West's use of slang, however, has also dated the book, making it somewhat challenging for modern readers to understand some of the language.

Of all the book's characters, Faye seems to use slang the most, possibly because she is the youngest adult character. Much of her slang is used in a way that sounds flirtatious and teasing, especially toward men. When Tod tries to kiss her after listening to her feeble ideas about a screenplay, she lets him but pushes him away when he tries to keep his arms around her for too long. "Whoa there, palsywalsy," Faye warns, "Mama spank."

Historical Context

Hollywood's Golden Age

Many film historians and critics consider the 1930s to be Hollywood's golden age. Though much of the world, including the United States, was

Compare & Contrast

- **1930s:** Hollywood movie studios have a huge amount of control over their actors, even the stars. Actors sign multi-movie contracts that limit their ability to select the films in which they appear, and their private lives are governed by strict codes of behavior.

  Today: Movie stars have unprecedented freedom to choose their work and in some cases play a role in the producing or directing of their films. Studios regularly pay stars millions of dollars for their work in only one film.

- **1930s:** With the Great Depression taking a toll on families' budgets, multiple generations living under the same roof, or doubling-up, becomes the norm again. In West's novel, Faye and her father share an apartment.

  Today: The post–World War II housing boom launched a series of generations that never expected to live with their parents after they left home for school or work. A trend has emerged, however, in which more and more young, post-college adults are moving back home. Some explain that these young adults are choosing their parents' homes over their own apartments because of the rising cost of living, while others believe the trend is linked to a rising first-marriage age.

- **1930s:** Hundreds of thousands of people from the American Midwest, whose farms have turned into dust because of poor farming prac-

  tices and freakish weather, travel to California in search of jobs and new lives. Unfortunately, conditions are not quite what they hoped; jobs are scarce and many Californians are not happy about competing for what jobs there are. Close to six million people live in California.

  Today: California is still a popular place to live; its population is now more than thirty-four million. Demographers estimate that California's population grows by sixty people every hour of every day.

- **1930s:** Hollywood film technicians are making huge strides in adding sound and color to movies. Special effects are improving, but they are usually achieved by technicians creating tiny models and using stop-action film—a painstaking process in which the filmmakers stop each frame of the film and move the model to its next position before they shoot another frame.

  Today: Most special effects are done by computer. Sometimes the images seen in films are completely computer-generated, and other times they involve the use of as many as thirty individual still cameras to capture an image and manipulate it. For example, the film *The Matrix* features a sophisticated technique using multiple still cameras and computers so that actors appear to be hanging in space, moving in slow motion while the camera circles around them.

suffering from economic depression and high unemployment, the movie industry flourished both technically and artistically. In fact, 1939 saw the release of two of the American Film Institute's ten most popular movies: *Gone With the Wind* and *The Wizard of Oz*.

By 1932 technicians had solved most of the early problems associated with adding sound to film, and nearly all Hollywood films included voice and music. The thirties also saw the use of color in

filming, and by 1939 the Technicolor Corporation had dramatically improved the industry's techniques such that colorized film no longer looked so artificial. This decade saw the birth of improved special effects, as well, with the release of *King Kong*. In the movie, the giant ape was actually a tiny metal skeleton covered with rubber and, for its close-ups, a huge mechanized ape head with only shoulders. The ape's filmed movements were carefully shot using such techniques as stop-action photography—a painstaking process in which the film-makers stop each frame of the film and move the model to its next position before they shoot another frame. Films featuring special-effects dinosaurs also became popular at this time.

The 1930s saw the dawn of hugely popular movie stars who became Hollywood's royalty. As depicted in the final scene of West's novel, thousands of fans would stand in line for hours for a chance to glimpse their favorite actors. Greta Garbo, a cool and sleek star with an air of mystery, and Clark Gable, a handsome leading man who always got the girl, were two of the most popular movie stars of the decade. Studios made huge profits even during the troubled economic times, mostly by making fun, escapist movies. Patrons seeking relief from their daily lives flocked to Westerns, musicals, comedies, and gangster films. The comedy of the Marx Brothers found a large audience; many of their films used slapstick humor to poke fun at businessmen, politicians, and such institutions as capitalism.

The Great Depression

On October 29, 1929, the New York Stock Market crashed when investors sold sixteen million shares in just one trading day. Just a year before, Herbert Hoover had been elected U.S. president, and the nation was basking in the glow of an unprecedented economic boom. Some sectors of the economy, however, had experienced a slowdown during the latter 1920s, particularly agriculture. The stock market collapse placed the nation on the road to the Great Depression and by 1933, the unemployment rate was at about 25 percent. Historians and economists disagree over the cause of the depression: some maintain that the crisis was a global event, exacerbated by Germany's inability to pay the reparations that England and France demanded for its role in World War I; others blame a decline in consumption by Americans; still others point to overvalued stocks as the culprit.

The stock collapse did not affect the nation's economy all at once. Gradually, businesses closed, banks failed, and savings and investments disappeared. Fewer families could afford a new car, and spending on new construction in 1933 fell to one-sixth of its pre-depression level. Shantytowns, called "Hoovervilles" after the president, appeared on the outskirts of large cities and became places where men who had lost their jobs and homes could congregate. In West's novel, Miguel and Earle live in a small encampment on the edge of the city, where Earle traps small game for his meals and

Miguel raises fighting roosters. Homer lets them live in his garage because, he tells Tod, they are "just down on their luck, like a lot of people these days, you know."

The nation had experienced prior cyclic economic depressions, occurring every eight to twelve years and each lasting a couple of years. At first, many businessmen and politicians saw the 1930s depression as part of an expected business cycle, but by the early 1930s, most realized that this depression was more widespread and intense than previous slumps. A series of disastrous economic decisions by Hoover resulted in Franklin D. Roosevelt's 1932 presidential victory. Almost immediately, Roosevelt launched a series of federal economic recovery programs referred to as the New Deal.

By 1937, signs indicated that the depression was loosening its grip on the nation. Many credit the start of war in Europe in 1939 with stimulating the world and national economies and ending the Great Depression, while others claim that the depression's end came only because the New Deal programs helped to strengthen the American people's confidence in the nation's economy.

Critical Overview

When he died at thirty-seven, West left a relatively small body of work: four novels, a few essays, a play, and some movie scripts. Critics differ on whether West had just begun to reach an advanced level of writing with the publication of his last novel, *The Day of the Locust*, or whether this work indicated merely an average talent with little more to offer.

Algis Valiunas, writing in *Commentary*, weighs in on the side that has never been particularly impressed with West and his style of writing. In his review of the 1997 Modern Library collection of West's work, *Novels and Other Writings*, Valiunas notes that other critics have called *The Day of the Locust* the best novel ever written about Hollywood, but he wishes there were a better one to consider. West "wrote about emotional, moral, and spiritual coarseness, and, notwithstanding his considerable learning, style, and wit, he wrote about them coarsely," charges Valiunas. He accuses West of cowardice for leaving out of *The Day of the Locust* the studio heads and other characters who, in real life, "were the ones doing the real

Still from the 1975 film version of the novel

destroying." Through this omission, West "missed a great opportunity," according to Valiunas.

Stanley Edgar Hyman, in *American Writers*, is equally critical of West and his writing abilities. While crediting West with a number of "very powerful scenes" in *The Day of the Locust*, he believes that the book "ultimately fails as a novel. . . . [I]t has no dramatic unity, and . . . it has no moral core." The characters in the novel "tend to be symbolic abstractions," Hyman asserts, pointing out that the character of Tod never quite "comes to life," primarily because of West's obvious struggle to keep him from being completely autobiographical.

Randall Reid, however, argues that those who expect straightforward realism will be disappointed with West's prose. "[T]hose who believe that the novel must portray with detailed fidelity the surface of life—whether natural or social—must necessarily feel that West fails as a novelist," he writes in his book, *The Fiction of Nathanael West: No Redeemer, No Promised Land*. West is a difficult author to read, Reid claims, because he "frustrates too many of the common motives for reading." West's style was simple, tending toward parody, and he found himself more interested in "the power latent in mass discontent," according to Reid, than in trying to make his reader comfortable.

Other critics have been more positive about *The Day of the Locust* without completely agreeing about it. I. B. Nadel in *Reference Guide to American Literature* considers the book "a realistic novel about an unreal city." West's prose in the novel is "relentless in its exposure of decay and violence," comments Nadel. Others focus on the dream-like atmosphere of the book, such as Earl Rovit, also writing in *Reference Guide to American Literature*. He compares West's last novel to T. S. Eliot's *The Wasteland*, calling it "equally hallucinatory and probably more pessimistic, as well as more comic."

Some critics have focused on West's influences. In her article in *Studies in Short Fiction*, Diane Long Hoeveler argues that West was influenced by Henri Bergson, a French philosopher who depicted modern industrial society as a pawnshop. According to Hoeveler, West created his characters with this philosophy in mind, as he has them living lives that are "ludicrously machine-like, commodified, and objectified." In doing so, "West condemns the schizophrenia and alienation that capitalism has produced in its modern victims," she writes. Richard Keller Simon, writing in *Modern Language Quarterly*, believes that in his final novel, West was attacking the 1930s movie director Frank Capra while also using many of Capra's storytelling techniques. *The Day of the Locust*, according to Simon, contains many story elements found in Capra's 1936 blockbuster, *Mr. Deeds Goes to Town*, but turns Capra's happy ending on its head. He also argues that the German essayist and philosopher Theodor Adorno informed West's novel, noting that much of the argument in Adorno's 1938 essay on popular music reappears as social criticism in the book. "Once placed within these contexts [Capra and Adorno]," Simon writes, *The Day of the Locust* "can be recognized as one of the first complex analyses of modern mass culture written in America . . . as well as one of the first major works of modern literature to rework the conventions of mass culture."

Criticism

Susan Sanderson

Sanderson holds a master of fine arts degree in fiction writing and is an independent writer. In this essay, Sanderson examines images of nature, impotence, and violence in West's The Day of the Locust, *and how they relate to the novel's curious title.*

West's final novel before his death, *The Day of the Locust*, immediately presents the reader with a question: What does this curious title refer to? Even after a person reads the book, the title's appropriateness to the novel's contents may not be immediately apparent. There are no locusts in the book and, in fact, nature as it is commonly perceived seems to have been almost completely left out of West's image of a city defined by artificiality.

The most famous literary or historical reference to locusts is in the book of Exodus in the Bible, in which God sends a plague of locusts to the pharaoh of Egypt as retribution for refusing to free the enslaved Jews. Millions of locusts swarm over the lush fields of Egypt, destroying its food supplies. Destructive locusts also appear in the New Testament in the symbolic and apocalyptic book of Revelation.

West's use of the locust in his title, then, calls up images of destruction and a land stripped bare of anything green and living. Certainly, the novel is filled with images of destruction: Tod Hackett's painting entitled "The Burning of Los Angeles," his violent fantasies about Faye, and the bloody result of the cockfight, just to name a few. A close

> " West's use of the locust in his title, then, calls up images of destruction and a land stripped bare of anything green and living."

examination of West's characters and his selective use of natural images, which include representations of violence and impotence—and which are therefore contrary to popular images linking nature and fertility—reveals that the locust in the title refers to the character of Tod.

In his essay in *American Writers*, Stanley Edgar Hyman notes that while Faye Greener's character may represent nature, she is a version of nature that is "deceptive." Her last name may signify lushness and prosperity, but in reality Faye embodies neither. The photograph that Tod keeps of her displays a Faye who, with her "moon face," looks at first as if she is "welcoming a lover." But when Tod looks closely at the photograph, he sees a woman whose "invitation wasn't to pleasure, but to struggle, hard and sharp, closer to murder than love."

In the novel, then, nature, like humanity, is deceptive. Even the few animal images are presented as damaged or artificial. For the cockfight, Miguel chooses a rooster for Claude that looks like "an ordinary barnyard fowl," even though the bird has fought before. Upon closer inspection, Abe discovers that the rooster's beak is cracked, making him nearly useless in a fight. At Claude's party, a rubber horse floats in the swimming pool for the supposed amusement of his guests.

In fact, almost everything in the novel's Hollywood is falsified. Homer's Irish-style cottage contains a New England-style bedroom in which there is a bed with an iron frame that has been manufactured to look like heavily grained wood. Tod works at a movie company where he must walk through acres and acres of fake ocean liners, Western saloons, and even Egyptian sphinxes, all made from flimsy plywood and plaster and forming a sort of hallucinatory neighborhood. This is what passes for a natural landscape in West's novel.

Alongside these images are representations of impotence—the very antithesis of nature's energy and fertility. Despite the numerous references to sex in the book, all but one ultimately point to failed efforts. West sets a scene in a whorehouse, where a projector screening a dirty film gets jammed just before it gets interesting. "The old teaser routine!" shouts one of the patrons. Homer approaches a woman sitting on her bed who seems somewhat interested in receiving his advances, but he freezes because he has no clue about what to do next. The closest he can get to a sexual relationship with Faye, the woman of his dreams, is to buy clothes for her and allow her to live in his house as part of a "business agreement." Faye, of course, presents the men in the story with everything they want but cannot have. Earle tries to court her but he is physically too clumsy, and Tod's advances are firmly brushed off, even when he begs or offers money.

Tod's response to Faye's rejection is twofold. Sometimes he imagines her in his painting, fleeing both the bloodthirsty mob about to destroy Los Angeles and a woman about to hit her with a rock. Faye is frightened but exhilarated by the chase, "enjoying the release that wild flight gives in much the same way that a game bird must when, after hiding for several tense minutes, it bursts from cover in complete, unthinking panic." Other times, Tod dreams of raping Faye, a fantasy in which Tod chases after her and brings her to the ground but is never quite able to complete the crime. Tod acts out part of these fantasies in real life when Faye flees the scene of Earle and Miguel's fight. Tod tries to grab her, but she is too fast; nevertheless, he lies down feeling "comfortably relaxed, even happy."

The only scene in the book in which the sex act is completed takes place between Faye and Miguel. At first, their coupling may seem to be a fluke, but there is more to Miguel than is immediately apparent. In Hollywood, where everyone is from somewhere else and there does not appear to be any indigenous culture, Miguel is about as close to a local as West gets. Miguel is Mexican, still living on the land taken from his ancestors centuries before. His connection to the dirt beneath his feet gives him power over those who have come to California from the East coast, like Tod, or the Midwest, like Homer. This man, who is still in touch with something natural, however fractured, is the only one Faye will allow into her bed.

There are, of course, nonsexual representations of impotence and failure in the book, especially for

Tod. Tod's last name is a reminder, for example, that he is a failure at most things he tries. He is a "hack" artist, paid to produce something that has commercial, but not artistic, value. While Tod thinks quite a bit about his painting, usually imagining the violence it will portray, West never shows him actually creating the painting.

Tod's failures drive him to imaginary violence. His violence is never acted out but is always just beneath the surface of everything he does and thinks. Even though Faye is a coarse likeness of nature, Tod still wants her and wants to plunder the natural world that she represents. He describes his fantasy sex with her in almost hyper-violent terms. "If you threw yourself on her, it would be like throwing yourself from the parapet of a skyscraper," he visualizes. "You would do it with a scream. . . . Your teeth would be driven into your skull like nails into a pine board."

Tod is violence and destruction personified, much like a locust. He is entranced by the possibilities of violence, as pictured in his plan for his painting, where a great mob of dissatisfied and bored people attempt to destroy the city. Like Tod, they came to Hollywood to find something that would make their lives whole and exciting. "Once there, they discovered that sunshine isn't enough. . . . Their boredom becomes more and more and terrible. They realize they've been tricked and they burn with resentment," the narrator says. In Tod's painting, they explode and take out their frustrations on the city and everyone around them.

Like a locust, Tod is intent on destroying and plundering everything he sees, including Faye. But a single locust is nearly harmless; it is only when they swarm that they do real damage. Tod has spent the entire novel observing the people he thinks have "come to California to die," considering how he will fill his canvas with them and have them do the destruction he so desperately wants to see. Through his act of observation, Tod has set himself apart from them. But by the novel's final scene, it is clear that he is no less angry than they are and no less willing to be a part of their violence. Before he is swept up in the movie theater mob, Tod walks in front of the crowd, protected by a velvet rope, almost taunting, but certainly considering whether he will join them. After Homer bludgeons the young boy, the mob makes Tod's decision for him and sweeps him up.

Tod becomes a locust in fact—a part of the destruction he has craved—when the mob carries him away, and he seems happy, almost satisfied. He is able to close his eyes and mentally work on his painting, one flame at a time. The day Tod becomes part of the mob is truly the day of the locust.

Source: Susan Sanderson, Critical Essay on *The Day of the Locust*, in *Novels for Students*, The Gale Group, 2003.

I. B. Nadel

In the following essay, Nadel suggests that The Day of the Locust *is "relentless in its exposure of the decay and violence that comes from the betrayal of dreams."*

Nathanael West's *The Day of the Locust* is a realistic novel about an unreal city. Centered in Hollywood and the world of movie-making, the story avoids the glitter of stardom to concentrate on the life of the disenchanted. It presents the disillusioned, those who find themselves cheated of the glamour their fantasies promised and the movies provided. The novel emphasizes the spiritual and moral death of the city, symptomatic of the condition within the country as a whole. Focusing on the despair of out-of-work bit actors, the illusions of romantic but untalented actresses, the unhappiness of once-successful vaudeville comics, the paralysis of those who journey to the coast, the novel stresses the death of dreams and culminates in a fiery riot of frenzied movie fans at a Hollywood premiere. This scene, which ends the novel, embodies the efforts of the protagonist, Tod Hackett, to finish his panoramic painting recording life in the city which he titles *The Burning of Los Angeles*. With the Old Testament allusion of its title and it apocalyptic ending by fire, the novel stands as a unique indictment of romance and its destruction in modern America. This intensely moral work, displaying characters entrapped between their idealism and corruption, initiates a series of Hollywood novels which extend West's satire. F. Scot Fitzgerald's *The Last Tycoon*, Budd Schulberg's *What Makes Sammy Run?*, and Joan Didion's *Play It As It Lays* are three distinguished examples.

The principal themes of *The Day of the Locust* are the tension between disillusionment and romance and the reaction to recognizing the absurdity of everyday life. The clearest demonstration of the conflict occurs in chapter 18 when Tod Hackett wanders about a studio lot in quest of Faye Greener, the lustful but elusive *femme fatale* he has met earlier in the book. Believing she is an extra in an epic entitled *Waterloo*—the title itself symbolic of the imminent downfall of Hollywood—he follows a group of *cuirassiers* heading for the set

in search of her. He quickly loses them but encounters in succession a painted ocean liner, a papier-mâché sphinx, a desert, a western saloon, a jungle, a Paris street, a Romanesque courtyard, a waterfall, a campy resort, and a Greek temple where the god of Eros "lay face downward in a pile of old newspapers and bottles." Such is the fate of love in the novel—lost, discarded and impotent. Before he actually witnesses the literal collapse of a cardboard Mont St. Jean when hundreds of soldiers enter a mock battle but unexpectedly crash through canvas, cardboard, and plaster, Tod glimpses an adobe fort, a wooden horse of Troy, a set of baroque palace stairs, a Dutch windmill, and the bones of a dinosaur. In this pivotal chapter, West emphasizes the riot of scenes and fraudulent quality of history when placed in the hands of the image makers. But the chapter also echoes the illusionary lives all the characters lead in a city that is itself a jumble of architectural and life styles and which values masquerade over authenticity. In Hollywood, West emphasizes, the natural is the artificial.

The unusual characters in the novel parallel the melange of styles and values depicted. A dwarf, a painter, a bookkeeper, a family of Eskimos, a cowboy, a vaudeville comedian, and an untalented actress/prostitute are the principals. But their mixture expresses the frustration rather than achievement of talents. The life of these extras, movie fans, would-be stars, screenwriters, and hangers-on is one of boredom, suffering, and impotence repeated thematically and symbolically throughout the novel. Sordid rooms, sterile landscapes, and dead-end streets project the empty lives in Los Angeles. Promised romance and stardom, adventure and sex, the figured discover only the artificial world of make-believe. And for West's characters, resentment at this discovery unleashes violence. Not surprisingly, the original title of the novel was *The Cheated*.

Faye Greener, the heroine, embodies many of the contradictions of the city. Pursued by all, obtained by none, she is a kind of bitch goddess (like success) who will be possessed only by those who can pay for her. But like the image on a screen, she remains untouchable, a fantasy. She becomes a phantom bride not only for Tod Hackett and Homer Simpson, the retired bookkeeper, but also for the seedy cowboy actor Earle Shoop and the brutal but sexual Mexican Miguel. Faye remains elusive, the dream of love that is unattainable for the nation but which it continues to desire. "Her invitation

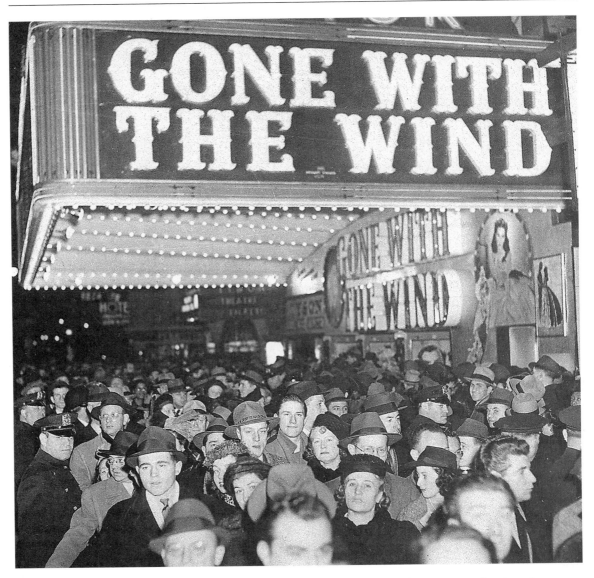

Crowd gathered for the 1939 premier of Gone With the Wind, *one of the most popular American movies and the epitome of the Golden Age of Hollywood*

wasn't to pleasure," West writes, "but to struggle, hard and sharp, closer to murder than to love."

The Day of the Locust is relentless in its exposure of the decay and violence that comes from the betrayal of dreams. Yet West exhibits supreme control in the telling of his story, despite the continued division between the idealism and actuality of Hollywood life. Adjusting to the discrepancy between the imagined and the real, Hackett becomes both an artist fashioning a new future and a Jeremiah predicting doom. The novel is a remarkable satire of America and its dreams, providing a dis-

turbing portrait of its fantasies evoked through language, symbol, and character. And at the core of these desires is violence which for West is idiomatic in America. When the masses discover that "they haven't the mental equipment for pleasure," their only recourse is to destroy. Boredom and disappointment make them savage, as Hackett experiences when he is caught in the mob scene at Kahn's Persian Palace Theatre which ends the novel. But the event paradoxically allows him a vision of his completed painting which he has been unable to finish until that moment.

Just before the climactic riot, Hackett remarks that "at the sight of their heroes and heroines, the crowd would turn demonic." The frustrations beneath the surface of wish-fulfillment and dream-seeking sharpen the theme of middle-class dissatisfaction, creating a startling work of fiction. In its presentation of divided characters, split between their desires and actions, in its rendering of anguish-ridden romantics surrounded by indifferent pragmatists, the work conveys the dilemma of the modern American psyche. And in its accuracy in showing "all those poor devils who can only be stirred by the promise of miracle and then only to violence," the novel has a remarkable contemporary quality. For West, life as illusion masks discontent, although awareness of this condition ironically intensifies the need for fantasy. Difficult to control and uncertain in their goals, the masses feel threatened by their idols and are prepared to destroy them when they fail to gratify their dreams. In the neo-Gothic world of his California, West creates a riveting but profoundly disturbing fiction.

Source: I. B. Nadel, "*The Day of the Locust*," in *Reference Guide to American Literature*, 4th ed., edited by Jim Kamp, St. James Press, 2000, pp. 988–89.

Kingsley Widner

In the following excerpt, Widner examines the Hollywood setting and culture that underpins West's novel.

The Greener Masquerading

Early in the novel, West makes a distinction between the "masqueraders," the costumed role-players characteristic of Hollywood (and, more generally, of the manipulative, shifting, and anomic southern California culture and society), and those retirees and other refugees, mostly from mid-America, who have "come to California to die," They, representing the broader American society, provide the audience of the masqueraders. Several things, as we will see, go novelistically wrong with this division, but let us first consider the Greeners, Harry and Faye, as epitomizing the masqueraders.

Harry is a clown. Clowning often serves as a combination of the self-protective and the self-punitive masquerade (as we often recognize in the adolescent "class clown"). But clowning can become compulsive, the masquerade turning into an entrapping mechanism. West dramatized some of this with Beagle Darwin and Willie Shrike in his first two books and again in *Locust* with his most carefully detailed clown, Harry Greener, aging ex-vaudevillean, burlesque stooge, and sometime Hol-

> " The Hollywood 'dream dump' is where every fantasy will be exploited and washed up."

lywood bit player who makes his depression living huckstering with phony acts door-to-door a dubious homemade silver polish. "When Harry had first begun his stage career," forty years before, ruminates Tod, "he had probably restricted his clowning to the boards, but now he clowned continuously. It was his sole method of defense. Most people, he had discovered, won't go out of their way to punish a clown." His most successful professional role had been as a "bedraggled Harlequin" taking punishment from a group of acrobats (partly like Lem in the final scenes of *A Cool Million* playing masochistic stooge for the audience's sadistic guffaws). Now Harry specializes in burlesque pitifulness, playing the victim whenever he is "on," and overplaying the reverse, the rather nasty wise guy, when supposedly not masquerading. He dramatizes himself as the give-away fake, "dressing like a banker, a cheap unconvincing imitation" which by fooling no one "slyly" fools his auditors into sympathy. The "act" has become automatic.

Tod realizes this when in sickroom conversation Harry starts one of his compulsive routines and the auditor has "to let him run down like a clock." Though Harry's illness is "real," a heart attack which will shortly kill him, he "groaned skillfully. It was a second-act curtain groan, so phony that Tod had to hide a smile. And yet the old man's pallor hadn't come from a box." The only way Harry knows to express suffering is by exaggeratedly pretending it. His face, grotesquely overdone "like a mask" from the ravages of years of overacting, can never "express anything either subtly or exactly … only the furthest degree." (Historically, it has become unfashionable in fictions as well as in life to find revelations of character in physiognomy or illness, but West repeatedly points to the old existential truth that we really are what we have done and do, not least the counterfeiting.) Harry's once-chosen role as victim has also fixated the pleasure in his suffering, though, of course, "he only enjoyed the sort that was self-inflicted." Harry inflicts on any and every one his life story, an unstoppable jokey-piteous charade of doggerel, mimicry, melodrama, bombast, and self-parodying comic patter. Hamming up his life has, in fact, become his life.

Earlier, we see him peddling his misery act and polish when (at Homer's house) he has a real heart attack. He acts hurt, and does hurt, "wondering himself whether he was acting or sick." The high point of his routine is his "victim's laugh" which he uses to victimize others. His intended sales victim (Homer) tries to stop Harry:

> But Harry couldn't stop. He was really sick. The last block that held him poised over the runway of self-pity had been knocked away and he was sliding down the chute.... He jumped to his feet and began doing Harry Greener, poor Harry, honest Harry.... At the end of the pantomime, Harry stood with his head thrown back, clutching his throat as though waiting for the curtain.... But Harry wasn't finished. He bowed, sweeping his hat to his heart, then began again. He didn't get very far this time and had to gasp painfully for breath. Suddenly, like a mechanical toy that had been overwound, something snapped inside him and he began to spin through his entire repertoire. The effort was purely muscular, like the dance of a paralytic. Hie jigged, juggled his hat, made believe he had been kicked.... He went through it all in one dizzy spasm, then reeled to the couch....

As real victim he was "even more surprised" than his ostensible victim-audience; though "really sick," he can only think and respond in terms of "performance." While playing faint, he shockingly discovers that he really "is faint." Having role-played so much, he can no longer tell when his is acting pain and feeling pain, pretending suffering and really suffering. In role-playing desperation, like the poseur-poet in *Balso Snell*, his posing act takes over on its frenziedly mechanical own. The masquerade has become all.

The narrator's (and author's) detailed fascination with the Greener role-playing may be because Harry is a genuine fake, all pose with little person left over. So, too, with his daughter, Faye Greener, central idol in most of the violent masquerade of West's mock-scenario of Hollywood eroticism. From the second chapter to concluding riot-rehearsal, Faye is the unmoved mover of the obsessional sexual fantasies of all the particularized males in the novel. An unloving parody love goddess, she provides another masturbatory rape image of the long-dominant Hollywood fantasy type (Harlowe, Monroe, et al). A pretty would-be starlet, tall ("with sword-like legs"), wide chested and high breasted, "platinum" blonde seventeen year old (she usually looks even younger), she is "taut and vibrant" with a constant sexual come-on. Analyzing his own longings for Faye, Tod realizes her appeal "wasn't to pleasure" but to something else, "closer to murder than to love." In further images, coupling with Faye becomes an act of mindless self-immolation, an almost inverted mystical experience, which is much of what media eroticism is about. Even doltishly passive Tod has repeated visions of raping Faye.

The erotic deity is peurile and mannered, with a "subtle half-smile uncontaminated by thought," sexual fantasy unencumbered by other human dimensions. Her compulsive sexual gestures were "so completely meaningless, almost formal, that she seemed like a dancer rather than an affected actress," which she was badly imitating. Much of the time she mechanically, self-lovingly, postures before mirrors. Even to tasteful Yalie Tod, her "affectations" were "so completely artificial that he found them charming." Like Harry's, Faye's role-playing works by not fooling anyone; instead, it was "like being backstage during an amateurish, ridiculous play." The very totality of her absurdity takes people in, with a knowing smile but none the less caught. For example, we several times see one of her "most characteristic gestures" of erotic signaling "with a secret smile and the tongue caress" of her parted lips: "It seemed to promise all sorts of undefined intimacies, yet it was really as simple and automatic as the word thanks." But that very impersonality, the unencumbered sexual come-on, is the appeal.

Faye constantly turns and twists her well-shaped body in sexual automation. Even the sophisticatedly blasé screenwriter, Claude, is mesmerized by it. He eagerly listens to her expound on Hollywood as she jumbles "bits of badly understood advice from the trade papers . . . fan magazines and ... legends"—all "nonsense"—but, like most of her auditors, he is "busy watching her smile, laugh, shiver, whisper, grow indignant, cross and uncross her legs, stick out her tongue, widen and narrow her eyes, toss her head . . . ." It is a weirdly dissociated performance of gestures and words. Like other perhaps sincerely fraudulent people (Richard Nixon provides a famous example), her body language disconnects from her words, "her gestures and expressions didn't really illustrate what she was saying. They were almost pure. It was as though her body recognized how foolish her words were . . . ." But most of the listeners are not really connecting with her body, but with the fantasy of using it. Faye, an automated sexual charade, is as bad an actress otherwise as most popular media figures, existing only as crude fantasy image.

And that does express her. She lives in fantasy. In a scene of careful dramatization, West shows her choosing her "stories," running through stock fantasies as if thumbing a deck of cards. She takes them earnestly, wholeheartedly, sincerely stupid and ungenuine, proposing to friend Tod, whom she uses but never sexually, various garbled but literal-minded "B" movie scripts of the time—"a South Sea tale," a "familiar version of the Cinderella theme"—as something that would make them successful and rich. As so often in *Locust*, Tod summarizes the quality in a painting analogy: "Although the events she described were miraculous, her description of them was realistic. The effect was similar to that obtained by the artists of the Middle Ages, who, when doing a subject like the raising of Lazarus from the dead or Christ walking on water, were careful to keep all the details intensely realistic." (So does West with his fantasy figures.) Faye's literalism thus achieves a naive power. And a deeper irony since her faith is not cosmic Christianity but Hollywood shoddy, the crassest commercial-romantic junk, in which she is a true believer, an erotic nun of masturbatory dreams. It is "these little daydreams of hers" which "gave such extraordinary color and mystery to her movements," a tumescent holiness total in its human counterfeit. Faye is a mystical vibrating machine. And it seems to be this autoeroticism which leads to the male audiences' rape-longings against her mad "completeness, egg-like self-sufficiency," that makes even Tod "want to crush her," or throw "her down in the soft, warm mud" of the fantasy swamp that she lives in. This is violating, as an old form of pornography emphasized, the nun, only this time of Hollywood fantasy-piety.

Faye's tormenting aroused males, fighting with her father (she counters his maniacal "victim's laugh" with mechanically lascivious singing of "Jeepers-Creepers"), or setting off violence between her incidental lovers (Earl, the drugstore cowboy, Miguel, the Mexican cockfighting primitive), do not really affect her. Nor apparently does her complacent whoring. It cannot faze her, Tod concludes, because "her beauty was structural like a tree's, not a quality of her mind or heart." She is simply not a real person.

When Harry dies, Faye, who has been treating him meanly, decides to role-play, rather forcedly, the devoted daughter. She will provide a proper funeral. And for that, within a few paragraphs, her

What Do I Read Next?

- F. Scott Fitzgerald died just one day before West in 1940 and before he could finish *The Love of the Last Tycoon: A Western*. It is the story of a young Hollywood film executive and an exposé of the Hollywood studio system in the 1930s. In 1995, Scribner released an edition that restores the 1940 version (published as *The Last Tycoon*) and includes Fitzgerald's manuscripts, drafts, and working notes.

- Horace McCoy's 1935 novel, *They Shoot Horses, Don't They*, presents a picture of 1930s Hollywood every bit as cynical as the view West offers. A couple who take part in the depression-era craze for weeks-long dance marathons, in hopes of earning some money, become pawns in a Hollywood publicity stunt.

- John Steinbeck's 1940 Pulitzer Prize–winning novel, *The Grapes of Wrath* (1939), gives a very different picture of 1930s California than the one seen in West's *The Day of the Locust*. The story chronicles the journey of the Joad family from Oklahoma, where the bank has foreclosed on their farm and the wind has carried away most of the topsoil, to California, where they hope to start a new life picking fruit.

- *A Cool Million*, published in 1934, was West's third book. It is a satiric rags-to-riches story about a young man struggling to fulfill his American Dream, set during the Great Depression.

language switches from stock sentimentality to tough-broad slang as she plans to earn the funeral money on her back—call girl for Mrs. Jenning's high-class establishment. After all, it is just another role-playing. Indeed, when she takes on a role that bothers her, as does her chaste moving in with middle-aged Homer as a "business arrangement" to provide her with the clothes, convertible, and other fetish accoutrements that will certify her stardom, she finds the doggily devoted dope shame-arousing, and so decides to cancel the role. While Faye gets carefully delineated with touches of shame, anger, geniality, even lasciviousness, and a "viper" high (from the song she sings, earlier slang for a "stoner" or "pothead"), these can only be incidental to her masquerading, which is most of the essential self she has.

Tod's final vision of Faye, after the day of a gruesome and fraudulent cockfight in the garage and then a parallel stud fight in Homer's living room between Faye's sexually teased admirers, provides a metaphoric summary. He wonders if she has gone off with Miguel, whom she went to bed with the previous night, or, more likely, back to whoring for Mrs. Jenning:

> But either way she would come out all right. Nothing could hurt her. She was like a cork. No matter how rough the sea got, she would go dancing over the same waves that sank iron ships and tore away piers of reinforced concrete. He pictured her riding a tremendous sea. Wave after wave reared its ton on ton of solid water and crashed down only to have her spin gaily away.... a pretty cork, gilt with a glittering fragment of mirror set in its top. The sea in which it danced was beautiful, green in the trough of the waves and silver at their tips. But for all their moon-driven power, they could do no more than net the bright cork for a moment in a spume of intricate lace. Finally it was set down on a strange shore where a savage with pork-sausage fingers and a pimpled butt picked it up and hugged it to his sagging belly. Tod recognized the fortunate man; he was one of Mrs. Jenning's customers.

The passage serves to again reveal Tod's own passive fantasy indulgence, but it also does other things. In this vintage West, an extended conceit, we see the intentional yoking of incongruities—gilt cork and concrete pier, intricate lace and pimpled butt, lyrical nature poetry and crude human grotesquery, wild vision and hard-nosed cynicism. But the larger significance may be seen in the final judgment of Faye-as-cork: narcissistic (the fragment of mirror on top), partially exempt from the natural order in her very denaturing (uncapturable by the destructive sea), subject only to one of her parodistic South Sea romance scripts, turned back into properly whorish reality. Faye, as person and type, is invulnerable, not only in her metaphoric journey here but in her "life" in the novel as well as in her final symbolism as a figure in Tod's painting, "The Burning of Los Angeles" (running ecstatically ahead of the ravaging locust-mob, who revengefully pursue the masqueraders who have helped cheat them of genuine life).

Faye is unfazable. But that also means she floats invulnerable to most human possibilities, always in bouncing escape, only momentarily netted in the spume. Neither tragic nor comic, Faye remains unarousable to fuller life, just a dancing cork in a kaleidoscopic masquerade of autoeroticism. Though bemused in tone, the passage may be read as propounding West's devastating view of the consequences of endless role-playing. With Faye always bouncing free to continue in her fantasies, or Harry not knowing what he feels because clownishly playing his disguised self, the Greeners show that for compulsive masqueraders little authentic life is possible. It is a disease of unreality as bad as religion. What "Hollywood" means, then, is not just the obvious grossness and corruption but the "greener" fantasy masquerading of life and self—and all America.

West's compassionate handling of the Greeners, and indeed of the whole masquerading ambience, should not detract from the sense of horror. Here, as he wrote in *Miss Lonelyhearts*, we can see some of the great "betrayal" of human dreams. Since West's time, our exploitative technocratic popular culture has extended, increased, and intensified; larger realms of daily activities—politics, religion, schooling, social responses, culture—have more fully merged into the masquerades. The probabilities can hardly be less than apocalyptic.

Machined Fantasies

Though not much of *The Day of the Locust* concerns cinema production, West seems to have perceived that an essence of the Hollywood "art" was to provide mechanical fantasies of violent eroticism for repressed mass America. His imagery for Los Angeles insists strongly on machined fantasy, fabricated dreams which become grotesque monstrosities. So, too, with his often wryly amusing descriptions of his caricature people. For example, Earl Shoup, Faye's stud and a minor cowboy actor, costumed in Western clothes, gestures, and clichés, "had a two dimensional face that a talented child might have drawn with a ruler and a compass." The flat symmetry of features and the coloring like a wash "completed his resemblance to a mechanical drawing." A mechanical and two-dimensional persona, his responses, mostly laconic posing and sex and violence, lack most fuller human depth.

Throughout the fiction, West plays variations on the mechanical phantasm. Tod goes to a party at the imitation Mississippi mansion in Los Angeles of successful screen writer Claude. His host has made masquerading into an infinite regress of mockery, such as calling to his butler, " 'Here you black rascal! A mint julep.' A Chinese servant came running with a Scotch and soda." A more simple mechanism, a floodlighted "conversation piece" (as it was later to be called by similar affluently bored people), is a "dead horse" in his swimming pool, "or, rather, a life-size, realistic reproduction of one. Its legs stuck up stiff and straight and it had an enormous, distended belly. Its hammerhead lay twisted to one side and from its mouth, which was set in an agonized grin, hung a heavy black tongue." Why is this grotesque mechanism there? "To amuse."

Claude also jokes with a parody rhetoric "that permitted him to express his moral indignation and still keep his reputation for worldliness and wit." So did Nathanael West, and other characters in his fiction such as "joke machine" Shrike, in a desperate effort to amuse, to mask horror and emptiness. Claude wants Tod to join the party in visiting Audrey Jenning's classy whorehouse to watch what turns out to be a blandly obscene movie of polymorphous sex. Tod demurs. Claude explains that the cultivated madam—"refined," she "insists on discussing Gertrude Stein and Juan Gris"—"makes vice attractive by skillful packaging. Her dive's a triumph of industrial design." "I don't care how much cellophane she wraps it in," Tod counters, "nautch joints are depressing, like all places for deposit, banks, mail boxes, tombs, vending machines." With cynical playfulness, Claude picks up the mechanical metaphor: "Love is like a vending machine, eh? Not bad. You insert a coin and press home the lever. There's some mechanical activity inside the bowels of the device. You receive a small sweet, frown at yourself in the dirty mirror, adjust your hat . . . and walk away, trying to look as though nothing had happened. It's good, but it's not for pictures." For instead of this mechanical autoeroticism, after all, the "barber in Purdue" wants an even more counterfeit mechanism of "amour and glamor." But all possibilities remain "industrial design."

So does most of the southern California scene, including the fantasy ersatz ("plastic," people in the 1970s would say) styles of housing and decorating and costuming: sports clothes which were "really fancy dress"; imitation northern European cottages (Homer's is described in ugly detail) for a Mediterranean climate; plants made of "rubber and cork" mixed with real ones; everything painted and plastered and stamped to pretend to be something else (the "surfeit of shoddy" of *A Cool Million*, the violation of function and the nature of materials). By

contagion, apparently, even nature appears as machined artifice. In truly apt metaphors, we get the night scene in Los Angeles in which, amid Claude's mimosa and oleander, through "a slit in the blue serge sky poked a grained moon that looked like an enormous bone button." That metaphoric direction had been set in the opening chapter with images of dusk with its semidesert purplish tones in which "violet piping, like a Neon tube, outlined the tops of the ugly, humpbacked hills." Much later in the story, it becomes "one of those blue and lavender nights when the luminous color seems to have been blown over the scene with an airbrush." The Westean twist to grotesquery almost convinces the reader that the hills are crippled and all the natural ambience tasteless machine work. Yet in comparison with the hard industrial and class impositions on nature in the East, it has crass charm.

West's stylistic problem is to find the metaphors which will meaningfully encompass the crippled beings within the mechanical artifice. He uses painting styles as analogues, in the first chapter having Tod announce his turn away from the positive Americana of Homer and Ryder for the sharper nineteenth-century European mockeries of Daumier and Goya. Somewhat after the middle of the novel, Tod favors the eighteenth-century picturesque painters of decay, such as Rosa and Guardi. Later, observing the Hollywood cultists, he turns to the tortured mannerism of Magnasco. Tod's projected painting, "The Burning of Los Angeles," suggests a combination of Ensor's early twentieth-century apocalyptic symbolism, surrealist incongruities (as do the machined nature descriptions quoted above)—and perhaps rather too much disaster-epic illustration, Hollywood style, since popular culture usually shows an exploitative willingness to mask cheap sensationalism and emptiness as portentous apocalypse.

An obvious part of the machined-fantasy conception comes out in the prop versus reality studio scenes where the mechanisms, and false facades, of dreams are so evident. The studio backlot serves as a "dream dump" for discarded sets and props. It is compared to T. A. Janvier's [*In the*] *Sargasso Sea* (a novel [1898] drawing a mythic illustration of the mid-Atlantic doldrums which collect flotsam and jetsam—and in legend, the Flying Dutchman and the Ancient Mariner). The studio, then, is "a Sargasso of the imagination!" (The metaphor had been used earlier in Ezra Pound's satiric portrayal of a culture-vulture rich lady, "Portrait d'un Femme".) The Hollywood "dream dump" is where every fantasy will be exploited and washed up.

This includes the costuming of history as well. Returning (Chapter 18) to his opening studio scene of the filming of "The Battle of Waterloo," we get ironic play on defeat—for the historic Napoleon because of a collapsed cavalry charge at Mont St. Jean, for the movie production because of the collapsed (unfinished) wood-canvas-plaster set of Mont St. Jean. Real people get hurt in the collapse, though they express, depression style, pleasure at the likelihood of injury compensation. The traditional mock-heroic provides the method here: great event, shoddy mechanical imitation, practical human point.

But much of West's treatment develops from more direct realism than these highlighted allusions and metaphors would suggest. Simply presenting actual southern California scenes and types gives more than enough of the bizarre. Note, for example, a comic-gruesome set piece: Mrs. Loomis comes upon Tod and Homer while searching for her darling child, Adore, talks to Tod of California as a "paradise," of her faith in raw vegetables (following one "Dr. Pierce . . . 'Know-All Pierce-All' " in "the search for Health along the Road of Life"), and of her obsessional displaced ambitions to make her child a screen star (the widespread "Squirrely Temple" craze as it was sometimes called in the 1930s). Adore, an artificially manner little boy of eight, appears, "with a pale, peaked face and a large troubled forehead . . . staring eyes . . . eyebrows . . . plucked and shaped . . . dressed like a man." Already full of horrific psychological tics, he makes faces; his mother apologetically explains that he thinks he is the "Frankenstein monster"—and so he is! She forces her machine-fantasy monster-child to perform, "expertly" singing a semiobscene hyped-blues, "Mamma Doan Wan' No Peas," while imitatively writhing with "a top-heavy load of sexual pain." (Such grotesque role-playing, of course, continues and expresses an all-American ideal of the "loving" ambitious parent, as with those tens of thousands of petit bourgeois ones who drive their daughters to be competitive and posturing baton twirlers, cheerleaders, fashion models, and other mechanically tuned and costumed obscenities, and their sons to be jocks.) Not at all incidentally, Adore breaks through his imposed role with inevitable violence, later throwing a stone at the near-psychotic Homer, which starts the mass violence of the final riot scene in the novel. West several times stresses the point that the role-players, by the obvious psychological mechanisms of repression and release, turn nasty.

Not quite all the masqueraders come out as such inhuman "automatons." Almost sarcastically, West presents as the most naturally spontaneous and responsive a three-foot dwarf, "Honest Abe Kusich," racetrack tout, pugnacious friend of whores and Tod, earnest handler of the losing bird in the rigged cockfight, and crusher of Earl's testicles when monopolizing Faye's attentions at the following part. Indomitable midget, Abe masquerades as a big macho tough guy, and in a not altogether ironic sense really is. But West, with a natural taste for the grotesque (as Balso Snell in his first fiction had a taste for cripples), perhaps expands too much on the role-playing of the dwarf, of Harry Greener, and of other grotesqueries such as a satire of a performing transvestite (a man who badly imitates a man). The author performs rather too much as transfixed Eastern aesthete with the Southland decor. Some of this, of course, may be attributed to writing in the rather documentary form of the "Hollywood novel" and its emphasis on bizarre detail. Postsick and black humor, which it foreshadows, it may have lost some of its shock and comic effects. But perhaps more generally West's fiction can be taken as implying what was to happen: the machined fantasies represented by Hollywood in an earlier period were to invade the repressed American character. But the result was to be less the violent upheaval with which West concludes his story than the Hollywoodization of everything until an amorphous counterfeit culture provided a technocratic masquerade of a civilization.

Source: Kingsley Widner, "The Hollywood Masquerade: *The Day of the Locust*," in *Nathanael West*, Twayne Publishers, 1982, pp. 67–94.

Sources

Gehman, Richard B., "Introduction," in *The Day of the Locust*, Aeonian Press, 1976, pp. ix–xx.

Hoeveler, Diane Long, "In This Cosmic Pawnshop We Call Life: Nathanael West, Bergson, Capitalism and Schizophrenia," in *Studies in Short Fiction*, Vol. 33, No. 3, Summer 1996, pp. 411–12.

Hyman, Stanley Edgar, "Nathanael West," in *American Writers*, Vol. 4, Charles Scribner's Sons, 1974, pp. 285–307.

Nadel, I. B., "*The Day of the Locust*: Overview," in *Reference Guide to American Literature*, 3d ed., edited by Jim Kamp, St. James Press, 1994.

Reid, Randall, *The Fiction of Nathanael West: No Redeemer, No Promised Land*, University of Chicago Press, 1967.

Rovit, Earl, "West, Nathanael," in *Reference Guide to American Literature*, 3d ed., edited by Jim Kamp, St. James Press, 1994.

Simon, Richard Keller, "Between Capra and Adorno: West's *Day of the Locust* and the Movies of the 1930s," in *Modern Language Quarterly*, Vol. 54, No. 4, December 1993, pp. 513–24.

Valiunas, Algis, "Review of *Novels and Other Writings*," in *Commentary*, Vol. 104, No. 5, November 1997, pp. 64–66.

Further Reading

Bergman, Andrew, *We're in the Money: Depression America and Its Films*, Ivan R. Dee, 1992.

This books looks at how Hollywood films in the 1930s helped support various American institutions and myths, such as individual success and capitalism.

Perelman, S. J., *Acres and Pains*, Burford Books, 1999.

The humor writer S. J. Perelman was West's brother-in-law and financially supported West during some of his leaner years. In this book, originally published in 1947, the author pokes fun at himself and his attempts to adjust his city-boy ways to life in the country.

Sklar, Robert, *Movie-Made America: A Cultural History of American Movies*, Vintage Books, 1994.

When this book was originally published in 1975, critics hailed it as the ultimate source on the history of American films and how films have shaped American values. The author has revised and updated the content for this edition.

Terkel, Studs, *Hard Times: An Oral History of the Great Depression*, New Press, 2000.

Originally published in 1970, Studs Terkel's book chronicles the effect the Great Depression had on dozens of ordinary people (and a few famous ones), using their own words.

The End of the Affair

Graham Greene

1951

Graham Greene's novel *The End of the Affair* was first published in 1951 in England. The events of the novel concern an adulterous affair in England during World War II. With the war and the affair over, Maurice Bendrix seeks an explanation of why his lover, Sarah Miles, broke off their relationship so suddenly. Greene's contemporaries could relate to the setting of the story, as the war was fresh in their memories and they were living in the same postwar period as the characters. Within this setting, Greene explores themes of love and hate, faithfulness, and the presence of the divine in human lives. Critics have been generally positive in their reviews and analyses of the novel, and readers have embraced it for more than fifty years. One of Greene's early admirers was William Faulkner.

Critics consider *The End of the Affair* the last in Greene's Catholic tetralogy. In the first three books of the four, *Brighton Rock*, *The Power and the Glory*, and *The Heart of the Matter*, Greene depicts God as a source of grace in people's spiritual lives, but in *The End of the Affair*, Greene presents a more active, involved God who is a force in people's earthly lives (performing miracles through Sarah, for example). All four novels address the ideas of mortal sin and redemption. To many critics, *The End of the Affair* is the most obviously Catholic of Greene's novels, due in large part to the apparent sainthood of the heroine, whose death is followed by a series of miracles.

Author Biography

Graham Greene was born in Hertfordshire, England, on October 2, 1904, to Marion Greene (first cousin of the writer Robert Louis Stevenson) and Charles Henry Greene, a school headmaster. An introverted and sensitive child, Greene's had difficult early years because of his strict father and boarding school bullies. At sixteen, Greene suffered a breakdown and went to London for treatment by a student of Sigmund Freud.

While in London, Greene became an avid reader and writer. Before leaving, he met Ezra Pound and Gertrude Stein, who became lifelong literary mentors to him. His other influences were Henry James, Joseph Conrad, and Ford Madox Ford. After graduating from high school in 1922, Greene attended Oxford University's Balliol College, where he received a degree in history in 1925. While at college, Greene became interested in politics, especially Marxist socialism (but not communism). This interest sometimes created tension in Greene's friendship with the conservative writer Evelyn Waugh, although the two remained steady friends for many years.

In 1926, Greene converted to Catholicism for his fiancée, Vivien Dayrell Browning, whom he married the following year. The couple eventually had two children. Greene is generally considered a Catholic writer despite his insistence that the conversion was not his greatest literary influence.

During World War II, Greene did intelligence work for the British government in West Africa. His experiences at home and abroad inspired works like *The Heart of the Matter* (1948). In addition to his novels of intrigue, peopled with spies, criminals, and other colorful characters, Greene wrote short stories, essays, screenplays, autobiographies, and criticism. His literary reputation rests primarily on what are termed his Catholic novels, *Brighton Rock* (1938), *The Power and the Glory* (1940), *The Heart of the Matter* (1948), and *The End of the Affair* (1951); and his Cold War-era political novels, which include *The Quiet American* (1955) and *The Comedians* (1966). Greene is considered one of the most important English writers of the twentieth century, and his honors include consideration for a Nobel Prize. His works are popular with critics and readers, and they have been translated into twenty-seven languages and have sold more than twenty million copies.

Greene died of blood disease in Vevey, Switzerland, on April 3, 1991.

Graham Greene

Plot Summary

Books 1–2

As *The End of the Affair* opens, the narrator, Maurice Bendrix (called simply "Bendrix" by his friends) explains that he is a writer and thus is in control of the story he is about to tell. Although it is a true story, he determines how much of it he will tell—at what point he will begin his tale and at what point he will end it. He begins with the night he encounters Henry Miles, the husband of a woman with whom Bendrix had an affair in the recent past. Henry has no idea that Bendrix was once involved with his wife. The two men go to a bar to get out of the rain, and Henry reveals that he thinks Sarah (his wife) is seeing another man. Pretending to be a friend to Henry, Bendrix offers to secure a private investigator to find out the truth. In reality, Bendrix is jealous and wants to know for his own reasons if Sarah is seeing someone. Bendrix's affair with Sarah ended suddenly, and he is tormented by the breakup and longs to know why she ended the relationship. When Bendrix is talking to Henry, he mentions that a demon encourages him to be deceptive and false in pretending to be Henry's friend so that he can find out about Sarah. At various

Media Adaptations

- In 1955, *The End of the Affair* was adapted to film by Columbia Pictures. This production was directed by Edward Dmytryk and starred Deborah Kerr as Sarah, Peter Cushing as Henry, and Van Johnson as Maurice Bendrix.

- In 1999, Columbia Pictures again adapted the novel to film, this time directed by Neil Jordan and starring Julianne Moore as Sarah, Stephen Rea as Henry, and Ralph Fiennes as Maurice Bendrix. Moore received an Academy Award nomination and a Golden Globe award nomination for Best Actress, and the film was a Best Drama nominee for a Golden Globe award.

points throughout the novel, Bendrix mentions this demon, which represents his hate and selfishness.

Henry decides against hiring an investigator, but Bendrix does so anyway. A man named Mr. Parkis is assigned to the case. Parkis follows Sarah and reports back to Bendrix on what he sees, which is very little. When Henry finds out that Bendrix has hired a detective, he guesses that Bendrix's interest in Sarah means that they were once involved with each other. Bendrix admits this, and the two men talk calmly about it.

Parkis finds that Sarah has been visiting a man named Richard Smythe, so Bendrix creates a ruse in order to visit him. Smythe, a man with "livid spots" on the left side of his face, turns out to be a rationalist with an extensive library, and Sarah has been debating the existence and nature of God with him.

Books 3–5

Parkis takes Sarah's diary while posing as a party guest in the Miles's home, so Bendrix can finally know why she broke off their relationship. He reads Sarah's diary, reviewing entries about their relationship and her feelings for him. Then he finds the entry about their last day together. They had been in bed when bombs started to fall. Bendrix

went to see if the landlady had retreated to the bomb shelter. While he was looking, he was knocked unconscious. Seeing him in the hallway, Sarah thought he was dead or dying, so she went back to the bedroom and pleaded with God to let him live. She felt so strongly about this that she vowed she would give up her sinful ways, and Bendrix, if only he would live. When he walked in shortly thereafter, Sarah believed that her prayer had been answered. She broke off their relationship to keep her vow.

But Sarah's inner conflict did not end on the day of the air raid. She embarked on a spiritual journey of deep, painful struggle. She looked for ways to rationalize recommencing a relationship with Bendrix. She felt love and hate for God, but ultimately made peace with the situation. At the end of her struggle, she feels the power of God's love in her life, and she dedicates herself to Him. She reinterprets her relationship with Bendrix as a precursor to the deeper, purer love of God, and she asks God to give Bendrix the peace she now enjoys. From her pain comes faith in, and love for, God.

After reading Sarah's diary, Bendrix is convinced that she still loves him and that he can offer her real, tangible joy, not the kind of abstract happiness of spirituality. He calls her, but she says she does not want to see him. When he insists on seeing her, she leaves the house, running through the cold and sleet to evade him. She does not know that he is following her, but she keeps running. Finally she collapses, coughing and clutching her side. He rushes to her, and as he tells her of his plans to run away together, she insists that she does not want to go. He can see that she is exhausted and ill, so he tells her to go home and to call him when she feels better. Eight days later, Bendrix receives a call from Henry. Sarah has died of pneumonia.

Bendrix and Henry find themselves surprisingly close as they grieve the loss of Sarah. Although Sarah had expressed a desire to become Catholic, Henry and Bendrix decide against giving her a Catholic burial. In fact, when visited by a priest, Bendrix makes it clear that Sarah will be cremated, despite the Church's objections.

On the day of the funeral, Bendrix first meets with Waverly, a writer who is working on an article about him. After a brief exchange, Bendrix must leave for the funeral, and he takes Waverly's girlfriend with him. Bendrix does not like Waverly, and he feels powerful in taking his girl from him.

Realizing that he does not actually want the girl along, he says a prayer to Sarah to help him out of the situation. Sarah's mother arrives, and Bendrix has an excuse to ask the girl to leave. Over dinner, Sarah's mother explains to Bendrix that Sarah was actually Catholic all her life, having been baptized as such at the age of two.

A series of miracles is attributed to Sarah in the days following her death. First, Parkis's son is cured of appendicitis after being given a book that belonged to Sarah. The spots on Smythe's face clear spontaneously. At the end, Bendrix and Henry are walking arm in arm as Henry declares how much he looks forward to their walks. Bendrix agrees. Silently, he tells God that he is tired and old, and he implores God to leave him alone.

Characters

Maurice Bendrix

Maurice Bendrix is the story's narrator. He is an unreliable narrator and a selfish, immature, insensitive, and cynical man. He is a moderately successful writer who met Sarah Miles while doing background research on her husband for a novel he wanted to write. As a writer, he has a following, is somewhat well known, and makes a living at his craft, but he is unable to become truly great in the eyes of critics because his work is too polished. His control over his fiction mirrors the control he strives to have in his life. What he fails to understand, however, is that people in his life are not characters he can create and manipulate at will. He finds this lack of control frustrating and unfair.

Bendrix claims not to be impressed when he first meets Sarah. His physical imperfection—one leg is shorter than the other—prompts him to reject people before they can reject him. He almost always seeks to assert superiority over people because of his self-consciousness about his leg. Sarah's beauty overwhelms him when they meet, stirring his insecurities, so he conjures his superiority by trying to forget her. Eventually, they begin to see each other romantically, and his shaky self-esteem takes the form of jealousy. Emotionally, Bendrix is an extremist. He lacks the emotional maturity to feel anything moderately; he is either madly in love with Sarah or he hates her passionately. The only topic about life to which he is indifferent is religion.

Bendrix's arrogance is apparent throughout the novel. It is evident in his dealings with people, and it is also apparent in his assumption that because God is his rival for Sarah's affections, he can easily win her back. He believes that the tangible love he can offer will be more appealing than abstract promises of salvation or redemption.

Henry Miles

Henry is Sarah's hapless husband. Bendrix originally wanted to research Henry's life as a civil servant for a book he was writing, but the book was never finished. Henry is oblivious to his wife's affair until Bendrix has her investigated by a private detective. When Henry figures out that his wife and Bendrix were once involved with each other, his response is calm disappointment. Upon Sarah's death, Henry calls Bendrix and the two become unlikely friends. Henry is a pleasant, but introverted man who lacks the passions that color Bendrix.

Sarah Miles

Sarah is Henry's wife and Bendrix's lover. Her love relationship with Bendrix is complicated. She is hesitant to talk of their love when he asks, yet she sometimes surprises him by saying that she loves him deeply. While she seems to find in Bendrix what is missing in her marriage with Henry, she is not open about it.

Sarah is a person of pleasure and selfishness until she has a traumatic experience during which she vows to God that she will be virtuous if He will save Bendrix. While before this experience she thought little of how her affair might hurt her husband, her bargain with God forces her to look deep inside her morality. She emerges from her spiritual struggles a stronger, more loving and virtuous woman. Not only does she refuse Bendrix's advances after her vow, she also prays that he will be given the same spiritual peace she has found.

After attaining spiritual resolution, Sarah seeks to deepen her faith. She debates with a rationalist man about the existence and nature of God, and she tells a priest that she wants to become Catholic. Her personal growth is cut short, however, when she dies from pneumonia after fleeing into bad weather to escape Bendrix. After her death, a series of miracles are attributed to her, and she ascends to the level of saint in the eyes of those who knew her. Critics have commented that Sarah's life story reads like that of a saint's life; she abandons a life of mortal pleasures to devote herself to God, dies unjustly, and performs loving miracles on Earth.

Topics for Further Study

- People in frightening situations often bargain with God, promising to become better people in return for divine favor in the situation. Sarah makes this bargain and keeps her promise. Do you think that most people follow through as she did? Explain your answer.

- Greene mentions a stairway at various points throughout the story. What is the symbolic meaning of the stairway? How does it enhance the story, and do you think that Bendrix realizes that it is meaningful when he includes it in his telling of the story?

- During and after times of crisis, attendance at churches, synagogues, mosques, temples, and other places of worship tends to increase. Was this the case during and after World War II in England? Research the role of religion in wartime and post-war England and present your findings in an essay.

- Bendrix mentions that he and Sarah had "become unused" to air raids because of their infrequency compared to the recent past. What do you think it would be like to live in a time and place where bombing was frequent and might begin at any time? Pretend that you are Sarah and write a diary entry for a day (or night) in 1940 when an air raid took place.

- Sarah's mother, Mrs. Bertram, tells Bendrix that Sarah had a Catholic baptism as a child. What is the Catholic Church's position on baptism? What does this ritual mean to Catholics? What is the significance, in the story, of this information? Write a short script in which a priest explains these religious points to one of Sarah's friends who does not understand Catholic beliefs.

Lance Parkis

Mr. Parkis's son, Lance, accompanies Bendrix on his trip to the Smythe's house to try to discover the nature of Richard Smythe's relationship with Sarah. Because his father involves him in detective work, Lance is a suitable actor to pretend to be Bendrix's son. Lance is also the recipient of one of Sarah's miracles.

Lance is named after Sir Lancelot from Arthurian legend. Parkis named his son Lance because he mistakenly believed that Lancelot was the knight who found the Holy Grail.

Mr. Parkis

Mr. Parkis is hired by Bendrix to discover whether Sarah is having an affair. The investigation takes place after Sarah's relationship with Bendrix has ended. Parkis is congenial enough but inefficient. He involves his young son in his business, which creates comic moments in the novel.

Richard Smythe

Richard Smythe is an acquaintance of Sarah; she contacts him during her spiritual struggle. After her vow to give up her affair, she wants to rationalize a way to continue her relationship with Bendrix, so she contacts Richard. He is a rationalist (someone who believes only in what the intellect can perceive, not in tradition or authority) who has an impressive library and engages in spirited debates with her. His efforts to convince her that God does not exist, however, only serve to bolster her belief that He does.

Richard has "livid spots" on his left cheek, but they miraculously disappear after Sarah's death. Because this was something about which she felt compassion, he assumes that she is responsible for the miracle.

Themes

Love and Hate

The opposing themes of love and hate run throughout *The End of the Affair* as Greene sets them up to shed light on each other. Ultimately, he demonstrates that hate can be the surprising precursor to love. At the same time, he depicts the cruel realities often associated with love and hate. After all, Sarah chooses love (divine) and dies, but Bendrix chooses hate (earthly) and is still alive at the end of the novel. The choices these characters make represent the two kinds of love in the novel: divine love, which is selfless; and romantic love, which is selfish and can easily turn to hate.

Bendrix knows only romantic love, and he knows it only for Sarah. After she ends their relationship, he does not seek a new woman for his life. Instead, he alternates between love and hate for her. When they are involved, he loves her, but when she stops seeing him, he hates her. Then when he thinks he has a chance to win her back, he loves her again. When she dies, he claims to love her, but his actions tell a different story. His love is so confused by romantic selfishness that he ignores what he can infer about her burial wishes and insists that she be cremated, which according to Catholic faith, would be unpleasing to the God who took her from him.

Sarah, on the other hand, sacrifices romantic love for divine love. Although she began the affair in pursuit of romantic love, even at the cost of her morality, she is surprised to find herself giving it up to fulfill a desperate promise made to God.

Sacrificing the affair leads Sarah to the other kind of love presented in the novel, divine love. After an intense spiritual struggle to truly give up her romance with Bendrix, she finds herself at peace because she has accepted the love of God. She finds that this love renews her, whereas her love for Bendrix was sinful and unhealthy. In fact, she concludes that her love for Bendrix was merely a stop on the way to the divine love that awaited her. In her diary, she writes:

> Did I ever love Maurice as much before I loved you? Or was it You I really loved all the time? . . . For he hated in me the things You hate. He was on Your side all the time without knowing it. You willed our separation, but he willed it too. He worked for it with his anger and his jealousy, and he worked for it with his love. For he gave so much love and I gave him so much love that soon there wasn't anything left, when we'd finished, but You.

The Divine

Whether or not they are aware of it, the divine plays a role in the characters' lives. Sarah prays to God in a panicked moment, pleading for Bendrix's life and promising to abandon her immoral ways in return. When Bendrix walks into the room, she is convinced that her prayer has saved him and she makes good on her promise. For Sarah, this incident is unquestionably a moment of divine intervention. The spiritual struggle that follows is also an example of the divine shaping her life. She realizes that she cannot attain spiritual peace alone, and she submits to the will of God and feels the change in her life.

After Sarah's death a series of miracles occurs, seemingly because of her status in heaven. In the Catholic tradition, a person is not canonized (declared a saint by the Catholic Church) unless a miracle is attributed to him or her. This implies that Sarah is a saint or is eligible for such divine status. Her ability to perform miracles after her death represents her divine influence in the lives of the people she once knew.

The presence of Bendrix's demon also alludes to the divine world. As a devout Catholic, Greene is likely familiar with the position of St. Augustine, a first-century bishop and theologian whose teachings are regarded as among the most important in Catholic theology. Augustine taught that evil is present in the mere absence of God. This is relevant to Greene's novel because Bendrix makes repeated references to his demon, which seems to appear and talk him into doing and saying things that are hateful. According to Augustine, the intervention of this evil presence would be evidence of Bendrix's separation from God.

Style

First-Person Narrator

Bendrix narrates in first-person for most of the story, acknowledging that he alone holds the power to tell the story and that he will control its presentation. At the beginning of the book, he explains that he is shaping what is purported to be a true story. However, interpreting situations according to his personal feelings and cynicism renders Bendrix an unreliable narrator. He allows his negative feelings to color his telling of the story at almost every turn.

As the story unfolds, then, the reader may sense that Bendrix is working out his feelings and processing his experience. This suggests that Bendrix only thinks he is controlling the plot, when in fact his emotional response to the events of the book evolves from hatred to understanding as he reflects on the details. The best example of Bendrix's progression is his assertion that the book is a record of hate, a claim he makes at the beginning of the book. His perspective changes, however, as he gets deeper into the story. For example, in book two, chapter two, he admits, "When I began to write I said this was a story of hatred, but I am not convinced. Perhaps my hatred is really as deficient as my love." Later in book four, chapter one, he writes:

> When I began to write our story down, I thought I was writing a record of hate, but somehow the hate

has got mislaid and all I know is that in spite of her mistakes and her unreliability, she was better than most." By the end, he is hopeless, filled with resignation rather than hate.

Once it is clear that Bendrix is less reliable than he thinks he is, the reader is able to begin drawing independent conclusions. The reader questions Bendrix's version of events in the story. Furthermore, Greene provides other narrative forms within Bendrix's first-person account. This enables the reader to better understand the themes and conflicts of the novel, of which Bendrix is only part. These techniques include flashback, letters, Sarah's diary, and dreams to help the reader see beyond Bendrix's perspective.

Sarah's diary is an important part of the narration because it forms a first-person narrative within the first-person narrative. Presumably, Bendrix is deciding which passages he will reveal to the reader, but Sarah's voice and her side of the story still come through. Her struggle, her pain, and her honesty assure the reader that she is a reliable narrator. Because it is a diary that was intended to be private, it contains truthful versions of Sarah's thoughts and experiences. Having no close friends and unable to confide in either her husband or her lover, Sarah turned to her diary to express and explore her feelings.

Time Shifts

Greene uses time shifts to put his story in a broader chronological context and to offer the reader background information and Sarah's point of view. The novel itself is a time shift, as the narrator is telling the story of events that happened in his past. Within the story, the narrator also uses flashbacks to tell the reader about his romance with Sarah and his emotional reaction to their breakup. In addition, Sarah's diary and her letter to Bendrix are time shift devices that allow the reader to understand the inner experience of a character who has died by the time Bendrix is telling his story. Without Sarah's writings, the reader would never know about her deep personal struggles and her profound sense of peace.

Historical Context

Modernist Period in English Literature

The modernist period in English literature began in 1914 with the onset of World War I and extended through 1965. It is a literary period that reflects the nation's wartime experiences (World War I and World War II), the emerging British talent of the 1920s, and the economic depression of the 1930s. Toward the end of the period, literature and art demonstrated the nation's growing uncertainty, which became especially pronounced after World War II; this uncertainty would give way to hostility and protest in the postmodernist period.

During the early years of the modernist period, the foremost writers were English novelists E. M. Forster, Joseph Conrad, Ford Madox Ford, Virginia Woolf, and Somerset Maugham. One of the major accomplishments of this period came from Ireland with the publication of James Joyce's *Ulysses*, a work that continues to be respected as a masterpiece of twentieth-century literature. In the 1920s and 1930s, the novels of D. H. Lawrence and Evelyn Waugh were harshly critical of modern society, an attitude shared by many English men and women of the day. In the 1930s and 1940s, novelists such as Greene wrote traditional fiction that was well-crafted enough both to stand up to innovative fiction of the day and to gain a wide and loyal audience.

Many writers of this period (Greene included) were born at the turn of the century, near the end of the Victorian era. These writers were reared in an environment of romanticism, which often meant leading a relatively sheltered childhood that left them ill-prepared for the realities of adult life. This background, combined with events of the first half of the twentieth century, led writers such as Greene to question the values of their past and to reevaluate the world in which they lived as adults. This is seen in Greene's fiction as he explores morality and creates characters who possess the capacity for both virtue and vice.

The Battle of Britain

By the summer of 1940, German Chancellor Adolph Hitler had conquered most of Europe. Britain, however, refused to yield. Under the new leadership of Prime Minister Winston Churchill, Britain was determined to fight Germany, despite heavy losses of artillery and the unwillingness of Russia to get involved. After Germany took France, the United States, not yet involved in the war, began fortifying its military personnel and budget. In June, Germany initiated submarine warfare to prevent goods from going into or out of Britain. Hitler planned to invade Britain but would not do so until the British air force had been substantially weakened. In August 1940, the Battle of Britain began, with Germany hoping to decimate the British mil-

Compare
&
Contrast

- **1940s:** The Catholic Church still forbids cremation as a means of disposing of a dead body. Catholics are buried in the ground or in tombs. This is a tradition from the days of the early Christians.

  Today: As of 1963, Catholics are permitted to choose cremation as an alternative to traditional means of burial. The Church still encourages keeping the body intact, and, if the body is to be cremated, the Church prefers that it be done after the funeral liturgy so that the body may be present for the ceremony. Still, Catholics are not forbidden to be cremated or to have the cremated remains present at the ceremony.

- **1940s:** Penicillin has recently been made widely available and is used to treat a wide variety of illnesses, including pneumonia. Because pneumonia is a major health concern, doctors are relieved to be able to reduce the number of mortalities by administering the antibiotic.

  Today: Antibiotics such as penicillin are still used to treat pneumonia. More people are aware of its benefits and tend to see the doctor sooner when they are seriously ill. Pneumonia continues to be a major health concern for people in England; it is the fifth leading cause of death in the United Kingdom.

- **1940s:** Air raids in the early and mid-1940s, along with the general threat posed by World War II, lead to heightened security in England. England experiences what it is like to be attacked on its own soil, and the escalation and immediacy of the war are frightening.

  Today: In September 2001, the United States is attacked by terrorists who hijack passenger airplanes and use them as giant bombs to destroy the World Trade Center towers and to attack the Pentagon. England is among the first nations to rally to the Americans' cause against terrorism. This public declaration of support, along with the international nature of the terrorist threat, leads to heightened security at England's airports.

---

itary and British resistance to keep control of their land. The Germans began with daytime air raids of ports, radar stations, and airfields, moving to inland cities in late August. The first targets of inland raids were Royal Air Force installations and aircraft manufacturers. Germany had hoped to draw out the English military and destroy it, but the combination of radar technology and the ability of the English to see German planes in the daylight compromised their objectives. Germany's failures with daytime raids led them to begin nighttime raids on September 7. Such nighttime raids were very intensive, involving massive attacks from as much of the military resources that Germay could thrust at England. This type of concentrated, suprise offensive aimed at overwhelming the enemy with one big blow is known as a *blitzkrieg*.

The British fought hard and used new radar technology to strengthen their position. By the end of October, the German bombing of England diminished and eventually ended. The German military lost twenty-three hundred aircraft in the Battle of Britain; the British military lost nine hundred. The loss of this battle was the first important German loss in World War II. In the years following the Battle of Britain, the frequency of nighttime air raids on England was erratic. It was one of the later raids that occurred when Bendrix and Sarah were together and she thought he had been killed. The infrequency of the raids compared to the recent past is evident in Bendrix's comment: "We had become unused to air raids."

Critical Overview

Critical response to *The End of the Affair* has been overwhelmingly positive. Critics praise Greene's

Julianne Moore as Sarah Miles and Ralph Fiennes as Maurice Bendrix in the 1999 film version of the novel

complex thematic presentation, astute characterization, and complex narrative style. In a review that was printed the year the novel was published, George Mayberry of *New York Times* describes the novel as "savage and sad, vulgar and ideal, coarse and refined, and a rather accurate image of an era of cunning and glory, of cowardice and heroism, of belief and unbelief." Bruce Bawer in *The New Criterion* comments that the novel is

> exquisitely shaped and paced, the people and their relationships seem real, and both the passion and the bitterness ring true; though plenty of abstractions are brought into play, one does not constantly have the feeling that the characters serve merely as symbolic tokens.

Many critics comment on the novel's strong religious theme. Richard Hauer Costa in *Dictionary of Literary Biography*, Volume 15: *British Novelists, 1930–1959* asserts that the theological elements in the novel are intimately connected to the characters' human emotions. He writes that Green "can write a powerful love story on two levels—the earthbound and the divine—while making each level reinforce the other." Critics such as Costa and Bernard Bergonzi of *British Writers* observe that God is such a central player in the novel's action

that He essentially becomes a character. Costa explains, "The journal entries of Sarah Miles in *The End of the Affair* show her infidelity with Bendrix pitted against God's will in such a way as to make God an actual character."

Critics frequently remark on the strong Catholic nature of the novel. A. A. DeVitis in *Twayne's English Authors Series Online*, for example, finds it to be the most Catholic of Greene's books, "in the narrowest sense of the definition." The critic points to the saintly status of Sarah as evidence and the sensitive characterization of the priest as more than just a spokesman for the Church. Bergonzi also observes that the novel has a strong Catholic disposition, "disconcertingly so for some humanist readers, just as the emphasis on sex disturbs some of Greene's devout Catholic readers."

Besides the substance of the book, critics are also impressed with the style of the storytelling. Mayberry observes that because the main character and narrator is a writer, like Greene, the novel reflects a "command of language," adding, "His cocktail party chit-chat, his fumbling man-to-man conversations, his not-to-be-overheard mutterings between lovers are concrete and probably universal." DeVitis is particularly impressed with Greene's stylistic presentation of the story, making special mention of the dream sequences, debates, and time shifts, all of which give the reader unique and important insights into the characters' inner lives and struggles. DeVitis also praises the way Greene places characters in context with one another:

> Greene's use of the diary and of the journal allows him not only to characterize his people but also to portray the various levels of meaning of the spiritual drama enacted. Bendrix looks at Sarah; Sarah looks at herself as she looks at God. The Bystanders look at Sarah, and she leaves her mark on them.

Although critics deem the book a great accomplishment, they also note its shortcomings. In an analysis of the two main characters, DeVitis concludes, "One of the flaws of the novel is quite simply the fact, sexual matters excluded, that it is difficult to understand why Sarah loves [Bendrix]." Bawer, who praises some aspects of the book, finds the depiction of religion to be lacking. He writes that "Greene's fixation on suffering seems masochistic, morbid; certainly the notion that religion should be nothing but suffering is as distasteful as the notion that it should be nothing but sweetness and light." Orville Prescott comments in *In My Opinion: An Inquiry into the Contemporary Novel* that in *The End of the Affair*:

> Mr. Greene displays his usual distinctive flair for words and atmosphere. His precise, carved sentences fit together like stone blocks which require no mortar. But his author's hands jerking his puppet strings are always noticeable. He is not content to demonstrate his thesis with one religious conversion. He adds two more, both of them even more unlikely. He even makes use of several near miracles. It is too much. *The End of the Affair* is not only unconvincing; it is dull.

In *Graham Greene*, author Francis Wyndham finds substantial fault with the narrative style that so many other critics praise. Wyndham asserts that the first-person narration creates too narrow a view, preventing the reader from truly gaining a perspective on the story. He adds that the time sequences are hard to follow and, in a comment similar to that of Prescott's, that the miracles are neither believable nor necessary. In short, he concludes that "the book must be regarded as a stumble in Greene's progress."

Despite the faults found by a few critics, most scholars maintain that *The End of the Affair* is an important book in Greene's overall career. J. C. Hilson of *Reference Guide to English Literature* asserts that "Bendrix, the unsympathetic novelist-narrator,

is the precursor of the antiheroes of the later Greene." According to Costa, the novel's other main character, Sarah, also represents a turning point in Greene's fiction. He explains, "Until this book, the conversions of the good-bad characters in Greene have always been either tentative or ambiguous or both. Sarah Miles finds true reconciliation."

Criticism

Jennifer Bussey

Bussey holds a master's degree in interdisciplinary studies and a bachelor's degree in English Literature. She is an independent writer specializing in literature. In the following essay, Bussey maintains that Bendrix, the unsympathetic narrator of Greene's novel, is unlikely to reach the spiritual peace that his ex-lover, Sarah, attained before her death.

At the end of Greene's *The End of the Affair*, the narrator, Bendrix, seems unaffected by the profound spiritual transformation of Sarah, the woman he claims to love. Although he has read her diary and a moving letter she left for him before she died from pneumonia, he feels none of the spiritual urgency that she felt. Bendrix is a hateful man, and his hate overtly extends to God. Many critics contend that because love and hate are so close together (both are the product of passionate beliefs and indicate caring deeply one way or the other about something personal), Bendrix is well on his way to experiencing the same spiritual transformation that Sarah experienced. Because of the fundamental differences between the two characters and Bendrix's last-minute shift to apathy, however, it is highly unlikely that he will ever change. Instead, he will probably continue to live as a bitter man, feeling wronged by the world and by the God who created it, sinking deeper into his cynicism.

Bendrix introduces his story by claiming that it is a record of hate. He returns to this claim throughout the book, usually to alter it. His stance softens as he relives his relationship with Sarah and the heartbreaks that followed their break-up and her death. He is determined to believe that he is writing the book out of a sense of hatred, and he is equally determined to convince the reader of that. His revisions to his original claim point to the fact that the hate he feels at the beginning of the book is toward Sarah. This is apparent because as his stance softens, it is always in reference to her.

> There could hardly be a more dramatic series of events so close to his heart, so it seems he has lost his only chance to find peace within himself and know the love of God as Sarah did."

In book 2, he claims that his hatred was perhaps as deficient as his love. Sarah is the only person he has ever loved, so he is obviously referring to his feelings for her. In book 4, he is more straightforward, admitting that his hate has been "mislaid" now that he realizes that "in spite of her mistakes and her unreliability, she was better than most." As he processes the experiences related in the book, he matures somewhat. He comes to understand that it was not Sarah that he hated, but his own inability to control a situation in which he was emotionally vulnerable. Once Sarah broke off the relationship with Bendrix, he grasped for any way to exert control, and hating her was his solution.

Bendrix's hatred of Sarah is important to understanding why he is unlikely to experience spiritual redemption because it shows how out-of-touch with his feelings he is and how little he actually knows himself. Many critics believe that Sarah is a role model who foreshadows what lies ahead in Bendrix's future when, in fact, the two characters are almost opposites. While Sarah has the capacity for selflessness, Bendrix is completely absorbed in his own feelings and desires. She loved Bendrix in an ultimately selfless way. Faced with the possibility that he might die, she makes a bargain with God. She promises to live a life of virtue, which means giving up her lover, if only he will live. She does this without thinking about it, without weighing her options, and without thinking of how painful it will be to lose him, but she does it with absolute certainty.

In contrast, Bendrix always thinks of his own feelings first. Perhaps the best illustration of this is that he has the opportunity to return the favor and try to save Sarah from dying, but he does not. He leaves her shivering and alone in the sleet, telling her to go home and call him when she is ready to run away with him. He is blind to her predicament because he believes—despite her objections—that they will be together again. Rather than try to help her and make sure she is going to be well, he happily returns to his home and awaits her call; he waits for her to fulfill his desires without any concern for her welfare or desires. When his phone finally does ring, it is news that she is dead.

Because of Bendrix's selfishness, he will never sacrifice his own happiness for the well-being of someone else, which is what Sarah did and what led her to spiritual redemption. He claims repeatedly that Sarah was the love of his life, adding that he will never again be able to be with a woman that he does not love. After she breaks off the relationship, he fixates on her, just as he did with his jealousy when they were together. If the intensity of this relationship was inadequate to conquer his selfishness and help him see that there is a spiritual aspect to true love, nothing ever will. There could hardly be a more dramatic series of events so close to his heart, so it seems he has lost his only chance to find peace within himself and know the love of God as Sarah did. Bendrix, unlike Sarah, is unwilling to suffer in the name of a higher aim. When he suffers, he does not look for the lesson in it but perceives himself as a victim of unjust circumstances.

There is a theological element in Bendrix's life in the figure of the demon that he claims whispers to him. It tells him cruel things to do and say, and Bendrix recognizes this demon as hate. His attitude toward this demon is cavalier, and he seems resigned to listen to it for the rest of his life. He does not love or hate the demon, so he is unlikely to either challenge or embrace it. Most likely, he realizes that he is the demon's creator. After all, Bendrix is a man who insists on being in control, which is not the sort of man who would be obedient to any voice that was not his own. He fails to recognize that he has an emerging spirituality, and it leans distinctly toward evil, not good. His casual attitude about it, however, makes it improbable that he will realize this about himself.

The three most revealing things about the future of Bendrix's spirituality come at the very end of the novel. This is where the reader would expect to find a glimmer of hope or some reason, however subtle, to believe that Bendrix is on his way to salvation. Instead, his spiritual doom is made clear. First, Bendrix is meeting his new best friend, Henry. In a sense, Henry will replace Sarah in his life. Henry and Bendrix have become friends through being in love with the same woman; neither has any spiritual leanings, and there is no reason to believe that either of them will feel compelled to pursue God. The second cue Greene provides at the end is Bendrix's comment, "I thought, in the morning I'll ring up a doctor and ask him whether a faith cure is possible. And then I thought, better not; so long as one doesn't *know*, one can imagine innumerable cures."

These statements represent Bendrix's conclusion that faith does not cure anything at all, but if he is never told that, he can always return to it as a last-resort explanation of phenomena like the miracles that seem to occur through Sarah. Bendrix is moving from hate to apathy toward God at this moment. He has just thought to himself that if Sarah could have her way—he would believe that God exists. But he rejects the idea that he will ever love God or ask Him for anything. Wondering whether faith cures are possible, he does not ask God or himself but instead considers asking a doctor for a scientific opinion. When he then makes the statement that he can imagine innumerable cures by believing in God, he makes room for the possibility that God can make things happen in people's lives. He just does not want God to make anything happen in his life.

This sets up the third indication of Bendrix's spiritual future in the last lines of the book, in which Bendrix thinks to himself, "I found the one prayer that seemed to serve the winter mood: O God, You've done enough, You've robbed me of enough, I'm too tired and too old to learn to love, leave me alone forever." Here, he makes a final decision that God exists, but that He offers nothing but pain. Bendrix gives up on finding love of any kind and wants to be left alone. This statement to God, along with his situation at the end of the novel and his lack of response to both his own evil nature and the example of Sarah's goodness, all ensure that Bendrix is not headed toward spiritual growth or transformation.

Source: Jennifer Bussey, Critical Essay on *The End of the Affair*, in *Novels for Students*, The Gale Group, 2003.

Laura Kryhoski

Kryhoski is currently working as a freelance writer. She has also taught English literature in addition to English as a Second Language overseas. In this essay, Kryhoski considers love as a religious experience in Greene's work.

What Do I Read Next?

- Greene acknowledged that he admired Ford Madox Ford's *The Good Soldier: A Tale of Passion* (1915) and read it repeatedly. Critics often comment on the influence of this novel on *The End of the Affair*. Considered by many to be Ford's masterpiece, it is the story of how indiscretions and lust destroy two couples who often vacation together.

- *The Power and the Glory* (1940) is among the four novels included in Greene's Catholic tetralogy. In this novel, one Mexican state has outlawed the Church and executed all priests save one, the whisky priest, who must run for his life. The priest is a divided man, torn between his own sinfulness and his compulsion to put himself in danger by doing the work of the Church.

- Francis Joseph Sheed's *Theology for Beginners* (1982) is an easy-to-understand introduction to Catholic doctrine. Insightful for Catholics and non-Catholics alike, this book explains the meanings and traditions behind Catholic beliefs and practices.

- Edited by Philip Stratford, *The Portable Graham Greene* (1994) is a valuable resource for new readers and long-standing admirers of Greene's work. It includes two complete novels, excerpts from ten other novels, short stories, essays, travel writing selections, and memoir excerpts, in addition to a thorough introduction and bibliography.

In Graham Greene's *The End of the Affair*, a lock of hair has the power to suddenly erase both physical and emotional scarring for a lifetime. The power of the lock is merely an expression of a higher love and its power to endure without end, a love akin to religious experience. Using religious iconography or symbolic references, Greene is able to convey the persistent, emotive power of love as one not only rivaling religious experience, but posing serious moral and emotional challenges.

> " Bendrix's love offering
> compels Sarah to seek refuge in
> the church but ultimately sends
> her to an untimely death."

Bendrix is the voice of the novel and the protagonist of the work. He talks of his relationship with Sarah at the beginning of the novel as being one affected by intense hatred, stating "I hated Henry—I hated his wife Sarah, too." Soon after this statement the reader discovers that Sarah is in fact a former lover of Bendrix's. As a result, Bendrix's hatred takes on a deeper connotation when he adds that "nothing would have delighted me more than to have heard that she was sick, unhappy, dying," imagining that "any suffering she [Sarah] underwent would lighten mine." The relationship is described with bitterness, like the lament for a relationship that once seemed to mean "complete love" for "hours at a time." The spirit of the first half of the novel is tainted with Bendrix's loathing or expressed hatred for his former lover, Sarah. These sentiments run deeply within his soul, so deeply that they are often times expressed as if they were bodily functions gone wrong. In one instance, Bendrix describes the nature of love and hate on a glandular level, stating that "hatred alone seems to operate the same as the glands of love: it even produces the same actions." He reacts to the emotive power of the situation as though such feelings are secreted from his body, a natural process he seemingly cannot control or begin to understand.

Bendrix's response to his lover dramatically shifts in the second part of the story, and it is a dramatic shift that mimics the course of troubled love in life. The author also uses these narrative techniques to successfully illustrate the somewhat irrational nature of the character, rendering the narrator unreliable but also vulnerable to his own human failings. At the outset of the novel, he is spurned, abandoned, burned by his lover's rejection, filled with hatred for both her and the affair. A simple contact between Henry and Bendrix ignites his obsession with Sarah again, compelling him to become a voyeur or intruder into the personal life of his ex-lover Sarah.

This dynamic emotional pattern exhibited by the narrator, moodily swinging back and forth from intense hatred to overwhelming admiration, on some level mirrors the conflicts also inherent in a relationship with a higher being whom one cannot touch, feel, see, or comprehend. Bendrix is only able to spiritually connect to Sarah with the aid of the journal, but even this medium for contact has been ill-gotten.

Furthermore, a perception of distance contributes to the overall assertions of the narrator, who at the start feels an unsettling sense of disconnection from the woman he loves. The following quote illustrates Bendrix's uneasiness: "I have always found it hard to feel sexual desire without some sense of superiority, mental or physical." He is instead amazed by the idea that "All I noticed about her that first time was her beauty and her happiness and her way of touching people with her hands, as though she loved them." Bendrix's feelings for Sarah are unfamiliar to him; they fall outside of the realm of sexual attraction. He is instead drawn to her in an intensely spiritual way. The interaction is not only foreign to him, but for Bendrix constitutes a very mystical experience.

At the core of Bendrix's attachment to Sarah lies an equation of feeling to that of religious experience. In fact, many of the spurned or neglected lover's assessments of the affair between hims and his former paramour or lover are related by way of sacred comparison. Assigning value to the relationship, for example, Bendrix poses that one's interpretation of the Passion is essential to understanding "from their actions alone whether it was jealous Judas or cowardly Peter who loved Christ?" The Biblical story of the Passion revolves around the betrayal of Jesus, and by extension, of God, by both Peter and Judas. Despite Peter's insistence that Jesus adopt his role as religious teacher, when Jesus is captured, Peter denies him three times. Judas Iscariot has been often characterized as being the "devil" among the apostles, identifying Jesus for the authorities by kissing him.

The use of Biblical allusion serves to emphasize the very nature of Bendrix's relations with Sarah by comparison. True to the text, Bendrix admits that he would open his heart to Sarah in one moment as easily and readily as he would refute or deny her in the next. Self-expression for Bendrix, in this instance, has created a soup of mixed emotion. Together the power to love and to hate form an interesting dichotomy or division of feeling into two opposing parts, perplexing emotions Bendrix claims he is prone to feel separately or in tandem (together) at any given time.

Greene's book is a story of human frailty, of human failings. It is a modern-day parable based on the perhaps most ancient and revered of all, the Biblical parables of the New Testament, stories which form the basis for the life and times of Jesus. Greene, in this sense, successfully conveys the human failings of Bendrix and others, connecting them to the demise of the Christ-like figure of Sarah. Early on in the work, the reader discovers Sarah's divine nature has driven her away from her lover. Claiming that "love doesn't end," Sarah explains away the abruptness of her departure, by attempting to minimize her choice to break up with Bendrix, explaining that her feelings for her lover are analogous to the love she harbors for God. She explains her sudden decision, stating, "People go on loving God, don't they, all their lives without seeing Him?"

When Bendrix reads her journal, Sarah is revealed to be a pious or devoted Christian. Her sacrifice, one of true happiness, is made real in her dialogues with "You," or God, rather, for whom she at times grudgingly suffers. At other times, the suffering expressed in Sarah's journal culminates in or becomes the highest expression of love. The reader discovers Sarah's relationship with God when Bendrix introduces the contents of the journal, selecting a passage in which Sarah characterizes her sacred moments with Maurice (Bendrix) in the context of her faith:

> You were there, teaching us to squander, like you taught the rich man, so that one day we might have nothing left except in this love of You. But You are too good to me. When I ask You for pain, You give me peace. Give it to him too. Give him my peace—he needs it more.

The "You" in the passage signifies a more personal relationship with God, in which Sarah has put her trust, faith, and appreciation, by willingly ending her relations with Bendrix. Sarah's conviction that her choice to step back from the union between her and her lover is a spiritual one; however, Bendrix discovers, in the end, that such a choice has become one of great personal sacrifice. The last entry he shares with the reader in his ongoing narration of the events surrounding the affair includes the following statement from Sarah: "I'm tired and I don't want any more pain. I want Maurice [Bendrix]. I want ordinary corrupt human love."

This portion of the entry has appeared before, and it is the first entry in its entirety to be revealed in the sequence of entries that follows it. The reappearance of the phrase "ordinary corrupt human love," works on several levels. First and foremost, it affirms the idea that Sarah has made her decision to sever relations with Bendrix based on a sense of moral responsibility to God. Second, it emphasizes that while Sarah has chosen to responsibly live her life according to the standards of her religion and her God, by denying her humanness, she has painfully sacrificed herself.

Christ indeed has been described as a man of two natures, both divine and human. In the New Testament, He is characterized not only as genuinely human, but the reality of His personal sacrifice serves to raise Him to divine heights. Sarah is described in terms of both natures, and by implication, she becomes a mythical, Christ-like figure by the end of the text. Bendrix, despite his shortcomings, also realizes this in Sarah, responding to her pleas for "corrupt human love" with a sense of pain and frustration all his own. He recognizes that he has failed Sarah, that for him divine love is not possible, that "corrupt human love" is "all I can give you. . . . I don't know about any other kind of love." Bendrix's love offering compels Sarah to seek refuge in the church but ultimately sends her to an untimely death.

In Greene's novel, Sarah clearly sacrifices her life for the sake of Bendrix's peace of mind. The idea of sacrifice and the religious and moral implications behind the nature of such a sacrifice also surface in Greene's novel *The Power and the Glory*. The martyr of the work is an alcoholic priest who gives his own life by execution in order to save career criminal James Calver. According to David Lyle Jeffrey, in the *Dictionary of Biblical Tradition in English Literature*, the novel draws some Biblical parallels similar to that of *The End of the Affair*. He states that in *The Power and the Glory*, "Peter's denial of Jesus is symbolized by Padre José, who refuses to hear the whiskey priest's confession, and Judas, is represented by the mestizo, who in effect causes the hero's arrest."

Graham Greene's *The End of the Affair* is an exploration of love and the social ramifications of acting upon love born of an illicit affair. Greene uses the Christ-like Sarah to illustrate what happens when love, formed out of the best intentions, but straining ethical social limits, has the power to destroy those most insistent on its expression. For Sarah, love is physically fatal, for Bendrix, it becomes "a record of hate."

Source: Laura Kryhoski, Critical Essay on *The End of the Affair*, in *Novels for Students*, The Gale Group, 2003.

An area of London damaged by a German air raid during the London Blitz of World War II

Ronald G. Walker

In the following excerpt, Walker examines the structure of Greene's novel.

What are the thematic implications of such a variegated structure? I cannot hope to expatiate on all of them here, but there is one at least worth pursuing in some detail. Simply stated, it is the idea that reality is malleable not fixed and that what shapes it, continuously, is the sensibility of the human observer, itself always in flux and subject to influence from every quarter. Such a view is of course by no means original with Graham Greene. Writers from Plato on have expressed similar misgivings about the narrowness of the finite epistemologies of their day. But the familiarity of the idea makes it no less unsettling. The various reactions against it have been motivated, at bottom, by the need for ontological security. In self-defense, so to speak, man is forever fabricating alternative explanations which envision reality as fixed and finite and, therefore, more amenable to rational comprehension. But though (to paraphrase another line from Wallace Stevens) reality may in effect consist of the propositions made about it, the danger

is that in time these explanatory fictions may become reified and be taken literally as prescriptive guides to life.

This danger is amply represented in Greene's novel by characters who live according to rigid codes which reduce the multifarious complexities of human experience to a set of formulas and the fertile mystery of God to a "perfect equation, as clear as air". Thus for the effete literary critic Waterbury, life imitates art; art is a commodity that exists to be "ranked" by the cognoscenti; and artists are commodities to be "placed" according to which "school" they belong. For Parkis the detective, the aim of an investigation is to render "the exact truth," no less, and this can be accomplished by simply recovering scraps from certain wastepaper baskets, procuring appointment books and diaries from "the party" under surveillance, and bribing servants to divulge incriminating evidence about their employers. For Father Crompton, belief in God is a matter of receiving the sacraments of the Church or, failing that, at least what he calls "the baptism of desire." This doctrine is "produced [by] a formula," Bendrix notes. For Richard Smythe the rationalist pedagogue, not only religion but love can be defined in purely functional terms. Love is viewed clinically as the "desire to possess in some, like avarice; in others the desire to surrender, to lose the sense of responsibility, the wish to be admired. Sometimes just the wish to be able to talk, to unburden yourself to someone who won't be bored. The desire to find again a father or a mother. And of course under it all the biological motive."

As for Bendrix, though by both temperament and training he is responsive to the urgings of his own imagination, there are moments when he seems the most formula-bound character of the lot. When his creative "passion" flags, he resorts to the most mechanical sort of craftsmanship, turning out a novel every year by writing in daily five-hundred-word quotas. Similarly, when his romantic passion for Sarah turns to jealousy and pettiness, he helplessly capitulates to the reduction of love into a love affair, with a finite beginning and end. From this reductive point of view, he can even contemplate the resumption of the affair after its end in functional terms, comparable to Smythe's "biological motive": "If two people loved, they slept together; it was a mathematical formula, tested and proved by human experience." Where Bendrix turns, in periods of depression and doubt, to a defensive rationalism, Sarah records in her journal an alternative outlook tempered by the agony of her spiritual transformation:

> It's strange how the human mind swings back and forth, from one extreme to another. Does truth lie at some point of the pendulum's swing, at a point where it never rests—not in the dull perpendicular mean, where it dangles in the end like a windless flag, but at an angle, nearer one extreme than another? If only a miracle could stop the pendulum at an angle of sixty degrees, one would believe the truth was there.

Such quasi-mystical sentiments could scarcely be at further remove from the Bendrix of the quota for writing and the formula for loving, the Bendrix who places his trust in facts and who would reduce God to "a perfect equation."

But there is, fortunately, another side of Bendrix. His formulaic approach to writing and loving at any rate is more than balanced by other statements (and some of these are made very early on) indicating that, at his best and most characteristic, he values their complexity and in fact views them in something like mystical terms. Significantly, it is only his attitude toward God and religious belief that he—persists—up until the very end of the hunt—in his desperately narrow rationalism. As the evidence of Sarah's miraculous influence proliferates in the weeks after her death, he clings to what he calls, in an appropriately paradoxical phrase, his "faith in coincidence."

The end of this "faith" proves the beginning of another. In very general terms we may say that Greene's strategy, both narrative and rhetorical, is essentially designed to expose the sham of reductive fictions and their palliative function; at the same time, however, he relentlessly strives to create assent to a far more profound fiction whose function is anything but palliative as envisioned in *The End of the Affair*. This is of course the appalling mystery of divine grace moving through a fallen world, Heaven's Hound on the prowl for human prey: a version, in short, of what Kermode calls the fiction of immanent Apocalypse. We have seen how Greene manipulates the novel's structure into a complicated series of dynamic configurations—the parallel, the pendulum, the slack and the taut line, the circle—which, by their subtle interaction, tease and chasten the tendency on the part of both Bendrix and the reader to formulate facile end-expectations. Equally devastating is Greene's rhetorical assault on beginnings and endings and the finite view of time which relies on them. He paraphrases St. Augustine's famous dictum that time "came out of the future which didn't exist yet, into the present that had no duration, and went into

> " Both Sarah and Bendrix are recalcitrant to God's plot making (if not to Greene's), and both require more than their share of 'forcing.'"

the past which had ceased to exist." Of course a saint enjoys a kind of dual perspective; he can see the wholeness of time and still affirm its ceaseless fluidity because, though he has participated in the diachronous unfolding of human history, he stands "outside the plot, unconditioned by it." Ordinary human beings, however, are "inextricably bound to the plot, and wearily God forces [them], here and there, according to his intention." Both Sarah and Bendrix are recalcitrant to God's plot making (if not to Greene's), and both require more than their share of "forcing."

When Bendrix first meets her, Sarah is one for whom "the moment only mattered." "Unlike the rest of us she was unhaunted by guilt. In her view, when a thing was done, it was done; remorse died with the act." Bendrix, on the other hand, "couldn't bring down that curtain round the moment . . . couldn't forget and . . . couldn't not fear." He is time's victim: "to me the present is never here, it is always last year or next week." Yet, different as their attitudes toward time are, both accept the finiteness of its ultimate boundaries. Only in their stealthy lovemaking during the bombing raids do they contemplate the idea that "eternity might . . . after all exist as the endless prolongation of the moment of death," and at such moments "death" refers as much to their sexual abandonment as to their possible demise in a bombardment. But God the plotter is the master ironist, for it is at just such a moment that he chooses to end the affair and, in effect, to begin the process of severe privation by which both Sarah and Bendrix will come to the end of all endings.

The privation, of course, is double-edged. Sarah's vow to God restores Bendrix to life after the V-1 explosion, but it also necessitates their separation. Because of the separation, both their lives are made truly miserable, and yet out of this misery comes the loss of self necessary to the successful resolution of the divine plot. In the meantime, however, they are abandoned in a kind of purgatorial state, an alien region through which each must pass without benefit of a map, and with the hapless Henry as an additional burden. In her diary Sarah refers to this place as a desert in which "everything's over forever . . . [with] nobody, nothing, for miles and miles around." But "if one could believe in God," she wonders, "would he fill the desert?". For his part, Bendrix comes to realize this condition fully only after Sarah's death, when he and Henry become companions in bereavement. Faced with the mounting evidence of her saintly intercession, the concatenation of miraculous events which threaten his "faith in coincidence," he feels his defenses dissolving: "And with a sense of weariness I thought, how many coincidences are there going to be? [Sarah's] mother at the funeral, [Lance Parkis's] dream. Is this going to continue day by day? I felt like a swimmer who has overpassed his strength and knows the tide is stronger than himself." With only Henry as his ally "against an infinite tide," Bendrix's carefully bounded existence is doomed, and he knows it.

"Eternity," he notes in the novel which enacts that knowledge, "is said not to be an extension of time but an absence of time." This idea in turn reminds him of "that strange mathematical point of endlessness, a point with no width, occupying no space." Adrift in undifferentiated time and space, questing about for the fictive shape which will provide order and meaning and, perhaps, peace of mind—that is more or less the spiritual condition of the Bendrix who struggles to write this story with "no beginning or end," this novel whose last word is *forever*. Repeatedly he insists that he would "turn back time" to alter events such as the initial encounter with Henry on the Common; that he "knows" how the story of Sarah will come out when he does not; that he would end his novel with this scene or that one, only to proceed to another chapter. At the outset, he refers to the novel as "a record of hate far more than of love;" yet by the middle of Book IV, he admits that "somehow the hate has got mislaid." In short, the novel is beyond Bendrix's control: it is written through him but not by him, and like the other characters in it, he is "inextricably bound to the plot."

Bendrix's complaints notwithstanding, the maker of *this* plot knows his craft surpassingly well. For the beginning whose arbitrariness Bendrix protests, the ending whose outcome confounds his every expectation, and the middle whose failure "to take a straight course" prompts him to apologize, these provide us, after all, with the fictive consonance of which Kermode speaks. The book opens and closes with Bendrix and Henry together on the Common. The first time, they meet there by chance after a long absence, and as far as Bendrix is concerned, they meet as enemies. The last scene, in contrast, finds them walking arm in arm to a pub for an evening drink, and here Bendrix shows a solicitude toward his former enemy and victim that is further evidence of this being ultimately a record of love rather than of hate. As they walk over the Common, passing by the intersecting roads where lovers meet, Bendrix looks across to the other side toward his old flat in "the house with the ruined steps where He gave me back this hopeless crippled life." The novel thus finally turns back upon itself, conferring an almost wheellike pattern on the whole. The slightly off-center hub of the wheel is the sole diary entry in Book III, chapter 6. Though not precisely equivalent to "that strange mathematical point of endlessness . . . occupying no space," it is still the novel's smallest segment of textual space at the chapter level. The entry is dated January 10, 1946, that same black wet night on which the novel opens, with the lives of the three principal characters "intersecting" for the first time since the end of the affair nineteen months before. Moreover, the entry amounts to a crucial turning point in Sarah's passage through the "desert," when for the first time she feels—in words that anticipate the novel's final paragraph—"as though I nearly loved You [God]."

We can say, then, that the overall *design* of *The End of the Affair* is roughly circular. Its *rhythm*, consistent with its epistemological concerns, is a complicated juxtaposition of movements in time and space, the medial movement being the elaborate pirouette of Book III. And both of these narrative patterns, along with the rhetorical assault on beginnings and ends, function so as to frustrate facile expectations on the reader's part, forcing instead a redistribution of attention to the subordinate elements in their dynamic interaction. Finally, the novel affords a meaningful consonance not despite but *because* of these complications. And indeed, when we recall Kermode's account of the permutations of the apocalyptic myth into the modern myth of transition and immanent crisis, we may find some satisfaction in the corroboration of one of his main points: the remarkable tenacity and adaptability of the fiction-making impulse, which motivates not only plot making and reading, but also (to incorporate one of Greene's themes) loving. If in the modern age the myth of crisis has usurped the traditional role of Apocalypse, throwing the weight of our end-feeling onto virtually every moment, then we can fairly say that in *The End of the Affair* Greene has created a compelling version of that myth.

Source: Ronald G. Walker, "World without End: An Approach to Narrative Structure in Greene's *The End of the Affair*," in *Texas Studies in Language and Literature*, Vol. 26, No. 2, Summer 1984, pp. 218–41.

Sources

Bawer, Bruce, "Graham Greene: The Catholic Novels," in the *New Criterion*, Vol. 8, No. 2, October 1989, pp. 24–32.

Bergonzi, Bernard, "Graham Greene," in *British Writers*, Scribner Writers Series, 1987, pp. 1–20.

Costa, Richard Hauer, "Graham Greene," in *Dictionary of Literary Biography*, Vol. 15: *British Novelists, 1930–1959*, Gale Research, 1983, pp. 146–69.

DeVitis, A. A., "Graham Greene: Chapter Four: The Grand Theme," in *Twayne's English Authors Series Online*, G. K. Hall, 1986.

Hilson, J. C., "Greene, Graham," in *Reference Guide to English Literature*, edited by D. L. Kirkpatrick, St. James Press, 1991.

Jeffrey, David Lyle, ed., *A Dictionary of Biblical Tradition in English Literature*, William B. Eerdmans Publishing Company, 1992.

Mayberry, George, "Mr. Greene's Intense Art," in *New York Times*, October 28, 1951.

Prescott, Orville, "Comrades of the Coterie: Henry Green, Compton-Burnett, Bowen, Graham Greene," in *In My Opinion: An Inquiry into the Contemporary Novel*, Bobbs-Merrill, 1952, p. 108.

Wyndham, Francis, "Graham Greene," in *Graham Greene*, Longmans, Green, and Company, 1955, p. 24.

Further Reading

Bloom, Harold, and William Golding, eds., *Graham Greene*, Modern Critical Views series, Chelsea House, 1992.
    Noted literary scholars Bloom and Golding explore Greene's life and career in this installment of their Modern Critical Views series. Besides reviewing Greene's biographical information, the editors examine Greene's writings as a whole, commenting on themes, style, and influence.

Cassis, A. F., ed., *Graham Greene: Man of Paradox*, Loyola Press, 1994.
    This collection of fifty-seven essays and excerpts includes writings by the author, interviews, and writings about Greene by others, all of which give the reader a sense of what kind of man Greene was personally and professionally. Topics covered include writing, Catholicism, and the writer's role in modern society. Contributors include Evelyn Waugh and Anthony Burgess.

Clarke, P. F., and Mark Kishlansky, *Hope and Glory: Britain 1900–1990*, Penguin, 1997.
    This contribution to the Penguin History of Britain Series provides an overview of modern British history. Besides providing students with a better understanding of the events leading up to both world wars (and their aftereffects), this book provides commentary on religious, social, and intellectual changes over the past century.

Sherry, Norman, *The Life of Graham Greene*, Vol. 1, *1904–1939*, Viking Penguin, 1989.
    This biography covers the early years of Greene's life up to 1939, exploring his influences and preoccupations that would later characterize his writing. To complement the biography, Sherry includes photographs.

————, *The Life of Graham Greene*, Vol. 2, *1939–1955*, Viking Penguin, 1996.
    In this second volume of Greene's biography, Sherry relates the events of the author's life from 1939 to 1955, with special emphasis on the autobiographical nature of Greene's fiction. This volume also contains photographs.

Evelina; or, The History of a Young Lady's Entrance into the World

Fanny Burney

1778

Fanny Burney's *Evelina; or, The History of a Young Lady's Entrance into the World* is a fascinating and funny look at high society in late eighteenth-century Britain. Through a quite extensive collection of letters, the story unfolds and the reader is welcomed into the evolving world of a young, innocent country girl as she learns the ways of her society through misunderstandings and embarrassing social errors. Evelina's innocence is matched in equal measure with the lies and pretenses of egocentric characters who make fools of themselves in their attempts to win influence.

With twists and turns, misunderstandings, and false identities, Burney tells a story that is reminiscent of Shakespearean comedies. When *Evelina; or, The History of a Young Lady's Entrance into the World* was first published, Kate Chisholm writes in an article for the *Guardian*, "everyone wanted to know who had written such a wickedly funny satire on fashionable society." This book marked the beginning of Burney's very successful career as a writer, as well as the birth of one of England's most famous female novelists. Her books were the talk of the town, and people impatiently waited for each new book to appear. Burney's writing was, according to Lauren Goldstein, writing for *Time Europe*, "more widely read than Jane Austen's" during her time.

Evelina; or, The History of a Young Lady's Entrance into the World is the kind of book that is hard to put down. Even if the reader suspects how the book will end, the writing is so compelling and the story so convoluted that trying to figure out what will happen next keeps the reader turning the pages. The book was audacious in Burney's time. Today it is a fascinating look into the eighteenth century through the eyes of an intelligent and witty woman.

Author Biography

Fanny Burney was born on June 13, 1752, in King's Lyn, Norfolk, England. She was the daughter of Esther Sleepe and Charles Burney, who held a doctorate in music history. Her biographers claim that she was a very intelligent young girl who began writing odes, plays, songs, and farces at a very early age. Most of these early works were lost when Burney decided, as a teenager, to burn them. However she began to keep a diary around the age of fifteen, in which she recorded both typical, personal concerns of a young girl as well as anecdotes about her unusual experiences in court from the reign of George III to the beginning of the Victorian Age. Some of the incidents that Burney recorded and published in her *The Early Diary of Frances Burney 1768–1778*, were referred to for the 1994 movie *The Madness of King George*. Burney had served as lady-in-waiting to the king's wife, Queen Charlotte.

At the age of twenty-six Burney published her first novel, *Evelina; or, The History of a Young Lady's Entrance into the World*, anonymously in 1778. Although her father disapproved of her attempting to be published, he reconciled with his daughter after the novel became a huge success. From her popularity, she gained access to literary circles, including acquaintance with noted authors Samuel Johnson and Richard Sheridan. In 1782, Burney's second novel, *Cecilia; or, Memoirs of an Heiress*, increased her fame. Author Jane Austen is said to have studied Burney's works, which became such a strong influence on her writing that literary critics contend that Austen's *Pride and Prejudice* has some very noticeable similarities to Burney's style of writing. The title of Austen's book is actually taken from the last chapter of Burney's *Cecilia; or, Memoirs of an Heiress*. Historians have also recorded that Napoleon read Burney's books and sent his compliments through Burney's husband, General Alexandre d'Arblay, whom Burney married in 1793.

Burney's third novel, *Camilla; or, A Picture of Youth*, was published in 1796 and it also enjoyed

Fanny Burney

incredible success. A few years after this publication, General d'Arblay moved his family back to his homeland of France in an attempt to regain property he had abandoned there years before. The family remained in France for ten years, during which time Burney had to have an operation to remove a cancerous breast, which she suffered without anesthesia. She chronicled this experience in her diary, and for some people, this became her most famous writing. Burney's last novel, *The Wanderer; or, Female Difficulties*, was published in 1814 after she had moved back to England.

Although Burney wrote several plays, none of them were produced during her lifetime. Writing novels was at first considered a dishonorable occupation for women. Burney's success helped to change the attitude of most people in this respect. However, the theater remained, according to Kate Chisholm, writing for the *Guardian*, "an unsuitable occupation for ladies of a certain class." Not until 1993 did one of Burney's plays reach the stage. Since then Burney's material has been rejuvenated, culminating in not only having her plays produced but having a play written about her. In June 2002, in Westminister Abbey, on the 250th anniversary of her birth, Burney was commemorated in Poets' Corner, joining Jane Austen, George Eliot, and the Brontë sisters as the only women so honored.

Burney enjoyed a long life, almost doubling the average life span of her contemporaries. She died at the age of eighty-eight in 1840.

Plot Summary

Letter I–Letter IX

Fanny Burney's story *Evelina; or, The History of a Young Lady's Entrance into the World* opens with a letter from Lady Howard to the Reverend Arthur Villars in which she complains about the rudeness of Madame Duvall. Lady Howard then continues the letter inviting Evelina to stay at Howard Grove for a brief period of time. The reverend agrees to send Evelina to Lady Howard so she can enjoy the company of Maria Mirvan, Lady Howard's granddaughter and a childhood friend of Evelina's. Shortly after Evelina arrives, Lady Howard sends another note to the reverend asking his permission to allow Evelina to accompany Maria and her mother to London to await the arrival of Captain Mirvan, Maria's father, who is returning from sea duty. The reverend agrees and Mrs. Mirvan, Maria, and Evelina set off for London.

Letter X–Letter XXIII

During their stay in London, Mrs. Mirvan decides to take the two young girls to a ball. At the ball, Evelina dances with Lord Orville. This is the first ball that Evelina ever attended, and she makes many social errors, including insulting a man with whom she refuses to dance and becoming somewhat dumbfounded by the presence of Lord Orville. Maria overhears Lord Orville describe Evelina as "a poor weak girl!" However, when the man with whom she refused to dance refers to Evelina as being ill bred, Lord Orville comes to her defense and states "that elegant face can never be so vile a mask!"

Evelina is somewhat intrigued by Lord Orville, but she does not like that he has referred to her as a weak girl, and every time she sees him afterward, she tries to improve his image of her, but she always finds herself at a loss for words because she is so awed by him.

While in London, the Mirvans accidentally bump into Madame Duvall who is on her way to stay with Lady Howard. Captain Mirvan makes fun of Madame Duvall at every opportunity. Madame Duvall, for her part, continually exposes her lack of social grace and intelligence. Eventually, everyone returns to Howard Grove.

Letter XXIV–Letter XXXIX

Back at Howard Grove, Evelina remarks that the atmosphere has changed so much with the presence of the Captain and his constant disapproval of Madame Duvall that she is uncomfortable there. Madame Duvall then informs her that she is writing to Sir John Belmont to find out if he would acknowledge Evelina as his daughter. If all else fails, Madame Duvall is willing to bring a lawsuit against Sir Belmont, something that everyone at Howard Grove finds disgraceful except for Madame Duvall. To soften Madame Duvall's crude attempts to win Sir Belmont's support of his daughter, Lady Howard writes a letter to Sir Belmont, asking that he allow Evelina to visit him. Sir Belmont writes back, refusing.

Sir Clement Willoughby visits Howard Grove and continues his aggressive pursuit of Evelina. Willoughby also schemes with the Captain to further antagonize Madame Duvall, by sending her off on a wild goose chase for her companion Monsieur DuBois and then faking a robbery of some of her goods. Madame Duvall leaves Howard Grove and visits with the Reverend Villars in an attempt to get him to concede to her taking Evelina back to Paris with her. In concession, he does agree to allow Evelina to stay with Madame Duvall for a short while in London.

Letter XL–Letter LVI

Evelina stays with Madame Duvall in London. She remarks that the London she had visited earlier with Mrs. Mirvan and Maria is totally different from the London that she is now experiencing. Madame Duvall introduces her to the Branghtons, relatives of Madame Duvall. For the entire length of her stay with Madame Duvall, the Branghtons are constant companions. On occasions when they go out, Evelina bumps into Lord Orville and Sir Willoughby, and she is disgraced by her companions' reactions to them. One night while they are out, Polly and Biddy Branghton take Evelina for a walk down a dark street, where they encounter a group of men who harass them. Sir Willoughby rescues Evelina.

It is during this time that Evelina meets Mr. Macartney, described as a poor Scottish poet. He is so depressed that one day Evelina finds him sitting in his room with a revolver in his hand. She stops him from committing suicide. He then is forever indebted to her kindness.

Before leaving Madame Duvall, Evelina has several men vie for her hand. These include Tom

Branghton, Mr. Smith, and Monsieur DuBois. Evelina also runs into Lord Merton, who praises her beauty and flirts with her. Sir Willoughby finds out where she is staying and often visits her house.

Just before leaving, Lord Orville makes a presence. When Madame Duvall and the Branghtons realize that Evelina knows someone with as much money and great social standing as Lord Orville, they try every chance they get to take advantage of the acquaintance. At one point, they even borrow his coach by using Evelina's name. In the process, young Tom Branghton breaks one of the windows in the coach. Evelina, in an attempt to explain that she had nothing to do with this, writes Lord Orville a letter. Sir Willoughby intercepts the letter and writes a response, in Lord Orville's name. The letter is rather crude, giving Evelina a negative impression of Lord Orville. She leaves London and returns to Berry Hill and the reverend.

Letter LVII–Letter LX

Evelina is heartsick. The reverend sees that she is depressed, but he cannot get her to open up to him. Evelina does not want to talk about Lord Orville because she is so disappointed by him because of the letter that she believes he sent her. Instead of talking to the reverend, she writes to Maria, pouring out all her disappointments and confusion. She is in pain not just because of her broken heart but also because she does not know how to talk to the reverend about what is bothering her. When she finally tells the reverend what is bothering her, she shows him the letter she received. The reverend says that the only way to explain the sudden change in Lord Orville is that he must have been intoxicated when he wrote it. This softens the letter a little, but Evelina is still disappointed that he would have written to her in that state.

Because of her depression, Evelina's health fails. In order to correct this, the reverend suggests that she go with Mrs. Selwyn to a health resort in Bristol. Evelina agrees to this, and she and Mrs. Selwyn set off for Bristol Hotwells.

Letter LXI–Letter LXIV

At Bristol, Evelina's health slowly returns. While strolling on the grounds of this health spa, Evelina comes in contact with several men who flirt with her. Among them is Lord Merton, whom she learns is pursuing Lady Louisa Larpent, the sister of Lord Orville. Someone informs Evelina that Lady Louisa and Lord Orville are planning a visit at the house of Mrs. Beaumont, a friend of Mrs.

Media Adaptations

- In the spring and summer of 2000, the Argonaut Theatre Company in Britain produced a one-woman play based on Burney's journals. Karin Fernald was the actress who starred in this play. Reviews and more details about this production and the reviews it received can be found at http://www.karinfernald.ukf.net/.

Selwyn's. Circumstances once again throw Lord Orville and Evelina together.

The first time that Evelina meets with Lord Orville, she is happy to inform the reverend that Orville is still very much a gentleman. When he finds that Evelina is being mostly ignored by his sister and her friends, he sits next to Evelina and strikes up a conversation. Evelina, however, tries very hard not to allow her emotions to flare. She tries to keep calm and she does this by remembering the crude letter that he sent to her. Although he is friendly with her, she is "grave and distant." She writes, "I scarce looked at him when he spoke, or answered him when he was silent." Mrs. Selwyn is very impressed with Lord Orville, describing him as such: "there must have been some mistake in the birth of that young man; he was, undoubtedly, designed for the last age; for he is really polite!" With this sentiment from Mrs. Selwyn, Evelina starts to weaken. She asks, in a letter to Reverend Villars: "And now, my dear Sir, do not you think, according to the present situation of affairs, I may give up my resentment, without imprudence or impropriety?"

Letter LXV–Letter LXXXIV

Mrs. Selwyn and Evelina are invited to stay at Mrs. Beaumont's home. This provides further opportunity for Lord Orville to continue to impress Evelina as they eat their meals together and go for walks in the garden alone. Shortly after Evelina moves into the Beaumont home, Mr. Macartney shows up, meeting Evelina in the garden one morning when she went out by herself to walk. Lord Orville comes upon them quite unexpectedly and suspects that Mr. Macartney might be a love of Evelina's. Evelina feels compelled to keep much of Mr. Macartney's story untold because the details are so very personal. Lord Orville is a bit jealous but overcomes this because he knows of Evelina's honesty and integrity.

Mr. Macartney reveals to Evelina that he is there to confront Sir John Belmont. He has discovered, from a letter that his mother sent to him from her deathbed, that Sir Belmont is his father; Sir Belmont having had an illicit affair with Mr. Macartney's mother. Of course, this makes Mr. Macartney Evelina's half-brother.

Another guest arrives, a young woman the same age as Evelina, to whom people refer as the daughter of Sir John Belmont. Mrs. Selwyn and Evelina investigate the background of this woman and discover that Evelina's first nurse maid, Dame Green, switched her own baby for Evelina upon Evelina's mother's death, and presented the baby to Sir John Belmont as his child. Sir Belmont sent the baby to a convent in France where she was raised and educated. She has now come home to claim her inheritance. As coincidence would have it, this is the same woman that Mr. Macartney fell in love with while he was in Paris.

Mrs. Selwyn, in an attempt to clear this story up, takes Evelina to Sir John Belmont and insists that he at least see her. He agrees. Upon looking at her face, he knows at once that this is his child, because she looks so much like her mother, whereas the other young woman, whom he thought was his child, shows no resemblance to either her supposed mother or father. In an attempt for everyone to save face in this situation, Sir John Belmont suggests that the false Miss Belmont immediately marry Mr. Macartney, whom he has admitted is his son, and that Lord Orville and Evelina should also be married in a quiet ceremony. In this way, Sir John Belmont can make a simple and truthful public statement that his daughter has been married.

The story concludes with Sir Clement Willoughby confessing that it was he who wrote the crude letter and signed Lord Orville's name; and Willoughby then dismisses himself from the scene. Evelina and Lord Orville gain the reverend's blessing for the marriage, and everything ends happily.

Characters

Evelina Anville

Evelina is the protagonist of this story. Although the Reverend Villars tells Lady Howard that he has always referred to her as Evelina Anville, there is no explanation given for her last name. Evelina is the main correspondent in the series of letters that makes up this story. In these letters, she recounts her experiences from the time she is first introduced into society to the days before her wedding to Lord Orville.

Evelina is described as "innocent as an angel, and artless as purity itself." She is also said to be very beautiful. She attracts a lot of attention wherever she goes, mostly from men who want to be near her for her beauty and youth. Some men make fun of her innocence, with Lord Orville one of the few who appreciates the freshness and openness of her demeanor.

In the beginning, Evelina, through her lack of experience, makes certain social blunders. Because of these errors, some people laugh at her. Even Lord Orville wonders, in the beginning, if she lacks intelligence, due to the fact that she is so in awe of him she can barely speak. When other men force their attentions upon her, she is often left without a means of getting rid of them.

She goes from the loving home of the Reverend Villars and eventually ends up in the chaos and chicanery that seems to permeate the dwelling of Madame Duvall. After suffering through the whims of Madame Duvall, Evelina escapes back to the world of the reverend. She feels that her hopes of ever being accepted by her father and being loved by Lord Orville are all in vain. However, in the end, her innocence and honesty are well rewarded.

Mrs. Beaumont

Mrs. Beaumont owns the house at Clifton, where most of the characters meet at the end of the story. She is a shallow woman whose main interest in life is to associate with aristocracy. She is a minor character who only appears at the end of the story and whose only reason for being in the story seems to be to provide a place for the major characters to meet at the climax.

Sir John Belmont

Sir John Belmont met Caroline Evelyn in France and secretly married her. When he returned to Britain, he denounced her and the child to whom she gave birth. Later, when Lady Howard and Evelina's grandmother, Madame Duvall, write to him to ask him to receive Evelina, Sir Belmont refuses. Not until the end of the story, when Evelina chances to meet a young woman her own age, who is referred to as the daughter of Sir Belmont, is the reason for Sir Belmont's refusal to accept Evelina made clear. In the end when he sees Evelina, who resembles her mother, Sir Belmont repents all the injustice that he made Caroline endure and accepts Evelina as his true daughter.

Lady Belmont

See Miss Caroline Evelyn

Miss Belmont

Miss Belmont is Dame Green's daughter. As a baby, Dame Green presented her daughter to Sir John Belmont, telling him that she was his daughter. Miss Belmont is sent to France and raised in a convent, where she is well taken care of and educated. Mr. Macartney meets Miss Belmont during a visit to France and falls in love with her. Upon discovering the affair, Sir Belmont refuses to allow Mr. Macartney to see his daughter again. Miss Belmont shows up at the end of the story, to the surprise of Evelina, claiming to be the daughter of Sir John Belmont, heiress to his fortune. By the end of the story, when the details of the switched babies are cleared up, Evelina embraces Miss Belmont, claiming that she will treat her as a sister. Sir John Belmont, in an attempt to not embarrass Miss Belmont, does not refute her. He does, however, quickly marry her off to Mr. Macartney.

Biddy Branghton

Biddy is the older of the two daughters of Mr. Branghton. There is very little said about her, but she is often included in a crowd of people who go out in the evening with Madame Duvall. She would like to marry Mr. Smith and becomes jealous of Evelina when Mr. Smith proposes to Evelina.

Mr. Branghton

Mr. Branghton is a relative of Madame Duvall's. He lives in London and owns a silversmith shop. His children live with him above the shop, as does Mr. Macartney. He proposes that Evelina marry his son, Tom, a plan that Evelina scoffs at.

Polly Branghton

Polly Branghton is the younger of the two daughters of Mr. Branghton. She is crude and wild and at one point nearly gets Evelina in trouble by taking her out walking at night alone. Evelina often catches Polly kissing with Mr. Brown, a man whom Polly hopes to marry, not for love but to be married before her older sister.

Tom Branghton

Tom is the son of Mr. Branghton. He often makes fun of his sisters and tries to embarrass them. He develops a crush on Evelina while she is staying with her grandmother, Madame Duvall. He asks Madame Duvall and his father to make arrangements for him to become engaged to Evelina. He is confused and disappointed when Evelina turns him down.

Mr. Brown

Mr. Brown often visits the Branghton home and is attracted to Polly Branghton.

Mrs. Clinton

Mrs. Clinton was the second nursemaid to Evelina when she was a baby. She is also the housemaid of Reverend Villars. Mrs. Clinton accompanies Evelina when she travels unescorted.

Monsieur DuBois

Monsieur DuBois is Madame Duvall's traveling companion when she visits England. He speaks very little English and plays a minor role in the plot. Often, while in the care of Madame Duvall, Evelina turns to Monsieur DuBois for company, partly because he does not speak English and partly because he is the most decent person in the crowd who hangs around Madame Duvall. Before Evelina leaves Madame Duvall, Monsieur DuBois throws himself at Evelina's feet and declares his love for her. This embarrasses Evelina and surprises Madame Duvall.

Madame Duvall

Madame Duvall is described by both Lady Howard and Reverend Villars, in the opening letters of this story, as being "vulgar and illiterate" and "uneducated and unprincipled; ungentle in temper and unamiable in her manners." Madame Duvall was a "waiting girl" at a French café when Mr. Evelyn first met her. She and Mr. Evelyn were married only two years before Mr. Evelyn died. They have a child, Caroline Evelyn. Madame Duvall next marries Monsieur Duvall and sends Caroline to the Reverend Villars, according to Mr. Evelyn's will, to be raised. Upon Caroline's eighteenth birthday, Madame Duvall sends for Caroline for the purpose of marrying her to Monsieur Duvall's nephew. Caroline refuses, so Madame Duvall disowns her.

Likewise, when Evelina, Madame Duvall's granddaughter, is nearing her eighteenth birthday Madame Duvall once again becomes involved in her granddaughter's life. There are rumors that she is doing so in order to take advantage of Sir John Belmont, should he acknowledge Evelina as his daughter and therefore give her an inheritance. When this plan fails, Madame Duvall tries to marry Evelina to another of her nephews.

Madame Duvall is an embarrassment to Evelina. She is crude and has little understanding of society. Her clothing is gaudy, her manners are boorish, and her main purpose in life is the accumulation of money and status. She also likes the attention of men and often makes a fool of herself at the dances she attends. When Monsieur Dubois, a male companion of hers, falls in love with Evelina, Madame Duvall is insulted. Although she is Evelina's grandmother, she represents the exact opposite of someone upon whom Evelina would model herself.

Monsieur Duvall

Very little is known about Monsieur Duvall except for the fact that he is Madame Duvall's husband.

Miss Caroline Evelyn

Caroline Evelyn, also referred to as Lady Belmont, was the daughter of Madame Duvall and Mr. Evelyn. She was also the mother of Evelina. She was raised by the Reverend Villars and then sent to her mother upon her eighteenth birthday. When she refused to marry a nephew of Madame Duvall's, her mother disowned her. She then met Sir John Belmont and eloped with him. Sir Belmont left France and while in England, he denied that he had married Caroline, leaving her pregnant and without any support. Caroline grew ill and died in childbirth.

Mr. Evelyn

Mr. Evelyn is Evelina's maternal grandfather. He dies very shortly after marrying Madame Duvall but has the foresight of bequeathing his daughter to the care of the Reverend Villars, who was once Mr. Evelyn's tutor.

Mrs. Evelyn

See Madame Duvall

Dame Green

Dame Green was the nursemaid of Evelina. She had a daughter who was only a few weeks older than Evelina and upon the death of Evelina's mother, Dame Green became aware of the fact that Evelina's father was Sir John Belmont, a man who has promised to secure Evelina's financial and educational needs for the rest of her life. Upon learning this news, Dame Green takes her own daughter to Sir John Belmont, pretending that her baby is in fact his daughter. At the end of the story when this incident is brought to light, Dame Green at first lies about switching the babies but eventually owns up to the truth.

Lady Howard

Lady Howard opens the story with the first letter. Her character is only minimally developed after that. She is the mother of Mrs. Mirvan and grandmother of Maria Mirvan. She owns the home at Howard Grove where Captain and Mrs. Mirvan live. It is at this home that Evelina often spent her summers. Lady Howard convinces Reverend Villars to allow Evelina to travel with Mrs. Mirvan to London.

Lady Louisa Larpent

Lady Louisa Larpent is Lord Orville's sister. Her character is quite the opposite of Lord Orville's. She is loud, selfish, inconsiderate, and insecure. She likes the attention of men but chooses one of the worst of the male characters in the story for a prospective husband, Lord Merton. She ignores Evelina until Evelina's true identity is finally made known. Her major appearance is at the end of the story, when everyone meets at Mrs. Beaumont's house.

Mr. Lovel

Mr. Lovel is the first man to ask Evelina for a dance at her first London ball. She refuses him because he is very unattractive to her. However, later, when she accepts Lord Orville's invitation to dance, Mr. Lovel is offended. Apparently, Evelina has broken a social rule by doing this. This is the first appearance of Mr. Lovel. He flows in and out of the story, and every time that he does, he finds some way to make a fool of himself. At one point Captain Mirvan makes fun of Mr. Lovel for his lack of knowledge about the opera that they all are attending.

Mr. Macartney

Mr. Macartney is described as a poor man from Scotland. He is a poet who happens to be renting a room at Mr. Branghton's home when Evelina revisits London with Madame Duvall. Evelina sees Mr. Macartney sitting in his room with a loaded pistol one day, and she stops him from committing suicide. Eventually Mr. Macartney tells Evelina the story of his circumstances. At the end of the story, it is divulged that Mr. Macartney is the illegitimate son of Sir John Belmont. This makes him Evelina's half-brother. Evelina claims that she must have known it intuitively because she was drawn to him from the first time she saw him. Mr. Macartney falls in love with the false Lady Belmont, and in the end he marries her.

Lord Merton

When Evelina goes to London during the course of one of her evenings out, she meets Lord Merton, although she does not learn his name until the last quarter of the story. Lord Merton is a lecherous and insincere man. He flirts with Evelina, attracted to her because of her beauty. He cares little for her mind or her thoughts. He pretends to befriend her, but when they meet at Mrs. Beaumont's house at the end of the story, he totally ignores her, at least while he is in the presence of Lady Louisa Larpent. He is courting Lady Louisa and hopes to win her approval in order to gain a hold on Lord Orville's estate and social status.

Captain Mirvan

Captain Mirvan is Mrs. Mirvan's husband and Maria Mirvan's father. He is also the son-in-law of Mrs. Howard. At the beginning of the story, he was on duty with the British Navy. His return is the reason that Mrs. Mirvan, Maria, and Evelina travel to London. Captain Mirvan has few social skills and is very abusive toward Madame Duvall, Evelina's maternal grandmother. He is often rude and likes to play childish pranks.

Maria Mirvan

Maria Mirvan is Mrs. Mirvan's and Captain Mirvan's daughter. Since Mrs. Mirvan had been a friend of Evelina's mother, Caroline, she invites the Reverend Villars and Evelina to her home every summer. In this way, Maria and Evelina develop a relationship. At the beginning of the story, Evelina and Maria come together after an absence of four years. They go to London together and share their mutual introduction to London society. When Evelina must leave Maria to stay with Madame Du-

vall, she writes letters to Maria. Maria reappears at the end of the story just as Evelina is enjoying having been accepted by her father and having become engaged to Lord Orville.

Mrs. Mirvan

Mrs. Mirvan is the wife of Captain Mirvan and the daughter of Lady Howard. She was a friend of Caroline Evelyn, Evelina's mother, and has maintained a close relationship with Evelina because of that. Maria Mirvan is Mrs. Mirvan's daughter. Mrs. Mirvan is responsible for Evelina when they travel to London for the first time. She tries to educate Evelina in the ways and manners of London society. She refers to Evelina as her child; and at one point, Evelina calls her Momma. She is very patient with her sometimes obnoxious husband and is very loving toward Evelina.

Lord Orville

Lord Orville stands out as a man among men. Most of the other male characters, except for Reverend Villars, are buffoons of one sort or another. Lord Orville is gracious, warm, and distinguished, and Evelina falls in love with him from the first moment she sees him.

Although Lord Orville is attracted to Evelina, he keeps his distance. This detachment keeps Evelina perpetually wondering about him. He often visits wherever Evelina is staying, to ask about her; but their conversations are very short and he does not reveal his attraction to her. Throughout the story his presence is felt, but he is always in the distance. He is used as the model upon which Evelina judges all the other men, with no one ever matching him.

Only near the end of the story does Lord Orville admit his feelings toward Evelina; and once he does this, the emotions between the two of them quickly develop, but not without hesitations and detours. In the last quarter of the story, he first requests that Evelina consider him a friend. Later he asks that she cherish him as a brother. Finally, he lets it be known that he wants to marry her.

Mrs. Selwyn

Mrs. Selwyn is an old trusted friend of Arthur Villars. She accompanies Evelina to Bristol Hotwells in order to help Evelina regain her health. While there, she takes Evelina to Mrs. Beaumont's house where she and Evelina eventually end up staying. Mrs. Selwyn is described as having a very dry and sarcastic sense of humor. She is, however, a lot more rational than most of the characters in this story. It is through Mrs. Selwyn that Evelina is reunited with her father, Sir John Belmont. Lord Orville also uses Mrs. Selwyn as a surrogate parent of Evelina when he wants to ask for Evelina's hand in marriage.

Mr. Smith

Mr. Smith rents a room at the Branghton home. He falls in love with Evelina but is turned down by her.

Reverend Arthur Villars

Reverend Villars was the tutor of Mr. Evelyn, Evelina's maternal grandfather. Upon Mr. Evelyn's death, he leaves his daughter, Caroline, to the care of Reverend Villars. Reverend Villars raises Caroline until she is eighteen years old, at which time her mother insists that she return to France. When Caroline is rejected by her mother, she returns to England and gives birth to Evelina and asks that the reverend take care of her.

Reverend Villars takes Evelina into his home and raises her until she is seventeen, which is the point at which the story opens. Most of Evelina's correspondence is written to Reverend Villars. In the letters Evelina exposes her most tender feelings for the reverend, and he likewise shows his strong emotions for her. Evelina returns to the reverend after parting company with Madame Duvall. She stays with him for a short period of time trying to regain her health. She had become ill with emotional confusion over her feelings for Lord Orville. The reverend suggests that Evelina travel with Mrs. Selwyn in order to regain her health. In the end, Lord Orville and Evelina ask for the reverend's blessing on their proposed marriage.

Sir Clement Willoughby

Sir Clement Willoughby is aggressive in his attempts to court Evelina. He often breaks social rules of etiquette and takes advantage of Evelina's innocence. It is not clear that he loves her, but it is obvious that he wants her. When he suspects that it is Lord Orville to whom Evelina is most attracted, Sir Willoughby steals a letter that Evelina has written to Lord Orville and then responds to Evelina in another letter, pretending that it is Lord Orville who is writing. He does this in order to make Lord Orville look suspicious in Evelina's eyes. When his plan fails, it is not certain whether his heart is broken or that his pride is crushed.

Themes

High Society Manners and Foibles

The overall purpose of this novel is to expose the silliness of the mannerisms as well as the vulgarities of high society in England during the latter part of the eighteenth century. Burney's astute eye and sense of humor, as well as her in-depth acquaintance with high society, and her intelligence and gift for writing, all come together in her first novel to create a rather scathing account of the absurdities of the unwritten social rules as seen through the eyes of an innocent country girl.

As a young woman who was raised in the country, Evelina is at first thwarted and discouraged by all the social rules. As she becomes accustomed to the rules and gains confidence in her own interpretation of them, she begins to see the ludicrousness present in the social manners. It is through these eyes of innocence that Burney creates her comedy. She imbues Evelina not only with innocence but also with a strong desire to be truthful. While everyone around Evelina is scheming for money or power or a rewarding marriage, Evelina searches for honesty, dignity, intelligence, and love. In the process, she stumbles over the rules a few times, embarrassing herself and sometimes infuriating those around her. Only the most noble appreciate her good character and join her in scorning those who do not enjoy the higher standards that she has set for herself. Evelina becomes the model against which all other characters are judged. Most of them fail, for they are caught up in their egocentric passions to finagle and impress or lie and steal their ways up the social ladder.

The most obvious example of the fool is Mr. Lovel, who attends the opera to impress the people who are seated in the audience. He knows little about the opera before he attends, and while he is there he pays more attention to the people sitting in the boxes than he does to the actors on stage.

Then there is Madame Duvall, who started out as a waitress and worked her way up the social ladder through her marriages and her attempts to marry off her daughter and granddaughter. Another contemptible character is Lord Merton, who schemes to marry Lord Orville's sister because he has already wasted half of his inheritance and wishes to claim more. He feigns love for Lady Louisa but behind her back, he flirts with Evelina. Mrs. Beaumont also spends most of her life entertaining people at her house because she wants to rub elbows with the elite. She ignores Evelina until it is exposed that Evelina is the daughter of Sir Belmont.

Captain Mirvan is a special character. He has rank and has married into a family of money. Unfortunately, he appears as one of the elite who is bored. In order to entertain himself, he takes out all his fury in adolescent pranks against Madame Duvall, whom he dislikes because she is French and because she puts on false airs. He makes fun of her accent, her clothes, and her lack of education. He creates ridiculous farces, which Madame Duvall readily falls into as victim.

Sir Clement Willoughby is also very different from all the other characters. At times he appears genuine in his pursuit of Evelina. It is never made clear what his intentions or motives are. He disregards social customs in attempts to engage Evelina and he might do so, knowing that she is unaware of the rules. He lies and cheats but somehow seems to rationalize it as necessary in order to gain Evelina's hand. There are many incidents when he actually comes to her rescue. However, there are an equal number of incidents when he is the cause of her discomfort and frustration.

Burney also points out the double standards employed in society in relation to the freedoms enjoyed (or the lack of them) between the sexes. For instance, women were considered fair game if they were found walking by themselves. This is observed in the scene in which Polly and Biddy take Evelina away from their party and walk with her down what is called a dark alleyway or street. The three women are quickly surrounded by a group of rowdy men. The women are toyed with and become frightened. Their only defense is to stay together. When they are separated, their fate worsens. They are at the mercy of these scoundrels until a decent man come to their rescue.

Poor people are also fair game. Burney demonstrates this through the character of Mr. Macartney. In a very simple scene in which several people are gathered in a room, Burney creates a dialogue that reflects the lack of concern for Mr. Macartney's need of a chair. Everyone in the room finds a chair for themselves, and when it is noticed that Evelina does not have a place to sit, they demand the Mr. Macartney give up his chair. The implication is that he is not worthy of it. Another time when the same group of people is together, they take a vote as to where they want to go that evening. Mr. Macartney is present in the room and when Evelina sug-

Topics for Further Study

- Write a short account, either as a letter, a short story, or a journal entry, about a time when you did something quite innocently, but also quite embarrassing, in public. Who were the people involved? What were their reactions? How did it make you feel? Were you able to save face?

- Lord Orville's thoughts are never realized in this story. Write several letters for Lord Orville about Evelina at different stages of the story's development. Make a point of contrasting some of Evelina's interpretations of the events. What do you think he was doing or thinking about when he was not with Evelina? How do you think he reacted to seeing her with Madame Duvall in London? What were his feelings when Tom Branghton broke the window in his carriage and then insisted on visiting him at his home, using Evelina's name to gain entry?

- Read Jane Austen's *Pride and Prejudice*, a book that is said to have been heavily influenced by Burney's writing. How does Austen's book compare to Burney's? Are the plot lines similar? Are there any characters in Austen's book that remind you of the characters in Burney's?

- Write a paper on contemporary social customs. Which do you find the most humorous? If you could, how would you change them? After your paper is complete, find one or two classmates to act out some of these customs. Create skits, such as on *Saturday Night Live*, satirizing the customs that you find most annoying.

gests that Mr. Macartney should also vote, she is laughed at. Evelina also receives similar treatment when she stays at Mrs. Beaumont's house. Everyone but Lord Orville and Mrs. Selwyn ignores her when Evelina enters a room. She is not included in any of the conversations, and no one says goodbye to her when they leave. Only after they discover that she is about to inherit a title and a fortune do they pay any attention to her.

Style

Epistolary Novel

The epistolary novel, a novel told through a series of letters written by one or more characters, was very popular in the eighteenth century. During this time period, letter writing was used to convey new scientific discoveries, to reflect on philosophical thoughts, and, of course, for personal communications. The form of the epistolary novel is claimed to have been first used by Samuel Richardson (1689–1761), most famously in his books *Pamela* (1740) and *Clarissa Harlow* (1747–1748). Richardson was a printer and upon retiring, he was asked to write a book as guidance for young women on how to properly write letters. Instead, Richardson was inspired to use the letter form to write a story. Other authors who have used the form include Johann Wolfgang Goethe in his book *The Sorrows of Werther* (1774) and Jane Austen in her *Love and Friendship* (1790). A more contemporary version of the epistolary novel is Alice Walker's *The Color Purple* (1982).

This form of novel allows the reader a more intimate glimpse into the character's thoughts. It also is an excellent way in which to portray a sense of immediacy, as the reader senses the tension and expectancy of the writer in the present as he or she is thinking through experiences that have just recently happened or anticipating those that are about to occur. The limitation of this form is that the reader watches the story unfold through the limited vision of those characters who are involved in the letter writing. In *Evelina; or, The History of a Young Lady's Entrance into the World*, most of the letters are written by Evelina. A few more letters in response to hers are written by Reverend Villars. One or two more are composed by Lady Howard. The reader is never privy to the thoughts of any of the other characters.

Comedy of Manners

Comedy of Manners is a witty and intelligent form for writing dramatic comedy and was often used for plays during the eighteenth century. Among the most popular works from this period are William Congreve's *The Way of the World* (1700), Oliver Goldsmith's *She Stoops to Conquer* (1773), and Richard Sheridan's *The School for Scandal* (1777). Richard Sheridan was a friend of Burney's and he often asked her to write screenplays, recognizing her skill of creating dramatic affects.

Comedy of Manners is often used to satirize the ways of a contemporary society by setting up the social standards of the day and then pitting the characters against those standards to see if they stand up to them. The comedy occurs in either the attempts of the characters to try to meet those standards or in the ridiculousness of the standards themselves. One of the biggest buffoons in *Evelina; or, The History of a Young Lady's Entrance into the World* is Madame Duvall. She is uneducated and has no training in social skills. Her assumptions about dress, manners, and proper conversation are totally inept. She makes things worse for herself by putting on airs.

A type of modern Comedy of Manners can be seen on the weekly television program *Saturday Night Live*, which uses comedy to satirize political and social manners.

Historical Context

Reign of George III

King George III (1738–1820) reigned during turbulent times, while suffering an illness that was slowly decaying his mental faculties. He married Charlotte of Mecklinburg-Strelitz in 1761, and together they had fifteen children. At one point in time, Burney would serve Queen Charlotte, a role she would come to dislike.

King George was afflicted with a disease known as porphyria, a disorder that causes an overproduction of the chemical porphyrin, which can lead to madness. Often, King George, while conducting official business as well as in his personal life, would lose his grip on reality, seeing things that did not exist, saying things that did not make sense.

It was during the reign of King George III that the American Revolution occurred. He insisted on taxing the new colonies and when finally engaged in a war with America, refused to give in until his troops were completely defeated. This caused him a loss of support in his own country.

War also raged on the European front during his reign, as Napoleon sought to win control of all of Europe. Although the British Navy at that time had complete control of the water, Napoleon's army was the most powerful force on land. As King George began his rule, the Seven Years' War with France was just ending. There was a very strong dislike of the French in Britain and anti-France pol-

Compare & Contrast

- **Nineteenth Century:** England's Royal Navy uses balloons and kites to send propaganda leaflets to the French people to help turn the tide of Napoleon's army.

  Twentieth Century: During World War I, Britain drops over nine million pamphlets into the German trenches to try to change the attitude of Hitler's troops.

  Today: The United States drops messages to the people of Afghanistan in order to persuade them to help get rid of the ruling Taliban government, which is supporting terrorists.

- **Nineteenth Century:** The Industrial Revolution begins and is at its height in Great Britain with masses of people moving off the farm and into the city to take jobs in factories. The population of London dramatically increases.

  Twentieth Century: The Industrial Revolution slowly crosses the Atlantic Ocean and affects the United States, where the automobile becomes the prominent means of transportation.

  Agriculture is superseded by the manufacturing industry.

  Today: Globalization is the new buzzword around the world as industry affects every nation. Controversy arises as third world countries become a source of cheap labor for the leading industrial nations such as those in Europe, the United States, and Japan.

- **Nineteenth Century:** Women in England and the United States gain strength by organizing in groups to demonstrate for their rights.

  Twentieth Century: Both England and the United States governments give women the right to vote.

  Today: Women from all over the globe gather in conventions, such as the Feminist Expo in Baltimore, to share strategies and fuel the women's movement. Topics include abortion, political involvement, and globalization and its effect on women.

---

itics prevailed. The peace with France did not last very long, as Napoleon continued to conquer European countries and eventually threatened Britain once again. The British eventually defeated Napoleon in 1814.

King George's health deteriorated and eventually his oldest son, George, attempted to reign, but he was often thwarted by the irrational will of his father. King George's illness deemed him so unfit that eventually he stepped down and gave full power to his son. He died in 1820, blind, deaf, and mad.

Literary Influences

Burney was influenced most profoundly by her friend and dramatist Richard Brinsley Sheridan (1751–1816). Born in Ireland, Sheridan moved to London and lived out his remaining years there. He began writing plays and in 1775 produced his first, *The Rivals*, which was not an immediate success,

but upon revision it became one of the most popular comedies in Britain. His most famous work, *The School for Scandal* (1777) likewise was a major hit.

Sheridan did not remain a writer for very long. Instead, he moved into politics and became known as one of Britain's finest orators. Sheridan was also considered a radical for supporting the American Revolution as well as the revolution in France. He was also an outspoken proponent of a free press and the right of people to openly criticize their government. Toward the end of his life, Sheridan fell in disfavor with the local politicians and died a very poor man.

Aphra Behn (1640–1689) lived a century before Burney, but she was one of a very few female authors of any influence that Burney could have turned to as a model. She is considered the first professional English female author, known for her poetry, plays, and novels. Her most famous novel

A scene from the novel as depicted by the author's cousin, Edward Francesco Burney

was *Oroonoko; or, the Royal Slave* (1688), said to be one of the first philosophical novels ever written. Behn, at one time, enjoyed royal patronage. She was even asked by King Charles II to spy for Britain in the war against the Dutch. She was never paid for her services and ironically, when she returned home from Antwerp, she was briefly imprisoned for debt. Her works became very popular during the movement, in the 1970s, of feminists searching for literature written by women. She remains one of the most popular authors of her time.

Critical Overview

Fanny Burney was a popular success in her time. However, history did not look on her with favor. Her books were buried beneath the fame of other popular writers, and not until recently have her works been rediscovered.

Critics remain puzzled over the fact that Jane Austen and Emily Dickinson, who read and were influenced by Burney's works, have always enjoyed continual reprints of their works while Burney's books seemed to have lost favor with publishers. Some critics believe that Burney was remembered as a diarist by most people, and her novels were forgotten.

All of this changed in 1993 when Joyce Hemlow, a scholar devoted to Burney's works, discovered a play of Burney's and realized that it was better than anything Richard Sheridan, a popular playwright and friend of Burney's, had ever writ-

ten. Hemlow pushed to have the play *A Busy Day* produced, and the rebirth of Burney began. The director of that play, Alan Coveney, is quoted as describing Burney's work, in Kate Chisholm's article for the *Guardian*, "Because she does not rely on gags for comic effect, but on the interplay between the characters, her comedy is as relevant today as it was when she wrote it."

In trying to answer why Burney's works have experienced a rebirth, Lauren Goldstein, writing for *Time Europe*, states that it is "perhaps . . . because there are so many remarkable parallels between Fanny Burney's turbulent times and ours." In that same article, Goldstein quotes Paula Stepankowsky, the president of the Burney Society, as saying: "[Jane] Austen may have done it better, more elegantly, have been more polished, but Fanny did it first." And so the love affair between the public and Burney continues.

Daniel McCabe is a writer for the *McGill Reporter*. He starts a recent article with: "When it came to 18th-century England, Fanny Burney had a front row seat." Later, McCabe quotes English professor Lars Troide: "As a chronicler of her times, Troide says, 'nobody comes close to Burney.'" McCabe again quotes Troide: "'She had a very keen eye for the physical world,' says Troide. 'She also had a tremendous gift for capturing character in only a few words.'"

In the *Observer*, Andrew Marr reviews Claire Harman's biography of Burney and summarizes some of the content with these remarks:

> She was a superstar of literary London who, in her heyday, enthralled the reading public, was admired by such formidable intelligences as Johnson and Burke and whose influence on Jane Austen, Thackeray, and even Dickens is indisputable.

Criticism

Joyce Hart

Hart holds degrees in English literature and creative writing and focuses her writing on literary themes. In this essay, Hart looks at Burney's portrayal of women and the restrictions upon them in eighteenth-century England.

Even if readers had no previous knowledge of the customs and manners of eighteenth-century England, Fanny Burney's story *Evelina; or, The History of a Young Lady's Entrance into the World* would provide them with enough information and detail to give them a fair description. Burney's books were hot sellers in her time for many reasons. She had a knack for creating humorous and convoluted plot lines that kept her readers engaged; and she had an astute understanding of high society gathered from her own personal experiences in court. However, one of the more significant explanations for her popularity is the fact that she had a keen understanding of the role of women, and she eagerly exposed all the most exaggerated restrictions upon her sex as well as many of the more subtle ones. Not everyone appreciated the way she poked fun at her society, but despite themselves, they anxiously anticipated all her new books, impatient to see their way of life through the vision of Burney.

Burney has written that she liked creating female protagonists who were raised in some quiet manner, usually as orphans, and then put out into society without benefit of a mentor, having to make it or break it on the merit of their own wit and courage. This was the premise of most of her novels, the material upon which she created her most intriguing plots. Burney's heroine Evelina is a perfect example, as she represents all that is innocent, pure, and beautiful. She is every father's dream; every suitor's fantasy; every mother's pride. She is the epitome of Woman, at least Woman of her time. The only thing that she lacks is the knowledge of high society's unwritten code of conduct, or manners. This does not infer that she lacks social grace, for she is most honest, most compassionate, and most noble. These traits, however, sometimes clash with the prescribed manners of the elite; and so Evelina often finds herself embroiled in controversy.

Thrown out into the world without benefit of a mother or father as models, Evelina must lean upon the loving care that she received from her adopted father, the Reverend Arthur Villars, and from a close friend of her deceased mother, Mrs. Mirvan. However, the reverend is ill and remains in his home in the country when Evelina first ventures out; and Mrs. Mirvan sometimes forgets that Evelina, as intelligent and beautiful as she is, has had no experience in courtship manners. These manners are very formal for young women, and those who are ignorant of them stand to be disgraced, or worse, man-handled and disrespected.

Women were expected to be educated, at least in the art of conversation. From the beginning pages of this story, even noble Lady Howard has trouble being graceful toward Madame Duvall,

> **Underlying many of the customs is the belief that women must always remain accessible to men and that they have no right to choose what they want. They are there for the enjoyment of the men."**

whom she finds to be "vulgar and illiterate." Likewise, when Evelina attends a ball and is so flabbergasted by the pomp of the London affair that she is unable to grab her wits and say anything intelligent while dancing with Lord Orville, she too is at first looked down upon. Even Lord Orville, described as a very compassionate person, first describes Evelina in a derogatory tone as being a weak country girl, simply because she was unable to carry on a conversation. Although women were supposed to be educated or at least sound intelligent, their schooling was almost always carried out only in the home. So it is not the education, per se, that young men are expecting from the women that they court, but rather that the young woman be capable of entertaining them.

Evelina was also ridiculed because she chose not to dance with a man she found unattractive. The proper way of turning someone down was to then turn down every man who came over and asked her to dance. If she did not follow this custom, she was considered rude. This put women in an awkward position. They had to oblige themselves to every fop and brute in order to remain eligible for the men capable of affecting their hearts. Underlying many of the customs is the belief that women must always remain accessible to men and that they have no right to choose what they want. They are there for the enjoyment of the men. If they refuse one, they might as well go home.

Evelina may have had no say in the matter when it came to choosing her dance partners, but one could argue that she had little say about anything in her life. She goes where the Reverend Villars sends her, or else she goes with Mrs. Mirvan, or Madame Duvall. If she wants to stay at home because she is tired of being seen with the company that attends Madame Duvall, she is considered rude. If she wants to go for a walk by herself, she is considered vulgar or stupid. Granted there are good reasons behind some of these restrictions, for it appears that a woman on her own is considered fair play by any man who happens to find her. It's difficult to understand that even when three women walk alone, they can be assaulted, and not by gangsters or thieves, but by men of their own station. In an age when even taking a woman's hand is considered forward, one has to wonder how these manners are completely discarded when a group of men encounters women who are not chaperoned and think nothing of taunting them to the point where the women become fearful of the harm that these men can do to them.

Another overall theme in this story is that of the importance of money and family heritage. Without these, no matter how beautiful or intelligent the woman might be, society diminishes her worth to the point that she may find herself without a husband and be forced to take on extremely minimal jobs, such as a housekeeper, in order to keep herself alive. This threat is most obvious to Dame Green, who sacrifices her daughter by giving her up to the whims of Sir John Belmont in the hopes that the young girl will be educated and financially taken care of for the rest of her life. It is a very difficult thing for a mother to give away her baby no matter what beneficial circumstances may follow. However, Dame Green was a nursemaid. She had no future to offer her daughter. The sacrifice was necessary to give her daughter a chance for a husband, the only reward women of this time had to look forward to.

Of course, Evelina was in a similar position. Without Sir Belmont acknowledging her as his daughter, not only does she not gain his social status or inherit his fortune, she does not have a legitimate name. If Sir Belmont does not claim her, she is seen in society as a bastard. No matter how much love the Reverend Villars rains down on her, he cannot protect her from her situation. Her choice is to accept her position or go with Madame Duvall and be married to some distant cousin. Since the reader is not privileged to Lord Orville's thoughts, it is not known if he is willing to marry her no matter what her background is. Were he to be informed of her sketchy heritage, he might not have been so attracted. He is noble, but he, too, has family he must be concerned with.

Readers can surmise through the Reverend Villar's warning to Evelina, that society in which

Evelina lived did not hold out too much promise. "Could I flatter myself that Lord Orville would, indeed, be sensible of your worth," the reverend writes, "and act with a nobleness of mind which should prove it congenial to your own," then the reverend states that he would have no worries about Evelina. Instead, he tells Evelina to come home, to quit the fantasies she holds, to leave the world of high society, in which, he implies, Evelina does not belong.

Evelina, although run down from all the emotions that she has endured, has spunk. Although, on her own, she is willing to accept the reverend's decree and give herself up for the life of a spinster, stuck away in some isolated country manor, she jumps at the chance to avoid this when Mrs. Selwyn suggests that she stay and fight for her rights. Regardless that Mrs. Selwyn, it must be pointed out, is one of the most courageous, rational, and out-spoken women in the novel, most often she is described in a negative tone for her "propensity to satire," which is, of course, Burney's own sense of irony, since she is writing satire. Interestingly, too, Evelina, when she compliments Mrs. Selwyn for being very clever, follows this statement with "her understanding, indeed, may be called *masculine*." Evelina continues that in Mrs. Selwyn's attaining her gifts by studying men so closely, she has sacrificed her feminine side and "has lost all her softness."

For Evelina, gentleness is an essential virtue "of the female character." It can then be assumed from these observations that women must be reticent, and must stay in the background of life. That they must be soft could be interpreted as they must be elastic, giving in to men. Mrs. Selwyn is blunt in her conversations. She stands up to men, refusing to take a back seat. She takes their language and turns it back on them, exposing their weaknesses and refusing to be defined as a toy to be tampered with. Upon reflecting more closely on Mrs. Selwyn, readers might come to the conclusion that she most closely reflects the sentiments of the author. It is Mrs. Selwyn, after all, who saves the day, saves the whole comedy; for without her, Evelina would have floated away into obscurity, and that would not have been a happy ending at all.

Source: Joyce Hart, Critical Essay on *Evelina; or, The History of a Young Lady's Entrance into the World*, in *Novels for Students*, The Gale Group, 2003.

Joanne Cutting-Gray

In the following excerpt, Cutting-Gray discusses the themes of innocence and experience in Burney's novel.

> *Thus ought a chaste and virtuous woman ... lock up her very words and set a guard upon her lips, especially in the company of strangers, since there is nothing which sooner discovers the qualities and conditions of a woman than her discourse.*
>
> —Plutarch

A worldly wise, often subversive, journalist-narrator who represents herself as an inexperienced young rustic has intrigued, if not puzzled, the readers of Burney's first novel, *Evelina*. The fact that Evelina's innocence can only be seen from the narrator's perspective beyond innocence, that innocence is a reductive concept within the broader, reflexive context of writing is an important clue to the quixotic conduct of Burney's first heroine. If, as T. B. Macaulay notes, "novel" was a name that produced shudders from respectable people so that a novelist sometimes risked social ostracism, then a female novelist, much like her fictional counterpart, risked even more. It is no wonder then, that young Burney, single, genteel, and shy, kept her authorship a secret. No one, except perhaps her father, was more astonished than she at the immediate popularity of *Evelina*.

Aside from its popular reception, Burney's first novel also charmed the arbiters of eighteenth-century taste—Johnson, Reynolds, Burke, and Sheridan—and delighted Mrs. Thrale and Lady Mary Montagu. Mrs. Thrale, relieved to discover that *Evelina* was not "mere sentimental business," commented that "it's writ by somebody that knows *the top and the bottom*, the *highest* and *lowest* of mankind." Early reviewers of *Evelina* praised its charming, unaffected glimpse into the social life of London, its satire of class and individual character and its broad humor and pathos even as they cited its contrived plot and flatly conceived heroine as instances of its conventionality. Modern commentary, however, is more likely to laud *Evelina*'s publication in 1778 as a frontier: "Behind it are centuries of silence; in front of it, that 'damned mob of scribbling women' who seized upon the novel as a means of subsistence and self-expression and thereby challenged the masculine perspective that had previously dominated literature."

As circumspect forerunner of what was called that "mob of scribbling women," Burney explained the innocent character of Evelina to her sister Susan by saying that she "had been brought up in the

> " As long as woman lacks a voice in the sense of sharing in the cultural figuration of who she is, she can never be an active conveyor of meaning."

strictest retirement, that she knew nothing of the world, and only acted from the impulses of Nature." Quoting from her own preface, she added that the heroine was the "offspring of Nature in her simplest attire." Though Evelina incarnates artlessness in a world of duplicity and evil, she nonetheless requires "observation and experience" to make her "fit for the world." Evelina under the guardianship of the Reverend Mr. Villars is the innocent in a private world of innocence until she sallies forth into a disjunctive, public world where, affronted by male assertiveness, she, as female, becomes a problem to herself. Unless one hears in Evelina's discourse a misguided effort to maintain the "simplest attire" of innocence, one will too often see only female compliancy. As long as she insists upon preserving her innocence-passivity (a symbol for the stasis of her being), she cannot assimilate experience. Compliancy thus becomes for Evelina a deviant form of prudence that violates any practical wisdom.

Knowing nothing of the world suggests a state of unreflective union with nature prior to knowledge. This state of unselfconsciousness contrasts with a succeeding stage of irretrievable loss in which the emergent self stands over against the world. Indeed, to act only from the "impulses of Nature" accords with those older patriarchal notions of the feminine as well as our common sense precept of innocence ("Nature in her simplest attire"). Within such a limited, cultural stereotype for female behavior Evelina authors her journal-diary and retrieves in the act of writing a richness of experience otherwise denied to her. In the gap between her speech and action, between her disclaimers of experience and her writing of a journal-diary, one can hear a frustrated desire that seeks to be recognized: what will emerge as both problem and promise is Evelina's namelessness as a metonym for her absence from patriarchal language. Through the social void opened up by that gap, Evelina discovers that both she and her history can be (re)figured by her own act of writing. For that reason, writing an account of her experiences shatters the rigid concept of woman that she begins with. Writing her journal-letters will liberate Evelina from the alienating self-consciousness that divides her from herself; it will release her to the company of the two-in-one of thought—a process denied the rest of Burney's represented heroines.

What needs to be carefully traced before one can understand the significance of Evelina's journal is how, at first, she relinquishes experience for the sake of concealing herself in innocence. In her early forays into the world, the assailed heroine's intentional focus upon artlessness obscures the transparency of the natural self that she wishes to project. In effect, to act only from "the impulses of Nature" is to perform, as well as to invite, oppression. Furthermore, any binary economy of female innocence—male oppression overlooks Evelina's calculated innocence and concealed experience. Only at a point of crisis near to hysteria, when she is forced to write on her own behalf, does Evelina begin to understand how concealment does not prevent her from revealing herself—to herself, as well as to others. Even as Evelina narrates a representational myth in which the one narrated is caught in the female self-identity/male repression dichotomy, as writer she questions the essentialism underlying that binary economy.

The novel opens with the cultural definition that outlines Evelina's intrinsically innocent character. Reverend Villars describes his adopted ward, setting forth in little the problem of the female in eighteenth-century society: "This artless young creature, with too much beauty to escape notice, has too much sensibility to be indifferent to it; but she has too little wealth to be sought with propriety by men of the fashionable world." He explains the "peculiar cruelty of her situation" as "only child of a wealthy Baronet, whose person she has never seen, whose character she has reason to abhor, and whose name she is forbidden to claim; entitled as she is to lawfully inherit his fortune and estate, is there any probability that he will *properly* own her?" Artlessness and beauty without wealth and name is not only Evelina's global condition; it is also the charm of her appeal, the only marketable asset she has, and the greatest danger to her character.

Evelina's social position teeters precariously between legitimacy and bastardy; although she is the legitimate daughter of a baronet, her mother's legal marriage remains unacknowledged by her father. Adopted by a country parson, she can't claim social rank with such modest means. Her namelessness—a form of social silence—creates the conflict in the novel. More than a social deficiency, namelessness functions symbolically for the patriarchy that constitutes the "named." As a metonym for woman, it stands in the way of Evelina's social acceptance and inhibits her ability to name herself other than within the category of innocence, the character given to her by her culture.

The question of character and its rival conceptions immediately emerge. Is Evelina to be described as a traditional fictional entity created and controlled by an author—even an author in the form of a dominant culture who authors her? Is she an autonomous person, a "real identity," who speaks and acts by her own authority? Is she a purely linguistic construction? Each of these notions of character fails to describe adequately the generative power of naming that multiplies the company of Evelina within the free play of writing.

Preserving Evelina's singularly innocent name seems mandated by all those in the novel concerned with the continuity of the social order. For example, Villars's wish to have Evelina returned from her social experiences unchanged, still "all innocence," implies sacrificing the seasoning of practical knowledge on the patriarchal altar of pristine ignorance. All he asks from Lady Howard in sending her his Evelina as "innocent as angel, and artless as purity itself," is that she will return his child "as you receive her." Lady Howard reassuringly agrees with Villars that Evelina is indeed "truly ingenuous and simple" with "a certain air of inexperience and innocency." Launched into the world, Evelina should somehow expand her experience, but without the loss of her intrinsic, encapsulated innocence. "The world," says Villars to Evelina, "is the general harbour of fraud and of folly, of duplicity and of impertinence" where "the artlessness of your nature, and the simplicity of your education alike *unfit* you for its thorny path" (emphasis added). A properly feminine, bourgeois "education" assures one of a perspective "unfit" for the intrigues of society. Villars holds an unshakable belief in Evelina's essentialistic innocence and hopes that she may be an "ornament" of delight to family, friends, and neighbors, "employing herself in useful and innocent occupations." Above all else, he cautions her to retain her "genuine simplicity."

What Do I Read Next?

- For a contemporary look at the epistolary novel, one can read John Barth's *Letters* (1997). Barth sets this novel in 1960s during a time of revolution and rebellion and, through some friends writing letters, compares the 1960s to the time of the American revolution.

- Alice Walker also uses letter writing to tell a story in *The Color Purple* (1982), in which the character Celie writes letters to God, explaining her feelings and experiences.

- The novel *Love* (1993), by Paul Kafka, won the *Los Angeles Times* Book Prize for best first fiction. Kafka (a distant relative of the novelist Franz Kafka) also writes in the epistolary form about a young man in Paris who has hopelessly fallen in love.

- For background information on Fanny Burney, one can read *World of Fanny Burney* (1993) by Evelyn Farr. Another biography, *Frances Burney* (1988), by Margaret Anne Doody, is also highly recommended.

- *Their Faithful Handmaid: Fanny Burney at the Court of King George III* (2000), by Hester Davenport, will give the reader a more concentrated study of Burney's time spent with the aristocracy of Britain.

- For Burney's own account of her early life, one can read *Early Journals and Letters of Fanny Burney, 1774–1777* (1991), edited by Lars E. Triode.

- Burney's own *The Wanderer; or, Female Difficulties* was republished in 2001. This story traces the life of a French émigré who has escaped the French Revolution and gone to Great Britain. She does not find life much better there, as Burney tells it, exposing the eighteenth-century, English middle-class's poor attitudes toward women.

- In 1782, Burney wrote *Cecilla: Memoirs of an Heiress*, which has recently been republished in 1999. This story is similar to *Evelina; or, The History of a Young Lady's Entrance into the World* in that it is a love story told through social criticism.

But we will see by Evelina's own account of her first social forays that she is not as devoid of practical wisdom or as unfit for society as she, and everyone else, assumes.

In writing about her first ball to Villars, Evelina finds male behavior so "provoking" that she determines not to dance at all rather than seem to be "humouring" male condescension. Her reaction is more than the shock of innocence at the disportment of behavior outside the bounds of her experience, for she interprets what she sees as an assumption of superiority toward women. Rather than lacking awareness about the situation at hand, she is lacking information about social propriety. The fact that her account to Villars focuses not on ignorance of social sanctions but on her interpretation of human incivility proves this point. In this respect, her response is spontaneous but not discriminating, intuitively just, but not socially correct.

Evelina's reflexive ability to read more than one possible meaning in otherwise socially correct behavior refutes any Lockean notion that innocence is a tabula rasa upon which an accumulating experience is engraved. Although Evelina recognizes hypocrisy (Mr. Lovel), bad taste (the Branghtons), male impertinence (Willoughby), and female constraints (codes of propriety), time and again she retreats into the blankness of self-conscious confusion, silence, and the unformed feature of innocence, as when she meets Lord Orville:

> How will he be provoked, thought I, when he finds what a simple rustic he has honoured with his choice!

one whose ignorance of the world makes her perpetually fear doing something wrong!

But while castigating her own behavior, Evelina exhibits an assimilative, interpretive grasp, as when the thought occurs to her that Orville did choose her, "insignificant as I was, compared to a man of his rank and figure." This ready adaptability to fit herself to new social situations is belied by the way her letters attire her in an innocence bordering on the hysterical. Furthermore, that correct social appearance includes a contradictory comportment of innocence: unworldly enough to appear guileless or diffident, yet sophisticated enough to recognize dissimulation and artifice; subtle enough to discern deception and fraud, and poised enough to withstand male aggression.

From Evelina's writing about her very first ball, we can see that though ignorant of social decorum, she is not devoid of perception. We are led to think otherwise when Villars's letters array her in artlessness. Whenever Evelina is abashed with shyness or outraged at male impropriety toward her person, she does the same. On such occasions, she cloaks her feelings in the more artless raiment of silence even as she discloses them in her writing: "But I was silent, for I knew not what I ought to say." As she enters an already established symbolic order and submits her desire to the pressures of that order, adopting a conventional conceptual wardrobe, furnishing herself with a language that has already determined who she is, she allows her reflections to be covered over by the veneer of naïveté.

This acquiescence, a very imprudent prudence, precipitates her disasters. Lord Orville's attentions, in part an attempt to test her capability to speak, merely create a restraint that causes her to lapse into silence. Ignorant of the impropriety entailed in refusing one dance partner and accepting another, Evelina generates male judgments ranging from "beautiful" to "ill-bred," "intelligent" to " rustic," or in Orville's case, from "ignorant or mischievous" to "a poor weak girl." To submit to the pressure for female silence contributes to her appearance of artlessness, a commodity valuable to the patriarchal appetite for the natural, as, for example, when Orville later says of Evelina that "she is too young for suspicion, and has an artlessness of disposition I never saw equalled." She discovers early, however, that an uncalculated artlessness is unreadable by others without the accompanying signs of reflection in her that would prevent misreading *artless* for *artifice*. Smarting from the effects of her own innocent guise, Evelina writes that she wishes to flee London, convincing herself that she now finds it "tiresome."

If Evelina's inexperience causes her embarrassment and real anguish, so does pretending to an experience that would conceal her genuine lack of worldly tempering. This posturing reveals itself when she attempts to elude the impertinent attentions of the lecherous Sir Clement Willoughby. She imitates fashionable manners, but her artifice cannot match Willoughby's rakishness. Here is a much keener male adversary than any she has met before, and one who epitomizes the fraud and duplicity Villars worries about. Her "peevish" indignation only charms the rake into further importunities toward one whose "airs" heighten her beauty. Merely exchanging innocence for sophistication does not solve the problem of being turned—or turning oneself—into an object for exploitation.

Evelina concludes her London letters to Villars with the plaint: "I am too inexperienced and ignorant to conduct myself with propriety in this town, where everything is new to me, and many things are unaccountable and perplexing." Though her comment testifies to the inadequacy of *any* concept of female innocence that excludes an experiential understanding, it also clearly demonstrates a view that oscillates between the perspectives of innocence and experience. Claiming confusion admits to an articulated need for understanding experience—and therefore admits to how much she already understands it.

Even when displeased with her narrated ignorance, Villars is quite aware of Evelina's narrative understanding; her persuasive writing is enough to convince him of her budding wisdom. Nevertheless, he answers her letter with a postscripted prayer that artlessness or "gaiety of heart" will remain hers. It is not only Evelina who feels compelled to overwrite her experience with the inscription of innocence—it is Villars's religious and moral clothing as well.

The contrast between Evelina's practical wisdom and others' dullness sharpens when she meets her wealthy but vulgar grandmother and her middle-class shopkeeping relatives. The Branghtons display all the ignorant excesses of grasping bourgeois social climbers without any of the intelligence that could redeem them. Their vulgarity and lack of manners vividly contrast Evelina's grace, refinement, modesty, and quickness. Willfully ignorant of decorum governing opera, they embarrass Evelina with their stingy selection of seats, lack of civility and proper attire. Offensive at every turn, they even arouse our sympathy for her when she rushes into Willoughby's arms to escape them. At the same time, however, the Branghtons' doggedly unrefined appetites attest to Evelina's fuller understanding of those social nuances that remain unarticulated. Indeed, such outrageous, low, and vulgar behavior spontaneously prompts her will, passion, and tongue: "This family is so low-bred and vulgar, that I should be equally ashamed of such a connection in the country, or anywhere."

When straining to recommend herself to males, however, Evelina postures in the language and comportment of the idealized female for whom discrimination is forbidden. She fails to distinguish between acquiring the accoutrements of innocence and *being* innocent, a standard that forces her into an anxious mode and wears away her spontaneity. Even though Evelina can understand a bold stare, even from a mighty lord, to be a "look of libertinism toward women", she seems almost willfully to overlook sexual dangers. Her awareness, significantly, does not extend to the sexual-social threat in accepting, although under some duress, Willoughby's offer to drive her home unescorted or in accompanying the Branghton girls into the darkened alleys of Vauxhall. This gap in her understanding points to the broader issue of how the conceptual model of vulnerable innocence conceals from a female not only her own sexual desire but her sexual power as well. The patriarchal model for female virtue appears to posit innocence merely in order to assault it, so that lecherous Willoughby can silence Evelina's objections by invoking the patriarchal code designed to protect her. Thus, when Orville discovers her alone with the rake, she "was not at liberty to assign any reason" for her ambiguous behavior. An unarticulated injunction against understanding, as well as interpreting, herself to others lies at the core of her repressed desperation and anguish. Merely deferring to male authority encourages misinterpretation, accedes to an unconscious presumption of her own innocence, and attests to the ambiguity inherent in consciously maintaining a vicious form of female virtue: permanent naïveté.

We learn then, very early in the novel that Evelina is persuasively observant, often aware of the role she plays in creating equivocal situations. Evelina and those representing her culture have mutually, though not always overtly, collaborated to grant her a character that denies the richness of archetype by confining it to stereotype. Above all else, reflective thought must be excluded from a conception of female virtue. It is no surprise then that attending Congreves's *Love for Love* puts her out of countenance, paralyzes her with silence, prevents her from observing. This is not a play, Orville says, that "can be honoured with their [the ladies'] approbation"; the young ladies in question must keep their observations to themselves in order to keep their innocence intact. Despite Orville's injunction against honoring the risqué play with female approbation, Evelina *writes* that it was "fraught with wit and entertainment." She also admits to Villars in another letter how her own virtue "must seem rather to invite than to forbid the offers and notice I received; and yet, so great was my apprehension of this interpretation, that I am sure, my dear Sir, you would have laughed had you seen how proudly grave I appeared."

In spite of such astute reasoning, in every situation where Lord Orville sees but does not hear her, her represented (cultivated) artlessness veils her in an ambiguous silence that invites attack. Overlooking the obvious sexual threat, Evelina reluctantly agrees to accompany the vulgar Branghton girls into the darkened alleys of Vauxhall. Accosted by a group of rowdy wags bent upon the plunder of innocence, Evelina once again flies off with Willoughby into an even darker alley. Although outraged at his predatory impertinence, at the implied sexual innuendo that seeks to cut off her response, she cannot refute the stinging correctness of his satire: "Is this a place for Miss Anville?—these, dark walks!—no party! no companions!" Mr. Branghton puts it more bluntly: "You must all of you have had a mind to be affronted." "A mind to be affronted" rationalizes its complicity by taking refuge in the role of female victim. We can be outraged at Willoughby's verbal power play, but we cannot discount the truth of what he says. Willoughby himself testifies to Evelina's wisdom: "Let Miss Anville look to herself; she has an excellent understanding, and needs no counselor." But the weight of social codes and conceptual models is too much for someone who must adhere to a narrow female standard.

Whenever Evelina relinquishes the authority of her own experience in favor of a naive sexual facade, she draws from others an opposing aggressiveness. After a fireworks display at Marybone Gardens, Evelina once again rushes off in a fright, heedless of remaining with her companions. Various "bold and unfeeling" men accost her, and she runs hastily to some questionable women for refuge. It is revealing that she protests her inability to free herself from their strong grip, and yet as soon as she is recognized by Orville, she finds the strength to tear herself away. With consternation and a measure of disingenuousness she later writes, "How strangely, how cruelly have all appearances turned against me! Had I been blessed with any presence of mind, I should instantly have explained to him the accident which occasioned my being in such terrible company:—but I have none!" If courage has deserted her in this incident, so has the memory of similar experiences. To Villars, she deplores her lack of "presence of mind," while forgetting that "presence of mind" responds spontaneously to the situation at hand, but persistently believing what she ought to be supersedes what she needs to do. If further proof that Evelina has guessed full well what kind of "ladies" she has been with is needed, she provides it when amused at Madame Duval's ignorance of them: "Indeed, it is wonderful to see how easily and how frequently she is deceived."

Doomed to fly from one dangerous and improper situation into another, Evelina seems inflexibly passive in her resignation to "properly own" the female name she has adopted, in spite of growing experiental evidence that this name does not serve her best interests any more than her namelessness does. If Evelina needs to learn to overcome a passive role, she also needs to acknowledge that passivity and innocence are anything but powerless. Mrs. Selwyn, a delightfully satirical version of woman, comments that Evelina's appearance seems coquettish and creates confusion: "You, innocent as you pretend to look, are the cause." When Evelina departs from Clifton in order to flee Orville, the same event viewed from Mrs. Selwyn's perspective is seen as "the logic of coquetry" crafted to captivate Orville. Seeing herself as a victim only, that is, as an unaccountable participant, however involuntary that participation may be, reduces the richer possibilities for action that would fit Evelina *for* the world and not just *to* it. In the social arena where she must display herself as a nameless (valueless) commodity until she can acquire nameability, however, she is often overwhelmed by the harshness of a world based upon a conceptual model that categorizes her by gender, calculates her visible worth, names her as nameless, and thereby condemns her to a passive silence by speaking for her.

The Evelina so named (represented) in the journal, however, is not the one who intrigues us as much as the who that narrates and orders the events by writing about them. The Evelina who writes reveals a much more evaluative knowledge of her world than the Evelina she writes about. As the account of Mrs. Stanley's ball has shown, Evelina is not without judgment, wit, and quick intelligence. As her accounts of the Branghtons show, she is brighter, more sensitive, and perceptive than they could ever hope to be. Her journal reveals that the most intelligent men, Orville and Willoughby, do appreciate her understanding in spite of her inexperience. Furthermore, when describing the witty Mrs. Selwyn's satirical forays, the Evelina who writes is more discriminating than the older lady who seems unaware of the censure her bent for irony invites. The ability to converse by writing to "two in good company," the oneself who asks and the oneself who answers, by traveling back and forth through the gap created by speech and writing, enables Evelina to find a path through the horrific void that namelessness implies.

A central episode involving the use and authority of Evelina's name marks a turn in her understanding of herself, a turn away from any self constructed as a singular entity, and also marks the intersection between the Evelina narrated and the who that narrates. The Branghtons learn of her acquaintance with Lord Orville and insist upon taking advantage of that relationship in order to usurp the social meaning of her name when they call on Lord Orville to solicit his business for the family shop. She writes to Villars: "I could have met with no accident that would so cruelly have tormented me." This threat is even more serious than the sexual dangers she has encountered. Until now, Evelina's own essentialistic awareness of herself as an innocent has prevented her from fully recognizing the self-objectification enforced by that definition. The overt reification of her as a "device" available to the utility and consumption of bourgeois economy, another form of namelessness, presses upon her what she would otherwise wish to conceal from herself. She cries out: "By what authority did you take such a liberty," and, "who gave you leave?—who desired you?" At this instance the subdued and repressed hysteria percolating at the edges of the narrative boils to the surface. For perhaps the first time in the novel, Evelina claims her own right to the disclosing as well as the concealing power of name and discourse. To speak importunately to Orville "as comes from one Miss Anville", makes her name an item in the Branghton trade. It forces her to act to lay aside the disguise of female passivity.

Usurping and reifying Evelina's name graphically illustrates how a narrowly defined, passive female role but poorly serves her, causing her to forfeit Orville's good opinion and giving him "reason to suppose I presumed to boast of his acquaintance!" "Half frantic," driven "wild," suffering an "irreparable injury," Evelina eschews the codes of both female decorum and virtue and writes to Orville directly. Forced to assert herself to prevent an inauthentic mode of discourse, namely reification, she nonetheless is impeded when her status as a nameless female undercuts her authority to name, that is, to articulate and interpret herself to others. To the Branghtons she may insist, "I must take the liberty to request, that my name may never be made use of without my knowledge," but in experience her name as female consists of those qualities and traits attributed *to* her rather than *by* her. Evelina closes her letter to Orville with a plaintive acknowledgment that she was used as the "instrument, however innocently, of so much trouble." When the letter is purloined by Willoughby just as her name was usurped by the Branghtons, it erupts from the silence relegated to a female; domestic circle of family and friends and into the din of a male, public circulation. The letter and its erratic and unforeseen postings radically alter the message Evelina has been sending about herself—to others as well as herself.

II

This central episode introduces the purloined letter and the forged reply. The letter never reaches Orville because Willoughby purloins it, forges an impertinent answer, and signs Orville's name. Woman's letter, her "name" is purloined through Willoughby by the patriarchal "name of the father."

When Evelina's letter is diverted from its path, it becomes purloined in another sense. *Pur-loigner* in the French means to put aside or put amiss, to suffer, a letter in sufferance trapped in a discourse it does not initiate, a letter effectively silenced. So trapped, Evelina herself becomes a letter in sufferance. Nonetheless, when the letter is diverted from its "proper" course, it does not cease to function. Evelina's letter overreaches authorial intention and male possession, initiating a chain of unpredictable changes in whoever comes to read it. She intends her letter to represent her "truely" to Orville, whereas Willoughby intends his letter persuasively to present Orville as different from the man himself. In each case, the one who comes to possess the letter is determined by it. Although the forged reply at first delights Evelina, Evelina's letter comes to possess Willoughby. In holding her letter, Willoughby hides her and her possibilities and becomes possessed by what he possesses without

authority. In holding the false letter, Evelina comes to a clearer understanding of the real Orville. The letter stirs desire and, in some sense, rewrites all their lives. Even at the end of the novel, Evelina's letter still has the power to cost someone's life in a duel.

At first perusal, as Evelina ruefully admits, the forged reply delights her. She marks only its expressions of regard because they answer to her own desires:

> It gave me no sensation but of delight. . . . I only marked the expressions of his own regard . . . repeating to myself, 'Good God, is it possible?—am I then loved by Lord Orville?'

In a second reading, "every word changed,—it did not seem the same letter." She recalls, furthermore, the circumstances surrounding the receipt of the letter:

> Had this letter been the most respectful that could be written, the clandestine air given to it, by his proposal of sending his servant for my answer, instead of having it directed to his house, would effectually have prevented my writing.

In the forgery, Willoughby speaks for Orville, in his name, to discredit his authority and to conceal Evelina's "capacity": "I concealed your letter to prevent a discovery of your capacity; and I wrote you an answer, which I hoped would prevent your wishing for any other." It bears a "clandestine air" because it tries to divert her response, to prevent her from "having it directed to [Orville's] house." Once again the forged letter conceals Evelina, requiring her to envelop herself in innocence, to post herself into danger. In purloining her letter he silences her, denies her voice and name.

Nevertheless, words are changed by changing contexts, and when she and Orville meet in Bristol, Evelina rejects the forgery, rejects Villars's abstractions about character, and lets observation guide her judgment. Accordingly, she can interpret the letter more accurately in writing about it. Evelina recognizes in this concrete event how innocence can be a "false delicacy which occasioned my silence." Writing opens to her a horizon of experience beyond the literal reading of the text, beyond the sense corresponding to her desire, beyond the sense of the "Orville" presented to her. Although the words in the forged letter remain unchanged, the meaning of them does not. When she rethinks the situation by writing about it, Villars's reply and Orville's past actions change the significance of the false letter.

When Evelina meets Orville face to face, her proper, intended coldness and reserve melt away and she writes Villars:

> It was my intention, nay, my endeavour, to support them with firmness: but when I formed the plan, I thought only of the letter,—not of Lord Orville.

In rejecting the false letter as a misrepresentation of Orville, Evelina acts from the stronger conviction that she knows him through a broader context of experience—character, regard, comportment.

The meaning, then, of the letter resides in the relations among sender, receiver, and holder, a communal bond that enmeshes in its web whoever comes in contact with it. When Willoughby purloins Evelina's letter, he is only the most outrageous (and hence useful) instance of a social order that in speaking for her, in owning the signs that signify her, in using namelessness as a sign of woman as currency, purloins her letter. In *The Rape of Clarissa*, Terry Eagleton conjoins writing and woman:

> The problem of writing is in this sense the problem of the woman: how is she to be at once decorous and spontaneous, translucently candid yet subdued to social pressure? Writing, like women, marks a frontier between public and private, at once agonized outpouring and prudent stratagem.

Through the dialogic agency of a letter as both "agonized outpouring and prudent stratagem" and of her own journal, "decorous and spontaneous, translucently candid yet subdued to social pressure," Evelina better understands the consequences of her misrepresentation. Moreover, she recognizes that silence transforms her into a victim and exacerbates her sufferings; silence does not prevent her self-revelation when she admits that behavior, mood, and other nonverbal gestures create a horizon of possible meaning for Orville to interpret: "I tremble lest he should misconstrue my reserve for embarrassment!" And again, "I could not endure he should make his own interpretation of my silence".

Writing gives Evelina an opportunity to speak, lending her a voice that the world not only denies but insists she doesn't have. She does not simply record what confounds her in London—a form of spectatorship—she participates in reordering what puzzles and frightens her. In writing, Evelina learns that she is capable of thought and therefore capable of speech, and she says this in the very process of denying it: "I will talk,—write,—think of him no more!" These disclaimers cause Villars to miss the strength and achievement of Evelina's letters.

He unwittingly acknowledges their authority by simply accepting them as representational, as veridical accounts. The persuasive power of her narration compensates for the authority that silences her. She corresponds because her experiences do not—*discordia concors*.

At times the dazzling power of narration causes Evelina to fall back upon that reductive concept of female innocence, laying claim to the unambiguous and literal, draping herself in self-illusion. To discover that writing uncovers what has been carefully concealed from oneself can be very disconcerting: "I will not write any longer; for the more I think . . . the less indifferent . . . I find myself." Writing begins to find for her, her self. What she cannot see, perhaps what at times she *will* not see is that transparency and innocence are available only within experience. The greater her vocabulary of experience, the broader her perspective on a situation, the more she understands the power and attendant dangers of innocence. Writing enables Evelina to share in the composition of her own destiny, to see that the role of innocent bystander is often complicitous with that of active participant.

Writing as act precludes her being a passive spectator: she is enmeshed in a web of discourse that calls for her response, that connects her to her particular place in culture. Writing reliably guides or opens her to possible modes of female conduct. When Villars warns Evelina against "those regions of fancy and passion whither her new guide conducted her," he also implies that writing informs experience, since her new "guide" is her imaginative pen—not patriarchal advice. Since the letters themselves not only reside in but *are* the "regions of fancy and passion," they are not as easily subject to the discursive control of patriarchal logic. Neither are they limited to the linear movement of a conventional plot, a sending that asks for no reply. In fact, the episodic zigzag movement of epistolary narrative resists any overarching structure targeted as plot. The epistolary shapes pathos, terror, emotion in such a way as to discourage the reader from building theoretical constructions of analysis upon it. Her letters are not a form for imperatives, statements of facts, or assertions. The indirection of the culturally unsayable opens "regions of fancy and passion."

Feelings are less a subject Evelina takes *up* than an affective condition that takes *her*. "I made a resolution, when I began, that I would not be urgent; but my pen—or rather my thoughts, will not suffer me to keep it—." Writing does not merely record her feelings for Orville, it shapes them, gives space for the feelings that draw her into dark alleys. Writing reveals to her—and others—the pattern of her desires. Villars, Maria, and we are sure she is in love, even though she has never admitted to it openly: "Long . . . have I perceived the ascendancy which Lord Orville has gained upon your mind." Evelina writes to Villars but finds herself addressing Orville:

> Oh! Lord Orville!—it shall be the sole study of my happy life, to express, better than by words, the sense I have of your exalted benevolence and greatness of mind!

As Evelina's writing becomes a displacement for her concealed desires, it opens her to more than one identity, more than one version of character. It draws her out of the stifling closet of female reserve and into multiple chambers of thought.

The company of thought is available to Evelina through the conversation of her writing. This conversation enables Evelina to discover a counter-authority to that of the patriarchy. Usually when Evelina's discourse falls silent due to lack of authority, it is Villars, much like Burney's father, who feels authorized to speak for her. His letters to Evelina are filled with maxims, exhortations, and the highest sentiments of concern and moral propriety. Ever admonishing, he simply cannot forbear talking about "the right line of conduct," the same for both sexes, "though the manner in which it is pursued may somewhat vary." The varied "manner" in which "the right line of conduct" is pursued not only attests to the inadequacy of any "right line of conduct" as a guide for females but also to the impossibility of only one "right line." Nonetheless, even Villars is persuaded by Evelina's narrative power so that, when she writes about male importunity, he admonishes her to take authority in the sense of responsibility to her own experience to learn from it:

> But you must learn not only to *judge* but to *act* for yourself; if any schemes are started, any engagements made, which your understanding represents to you as improper, *exert* yourself resolutely in avoiding them; and do not, by a *too passive* facility, risk the censure of the world, or your own future regret. (emphasis added)

In an astonishing admission, Villars explains to Evelina that innocence *conceals* the approach of duplicity: "Guileless yourself, how could you prepare against the duplicity of another? Your disappointment has but been proportioned . . . to the innocence which hid its approach." He repines: "That innocence . . . should, of all others, be the blindest to its own danger,—the most exposed to treachery,—and the least able to defend itself, in a world where it is little known, less valued, and perpetually deceived!" Innocence, he implies, nurtures hysteria. Evelina's persuasive narration holds an authority that forces Villars to redefine his cherished concept of female innocence.

The dialogue generated by these letters shows how writing addresses an important issue far beyond the need to express or the purpose of guidance—especially since Evelina often does not respond in her letters to the advice he gives. Her realistic descriptions and astute assessments of human behavior convince Villars of the authority of her writing even as he tries to maintain the fiction of her artlessness. He consistently displaces Evelina's authority, standing *in* for her but not letting her stand *up* for herself. Renouncing such a patriarchal version of authority can be the means for woman to name herself rather than let others name her.

Although Villars may speak for Evelina when she cannot, *speaking for* is not the same as *letting* speak. Evelina's letters are authoritative precisely to the extent to which they are filled with concrete, but ever-changing, interpretations of particular events. When pressed by Evelina's details concerning actual events, Villars is forced to relinquish his abstractions for more practical considerations that are attuned to the present need. Her authority corresponds to the way her letters say what is rather than what ought to be. Evelina's letter about Willoughby is so persuasive that it even moves Villars to relinquish the patriarchal mandate for female reserve:

> It is not sufficient for you to be reserved: his conduct even calls for your resentment; and should he again, as will doubtless be his endeavour, contrive to solicit your favour in private, let your disdain and displeasure be so marked, as to constrain a change in his behaviour.

In other words, female virtue encompasses more than a silent reserve; virtue takes the active form of a disdain and displeasure so marked that it will force a behavioral change in others. Concealing the strength of a woman's own desires and intelligence diminishes her human richness; she remains one-dimensional as long as she is complicitous with the representational model.

In writing, Evelina finds the connections, the parallels, and the patterns of events that shape her experience to herself and her corespondents. In writing, Evelina can explain and defend how she behaved at her first ball, although she could never do so by speaking directly to those who received a wrong impression of her. In a letter she can discuss her disapprobation of people, places, and events, expressing attitudes and opinions that she must otherwise hide or dissemble. The letter privately gratifies, frees her discourse from what must otherwise adhere to social strictures. Eagleton states that a decorum of who may write to whom, and under what conditions, provides an internal censorship, since the epistle is at heart an appeal to another. Since Evelina writes the bulk of her letters to Villars who represents the authority of patriarchy, she allows the dialogue to speak for her rather than give him the impression she is making judgments. By seeming to record whole conversations, she lets the rhetoric of the letter ameliorate the impertinence of its own intimate revelation. Her epistles subversively charm more than her strained efforts to be artless; the more her letters express a deeply felt private sentiment, the more they snare the reader into a reciprocal intimacy.

Evelina allows the dialogue to speak indirectly for her rather than playing author in the patriarchal sense. She criticizes the authorial model, nonetheless, when she, like Burney, deliberately conceals her authority by editing or merely recording events in the form of private letters. Evelina's (non)authority becomes a viable alternative not only to the power exercised by males, but to that of the other women as well. Madame Duval's access to society rests entirely upon her patrilineal name and money, for which she is more tolerated than accepted. Lady Howard can speak with the authority of the patrilineal name, money, and position. She therefore does not test the limits of masculine authority. Though Mrs. Selwyn thrives on satirical challenges to authority, she is indulged for the sake of name and position. These versions of female power rely on an idea of identity coextensive with patriarchy. The forced race of the nameless old women servants, so often puzzling to readers, demonstrates the plight of woman without resource to male legitimation. The argument here is that Evelina, by contrast, opens up a non-patriarchal path for identity and authority through the company of the letter's conversation.

The novel is about sendings, letters; hence a novel without author(ity), only an editor. In both Burney's preface and Evelina's narrative, authority is renounced. What is true of the letters is true of the novel: neither Evelina, the one narrated and the one narrating, nor Burney authors it in the sense of origin and closure. They send letters—one sends

to Berry Hill, one into the world—but they do not speak for others. They let others speak for themselves and keep the conversation going. They listen to the world and send letters as a function of listening. Evelina narrates: in letting the others speak she must listen and understand them better perhaps than they understand themselves. She makes Mrs. Selwyn's irony her own, makes Branghton vulgarity part of her world even as she dismisses it; she even assimilates the aggression of the male and the displacement of woman to this narrated world. She is author in the ancient sense of *auctor*, one who augments the conversation underway, one who need not command or coerce to make herself heard.

With the help of her new guide, Evelina discovers how she can resist any "plot" ready formed for her. It enables her to say who she is in spite of cultural limits upon her discourse. The intimacy of the letter creates the impression of saying what was not intended to be heard, what she is not authorized to say. Thus, she can use writing as a form of cultural power to disarm cherished notions rather than wresting them from the grip of the opposition. The patriarchal authorities, those "magistrates of the press, and Censors for the public" (original preface), merely assert what ought to be, while Evelina describes what is, that is, what appears. This opening for what appears, for further dialogue, prevents any determinant meaning. The Evelina narrated and the one who narrates, Villars, Maria, Burney, and imagination, the new guide, all symbolize the intersubjective relations that expropriate the individual.

Narrating names who she is long before her father or her husband give her an authorized, patrilineal name. But the narrative is not public, else it couldn't be written—or is public only by editorial intervention. Like Evelina's unauthorized being, her letters are unauthorized, private appeals to another, protected by an internal censorship:

> I gave over the attempt of reading ... and, having no voice to answer the enquiries of Lord Orville, I put the letter into his hands, and *left it to speak both for me and itself.* (emphasis added)

Otherwise they would be indecorous, even impertinent. Thus the narrating Evelina outgrows the already narrated innocent angel whom others wish to preserve.

Burney may purloin Evelina's letters by editing them, and we may eavesdrop. Like Willoughby, we may be claimed, drawn into the narrative conversation by overhearing her, but she does not intend the world to hear what she is not authorized to say. Instead, Evelina's authority is revealed as that of character in the ancient sense of ethos. It is based upon everything we as readers know about her: her represented and representing self, her shrewdness in oscillating between those two selves. Ethos emerges as a provisional identity, in between the narrator/narrated, in between author/editor Burney, between the different sendings. Burney's narrative about Evelina writing a narrative about herself is not properly named or fathered; like that of Evelina, it is "unnamed, unknown without any sort of recommendation" (original preface), an "other" message. Evelina's letter was purloined at birth, and her search is for a legitimate name, a voice that is authentically her own.

Evelina cannot authenticate her own narrative according to the patriarchal standards for authority and legitimacy. To do so would open her to dangers which patrilineal name, position, and money would otherwise circumvent. It would also open her to the censure that Mrs. Selwyn's irony receives. Jean-François Lyotard helps us say what is at stake in this narrative at a high level of generality, and hence, at a broad level of applicability. Legitimation, he observes, is the process of deciding the true and the false. Representation and its rational criterion of adequacy or accuracy is masculine—an Enlightenment ideal. In the Enlightenment culture of Burney's age, narrative knowledge lacks legitimacy and belongs to "fables, myths, legends, fit only for women and children." However, narrative knowledge lies behind, is presupposed by, such rational discourse. It reveals the significant shape of human life in that all questions of truth are situated in events that have enough coherence to be told as a narrative. The events and their connections are not veridical; rather they are events of vision, the a priori context for representational discourse.

It is no accident that women who, like Evelina, cannot control signification write letters that forestall closure and keep the conversation in good company. As Evelina's letters displace her as a constituted entity, they become communally constitutive. Each sending replaces the previous one so that ideological structures cannot censor them. Thus they mediate all conceptual boundaries—public, private, self, world. Instead of embalming the world in patriarchy's sterile discourse, the name of the father, these generative women—Evelina, Caroline Evelyn, Fanny Burney—give it birth, even beyond their own mortality.

Women's purloinable letter, like an unnamed child without a legitimating birthright, reveals there is no fixed identity at either end of the correspondence. Evelina's birthright cannot be subject to such a public or legal claim, for if it were, it would violate the rule of female propriety, damage her father's honor, and call her own legitimacy into question. She must rely, instead, on private intercession by others who speak on her behalf. Yet, what convinces Sir John Belmont that Evelina is his daughter is not Mrs. Selwyn's argument, not a legal claim, not even an appeal to pathos. It is Evelina's resemblance to her mother, a truth that destroys his narrative by substituting another—by refiguring his life. That is, her most convincing proof is neither a document nor a form of patriarchal speech that bears the silencing authority of a truth statement. She posts a likeness of her mother that lacks any of those patrilineal seals of legitimation. Caroline Evelyn's letter, read by John Belmont years after her death, is shattering: "Ten thousand daggers could not have wounded me like this letter." Evelina's legitimacy rests on a revolutionary displacement of the criterion of legitimacy inherent in patriarchal culture. It rests upon her own renunciation of the patriarchal authority that diminishes rather than augments when it insists upon power over discourse. Though she seems to sink into the conventional patrilineal family and ends her story, "I have time for no more [writing]," her lack of name and of the means by which her name is recovered opens a countercultural possibility for narrating ourselves without the authoritative subject at either end of the writing and conversing process. The representative heroine is subverted by her own act of representing.

We have seen that any notion of the female as a singular, stable entity is radically altered by Evelina's writing. In writing, the representational Evelina is exposed as a reductive concept, a product of the narrowly mediated, patriarchal code. Uncritically assuming that the individual is fully present as given, that representation is the ontological determination of woman, ensures an utterly predictable crisis for, and plot against, women. That plot, woman's silence, her repressed hysteria, hides possible self-discovery when it makes her nameable, sayable only by the linguistically mediated form available to her. As long as woman lacks a voice in the sense of sharing in the cultural figuration of who she is, she can never be an active conveyor of meaning. Indirection by means of writing without closure allows the forbidden unsayable to be said. Julia Kristeva writes: "In 'woman' I see something that cannot be represented, something that is not said, something above and beyond nomenclature and ideologies." Yet, every time "nomenclature and ideologies" fail women, they speak indirectly of woman's inexhaustibility and subvert their own representation of woman. Revealed and concealed in any concept of woman is the open possibility for an ongoing, ever incomplete and incompletable identity. That possibility lies in writing, for, more than marks upon a page, writing calls forth the generative power of name— all that woman is and can be and is not yet; all about her that has been overlooked and yet is to be said.

Source: Joanne Cutting-Gray, *"Evelina:* Writing between Experience and Innocence,'' in *Woman as "Nobody" and the Novels of Fanny Burney,* University Press of Florida, 1992, pp. 9–31.

Edward A. Bloom

In the following excerpt, Bloom gives an emcompassing critique of Burney's novel.

II

When Evelina, in the sentimentalized words of her creator, made 'her first appearance upon the great and busy stage of life', she had 'a virtuous mind, a cultivated understanding, and a feeling heart'. At the same time, she revealed an 'ignorance of the forms, and inexperience in the manners, of the world'. Fanny Burney thus allowed her beautiful heroine (aged seventeen) about seven months in which to discover herself; to relate herself to the external demands of society and confirm the incorruptibility of disciplined innocence. Towards the achievement of this victory, as much social as moral, Evelina can draw upon dual resources: her own nature and the guidance of such high-minded teachers as the Reverend Arthur Villars and Lord Orville. Throughout the novel, indeed, there is little doubt that she will succeed. The suspense—from incident to incident—inheres in the means, since the successful resolution of the conflict is assumed from the start.

Fanny Burney therefore built her novel upon a series of 'little incidents' which test Evelina's response to the newly found joys and frustrations, the tensions and satisfactions of worldliness. Although the situations are entertaining in and of themselves, their appeal is as much to the moral sense as to the imagination. Each episode becomes a tutorial adventure, providing Evelina with new experiences 'in the manners of the world'. These she must as-

similate in a way that will bring wisdom to herself and honour to her teachers. More protected and so more fortunate than other fictional young women who had gone into the world—Defoe's Moll and Roxana, Marivaux's Marianne, or Richardson's Pamela—Evelina is never far from benign counsel or a sheltering friend. When distance reduces Villars's influence to affectionate abstraction, there are always Mrs. Mirvan and Lord Orville to abet her instinctive goodness with practicality.

Like any education, hers is cumulative, with virtue and self-awareness directed to social fulfilment. Being already endowed with virtue, she must now assure its preservation by storing up and applying the lessons of her moral odyssey. By the end of seven months her education, if not complete, has prepared her to take on the responsibilities of adulthood. No longer a child, she has come to learn— often painfully—the value of prudence. And all of the incidents in the novel, all of the concern with setting and manners, corroborate the means by which the prudent individual may attain harmony with himself and his social group.

That Evelina has reached this enviable state is symbolized in her marriage, which guarantees feeling as well as status and security. Not that she is now invulnerable to all temptation. She has, however, come to appreciate the efficacy of prudence in human affairs. And while she will doubtless err from time to time, her educational progress is certain: Orville, who is now her guide, is a paragon of wise, deliberate conduct; and Villars, as the final letter makes amusingly plain, will not relinquish his spiritual guardianship simply because Evelina is married.

The plot, disarmingly simple, is an effective vehicle for the subject of initiation. Like most eighteenth-century fiction the story is enlivened by variety of incident, contrivance, and mood; yet the plot moves steadily towards the inculcation of its moral premise. Almost from the beginning, Fanny Burney employs a double narrative vision: that of Villars, who supplies expository details as well as moral reflections; and that of Evelina, who in her dramatic movement gives Villars the bases for exhortation and advice. However reluctant he had been to release her from Berry Hill, he understood in the spirit Johnson's Imlac that 'the time draws on for experience and observation to take place of instruction'. As she tests her values empirically, discarding the naïve for those more sophisticated, she shares with her guardian the responsibility for confirming the worth of prudence. At the outset, in other words, Villars establishes the problem as in the opening act of a drama; thereafter Evelina takes a dominant position, involving herself in complications, being involved in them, and generally creating a climate of discovery.

She is not only an individual, however; she is a representative of feminine decorum, so that Villars may admonish her, 'nothing is so delicate as the reputation of a woman: it is, at once, the most beautiful and most brittle of all human things'. It is her duty to protect such fragility, and social induction puts her to the proof. Her entrance into the world parallels the temptation of Eve; unlike the biblical figure, however, she will be able to bridle her impulses and thus reach for prudential maturity. But initially the confusion and the wavering are there. Because of the 'artlessness of [her] nature, and the simplicity of [her] education', she is weak enough to enjoy flattery. She is young enough to relish the social round, to implicate herself in white lies and desires that strain against caution. She herself, aware of her occasional immoderacy, is troubled by 'heedless indiscretion[s] of temper' which balk discipline. Yearning for the revels of Ranelagh and the Pantheon, she writes to Villars: 'I believe I am bewitched! I made a resolution when I began, that I would not be urgent; but my pen— or rather my thoughts, will not suffer me to keep it—for I acknowledge, I must acknowledge, I cannot help wishing for your permission.'

This is the credible reaction of a naïve but obedient girl. That she is not ready for the lures of a false Eden is obvious; that she is moving towards sophisticated prudence is equally obvious. In time her experiences increase. Proportionately her vulnerability and dependence diminish; her capacity for sound judgement grows. Throughout the dramatic story of Evelina's evolving education, there runs a moralistic leitmotive which never alters: judicious conduct offers safety and sound reputation; intemperance only uncertainty and sorry consequences.

Villars's letters, as a result, are crucial both to the structural and thematic development of the novel. At the first level they are the link between the social universe Evelina has just entered and the world of Berry Hill. They assure the permanence of affection and prudential order; and they help Evelina to widen her vision, to exemplify, her own understanding of incident and character. To this extent, the Villars-Evelina correspondence is integral to the plot. At the second level, however, his correspondence with Lady Howard—though still

> **The plot moves steadily against a background of social extremes, comic mishaps, and near-tragedy."**

within the framework of the plot—serves a frankly hortatory function. These observations sometimes go beyond the immediate range of Evelina's adventures. And because they are addressed to another adult rather than to an impressionable child, their contents—unlike the euphemisms which fill his letters to Evelina—are more forthright. They stress without camouflage the necessity of prudence.

For instance, he is restrained in acknowledging Mme Duval's faults to Evelina and insists upon the former's right to her granddaughter's respect. But in writing to Lady Howard, he is vehement about the Frenchwoman's impertinence and prejudices, her 'unruly and illiberal passions', which are the antitheses of prudence. It is to Lady Howard that he speaks of the tragic consequences to 'the mother of this dear child,—who was led to destruction by her own imprudence, the hardness of heart of Madame Duval, and the villainy of Sir John Belmont'. The sharp tonal differences between his letters to Evelina and those to Lady Howard give breadth to the novel. They also illuminate the character of Villars, and, perhaps above all else, impress upon the reader more stringently than is possible in general discourse with Evelina the author's pervasive moral intention.

That intention is best summed up by Evelina herself: 'Alas, my dearest Sir, that my reflections should always be too late to serve me! dearly, indeed, do I purchase experience! and much I fear I shall suffer yet more severely, from the heedless indiscretion of my temper, ere I attain that prudence and consideration, which, by foreseeing distant consequences, may rule and direct in present exigencies.' Prudence thus relates the individual to what Johnson (in *Idler*, No. 57) called the 'cursory business of common life', sensible preparation for everyday existence. But for Johnson, and for Fanny Burney as well, prudence was more than merely pragmatic. An intellectual faculty also, it was (as in Aristotle's *Ethics*) 'practical wisdom' and so a guard to virtue. To pursue the Aristotelian by definition, 'a man has practical wisdom not by knowing only but by being able to act'. And proper action is inseparable from a capacity for proper judgement.

That is why Villars persistently reminds Evelina that she must learn to judge and act for herself. Now judgement entails two collateral powers: inner understanding or self-knowledge, and apprehension of external reality, the 'forms' and 'manners, of the world'. Evelina gropes toward this complex goal and—despite near-disastrous blunders—she preserves her reputation and finds her way. She comes to learn that self-concealment is 'the foe of tranquility', that appearances often belie reality, that the 'amiable' is not necessarily the 'good'. She learns to discriminate between what is lasting and worthy and what is transient and meaningless, not by the promptings of the heart but by the discipline of the mind, by the training of 'discretion' and 'thought'.

From the beginning her education has aimed at the achievement of virtue in action; that is, the moral sense at work in diverse social relationships. Its truths unfold gradually for her. Each new situation or individual she meets enlarges her capacity to make ethical judgements or choices; exposure negative activity is paradoxically as essential to her development as the positive. Thus, once in the glittering atmosphere of London and Bristol Hotwells, she is introduced to varieties of imprudence: the ill temper of Mme Duval, the vulgarity of the Branghtons and Smith, the crudity of Captain Mirvan, the passion of Willoughby, the foppishness of Lovel, the 'villainy' of Belmont. She recognizes that these people have imperfections which she cannot always escape and which she must, therefore, endure, transcend, and in the case of her father forgive. But in this same world, so dynamic after Berry Hill, is Orville, who by loving example teaches her that virtue may flourish in sophistication as well as in rustic simplicity.

'Generous, noble Lord Orville!' she describes him, 'how disinterested his conduct! how delicate his whole behaviour!' And how passionless the attraction between them. Evelina, indeed, thinks of him as brother and father; he calls her 'sister'. Sensuousness is in tact erased by spiritual compatibility. She—meek, obedient, chaste, forgiving—has the traits, despite minor venial failings, of a Christian heroine. Through her idealizing vision he takes on the superior virtues of a Christian hero—'civility, courtesy, obligingness'. He is the rational al-truist, offering 'compassion' and 'service even to people unknown'. Although he controls his passions and so every situation, he escapes self-righteousness; he conducts himself with a good nature which 'knows no intermission, and makes no distinction, is as unassuming and modest, as if he had never mixed with the great, and was totally ignorant of every qualification he possesses'.

Evelina is no philosopher, of course; but she does intuit Orville's consummate goodness in action. Socially pre-eminent and worldly, as Villars is not, he nevertheless translates all of the older man's admirable qualities into a secular context. As an exemplar of moderation, he is the enemy of cruelty and injustice. On the occasion of the footrace between the two ancient women, for instance, he shows in his inimitably reserved way that he can be 'angry at the right things and with the right people'. As a lover he is notable for propriety if not for ardour. His declaration of line, when it finally comes, is correctly ritualistic. It is a social form to be enacted on bended knees, and the sardonic interruption of Mrs. Selwyn barely disturbs his aplomb. Even jealousy does not provoke him into being other than polite and restrained.

Among readers to whom such exquisite sensibility is two hundred years removed from their coarser reality, Orville is almost incredibly perfect. And to be sure he does border upon a stereotype of consideration and social finesse. Some allowance must be made for Fanny Burney's reticence and inexperience, that is, her limitation in painting a masculine portrait whole. But even as she created him, he is the ideal companion for Evelina while she learns the rules of discretion. For her he is as much mentor as lover, a sentimental guide who gladly assumes the task of ordering her 'feeling heart' with wisdom, of refining the lessons of prudence which Villars had begun years before in Berry Hill.

III

A novel, according to Fanny Burney, 'is, or it ought to be, a picture of supposed, but natural and probable human existence. It holds, therefore, in its hands our best affections; it exercises our imaginations; it points out the path of honour; and gives to juvenile credulity knowledge of the world, without ruin, or repentance; and the lessons of experience, without its tears'. Although she published this statement in 1814, when dedicating *The Wanderer* to her father, she could have attached it just as readily to *Evelina* thirty-six years earlier. In her theory of fiction, as in her novels, she indicates a proper respect for the inventive faculty but nothing which suggests a depth of aesthetic and technical concern. Rather, very much in tune with eighteenth-century moralism, she saw the novel as a preceptive vehicle. That is why she insisted, 'whatever, in illustrating the characters, manners, or opinions of the day, exhibits what is noxious or reprehensible, should scrupulously be accompanied by what is salubrious, or chastening'.

The fictional intention of *Evelina* evolved from the orderly pattern of a tranquil existence. The standards clearly delimited in the 'Author's Preface' are probability, reason, and natural simplicity; and these not unexpectedly obviate the Fantasy of romance. Furthermore, because Fanny wished to enlarge and generalize the implications of her narrative materials, she deliberately chose to draw social types, 'characters from nature, though not from life, and to mark the manners of the times'.

Her first novel is the product of a singularly uncomplicated personality. Long before writing *Evelina*, when Fanny was sixteen, she was shocked by the pessimism of *Rasselas*; but (after initial misgivings) she was intrigued by the 'rural felicity' of *The Vicar of Wakefield*. Unrelieved human wickedness, such as she found in Walpole's *Mysterious Mother*, was to her at once incomprehensible and unbearable. Always pronouncedly affective in her response to literature, she made her own writings a register of personal emotions and values. Realism, which she consequently related to her early serenity, becomes a triumph of benevolence with social propriety and unaffected goodness inseparable virtues. In her fictional practice, hence, she worked from a broadly humanistic base while at the same time symbolically projecting her own optimism.

The comic spirit which has pleased readers of *Evelina* for almost two centuries is a by-product of that optimism. It would be wrong, however, to assume (as does an uncomprehending moralist like Mrs. Barbauld) that her comedy either bars or corrupts serious purpose. *Evelina* is, in fact, a serio-comic novel which partakes of two narrative movements, one intellectual or thematic and the other situational or structural, but both operating at the same time. In its thematic movement *Evelina* focuses upon the adventures of its heroine: and though many of them are laughable, they often bring her perilously close to disaster. Through it all she manages to skirt the pitfalls. Each escape, in short, becomes one more step in her progress towards self-knowledge and in the assurance of a

happy resolution. In its structural movement the novel is neatly—too neatly—defined by a system of balance and counterbalance, point and counterpoint. No amusing episode is contrived for its own sake; rather, each is juxtaposed to another that is notable for its serious implications, or it is followed by an edifying, hortatory statement. Whatever is 'noxious', or at least deserving of censure, is 'scrupulously . . . accompanied by what is salubrious, or chastening'.

This controlled tidiness of meaning and plot is complemented by settings which blend with but never dominate actions or characters. While Fanny Burney gives impressions of tangible locations, she seldom if ever provides minute details. Critics like Paul Elmer More and Austin Dobson were perhaps right in complaining about her visual deficiency, but there are compensations in this lack which they failed to take into account. By suggesting rather than delineating place, Fanny keeps her people in the foreground at all times and lets them play their roles in appropriate but muted settings. We may regret the absence of vivid pictures, but the narrator's hints, flurries of action, and dialogue stimulate our own imaginations to fill in the outlines. If we do not really see place, we are always aware of it as a social force. As a novelist Fanny appreciated setting, but she thought it less important than her shifting clusters of people and their interaction.

She was nevertheless carefully selective in matching character or situation with place. The vaguely pastoral Berry Hill, for example, is an appropriate environment for elderly, slow-paced wisdom. Howard Grove, though also rural, emphasizes a lively, youthful prelude to the city. Here too we find the seeds of contrast and conflict; these anticipate and vivify the London experiences as Captain Mirvan and Mme Duval disrupt the order of the country with their brawls. On a more radical scale London is a kaleidoscope of confusion and gaiety—sparkling and sordid, artificial and dirty, treacherous and wanton. In a welter of topsy-turvy values the opera is a place where one goes to be seen, the parks playgrounds for would-be seducers. The disorder of the city is symbolized by the untidy Branghton house, the broken carriage, the muddy and rain-drenched streets. Yet urban life is not all bad: the London round has its charms, and it has Orville too. Furthermore there is the provincial setting—in some ways the most important in the novel—of Bristol Hotwells and Clifton, where town and country meet on elegant terms. Against this fashionable but faintly drawn backdrop Evelina undergoes her final tests and resolves all her problems.

Even as setting reinforces the schematized balance of *Evelina*, the precisely ordered structure as a whole contributes to the same effect. Coincident with the division of the novel into three volumes, the narrative centre is tripartite. Three units, comparable in length, are separated by actions of less magnitude, entr'actes that provide useful moments of contrast and stasis. Part one is preparatory, with Evelina's visit to the Mirvans logically succeeded by the first trip to London; here she discovers high and low social groupings, the modish set and the vulgar one of Mme Duval and the Branghtons. The climax of part one, vividly told by Evelina (16 April, Letter XXI), is the embarrassing episode at the opera. An interval at Howard Grove juxtaposes the rough-house comedy of the Captain (assisted by Willoughby) and the refinements of London society. The main action of part two then returns Evelina to London (beginning with the letter of 6 June) and emphasizes her exposure to the coarseness of Mme Duval and her mercantile relatives. The climactic episode (described in the letter of 3 July) deals with the former's impertinent appropriation of Orville's coach and ends in Evelina's imprudent letter of apology to Orville. This misadventure leads to the dark interlude at Berry Hill (starting with the letter of 14 July). Here, upon receipt of the false love letter supposedly from Orville, Evelina broods over the unreliability of appearances. Part three is centred in Bristol Hotwells and Clifton where she goes to recover from the deception. At the spa ferocity is camouflaged by gentility, and Evelina encounters decadence at its worst; in this setting she is also at the lowest point in her search for familial identity. Now, however, the wheel is turning upward, and she is about to enjoy her greatest triumphs: she and Orville come to recognize their love—that is, their mutual esteem; she discovers a father and a brother.

Climax thus builds upon climax, advancing through a series of misunderstandings, discomfitures, and complexities. The plot moves steadily against a background of social extremes, comic mishaps, and near-tragedy. The search for a father, while a necessary complication which threads its way through the entire novel, is less significant than the search for practical wisdom and its correlative, the pursuit of a 'proper' marriage. In its serio-comic theme, then, *Evelina* at least partially fulfils Lionel Trilling's concept of the novel as 'a perpetual quest for reality, the field of its research being always the social world, the material of its analysis being always manners ["a culture's hum and buzz of implication"] as the direction of man's soul'. To develop the tensions which are the measure of her own quest for reality, Fanny Burney methodically set the comic against the serious. The result, if one were to make a chart of the double movement, might look like this: the thematic strain, pervading the entire book, would be represented by a single, continuous line, its course gradually upward; the structural elements, enforcing the thematic, would appear to be a pendulant line swinging with more or less regularity from a fixed point between the serious and the comic.

Once the thematic direction of *Evelina* is understood—and this is early in the novel—it does not invite particularly subtle analysis; it is ingenuously straightforward. The situations may oscillate between the grave and the amusing; but they are tightly controlled by the stability of the argument. For example, Evelina's letter of 27 June is a grateful confirmation of her respect for Villars. After a hiatus of two days, however, she renews her letter with an abrupt shift in mood from her sober reflections to a dramatization of the vulgar conduct of Smith, Mme Duval, and the Branghtons before and at the Hampstead Assembly. On the surface, as Evelina describes their speech and actions, they are ludicrous figures, ridiculous copies of their social betters. Their apishness, as the core of a narrative situation, is exploited for its comedy. And in so far as they can be divorced from Evelina, their antics provoke involuntary laughter. Our sympathies, however, are so closely bound with her that even while we laugh we see them through her disapproving eyes as vulgarians who deny decorum and, hence, moral substance. In this way, through a reversal of approved values, the theme is corroborated. The overtly serious mood is then quickly restored by Macartney's letter; this not only has melodramatic overtones and conveniently implies his blood relationship with Evelina, but also points up the consequences of his own imprudence.

The device of balance and reversal occurs so frequently in *Evelina* as to be almost mechanical. That the comic will be succeeded by the serious is a constant expectation, and as a result the moral purpose pre-empts a large portion of the reader's attention. Even when the author refrains from explicit statement, irony of situation supplies the missing hortatory element. The first letter of 16 April, for example, centres in the Captain's crudely amusing torment of Mme Duval. The initial impression is farcical because we have no reason to mind seeing her mauled by the rough nationalist.

But Willoughby's mannered subtlety emphasizes the ill breeding of the sailor, and—more significantly—implies that his own good breeding is illusory. This alliance of two disparate social types thus converts broad comedy into an ironical censure of indecorous behaviour. The point is underscored in the next letter with the appearance of Lovel and Lord Orville. The former, of course, adds to Evelina's distaste for bad manners, while his lordship clarifies for her the nature of rational gentlemanliness.

Without such balance the humour and horseplay which abound in the novel would be aimlessly cruel and even awkward. Unlike Smollett, whose influence lurks behind the farce of *Evelina*, Fanny Burney does not have a talent for sustaining boisterously savage exchanges. More like Fielding, she is at her best in the controlled play of social affectation, in the adumbration of what is ridiculous and not painful. Generally, thus, her comic scenes are intervals between the grave ones; and not only do they serve her thematically through ironic reversal, but they often contribute to structural development. The comic introduction of Mme Duval, in the letter of 13 April, is replete with Captain Mirvan's anti-Gallicisms. The real issue, however, is Evelina's shocked discovery of her grandmother. Comparably, the footrace between the two old women will seem to most modern readers questionable fun. Yet by contrasting the cruelty of Lord Merton and Mr. Coverley with the benevolence of Lord Orville, Fanny tightens the affinity between the latter and Evelina.

Apart from the thematic interest of the novel, much of its lasting appeal derives from both characterization and particular comic scenes. The value of the moral lessons depends upon the immediate, subjective relevance of the people who enact them. According to Fanny's own terms, ideas must be exemplified. Once she questioned philosophy as 'an endurance of events in which we have no share—any thing, every thing—but Feeling and Nature!' Without a capacity for philosophical abstraction, she none the less had ideas which, with a sensitivity for 'Feeling and Nature', she incorporated in her characters. Most of them—even within the confining limits of what they represent—provoke us to a response, whether it be to their hypocrisy and vanity or to their good nature and charity. The characters of worth are paradoxically less interesting than those who perform with eccentric crudity or selfishness. Such goodness as we see in Villars, Orville, Macartney, Evelina herself, often taxes even the latitude implicit in moral realism. The fops

and posturers are likewise exaggerated, but their credibly comic dialogue and actions soften didactic intention. Human imperfections, if we allow for the author's inflation, are more assimilable than superhuman virtues. But the bad and the low are as necessary to Fanny's scheme as the good and the high.

In the creation of her comic characters she observed a precedent set by Fielding. That is, she too—without his consciously satiric thrust—recognized affectation as the 'source of the true Ridiculous'. Plot—and hers is a frail one—was ultimately less important to the intention of *Evelina* than characterization. More precisely Fanny was absorbed in the problem of making her heroine see and come to grips with varieties of personality and behaviour. Such preoccupation tends to produce type-figures, two-dimensional or 'flat' figures (as E. M. Forster would have it) who exist for their predominant traits. Yet out of the interplay of types—the balance of attitudes—emerges Fanny Burney's distinct if contracted image of humanity.

There are times when we wish the 'flatness' to be less pronounced: sometimes the triflers are too trifling, the vulgarians too vulgar, the snobs too snobbish. The occasional inadequacy of portraiture is one of execution (and perhaps even of experience) rather than of intention, for Fanny herself thought her portraiture was realistic. A common complaint in her own day, for instance, was that Captain Mirvan's grossness went beyond credibility. In her *Diary* she comforted herself with the retaliatory thought, 'that the more I see of sea captains, the less reason I have to be ashamed of Captain Mirvan; for they have all so irresistible a propensity to wanton mischief,—to roasting beaux, and detesting old women, that I quite rejoice I showed the book to no one ere printed, lest I should have been prevailed upon to soften his character'.

Narrative writing was almost second nature for Fanny Burney, whose diaries, letters, and scrapbooks give the impression of one who is always self-consciously playing the author. During a visit to the country in 1777, for instance, she wrote to Susan: 'Indeed, for the future, I must beg leave to visit places with which you are wholly unacquainted; for here my genius is perpetually curbed, my fancy nipped in the bud; and the whole train of my descriptive powers cast away, like a ship upon a desert island! . . . a marvellous good simile!' Descriptions of people and events—particularly the odd and eccentric—are confided to these private pages: a marriage between the family cook and a glassblower (or polisher) much her junior; a masquerade; a coach accident in London; a sea-storm; a pig race and a rowing match between women (germs perhaps of the footrace in *Evelina*); visits to the theatre. On other pages she captured social types—coxcombs, gentlemen, fops, ardent suitors—traces of whom appear in the novel. Or occasionally she tried her hand at vignettes which emphasize female vanity: Miss Pogelandel, Miss Digget, Miss Hasty. The last, a seventeen-year-old girl, is intriguing as the antithesis of Evelina. Through these early jottings Fanny shows herself to be adept in the rendering of suspense, responsive to the minutiae of character and episode.

Her creative imagination led her inevitably to *Evelina* and a firm place in the tradition of eithteenth-century fiction. As a bridge from the earlier novelists—Fielding, Richardson, Smollett—to Maria Edgeworth and Jane Austen, she served both as pupil and teacher. Under the influence of Fielding, she refined her comic and social perceptions; even her thematic interest owes much to him. Her purpose in *Evelina* is not unlike Fielding's in *Tom Jones*. 'I have endeavoured', he wrote in his dedication to George Lyttleton, 'strongly to inculcate that virtue and innocence can scarce ever be injured but by indiscretion; and that is this alone which often betrays them into the snares that deceit and villainy spread for them.' From Fielding also she doubtless learned a good deal about the careful ordering of plot. But there were additional lessons for her in the epistolary techniques of Richardson and Smollett, to say nothing of the violent comedy of the latter and the moral, sentimental gravity of the former. To these debts, of course, must be added those which she herself ascribed to Rousseau, Johnson, and Marivaux.

Looking ahead to those who followed her closely in time, we see the resemblance of Maria Edgeworth's Lord Colambre and Grace Nugent (of *The Absentee*) to Lord Orville and Evelina. That the line of influence culminates superbly in Jane Austen is a critical commonplace which needs no enlargement. With her superior comic vision, acute psychological understanding, and sheer craftsmanship Jane has overshadowed her predecessor. But it is pleasant to realize that Fanny, though somewhat obscured by Jane's lustre, continues to glow softly in the light of her own memorable achievement.

Source: Edward A. Bloom, Introduction, in *Evelina*, Oxford University Press, 1968, pp. vii–xxxi.

Sources

Chisholm, Kate, "Return of the Wanderer," in the *Guardian*, April 19, 2000.

Goldstein, Lauren, "Move Over Austen," in *Time Europe*, Vol. 155, No. 19, May 15, 2000.

Marr, Andrew, "Burney Peculiar," in *Observer*, July 9, 2000.

McCabe, Daniel, "The World according to Fanny," in *McGill Report*, Vol. 33, No. 3, October 5, 2000.

Further Reading

Bilger, Audry, *Laughing Feminism: Subversive Comedy in Frances Burney, Maria Edgeworth, and Jane Austen*, Humor in Life and Letters series, Wayne State University Press, 1998.

> The title of this work says it all. This is an interesting look into early women's writing about the female situation of their times.

Cutting-Gray, Joanne, *Woman as "Nobody" and the Novels of Fanny Burney*, University of Florida Press, 1992.

> This is a study of Burney's writing through a feminist eye.

Daugherty, Tracy Edgar, *Narrative Techniques in the Novels of Fanny Burney*, Peter Lang Publishing, 1989.

> This provides a close study of the writing techniques that Burney employed. It is a good book for anyone interested in writing.

Gill, Pat, *Interpreting Ladies: Women, Wit, and Morality in the Restoration Comedy of Manners*, University of Georgia Press, 1995.

> Gill focuses on such early playwrights as William Congreve and Aphra Behn to explore the roles and function of female characters in eighteenth-century plays.

Volansky, Michele, and Michael Dixon, eds., *Kiss and Tell: Restoration Comedy of Manners: Monologues, Scenes and Historical Context*, Smith & Kraus, 1993.

> This is a handbook for actors but also a synopsis of some of the best scenes from Comedy of Manners plays. It provides a good examination of some of the verbal wit used in the most popular plays of that time.

Fathers and Sons

Ivan Turgenev
1862

Ivan Turgenev's *Fathers and Sons* was originally published in 1862 in the Russian magazine, *Russkii vestnik* (*The Russian Herald*), under the title, *Ottsy i deti*, and is also known as *Fathers and Children* in some translations. Even before its publication, the novel ignited controversy. The generation gap between the fathers and sons in the story neatly symbolized the current political debates between the older reactionaries and the younger radicals. The character of Bazarov, a young radical who declares himself a "nihilist," somebody who accepts nothingness, particularly inflamed both sides. Although Turgenev claimed at one point that he meant the book to be a favorable depiction of the young radicals, this group viewed Bazarov as a spiteful caricature of them. Many of the older liberals did not understand the book and were also very upset at the influence that it had on the young radicals, who claimed the term "nihilist" for themselves, and used it in their violent protests.

Despite the initially scathing reviews, the book has stood the test of time, and many regard it as Turgenev's best. The book also represents the times, depicting the social unrest that was present in Russia just prior to the historic 1861 emancipation of the serfs—Russian slaves that were owned by the landed nobility—by Alexander II, as well as the various reforms that were in place at the time.

Ivan Turgenev

Author Biography

Turgenev was born on October 28, 1818, in Orel, a provincial town in Russia. His mother, Varvara Petrovna, had inherited a large amount of land, and the estate of Spasskoe-Lutovinovo was the largest and most impressive of her holdings. It was here that Turgenev's family stayed for the first few years of the author's life. Although they left the estate in 1822 to travel through Western Europe for a year, and then moved to Moscow in 1824, Turgenev would always be attached to Spasskoe. Turgenev received his education through a series of formal schools and private tutors and was educated in many languages. In 1833, Turgenev's father petitioned Moscow University to waive the age requirement and let Turgenev take his entrance exams early, which he eventually did.

Turgenev was well-read as a child, and became interested in literature very early. His first publication was a poem, "Vecher," which he published in the 1838 issue of *Sovremennik* (*The Contemporary*). In the same year, Turgenev left for Germany, where he stayed until 1841. During this time, he made friends with several other Russians and he continued to send his poetry back to Russia for publication. In 1843, when Turgenev was back in Russia, Turgenev's narrative poem, "Parasha," was

published, and the author began to be noticed—so much so, in fact, that he never finished his dissertation for his degree, which would have allowed him to teach. The same year, Turgenev was appointed to a post in the Ministry of Internal Affairs, which he left two years later to pursue his writing.

In 1845, Turgenev stepped up his literary efforts, taking part, along with other writers, in the publication of *Sovremennik*, which was under new management. In 1847, he returned to Berlin, although he continued to work on his writing and send selections back to *Sovremennik*. Turgenev returned to Russia in 1850, and the following year, he was imprisoned in St. Petersburg for trying to publish in Moscow an obituary of a fellow writer, Gogol, which had been banned by the St. Petersburg censors. Turgenev's jail time was not long, but he was sent into exile for what turned out to be a two-year term at his Spasskoe estate.

In 1856, Turgenev's first novel, *Rudin*, was published in *Sovremennik*, in two issues. In 1858, he published his short story, "Asia," in *Sovremennik*. The story was one of the first that marked Turgenev as a liberal from the 1840s, and it was this, along with other works, most notably *Fathers and Sons* in 1862, led to a break with *Sovremennik* and with the young radicals.

The novel depicts the problems inherent with the emancipation reforms that freed the Russian serfs. The backlash from the novel's reception discouraged Turgenev from pursuing any major works until 1865, when he began writing his fifth novel, *Dym*, which was published in 1867. Although he would eventually be overshadowed by Tolstoy and Dostoyevsky, Turgenev was still the first Russian writer who was known worldwide. Turgenev died on August 22, 1883, in his chalet at Bougival.

Plot Summary

Chapters I–III

Fathers and Sons starts with Nikolai Kirsanov eagerly waiting at a posting station—a depot for horse carriages—for his son Arkady, who has just graduated from school. When Arkady arrives, however, his father is surprised to see that he has brought a friend, Bazarov, to stay with him at their farm. Bazarov is an older medical student who serves as Arkady's mentor. He is calm, cool, and dispassionate.

Chapters IV–XI

They reach the farm where Arkady's uncle, Pavel Kirsanov, is happy to see him. Pavel does not care for Bazarov, however, and makes no effort to hide his distaste. Nikolai tries to bring up the subject of his mistress, Fenitchka, delicately, but Arkady charges off to see her, finding out in the process that he has a new baby brother. It does not take long before the two generations start clashing, mainly due to Bazarov's nihilistic ideas, a type of scientific materialism that advocates believing in nothing. These ideas, which Arkady mimics in their conversations, distress the older Kirsanovs, who realize that there is a large generation gap between them and the young men. Nikolai is sad, feeling his son slipping away from him, while Pavel is angry and gets into heated debates with Bazarov. After Nikolai and Pavel decline an invitation to go see their cousin in another provincial town, Bazarov and Arkady accept in their place.

Chapters XII–XV

In the town they meet Matvy Ilyich Kolyazin, Nikolai's cousin, who is an important official. Like Pavel, Kolyazin does not like Bazarov, although he invites both young men to the Governor's Ball. On the road they run into Victor Sitnikov, another one of Bazarov's disciples, who convinces them to pay a visit to Evdoksya Kukshin. Bazarov finds her boring, but still drinks her champagne. Kukshin tells them they should meet Anna Odintsov, a rich young widow, at the Governor's Ball. At the ball Arkady meets Anna and instantly falls in love with her, but she treats him like a friend and asks about Bazarov. After the dance, Arkady lets Bazarov know that Anna is interested in meeting with him and they visit at her hotel. Bazarov is uncharacteristically nervous in her presence. Anna suggests they come see her at Nikolskoe, her country estate, which they do a few days later.

Chapters XVI–XVIII

At Nikolskoe, Anna introduces the two young men to her sister Katya. Bazarov and Arkady stay at the estate for a fortnight, during which time Arkady slowly builds up a friendship with Katya, which starts to blossom into love and override his nihilism. In the meantime Bazarov is in the throes of a passionate love for Anna, which he finally confesses to her at the end of his stay. However, even though she has been flirting with him, he is dismayed when she spurns his advance. Relations are awkward with all of them until Bazarov and Arkady

Media Adaptations

- *Fathers and Sons* was adapted as an audio book by The Audio Partners Publishing Corporation in 1998 and read by David Horovitch.

- *Ottsy i deti* is the Russian version of *Fathers and Sons*. It was adapted as a film in 1959. It was produced by Lenfilm Studio and distributed by Artkino Pictures.

leave shortly thereafter for Bazarov's parents' house.

Chapters XIX–XXII

Bazarov's parents have not seen him for three years and are expecting a long stay. However, they smother him with affection, which makes him uncomfortable, and he and Arkady stay only three days, much to their dismay. They get on the road to go back to Maryino and pick up Bazarov's scientific instruments but on a whim, Arkady decides to have them go back to Nikolskoe. Anna is not expecting them, and does not seem pleased to see them. They quickly make an excuse, saying that they were not intending on staying and that they have just stopped in on their way to Maryino. Bazarov and Arkady surprise everyone at Maryino, who also were not expecting them back so soon. However, they are glad to see the two young men. Arkady is not long at home, however, before he finds out from his father that he has letters from Katya's mother, who used to write to Arkady's mother. He decides to use the letters as an excuse to visit Nikolskoe again, but this time, he is received warmly by Katya.

Chapter XXIII–XXIV

While Arkady is at Nikolskoe, Bazarov busies himself with his scientific experiments at Maryino. He also starts to spend more time with Fenitchka, Nikolai's mistress, under the pretense of offering doctor's remedies to their child. One day, when he is alone with Fenitchka in the garden, he kisses her, and Pavel sees. Shortly thereafter, Pavel challenges him to a secret duel and Bazarov accepts. Bazarov is unharmed, but shoots Pavel in the leg, then bandages the wound for him and stays with him until another doctor comes to relieve him. Bazarov leaves.

Chapters XXV–XXVI

Meanwhile Arkady is starting to express his feelings for Katya, but cannot quite tell her he loves her. Bazarov arrives and stays for a few days. Arkady again tries to express his love for Katya in the garden but is interrupted when they hear Bazarov and Anna walking by, talking about their own failed relationship. They leave and Arkady finally tells Katya he loves her. She returns the sentiment and shortly thereafter, Arkady asks Anna for her sister's hand in marriage. Bazarov leaves.

Chapter XXVII

Bazarov's parents are overjoyed to see him, especially when he tells them that he will be there for six weeks. He is noticeably changed from his experiences. Although he tries to busy himself with his experiments, he finds himself getting more social, talking to peasants, and begins to help his father, another doctor, with his patients. After a patient dies of typhus, Bazarov performs an autopsy, cutting himself in the process. The typhus infection quickly overcomes him, and he dies shortly thereafter. On his deathbed, he sends for Anna, who is with him when he collapses into his final unconscious state before death.

Chapter XXVIII

Six months pass, and in January, both Arkady and his father marry their respective loves. Pavel leaves on the day of the wedding to seek his fortunes abroad. Turgenev addresses the reader, saying that he will give a short synopsis of how everybody is doing in the present. Anna gets married, but not out of love; instead, it is out of the same practical good sense that she has always followed. Arkady, his father, and their respective families live at Maryino, where Arkady is running the now-prosperous farm, while Nikolai helps to institute the upcoming emancipation reforms that will revolutionize Russian society. Pavel spends his time first in Moscow before settling in Dresden, Germany. Finally, Bazarov's parents weep at his grave often, mourning their lost son. Turgenev offers one final thought, saying that love is not hopeless, and that in the end, even Bazarov will have eternal reconciliation and life without end.

Characters

Father Alexey

Father Alexey is a nice priest who comes to visit Bazarov's parents; he wins money from Bazarov at whist, a card game.

Arisha

See Arina Vlasyevna Bazarov

Arkasha

See Arkady Nikolaitch Kirsanov

Arina Vlasyevna Bazarov

Arina Vlasyevna, Bazarov's mother, adores her son and is crushed at his tragic death. When she was younger, Arina was part of the Russian minor nobility, but since she has married, she has turned over all of her affairs to her husband, Vassily. She is still horrified at the upcoming reforms, however, which will divide up the land of the nobility. When Bazarov comes home to visit for the first time in three years, she smothers him with attention, and, as a result, he leaves after three days. When Bazarov comes back for a longer stay, she is more discreet and does not bother him as much. Vassily does not tell Arina about Bazarov's typhus until he is sure his son is infected. After Bazarov's death, his parents visit his grave often, weeping for their son.

Vassily Ivanovitch Bazarov

Vassily Ivanovitch is Bazarov's father and like his wife, Arina, he adores his son. Vassily worked as an army surgeon under Arkady's grandfather, who was a general at the time. In his retirement, Vassily and his wife live in a small country homestead, where Vassily still administers treatment to the peasants for free. When Bazarov comes home, it is the first time he has seen his son in three years, and Bazarov only stays three days, a fact that makes Vassily very sad. When Bazarov comes back, Vassily is overjoyed to hear that Bazarov will be staying for six weeks. Bazarov starts helping his father with his patients, and in the process takes the opportunity to dissect a man who has just died from typhus. When Vassily sees the cut on Bazarov's finger that he gets during the autopsy, he is frightened that his son has caught the disease. A few days later, Bazarov dies, and Vassily's fears come true.

Yevgeny Vassilyev Bazarov

Bazarov, as he is known throughout most of the work, is the friend of Arkady, and he dies at the end of the novel from a typhus infection. Even from the beginning of the novel, Bazarov, a young medical student, is expected by almost everybody to do great things. His unflinching manner and severe conviction to the strict tenets of nihilism—a type of scientific rationalism—have given him many disciples, of which Arkady is one. At the beginning of the book, Bazarov comes to stay with Arkady and his father at Maryino. The visit is full of conflict, as Bazarov's harshly radical ideas clash with Nikolai's brother, Pavel. Bazarov is completely unapologetic, even when Arkady tries to appeal to him. In fact, even though he wounds his friend with his sarcasm, Bazarov does not make amends. He states to all that he does not believe in his own emotions and should not therefore spare others. Bazarov and Arkady leave for a provincial town to meet Arkady's second cousin, who invites them to the Governor's Ball, where Arkady meets Anna Odintsov. The lady has more interest in Bazarov, however, and soon Arkady and Bazarov are staying with her at her country estate.

Although he tries to deny his feelings for Anna, they overcome Bazarov, who professes his love to her on the eve of his departure. She shuns him, however, and he goes instead to stay with his parents. They smother him with their emotion, and he leaves after three days, eventually going back to Maryino. Although he is content at first to busy himself with his scientific experiments, his eyes begin to stray, and at one point, he kisses Fenitchka, Nikolai's mistress. She is not interested in his affections, however, even though she was friendly with him. Pavel sees the kiss and challenges Bazarov to a secret duel. Bazarov accepts and walks away unharmed, although he shoots Pavel in the leg. Bazarov immediately takes care of the wound. He leaves Maryino shortly thereafter, and, after one more brief visit to Nikolskoe to see Anna, he bids his farewell to Arkady and goes to his parents' home. He tries to busy himself with his experiments, but finds himself being more social instead. He also starts to help his father, a retired army surgeon, with the peasant patients who come to him. In the course of performing an autopsy on a typhus victim, he cuts himself and gets typhus himself, which kills him a few days later. On his deathbed, he sends for Anna, who sees him before he dies.

Enyusha

See Yevgeny Vassilyev Bazarov

Fenitchka

See Fedyosa Savishna

The Governor

The Governor throws the ball where Arkady meets Anna Odintsov. He is also the employer of Arkady's second cousin, Matvy Ilyich Kolyazin.

Princess Avdotya Stepanovna H——

Princess H—— is the rich and grumpy aunt of Anna and Katya, who comes to live with them after their father dies. Nobody likes her, and nobody remembers her when she is dead.

Katya

See Katerina Sergyevna

Arkady Nikolaitch Kirsanov

Arkady Kirsanov is Bazarov's friend, Nikolai's son, Pavel's nephew and eventually, Katya's husband. When the book begins, Arkady, who is quite impressionable, is under the influence of Bazarov, and is trying desperately to adopt his friend's nihilistic ways. However, it is apparent from very early on that, although Arkady thinks he wants to be a radical, he still enjoys music, nature, and other "irrational" pursuits that distance him from Bazarov and nihilism. In fact, he and Bazarov get in many arguments throughout the novel about their conflicting beliefs. Still, in most cases, Arkady is willing to follow his mentor and does so to many destinations. At the Governor's Ball, it is Arkady who first meets and makes the acquaintance of Anna Odintsov. However, even though he is smitten with her, she only has sisterly love for him, and wants to meet Bazarov. As the two young men stay at Nikolskoe, Anna's country estate, the divide between them grows deeper, as Bazarov spends more time with Anna, and Arkady finds himself increasingly more attracted to Katya.

When Bazarov gets ready to leave Nikolskoe, Arkady is torn. He wants to follow his friend, but he also wants to stay with Katya. He follows his friend, first to Bazarov's parents' house, and then back to Maryino. However, Arkady cannot sit still for long. Finding an excuse to visit Nikolskoe again, he does so, where he finds Katya overjoyed to see him. After staying there for a little longer, Arkady finally gets up his nerve to propose to Katya, which he does after a few attempts. She happily accepts. When Bazarov shows up at Nikolskoe and says his farewell to Arkady, he tells him that he never would have made a good nihilist, and that he should pursue family life. Arkady and Katya are married in a ceremony with his father and Fenitchka. After this, they move into Maryino with the other couple, and Arkady takes over the management of the farm, whipping it into a profitable enterprise once more. At the end of the story, Arkady and Katya also have a son, Nikolai.

Marya Kirsanov

Marya Kirsanov is Nikolai's deceased wife and Arkady's deceased mother. Nikolai names his estate, "Maryino," after her.

Nikolai Petrovich Kirsanov

Nikolai Kirsanov is Arkady's father and Pavel's brother. Nikolai and Pavel's father was a general, so they were both expected to go into military service, which Pavel does. Nikolai, however, breaks his leg on the day he is supposed to leave for service, and is unable to serve. Instead, Nikolai gets his university degree and then works in the civil service position that his father finds for him. However, directly after the mourning period for his parents' deaths, Nikolai quits the civil service position, marries Masha, the daughter of his landlord—something his parents did not approve of—and moves to his country estate to live. When their son Arkady is born, they are joyous but ten years later, Masha dies. Nikolai spends more time with his son, even going to stay three years in town to be by his son while he is attending college, getting to know his son's friends.

For his son's last year, however, he does not stay, so he is surprised by the arrival of Bazarov at Maryino when Arkady graduates and comes home. Nikolai is gracious to Bazarov, but is also distressed at the young man's nihilistic views. Nikolai feels the generation gap widening between him and his son. Meanwhile, he has had a child with Fenitchka, the young daughter of his old housekeeper. Although he has held off from marrying her out of respect for his brother, Pavel, whom he does not think believes in marriage. Pavel eventually encourages him to marry. Nikolai gets married to Fenitchka in the same ceremony where Arkady marries Katya. This double wedding, and Arkady's choice to start running his father's farm, helps to close the generation gap.

Pavel Petrovich Kirsanov

Pavel Kirsanov is Nikolai's brother, Arkady's uncle, and Bazarov's opponent; when he challenges Bazarov to a duel, the younger man wounds him, then tends to the wound. When he was younger, Pavel had a promising military career, which he ruined when he resigned his commission to chase after a married woman, Princess R——. Although the two do have an affair, it is torturous for both and she eventually ends it, after he has chased her through many countries, and they have one final meeting. Pavel tries to resume his normal life but he is a broken man. The only remnant of his disciplined officer days are the smart clothes and nail polish that he wears, even when lounging casually around Maryino, Nikolai's home, where he lives. Pavel occasionally bails Nikolai out when he has money problems.

When Pavel first sees Bazarov, he does not like him, an animosity that grows as Bazarov gives his nihilistic beliefs. They get in many arguments and on Bazarov's second visit, they appear to be at peace. When Pavel catches Bazarov kissing his brother's mistress, however, he challenges Bazarov to a secret duel with pistols. Bazarov accepts and walks away unhurt. Pavel, however, gets shot in the leg. Through the experience of getting shot, getting tended by Bazarov, and recuperating in Maryino, Pavel is able to finally put his past behind and get on with his life. After the dual wedding of his brother and nephew, Pavel goes to Moscow, then finally settles in Germany, where he renews his old social habits for which he was famous as an officer.

Ilya Kolyazin

See Matvy Ilyich Kolyazin

Matvy Ilyich Kolyazin

Matvy Ilyich Kolyazin is Arkady's second cousin, a high-ranking official and the one who invites Arkady and Bazarov to the Governor's Ball where Arkady meets Anna Odintsov. Kolyazin is the cousin of Nikolai and Pavel, and originally extends the visitation invitation to them, but they turn it down. Arkady and Bazarov go in their place.

Madame Evdoksya Kukshin

Madame Kukshin is a friend of Victor Sitnikov, who tells Arkady and Bazarov they should seek out Anna Odintsov. Arkady and Bazarov only agree to meet Kukshin with the promise by Sitnikov of free alcohol. Kukshin tries to impress Arkady and Bazarov with her advanced ways of thinking. She is an independent woman who runs her own affairs now that she is separated from her husband. At the end of the novel, she goes to Heidelberg, Germany to study architecture.

Sergay Nikolaevitch Loktev

Sergay Loktev is Anna Odintsov's father, who loses much of the family fortune playing cards, prompting Anna to marry for money after his death.

Masha

See Marya Kirsanov

Mitya

Mitya is the child of Nikolai and Fenitchka. The child is born out of wedlock, but the couple marries by the end of the story.

Nellie

See Princess R——

Avdotya Nikitishna

See Madame Evdoksya Kukshin

Fedyosa Nikolaevna

See Fedyosa Savishna

Madame Anna Sergyevna Odintsov

Madame Anna Odintsov is the love interest of both Arkady and Bazarov, and ends up shunning both. Anna acts like a mother to her sister Katya, ever since their father's death. After his death, Anna marries a wealthy man to better her financial position and she and Katya retire to Nikolskoe where they live in isolation. Anna's neighbors do not like her because of the rumors that surround her and her father's scandalous gambling debts. Shortly after they move into Nikolskoe, their aunt Princess H——, a surly woman whom nobody likes, moves into Nikolskoe. Anna takes it all in stride and sticks to her principles of keeping everything orderly, including people.

Anna first meets Arkady at the Governor's Ball, where he talks to her at length, but she shows only sisterly interest in him. She does, however, ask to meet Bazarov, and does shortly thereafter when Arkady and Bazarov come to her hotel room. While she is calm, Bazarov is struck by love and behaves irrationally for perhaps the first time in his life. She invites them to come see her at Nikolskoe, her country estate, and they do so a few days later. Although Anna, Katya, Arkady, and Bazarov start out in each other's company, over the next fortnight they split into two couples—Anna and Bazarov; Katya and Arkady. When she is alone with Bazarov, Anna flirts with him, but then rejects

his advances when he professes his love for her. She is scared of his passion and wishes to live her orderly life. After she approves of Katya's marriage to Arkady, Anna eventually remarries also, this time to a politically powerful lawyer—as before, it is out of opportunity, not love. She responds to Bazarov's deathbed summons, seeing him one last time before he dies.

Piotr

Piotr is one of the few freed serfs that Nikolai keeps employed at Maryino. Piotr also serves as the witness at the duel between Bazarov and Pavel.

Porfiry Platonitch

Porfiry Platonitch is the card-playing neighbor of Anna Odintsov's, and one of few regular visitors to Nikolskoe.

Princess R——

Princess R—— is the woman with whom Pavel Kirsanov falls in love. Both are tormented by the relationship, which she finally ends by running away from Pavel. On her deathbed, she sends Pavel back his ring.

Fedosya Savishna

Fedosya Savishna, also known as Fenitchka, is Nikolai's mistress. Fenitchka is the daughter of Nikolai's housekeeper, who comes to live with Nikolai while Arkady is at school. Although she is shy around Nikolai at first, at one point, he helps to heal her eye from a spark that has flown into it. After this, she starts to warm up to him. When her mother dies from cholera, Nikolai begins to have his affair with her, which results in the birth of Mitya. When Arkaday comes home from school, he has heard about Fenitchka, but has not met her. Although Fenitchka is shy around him, and indeed around everyone, she gradually starts to open up. Bazarov introduces himself as a doctor, after which she comes to see him for various questions about Mitya. At one point, in the garden, Bazarov oversteps his bounds and kisses her. Although they had been having playful conversation, she did not want this, and lets him know. Pavel witnesses the incident, and later confronts her on it, but it is only to make sure that she is truly in love with Nikolai. Pavel encourages Nikolai and Fenitchka to get married, which they do with Arkady and Katya. At the end of the book, Fenitchka loves nothing more than conversing with her daughter-in-law, Katya.

Katerina Sergyevna

Katerina Sergyevna, also known as Katya, is the sister of Anna Odintsov, and marries Arkady Kirsanov. When Anna first introduces Katya to Arkady and Bazarov, neither one is interested in her. They are both in love with Anna. Bazarov views her as a pupil, who could be molded into whatever they want. However, after a while, Arkady's love for Anna fades, and, through a slow but steady friendship at Nikolskoe, Arkady falls in love with Katya, denouncing many of his nihilistic beliefs in the process. When he proposes to her, it takes him a few tries to get the words out, but she gives him an immediate "yes." Katy and Arkady are married in the same ceremony as Fenitchka and Nikolai.

Victor Sitnikov

Victor Sitnikov is the overeager disciple of Bazarov, who introduces Arkady and Bazarov to Evdoksya Kukshin. Sitnikov wants to be a true nihilist, but shows too much emotion for Bazarov's taste. For their part, both Arkady and Bazarov treat Sitnikov badly, ignoring him, making sarcastic remarks, and deliberately taking a carriage other than his.

Vasya

See Vassily Ivanovitch Bazarov

Themes

The Generation Gap

The very title of the novel indicates one of the major themes. The gap between the older and younger generation is very pronounced, especially between fathers and their sons. Nikolai Kirsanov notes to his brother, Pavel, how they are "behind the times" and that the younger generation has surpassed them. He is wistful, however, at the implications of this gap: "I did so hope, precisely now, to get on to such close, intimate terms with Arkady, and it turns out I'm left behind, and he has gone forward, and we can't understand one another."

Bazarov's father makes a similar observation, when he gets into a discussion about new versus old ideas: "Of course, gentlemen, you know best; how could we keep pace with you? You are here to take our places." This gap seems to grow between them as they talk, and the old man tries to fit in by telling a funny story: "The old man was alone in his laughter; Arkady forced a smile on his face. Bazarov simply stretched. The conversation went on in this way for about an hour." When Bazarov's father complains about this fact to his wife, she tells him that there is "no help for it, Vasya! A son is a separate piece cut off."

Although Bazarov's early death prevents him and his father from closing their generation gap, the case is different for Arkady and Nikolai: "A week before in the small parish church two weddings had taken place quietly. . . . Arkady and Katya's, and Nikolai Petrovitch and Fenitchka's." The double wedding leads to Arkady and Katya staying at Maryino, where Arkady eventually pitches in and runs his father's estate for him. As Turgenev's narrator says, "their fortunes are beginning to mend."

Poverty

Poverty is a very real issue in the story, even for formerly wealthy landowners like Nikolai. In the beginning, when Nikolai's farm, Maryino, is described, the peasant's portion is depicted as follows: "the peasants they met were all in tatters and on the sorriest little nags; the willows, with their trunks stripped of bark, and broken branches, stood like ragged beggars along the roadside." The peasants are not the only ones who feel the pinch. Nikolai often "sighed, and was gloomy; he felt that the thing could not go on without money, and his money was almost spent." For these reasons, Nikolai's farm is infamous; "the peasants had nicknamed it, Poverty Farm."

Bazarov's parents are even poorer. When Arkady first arrives at the residence, the reader sees that "his whole house consisted of six tiny rooms." And, as Vassily Ivanovitch notes: "I warned you, my dear Arkady Nikolaitch. . . . that we live, so to say, bivouacking." This military term, from Vassily's time in the military service, denotes a rougher lifestyle akin to camping in the rough.

Nihilism

In the story, Turgenev sets up a conflict between the older generation of fathers who believe in art and other irrational activities, and the nihilists—scientific materialists like Bazarov who accept nothing. Bazarov is very critical of anything that does not serve a purpose, especially art. "A good chemist is twenty times as useful as any poet," Bazarov tells them.

For their part, the older generation of Kirsanov men does not agree. Says Pavel to Bazarov, "If we listen to you, we shall find ourselves outside humanity, outside its laws." Furthermore, Nikolai tells Bazarov that he does more than "deny everything . . . you destroy everything. . . . But one must construct too, you know." For Bazarov and other nihilists, leveling society and starting with a clean slate is the only way to get rid of "our leading men, so-called advanced people and reformers," who "are no good." Being a liberal himself, Nikolai understands his son's desire for reform, but cannot understand the total exclusion of the arts: "But to renounce poetry? . . . to have no feeling for art, for nature?"

As for Arkady, Bazarov's disciple, he finds it tough to maintain his nihilistic attitude as the novel goes on: "In his heart he was highly delighted with his friend's suggestion, but he thought it a duty to conceal his feeling. He was not a nihilist for nothing!" By the end of the novel, Arkady has totally forsaken his nihilistic beliefs for marriage, music, and nature, three ideas that nihilism does not allow. Bazarov also experiences a change by the end of the novel. After he is slighted by Anna following his unprecedented profession of love, he tells her, "Before you is a poor mortal, who has come to his senses long ago, and hopes other people, too, have forgotten his follies."

Bazarov has started to realize the error of his ways. While he is staying with his parents, they notice it too. "A strange weariness began to show itself in all his movements; even his walk, firm, bold and strenuous, was changed. He gave up walking in solitude, and began to seek society." And when he is dying from typhus, he encourages his parents "to make the most of your religious belief; now's the time to put it to the test." Although, it is telling that when Bazarov has the chance to try to save his soul with his parents' religion, he declines. Even though he has changed, allowed himself to love, and admitted the folly of some of his ways, he is not ready to embrace religion even on his deathbed.

Love

The idea of romantic love permeates the novel and is most apparent with Arkady and Bazarov, who experience two different types of love. Arkady experiences a love that is based on friendship. Before he even meets his true love, Katya, he is smitten by Madame Anna Odintsov. Unfortunately, the older woman looks at him "as married sisters look at very young brothers." With Katya, however, the situation is different, even from the start. He "encouraged her to express the impressions made on her by music, reading novels, verses, and other such trifles, without noticing or realizing that these

Topics for Further Study

- Research the specific beliefs of both the young radicals from the 1860s and the older liberals from the 1840s in Russia. Create a picture, story, or some other sort of artistic effort in which half of the item represents the ideas of the radicals and half represents the liberals. Somewhere on this item, indicate the qualities you are trying to demonstrate for each half.

- Read Albert Camus's *The Stranger* and compare Camus's existentialist narrator to Bazarov. What are the similarities and differences between nihilism and existentialism?

- Research the current state of affairs in Russia, noting any particular reform efforts that are going on. How do these differ from reforms that were happening in the mid-1800s?

- Research Russian art from the mid-1800s until the end of the nineteenth century and discuss whether it did or did not take a revolutionary approach, like much literature did. In either case, find one painting that you like and write a report giving your interpretation of what the painting means, as well as any historical significance it may have.

- Research the complex history surrounding the emancipation of the serfs in Russia in the 1860s and their gradual establishment as landowners. Write a journal entry from the perspective of either a recently freed serf or a former member of the landed aristocracy, describing your views on the emancipation reforms. Incorporate your research into your entry where necessary.

- Suppose Bazarov had not died from typhus at the end of the book and an extra chapter had been added on to talk about what happened to him in the end. Based on the transformation he undergoes in the novel, how do you predict he would have spent the rest of his life? Write a short plot summary detailing what would take place in this extra chapter.

trifles were what interested him too." From this tentative friendship, their love starts to blossom, and Arkady's love for Katya starts to replace his love for Madame Odintsov: "He began to imagine Anna Sergyevna to himself, then other features gradually eclipsed the lovely young image of the young widow."

The night before Arkady plans on leaving Nikolskoe with Bazarov, he is distraught: "I'm sorry to lose Katya too!" Arkady whispered to his pillow, on which a tear had already fallen." Eventually Arkady becomes so attached to Katya that he is ecstatic when he arrives unannounced and sees her first: "His meeting with her struck him as a particularly happy omen; he was delighted to see her, as though she were of his own kindred." Finally, Arkady owns up to his feelings, and eventually lets her know that "My eyes have been opened lately, thanks to one feeling." The feeling is love, but in Arkady's case, it is a love that builds slowly from friendship.

For Bazarov, on the other hand, the love is more passionate, forceful. Bazarov shows the signs of an irrational love at his first meeting with Anna. While she is sitting calmly, "leaning back in her easy-chair," and "He, contrary to his habit, was talking a good deal, and obviously trying to interest her—again a surprise for Arkady." As Bazarov stays at Nikolskoe, he begins to exhibit "signs of an unrest, unprecedented in him. . . . and could not sit still in one place, just as though he were possessed by some secret longing."

For her part, Anna gives Bazarov her terms for love: "My idea is everything or nothing. A life for a life. Take mine, give up thine, and that without regret or turning back. Or else better have nothing." Bazarov takes these conversations as a sign that Anna loves him and on the eve of his departure, lets her know that "I love you like a fool, like a madman . . . There, you've forced it out of me." However, Anna's intentions are not amorous, so her words are crushing to the passionate lover who has let his emotions overtake him for the first time: "You have misunderstood me."

Style

Setting

The setting in *Fathers and Sons* is crucial to the effect of the novel. The various provincial settings—Maryino, Nikolskoe, Vassily Ivanovitch's unnamed homestead—are seen as backward and uneducated when compared with the cities, which are vibrant with new ideas and scholarship. As Bazarov notes to Arkady at one point, if they were to look at their fathers' country existence from a certain perspective, it could be seen as enjoyable, having a routine to keep busy: "When one gets a side view from a distance of the dead-alive life our 'fathers' lead here, one thinks, What could be better?" However, for Bazarov, this life could only ever be "dead-alive," unlike Arkady. On a different occasion, Arkady, who likes the nature one finds in the country, challenges Bazarov: "And is nature foolery?" Arkady hopes to stump Bazarov, but the nihilist is not disturbed and as always, has an answer: "Nature, too, is foolery in the sense you understand it. Nature's not a temple, but a workshop, and man's the workman in it." For Bazarov, nature is something to be dissected as he does with the frogs, or otherwise observed from a scientific viewpoint. Arkady cannot do this, however, and he eventually comes to prefer the country, moving into Maryino with his new wife and his father's family, where Arkady becomes "zealous in the management of the estate" and turns it into a prosperous affair.

Irony

A situation is ironic when its outcome is contrary to what the character and reader expects. In Turgenev's novel this happens many times. For example, Vassily Ivanovitch describes the bitter irony of the generation gap when talking to his son and Arkady about a philosopher of whom they are enamored: "you bow down to him, but in another twenty years it will be his turn to be laughed at." Bazarov and Arkady feel strong and invincible in their youth, as if their ideas are the only ones and they will never be refuted. However, when Arkady's son grows up, Arkady will no doubt realize, as Nikolai does, that aging and the decline of one's ideas is "a bitter pill" and that every new generation is ready to tell the old to "swallow your pill."

Other ironic situations are introduced in the character of Bazarov, whom the reader is led to believe from the beginning cannot be swayed to love. Bazarov is against love because there is no control over it, and it overpowers the senses that he holds dear and by which he rules his life. It is ironic, therefore, that Bazarov is stricken blind with love for Anna, and admits to her, "I love you like a fool, like a madman." It is also ironic that Bazarov, the character who is depicted in an almost god-like, invincible light, is refuted in his advance, from Anna, who seems on the verge of giving her heart to Bazarov.

The cruelest irony of the novel, however, is the death of Bazarov. The young nihilist who appreciates the hard sciences more than anything else goes to the village, "where they brought that peasant with typhus fever." Although there is a doctor there who is going to dissect the body, Bazarov, always eager for scientific knowledge, offers to do it. Unfortunately, in the process, he makes a careless mistake and cuts himself, contracting the infection that soon kills him. It is tragically ironic that Bazarov's quest for knowledge is the thing that kills him in the end.

Point of View

The novel is told by a third person omniscient, or all-knowing, narrator who has the power to go within any character's mind and display their thoughts. For example, when Bazarov and Pavel get in their first argument over their beliefs, Nikolai thinks to himself, "You are certainly a nihilist, I see that," although what he says aloud is "Still, you will allow me to apply to you on occasion." This is the style for most of the novel. However, there is a notable exception in the narration: at times, the narrator speaks directly to the reader, as when the narrator introduces Nikolai: "We will introduce him to the reader while he sits, his feet tucked under him, gazing thoughtfully round." This style is also used at the end of the novel: "But perhaps some one of our readers would care to know what each of the characters we have introduced is doing in the present." By book-ending the story with these two references that draw attention to the narrator, readers are reminded that they are reading a work of art and are encouraged to focus on the realities of the social situation the book describes—instead of just getting caught up in the story.

Historical Context

Fathers and Sons is tied to Russia's history, particularly to the period of social unrest and reform that began to come to a head with the rule of Alexander II. Following the Crimean War, during which Alexander came to power in 1855, Russian society—and Alexander himself—was made painfully aware of Russia's backward place in the world. These were old concerns that were reawak-

ened with the loss of about 250,000 men and some of Russia's land.

This war was not received well in society and as a result, Alexander, who had been taught by an artistic, romantic tutor, and who was sympathetic to liberal concerns, sought reform. Pitting himself against the landowners who owned serfs, Alexander began to talk about abolishing serfdom. Says Victor Ripp, in his *Turgenev's Russia: From "Notes of a Hunter" to "Fathers and Sons"*: "The Emancipation Act was signed by Alexander II on February 19, 1861, a little less than five years after he had openly declared his support for the abolition of serfdom." In the time between Alexander's announcement of the abolishment and the actual abolishment, Russia underwent some drastic changes as the nation prepared itself for reform.

In this time of uneasiness, Turgenev chose to set his book. As Ripp notes, "it is the spring of 1859, and the emancipation of the serfs, with all its uncertain consequences, is only two years ahead." Even two years before this historic event the effects could be seen in many locations. Nikolai Petrovitch, a more liberal landowner, has already freed his serfs before he is required to, although he is wary about giving his former slaves any control in any major business affairs. Says Nikolai: "I decided not to keep about me any freed serfs, who have been house servants, or, at least, not to intrust them with duties of any responsibility."

Not everybody was as enlightened as Nikolai, however. Some, especially the older Russian nobility with much land to lose, decried the reforms, like Bazarov's mother. She used to be a member of the landed gentry, but turned her land over to the care of her husband, a poor, retired army surgeon. She "used to groan, wave her handkerchief, and raise her eyebrows higher and higher with horror when her old husband began to discuss the impending government reforms."

However, those who observed the decline of Russia, as Arkady does in the novel, realized that reform was sorely needed: "this is not a rich country; it does not impress one by plenty or industry; it can't, it can't go on like this, reforms are absolutely necessary." Of course, as Arkady notes shortly thereafter, "how is one to carry them out, how is one to begin?" There seemed to be no clear answer to that, since Russia was mired in corruption, which, even though it started at higher levels, worked its way down. As the narrator notes of the young governor's official sent to a provincial town, he "was a young man, and at once a progressive

Compare & Contrast

- **1860s:** Under the leadership of Alexander II Russia embarks on a number of social reforms, including abolishing serfdom and improving communications, such as establishing more railroad lines.

  Today: Russia remains a poor and unstable country after the fall of the Soviet Union at the end of the twentieth century. In the wake of the brutal dictatorial regime that ruled "communist" Russia and other Soviet countries for much of the twentieth century, the plight of many Russians has worsened.

- **1860s:** Like those in other countries, many of Russia's youth adhere to a scientific materialism philosophy, questioning everything with a strict rationalism and not letting any "irrational" behavior overcome them.

  Today: In many civilized countries there is a resurgence in art, nature, and other humanistic pursuits, due in large part to humanity's increasing dependence upon technology.

- **1860s:** Although modern medicine is improving with the such developments as vaccines, the "germ theory" of disease, and improved sanitation in hospitals, doctors are largely powerless. When cholera sweeps across Europe and Russia, many are killed.

  Today: In most modernized countries, cholera and typhus, which are usually prevalent in poor, unsanitary areas, have been wiped out. Epidemic typhus persists in countries that experience famine, crowded living conditions, and other areas where sanitation is an issue. Cholera, on the other hand, has been largely dormant, and has not seen a major outbreak for more than a decade.

and a despot, as often happens with Russians." This young man is both a sympathetic liberal and a tyrant when he is given the power to abuse. The same was true about the behavior of the lower classes. When given any power at all, they abused it, as Nikolai's farm manager does: "The overseer suddenly turned lazy, and began to grow fat, as every Russian grows fat when he gets a snug berth." Likewise, once Nikolai puts the peasants on a rent system and does not enforce it, he has problems. "The peasants who had been put on the rent system did not bring their money at the time due, and stole the forest-timber."

Even when the serfs were about to be emancipated in 1861, the actual Emancipation Act caused much confusion. As Ripp notes, "In its efforts to please all factions, the Editing Committee produced an immensely complicated document." This general feeling of failure on the part of the Emancipation Act is expressed in the novel through the character of Nikolai, who is entrusted to carry out the upcoming reforms at the end of the novel.

He drives around his district, giving long speeches that say the same thing over and over again, but as Turgenev's narrator notes, "to tell the truth, he does not give complete satisfaction either to the refined gentry. . . . nor to the uncultivated gentry. . . . He is too soft-hearted for both sets." Neither the landed class nor the lower classes wanted a hesitant legislation, but unfortunately, in its attempts to please everyone, the Emancipation Act pleased almost no one and eventually led to more unrest. As Ripp notes, Turgenev is aware of all of this as he writes the book in 1862, a year after the act has been implemented: "Turgenev wrote *Fathers and Sons*, his greatest novel, while directly under the influence of the crisis caused by the Emancipation Act."

Critical Overview

In 1862, when Turgenev first gave the manuscript for *Fathers and Sons* to his editor Mikhail Niki-forovich Katkov, the *Russkii vestnik* (*Russian Her-*

Russian serfs receiving their freedom as a result of Alexander II's Emancipation Act

ald) editor was concerned about the potential backlash over the novel.

Katkov had reason to be concerned. As Edward Garnett notes in his *Turgenev*, "the stormy controversy that the novel immediately provoked was so bitter, deep, and lasting that the episode forms one of the most interesting chapters in literary history." The controversy originated in the interpretation of the novel by the two main political forces in Russia at the time—the older liberals, or reactionaries, from the 1840s who were of Turgenev's generation, and the younger radicals—whom Turgenev called "nihilists" in the novel—of the current, 1860s generation. It was with this second group that Turgenev had found favor with through the publication of some of his earlier works in *Sovremennik* (*Contemporary*). However, the same critics who had praised Turgenev's earlier works now offered harsh criticism for *Fathers and Sons* as they had for Turgenev's previous novel, *Nakanune*. One of the most vocal critics from *The Contemporary* was M. A. Antonovich, who remarked that Bazarov "is not a man, but some horrible being, simply a devil or, to express oneself more poetically, a foul fiend."

Another radical critic, A. I. Gertsen, notes that in the book, "gloomy, concentrated energy has spoken in this *unfriendly* attitude of the young gener-

ation to its mentors." The overwhelming majority of criticisms, both good and bad, concerned the character Bazarov. D. I. Pisarev, another of the younger radicals, was the only critic from his political party who did not describe Bazarov as a "vicious caricature" of the radicals, as Leonard Schapiro notes in *Turgenev: His Life and Times*. Instead, Pisarev writes to both radicals and liberals: "You may be indignant about people like Bazarov to your heart's content, but it is most essential to acknowledge their sincerity."

The book was also disliked by the liberals, many of whom blamed Turgenev's book for the violence exhibited by young radicals. Turgenev himself recounts what is now a famous anecdote from his life, when he returned to Petersburg in 1862 on the same day that young radicals—calling themselves "nihilists"—were setting fire to buildings: "the first exclamation to fall from the lips of the first acquaintance I encountered . . . was: 'Look what *your* nihilists are doing! Burning Petersburg!'"

The major problem in the book's reception was the fact that both radicals and liberals thought that the book was aimed against them, especially in the portrayal of Bazarov. This problem was underscored by Turgenev's own conflicting views on the character. Although he stated in a March 30 letter to Fyodor Dostoyevsky that "during all the time of writing I have felt an involuntary attraction for him," he stated in a different letter on April 18 to A. A. Fet: "Did I wish to curse Bazarov, or extol him? *I don't know that myself*, for I don't know if I love or hate him!"

In 1881, William Ralston Shedden-Ralston, one of Turgenev's English friends, publicized the author's upcoming visit by noting that Turgenev was "the wielder of a style unrivalled for delicacy and seldom equalled in force," and that "it will be easy to see that in his own field he stands alone." George Moore notes of Bazarov that "he is a real creation, not a modernisation of some Shakespearean or classical conception, but an absolutely new and absolutely distinct addition made to our knowledge of life." The famous American-born, English writer and critic, Henry James, notes the novel's "poignant interest," that is created by the "young world" smiting "the old world which has brought it forth with a mother's tears and a mother's hopes."

During the twentieth century, reviews were largely positive, as reviewers focused on Turgenev's artistic techniques and prophetic powers. Peter Henry notes that "it is a brilliant stroke of irony on Turgenev's part that Bazarov and Pavel Petrovich, so sharply contrasted in every way, are endowed with an essential identity as unsuccessful lovers." In his *Turgenev: The Man, His Art and His Age*, Avrahm Yarmolinsky says that "throughout, his craftsmanship is at its best. Even the minor characters are deftly sketched in." And Isaiah Berlin notes that today, "the Bazarovs have won," since the world is ruled by technology and empirical science.

Criticism

Ryan D. Poquette

Poquette holds a bachelor's degree in English and specializes in writing about literature. In the following essay, Poquette discusses the many views of women in Turgenev's novel.

In Turgenev's *Fathers and Sons*, women play very important and influential roles in the plot. Anna Odintsov attracts Arkady and Bazarov, who are both trying to remain true to their nihilistic beliefs, which attempt to deny love—an irrational force. This surrender to love shakes the very core of Bazarov's foundation. Eventually, he tries again

at love, stealing a kiss from Fenitchka, which leads to the duel with Pavel. In the meantime, Katya wins over Arkady. Women are at the center of just about every major plot point in the book. But what does Turgenev think about women in general? The author makes several contradictory statements—through his characters—about how women are viewed, but in the end, he indicates that women are a necessary force, and a saving and nurturing influence on men.

At the beginning of *Fathers and Sons* Turgenev introduces four men, all of whom are strong Russian males. Arkady comes home from school a graduate, and brings his friend Bazarov, a nihilist with very powerful views. Almost at once, this younger generation of men conflicts with the older generation—Arkady's father; Nikolai, a liberal landowner; and Arkady's uncle Pavel, a retired military officer. Pavel does not like Bazarov from the start, calling him an "unkempt creature" after his first meeting with the younger man. This tension escalates when the younger men start expressing their radical views. Arkady informs his father and uncle that nihilists regard "everything from the critical point of view," and in the conversations between the two generations over the next fortnight, the young men criticize many of the institutions that the older generation holds dear. Bazarov—backed by Arkady—denounces all irrational pursuits including art, claiming, "a good chemist is twenty times as useful as any poet." For their part, the older generation says that "If we listen to you, we shall find ourselves outside humanity, outside its laws." This struggle between the two generations, the main theme in the book, is depicted throughout in passionate and violent terms.

However, just as this struggle culminates in the silly and ineffectual duel between Bazarov and Pavel, the men's manly debates are also ultimately ineffectual. While these strong men argue about philosophy and art, they are being quietly conquered by women who, like Fenitchka, only seem meek and mild, as when Fenitchka brings in Pavel's cup of cocoa and "dropped her eyes" in the presence of the men. "It seemed as though she were ashamed of having come in, and at the same time felt that she had a right to come." Of course, the men do not always realize the power that the women contain. In fact, through his male characters especially, Turgenev expresses many of the views of women that were prevalent at the time. One of the dominant views was that women were not very smart and could not hold their own against literate men. As Bazarov notes to Arkady about his own mother, "If a woman can keep up half-an-hour's conversation, it's always a hopeful sign." Bazarov is similarly condescending to Madame Kukshin, an independent woman who has separated from her husband. When Kukshin learns that Bazarov is interested in chemistry, she thinks they have something in common: "You are studying chemistry? That is my passion. I've even invented a new sort of composition myself." However, Bazarov is skeptical in his reply: "A composition? You?"

Bazarov does not always think that an inferior, uneducated woman is a bad thing, as he notes to Arkady when discussing Anna Odintsov's sister, Katya: "She now is fresh and untouched, and shy and silent, and anything you like. She's worth educating and developing. You might make something fine out of her." However, while Bazarov thinks that Katya can be manipulated, he holds no such illusion over Anna, whom he refers to as "a stale loaf." This negative depiction of Anna is due to the fact that she has already started to affect him in ways that he does not like, such as the effect Anna has on Bazarov at their first meeting: "Bazarov himself was conscious of being embarrassed, and was irritated by it." Bazarov cannot handle feeling out of control, and so when he and Arkady discuss Anna and Katya, he is critical. Arkady remarks "what an exquisite woman" Anna is, while Bazarov says, somewhat condescendingly, "Yes … a female with brains. Yes, and she's seen life too." Although Bazarov tries to explain that he means this in "a good sense," he nevertheless describes Anna with the "stale loaf" reference.

Bazarov is afraid of Anna, both for the power she is beginning to hold over his heart and because he has very little power over her; he cannot manipulate her as he initially believes Katya can be manipulated. Hypocritically, Bazarov, who warms to the idea of manipulating women like Katya into an image that is pleasing to him, complains of the manipulative quality of women. When Arkady previously asked his mentor, "Why are you unwilling to allow freethinking in women?'," Bazarov replies: "Because, my boy, as far as my observations go, the only freethinkers among women are frights."

Bazarov's view of freethinking women is even worse after Anna has "forced" him to confess to her that "I love you like a fool, like a madman." Anna slights his charms, letting him know that she is not interested in him in this way, and Bazarov tells Arkady that, "to my mind, it's better to break

> In the past, Bazarov would have viewed this power as dangerous, fearing that Katya might manipulate men in a bad way. However, in the end, Bazarov, and indeed Turgenev, conclude that this manipulation is a good thing."

stones on the highroad than to let a woman have the mastery of even the end of one's little finger." Bazarov feels he has let his guard down and been manipulated by Anna and becomes bitter at the thought that he has been played in this way.

Besides being looked at as inferior or manipulative, Turgenev's characters also view some women as independent. In fact, before he is rebuffed by Anna, Bazarov agreed to some extent with a woman's right to advance her circumstances. As Bazarov notes to Arkady just prior to meeting Anna (and prior to being rattled by her): "to my mind, to marry a rich old man is by no means a strange thing to do, but, on the contrary, very sensible." If Bazarov had not been affected by his love for Anna, he might have still held this view, instead of denouncing women as manipulative. In fact, as Barbara Alpern Engel notes in her book, *Mothers and Daughters: Women of the Intelligentsia in Nineteenth-century Russia*, the nihilists in general were very supportive of women's rights, and "devoted considerable attention to women's problems." Engel notes that during the 1860s especially, these nihilists "tried to help women by encouraging them to become autonomous and by providing alternatives to the traditional family."

This is certainly addressed through the character of Madame Kukshin, who Sitnikov, a professed nihilist, adores for her independence: "She's a remarkable nature, *émancipée* in the true sense of the word, an advanced woman." Kukshin is proud of the fact that she has separated from her husband, and loves the power and responsibility she holds: "I manage my property myself." Kukshin states to her gathered men—Sitnikov, Bazarov, and Arkady—that Russia needs to change its education system, since "our women are very badly educated." In fact, Kukshin cannot stand the writings of women like George Sand, who Kukshin says "hasn't an idea on education, nor physiology, nor anything. She's never, I'm persuaded, heard of embryology, and in these days—what can be done without that?" Kukshin, like her young male counterparts, rests her hopes on objective fields like science in an attempt to be "advanced." In fact, Sitnikov also criticizes other women who are not at the same level of advancement as Kukshin, as when he describes Anna Odintsov: "Clever, rich, a widow. It's a pity she's not yet advanced enough."

The idea of a woman being "advanced" is not new at this point and is not attributed only to the nihilists. In fact, Nikolai, Arkady's father, fell in love with a smart woman: "She was pretty, and, as it is called, an 'advanced' girl; she used to read the serious articles in the 'Science' column of the journals." However, whereas the nihilist view called for new, autonomous relationships for advanced women that were outside of the family, in the end Turgenev seems to imply the opposite. The two symbolic weddings at the end of the novel do more than heal the rift between Arkady and Nikolai; they also indicate Turgenev's true view about the appropriate role for women—powerful matriarchs. At the end of the novel, Fenitchka, who was meek and mild in the beginning, is "different." As Turgenev's narrator notes, she is "respectful towards herself and everything surrounding her, and smiled as though to say, "I beg your pardon; I'm not to blame." And Anna Odintsov, who is portrayed throughout as the ultimate independent woman, remarries. As the narrator notes, "They live in the greatest harmony together, and will live perhaps to attain complete happiness . . . perhaps love."

Even Bazarov, who had previously denounced women as inferior and manipulative, has had a change of heart, as he indicates to Anna in his final visit to Nikolskoe: "Before you is a poor mortal, who has come to his senses long ago, and hopes other people, too, have forgotten his follies." This is a far cry from the person who was never concerned with the way that people viewed him. In addition, Bazarov is also respectful toward the institution of marriage, something which he has never appreciated before. In his final conversation with Arkady, he is complementary about Katya's power: "Many a young lady's called clever simply because she can sigh cleverly; but yours can hold her own." Whereas before, Bazarov viewed Katya as weak and impressionable, now he acknowledges her strength. In the past, Bazarov would have

viewed this power as dangerous, fearing that Katya might manipulate men in a bad way. However in the end, Bazarov, and indeed Turgenev, conclude that this manipulation is a good thing: "she'll have you under thumb—to be sure, though, that's quite as it ought to be."

Source: Ryan D. Poquette, Critical Essay on *Fathers and Sons,* in *Novels for Students,* The Gale Group, 2003.

David Lowe

In the following excerpt, Lowe traces elements of both comedy and tragedy in Turgenev's novel.

Sometime during the first months of 1862 Afanasy Fet sent Turgenev his reactions to *Father and Sons.* Fet's letter is not extant, but we do have Turgenev's reply, and it reinforces the often expressed conviction that one ought not to pay too much attention to what writers have to say about their own works. In the letter of April 6/18, 1862, Turgenev writes: "You also mention parallelism; but where is it, allow me to ask, and where are these pairs, believing and unbelieving?" . . . [In] spite of Turgenev's protests parallelism is one of the two basic principles at work in the novel. The other is contrast. No doubt there are few works in world literature that do not depend to some extent on parallels and contrasts for the building blocks that hold them together and give them coherence. In *Father and Sons,* however, their significance is all-inclusive and extends to matters of composition, characterization, and thematics. In *Father and Sons,* a novel whose very title both links and contrasts the generations, form and content are one. That pronouncement is not the pious repetition of a Formalist cliché. As the examination proceeds it should become increasingly apparent that in *Father and Sons* thematics determine form. As the first step in proving the validity of that contention, let us turn our attention to matters of composition and their relation to the novel's thematic concerns.

One way to look at the novel's structure is as a series of trips: Arkady and Bazarov are thus examined and illuminated in a variety of environments. At Marino Arkady is at home and Bazarov is the stranger. In town and at Nikolskoe, both Arkady and Bazarov are thrown into an unfamiliar environment, while at Bazarov's parents' estate Arkady is the stranger (though, paradoxically, he is less an outsider there than is Bazarov). Parallelism and contrast are immediately evident in such a scheme: Bazarov is the newcomer in one milieu, Arkady in another. But even within the series of trips we can establish cycles. Brazhe writes of two cycles of trips from Marino to Bazarov's home. Such a calculation takes into account only Bazarov's point of view. It would be more accurate to identify three cycles of trips. The interesting structural note here is that Arkady's and Bazarov's travels consistently dovetail with each other, even when the two protagonists are not together. In the first cycle, Arkady and Bazarov go from Marino to town to Nikolskoe to Bazarov's home and back through Nikolskoe to Marino. In the second cycle, Arkady goes to Nikolskoe on his own. In a later and parallel development, Bazarov arrives at Nikolskoe on his own. Finally, in the last cycle, Bazarov goes home alone, as does Arkady. Implicit in this view of the novel's structure is one of the novel's major themes: children cannot turn their backs on the world of their fathers. Imperfect as it may be, it represents the mainstream of humanity. Children ultimately do go "home" again, and willingly or grudgingly, they are reconciled to the family hearth. At that point, as Joel Blair notes, "the lives of the fathers become patterns for understanding the lives of the children."

A second way of viewing the structure is as a series of confrontations. Such an interpretation is particularly widespread, since it provides abundant opportunities to discuss the ideological battles of the 1860s. Thus, we can map out the structure of *Fathers and Sons* as a series of ideological duels between Bazarov and Pavel, the ideological duels then capped by a real duel in which politics and social issues are as much at stake as personalities. Doubling the ideological skirmishes is Bazarov's series of erotic clashes with Odintsova. All discussions of the structure of *Fathers and Sons* in terms of confrontations are ultimately spinoffs from Gippius' Formalist analysis of composition in Turgenev's novels. (Rarely are they acknowledged as such.) Gippius' analysis is quite sophisticated, and there will be a need to return to it in some detail. It is nonetheless limited because, like most analyses of *Fathers and Sons*, it proceeds from the assumption that the novel is a tragedy and that Bazarov is the novel's only significant protagonist. These assumptions lead critics to attempt to identify a single, all-embracing structural pattern in the novel, whether it be trips, confrontations, love stories, or whatever. But the assumption needs to be reexamined. *Fathers and Sons* is a novel wholly dependent upon parallels and contrasts for its composition, and its structure is dualistic: it involves two parallel but contrasting patterns. The first is that of tragedy, while the second is comedy.

Since many will probably find controversial the notion that *Fathers and Sons* is in any way comedic, let us begin with this, the less obvious structural pattern in the novel. In using the word comedy, what it intended is not comedy in the popular sense (a funny play with a happy ending), but in the Aristotelian sense, specifically in its modern formulation by Northrop Frye. Frye uses comedy as a term denoting a literary mode, as he calls it, not a genre. Thus, as defined by Frye, the term is equally applicable to drama and narrative prose.

Basing his treatise on Aristotle's *Poetics*. Frye suggests that comedies deal with the integration of society. The standard comedic formula involves a young couple—the technical hero and heroine—whose marriage is blocked by other members of the cast (society). In realistic fiction employing the comedic mode, the hero and heroine tend to be dull but decent people, while the blocking characters are the truly interesting ones. The blocking characters are normally, but not necessarily, parental figures. They are consumed by a single passion (usually absurdly so), and they are in control of the society into which the hero and heroine seek entrance. The blocking characters are likely to be impostors, as Frye calls them, people who lack self-knowledge. At the conclusion of comedy the blocking characters are either incorporated into or expelled from the society, as a result of which the hero and heroine are free to wed. Thus, comedies often conclude with a wedding and the birth of babies, and have a rural setting (an escape to a simpler, less corrupt society). At the conclusion of comedy the audience feels that justice has triumphed, that the people who should have been united have been, and that everyone will live happily ever after in a freer, more flexible society.

This is a rather bald reduction of Frye's Aristotelian description of comedy, but it should be sufficient to demonstrate that in, *Fathers and Sons* we are dealing in part with the comedic mode. However, Turgeneve spins some fascinating variations around the age-old comedic pattern.

Arkady is the technical hero about whom the comedic plot revolves. This is not to say that he is the novel's central hero. He is the *technical* hero of the comedic plot. Significantly, Gary Jahn notes that "Arkady *and* Bazarov are the organizational focus of the novel [Italics mine-DL]." And true to comedic type, Arkady is a rather bland but not unattractive personality. As in Roman comedy, we have not a single hero, but a pair of heroes. Instead of the typical pair of young heroes, however, Turgenev gives us a father and son, both of whose marriages are blocked, as is a genuine reconciliation between father and son. The blocking characters are Pavel and Bazarov, and consistent with the traditions of fictional comedy, both of them are considerably more interesting than the technical heroes and heroines, and both of them are removed from the stage at the culmination of the comedic plot line.

Bazarov's negative influence on Arkady forestalls an accomodation between him and his father, and it temporarily blocks Arkady and Katya's marriage, largely because Bazarov's attitudes, which Arkady attempts in vain to adopt, prevent the latter from coming to terms with himself and his true nature. In this connection, James Justus points out that "the battle is not just fathers against sons, but sons against themselves." Bazarov's obstructing influence is apparent as early as the third chapter. Arkady, riding along in a carriage with his father, waxes lyrical, thus betraying his "unnihilistic" enthusiasm for the beauties of nature. He abruptly breaks off in mid-sentence. "Arkady suddenly paused, glanced back obliquely and lapsed into silence." Bazarov's presence prevents Arkady from being himself, and as a result the relations between father and son are strained. Bazarov is a blocker, and his status as an obstacle to reconciliation between father and son is emphasized in several of the novel's passages. Just after the scene in which Bazarov suggests that Arkady wean his father away from Pushkin by giving him more adult food for thought, i.e., Büchner's *Stoff und Kraft* (sic), we discover Pavel and Nikolay in conversation:

> "Well, you and I," Nikolay Petrovich, sitting in his brother's room the same day after dinner, said to Pavel, "have fallen into the ranks of the retired, our song is sung. What's to be done? Perhaps Bazarov is right; but I confess that one thing pains me: I was hoping just now to become close friends with Arkady; but it turns out that I have lagged behind, he has gone forward, and we cannot understand each other."

By the end of the novel there is no doubt that it is precisely Bazarov's sway over Arkady that temporarily thwarts mutual understanding between father and son. Furthermore, Arkady's distorted image of himself as a fire-breathing, militant disciple of Bazarov's impedes his progress toward the realization that his love is not for Odintsova, as he imagines, but for her sister Katya. It is Katya who articulates what the reader has sensed all along—Arkady has been under Bazarov's thumb. "My sister was under his [Bazarov's] influence then, just

as you were," Katya tells Arkady. She goes on to inform Arkady that he has nothing in common with Bazarov. When Arkady protests, saying that he wants to be strong and energetic like his friend, Katya lectures him: "You can't just wish that. . . . Your friend does not wish for it, it's just there in him." Here Katya sounds another of the novel's major themes: one cannot be what one is not. That Arkady's attempt to play the nihilist causes him to be untrue to himself is made explicit when Bazarov suggests that they go to town:

> ". . . Well, what do you think? Shall we go?"
>
> "I guess so," Arkady answered lazily.
>
> In his soul he rejoiced at his friend's suggestion, but felt obliged to hide his feeling. Not for nothing was he a nihilist!

Arkady's transition from his false role as Bazarov's protegé and a rival for Odintsova to his true status as his father's son and claimant for Katya's hand is signalled in a scene at Nikolskoe:

> They did not find him [Arkady] soon: he had taken himself off to the most remote part of the garden where, resting his chin on his folded hands, he sat, sunk in thought. [Cf. Nikolay's penchant for garden meditation.] They were profound and important, these thoughts, but not sad. He knew that Anna Sergeievna was sitting alone with Bazarov, and he did not feel jealousy, as had happened in the past; on the contrary, his face shone quietly; it seemed that he was surprised at something and gladdened, and that he was deciding on something.

It is appropriate that Arkady should come to such self-knowledge in the garden. Alexander Fischler has noted that the architecture of *Fathers and Sons* is linked to a garden motif, and that "the garden is a microcosm of nature, foreshortening its laws to uphold *what ought to be*." Arkady's post-garden proposal to Katya is a symbolic declaration of what he must be—independent from Bazarov: Arkady is now free to be himself, to express his true feelings. Bazarov's dramatic farewell and rejection of Arkady are really no more than a recognition on the former's part that he no longer has any influence over Arkady. Bazarov then retires to his father's house, removing himself from the comedic plot line and freeing Arkady to marry Katya and to be reconciled with his father.

Pavel is a blocking character vis-à-vis Nikolay [Nikolai] and Fenchka [Fenitchka]. His presumed hostility to the idea of their marriage dissuades Nikolay from regularizing his liaison with Fenechka. Note Nikolay's reaction when Pavel asks him to marry Fenechka:

Nikolay Petrovich took a step back and threw up his hands. "Is that you saying this, Pavel? You, whom I have always considered an implacable foe of such marriages? . . . But don't you know that it was only out of respect for you that I haven't fulfilled what you so rightly call my duty!"

So Pavel encourages Nikolay to marry Fenechka—an act that will assuage Nikolay's guilty conscience and allow him to feel more at ease with his son.

Then, at the culmination of the comedic plot line the blocking characters have been expelled (or have expelled themselves): Pavel prepares to spend the rest of his days in Europe, where he will continue his superfluous existence, while Bazarov retires to his father's home, and the pairs who belonged together all along are at last united.

Some critics have noted the importance of couplings, uncouplings, and recouplings in the novel. [F. R. Reeve] writes:

> Characters in pairs . . . relate each to the other through a succession of still other people, each relationship forming a temporary triangle, each triangle imperfect. . . . The third person's action always in some sense splits the original pair.

Or, as Blair formulates it:

> The principle of composition operating in the novel is the grouping and regrouping of characters; our understanding of the novel develops as we observe the initial groups of characters dissolve and perceive the formation of new pairs. Eventually, those characters who seemed most unalike are aligned; their similarities become more important than their differences.

This general movement toward the final, "inevitable" pairings is the stuff of comedy. The double wedding noted in the epilogue underscores the emergence of a new, pragmatically freer society, a salient feature of comedy. The crystallization of this less rigid society is underlined by Pavel when he urges Nikolay to marry Fenechka: "No, dear brother, enough of high-mindedness and thinking about society: we're already old and peaceful people; it's time we put aside empty pretense." The new society, though not earthshakingly different from the old, is a little less rigid, a little more spontaneous: Nikolay, a member of the gentry, has become free to take Fenechka, a peasant, as his lawfully wedded wife. In this respect [Viktor Shklovsky,] overstates the case in arguing that "What is new in Turgenev's novel was that he understood the love story as the confrontation of new people with a world built on old principles." It is really Nikolay and Fenechka who confront old social values with new ones, Arkady and Katya's thoroughly conventional marriage with their own

What Do I Read Next?

- Fyodor Dostoevsky's *The Idiot*, originally written in 1868, is about the struggle that eccentrics face in an elite society that is both emulating contemporary Europe and drowning in Western materialism.

- *Up from Serfdom: My Childhood and Youth in Russia, 1804–1824*, by Aleksandr Kikitenko, written in 1851—but not published until 1975—is a famous personal account from a young serf who describes what it was like as a member of the slave class, working at the mercy of Russia's wealthiest landowner. Although Kikitenko educates himself and becomes a teacher, he still faces the yoke of serfdom.

- *Anna Karenina*, originally published serially from 1875 to 1877 by Leo Tolstoy, is a story of a married woman who has an affair with a count. The story revolves around the relationship she has with the two men and the social standards that they break in the process.

- *Sketches from a Hunter's Album*, by Ivan Turgenev, is about the author's travels through Russia and his personal accounts with peasants who suffer because of their repression. When the sketches first appeared in book form in 1852, the author was put under house arrest for their political tone. Eventually, the sketches helped bring attention to the issue of emancipating the serfs.

- *Vicissitude of Genre in the Russian Novel: Turgenev's "Fathers and Sons," Chernyshevsky's "What Is to Be Done?," Dostoevsky's "Demons," Gorky's "Mother"* (2001), by Russell Scott Valentino, talks about these authors' works and how this genre of "tendentious novels" became the most influential genre in Russian literature in the 1860s.

- First published in 1842, *Dead Souls*, by Nikolai Vasilevich Gogol, is a story of a man who moves to an unknown town, wins the people's approval, and then plays out a scheme that involves buying the souls of all the recently deceased peasants.

socially "progressive" one. Shklovsky's assessment nonetheless shows that he perceives a comedic base in the novel. Fischler, who emphasizes the classical bases of *Fathers and Sons*, also sees comedy at work here. He writes of the epilogue as "*prostodushnaia komediia*, 'artless comedy'—life itself or a play in which the author's strings no longer matter. In such comedy, the naive pursuit of happiness by the characters remaining on the stage blends with the timeless designs, overwhelming what momentarily stood out and was disturbing because of its alien, fortuitous or fateful appearance."

What are the implications of the novel's comedic structure? One, obviously, is that the comedic mode is extraordinarily hardy and adaptive. But, more importantly, an analysis of *Fathers and Sons* in terms of comedy explains in generic terms why many critics read the novel as an affirmative one—one that celebrates life and nature (or, more accurately, Life and Nature). Strakhov, for instance, argues: "Although Bazarov stands above everyone in the novel, life stands above him."

But what kind of life stands above Bazarov? Some critics dismiss the life led by Katya, Arkady, Nikolay, and Fenechka as banal, mediocre, *poshly*. Pisarev, for one, suggests: "The life of a limited person always flows more evenly and pleasantly than the life of a genius or even just an intelligent person." [G. A. Byaly] asserts that Pavel and Nikolay are "finished" (*konchenye liudi*), that "life is passing them by." . . . Thus, for Byaly, Nikolay is not even involved in life.

Do Nikolay and Arkady and their wives represent mediocrity? Yes, but not in a negative sense. Their mediocrity is that of the middle way, the golden mean. Arkady and Nikolay may be ordinary, but, as Paul Bourget suggested, nearly a century ago, there is something fresh and appealing about Turgenev's average man. Turgenev himself spoke of Goethe's Faust as the defender of "the individual, passionate, limited man" who still has the right and the opportunity to be happy and not be ashamed of his happiness." Boyd writes: "The love of Arkady and Katya gives a healthy, optimistic balance to the novel. [A. Batyutor] calls the novel's love scenes life affirming. And Vinogradov writes:

> The novel in essence is a battle of "cerebral" negative theories with the mighty power of love, with the inexpressible beauty of nature, with all the intermix of human feelings which, though "old," are alive and warm—a battle that ends with the triumph of "humanness," "nature," "beauty," over "nihilism."

The comedic couples may be limited, but they are hardly vegetables, nor is their existence gray. Arkady is a competent estate manager, and all the Kirsanovs' lives, ordinary as they may be, are enriched by an instinctual and profound attraction to nature, art, and their fellow man. They represent an ideal that Turgenev himself was unable to attain. While working on *Fathers and Sons*, he wrote a letter to K. N. Leontiev in which he confessed:

> And that I, as you write, have lately become gloomy, there's nothing surprising in that: I will soon be 42 years old, but I haven't made a nest for myself, haven't secured any spot for myself on earth: there is little cause for joy in that.

It must be admitted, however, that Turgenev claimed (*post-facto*) that in *Fathers and Sons* he had taken a contemptuous, despairing attitude toward bourgeois domesticity. In a letter of April 14/26, 1862, to Sluchevsky, Turgenev responds to what seems to have been Sluchevsky's summary of the reactions of Russian students in Heidelberg to *Fathers and Sons* (no letters from Sluchevsky are extant). The students' reactions are indicative, as is Turgenev's reply:

> What was said about Arkady, about the rehabilitation of the fathers, etc., only shows—forgive me!—that I haven't been understood. *All my povest* [short novel] *is directed against the gentry as a progressive class.* Examine closely Nikolay Petrovich, Pavel Petrovich, Arkady. Weakness, flabbiness (*vialost*), or limitedness (*organichennost*).

Later in the same letter Turgenev expresses bewilderment at the Heidelberg students' having found Arkady "a more successful type." Thus we have Turgenev's own testimony that he did not intend to portray Arkady or Nikolay in a positive light. But an author's intentions are one thing, the reader's perceptions quite another. In spite of scornful depictions of "blissful" marriages in other Turgenev works, such as *"Andrey Kolosov," "Two Friends,"* and *"The Country Doctor,"* and Turgenev's protestations to the contrary, Nikolay, Arkady, and their wives add a healthy, optimistic note to *Fathers and Sons*. In this connection Gippius, discussing groups of *poshly* characters in *Smoke* and *Nest of Gentlefolk*, points out that these characters are "portrayed with exaggerated distortion, not at all as in *Fathers and Sons*, where the corresponding characters are presented in a significantly muted (*smiagchenny*) form, almost idealized, no matter how much Turgenev himself denied it."

Arkady and Nikolay are not men of great stature, they are not great thinkers, but Turgenev's having infused them with love of Schubert, Pushkin, evening sunsets, their families, and their fellow man makes it difficult to conceive of them and the life they lead as *poshly*. Turgenev portrays the Kirsanovs in a positive, if subdued light. And he does so within the context of a comedic structure, one that invariably leads the audience at the conclusion to recognize that "this is how things ought to be." Bazarov's death is quite another matter, of course. That is the culmination of the novel's tragedic structure. But in the first part of the novel's epilogue, where life and love are celebrated at Pavel's farewell dinner, with its exaltation of marriage and family [as Strakhov writes] "Turgenev stands for the eternal foundations of human life, for those basic elements which may perpetually change their forms, but in essence always remain unchanged."

But of course not all critics find such positive notes in *Fathers and Sons*. Most would probably argue that the novel is a tragedy. Such an analysis should surprise no one—it is a bromide of Turgenev criticism. But how and why *Fathers and Sons* is a tragedy—these are questions that until recently have remained largely unexplored. Once again Northrop Frye provides useful tools for analysis. The basic movement of tragedy, according to Frye, is toward the exclusion of a hero from a given society, with an emphasis on the hero's tragic isolation. It is in this connection that Gippius' analysis of the structure of *Fathers and Sons* is particularly apt. He perceives the novel's "dynamic highway" in this way: "Having cast himself off from the elements of his milieu, the obviously hostile ones as well as the pseudo-friendly ones, the hero remains tragically alone." Yury Mann sees a similar pattern, which he calls "one against all."

According to Frye, the tragic hero must be of heroic proportions: "The tragic hero is very great as compared with us, but there is something else, something on the side of him opposite the audience, compared to which he is small." Surely this is the case with Bazarov, whose greatness (implied, rather than shown) is, as Strakhov argues, less than the sum of life forces represented by the Kirsanovs and their spouses.

In addition, Frye conceives of the tragic hero as an impostor, someone who is deceived about himself, who plays a role that is not his to play. Significantly, Charles Bachman writes of "tragedy and self-deception" in *Fathers and Sons*, pointing out that "false self-images are crucial to the tragic view which the action of the novel seems to de-

> in *Fathers and Sons* the portraits of the Kirsanovs, their babies, their joyful participation in the natural cycle, all lead the audience to infer that all's right with the world."

mand. . . ." Most of the characters in the novel suffer from identity crises: this is true not just in the case of the strong characters, as Bachman suggests, but also of such a person as Arkady. But Bazarov's self-deception is the most extreme and his journey toward self-discovery the most painful and tragic. He dismisses the laws governing human life; his fatal infection, leading him to summon Odintsova for a last meeting in which he confesses that he is not the giant he had imagined himself to be, demonstrates that finally he understands the extent of his self-delusion.

The movement toward tragedy is generally toward a revelation of natural law, "that which is and must be," so that the audience's reaction to the hero's fall is paradoxical: we feel a sense of rightness (the tragic hero represents an imbalance in nature and thus must fall) and horrible wrongness (how sad that this man must fall). Such indeed is our reaction to Bazarov's death. Poignant as it may be, we nevertheless perceive, as Richard Freeborn formulates it, that Bazarov is a

usurper of divine right, whose arrogant self-will proclaims for itself a self-sufficiency in life which contravenes the limits of human experience and gives rise to a dilemma which is only to be resolved in death.

Fischler's approach to the question of Bazarov throws additional light on Turgenev's reliance on classical tragedic models:

One must first note that Bazarov belongs to a special category of protagonists, the tragic protagonist or even the nature hero. He fits there less because of his famous assertion that nature is his "workshop," than because of his repeatedly underlined mysterious bonds with his natural surroundings. He is associated with nature not only by brute strength and passion, but by vaguer, though not necessarily less awesome bonds of sympathy: the world responds to him, follows him, at least so long as he chooses to practice and accept association, that is, throughout the first part of the novel. He is born with a gift for harmony with the creation, yet, as he himself points out to Arkady, it is a gift of limited usefulness: one may derive strength from nature so long as one yields to it through naive faith, so long as one is willing to believe in the talismanic virtue of an aspen tree by a clay pit; but, when the magic is lost, one must drift to the inevitable end. Nonetheless, even when Bazarov's bond to nature ceases being a means for coping with the world, his fate remains associated with it by the structure of the novel. He is a nature hero, and, by ironic extension, he is even a nature "god"; he appears on the stage in spring (May 1859) to offer the traditional challenge to an existing order already undermined by inner and outer turmoil; he is defeated (expect perhaps in the duel with Pavel Kirsanov, the living-dead representative of the older order who, in many respects, is a projection of himself); then, largely through his own acquiescence and even complicity, he dies in August, at the height of summer, a traditional time for the death of gods. . . .

Comedy and tragedy coexist in *Fathers and Sons*. It is of course the novel's tragic side that impresses us most deeply. Such is human nature. Moreover, Turgenev takes pains to reinforce the novel's tragic overtones by placing the description of Bazarov's aged parents weeping inconsolably at their son's grave as the last element in the novel, the final chord of a tragic symphony, as it were. And yet, if we look closely at the very last lines of *Fathers and Sons,* we see that the narrator holds out a certain note of optimism, ambivalent as it may be:

> Can it really be that their prayers and their tears are fruitless? Can it really be that love, sacred, devoted love is not all-powerful? Oh no! No matter what a passionate, sinful, rebellious heart may be hidden in the grave, the flowers that grow on it look at us serenely with their innocent eyes; they speak to us not only of eternal peace, of that great peace of "indifferent" nature; they speak as well of eternal reconciliation and of life eternal. . . .

But what does Turgenev mean by "life everlasting"? The life of nature, which renews itself annually? The life of humanity, which is everlasting inasmuch as a new generation always takes the place of the dying one? Does the narrator really have in mind the Christian notion of the immortality of the soul? He is purposely vague in this quasi-pantheistic, quasi-Orthodox formulation. What is clear is that life goes on. Bazarov is dead, but Nikolay and Fenechka, along with Arkady and Katya, are multiplying and bringing forth much fruit.

The novel's tragic side predominates, but it does not overwhelm. Significantly, critics who write of *Fathers and Sons* as a tragedy often stop short of calling it a tragedy, pure and simple. Charles Bachman calls it "a basically tragic novel." Helen Muchnic describes the novel as "tragic in its implications, but not in its tone." Such hesitation can be accounted for on the formal level by the recognition of coexisting comedic and tragedic modes within the novel. Observing this relationship helps us to understand—in formal terms—the initial and continuing furor created by *Fathers and Sons*. In *"Apropos of Fathers and Sons"* Turgenev writes that he has an interesting collection of documents and letters from readers who accuse him of doing totally contradictory things in his novel. This is hardly surprising, since Turgenev *is* doing what seem to be contradictory things within the work. By combining the tragedic and comedic modes he seems to stand behind two diametrically opposed views of life at one and the same time. If we take the novel's comedic structure out of context, we conclude that life is triumphant, rewarding, and meaningful. Such is the conclusion that any comedy forces upon us. And in *Fathers and Sons* the portraits of the Kirsanovs, their babies, their joyful participation in the natural cycle, all lead the audience to infer that all's right with the world. On the other hand, if we take the novel's tragedic side out of context, we are led to the view that life, which is ruled by fate and the irrational, is essentially meaningless: death is triumphant. Where does Turgenev stand? "Where is the truth, on which side?" We may ask, as does Arkady. And Bazarov's answer is most appropriate: "Where? I'll answer you like an echo: where?" An analysis of the novel's dualistic structure shows that the truth is on both sides. Or, as Fischler argues, the problems raised in *Fathers and Sons* are insoluble and the rifts revealed can be mended only by time. This conclusion is supported by one of Turgenev's letters to Annenkov, in which he writes: "I know that in nature and in life everything is reconciled one way or another. . . . If life cannot [do the reconciling], death will reconcile." Thus Turgenev's own view of life is dualistic, but not contradictory, and this dualism lies at the heart of *Fathers and Sons*: as we have seen in this [essay], it accounts for the novel's structure.

Source: David Lowe, excerpt, from his *Turgenev's "Fathers and Sons,"* Ardis, 1983, pp. 15–27.

Charles R. Bachman

In the following essay, Bachman describes how false self-images contribute to the tragedy of Fa-thers and Sons.

Though Ivan Turgenev dealt with self-deception in a number of his works, nowhere is the theme more pervasive, or more subtly or convincingly handled, than in *Fathers and Sons*. Here false self-images are crucial to the tragic view which the action of the novel seems to demand, a view which in turn helps make it probably Turgenev's greatest work. This self-deception is most obvious in the case of certain minor characters. Peter (Piotr), Nikolai Kirsanov's "progressive" servant, is "a man whose whole merit consisted in the fact that he looked civil," and he obviously believes himself so, even though his civility is little more than an appearance. The progressive dandy, Sitnikov, is a sycophant who believes himself brave and definite when he feels the support of his idol, Bazarov, Madame Kukshin compensates for feminine plainness and frustration with the self-image of a woman of "advanced" views, and Matvey Ilyich Kolyazin, Arkady's relative who is sent to the town of X— to investigate the governor, is a "progressive" who "had the highest opinion of himself," whose slogan was *l'énergie est la première qualité d'un homme d'état*; and for all that, he was usually taken in, and any moderately experienced official could turn him round his finger."

These characters help exemplify Turgenev's satire on a society which wished to believe itself progressive; but they also reflect, in miniature as it were, the basic problem of self-identity of the three strong characters of the novel: Evgeny Vassilyich Bazarov, Pavel Petrovich Kirsanov and Anna Sergeyevna Odintsov. Turgenev distinguishes them as strong by giving them poise and self-confidence. They seem to feel superior to those around them, and have enough pride to trust their own personalities and judgements in social intercourse. By contrast Arkady, his father Nikolai, Bazarov's parents and Sitnikov are more typical of Turgenev's male figures: pliant and anxious to please. Arkady, for example, like Sitnikov, appears strong mainly when he senses Bazarov's support, and Turgenev implies that he will always be a follower.

In the novel strength of personality causes both attraction and repulsion, so that the points of greatest tension occur when the strong characters interact: the debate over nihilism, Bazarov's infatuation for Anna and the duel. These provide the major occasions through which Bazarov, Pavel and Anna each discover that the self-identity which formed the basis for their inner poise had been an illusion.

The chief encounter is that of Bazarov and Pavel, who at first appear to be opposite in several

> **As in Sophoclean tragedy, pride in Turgenev's novel is both a source of greatness and a tragic flaw."**

significant ways. The former is young, plain-featured, gruff and rude in manner, disrespectful of tradition and the humanities, and unconcerned with form, social and otherwise. Pavel is past middle-age, strikingly handsome, sensitive and careful in manner, strongly in favor of tradition and the humanities and over-concerned with form in dress, speech and behavior. While Arkady echoes Bazarov and Nikolai tries to be polite, the two main antagonists clash over the arts, tradition and nihilism. Their seemingly opposite attitudes and temperaments, however, and their contemptuous references to each other as "An antique survival" and "That unkept creature" can become the occasion for open conflict only because they are depicted as so similar in their egoism and their strength of personality. Both are accustomed to being deferred to, and cannot tolerate a lack of respect for themselves. Pavel is especially defensive. He ". . . had grown to detest Bazarov with all the strength of his soul; he regarded him as stuck-up, impudent, cynical and plebian; he suspected that Bazarov had no respect for him, that he had all but contempt for—him. Pavel Kirsanov!"

The most basic reason for Pavel's antagonism, however, lies deeper, and concerns his self-image. The great love affair of his life had been with the Princess R—, the glance of whose eyes was "swift and deep." Her reply to Pavel's statement that she was a sphinx indicated her intelligence: "'I?' she queried, and slowly raising her enigmatical glance upon him. 'Do you know that's awfully flattering?' she added with a meaningless smile, while her eyes still kept the same strange look."

In becoming infatuated with the Princess, Pavel had fallen in love with stupidity unconsciously masking itself as depth, and his tragedy in this affair had a conscious and an unconscious aspect. His whole personality was so bound up with her love that when she lost interest he became disillusioned with life. But a major reason for his being attracted to her in the first place would seem to have been that, like the Princess, Pavel himself had grown accustomed to depending for his sense of identity upon the esteem and expectations of others—an esteem based upon his impressive mask of manners and physical appearance. His response to the Princess had a quality of desperation. Thrust by handsome looks and a dashing manner into the role of a romantic, Pavel came to believe the role himself. His pride grasped at it as a self-identity which seemed as impressive as was his appearance. "Much admired in society," he "had read in all five or six French books." "... a brilliant career awaited him. Suddenly everything changed." The most ironic aspect of this change was that in becoming ensnared in the deep but "meaningless" gaze of the Princess' eyes, Pavel had, not unnaturally, fallen victim to the same kind of deception as had the society which admired him. While he had perhaps read "five or six" more French books than the Princess, his statement that she was a sphinx was almost as unperceptive as her inane but pretentious reply.

After being deserted, and unaware of the irony implicit in his love, Pavel settled at Marion, where "he arranged his whole life in the English style." Of course Turgenev is satirizing in this "man with the fragrant mustache" the snobbishness and artificiality of the Russian gentry. But the satire is mixed with sympathy, since Pavel's artificiality and need for a style of life are largely unconscious attempts to retain in a new setting the romantic self-image with which he has so long identified himself. While Pavel and his brother are standing outside at night, however, and Nikolai "had not the force to tear himself away from the darkness, the garden, the sense of the fresh air in his face, from that melancholy, that restless craving," Pavel's feelings are similar to what would have been expected from Bazarov: "... he too raised his eyes towards the heavens. But nothing was reflected in his beautiful dark eyes except the light of the stars. He was not born a romantic, and his fastidiously dry and sensuous soul, with its French tinge of misanthropy was not capable of dreaming ...."

Pavel's view of himself as a romantic, then, is quite obviously a self-deceptive illusion. In view of this, the underlying motive for his resentment of Bazarov would seem to be that he sensed in the younger man a rather complete image of his own genuine temperament: not only his egoism and pride, but his misanthropy and lack of romanticism as well. During the first argument (Chs. V and VI), his defense of nature, art and poetry against

Bazarov, who refuses to acknowledge their value and is even "indifferent to the beauties of nature," actually conceal an insensitiveness to the things Pavel is defending. His staunch support of "the traditions accepted in human conduct," and of "personal dignity" and firmness of character as the "foundation for ... the social fabric" are an overcompensation for the fear that in his encounter with Bazarov he is losing the basis for his own firmness of character—the image of self which he had so carefully though unconsciously created.

The duel not only forces the two antagonists into a grudging respect for each other's courage, but also reveals that they seem to hold similar attitudes toward Nikolai and the peasants. Pavel believes that Bazarov "behaved honorably," and they have a similar estimate of Nikolai's character:

"There's no deceiving my brother; we shall have to tell him we quarreled over politics."

"Very good," assented Bazarov. "You can say I insulted all Anglomaniacs."

"That will do splendidly."

Pavel is surprised at Bazarov's statement that the Russian peasant does not understand himself, because he obviously shares this belief: "Ah! so that's your idea! ... Look what your fool of a Peter has done!"

These similarities, however, only further convince Pavel of the extent to which his self-image has been an illusion, and his joking with Bazarov is probably a cloak for this realization. What is even more significant is the major cause of the duel itself: Pavel's feelings for Fenichka. Before the duel, Fenichka had become "more afraid of Pavel Petrovich than ever; for some time he had begun to watch her and would suddenly make his appearance as though he sprang out of the earth behind her back, in his English suit, with his immovable vigilant face ...." After the duel, while mildly delirious, Pavel states that he sees a physical resemblance between the Princess R— and Fenichka, thus acknowledging that the latter has replaced the former as the symbol of his romantic illusion. The exclamation, "Ah, how I love that light-headed creature!" seems to refer to the Princess, but the object of Pavel's subsequent threat is omitted by Turgenev: "I can't bear any insolent upstart to dare to touch ..." Both the Princess and Fenichka are meant, just as whatever rival had robbed Pavel of the Princess seems to be identified with Bazarov. By threatening the object toward which Pavel felt himself romantically inclined, both rivals have also threatened his careful illusion that he has a romantic temperament. His reaction in both cases is similarly desperate: in the first, disillusionment and exile from the Princess' scene of activity; in the second, the challenge to a duel and subsequent disillusionment and exile from Fenichka's scene of activity. After Bazarov's departure, Pavel tries to convince Nikolai that he should marry Fenichka: "I begin to think Bazarov was right in accusing me of being an aristocrat. No, dear brother, don't let us worry ourselves about appearances and the world's opinion any more; we are old folks and resigned; it's time we laid aside vanity of all kind." In laying aside "appearances and the world's opinion," Pavel is acknowledging the falseness of the only self-identity he has consciously known, and the tear that rolls down his cheek as he exhorts Fenichka to love Nikolai is partly one of regret that the waste caused by this false self-identity is irrevocable. His suggestion that Nikolai marry Fenichka is really an act of despair. It is after the marriage that Pavel goes abroad, spiritually "a dead man."

The most ironic aspect of Bazarov's effect on Pavel is that the former's anti-romanticism and cynicism, which have made Pavel aware of these qualities at the heart of his own personality, are also an appearance concealing a different kind of person than Pavel ever realizes. Bazarov's profession of physician and his intense faith in the validity of experimental research are in direct contradiction to his statements that as a nihilist he believes "in nothing." But his infatuation with Anna is the chief event which reveals the romantic and at times lyrical sensibility beneath the gruff exterior. This is an ironic reversal for one who has characterized love as "romanticism, nonsense, rot, artiness." His overt scorn of poetry rings false when he quotes a line of "Der Wanderer" to Anna, and in his lyrical recollection of childhood in his later conversation with Arkady:

"That aspen," began Bazarov, "reminds me of my childhood; it grows at the edge of the claypits where the brick-shed used to be, and in those days I believed firmly that that clay-pit possessed a peculiar talismanic power . . ."

When alone, Bazarov "recognized the romantic in himself." One probable reason for his resentment of Pavel, then, is also an insecurity with his own self-image—a fear that his real temperament contains some of the romantic idealism which Pavel avows.

A further irony is that Bazarov has criticized Pavel for allowing his whole life to become dependent upon his passion for the Princess: "Still, I must say that a man who stakes his whole life on one card—a woman's love—and when that card fails, turns sour, and lets himself go till he's fit for nothing, is not a man, but a male." Yet after being rejected by Anna Sergeyevna, Bazarov himself loses most of his own drive and sense of direction. He visits his parents, but feels dissatisfied and bored. After three days he impulsively visits Anna again and returns to Marino, where he conceals his romanticism from all but Arkady and Fenichka.

The source of Bazarov's disillusionment, however, is not only his discovery that his own self-image was an illusion. Anna's poise and serenity, which had attracted him and seemed to suggest genuine emotional depth, were actually manifestations of an emotional lethargy, an inability to feel deep passion. After Bazarov departs she begins to realize that there is something false about her conception of herself: "Under the influence of various vague emotions, the sense of life passing by, the desire of novelty, she had forced herself to go up to a certain point, forced herself to glance behind it, and had seen behind it not even an abyss, but a void . . . or something hideous."

Bazarov realizes that, like Pavel, he has become infatuated with a deceptive appearance. He turns to Fenichka partly because he senses that in her there is no illusion of self, and therefore no false mask. His declaration to her that "I live alone, a poor wretch," indicates the extent of both his trust in her and his disillusionment. The duel severs both him and Pavel from Fenichka, and Bazarov also becomes virtually a dead man, telling Arkady that "there seems to be an empty space in the box, and I am putting hay in; that's how it is in the box of our life; we would stuff it up with anything rather than have a void." He pays Anna one last visit, and the attempted casualness of their conversations cannot conceal the fact that they both feel ill at ease and empty. Feeling again "dreary boredom or vague restlessness," Bazarov finally returns home, and his death by typhus, like the demise of several of Thomas Hardy's heroes, is no artistic flaw in the novel, but an anticipated symbol of the death of his spirit which has already taken place.

Bazarov's tragic dilemma approaches the perspective which Turgenev invites the reader to share. The social class in the novel which suffers least from self-deception is the one to which Bazarov, in a last fruitless attempt to reestablish an identity, instinctively returns: that of the peasants and small rural landowners. The aristocracy, on the other hand, which wishes to believe itself progressive, is the class which as a whole suffers most from self-deception. In spite of disclaimers of didacticism Turgenev stated in a letter [dated 14 April 1862] to the poet K. K. Sluchevsky that "My entire tale is directed against the nobility as a leading class." Bazarov, however, like the, reader, has seen that not only "aristocrats" such as Pavel and Anna, but also all pseudo and genuine intellectual sophisticates, including himself, have been deceived as to their identity. Even Arkady, before his relationship with Katya, has had such illusions. As in Thomas Hardy, the gain of awareness has brought an inevitable loss of a sense of integrity—a dilemma which foreshadows the questioning of the very possibility of self-identity so prevalent in post-Freudian literature and society. But *Fathers and Sons*, though lacking the detailed psychological penetration present in the greater works of Tolstoy and Dostoevsky, nonetheless moves beyond the depiction of a pathetic paradox toward genuine tragedy; and perhaps the most fruitful method of discussing the tragic quality of this novel is by comparison with tragic drama.

As in Sophoclean tragedy, pride in Turgenev's novel is both a source of greatness and a tragic flaw. Because their pride is their own responsibility it becomes the main source of our admiration for Anna, Pavel and Bazarov, helping to give them magnitude and significance. Yet in contributing most to their perseverance in believing in and sustaining illusions of the self, their pride is also the major reason for their fall. Their own proud reserve and the modern universe in which they live prevent them from railing at the gods as did Lear, or examining the fatefulness of life as did Oedipus, Hamlet or Phèdre. But the questioning of the justice of fate, and the violent fall or destruction usually demanded by Sophoclean, Shakespearean and Racinian tragedy has become in *Fathers and Sons* the loss of self-identity: a paradox and a catastrophe which may well be as potentially tragic for modern man. This loss of self-identity, however, can be tragic rather than pathetic only if it involves a genuine, forceful and courageous internal and external struggle to maintain a sense of self. Necessary are both awareness and sheer stubbornness—which is presented rather than analyzed away. Through it would be foolish to argue equivalencies, this dilemma, which characterizes Bazarov and Pavel, and to a lesser degree Anna, is also that of Oedipus. The pride with which Bazarov and Pavel assert themselves so forcefully as compensation for an unconscious insecurity is unexplained; the forcefulness does not depend on the insecurity. Sitnikov is also insecure, but weak.

This unexplained but human dignity of pride which "goeth before a fall," combined with the seeming injustice—but not absurdity—of the fall, make it valid to classify *Fathers and Sons* as a basically tragic novel. The view of society and fate invited by the novel depends not upon Turgenev's final phrases concerning "eternal reconciliation," but upon the fact that for the strongest characters there has been no earthly reconciliation. In typical Turgenev fashion, the most assertive figure is killed off. The probability that the novelist's compulsion to destroy such heroes was motivated by his own pliant personality is only relevent to Turgenev's psychology, however. It does not affect the essential tragedy of *Fathers and Sons*, which lies in the fact that not only Bazarov, but all three strong characters in the novel have had self-images so dangerously false that, when uncovered, their personalities have been left shattered, dead of vitality or genuine hope.

Source: Charles R. Bachman, "Tragedy and Self-Deception in Turgenev's *Fathers and Sons*," in *Revue des langues vivantes*, Vol. XXXIV, No. 3, 1968, pp. 269–76.

Sources

Antonovich, M. A., "Asmodey nashego vremeni (An Asmodeus of our Time)," in *Fathers and Children*, edited by Patrick Waddington, Everyman, p. 253, originally published in *Sovremennik (The Contemporary)*, No. 3, 1862.

Berlin, Isaiah, Lecture on *Fathers and Children*, in *Fathers and Children*, edited by Patrick Waddington, Everyman, p. 272, originally published in *"Fathers and Children": the Romanes Lecture, delivered in the Sheldonian Theatre, 12 November 1970*, Oxford University Press, 1972, pp. 55–56.

Engel, Barbara Alpern, Excerpt, in *Fathers and Children*, edited by Patrick Waddington, Everyman, p. 273, originally published in *Mothers and Daughters: Women of the Intelligentsia in Nineteenth-Century Russia*, Cambridge University Press, 1983, p. 63.

Garnett, Edward, *Turgenev*, Kennikat Press, 1966, p. 110.

Gertsen, A. I., "Yeshchéraz Bazarov (Bazarov Again)," in *Fathers and Children*, edited by Patrick Waddington, Everyman, p. 257, originally published in *Polyarnaya zvezda (The Pole Star)*, 1869.

Henry, Peter, "I. S. Turgenev: *Fathers and Sons*," in *Fathers and Children*, edited by Patrick Waddington, Everyman, p. 277–78, originally published in *The Monster in the Mirror: Studies in Nineteenth-Century Realism*, edited by D. A. Williams, Oxford University Press, 1978, pp. 55–56.

James, Henry, "Ivan Turgéenieff," in *Fathers and Children*, edited by Patrick Waddington, Everyman, p. 267, originally published in *North American Review*, Vol. CXVIII, April 1874, pp. 326–56.

Moore, George, "Turgueneff," in *Fathers and Children*, edited by Patrick Waddington, Everyman, p. 265–66, originally published in *Fortnightly Review*, n.s., Vol. XLIII, February 1, 1888, pp. 244–46.

Pisarev, D. I., "Bazarov," in *Fathers and Children*, edited by Patrick Waddington, Everyman, p. 255, originally published in *Russkoye slovo (The Russian Word)*, No. 3, 1862.

Ripp, Victor, *Turgenev's Russia: From "Notes of a Hunter" to "Fathers and Sons,"* Cornell University Press, 1980, pp. 187, 190–91.

Schapiro, Leonard, *Turgenev: His Life and Times*, Random House, 1978, p. 185.

Shedden-Ralston, William Ralston, "Ivan Turguenief," in *Fathers and Children*, edited by Patrick Waddington, Everyman, p. 265, originally published in *Saturday Review*, October 22, 1881, p. 509.

Turgenev, Ivan, *Fathers and Sons*, Barnes & Noble Classics, 2000.

————, "Letter to A. A. Fet, Paris, 16 April 1862," in *Fathers and Children*, edited by Patrick Waddington, Everyman, p. 246, originally published in *Literaturnyye i zhiteyskiye vospominaniya* (Memories of Life and Literature), 1869, and subsequently translated into English and published in *I. S. Turgenev, Complete Works and Letters in 28 vols*, Moscow and Leningrad: Nauka, 1960–1968 (Letters), Vol. IV, p. 371.

————, "Letter to F. M. Dostoyevsky, Paris, 30 March 1862," in *Fathers and Children*, edited by Patrick Waddington, Everyman, p. 245, originally published in *Literaturnyye i zhiteyskiye vospominaniya* (Memories of Life and Literature), 1869, and subsequently translated into English and published in *I. S. Turgenev, Complete Works and Letters in 28 vols*, Moscow and Leningrad: Nauka, 1960–1968 (Letters), Vol. IV, pp. 358–59.

————, "On *Fathers and Children*," in *Fathers and Children*, edited by Patrick Waddington, Everyman, p. 251, originally published in *Literaturnyye i zhiteyskiye vospominaniya* (Memories of Life and Literature), 1869, and subsequently translated into English and published in *I. S. Turgenev, Complete Works and Letters in 28 vols*, Moscow and Leningrad: Nauka, 1960–1968 (Works), Vol. XIV, pp. 97–99, 103–05.

Yarmolinsky, Avrahm, *Turgenev: The Man, His Art and His Age*, Collier Books, 1959, p. 199.

Further Reading

Costlow, Jane Tussey, *Worlds within Worlds: The Novels of Ivan Turgenev*, Princeton University Press, 1990.

Turgenev's books are well known for the accurate portrayal of life within his time. The author discusses this aspect of his writing combined with his exquisite style for words.

Freeborn, Richard, *The Russian Revolutionary Novel: Turgenev to Pasternak*, Cambridge University Press, 1985.

Turgenev and Pasternak are just two of the Russian writers who faced persecution for their revolutionary works. One of the richest periods in Russian literature spans from the novels of Turgenev's time in the middle of the nineteenth century to those of Pasternak in the middle of the twentieth century.

Hayek, F. A., *The Road to Serfdom*, University of Chicago Press, 1994.

Ahead of its time when first published in 1947, this book discusses the dangers to a society when the government gains increasing economic control. Hayek focuses mainly on the tyrannies of his time in Germany, Italy, and Soviet Russia, which were based on National Socialism. In this classic text, Hayek foresaw the failure of socialism.

Kolchin, Peter, *Unfree Labor: American Slavery and Russian Serfdom*, Belknap Press, 1990.

Kolchin's acclaimed comparative history study examines the institutions of slavery and serfdom in America and Russia respectively, including the emancipation efforts.

Lowe, David A., *Critical Essays on Ivan Turgenev*, Macmillan Library Reference, 1988.

This book contains reprinted criticism—reviews and essays—that was originally published in the early to late twentieth century. The criticism was originally published in English, German, and Russian.

Roosevelt, Priscilla, *Life on the Russian Country Estate: A Social and Cultural History*, Yale University Press, 1997.

The author gives a historical account of the rural, Russian aristocratic landowner class, which survived the emancipation of the serfs and was visible even at the end of the century. The book features many images and illustrations of a cultural world that has since vanished.

Waddington, Patrick, *Ivan Turgenev and Britain*, Berg Publishers Incorporated, 1995.

This book discusses the influence that Britain had on Ivan Turgenev. The author visited England often and associated with many of the English literary class, including Tennyson and George Eliot. The book also reprints some previously unpublished articles and features an extensive bibliography.

The Fountainhead

Ayn Rand

1943

After Ayn Rand finished writing *The Fountainhead*, the manuscript was rejected by twelve publishers who claimed, as Laurence Miller notes in an article on the author for the *Dictionary of Literary Biography*, it was "commercially unsuitable because it was too politically and philosophically controversial, too intellectual, too improbable a story, too long, poorly written, and dull, and because it employed an unsympathetic hero." After Rand submitted it to Bobbs-Merrill, editor Archie Ogden recommended that the book be published. When his superiors disagreed, Ogden countered, "If this is not the book for you, then I am not the editor for you." This was enough to convince them to publish the novel in 1943.

While initial reviews were mixed, the public's approval grew each year until 1945, when it stayed on the best-seller list for twenty-six weeks. Sales are currently near three million copies. Readers responded not only to the story of brilliant architect Howard Roark's struggle to gain success in New York City; they also became intrigued with the philosophy Rand outlined through the characters and their interactions. Many readers became devoted followers of objectivism, Rand's vision of how to achieve an ideal self as expressed in the novel. Nathaniel Branden, who would become her protégé, claimed, as quoted by Miller, that the novel gave him "the sense of a door opening, intellectually, spiritually, psychologically—a passageway into another dimension, like a summons from the future." Miller notes that *The Fountainhead* helped

to ensure Rand "a place as one of the most controversial, colorful, and influential writers of the twentieth century."

Author Biography

Ayn Rand was born Alisa Rosenbaum in St. Petersburg, Russia, on February 2, 1905 to Fronz (a chemist) and Anna. Alisa taught herself to read at age six and by age nine, she determined that she would become a writer of idealist heroes like those created by Sir Walter Scott and Victor Hugo. The family fled the Bolshevik Revolution soon after it began in 1917 and relocated to the Crimea. The Communists confiscated her father's business and, as a result, the family was thrown into poverty. During this period she studied American history and became enthralled with the democratic system, which would have a profound effect on her fiction. When she and her family returned to Russia, she began studies in philosophy and history at the University of Petrograd where she graduated in 1924. That same year, her passion for films prompted her to enroll in the State Institute for Cinema Arts where she studied screen writing.

In 1925, she was granted permission to leave Russia to visit relatives, but she would never return to her homeland. She stayed in New York City for six months, extended her visa, and then moved to Hollywood where she changed her name and hoped to start a career as a screenwriter. Rand met Cecil B. DeMille on her second day in California, and the movie mogul immediately offered her a job as an extra and then a script reader on his film *King of Kings*. A week later she met actor Frank O'-Connor, who became her husband until his death fifty years later.

During the next few years Rand worked in various studio positions including in the wardrobe department until she sold her first screenplay, *Red Pawn*, to Universal Studios in 1932. Her play *Night of January 16th* was produced first in Hollywood and later on Broadway. In 1933, she completed her first novel, *We the Living*, which was rejected by several publishers until Macmillan agreed to accept the manuscript in 1936. The book, a fictional representation of her life in Russia after the communist takeover, was not well received by the public or critics. The previous year, she began writing *The Fountainhead*, determined to create her vision of an ideal hero. After twelve publishers rejected it, the novel was finally published in 1943, and within two years it had become a best-seller.

Ayn Rand

The Fountainhead, along with her popular last novel, *Atlas Shrugged*, expresses the philosophy she termed objectivism, which she would outline in lectures and essays from 1962 through 1976. During the last decades of her life she became a popular and controversial public philosopher, speaker, and cult figure. Her death in New York City on March 6, 1982 triggered new public and academic interest in her life, fiction, and her objectivist movement.

Plot Summary

Part I

The novel opens as the Stanton Institute of Technology is graduating its 1922 class. The dean has just informed Howard Roark that he is being expelled for "insubordination,"—for refusing to complete his assignments according to the standards of the college. Roark is not upset by the expulsion; rather, he admits that he should have quit the school long ago since he claims that he has learned very little there. Valedictory speaker Peter Keating, who has conformed to Stanton's rules, is considered by all to be the school's next success story. Yet Keating is unsure about his next move. He asks Roark's advice about whether to continue his studies in Europe or to accept a position with the Francon Architectural Firm in New York City. Roark tells him that he will learn nothing by studying the architecture of the past.

Both men move to New York City. Keating shows little creative promise but learns how to manipulate his employer, Guy Francon, and so quickly rises in the firm, becoming chief designer. Francon's beautiful daughter Dominique recognizes Keating's and her father's mediocrity and the pandering they must engage in to become successful. She openly criticizes them in her interior design column in *The New York Banner*. Overwhelmed by her beauty and commanding presence, Keating proposes marriage to her, but she refuses.

Roark becomes assistant to Henry Cameron, a renegade architect who once had enjoyed success for his innovative buildings, including the city's first skyscraper. When, however, the classic style came into vogue, Cameron refused to adapt and thus now receives few contracts. Roark works with the older man for three years, during which time he perfects his skills and establishes his architectural vision.

Keating's clever manipulation of others, coupled with Roark's willingness to assist in the improvement of his classmate's designs, affords him much success. When Keating determines to win a competition to design "the world's most beautiful building," he sees an opportunity to gain a partnership in the firm. He acknowledges, though, that he needs help from Roark, who cannot pass up any opportunity to create his own designs. Roark's plans, altered somewhat by Keating's addition of classical flourishes, win the award and Keating becomes a partner.

Part II

When Cameron retires, Roark accepts a job at Francon, but after refusing to work with others on his first design there, he is fired. He is later hired by another builder who lets him design independently but alters his work after it is completed. As a result, Roark determines to work for himself and is soon contracted by newspaperman Austen Heller to build his home. Roark cannot find other clients to appreciate his unique designs and so is forced to close his office and find work in a granite quarry in Connecticut, owned by Guy Francon.

That summer, Roark meets Dominique, and the two enter into an intense sexual relationship. He is soon called back to the city, though, to de-

sign an apartment building. After its completion, Roark gains recognition and more contracts. His success is noticed by Ellsworth Toohey, architectural critic for *The Banner*. Toohey, who has falsely assumed the role of humanist, feels threatened by Roark's individuality and so sets out to ruin him. On his recommendation, Roark is hired to build a "Temple to the Human Spirit," which upon completion, Toohey claims is heretical. As a result, Roark's career suffers.

Dominique marries Keating as an escape from her conflicted feelings about Roark, but the marriage lasts less than two years when she meets and decides to marry *Banner* publisher Gail Wynand. Recognizing and appreciating Roark's genius, Wynand hires him to build a house for Dominique, and the two men become friends. As Wynand uses his influence to get contracts for Roark, the architect's reputation grows.

Part III

In an effort to bolster his own reputation, Keating asks Roark to design a low-cost development called Cortlandt Homes. Roark agrees, with Keating's promise that he will not alter the plans. When Keating passes the design off as his own and allows it to be altered, Roark blows up the project with Dominique's help. When Roark goes on trial for the bombing, Wynand supports his friend, which turns public opinion against him. Toohey sees the situation as an opportunity for him to destroy Wynand, who has just fired him, and Roark. Toohey engineers a strike against the *Banner*. To save himself, Wynand writes an editorial condemning Roark, which salvages his career but breaks his spirit.

At his trial, Roark convinces the jury that he had a right to destroy his project and is found not guilty. Roger Enright buys Cortlandt Homes and commissions Roark to rebuild it. Keating's reputation is destroyed after the public discovers that he put his name on the designs. After Dominique divorces Wynand, she marries Roark, who agrees to build a skyscraper for Wynand, who tells him, "'Build it as a monument to that spirit which is yours . . . and could have been mine.'"

Characters

Henry Cameron

Roark seeks out Henry Cameron when he first comes to New York because of the architect's reputation as a man of independent vision. Unfortunately, Cameron's individualism has cost him a successful career. When Roark convinces Cameron to take him on as his assistant, the older man helps him develop his own style. Cameron is the first to recognize and help promote Roark's genius. At one point he tests Roark's resolve, suggesting that he sell out and give the public what it wants in order to gain approval and success. Roark's response, that he would rather starve, pleases Cameron and proves the older man's faith in him. Eventually, Roark must strike out on his own when Cameron cannot get enough contracts to keep his business going. Cameron's integrity represents the devotion to the individualistic spirit for its own sake, even in the face of social and economic failure, which is an important tenet of objectivism.

Lois Cook

Presenting herself as a nonconformist, Lois Cook breaks the rules of a society that she believes is trapped in conventionality. She does not try to fit standards of beauty or respectability. Yet her rebellion is shallow at heart. Instead of railing against social corruption or shoddy journalism, she instead chooses not to bathe regularly. She passes herself off as an intellectual but her writing, which breaks all the rules of grammar and form, ultimately is unintelligible.

Mike Donnigan

Working class electrician Mike Donnigan refuses to be swayed by public opinion. Though possessing only an average intelligence, he recognizes the quality of Roark's work and the mediocrity of Francon's and Keating's. His friendship with Roark develops through their mutual appreciation of well-constructed buildings.

Dominique Francon

Guy Francon's daughter, Dominique, is a troubled pessimist throughout most of the novel. She recognizes both the genius of men like Roark and the mediocrity of her father and Keating but is certain that the mediocrity will win out, especially under the influence of destructive men like Toohey. She falls in love with Roark, who represents to her the ideal man, yet she is convinced that he will ultimately be destroyed by a society that refuses to recognize and value his superiority. As a result, she tries to interfere with Roark's work before he is brought down by others.

Her feelings for Roark are further complicated by her determination that such a man will make too

Media Adaptations

- *The Fountainhead*, the film version of the novel, was released by Warner Brothers in 1949 and directed by King Vidor. The film stars Gary Cooper and Patricia Neal.

- An audio version of *The Fountainhead* was released by Blackstone Audio Books in 1995 and read by Christopher Hurt.

---

many demands on her. Thus she tries to protect herself by entering into relationships with inferior men. The characterization of Dominique turns troubling as she begins to exhibit masochistic tendencies. Rand suggests that Dominique punishes herself through degrading sexual experiences with men like Keating and Wynand because of her conflicted feelings about Roark. Yet her initial sexual encounter with Roark, which she thoroughly enjoys, also requires her submission.

Guy Francon

Keating works for Guy Francon, who heads the most successful architectural firm in the city. Francon has risen to the top not because of his talents, which are decidedly mediocre, but through the manipulation of others' abilities and through the development of keen sense of taste and style. Attuned to the latest trends, he gives the public what it wants, which is, when the novel opens, a reversion to the heavy ornamentation and flourishes of the classical era. His success has depended on his ability to copy that design. Although Francon is a second-hander, he does reflect positive social qualities: a sense of style and an appreciation of beauty, as his devotion to the classical age reflects. He also appreciates his daughter's independence and individuality. His ability to recognize the merit of these qualities prompts him to refuse to testify against Roark at his trial.

Catherine Halsey

Peter Keating becomes engaged to Catherine Halsey, Toohey's niece. When Keating drops her for Dominique she turns to a life of altruism under her uncle's direction, submerging herself completely in her duty to others. As a result of giving up a sense of selfhood, she becomes a bitter old woman. By the end of the novel, she is a mean-spirited Washington bureaucrat, barking orders— "not big orders or cruel orders; just mean little ones—about plumbing and disinfectants."

Austen Heller

Roark's benefactor, newspaper columnist Austen Heller, supports Roark's as well as others' individuality. He asks Roark to build a home for him and supports political prisoners around the world.

Peter Keating

Keating arrives in New York at the same time as Roark, but the two architects take very different paths. Keating achieves success rather quickly by learning, under Guy Francon's tutelage, how to manipulate others. Harboring no illusions about his lack of creativity, Keating easily accepts the help of others; in some cases he actually puts his name on others' work.

His lack of a clear vision of self is evident in his difficulty in making decisions, as he shows when he cannot decide at the beginning of the novel whether to continue his studies or to join Francon's firm. As a result of this insecurity and his desire for approval, he surrounds himself with things he thinks will help define him: expensive clothes, important friends like Ellsworth Toohey, and Dominique, his trophy wife. He subordinates any sense of self to his drive to succeed, evident as he discards Catherine Halsey, the woman he loves, for Dominique because of her beauty and stature in society. His refusal to develop his own identity results in his downfall when the public discovers that he has been claiming others' work as his own.

Kent Lansing

With "the patience of a Chinese executioner" and "the hide of a battleship," salesman Kent Lansing fights for what he feels is right. As a member of the board of advisors for the Aquitania Hotel, he hires Roark to finish the project because he recognizes the architect's integrity and talent. He serves as a middleman to help convince the public of Roark's gifts.

Steven Mallory

As his friend Roark notes, Steven Mallory's sculptures are "not what men are, but what men could be—and should be." Mallory's talents enable him to create "the heroic in man," similar to what Roark achieves in the construction of his skyscrapers. Mallory, like Cameron and Roark, has been unappreciated for his innovative vision and as a result, when Roark first meets him, he is bitter and cynical about ever achieving recognition. Unlike Roark, pubic opinion affects him. After continual rejections he turns to alcohol for escape. When Roark hires him to create a sculpture for the Stoddard temple, the architect helps him have confidence in his abilities without regard to others' judgments. As a result, he creates an exquisite sculpture of Dominique.

Howard Roark

Howard Roark is a brilliant architect whose innovative designs reflect his stanch individualism. At the beginning of the novel, he is expelled from school for his inability to conform to tradition. In her preliminary notes for the novel, Rand comments that Roark contains an "utter selfishness"— an "iron conviction" to "be himself at any cost—the only thing he really wants of life." He insists, "All that which proceeds from man's independent ego is good. All that which proceeds from man's dependence upon men is evil." What he wants is to be able to create his vision of the perfect building. He tells his mentor Cameron that he decided to be an architect because he does not believe in God. He builds, he claims, "Because I love this earth. That's all I love. I don't like the shape of things on this earth. I want to change them." He is willing to face criminal charges to maintain his integrity and his right to achieve his architectural vision.

His inability to compromise his ideals results in a difficult struggle to realize this vision. Society's rejection bothers him only in that it prevents him from this task, for he is never shaken in his confidence in himself and his abilities. In that sense, he is a static character in the novel. He learns a great deal about architecture during the course of the novel but nothing about himself, since he is fully formed when we first meet him after he is expelled from Stanton. Roark becomes a touchstone, however, for the other characters. As they come in contact with his overwhelming sense of integrity and individualism, readers measure the other characters against him.

Ellsworth Toohey

Ellsworth Toohey, the architectural critic for *The Banner*, promotes collectivism and so condemns Roark's display of individualism, insisting that the architect's sensibility is inherently selfish.

As a result, he attacks Roark in his column called "One Small Voice." Toohey claims humanitarian motives for his criticism of men like Roark. Yet his jealousy of their talent is the real cause of his efforts to destroy them. The narrator notes that when he was seven, Toohey had attacked a child who gained the attention he craved.

Toohey also tries to destroy Roark because the architect threatens the powerful position he enjoys. He has successfully passed himself off as a Marxist intellectual and has, as a result, developed a cult-like following. Toohey requires his disciples' blind obedience as he promotes his destructive form of communism, which requires a complete surrender of the self. Men like Roark whose success depends only on their own personal strength and vision point out the hollowness inherent in Toohey's philosophy.

Gus Webb

Another one of Toohey's followers, Gus Webb is, like Lois Cook, a shallow nonconformist architect. Unlike Roark, however, architect Webb has no creative spirit. He breaks the rules because he can, not because his vision compels him to. Devoted to the "international Style," he designs buildings that become a mere jumble of boxes without any structure or aesthetic value. He follows the rules of nonconformity as slavishly as traditionalists do. He does not wash regularly and breaks other accepted rules of behavior because that is what is expected of nonconformists. The shallowness of his devotion to "the workers' revolution" becomes apparent in his response to Roark's bombing of Cortlandt, when he comments, "I wish he'd blasted it when it was full of people—a few children blown to pieces—then you'd have something. Then I'd love it. The movement could use it."

Gail Wynand

Wynand is a powerful newspaper mogul who, like Dominique, has a pessimistic view of the world, even though he was able to successfully escape New York's Hell's Kitchen. He has built up his financial empire by "giv[ing] people what they want," with little regard for integrity. When he discovers that quality in Roark, Wynand determines to help him succeed. Wynand is convinced that he can manipulate public opinion, and so supports Roark when he is tried for the Cortlandt bombing. When the public subsequently turns against him, he tells himself, "You were a ruler of men. You held a leash. A leash is only a rope with a noose at both ends." Recognizing that his position is in jeop-

ardy, he writes an editorial condemning Roark, which salvages his career but breaks his spirit. Wynand is a truly tragic figure in the novel. He recognizes greatness but does not have the strength of character to become what he admires in Roark.

Themes

Reason

Rand believed that "reason is man's only proper judge of values and his only proper guide to action." She called her philosophy "objectivism" because she wanted to promote a sense of objective reality based on the power to reason. In the novel, Roark exhibits reason as he determines what nourishes his ego and thus sustains his life. The main quality that accomplishes these ends is his individualism. Throughout the novel, he continually refuses to allow others to alter his vision or to dictate the terms of his success.

Rand suggested that those who choose not to think rationally and look to others for guidance become second-handers as they refuse to take responsibility for their own lives. Peter Keating is the prime example of this type of individual. His insecurity prompts his lapses in reason as he tries to pass off Roark's work as his own. His inability to determine proper values and proper action results in his destruction.

Individualism versus Collectivism

Rand presents her philosophy of the merits of individualism and collectivism through two of her main characters: Howard Roark and Ellsworth Toohey. She champions individualism in her depiction of Roark, whose nobility rests in large part on his determination not to be influenced by others, especially in regards to his creative vision. Roark emphasizes that individuality fosters self-sufficiency, which enables him to successfully produce artistic architectural structures. Rand insisted in a 1934 letter to H. L. Mencken (as published in the *Letters of Ayn Rand*, edited by Michael S. Berliner), "I believe that man will always be an individualist, whether he knows it or not, and I want to make it my duty to make him know it" (Berliner, ed.).

Collectivism, which depends on self-sacrifice to the good of the group, becomes destructive in the characterization of Toohey and his followers. Toohey promotes this philosophy only to gain control of his followers who he has convinced to give

Topics for Further Study

- View the film version of *The Fountainhead* and critique it. Is Rand's philosophy of objectivism as evident in the film as it is in the novel? Are the characters believable? What changes would you make in the film to improve it?

- Compare Rand's political themes in her novel *We The Living* with the more social focus in *The Fountainhead*.

- Research the development of the skyscraper. Was there as much resistance to this new form of architecture as there is in the novel? Who were the innovative architects during the early part of the century in America? Did they also struggle for recognition and acceptance of their designs?

- In the novel, Rand condemns collectivism. Find arguments that support this movement and any examples that you can find of successful versions of it.

up their individuality in their devotion to the welfare of others. This exploitative system requires followers to subordinate themselves to the will of other people. The resulting self-abnegation undermines the honesty of the self and the human spirit.

Style

Structure

Rand was a great admirer of Aristotle, especially his literary theories. She believed that a novel should exhibit an Aristotelian logic, that all of its parts (plot, characters, and setting) should unite to reveal theme, reflected through and controlled by the imagination of the author. In her *The Romantic Manifesto*, she insists that these parts, or "attributes" as she calls them "unite into so integrated a sum that no starting point can be discerned." In a letter to Gerald Loeb she declares, "A STORY IS AN END IN ITSELF. . . . It is written as a man is born—an organic whole, dictated only by its own laws and its own necessity." Stephen Cox writes in his book on *The Fountainhead*, as noted by scholar Chris Sciabarra, that Rand's fiction reveals this "startling intensity of integration." *The Fountainhead* exhibits this organic unity as the characters, who reflect Rand's philosophy, come into conflict with each other that results in an ultimate justification of her beliefs in a setting that symbolizes those beliefs.

Symbols

The title of the novel symbolizes the character of Howard Roark and Rand's insistence that men like him should be considered the source of all human progress, as the fountainhead is the source of a river. She suggests that an independent spirit coupled with a creative imagination will produce an ideal man who will, through his inventions, help society prosper. Roark gains satisfaction by being true to his independent spirit, and at the same time, that spirit aids society as it creates functional and artistic buildings.

Rand employs the image of skyscrapers to suggest similar qualities. When Roark rejects the traditional stone and wood materials for glass and plastics, molding them into open, innovative designs, he becomes the symbol of progress. The fusion of the images of the fountainhead and the skyscraper occurs at the end of the novel when Roark is standing on the top platform at the construction site of the Wynand Building. His devotion to his individualism has propelled him to this height at the top of the skyscraper, as noted by Dominique who watches from below. She describes how he becomes a part of the landscape. Raising her eyes, she sees him high above the city where "there was only the ocean and the sky and the figure of Howard Roark."

Historical Context

The Great Depression

The Great Depression held America in its grip during the 1930s. The depression was a severe economic crisis that occurred in the United States after the stock market crash of 1929. The impact on Americans was staggering. In 1933, the worst year, unemployment rose to sixteen million, about one third of the available labor force. During the early months, men and women searched eagerly and dili-

Compare & Contrast

- **1930s:** Joseph Stalin is the oppressive dictator of the Soviet Union. His reign of terror lasts for two more decades.

  Today: In 1991, President Mikhail Gorbachev orders the dissolution of the Soviet Union, and a new Commonwealth of Independent States is formed by the countries that formerly made up the U.S.S.R.

- **1930s:** Germany invades Poland in 1939 and World War II begins.

  Today: George W. Bush declares a war on terrorism after the attacks on the Pentagon and the World Trade Center in September 2001.

- **1930s:** America and the world is in the grips of a severe economic depression.

  Today: America sees one of its strongest economic booms in the 1990s. At the beginning of the twenty-first century, that boom is now over, but, even on the brink of a recession, the economy is very stable.

---

gently for any type of work. However, after several months of no sustained employment, they became discouraged and often gave up. President Franklin Delanor Roosevelt's New Deal policies, which offered the country substantial economic relief, helped mitigate the effects of the depression, but the recovery was not complete until the government channeled money into the war effort in the early 1940s.

The Red Decade

During the Great Depression, impoverished Americans began to doubt whether they would ever attain the American dream of success. As a result, the traditional spirit of individualism began to be replaced by communal sentiment. This new *zeitgeist* (spirit of the age) had important political repercussions: the repeal of Prohibition, the rise of labor organizations, and the institution of social safety nets, most notable after the Social Security Act was passed. Social reformers such as Jane Addams and Florence Kelly, who had helped push through the Social Security Act, promoted a sense of society as a family rather than a group of individuals with self-serving goals. Many such reformers helped support Roosevelt's New Deal policy, with its implementation of social safety nets.

This new sense of community was in part inspired by the spread of socialism and communism in Europe and Russia. After prominent intellectu-

als lent support to these parties and engineered strikes and demonstrations throughout the country, historians labeled the 1930s "The Red Decade." The focus of many of these progressives was on class consciousness in America, especially on the plight of the working class as juxtaposed against the vast wealth and power of the industrialists.

World War II

The world experienced a decade of aggression in the 1930s that would culminate in World War II. This second world war resulted from the rise of totalitarian regimes in Germany, Italy, and Japan. These militaristic regimes gained control as a result of the depression experienced by most of the world in the early 1930s and from the conditions created by the peace settlements following World War I. The dictatorships established in each country encouraged expansion into neighboring countries. In Germany, Adolf Hitler strengthened the army during the 1930s. In 1935, Benito Mussolini's Italian troops took Ethiopia. From 1936 through 1939, Spain was engaged in civil war involving Francisco Franco's fascist army, aided by Germany and Italy. In March 1938, Germany annexed Austria, and in March 1939, occupied Czechoslovakia. Italy took Albania in April 1939. On September 1, 1939, one week after Nazi Germany and the U.S.S.R. signed the Treaty of Nonaggression, Germany invaded Poland and World War II began. On September 3, 1939, Britain and France declared

Gary Cooper as Howard Roark in the 1948 film version of the novel

war on Germany after a U-boat sank the British ship *Athenia* off the coast of Ireland. Another British ship, *Courageous*, was sunk on September 19th. All the members of the British Commonwealth, except Ireland, soon joined Britain and France in their declaration of war.

The Cold War

Soon after World War II, when Russian leader Joseph Stalin set up satellite communist states in Eastern Europe and Asia, the Cold War began, ushering in a new age of warfare and fear triggered by several circumstances: the United States' and the U.S.S.R.'s emergence as superpowers; each country's ability to use the atomic bomb; and communist expansion and U.S. determination to check it. Each side amassed stockpiles of nuclear weapons that could not only annihilate the other country, but also the world. Both sides declared the other the enemy and redoubled their commitment to fight for their own ideology and political and economic dominance. As China fell to the Communists in 1949, Russia crushed the Hungarian revolution in 1956, and the United States adopted the role of world policeman, the Cold War accelerated.

The Cold War induced anxiety among Americans, who feared both annihilation by Russians and the spread of communism at home. Americans were encouraged to stereotype all Russians as barbarians and atheists who were plotting to overthrow the U.S. government and brainwash its citizens. The fear that communism would spread to the United States led to suspicion and paranoia, and many suspected communists or communist sympathizers saw their lives ruined. This "red scare" was heightened by the indictment of ex-government official Alger Hiss (1950) and Julius and Ethel Rosenberg (1951) for passing defense secrets to the Russians. Soon, the country was engaged in a determined and often hysterical witch-hunt for communists, led by Senator Joseph McCarthy and the House of Representatives' Un-American Activities Committee (HUAC). In 1954, McCarthy was censured by the Senate for his unethical behavior during the Committee sessions. By the time of McCarthy's death in 1957, almost six million Americans had been investigated by government agencies because of their suspected communist sympathies, yet only a few had been indicted.

Critical Overview

Critical response to *The Fountainhead* after it was published in 1952 was decidedly mixed. Readers disagreed about the merit of the philosophy Rand expressed in the novel as well as her characterizations and writing style.

In "Ayn Rand's Neurotic Personalities of Our Times," Paul Deane notes that while "some critics have praised Rand for writing novels of ideas, calling her a thoughtful spokesperson for laissez-faire capitalism, many others have found her work too simplistic and didactic." Positive reviews include Dayana Stetco, who, in her overview of Rand for the *Reference Guide to American Literature*, claims that the novel is "a celebration of the self—a victory of individualism over collectivism." Chris Sciabarra in his article on Rand for *American Writers* insists that Rand has clearly and persuasively presented complex ideas" in the novel. Lorine Pruette's review for the *New York Times Book Review* commented that this "novel of ideas," unusual for a female author, revealed Rand to be "a writer of great power" with "a subtle and ingenious mind." Pruette favorably compared the novel to Thomas Mann's *The Magic Mountain* and Henrik Ibsen's *The Master Builder*. Her review, however, criticized the stance Rand took on the incompatibility of self interest and altruism.

Some reviewers find the characters in the novel to be merely mouthpieces for Rand's philosophy. In his article on the author for *National Review*, Joseph Sobran writes that Rand's "characters, on the page, often seem to be played by mediocre thespians who can't resist making their lines pat and their gestures extravagant." He adds that "every speech seems to hammer home Objectivist doctrine." Philip Gordon, in "The Extroflective Hero: A Look at Ayn Rand," insists that the novel's characters are "psychically stiff heroes" and that the author "presents nothing new with which to penetrate the legitimate and salient deliberation regarding connections of self to others."

Others, however, praise Rand's literary skills. Sciabarra argues that Rand is "in command throughout stylistically and intellectually" and that the novel is "remarkable in its literary style and plot, the complexity and interest of its several memorable characters, the interweaving of her philosophy within the framework of fiction, and its epic scope and grandeur." While N. L. Rothman in the *Saturday Review* criticizes Rand's negative position on collectivism, he applauds her characterization of Howard Roark. Pruette applauds Rand's "capacity of writing brilliantly, beautifully, bitterly."

Criticism

Wendy Perkins

Perkins teaches American literature and film and has published several essays on American and British authors. In the following essay, Perkins examines Rand's expression of her objectivist philosophy in The Fountainhead.

Ayn Rand presents Howard Roark, the main character in her influential novel, *The Fountainhead*, in an innovative way. Readers expect a main character to be fully rounded yet to develop in some way during the course of the story. Heroes, when faced with a conflict, usually reveal new aspects of their character that were previously unknown to them and to the readers. Often the thrust of the narrative involves the process of the main characters gaining valuable insight into their inner selves.

In *The Fountainhead* Rand rejects this traditional form of character development by presenting a hero who at the beginning of the novel is fully realized. Howard Roark knows exactly who he is when he is expelled from the Stanton Institute of

> In Gail Wynand, Rand traces the development of the novel's only truly tragic figure that has the potential to evolve into an ideal man, but whose inability to sustain a clear sense of self causes him ultimately to become a second-hander."

Technology for "insubordination," and Rand quickly outlines his character for her readers. Roark does not change during the course of the story or reveal new aspects of his personality. The conflicts he faces only reinforce the portrait of him that Rand has already presented. She has chosen Roark as her protagonist for a different purpose; his static character becomes a touchstone through which Rand expresses her philosophy of objectivism, especially as it concerns the definition of the self. Through her characterization of Roark and his interactions with the other characters in the novel, Rand presents her vision of the ideal man as well as the second-hander.

Rand's ideal man is assertive and aggressive in his drive for success and through his integrity becomes the fountainhead of human progress. His integrity stems from what Rand sees as the three cardinal values of objectivism: reason, purpose, and self-esteem, and their corresponding virtues: rationality, productiveness, and pride. In *Capitalism, the Unknown Ideal*, Rand explained that "production is the application of reason to the problem of survival." Yet the ideal man must also acquire "the values of character that makes [his life] worth sustaining." The most important value, that of self-esteem, translates into an ethic of rational selfishness. Rand insists in "The Objectivist Ethics" that the ideal man lives "for his own sake, neither sacrificing himself to others nor sacrificing others to himself. To live for his own sake means that the achievement of his own happiness is man's highest moral purpose."

Howard Roark becomes the embodiment of Rand's objectivist ideals. From the beginning of the novel, he displays a rational selfishness in his assurance of his own talents. This clear concept of self will not allow him to compromise his vision of creating the finest buildings in the city. At the end of the novel he justifies his bombing of the Cortlandt project when he insists to the jury, "the first right on earth is the right of the ego. Man's first duty is to himself. His moral law is never to place his prime goal within the persons of others." He argues that he had to destroy the project because others had taken it over and thus thwarted his prime goal—to realize his own architectural vision.

Rand places Roark into conflict with others in order not only to reveal the qualities of the ideal hero, but also to flesh out her concept of what she calls second-handers. She applies this term, which was her original working title for the novel, to those who lack clear convictions and a concept of self. As a result, they become destructive to themselves as well as the others who come into contact with them. Three characters in the novel, Peter Keating, Ellsworth Toohey, and Gail Wynand, all exhibit variations of Rand's definition of second-handers.

Throughout his career Peter Keating tries to pass off Roark's creative vision as his own since he can only accomplish a constant, mediocre replication of the designs of the past. Keating's lack of original thought and action independent of public opinion define him as a second-hander. His sense of inferiority creates a lack of integrity that allows him to let others control his life. He chooses his clothes, his wife, and his actions according to accepted guidelines rather than from a clear sense of individual need and desire. As a result, he helps to destroy the life of the woman he loves when he decides that she will not help him achieve his vision of success. Keating is ultimately ruined by his inability to establish his own identity when the public discovers that he has claimed Roark's design of the Cortlandt project as his own.

Ellsworth Toohey is a parasitic second-hander who contributes nothing to the society off of which he feeds. He displays a brute selfishness as he sacrifices others in his quest for power. Claiming to work toward creating brotherhood among men, he instructs his followers to "feel contempt for your own priceless little ego," for "only then can you achieve the true, broad peace of selflessness, the merging of your spirit with the vast collective spirit of mankind."

His true motive, however, emerges in his recognition that "every system of ethics that preached sacrifice grew into a world power and ruled millions of men" and concludes that "the man who speaks to you of sacrifice, speaks of slaves and masters. And intends to be the master." By appropriating a collectivist philosophy, Toohey hopes to wield absolute control over the lives of his followers as his promotion of selflessness obliterates their independent thoughts and actions. He attempts to destroy Roark because his success will contradict the collectivist philosophy he promotes, and therefore will strip him of the power he seeks.

In Gail Wynand, Rand traces the development of the novel's only truly tragic figure that has the potential to evolve into an ideal man, but whose inability to sustain a clear sense of self causes him ultimately to become a second-hander. Wynand had the ambition and resolve to pull himself out of the slums of Hell's Kitchen and become a successful newspaper magnate. Yet in his goal to "give people what they want," he has pandered to society's lowest tastes and as a result, his newspaper has become a vulgar tabloid. When he meets Roark, he recognizes the man's nobility and firmness of purpose and so determines that he will support him.

Wynand, ultimately however, has become a second-hander who has allowed the public to dictate the direction of his success. He assumes that he has power over public opinion when he throws his support to Roark during his trial, but his readers, made cynical over the years by his sensationalistic press, have lost their ability to appreciate true virtue. In an effort to save himself he gives into public opinion, recognizing the power he has granted them over his vision of success. The editorial he writes condemning Roark's action salvages his career but breaks his spirit.

In her outline of the principles of objectivism, Rand writes, "Art is a selective re-creation of reality according to an artist's metaphysical value-judgments," suggesting, as Leonard Peikoff notes, that its purpose is "to concretize the artist's fundamental view of existence." In the *The Fountainhead*, Rand has selectively recreated her vision of reality, structuring the characterizations in the novel to illustrate her unique concept of the self.

Source: Wendy Perkins, Critical Essay on *The Fountainhead*, in *Novels for Students*, The Gale Group, 2003.

Tamara Sakuda

Sakuda holds a bachelor of arts degree in communications and is an independent writer. In this essay, Sakuda contemplates Rand's book by examining an individual's selfish right to freedom of expression versus the rights of the collective.

Ayn Rand believed in the value of individual worth above all else. She felt the ideal man had a selfish desire to express his own truths no matter what the cost. Rand's novel, *The Fountainhead*, demonstrates the importance of man's struggle for independence and freedom from the tyranny of a collective society. The protagonist, or hero, of *The Fountainhead* is Howard Roark. Roark is a man of integrity who is driven to create by his values and his values alone. Other people's thoughts and criticisms do not sway Roark from his architectural dreams and he selfishly clings to these values. Throughout the book, his work is ridiculed and publicly condemned. His buildings are thought to be poorly designed and monstrous. Roark says the pain of criticism only reaches a part of him; it does not engulf him. The ability of Roark to withstand his detractors shows the strength of his ego. He has an absolute belief in the validity of his own ideas. As Mimi Reisel Gladstein states in *The Ayn Rand Companion*, "What Rand puts forth in *The Fountainhead* is a rationale for 'selfishness' or egoism as a moral good."

The Fountainhead opens with Roark contemplating his expulsion from the Architectural School of the Stanton Institute of Technology. Instead of being devastated by this, Roark laughs to himself as he remembers the actual meeting. Later as he enters the porch of his boarding house, his landlady extends her apologies, but the words do not register with Roark. He is not distraught by the expulsion. Roark's own belief in his talent arms him for the next phase of his career—a career as an architect. Although Roark is confident of his destiny, his dean and his landlady are convinced his judgment and values are flawed. In their view, Roark is doomed to fail.

Juxtaposed to the character of Roark is Peter Keating. He is the son of Roark's Stanton landlady. Just as Roark's character is used to represent the power of individualism, Rand uses Keating's character to represent the failure of collectivism. Keating is described as handsome and "president of the student body, captain of the track team, member of the most important fraternity and voted the most popular man on campus." Keating is a joiner or, as Rand describes him later in the book, a secondhander. Keating is someone who defines himself by what others believe. He has no true sense of self because he is too impressionable.

Keating graduates first in his class from the same school that expelled Roark. He is offered a job at the most prestigious architectural firm in

> " He is not sustained by the thoughts of others but by his own selfish need to create, to unleash the buildings that live inside his soul."

New York City. Instead of being overjoyed, Keating is full of self-doubt. Should he accept the job offer? Or should he accept a scholarship to study architecture in France? He turns to Roark for advice, which Roark refuses to give. As Keating readies himself for life in New York City, he is still full of doubt, although his mother and dean are convinced his judgment is sound. "But if that boy isn't the greatest architect of this U.S.A., his mother will want to know why!" says Mrs. Keating.

Roark and Keating begin their lives in New York. Keating tries to be all things to all people. He manipulates his co-workers to his advantage, flatters the ego of his boss, Guy Francon, and feigns an interest in rare porcelain to impress his boss's partner. His antics ingratiate him to his superiors. Keating quickly moves up the ranks in the firm. He is considered the golden boy of the architectural world—talented, successful, the man to emulate.

However, Keating still turns to Roark for advice on building design and hates himself for doing so. He is envious of Roark. Roark is not considered successful, but Roark also has no fears, no self doubts. As someone who depends on others for his self worth, Keating lives in fear: fear that his work will not be thought good enough, fear that he cannot measure up to what other expect of him, fear that someday his success will vanish. "Others gave Keating a sense of his own value. Roark gave him nothing. He thought he should seize his drawings and run. The danger was not Roark. The danger was that he, Keating remained."

Roark struggles in his early career. He seeks employment with the only architect whose work he admires, Henry Cameron. After an initial flush of success, Cameron's career spirals downward. When Roark finds him, Cameron is a tired, bitter man who is rejected by his peers. He initially refuses to hire Roark until he discovers the beauty and talent of Roark's drawings. Cameron's firm is a poor one financially, and he cannot afford to pay Roark a decent wage. This does not matter to Roark. He is content and learns a great deal from Cameron. Unlike Keating, the outward trappings of success do not matter to Roark. He is not sustained by the thoughts of others but by his own selfish need to create, to unleash the buildings that live inside his soul.

As Rand moves through the story of Keating and Roark, other characters are introduced who illustrate the continued theme of individualism versus collectivism. For example, Rand's selfish characters are those who do not depend on others for their self worth. They are driven to produce their life's work with no thought as to how it will be received by others. These characters are the creators in her story. Austen Heller, respected newspaper columnist, gives Roark his first commission and $500 to start an office. The house Roark designs and builds for Heller is ridiculed, but Heller does not care. He believes in Roark and remains a staunch defender throughout the story. Steven Mallory is a gifted sculptor who is rejected by the mainstream art world of New York. After Keating rejects Mallory's sculpture for his building, Mallory attempts to shoot a famous critic. In explaining his actions to Roark, Mallory delineates an important distinction in the struggle for the individual against the collective. He speaks of "poor fools" who cannot recognize greatness, but to Mallory the greater sin is "to see it and not want it." Mallory is speaking of the critic who recognizes great art but tries to destroy it so that the collective can be maintained.

Roark calls Rand's conformist characters "second-handers." These characters have no sense of self except what others give to them. Gordon Prescott is an architect who leads his public to believe he is a man of new vision and ideals. In reality, Prescott just puts old design techniques to new uses. Prescott fits Roark's definition of a second-hander because he "borrowed from others to in order to make an impression on others." Prescott's talent and thoughts are second rate and second hand.

Catherine Halsey is another second-hander. She is a timid wisp of a girl who is in love with Keating. However, Keating's mother and Catherine's uncle influence her against marrying him. Keating professes his love for Catherine but he ends up jilting her in favor of another woman with more status. Catherine then devotes herself to a life of social work, not because she wants this as a career, but because her uncle decides her path for her. Years later, Keating runs into Catherine and asks her to lunch. His attempts to apologize are brushed away. To Keating, his love for the timid Catherine was real. To Catherine, the bitter social worker, that love never existed.

Throughout the story, Roark is placed at odds with the second-handers. For instance, Cameron becomes ill and must close his office. Roark looks for work elsewhere. Keating hires him but Roark is soon fired because he refuses to compromise his ideals. This refusal creates setbacks for Roark. He is forced to work in a granite quarry. It is hard, manual labor. This shocks and saddens Roark's friends but not Roark. He continues to believe in himself, as he tells his friend Mike, "I'll save enough money and come back. Or maybe someone will send for me before then." Roark is not embittered by his outward situation. He is still an individual with value. His buildings are still there inside of him and he knows he will create them someday.

It is while working at the granite quarry, that Roark meets Dominique Francon. She is the daughter of Keating's boss and an ideal beauty. An explosive love affair soon follows. It is a difficult relationship. Mimi Reisel Gladstein in her book, *The Ayn Rand Companion*, characterizes Dominique as someone who is convinced that good does not stand a chance in this world and as a result does not let herself care about anything. Then she meets Howard Roark. Dominique vows to destroy Roark, even while admitting that she loves him, because she feels Roark and his work are too good for this world. Dominique is not a second-hander, but she does fear happiness. Roark amazingly takes Dominique's confession in stride. He sees the inner beauty and potential in Dominique. He is confident in his love for her, and he is confident that Dominique can come to love him openly on her own terms. Even when Dominque marries Keating, Roark tells her,

> You must learn not to be afraid of this world. Not to be held by it as you are now. Never to be hurt by it as you were in that courtroom. I must let you learn it. I can't help you. You must find your own way. When you have, you'll come back to me.

While Rand consistently pits second-handers like Keating against Roark, there is one character, which is a true villain in this story—Ellsworth Toohey. Rand describes Toohey as fragile looking, like a "chicken just emerging from the egg." Toohey is anything but fragile inside. He thrives on power and its accumulation. He purports to be a truly selfless hero: someone who cares for the masses and the struggles of the mediocre man. In reality he uses the weaknesses of others to control them. In his childhood, his aunt saw through him and said, "You're a maggot Elsie, you feed on sores." "Then I'll never starve," was his reply. He uses his positions of newspaper columnist, lecturer, and author to advance what he deems appropriate in art, architecture, novels, etc. It is through Toohey's control of collective opinion that he achieves power. As Roark's work begins to receive acclaim, Toohey looks for ways to destroy him. Toohey realizes the threat of a selfish, independent man. Men like Roark do not stand for mediocrity. Toohey cannot influence Roark. Even worse, if Roark achieves fame, then he will influence men, not Toohey.

The Fountainhead culminates with a trial. Roark is accused of blowing up a government housing project. He designed the project with the provision that it is built to his specifications. When the building is changed; he blows it up. Roark defends himself at the trial. It is Roark who chooses his jury. It is a panel made up of: "two executives of industrial concerns, two engineers, a mathematician, a truck driver, a bricklayer, an electrician, a gardener, and three factory workers." The jury is described as tough but Roark chose wisely. Most of these men have the capacity to create and be independent in their chosen work. These men know what it is like to experience the exhilaration of creation. Others on the jury, the factory workers, surely know how it feels to be yoked to the collective of mediocrity.

It is during Roark's final arguments that he emerges as a truly selfish hero. Roark speaks of those men who throughout the ages have been creators. "The great creators—the thinkers, the artists, the scientists, the inventors—stood alone against the men of their time." Roark talks of how all inventions were initially opposed or considered foolish. He speaks of the need for independence. "The creator lives for his work. He needs no other men. His primary goal is within himself. The parasite lives second-hand. He needs others. Others become his prime motive."

Roark believes that to be a hero he must be selfish. According to Mimi Reisel Gladstone in *The Ayn Rand Companion*, Roark believes that only by living for one's self can one accomplish the extraordinary. Roark also believes that man cannot share his intellect or his creative truths with others. He says there is no such thing as a "collective brain." Roark's buildings are his creations.

What Do I Read Next?

- The *Ayn Rand Lexicon: Objectivism from A to Z* (1990), edited by Harry Binswanger, is a collection of her writings that expresses her philosophy of objectivism.

- Rand's *Atlas Shrugged* (1957) presents another independent hero that lives by the author's objectivist philosophy.

- John Steinbeck's *The Grapes of Wrath* (1939) offers a compelling argument for collectivism, a movement Rand condemns in *The Fountainhead*.

- Rand's *We the Living*, her most autobiographical novel, presents her philosophy from a more political point of view.

They belong to him even though others can enjoy them. Rand then uses Roark to prove the primacy of the individual versus the collective. Rand is speaking directly through Roark when he speaks of what he deems a crowning achievement of his values, his country America. Roark believes America is the noblest country on earth. As a Russian immigrant, Rand believed this too. Roark states that American values are not based on the idea of selfless service, but rather on the idea that each man has a right to the pursuit of happiness. "His own happiness. Not anyone else's. A private, personal, selfish motive. Look at the results." Against all odds, the jury finds Roark, the selfish hero, innocent. His actions are vindicated.

At the end of the book, Dominique visits Roark, now her husband, as he is working on his greatest project, a skyscraper commissioned by Mr. Gail Wynand. It was to be a testament to Wynand's life but instead Wynand asks that the building be a monument to Roark's spirit—the spirit of a selfish hero who shows that the value of the individual is what truly matters.

Source: Tamara Sakuda, Critical Essay on *The Fountainhead*, in *Novels for Students*, The Gale Group, 2003.

> Through advertising, television, and films, the demand for conspicuous consumption keeps the desires pitched high."

Paul Deane

In the following essay, Deane praises the psychological realism of the characters in Rand's novel.

The philosophy of Ayn Rand, Objectivism, has been subject to intensive analysis and discussion. Interest in her theories has led critics to overlook largely her work as novelist. While it may fairly be said that her plots, except for *We the Living*, are amorphous and loose, that there is endless repetition in *Atlas Shrugged*, and that characters are generally two-dimensional vehicles for ideas, in *The Fountainhead* she has been almost totally successful in creating thoroughly realized characters whose motivations are psychologically valid. It is always dangerous to talk of "influences" on writers; it may be wiser to talk about "parallels." Howbeit, there are close resemblances between personality types described by Karen Horney in *The Neurotic Personality of Our Time* (1937) and by Ayn Rand in *The Fountainhead* (1943). Whether or not one can point to a definite knowledge of Horney and a deliberate use of her conclusions, it is clear that both psychologist and novelist-philosopher have been impressed by the same personality characteristics in American society.

Horney feels that when judgement is passed on individual "neurotics," in a real sense it is being passed on society at the same time. As *The Fountainhead* makes abundantly clear, a person may deviate from social norms without being neurotic— Howard Roark is a case on point; others, such as Peter Keating, Catherine Halsey, Gail Wynand, and Ellsworth Toohey, who have severe neuroses, may be accepted as fulfilling social values exactly. A neurotic is usually characterized by rigidity of behavior, by lack of flexibility: he has a limited number of options available in adjusting to a given situation. But rigidity may also not be "neurotic" unless it departs from the "normal" cultural pattern (i.e., rigid suspicion of everything new is a quality of small, isolated, peasant cultures; to be suspicious in these circumstances is "normal").

Karen Horney recognizes two major trends in neurosis in our time; both of them figure prominently in *The Fountainhead*. First is the excessive dependence on the approval or affection of others. Wishing to be liked is neurotic only when it is indiscriminate and out of proportion. Peter Keating, for instance, needs constant reassuring that his work is good, that he is valuable—from everyone. Feelings of inferiority seem to be among the chief evils of our day: Keating's neurosis is based on inferiority.

Though openly successful, Keating is actually a bundle of anxieties. These he attempts to obscure by amassing money, dressing in the prescribed way, following the proper opinions (those of Ellsworth Toohey). He has difficulties making decisions for himself and he hesitates to express selfish wishes. In important areas, such as marriage to Catherine Halsey, he lets himself drift. Without a clear conception of what he wants to do in his work, he ends by doing nothing. Envying everyone more secure and self-confident than himself, Keating becomes a parasite incapable of self direction. Dominique Francon marries him (he does not decide), Howard Roark gives him ideas for his work, Ellsworth Toohey directs his values.

Keating's need for approbation faces an additional cultural hurdle. Our society is based upon competition. This competition implies that each individual has to fight with others, and in any fight, inevitably someone loses. The result is a generally widespread hostility and tension, generated by fear of the potential hostility of others; fear of retaliation for one's own hostility; fear of failure, with resulting economic insecurity, loss of prestige; and fear of success, which, out of envy, may produce the hostility of others. Peter realizes that if he pursues his own desires and achieves success, others may retaliate and he will lose their approval. He sees that he must be modest, inconspicuous, and conventional; he must negate his potentialities; he must be "normal" in a society that paradoxically extols both competitive success and Christian self-sacrifice.

The quest for affection is one reassurance against fear mentioned by Karen Horney. The search for power, prestige, and possession (both of things and of people) is another. The wish to dominate, acquire, and be admired is as normal as the desire for approval. The feeling of power in a normal person may be a recognition of his superior strength (physical or mental). The striving for power may be connected with some cause: religion, patriotism, or work. The neurotic craving for power is born of anxiety, hatred, and feelings of inferiority. Thus "the normal striving for power is born of strength, the neurotic of weakness."

Comparative texts are sometimes revealing. From *The Fountainhead:*

> Ellsworth Monkton Toohey was seven years old when he turned the hose upon Johnny Stokes. . . . Johnny Stokes was a bright kid with dimples and golden curls: people always turned to look at Johnny Stokes. Nobody had ever turned to look at Ellsworth Toohey.

From *The Neurotic Personality of Our Time:*

> The quest for power is . . . a protection against helplessness and against insignificance. . . . The neurotic that falls in this group develops a stringent need to impress others, to be admired and respected. . . . Usually they have gone through a series of humiliating experiences in childhood. . . . Sometimes the ambition is not centered on a definite goal, but spreads over all a person's activities. He has to be the best in every field he comes in touch with.

From *The Fountainhead* descriptions of Gail Wynand:

> One day he walked up to the pressroom boss and stated that they should start a new service—deliver the paper to the reader's door . . . he explained how and why it would increase circulation. "Yeah?" said the boss. "I know it will work," said Wynand. "Well, you don't run things around here," said the boss. "You're a fool," said Wynand. He lost the job. One day he explained to the grocer what a good idea it would be to put milk up in bottles . . . "You shut your trap and go wait on Mrs. Sullivan there," said the grocer, "don't you tell me nothing I don't know about my business. You don't run things around here."

The name of Gail Wynand's boat is *I Do*. The *Neurotic Personality of Our Time* describes Wynand's character:

> Neurotic striving for power serves as a protection against the danger of feeling or being insignificant. The neurotic develops a rigid and irrational ideal of strength which makes him believe he should be able to master any situation. [*I Do*]. . . . He classifies people as either "strong" or "weak," admiring the former and despising the latter. . . . He has more or less contempt for all persons who agree with him or give in to his wishes.

In her chapter "The Meaning of Neurotic Suffering," Horney draws a solid portrait of Dominique Francon, the most interesting and unbearable character in *The Fountainhead*. Dominique's deliberate incurring of suffering accompanies "the realization of a growing discrepancy between potentialities and factual achievements"; Her suffering is "prompted by anxiety" and has "direct defense value against imminent dangers." Even stronger is Horney's suggestion that "having to realize a definite weakness or shortcoming of his own is unbearable for one who has such high-flown notions of his own uniqueness . . . abandoning oneself to excessive suffering may serve as an opiate against pain."

Dominique is in love with Howard Roark; she applauds his ideas. Yet she consistently tries to ruin him and thwart his projects. Through marriages to Peter Keating and Gail Wynand, she puts herself out of Roark's reach. Early in the novel she buys a beautiful statue, which she finds especially satisfying, but she flings it down an elevator shaft to smash it. These are all neurotic signs, but the reasons for them are more interesting than masochistic motives: they are explained by Horney. Dominique is afraid to believe that Howard Roark is as self-contained and dedicated as he seems, because such a person makes terrible demands on others; if she can find a flaw in him, she need not make an effort to be a complete individual. She also wants to take Roark out of a position where he can be hurt: i.e., if he is broken, if his ideals are gone and his work no longer his most important—and vulnerable—aspect, then the world cannot hurt him. By various experiences with men, she strives to humiliate herself in order to experience some of the pain she believes Roark is feeling. Sex for her is a degrading experience, a subduing one because carried on with inferior men.

Horney continues: "The obtaining of satisfaction by submersion in misery is an expression of the general principle of finding satisfaction by losing the self in something greater, by dissolving the individuality, by getting rid of the self with its doubts, conflicts, pains, limitations, and isolation." Roark will not have Dominique until she learns *not* to submerge herself, until she learns not to submit herself to something greater. He does not wish her to be Mrs. Howard Roark as much as he wants her to be Dominique first. *The Fountainhead* is a long account of the education of Dominique Francon.

As a foil for Dominique is Catherine Halsey, a tragic, beautifully drawn figure. She is what our society regards as the perfect social worker: a figure of utter altruism, of complete submersion in the lives of others. When she is first encountered in the novel, she is a delightful, open girl. After Peter Keating throws her over for Dominique, Catherine dedicates her life to serving others; in so doing, she impoverishes her whole personality, and becomes a bitter, prematurely old woman who worries about the bowels of her friends. Society, however, would applaud her dedication, failing to see that until she has a self of her own, she cannot possibly be of any value to others.

Howard Roark does not strictly speaking belong in a discussion of Ayn Rand's neurotic personalities, because he is not neurotic; he is, however, the touchstone for all the other characters in the novel and as such points up their particular neuroses. Roark needs no approval, acclaim, or admiration: whether he is liked is immaterial to him. He knows his work is good; no one needs to confirm the fact for him. He feels all the emotions except inferiority. While in social terms he is openly a failure, his inner calm and confidence belie the idea. Roark creates his own taste and follows none. In terms of fundamental values and ideals, his important decisions have already been made; he knows exactly what he wants to do, and for 754 pages of novel, expresses only his own selfish point of view. The potential hostility, retaliation of others do not affect him, nor does the prospect of success. And unlike a more typical romantic hero, he does not give up all for the woman he loves: his work and his integrity are more important.

The Fountainhead, chiefly through its characters, points up a number of paradoxes in our time and culture. There is first the paradox of the drive for competition and success on the one hand *vs.* the constant demand for brotherly love and humility on the other. On one side, the individual is spurred on to greater and greater heights of success, which means he must be assertive and aggressive, while on the other he is deeply imbued by the principle and ideal of unselfishness. A second paradox is that one's desires and needs are constantly kept stimulated, while the possibilities of fulfillment are slim or impossible. Through advertising, television, and films, the demand for conspicuous consumption keeps the desires pitched high. But for most the ability to realize this level is not commensurate with the wish, and there is a constant discrepancy between desire and achievement. The third paradox is that a gap exists between the alleged freedom of the individual and his actual limitations. One cannot choose his parents or his early environment, which limits his potential for meeting certain kinds of people. For the majority of people the possibilities are limited but not insurmountable. For the neurotic the conflicts are intensified, and as mentioned in regard to Keating, Toohey, and Wynand, a satisfactory solution is impossible.

The whole force of these paradoxes is to show that society as a whole is neurotic, in that its constitution encourages the neuroses found in *The Fountainhead*. If all society is faced with these paradoxes, and all the conflicts implied in them are essentially impossible to solve, then the Howard Roarks, the really well balanced and secure individuals, will be the ones considered neurotic by the society around them. Thus we end with a fourth paradox.

Source: Paul Deane, "Ayn Rand's Neurotic Personalities of Our Times," in *Revue des langues vivantes*, Vol. XXXVI, No. 2, 1970, pp. 125–29.

Sources

Berliner, Michael S., *Letters of Ayn Rand*, Plume, 1997.

Deane, Paul, "Ayn Rand's Neurotic Personalities of Our Times," in *Revue des langues vivantes*, Vol. XXXVI, No. 2, 1970, pp. 125–29.

Gladstein, Mimi Reisel, *The Ayn Rand Companion*, Greenwood Press, 1984, pp. 26, 36, 46, 56.

Gordon, Philip, "The Extroflective Hero: A Look at Ayn Rand," in *Journal of Popular Culture*, Vol. 10, No. 4, Spring 1977, pp. 701–10.

Miller, Laurence, "Ayn Rand," in *Dictionary of Literary Biography*, Vol. 227: *American Novelists Since World War II*, Sixth Series, The Gale Group, 2000, pp. 251–60.

Peikoff, Leonard, Afterword, in *The Fountainhead*, by Ayn Rand, Signet, 1993.

Pruette, Lorine, "Battle against Evil," in *New York Times Book Review*, May 16, 1943.

Rand, Ayn, *Capitalism: The Unknown Ideal*, New American Library, 1966.

Rand, Ayn, "The Objectivist Ethics," in *The Virtue of Selfishness: A New Concept of Egoism*, 1964.

Rothman, N. L., "H. Roark, Architect," in *Saturday Review*, May 29, 1943.

Sciabarra, Chris Matthew, "Ayn Rand," in *American Writers Supplement 4*, Scribners, 1966, pp. 517–35.

Sobran, Joseph, "Mussolini Shrugged," in *National Review*, Vol. XLI, No. 1, January 27, 1989, pp. 52–53.

Stetco, Dayana, "Rand, Ayn," in *Reference Guide to American Literature*, 3d ed., St. James Press, 1994.

Further Reading

Den Uyl, Douglas J., and Douglas B. Rasmussen, eds., *The Philosophic Thought of Ayn Rand*, University of Illinois Press, 1984.

This collection of essays presents a comprehensive statement of Rand's philosophy of objectivism.

Evans, M. Stanton, "The Gospel according to Ayn Rand," in *National Review*, Vol. XIX, No. 39, October 3, 1967, pp. 1059–63.

Evans evaluates Rand's philosophy from a conservative perspective.

Rosenbloom, Joel, "The Ends and Means of Ayn Rand," in the *New Republic*, Vol. 144, No. 17, April 24, 1961, pp. 28–29.

Rosenbloom presents a review of Rand's philosophy.

Smith, George H., "Atheism and Objectivism and Objectivism as Religion," in *Atheism, Ayn Rand, and Other Heresies,* Prometheus Books, 1991, pp. 181–92, 213–30.

This essay focuses on the religious aspects of objectivism.

A Gathering of Old Men

Ernest J. Gaines

1983

A Gathering of Old Men (1983) by Ernest J. Gaines is a novel about race relations in the American South. The action takes place over the course of one day in rural Louisiana. A white man has been shot dead and lies in the yard of a black man's house. Eighteen old black men gather at the house and each claims that he is responsible for the killing. The brutal white sheriff conducts his investigation as the old men await the revenge of the dead man's relatives, who have a fearsome, long-standing reputation for exacting vigilante justice against black people. By the end of the day, there have been many surprises, and many of the characters have changed in ways that they could not have imagined. The conclusion of the novel hints that although the wounds of the past run deep and still influence the present, times are changing, and in the future, black people can hold out hope for a new era in which everyone is treated equally under the law.

A Gathering of Old Men was Gaines's fifth novel. Gaines is an African American who was born and raised on a plantation in Louisiana, a fictional version of which is the setting for all of his work. His novels and short stories have been widely acclaimed for the accuracy with which he captures the language of rural African Americans in Louisiana, and the way he envisions the possibility of positive change for his characters, even those who are caught in the most difficult of circumstances.

Author Biography

Ernest J. Gaines was born on January 15, 1933, on the River Lake Plantation near New Roads, Pointe Coupee Parish, Louisiana. He was the son of Manuel (a laborer) and Adrienne J. (Colar) Gaines. As a boy, Gaines worked in the plantation fields near Baton Rouge, Louisiana. In 1948 he moved to Vallejo, California with his mother and stepfather, (Gaines's parents separated when he was young). Gaines read voraciously in the Vallejo Public Library but found nothing that resonated with his own experience of life, since all the writers he read were white and did not portray blacks accurately.

Gaines attended Vallejo Junior College before being conscripted into the army in 1953. He served until 1955, writing fiction during his off-duty hours. After military service he enrolled at San Francisco State College (now University), where he majored in English. His short story, "The Turtles," which appeared in the magazine, *Transfer*, was his first published work. Gaines graduated with a Bachelor of Arts degree in 1957 and was awarded the Wallace Stegner Creative Writing Fellowship, which enabled him to pursue graduate study in creative writing at Stanford University from 1958 to 1959.

Gaines continued to publish short stories, one of which, "Comeback," won the Joseph Henry Jackson Award from the San Francisco Foundation in 1959. His first novel, *Catherine Carmier*, set on a plantation in rural Louisiana, was published in 1964. A second novel, *Of Love and Dust*, with a similar setting, followed in 1967.

A collection of stories, *Bloodline*, appeared in 1968 and one of those stories, "A Long Day in November," was published separately as a children's story in 1971. In 1971 Gaines was a writer in residence at Denison University, Granville, Ohio, and it was during this year that his most well-known and widely acclaimed novel, *The Autobiography of Miss Jane Pittman*, was published. In 1972 the novel received an award from the Black Academy of Arts and Letters, and the fiction gold medal from Commonwealth Club of California. It was made into a television movie in 1974.

Gaines's fourth novel, *In My Father's House*, was published in 1978 followed by *A Gathering of Old Men* in 1983. The latter was made into a television movie in 1987.

More recognition came Gaines's way in 1987, when he received a literary award from the American Academy and Institute of Arts and Letters. He

Ernest J. Gaines

had already received honorary doctorates of letters from Denison University (1980), Brown University, (1985), Bard College (1985), and Louisiana State University (1987).

In 1983 Gaines became professor of English and writer in residence at the University of Southwestern Louisiana, Lafayette, Louisiana.

Gaines's 1993 novel is *A Lesson before Dying*, which won a National Book Critics Circle Award for Fiction in 1993 and was nominated for a Pulitzer Prize.

Plot Summary

The first narrator in *A Gathering of Old Men* is a black boy, Snookum. He says that Candy has instructed him to run and tell some of the local people to gather at Mathu's house. Snookum sees Beau lying in the yard, and Mathu tells him to go away. Snookum runs off on his errand.

At Marshall House, Jack Marshall is asleep and drunk on the porch, and his wife Bea is in the pasture. When Snookum arrives with his message, Janey, the housekeeper, calls Lou Dimes and Miss Merle. When Miss Merle arrives, Janey tells her there has been a killing. Miss Merle drives to Mathu's house where a group of men has gathered, some of them with shotguns. Candy tells her that she killed Beau, but Miss Merle does not believe her. Candy says that Mathu claims to have shot Beau and that two of the other old men also claim to have shot him. Candy asks her to get more people there with twelve-gauge shotguns and empty number five shells, so they can all claim they committed the killing.

Chimley is fishing with his friend Mat when they get the message to go to Mathu's house. They are scared because they know the whites will seek revenge for the killing of Beau. But they feel they ought to go to Mathu's since he was the only one they knew who had ever stood up to the whites. They agree to get a ride with Clatoo.

Mat waits for Clatoo to arrive and argues with his wife Ella. He tells her not to try to stop him from going to Marshall. Clatoo arrives with Billy Washington, Jacob Aguillard, Chimley, and Cherry Bello. As they head for Mathu's house with guns, they are scared but determined. They pick up Yank and Dirty Red. As they near Mathu's house, Clatoo lets them off and goes back for more men. They walk together and reach a graveyard, where each man visits his family plot. Clatoo returns with more men.

There are now eighteen old men at Mathu's house. Mathu says that when the sheriff arrives he will turn himself in, but all the other men claim that they are the killers. Reverend Jameson pleads with Mathu to turn himself in and tells the others to go home, but no one listens to him.

Lou Dimes arrives from Baton Rouge. Candy again claims that she killed Beau, but Lou knows she is lying. He tells her that Fix, Beau's father, will come looking for blood. Mapes arrives and he does not believe Candy either. He slaps Billy Washington and Gable, but both men still insist that they killed Beau. Then Mapes hits Reverend Jameson. Mapes believes that Mathu is the killer, but he cannot persuade anyone to change his story. Billy Washington says he did it because thirty years earlier, Fix's men had beaten his son. But Mapes knows that Billy cannot shoot a gun accurately.

Mapes questions Mathu, who admits his guilt but refuses to tell the other men to go home. Ding Lejeune says he killed Beau because of what the whites did to his sister's young daughter. Johnny Paul claims he did it to preserve the memory of his family who worked the fields with plows and mules before the tractors came. Tucker explains how all

the best land has been given to the Cajuns, and how Felix Boutan beat his brother Silas to death. Yank recalls how he used to break all the horses, but has had nothing to do since the tractors came. Gable tells how forty years ago, his sixteen-year-old son was sent to the electric chair for raping a white girl on questionable evidence. Coot, a veteran of World War I, tells of injustices against black servicemen.

Gil Boutan gets the news that his brother has been killed. It is the day before a big football game between Louisiana State and Mississippi. Sully drives him to where the old men are gathered, but Mapes tells Gil to go home. Miss Merle brings food and they all eat. She is bewildered by the strange situation in the house.

Sully drives Gil to his home where family and friends are gathered. Gil tells his father Fix that Mapes does not want him to go to Marshall until he is sent for. Luke Will and some of the others want to go there immediately and lynch Mathu. But Gil pleads with his father not to, because his own chances of making All-American at LSU will be shattered if he is involved in anything illegal. Gil's brother Claude says he will do whatever his father says, but another brother, Jean, agrees with Gil. Fix reacts bitterly and banishes Gil and Jean from his house. He tells the others there will be no lynch mob, although Luke Will does not accept his decision.

The narrative moves to Tee Jack's store, where there are several customers, including Jack Marshall and a quiet man who teaches at the University of Southwest Louisiana. Jack is uninterested in making conversation. Luke Will and his friends enter, and Luke hints at what they plan to do. When the teacher tries to persuade them not to, they force him to leave.

Back at the house, Mapes announces that Fix will not be coming, but at first the men do not believe him. Then Mathu says he will turn himself in, but Clatoo asks Mapes for a few minutes in which they can talk. Candy protests at being excluded, and Mathu tells her to go home. Lou hauls her off and throws her in the back of her own car. Mapes gives them fifteen minutes to talk. Clatoo says there is no one to fight and they should go home. The others protest and say they will go to jail with Mathu. Mathu says it is the proudest day of his life because he has finally seen the men stand up for themselves. He tells them to go home too, but then Charlie steps forward, saying Mathu does not have to go anywhere.

Lou and Candy return and hear that Charlie has confessed. He says that Beau attacked him with a stalk of sugar cane, and Charlie hit back. He ran to Mathu's house, and Mathu told him not to run from Beau, and gave him his own gun. Beau came into the yard, loading his gun, and Charlie shot him. Then Charlie ran away, asking Mathu to take the blame. But just before sunset he realized he must return. Mapes and Charlie step out onto the porch, only to hear Luke Will demanding that Charlie be handed over.

Mapes is wounded by a shot by Luke Will, and all the men except Jean Pierre and Billy Washington stream out of the house. They break up into three groups. There are several exchanges of gunfire, and one of the lynch mob is injured. Snookum tries to get out of harm's way. Outside, under the house, he sees that Mapes is unable to get up. Mapes tells Lou that he, Lou, is in charge.

Leroy Hall, the wounded man, snivels and pleads to give himself up. Luke Will kicks him and tells him to shut up. Luke asks Mapes to stop the blacks from shooting and he will turn himself in, but Charlie is in charge and refuses the offer. He heads for the tractor, which shelters Luke Will. There is more shooting, and Charlie and Luke Will are both killed.

For the trial that takes place later, the courthouse is packed, and half of those in attendance are from the news media. All the defendants, black and white, are put on probation for five years, and banned from possessing guns or being with anyone who has them.

Characters

Jacob Aguillard

Jacob is one of the old black men. His sister Tessie was killed by white men in 1947. He carries his gun like a soldier, and he takes part in the final shoot-out.

Robert Louis Stevenson Banks

See Chimley

Cherry Bello

Cherry Bello is a seventy-four year old black man who owns a liquor and grocery store. He is one of the men who gathers at Mathu's house.

Media Adaptations

- An audio tape titled *A Gathering of Old Men/ Readings* was produced in 1987 by Amer Audio Prose Library.

- Volker Schlöndorff directed a made-for-television adaptation of *A Gathering of Old Men* (1987).

Grant Bello

See Cherry Bello

Charlie Biggs

Charlie Biggs is a big, fifty-year-old black man. All his life he has been timid and submissive, but he finally learns to stand up for himself when he kills his employer, the abusive Beau, who is going to shoot Charlie. After the killing, Charlie hides for a while but finally realizes he must come back to face up to the consequences. He believes that by his actions he has finally become a man, and he insists on being called Mr. Biggs. He is killed in the shoot-out with the lynch mob.

Myrtle Bouchard

See Miss Merle

Beau Boutan

Beau is the aggressive, racist Cajun farmer who leases the plantation from the Marshall family. Beau attacks Charlie, who shoots him dead. He is mourned only by his own family.

Claude Boutan

Claude Boutan is one of Gil's older brothers. He drives a truck for an oil company. In the meeting at Fix's home, he says he will do whatever Fix decides.

Fix Boutan

Fix Boutan is the father of Beau. For many years he and his family and other like-minded whites have been able to take the law into their own hands. They have a long history of beating, killing, and abusing black people. As everyone expects, Fix wants to go to Marshall to lynch the killer of Beau. But two of his sons, Gil and Jean, oppose him, and Fix calls the lynching off. He says that the family must act as one, and if they disagree, he will not act. Fix says that he never wants to see his sons Gil and Jean again, but at the end of the novel there is a hint of reconciliation between Fix and Gil, as they sit together in the courtroom.

Gil Boutan

Gil is a student at Louisiana State University and he is an outstanding football player, the best fullback in the Southern Conference. Known as Salt because he plays so well with Cal, who is called Pepper, Gil desperately wants to be an All-American, like Cal. Unlike the rest of his family, he is not a racist, and after the killing of Beau he urges his father not to take the law into his own hands. He is bitterly upset when his father banishes him from the house.

Jean Boutan

Jean Boutan is one of Gil's older brothers. He is in his mid-thirties and owns a butcher's shop in Bayonne. Like Gil, he tries to persuade Fix not to send a lynch mob to Marshall, saying that they should allow the legal process to take care of the situation.

Sidney Brooks

See Coot

Matthew Lincoln Brown

See Mat

Cal

See Calvin Harrison

Candy

Candy is the strong-minded, independent, thirty-year-old niece of Jack and Beatrice Marshall. Her parents were killed in an automobile accident when she was five, and she was mostly raised by Miss Merle and Mathu. Her boyfriend is Lou Dimes. Candy is small and thin, with close-cropped hair. She wants to protect Mathu, and she insists that it was she who killed Beau. It is also her idea to summon the men to bring shotguns and empty number five shells, so that they can all claim to have killed Beau. When Mapes arrives, Candy is vigorous in her defense of the black men, and contemptuous of Mapes. Later, she becomes resentful when all the men want to discuss the situation in private. Mathu tells her to go home, and Lou bun-

dles her into the back seat of her own car. In the courtroom scene at the end of the novel, Mathu asserts his independence from her, while she and Lou are reconciled.

Chimley

Chimley is a seventy-two-year-old black man who is fishing with his lifelong friend Mat when he is summoned to Mathu's house. His first reaction is fear, remembering how the white people react after any violent incident, but he puts this aside and decides to go. Before he leaves he tells his wife to make sure his food is ready for him when he returns.

Antoine Christophe

See Dirty Red

Clatoo

Clatoo is one of the leaders of the black men. He drives many of them to Mathu's house in his truck, and he tells them to carry themselves like soldiers. He hates Fix because Fix's brother Forest tried to rape one of his sisters just before World War II. Like the other black men, Clatoo claims to have shot Beau. It is Clatoo who organizes the scheme whereby the men reload their shotguns, and it is he who stands up to Candy, telling her that the men are going to have a meeting without her. During the shoot-out, it is Clatoo who organizes the black men.

Coot

Coot goes to Mathu's house proudly wearing his World War I uniform. He says that when he got home from the war, a white man told him never to wear his uniform again, since people in that part of the world did not like black men wearing medals for killing whites. But the day of Beau's killing, Coot decided to wear his uniform and shoot anyone who laughed at him or told him to take it off. He claims he shot Beau when the Cajun would not stop coming toward him with his gun.

Lou Dimes

Lou Dimes is a white man who has been seeing Candy for three years. He works as a journalist for a newspaper in Baton Rouge, and appears not to share the racist attitudes of most of the white characters. He arrives at Mathu's house when Janey calls him and says that Candy needs him. Lou takes little part in the action himself but he closely observes and reports on what happens. In the shoot-out, the injured Mapes puts Lou in charge of the situation, and Lou unsuccessfully tries to negotiate a truce between Luke Will and Charlie.

Louis Alfred Dimoulin
See Lou Dimes

Dirty Red
Dirty Red, one of the old black men, always has a self-rolled cigarette hanging from the side of his mouth. He is the last of his family, and he has a reputation for laziness. But he acquits himself well in the shoot-out.

George Eliot Jr.
See Snookum

Griffin
Griffin is Mapes's young deputy. He is a slender, unimpressive man, ready to bully the defenseless but wary of anyone he thinks might fight back. Just before the shoot-out begins, he tells Mapes that he will not use his gun against white men in defense of black men.

Leroy Hall
Leroy Hall is a boy of seventeen who associates with Luke Will and his friends. He is wounded in the shoot-out and whines like a coward.

Calvin Harrison
Calvin, known as Cal, is a black football player who plays alongside Gil so well that the two of them are known as Salt and Pepper. Cal has been nominated for All-American.

Glo Hebert
Glo Hebert is the grandmother of Snookum, Toddy. and Minnie.

Herman
Herman is the coroner who collects Beau's body. He is in his mid-sixties.

Albert Jackson
See Rooster

Beulah Jackson
Beulah Jackson is Rooster's wife. She says she is ready to go to jail with the men.

Reverend Jameson
Reverend Jameson is the only black man who does not have a gun, and he is despised by the other men. He is short and bald, with a white mustache and beard. He is scared of what may happen and pleads with the men to go home, but no one listens to him. But even Reverend Jackson refuses to give Mapes the answers he wants, even when Mapes hits him.

Janey
Janey is the housekeeper at the Marshalls' house. She is scared when Snookum tells her about the killing, and repeatedly calls on Jesus to help her. Miss Merle bullies her into making a list of people who do not like Fix.

Bing Lejeune
Bing Lejeune is a mulatto who is one of the men at Mathu's house.

Ding Lejeune
Ding Lejeune is Bing's brother. He has a grudge against Fix because he believes his sister's child was poisoned by one of the Cajuns.

Mapes
Mapes is the white sheriff. He is in his late sixties, about six feet three, and heavy. He is a bully and starts his investigation by hitting three black men in quick succession. With the exception of Mathu, he does not respect the blacks. However, Mapes does try to avoid more bloodshed by instructing one of his men to keep Fix away from the house, and trying to persuade Mathu, whom he believes is guilty, to turn himself in. He also learns to respect Charlie Biggs. Mapes is slightly wounded in the final shoot-out, and has to sit on the porch, unable to get up. In the courtroom scene, he is embarrassed by having to admit his inability to do anything to stop or resolve the shoot-out.

Beatrice Marshall
Beatrice Marshall is Jack's wife. She shows no interest when she hears that Beau has been killed, since she has never liked him.

Jack Marshall
Jack Marshall owns the plantation but takes no interest in it, passing his responsibilities on to his niece, Candy. He drinks every day in Tee Jack's store, and seems to have no interest in anything in life. He knows that the situation at Mathu's house is dangerous but he refuses to do anything to defuse it.

Mat

Mat is seventy-two-years old; his closest friend is Chimley. He and Chimley decide that for once in their lives they are going to stand up for themselves against the whites. Mat refuses to tell his wife where he is going, and they quarrel. He weeps with anger over injustices that his family has suffered but he is determined finally to do something with his life.

Mathu

Mathu is a black man in his eighties. He is tall and dark-skinned, and is proud of having no white blood. His ancestors came from Senegal in Africa. Mathu is the only one of the blacks who all his life has stood up for himself, not letting the whites push him around. He once beat Fix in a long fistfight. This is why Mapes is so ready to believe that Mathu killed Beau, since Mapes does not think any of the other blacks would have been capable of it. Mathu helped to raise Candy, and that is why she tries to protect him, but he is willing to take the blame for the killing of Beau, even though he did not do it.

Miss Merle

Miss Merle is a family friend of the Marshalls. She helped to raise Candy and has known her for over twenty-five years. Janey thinks she is good-natured, but Miss Merle has a patronizing attitude toward the black men. When she takes sandwiches to the people in Mathu's house, she expresses anger to Candy and Mapes, and is bewildered by the strange situation.

Johnny Paul

Johnny Paul is one of the first of the old men to say he shot Beau. He reminisces about the past, when the blacks worked in the fields with hoes and plows from dawn to sunset, before the days of the tractor. He says he killed Beau to stop the tractors plowing up the graveyard and erasing all memory of his own people.

Pepper

See Calvin Harrison

Gable Raund

Gable Raund is one of the black men who claims he shot Beau, and he refuses to change his story even when Mapes hits him. He is angry because over forty years ago his sixteen-year-old son was sent to the electric chair after being unfairly convicted of raping a white girl.

Cyril Robillard

See Clatoo

Janice Robinson

See Janey

Rooster

Rooster is married to Beulah Jackson. Clatoo describes him as "yellow, with nappy black hair."

Rufe

Rufe is one of the first of the black men to arrive at Mathu's house and one of the first to claim that he shot Beau.

Russell

Russell is the deputy charged by Mapes to stop Fix coming to Marshall.

Salt

See Gil Boutan

Joseph Seaberry

See Rufe

Sharp

Sharp is one of the whites who accompanies Luke Will in the lynch mob. Like Luke Will, he is a truck driver.

Snookum

Snookum is the young boy who is sent by Candy to tell the neighbors to assemble at Mathu's house. He lives with his grandmother, Glo Hebert, and has a sister, Minnie, and a brother, Toddy.

Thomas Vincent Sullivan

See Sully

Sully

Sully is a friend of Gil and Cal. Like them, he is a football player, although a mediocre one. His main hobby is watching television. It is Sully who drives Gil to his father's house.

Tee Jack

Tee Jack owns a grocery and liquor store. He is a racist and does not care who knows it. He is intimidated by Luke Will and his friends when they come into the store, and he has to be careful of what he says in case they cause trouble.

Jacques Thibeaux

See Tee Jack

Horace Thompson

See Sharp

Cedric Tucker

Cedric Tucker is a quiet black man who usually keeps himself to himself. At Mathu's house, he tells the story of his brother Silas, who was the last black sharecropper at Marshall. Silas was killed by the whites in a fight after he had dared to perform better with his two mules than Felix Boutan did on his tractor.

Billy Washington

Billy Washington is one of the old black men. He is a terrible shot, and could not hit the side of a barn. The others tease him about it. Mapes hits him but he continues to insist that he shot Beau. He says it was because Fix and his men beat his son so hard his brain was permanently damaged.

Luke Will

Luke Will is a truck driver and a friend of Beau. He is big and rough looking, and is a racist who leads the lynch mob to Marshall. He is killed in the shoot-out.

Yank

Yank is one of the black men who go to Mathu's house. He is in his early seventies, and he used to break in the horses. He resents the whites because their tractors rendered horses unnecessary.

Themes

Racism

Racism pervades the novel, which shows that blacks have suffered discrimination and abuse for many generations. The racism continues even into the late 1970s. Many of the whites, including Luke Will and Tee Jack, routinely use the offensive word "nigger" to describe any black person. The Cajun Boutan family are guilty of innumerable ugly incidents involving blacks. The law either looks the other way or accepts a skewed version of events, as is revealed, for example, in the incident related by Tucker, in which his brother Silas was beaten to death by whites because he had dared to perform better with his mules than they did with their modern tractors. Tucker says, "Where was the law? Law said he cut in on the tractor, and he was the one who started the fight." In the story related by Gable, the word of a white girl of dubious reputation is enough to unjustly send a black boy of sixteen to the electric chair.

Topics for Further Study

- Have race relations improved in the United States since the 1970s? What are some of the problems associated with race relations and how can they be addressed in a constructive manner?

- Gaines is sometimes accused of creating negative stereotypes in his portrayal of white people. Is there any truth in this in *A Gathering of Old Men*? How are the whites such as Mapes, Fix Boutan, Gil Boutan, and Luke Will presented?

- What role do the black women play in the novel? Do they share in the empowering of the black men? What kind of relationship do black men such as Chimley and Mat have with their wives?

- Choose a character from the novel and write a narration of the trial scene from that person's point of view.

Sheriff Mapes's attitude when he first arrives at Mathu's house is testimony to the way whites treat blacks. When he does not get the answer he wants, Mapes resorts to beating three of the old men. That is the only way he knows how to deal with black people. When that does not work, he does not know what else to do.

As well as suffering abuse as individuals, blacks are also collectively discriminated against. When the white landowning Marshall family leased the land to sharecroppers (tenant farmers), they gave the best land to the Cajuns who had never been on the land before, and the worst land to the blacks even though the blacks had been working the land for a hundred years. This ensured the continuing poverty of the blacks.

There is also a hint that racism exists amongst the blacks as well. Mathu, who is very dark-skinned, prides himself on the fact that he has no white blood in him, and he looks down on others who have mixed blood, like Clatoo, who had a white grandfather and an Indian and black grandmother, and Rooster, who according to Clatoo is "yellow, with nappy black hair."

There are signs, however, that things are changing. Not only does the Boutan family decide not to seek vigilante justice as they did in the old days (even though family friends like Luke Will do not respect the decision), but Mapes develops a respect for a black man, Charlie Biggs, that he never had before. Finally, the close partnership between Cal and Gil, a black man and a white man, on the football field is a parable of how things might and should be between the two races. As Sully explains, they are of equal ability, and they work hard for each other:

> Wherever you went, people spoke of Salt and Pepper of LSU. Both were good powerful runners, and excellent blockers. Gil blocked for Cal on sweeps around end, and Cal returned the favor when Gil went up the middle.

Attaining Manhood

When the old black men decide to stand up for themselves after a lifetime in which they have passively endured humiliation and abuse, they finally become men in their own eyes. They face up to a challenge with courage instead of running from it or hiding.

Alone amongst the black men, Mathu has always managed to do this. He has always retained his dignity as a man and stood up to the whites. This has involved him in many fights, including one that Chimley recalls—a toe-to-toe fight between Mathu and Fix that broke out after Mathu refused Fix's request to return a bottle to the store. This is why Mathu is respected by Mapes, who regards him as a real man. It also explains why Mapes is so ready to believe that Mathu killed Beau, since Mapes does not think that any of the others would have had the courage to do it. Mapes does not regard the others as real men.

The theme of attaining manhood begins early in the novel, in the first sections narrated by black men. Chimley and Mat agree that this time it would take more strength to crawl under the bed than it would to stand up to Fix and his men. Mat says he has to go to Mathu's house because this may be his last chance to do something with his life. It must be remembered that the old black men are voluntarily walking into a highly dangerous situation in which they fully expect a lynch mob to appear at any minute to avenge a killing that each one of them is going to claim he committed. But they feel good and are determined to be courageous. As they approach Mathu's house, for example, "Jean Pierre, Billy Washington, and Chimley was doing all they could to walk with their heads up and backs straight."

When the men are interrogated by Mapes, they seem to get stronger every minute. They do not look down at their feet in a submissive posture but are able to look Mapes straight in the eye. They also talk back and mock him, to his bewilderment. They also mock Griffin, the young deputy, who, it is implied, has a long way to go before he attains real manhood. Griffin is ready to talk big and bully the defenseless but he has no real strength or authority. No one respects him, not even his boss, Mapes. And when Mapes tells him to stop Candy from blocking the door, Griffin backs off when he sees she is ready to punch him.

The theme of manhood becomes fully explicit in the character of Charlie. Charlie is the most timid of the black men. No one even considers that he might have been the killer. Although he has been bullied for years by Beau, he has never answered back or stood up for himself. Nevertheless, when Beau is ready to kill him, he finds the courage to defend himself. But Charlie's growth is not yet complete, because his first action is to run away and leave Mathu to take the blame. However, after hiding for a few hours, Charlie realizes what he has to do, and after he confesses to the crime he repeatedly exclaims his newfound self-respect:

> "I'm a man, Sheriff," Charlie said. "I want the world to know I'm a man. I'm a man, Miss Candy. I'm a man, Mr. Lou. I want you to write in your paper I'm a man."

Charlie's self-respect is also apparent in his request to be called Mr. Biggs. Mapes, who now has some respect for Charlie, is happy to oblige. From that point until Charlie's death, he is the man in charge of the situation, not Mapes, or Lou Dimes, and certainly not the would-be lyncher, Luke Will. When Charlie dies, leading a charge on the enemy, it is the death of a man, not a boy.

Style

Structure and Point of View

The novel is divided into twenty short chapters or segments, each of which is narrated in the first person. There are fifteen different narrators, ten black and five white (this is fewer than the number of chapters because Lou Dimes narrates four chapters, and Snookum and Sully two each). Dimes is given four chapters probably because Gaines thought him well suited, as a journalist, to report on events. Dimes supplies much objective information, since he adopts a fairly neutral stance, favoring neither the old men nor Mapes. The segments are also arranged with pacing and emotional tension in mind. Gaines stated in an interview that he tried to arrange the narratives of the different black men for variety. He wanted to avoid having two highly emotional segments following in succession.

Gaines's original idea was to have the novel narrated entirely by Lou Dimes, but he decided that this method was unsatisfactory because it could not capture the language that he wanted. The multiple narrative that he finally decided upon captures a variety of voices. Each narrator supplies not only his or her own point of view on the action but also an individual voice. The voice of Janey, for example, as she constantly appeals to Jesus for divine aid, is very different from that of the boy Snookum, who rushes off on his errand "spanking my butt the way you spank your horse when you want him to run fast." The language that Mat and Chimley use as they narrate their segments about fishing together is also very distinctive, with its use of black dialect that deviates from standard American English. It is quite different from the objective narrative of Lou Dimes, told in standard English, whose voice is in turn distinguished from the other white characters such as Tee Jack, Sharp, and Sully. In the long reminiscences and stories of the black characters in the segment narrated by Rufe, Gaines has also captured something of the quality of the oral tradition of storytelling that is a part of black culture in the region.

None of the major characters, such as Mapes, Candy, Mathu, Luke Will, Gil, Charlie, or Fix, is allocated a narrative segment. This means that these characters are revealed solely through what they say and do and what others say about them. The reader is given no direct insight into their thoughts (even though sometimes the narrators do offer comments on what Mapes is thinking, but that is still their opinion, formed from their perspective, not that of Mapes).

Gaines said he could not have Candy or Mathu narrate because they know too much about what happened, and this would have spoiled the effect for the reader. Mathu, for example, could hardly have avoided hinting that he did not kill Beau, but for the sake of telling a good story, Gaines wants this to come as a surprise to the reader. Saving this revelation for the end also helps to establish in the reader's mind the central idea that Charlie's act was not his alone. The accumulation of all the stories of racial injustice told by the other black men make it clear that everyone, black and white, is involved in the shared history of a single, albeit divided, community, and that everyone bears some responsibility for what finally happens.

Historical Context

Lynching in the South

The long list of injustices suffered by the old blacks in the novel, including the threat and the reality of lynching, is rooted in the real experience of black people in the South. According to Stewart E. Tolnay and E. M. Beck, in *A Festival of Violence: An Analysis of Southern Lynchings, 1882–1930*, there were 2,805 documented lynchings between 1882 and 1930 in ten southern states. Approximately 90 percent of the victims were African Americans. This means that on average, one black person was lynched by a white mob every single week from between 1882 until 1930, although in reality the lynchings reached a peak in the 1890s and declined afterwards. Victims were often tortured and mutilated before their deaths, and parts of their bodies were sold as souvenirs.

The four states with the worst records were Mississippi (463 lynchings, 1882–1930), Georgia (423), Louisiana (283) and Alabama (262). In Louisiana six lynchings occurred in Pointe Coupee Parish, where Gaines was born and raised, between 1881 and 1908. Some of these were "private" lynchings, carried out by relatives and friends of the victim; others were by a posse (groups of men appointed by the sheriff to track down suspects) or by a mass group. The last lynching in Louisiana, of a black man accused of intent to rape, occurred in 1946. The year 1951 was the first year since records began in 1882 when there were no lynchings anywhere in the south. The last officially recorded lynching in the United States occurred in 1968.

The fictional old men in the novel (which is set in 1979) were born sometime between the last years of the 1890s and the first decade of the twentieth century, making them well able to remember what happened to black people during this period. In the novel, Fix and his confederates are known and feared for their lynchings. In real life Louisiana in the 1920s and 1930s, eighteen men were lynched, fifteen of whom were black, including two men who were lynched on the same day in 1928, their only offense apparently being that they were the brothers of a murderer.

Tolnay and Beck list seventy-five reasons given for lynching black men. These included, in

Compare & Contrast

- **1930s:** The southern United States is a largely segregated society. Blacks face institutionalized discrimination in all aspects of their work and social life. They are excluded from positions of power and treated as second class citizens. Many are denied the right to vote.

  1960s: As the Civil Rights movement gathers momentum and affirmative action programs are introduced by private and public employers, a new era in race relations begins. However, there is a long way to go before the legacy of hundreds of years of injustice can be completely removed.

  Today: In terms of racial justice, southern states are almost unrecognizable from what they were fifty years ago. Alabama and Mississippi, for example, are now the two states with the highest number of African Americans elected to government offices. However, racism has not been eradicated, and problems in race relations remain.

- **1930s:** Capital punishment reaches a peak in the United States, with an average of 167 executions per year.

  1970s: In 1972, the Supreme Court declares the death penalty unconstitutional, but it is reinstated in 1976.

  Today: Many experts regard the death penalty as unfair because it affects black people disproportionately, reflecting conscious or unconscious racism in the judicial system. They point to the following statistics: Of the 752 (as of January 16, 2002) people executed in the United States since the death penalty was reinstated in 1976, 35 percent have been black, 7 percent Hispanic, and 56 percent white. Of those executed for interracial murder, only eleven were whites who killed blacks; 167 were blacks who killed whites. Those who murder whites are more likely to be sentenced to death than those who murder blacks.

- **1930s:** Although on the decline, lynchings still take place in the south. Five lynchings of black men occur in Louisiana.

  1980s: White supremacist groups are on the increase in the United States and incidents of violence against black people and other minorities show a corresponding increase.

  Today: Incidents of racial violence still take place. In 1998 James Byrd, a black man in Jasper, Texas, dies after being chained to a pickup truck and dragged behind it by three whites. Some see this case as a modern-day lynching.

addition to murder, robbery, and rape: acting suspiciously, gambling, quarreling, adultery, acting "improper" with a white woman, arguing with a white man, indolence, inflammatory language, being disreputable, being obnoxious, insulting a white man or woman (a black man named George Paul was lynched in Pointe Coupee Parish in 1894 for offending a white man), courting a white woman, demanding respect, trying to vote, voting for the wrong party, and unpopularity.

Some of these killings took place before the victim's arrest and some afterwards, often with the connivance of the authorities. Even if the black person accused of a capital offense was given a trial, the legal system was stacked against him. Although he would be given a lawyer, the lawyer was often inexperienced and given neither the time nor the resources to mount an effective defense. The verdict was often preordained, and was followed by swift execution.

Lynching, as well as other mob violence such as race riots, declined after World War II as the white supremacist group the Ku Klux Klan, which had peaked in membership in the 1920s, went into decline. By the 1950s, the Klan consisted mostly of poorly educated whites (like Luke Will in the novel).

Louis Gossett, Jr. (forefront) as Mathu, Woody Strode (left of Gossett) as Yank, and Julius Harris (right of Gossett) as Coot in the 1987 TV movie version of the novel

The Civil Rights movement of the 1950s and 1960s ushered in a new era in race relations in the south. It secured voting and other rights for black people and made discrimination illegal. In many parts of the rural south, however, change was slow, as the novel amply demonstrates. Tee Jack's bar, for example, has officially been desegregated for at least fifteen years, but blacks and whites still do not sit in the same place. Blacks buy a drink in the store and drink it outside, since Tee Jack and the white customers find many ways to make them feel unwelcome.

And even in the new era of civil rights, African Americans did not always have the full protection of the law. In an interview given in 1983, Gaines commented that old-style white vigilantism had ended but it was always likely to spring up in new guises. Now, "the Luke Wills are in the police department," he said.

Critical Overview

A Gathering of Old Men was received with unanimous praise by reviewers, who admired Gaines's ability to recreate once again, in his fifth novel, the texture of the lives of black and white people in rural Louisiana, especially the way the people actually spoke.

Reynolds Price, in *The New York Times Book Review*, drew attention to Gaines's "innovative method" of employing so many different first-person narrators, and the unexpected conclusion. He concluded that Gaines had constructed

> with large and single-minded skills, a dignified and calamitous and perhaps finally comic pageant to summarize the history of an enormous, long waste in our past—the mindless, mutual hatred of white and black, which, he implies, may slowly be healing.

Ben Forkner, in *America*, pointed out that the poor conditions under which the blacks live is not entirely due to racism. An underlying theme of the novel "is the simple, natural dispossession of old age, of the traditional and well-loved values of the past, the old trades and the old manners, forced to give way to modern times."

John F. Callahan, in *The New Republic*, described the novel as "a remarkably original gathering of voices," and praised Gaines's exploration of how the old ways and customs that operate between blacks and whites have changed and continue to do so. He also pointed out that Gaines "does not romanticize anyone, and even the deeply felt and deeply rendered recriminations of the old men are touched with occasional comic posturing, exaggerated emphasis, and obvious preaching."

Mary Helen Washington, in the *Nation*, wrote that the novel's greatest strength lay in its language, which recreated the past:

> These communal voices constitute a kind of collective revision of history, giving proof in their own words of the existence of ordinary people whom the world noticed only briefly in the long-gone era of the civil rights movement.

But Washington was also disturbed by the subordination of women in the novel. Candy, for example, although she is a strong woman, is finally shown as "just another threat to manhood. Women leading men is just another form of slavery, so Candy must be eliminated." Washington noted that black women were silenced also, and this meant that the novel underestimated the contribution made by women in shaping their own history.

The reviewer for *People Weekly* pointed out that although the novel has a serious subject, it "is often very funny." Later critics have examined Gaines's humor in the novel in more detail, as well as other aspects of his language, such as its roots in the oral traditions of southern black culture.

Criticism

Bryan Aubrey

Aubrey holds a Ph.D. in English and has published many articles on twentieth-century literature. In this essay, Aubrey discusses the theme of change in the novel.

Change is a prominent theme of *A Gathering of Old Men*. The old men change the habits of a lifetime and decide that this time they are going to stand up for themselves. Almost all the major characters undergo some decisive change in their attitudes or in their understanding of life. But although these changes happen quickly, the forces that lead to them have been building up for a long time. The origins of this momentous day in the history of the region lie in the changes in the methods of agricultural production that took place several decades previously, and which produced profound social as well as economic changes. In the novel, this is symbolized by the looming presence of Beau's tractor, which Snookum sees standing in front of Mathu's house at the very beginning of the novel, and which

also serves as the focal point of the final shoot-out. It is as if all the action takes place in the shadow of this giant piece of machinery.

It was the coming of the tractor to the Marshall plantation that changed everything. Before, there had been a sense of community amongst the black people who worked in the fields. They cultivated the land with mules, hoes, and plows, and there was a camaraderie amongst them, even though the work was hard. As Johnny Paul says in the moving chapter in which the blacks reminisce: "We stuck together, shared what little we had, and loved and respected each other." But in the late-1970s, the time in which the novel is set, that world has vanished. The houses where the black families used to live, the church where they used to worship and pray, have long gone, and all that is left are weeds, not the flowers that used to flourish in their yards. The process of change has come close to annihilating them, and Tucker fears that soon the tractors will reach the graveyard, where so many of their older relatives lie, and will tear it up, leaving no trace that he and his people ever existed.

Mapes asks if they have ever heard of progress, but the truth is that the process of agricultural mechanization was progress not for all groups equally. The blacks were exploited by an unjust, racist system that cared nothing for them as human beings and did not honor their long tradition of working on the land. Progress for some meant that others lost everything that gave their lives identity and meaning.

Gaines revealed in an interview that this aspect of the novel was exactly true to what happened in real life Louisiana when he was growing up. When he left the area for California in 1948, he says, the whites had tractors but he did not know a single black farmer who had one. The delicate, interdependent relationship between the blacks, their families, and the land that sustained them was broken, all in the name of superior technology. Eventually the black people were driven off the land altogether, and all the young blacks (many of whom had already left the area to serve in World War II) had to move north in search of work. The novel, Gaines explained, is all about "The ones who loved the land, worked the land, and then were kicked off the land."

For the blacks on the plantation, the processes of time and change, to which all humans are subject, have been especially cruel. It is perhaps not surprising that the old men live in the past, with their memories both of race-based injustice and of former intact families and communities. Most of the characters in the novel, white as well as black, live in the past also. Change has come, but they are unable to cope with it, or in many cases even acknowledge that it has happened. This includes Fix, who is unable to understand that the days of the lynch mob are over, and Mapes, whose way of conducting a police investigation is to hit people who give him an answer he does not wish to hear. It also includes Jack Marshall, who owns the land.

When Marshall drinks in Tee Jack's store, he always makes a point of facing the room that used to be reserved for the black customers in the days of segregation. In those days he used to order drinks to be taken in to the blacks. Tee Jack wonders whether Marshall is hearing ghosts singing as he stares at the door of that room. This is an apt metaphor for Jack Marshall, who lives entirely in the past. He has completely abdicated his responsibilities as landowner, which he never wanted in the first place, but which came to him only by inheritance. He takes refuge in drink and expresses no interest in anything, not even the death of Beau. He has failed to move with the times or exercise the social responsibility that his position of power and influence demands.

When Luke Will tells him that one of his "niggers" killed Beau, Jack Marshall says he does not have any because "They belong to her," meaning his niece Candy. He speaks like a slaveowner of old, to whom human beings are just pieces of property. His wife Beatrice has no sense of social responsibility either, even though the Marshall family is at the top of the social hierarchy. The two of them drink and nap their way through their days, together making fine symbols of an effete ruling class whose time has long past. The Marshalls have outlived whatever usefulness they may once have had and remain as relics of an unjust and obsolete power structure.

It is tempting to see the situation in Marxist terms as a class struggle in which economic relations between different classes determine relative power and social position. As in Marx's analysis of nineteenth-century industrial capitalism, the economic system revealed in the novel benefits the few and enslaves the many; it is based on class and race, on positions inherited rather than attained by merit. The terms of competition are weighted in favor of one group, the Cajuns, at the expense of the blacks. The lazy self-indulgence of the Marshalls is made possible only by their ownership of the land, even though they contribute nothing to the cultivation

> Letting go of the past is of course easier said than done. . . . But Gaines is careful to give each man, however humble, his moment of transformation."

and stewardship of it. The blacks, since they own nothing, are an oppressed class. (Marx advocated the abolition of private property, and held that the means of production, distribution, and exchange should be held in common, i.e., owned by the state. In the history of Marshall as depicted in the novel, this would have resulted in the common ownership of the tractors—the means of production—which, in theory at least, would have evened up the economic discrepancies between the Cajuns and the blacks.)

The other prominent member of the ruling, landowning elite is Candy. Candy is the opposite of her uncle and aunt (the Marshalls) in the sense that she cares about the blacks and takes their side. In political terms she might be thought of as the white liberal who embraces the causes of the oppressed, but can never really understand or be fully a part of their struggle. Candy has good reason to care about Mathu, since he, with Miss Merle, raised her, but she also makes the mistake of assuming that the blacks are weak and need her to protect them. Whatever her good intentions, she remains the representative of a paternalistic system that does not treat all people as equal in their humanity. And when the pressure builds up on Candy during the stand-off at the house, she reveals that she is not quite as benevolent and large-minded as she believes herself to be. When Clatoo tells her that the men are going to talk in private, without her, she becomes angry and orders Clatoo off the property, reminding him that she is the one who owns it. Rooster, who narrates this segment, notes that Candy glares at Clatoo in an attempt to get him to look down (as the blacks were accustomed to doing—before this memorable day—when spoken to by whites).

Under pressure, Candy reverts to the usual white attitude toward blacks. She too is living in the past, and she too must learn to change. And with Mathu's help, she does. It is Mathu, asserting his independence from her, who tells her to go home. Later, when the trial ends, Mathu is careful to distance himself from Candy. He declines her offer of a ride home, preferring instead to travel back with Clatoo and the others. Immediately after this, in the final sentence of the novel, Candy reaches out to Lou Dimes, her boyfriend; perhaps now she is ready to let the past go and live in the present.

Letting go of the past is of course easier said than done. For the blacks, bent low under the weight of the past, it is especially hard. But Gaines is careful to give each man, however humble, his moment of transformation. A case in point is Dirty Red. Dirty Red is one of the least significant of the black men. He has a reputation, even amongst his own people, for laziness, and he appears never to have done a day's work in his life. "Even to bat his eyes was too much work for Dirty Red," says Cherry. In the eyes of the world, Dirty Red amounts to very little. And yet near the end of the novel, as he lies next to Charlie in the darkness, he shows a strong desire to learn. He wants to know what has happened to Charlie, who has just been through an almost religious experience that has given him—after a lifetime of servility—pride, self-respect, and courage. Dirty Red wants to know what Charlie saw in those hours he spent in the swamps. Charlie does not answer him directly except to say that Dirty Red has seen it too. Then finally Charlie says, "You got it, Dirty. You already got it, partner." Like Charlie, Dirty Red too is changed; his moment has come, and he does what he has to do without fear.

Source: Bryan Aubrey, Critical Essay on *A Gathering of Old Men*, in *Novels for Students*, The Gale Group, 2003.

Mary T. Harper

In the following essay, Harper discusses the transformation of men into respected elders in Gaines's novel.

In *A Gathering of Old Men*, Ernest Gaines again returns to the Louisiana plantation, where he focuses on the black elders of a community who collectively are challenged to rise above their individual turmoil to confront an oppressive society—a group of men who develop from benign "men-children" to respected "fathers" and role models of the community.

As the novel opens, Beau Boutan, a Cajun farmer and boss of leased Marshall Plantation land, has been killed in the Quarters in front of Mathu's cabin. Determined to protect Mathu, the eighty-plus-year-old black man who helped rear her, Candy Marshall, the plantation's young white owner, persistently declares that she has shot Beau and summons Mathu's peers so that together they can form a united front against both Sheriff Mapes and the expected retaliation from Fix Boutan, the Cajun family patriarch.

Beau's death and Candy's summons set the stage for Gaines to present complex aspects of rural Louisiana life using a multiple first-person point of view. That is, the voices of eleven blacks and four whites reveal the ever-present social stratification and attitudes, especially the difficult acceptance of change. Certainly, these voices capture the richness—the humor and pathos—of folk life, centered on the introspection and actions of fifteen or more old men who answer Candy's summons, each bearing a twelve-gauge shotgun containing an empty number-five shell.

Candy Marshall's directive regarding the shotguns has several implications. First and most obviously, since Mathu has allegedly used such a weapon to kill Beau, pinpointing the actual killer will be difficult if everyone is similarly armed and admits guilt. Second but most important, an empty shotgun is a useless weapon just as the men possessing such weapons are harmless; hence, Candy becomes the protector. Regardless of her assertion that all black families have at sometime suffered Fix Boutan's wrath and that they now have an opportunity to confront both Fix and Mapes, this situation can be viewed as an example of the child-protector syndrome, with the thirty-year-old plantation mistress paternalistically and benevolently caring for her seventy-plus-year-old men-children. Adamantly, Candy tells Myrtle Bouchard (Miss Merle), the white neighbor and family friend who also helped rear her: "I will not let Mapes nor Fix harm my people . . . . I will protect my people. My daddy and all them before him did. . . ." Third, an empty gun is analogous to the lives these men have lived. Unlike the elderly Howard Mills of Gaines' *In My Father's House* who rejects his assigned social "place," or Ned Douglass, Jimmy Aaron, and Joe Pittman of *The Autobiography of Miss Jane Pittman* who face life fearlessly, realizing that they must risk death in order to live fully, these men—with the exception of Mathu—have faced life fearfully, refusing to take risks. Instead, they have become empty shells of men, regarded by whites such as Miss Merle as bedbugs—hidden, infesting insects—hidden in the tall weeds which presently mar the landscape of the Quarters.

Further, having seen how past fears have immobilized their elders, even the young blacks do not expect them to be other than elusive bedbugs. Gaines presents this negative image through the remarks of Fue, a somewhat effeminate but perceptive youth. After delivering Candy's message to seventy-two-year-old Robert L. Stevenson Banks (Chimley) and seventy-one-year-old Matthew Lincoln Brown (Mat), Fue sardonically reminds them of their alternatives: to act or "go home, lock y'all doors and crawl under the bed like y'all used to".

These words, demeaning in their implication of men crawling and hiding, serve as a catalyst, moving Mat and Chimley from idle reflection on their past to an assessment of their present and future. In spite of their visible but unspoken fears—for they know this is the first time a black man has actually killed a white man in their parish—they renew their dormant spiritual strength and rise to Fue's challenge. Gaines shows the beginning of this transformation in the men's conversation:

> Mat: He works in mysterious ways, don't He?
> Chimley: That's what they say.
> Mat: 'Bout that bed. . . . I'm too old to go crawling under that bed. I just don't have the strength for it no more. It's too low, Chimley.
> Chimley: Mine ain't no higher.
> Mat: I have to go, Chimley. . . . This can be my last chance
> Chimley: I'm going, too.

Determined, Mat returns home to prepare both himself and his wife Ella for this new action, an exchange Gaines again succinctly captures:

> Ella: You old fool. Y'all gone crazy?
> Mat: That's right. . . . Anytime we say we go'n stand up for something, they say we crazy. You right, we all gone crazy.

He describes feeling as if he'd "been running up a . . . steep hill, and now . . . had reached the top". With this description Gaines' images change from negative to positive—from crawling to running to ascending.

Reminding his wife of his years of unrewarding toil, of having cursed God and the world, of turning in frustration against her, of their son's death for lack of medical care because of his color, Mat restates his realization: "He works in mysterious ways. . . . Give a old nigger like me one more chance to do something with his life." Similarly, such introspection and reassessment seemingly characterize all the elders to whom Candy's summons has been directed, for Fue's comment to Mat and Chimley has symbolically echoed throughout

> **Just as skin color and personal motivation have separated the black community in the past, so do the social codes separate the whites."**

the parish challenging the men to act, as Mathu had bid them do in years past.

One of these men, Cyril Robillard (Clatoo) becomes a leader, tending men's spirits rather than crops. Instead of peddling his produce, the gardener Clatoo now uses his truck to transport this aged, scared, but proud group. In effect, he nurtures a rebirth of spirit as he picks up elders throughout the parish. Perceiving their need for unity, their need for sustenance, he directs them to assemble in the black graveyard so that together they may walk to Mathu's cabin.

Clatoo intuitively understands the significance of this gathering spot, for here past, present, and future merge. Each man searches among the unmarked graves for his family plot as if to draw strength from the ancestors, to recall how many of them had lived and suffered. This unkept burial ground, covered with weeds and grass like the landscape of the Quarters, also parallels the fear which stifles their lives. But among the weed-covered graves is life, for just as the abundant fruit from the nearby pecan tree covers the ground about them, providing actual physical nourishment, so too are their spirits nourished, even as they realize that their actions may result in their deaths. They are then ready to heed Clatoo's command as he tells them: "Heads up and backs straight. We going in like soldiers, not like tramps".

This transition from tramps to soldiers is a new experience, for much of their lives they have been trampled. Throughout the novel Gaines most poignantly allows the various voices to reiterate the many ills they have endured. He shows how their displacement, ill-treatment, and nonrecognition have resulted in a loss of pride, moving them towards invisibility, with little regard for their past efforts and creativity. Corrine, for example, one of the elderly women gathered to lend support to the men, bemoans her losses as she speaks of the St.

Charles River which they have been prohibited from using freely:

> That river.... Where the people went all these years. Where they fished, where they washed they clothes, where they was baptized. St. Charles River. Done gived us food, done cleaned us clothes, done cleaned us souls. St. Charles River—no more though. No more. They took it.

Their restricted use of the river with its nurturing, renewing, life-sustaining powers then becomes symbolic of all they have lost—physically, spiritually, and psychologically.

Gaines' voices make it clear that until the elders accept the challenge to unite at Mathu's cabin, they have mainly been old people recalling past years, looking down the empty Quarters deserted by the young for greener fields, looking at the weeds wondering what has happened to the roses, the four-o'clocks—the flowers of nature and the flowers of humanity that once kept the community vibrant. Gaines depicts this resurging vibrancy as Clatoo's "army" joins Mathu, Candy, and other men, women, and children already gathered. And though they at first have empty shotguns, like the soldiers Clatoo has commanded them to become, they indeed ready themselves for battle as they one by one load their guns with shells hidden behind Mathu's cabin.

Sheriff Mapes, however, remains unsuspecting. While he initially regards these elders as mere extensions of the Quarters' overgrown weeds, he does respect Mathu. He comments, "... I admire the nigger. He's a better man than most I've met, black or white". Mathu, still tall and straight, described by Gaines as "built like ... [an] old post in the ground," the only black ever to stand up to Fix Boutan, does not deny killing Beau. Looking Mapes directly in the eye, he tells him: "A man got to do what he thinks is right, Sheriff. . . . That's what part him from a boy".

The actions of the men reflect Mathu's words, for in spite of the tactics Mapes and his deputy employ, the men remain united, each steadily admitting guilt, with the exception of Rev. Jamison. Like the preacher in the dentist's office in "The Sky is Gray," he prefers passive acceptance to direct action. Philosophically outside the group, he is willing to surrender Mathu, afraid of their taking a stand primarily because he fears his personal loss, his own further displacement. He and Lou Dimes, Candy's fiancé, refer to the "wall of old black men with shotguns" as fools. But unlike the others, Rev. Jamison cannot withstand the physical abuse and

falls to the ground. Just as Rev. Phillip Martin of *In My Father's House* falls to the floor when confronted by his illegitimate son, so too is Jamison felled, not only by physical pain but also by fear and spiritual weakness.

Mapes's respect for the men grows, however, and as he converses with them, we see his awareness of changes wrought by time. The Lifesavers he continually sucks come to represent what he stands for—a saver of lives—for he, too, realizes that the vigilante tactics of Fix and his friends are outmoded. Accordingly, he disperses a deputy to dissuade the Boutan family from retaliating.

As the who-killed-Beau mystery unfolds, we learn that Charlie, the godson of Mathu, is the actual killer. Constantly humiliated by Beau's curses and threats to beat him no matter how diligently he works, he finally can take no more, and he and Beau fight in the canefield. Thinking he has killed Beau, he runs to his Parrain or godfather, Mathu, who gives him a gun as Beau approaches on a tractor. Then fearing for his own life, he shoots Beau; and as Candy approaches, he asks Mathu to take the blame while he runs.

His running, however, takes a new turn. Just as the cemetery renews the elders' spirits, so does Charlie experience a spiritual conversion as he hides among the cane and in the swamps. It is as if the spirits of those before him stop his running away from life. Returning just before Mathu surrenders to the sheriff, he recounts his experience: ". . . I heard a voice calling my name. I laid there listening, listening, listening, but I didn't hear it no more. But I knowed that voice was calling me back here". No longer does he see himself as "Big Charlie, nigger boy"; after fifty years of running he becomes Mr. Biggs and demands that Mapes address him accordingly. In effect, Charlie's process of unnaming and renaming signifies his self-liberation, his re-creation and reformation.

Gaines also shows the effect of change on others in this Louisiana setting. Just as skin color and personal motivation have separated the black community in the past, so do the social codes separate the whites. For example, Gil Boutan, Beau's brother, tells Candy of her attitude toward Cajuns:

> You never liked any of us. Looking at us as if we're a breed below you. But we're not, Candy. We're all made of the same bone, the same blood, the same skin. Your father had a break, mine didn't, that's all.

Ironically, these words also mirror black feelings.

Then there is Candy's Uncle Jack, aloof and nihilistic, uninterested in the present, one who closes his eyes to the controversy about him. Gaines allows Jacques Thibeaux, the white owner of the combination grocery and liquor store, to describe Jack Marshall:

> . . . he live on the land 'cause they left it there, but he don't give a damn for it. . . Get up and drink. Take a little nap, wake up and drink some more. . . . Don't give a damn for nothing. Women or nothing. . . . Politics or nothing. Nigger or nothing. . . . Things just too complicated. I reckon for people like him they have always been complicated—protecting name and land. . . . Feeling guilty about this, guilty about that. It wasn't his doing. He came here and found it, and they died and left it on him.

Marshall finds his refuge in drink, and though he curses the system that forces him to uphold its traditions, ironically, he still does not fully perceive of blacks as people; to him they are still possessions. To Luke Will's statement that Beau had been killed by "one of your niggers. . .", Jack replies: "I have no niggers. . . Never will have any niggers. They belong to her [Candy]".

Unlike her uncle, who abhors such possessions, Candy sees these black as extensions of the plantation's property and has difficulty understanding that she no longer owns them. Although Merle and Mathu have cooperatively reared her— "one to raise her as a lady, the other to make her understand the people who live on her place"—she fails to understand the changes that are continually occurring. For example, she becomes irate when the men exclude her from their conference inside Mathu's house, not understanding that their excluding her, their refusal of her paternalistic protection, is another meaningful step towards their manhood.

Gaines also uses Candy to illustrate the theme of racial interdependence when she tells Mathu that having known all of the Marshalls, he is the essence of the plantation's life. Recalling her forefathers' words, she tells him: "They said if you went, it went, because we could not—it could not—not without you, Mathu". But Lou, her fiancé, does understand both the changes that have occurred and the transformation the men are presently undergoing. He tells Candy that Mathu doesn't need her protection, that he must live his life "his own way".

The author again illustrates the same interdependence theme with Gil "Salt" Boutan, the Cajun LSU fullback, and Cal "Pepper" Harrison, the black LSU halfback. Together, they are a formidable team, a pair on whom both blacks and whites are

depending if LSU is to defeat "Ole Miss" in the football game scheduled for the next day.

Although distraught over his brother's death, Gil tells his father that he refuses to participate in the vigilante acts for which his family is known and further tries to explain how such acts will invalidate his chances to become an all-American and how he and Cal work together on the football field. Hurt and unable to understand Gil's point about black-white cooperation nor his refusal to protect family honor, Fix concedes—but not Luke Will, a fellow Cajun determined to avenge Beau's death and to control blacks. Fix, however, now as old as the blacks awaiting his arrival, refuses to support Luke, asserting: "I have no other cause to fight for. I'm too old for causes. Let Luke Will fight for causes. This is family". With such scenes, Gaines develops another dimension of Cajun life—their differing values and rationales for their actions, the conflicts they, too, experience as a result of change.

Thus, the confrontation between Cajun father and son culminates with Gil planning to play in the forthcoming game—a symbolic gesture to beat Luke Will and also symbolic of a changing South and hope for the future. Deputy Russell tells Gil: "Sometimes you got to hurt something to help something. Sometimes you have to plow under one thing in order for something else to grow. . . . You can help this country tomorrow. You can help yourself".

However, when Mapes informs the elders that Fix is not coming, they believe him to be lying. But he is happy that violence has been avoided, and drawing an analogy using Gil and Cal, he reminds them of the effects of change:

> No, y'all wanted them to play together. . . . Y'all the one—you cut your own throats. You told God you wanted Salt and Pepper to get together and God did it for you. At the same time, you wanted God to keep Fix the way Fix was thirty years ago so one day you would get a chance to shoot him. Well, God couldn't do both.

Mapes' joy is short-lived, for Luke Will and his friends, strengthened by liquor, arrive to avenge Beau's death.

Once children but now men, the elders bravely confront the enemy, led by Charlie and Antoine Christophe (Dirty Red)—all having been reborn in the plantation's swamps, canefields, and graveyard; having been infused with the spirit of their ancestors, a spirit that lives on just as the pecan tree continually bears fruit. Just before he stands and moves toward Luke, Charlie tells his friend Antoine that

Lynching victim

"life's so sweet when you know you ain't no more coward".

Once again, Gaines effectively depicts the trauma of change. Both Luke and Charlie kill each other—one dying trying to prevent change, the other having been changed. Charlie's act then culminates the transformation of "menchildren" to fathers, symbolizes a recognition by all that thwarted dreams can become present realities, that resignation can be replaced by renewed involvement and commitment, and that one's mortality need not preclude one's becoming a "new soldier" in the quest for manhood and dignity.

Source: Mary T. Harper, "From Sons to Fathers: Ernest Gaines' *A Gathering of Old Men*," in *CLA Journal*, Vol. XXXI, No. 3, March 1988, pp. 299–308.

Marcia Gaudet and Carl Wooton with Ernest Gaines

In the following interview, Gaines talks about the film version of his novel as well as music and writing.

After watching the movie version of A Gathering of Old Men, *what's your general response to what they did with the movie in relation to your book?*

Well, I think they did a pretty good job. The biggest change is the ending. When they came to Louisiana to shoot the film, the director told me they had changed it. He said, "I think it's for the best, and I think you'll like it."

Did you?

I don't know if I like it or not. I never argue with what they do in Hollywood. They have their own way of communicating with an audience, and I don't argue with it. Most people remember the film version of *The Autobiography of Miss Jane Pittman* by the ending—Miss Jane walking to the fountain—which I did not write. With *A Gathering of Old Men*, I was trying to prove a point—showing the old men standing. They brought guns, and I believe in the old Chekovian idea that if you bring a gun into the play, the gun must go off by the drop of the curtain. I don't know if there is any difference in the point made in the movie. They just didn't think they had to stick too close to Chekov.

I think if this film had been made for the theater, they could have done it better. Since it was done for television, maybe they didn't want a black and white shoot-out. I heard from some of the New York press that people were disappointed with the ending of the movie. They wanted to see the ending as I had written it.

How much of the filming of A Gathering of Old Men *did you get to watch?*

I went down to Thibodaux three weekends. I went on Saturdays and watched the shooting. Out of all the shooting, which took about a month, I saw about six days of it. There are lots of things you can criticize anytime someone makes something else out of your work. I'm sure Shakespeare could have criticized productions of his work, Tolstoy or Faulkner, you know, God with the Bible. Somebody is going to have to pay for it when they get up there with Him. They're going to have to pay for what they did. They'll line up and they'll have to pay Faulkner and Hemingway and Shakespeare for what they've done to their works.

It's a different medium. There's a story about Brahms. He saw one of his concertos being conducted by some crazy gypsy. This guy was just bouncing and jumping in the air directing the orchestra, and Brahms just sat there. At the end, someone asked him, "Herr Brahms, what do you think?" And Brahms said, "So, it can be done like that, too." And really, this is what you do. You say, "So, well, it can be done like that. I didn't know that." There are quite a few things they did that I didn't care about. They took liberties with dialogue, and they used their own dialects.

They changed names of characters. Instead of thirteen, or whatever number of old men I have speaking in the book, there are about six or seven speaking. They combined characters, taking the dialogue from two or three characters and giving it to one. They changed the clothes. They changed the size of the characters. In *A Gathering of Old Men* the character Mapes is big. Richard Widmark [who plays Mapes in the film] is thin.

Fortunately before we started shooting the film, the director [Volker Schlondorff] asked me to take him to the place where I had grown up. I showed him the house there so he could have an idea what the house looked like. I think he really recreated it. The house that they have in the film is just like the one that I showed him. The road is quite a bit like the rear road. The scenery is quite authentic. It was the dialogue which they tried to change a lot when they started combining things. When they started taking a few lines from here and a few lines from there and putting them together into one speech, and adding their own terms to it—that's when they took liberties I did not approve of. But as I said, I'm not part of it. I'm not in the filmmaking business.

Do you think they maintained the humor and the comic aspects?

That is one of the things I'm afraid does not really come through. Sometimes they don't speak the lines exactly the way I wrote them. For example, Widmark is supposed to say something that is very funny, but he does not say it funny. I told Volker, "I didn't hear any laughter," and he said, "Well, you can't hear laughter here because it was not meant for those people to laugh." And he said, "You'll hear laughter from the audience." And I said, "Ohhhh." I said, "I'm the audience now, and I didn't laugh, so I don't know whether or not I'll laugh later at the television screen."

I talked to a newspaper guy from Florida, and he questioned having a German director for the film. He said, "But does he know American humor? Does he know American mood?" You can't just bring in anybody and make this thing funny. You can make it dramatic, but you must know the subtleties to bring off the humor. The humor just didn't come off as it could have come off. Humor depends on that sense of pausing and understanding how the language is used. I don't think the director could handle this. He doesn't know the South. He did a better job with the drama. What went well was when he went into Fix's house. Stocker Fontelieu, who is from New Orleans, plays

Even with tough, hard men, whose lives are really rough, something funny at times can happen."

Fix. Oh, he was good at that. When he comes on the scene he knows what to do.

One thing that everyone seems pleased with was that Lou Gossett Jr. would play Mathu. How did you feel about it when you saw it being filmed?

I saw Gossett in a couple of scenes which were fantastic. One was the scene before Charlie returns and the old men gather in Mathu's house and he's telling them that they should go home. He's going to take responsibility. Gossett really speaks that scene very, very well. My main criticism is that at the very end he is supposed to have a long speech, and this is really minimized.

When I was told that he was in the film, I couldn't really imagine his being Mathu because Gossett is, I think, fifty and, what you could say, good-looking. But then Cicely [Tyson] was much younger when she played Miss Jane. Cicely was still in her thirties when she played someone who was 110. As soon as I saw Gossett in the makeup I knew he could do it because he had all the mannerisms of someone seventy years old. When Gower Frost, the producer, told me that Richard Widmark was playing Mapes, I thought, "Good Lord!" But then when you see it done, you can see that these guys are very good at it.

We were discussing characters one day before they started shooting. Gower Frost and I were talking about Charlie, and I was trying to show him how important it was that Charlie be big, so that when Charlie comes back, this huge guy comes back and people look up to him. And Volker—Volker's very short—said, "People can look at a short man the same way." And I said, "Well, I like bulk. Charlie should be bulk." And they did get someone like that: Walter Breaux. He is big. I have a picture of me standing between Walter and the guy playing Beau Boutan, the murder victim. These guys both weigh over three hundred pounds. I weigh 225, and I look small. These are huge men.

In the film made from "The Sky Is Gray," they used a corn field instead of a cane field, and the sky never was gray in the film. Do those kinds of changes bother you?

No, they don't bother me because by the time you make a film of a book, the writer—unless he's a one book writer—has just about forgotten that book and he's gone to something else. And it's a different medium altogether. You just feel like, okay, let them do what they want to do. You know, take the money and buy something. Invest the money if it's enough. If not, pay off the bills and hope that they'll make a decent film and the people will watch it and go out and buy the book. You're much more interested in selling the book than you are the film. Whether it's a good film or a bad film, people will go out and get that book. *Miss Jane Pittman* is a very good example. Before the filming, I think we'd had only about three printings in hardback and three or four printings in paperback. Since then, we've had, say, twelve printings in hardback and about twenty-two, twenty-three printings in paperback. Because of that film many colleges and high schools and universities have used that book. Even a bad film will get people interested in the book.

Were you pleased with the film versions of "The Sky Is Gray" and Miss Jane Pittman?

Let's say *Miss Jane Pittman* was maybe a five on a scale of one to ten and then "The Sky Is Gray" about the same. With *Miss Jane Pittman*, you could not get the entire story of a hundred years in two hours. You had to choose points, pieces, and then try to mold that into a whole. In "The Sky Is Gray," the main character is a little boy about eight years old, and they could not find a little boy eight years old to carry the story. So they had to get a larger boy about thirteen years old, and that makes a difference on the effect of the story.

The novel about Miss Jane uses the first person point of view. It's very difficult for the camera to look at the character and through the eyes of the character at the same time.

Something was said about the filming of Flaubert's *Madame Bovary*. In the book you can smell the cabbage cooking. In the film you never could smell the cabbage. There are certain things that you do capture, things that you do put on the screen. There are certain things in the book that you cannot put on the screen—many things. You can put action on the screen, but I don't know that you can put thoughts on the screen and dreams on the screen and really the depth of the personality on the screen. I don't know that you can put that on the screen, flash it on the screen.

You have said over and over again that you see yourself as a storyteller and that you came from a place that was oral, where people talked the stories. One of the things we see in your work is that you've taken an oral tradition of storytelling and you've transformed it into a literary medium.

Right, I try to do that. That's one of the hardest things in the world to do. You can go to any place, any bar on the corner out there and find people who can tell the greatest stories in the world—they can tell you some stories—but if you give one of them a pen and some paper and say, "Okay, write this stuff down," he'll run. He'll drop those things and start running. It's a tough thing to do, to try to recapture these things. But I try to do that, yes.

How do you make the leap from the oral storytelling tradition to the literary medium?

Well, I think it's a combination of things. I think Joyce does it. I think he does it in *Finnegans Wake*, and nobody can understand what the hell is going on there. I think he also did it in other stories. A good example would be "Ivy Day in the Committee Room." It's the old tradition of these old guys telling the story about the great fighter, the Irish patriot, Parnell, and Joyce can put this in literature because Joyce had such a great literary background. Faulkner does the same thing. "Spotted Horses" is nothing but a guy telling a story about some wild horses beating up on somebody, cutting people up and running people all over the place, and Twain does the same thing. Twain and Faulkner are the fathers of this, this combination of that oral tradition and then integrating it into a literary tradition. So it's something that I inherited from having that kind of background and then having studied literature.

Do you think it's possible for a writer to be able to do this if he's not, first of all, a part of that oral tradition?

I think a writer writes about what he is part of. He has to. I don't know that he could do it if he does not have this kind of background. I don't know that Faulkner could have written what he wrote if he had not come from that kind of background where people squatted around the place, around the stores or the courthouse square or wherever they did, and then did their work like that. I don't know if Twain could have done it had he not been part of that traditional Mississippi River storytelling crowd, and then knowing literature. And I don't know if you don't have that kind of tradition if you can do the same thing.

What you and Faulkner do is to add to the writing something to compensate for not having the audience and the sound and the performance there.

And then you leave off things, too. You leave out some of the things that they do tell you in order to make it in that literary form. You're transferring from the oral thing, a guy sitting there telling you a story. You have to take what he's telling you and use those twenty-six letters over here to put this thing down accurately. You try to put it down very accurately. But then you know you cannot do it because you cannot use all the gestures; you cannot use all the sounds of his voice, his improper syntax, whatever he does. That does not convey to the reader because the reader cannot understand what you're talking about.

For example, let's say we get someone who is a great Cajun storyteller. He can tell the greatest story in the world. You cannot write that! You better not try to write it. Nobody's going to read it. Nobody can understand it. Even someone who knows what he's talking about can't understand a thing, so you don't write it that way.

You can take what he told you and you say, I'm going halfway with what he told me, and I'm going to get what I've learned from all these years of reading. Then I'm going to use proper syntax; I'm going to use proper spelling; I'm going to do all those other little things. I'm going to take from what he gave me and I'm going to use from my background; I'm going to use something from over here that I have, and then I'm going to combine these things and then I'm going to put it out there and pray that someone will understand. I have to do something that can be recognized. I have to write the proper kind of dialogue that you can understand. I try to write in short sentences so you can grasp the dialogue. I try to make things as clear as possible. An actor or performer can make gestures or throw his voice out and cry and weep and do all sorts of things like that. What I have to do is use those twenty-six letters that tell you these things, so I can build up my scenes in that way.

You've talked before about models that you emulated, in the manner that Hemingway says he did Twain, and Norris did Zola.

You do emulate, you do, when you start out. I started out in the libraries, and I was just reading everything in my late teens in libraries. But I was fortunate when I came out of the army that I had some very good teachers who were just coming into

San Francisco at that time. They were eager to help, and they were just coming out from the Korean War. At that same time we had the Beat Scene going on in San Francisco, so we were reading a lot of books. Once my teachers saw what I wanted to write about—and that was about rural Louisiana, and this was in the mid-fifties, fifty-five, fifty-six— they encouraged me and recommended writers and stories to read.

I also discovered how music can help, and as Hemingway suggested, paintings can help, just by going to a museum or art gallery. Just look at paintings and see how you can describe a beautiful room with only two or three things, without having to go through everything in the room. Right now I'm thinking of Van Gogh's painting called "Vincent's Room"—it's the room where he used to live and sleep—and how he could do it so well with only two or three things or pieces of things.

I've also learned from the discipline of great athletes by just watching them. I ran a lot of track myself. I was the worst football player ever put a helmet on his head, but I was pretty good at track in college. I know about the discipline of athletes, and I know that same discipline must pertain to the writer, to the artist. He must be disciplined. He must do things over and over and over and over and over. And these kinds of things are also a great influence. The grace under pressure thing I think I learned from Hemingway. I've always said to students, especially black students, that somehow I feel that Hemingway was writing more about blacks than he was really about whites when he was using the grace under pressure theme. I see that Hemingway usually put his people in a moment where they must have grace under pressure, and I've often looked at black life, not only as a moment, but more as something constant, everyday. This is what my characters must come through.

I also learned how to understate things from Hemingway, and I learned from his structure of paragraphs, his structure of sentences, and his dialogue. Hemingway can repeat the lighting of a cigarette, the length or shortness of the cigarette, or the ash hanging, to show how time moves. He repeats little things throughout a scene to make you know the movement of time. Hemingway's importance to me is a combination of the language and that particular theme of grace under pressure. Of course there are also his drinking well and eating well. I like to do that, too.

I learned much about dialogue from Faulkner, especially when we're dealing with our Southern dialects. I learned rhythms from Gertrude Stein, learned to put a complete story in a day from Joyce's *Ulysses* or Tolstoy's "The Death of Ivan Ilych."

You have spoken before about how Russian writers influenced you.

Yes, I started out with form from Ivan Turgenyev. I was very much impressed, not only with form but with their use of peasantry. I think serfs are used much more humanely in their fiction than, say, the slaves were used, or the blacks were used, by many of the Southern writers. I remember Tolstoy says, "You just watch a serf, just watch him. He'll never tell you the truth." He says, now if you watch closely, you'll figure out the truth, but boy he's going to lead you all through the swamps, all through the woods, and then you get it. Then you get the truth out of him, and I learned that from just listening to these guys tell a story.

Many writers claim that one of the things they're trying to do is to create order out of all the chaos and disorder in the world. Do you have a sense of doing that?

I try. I think art is order. I think art must be order, no matter what you do with it. I don't care what Picasso did with twisted faces and bodies— all of that sort of thing. I think there has to be a form of order there or it's not art. The novel to me is art. The short story is art. And there must be order. I don't care what the chaos is. You must put it in some kind of decent form. When you leave this thing, you say you've gone through war, you've gone through hell, but this is not hell. This is a piece of art. This is work. This is a picture of hell. After reading this, you felt something very— not good about hell—something good about this piece of work. This is all it takes.

You said earlier that music also helped. How do you think that music helped you as a writer?

During the time I was writing *The Autobiography of Miss Jane Pittman*, I was playing Mussorgsky's "Pictures at an Exhibition." It's about someone going to a museum or art gallery and looking at pictures against the wall. There are different kinds of pictures: dramatic pictures, comic pictures, different colors, all depicted in sound. There is a common motif going through the whole thing. At one time when I was writing *The Autobiography of Miss Jane Pittman*, I was thinking about sketches of a plantation because I had been listening to that so much. I was thinking sketches, sketches,

sketches, and then I ceased thinking of sketches, for the autobiography.

Another thing about music: I think some of the best descriptions, especially dealing with blacks, some of the best descriptions of the big flood of '27, which most southern writers have written about, have been described better in music, especially by great blues singers like Bessie Smith, Josh White, Leadbelly, and many others. The whites did the newspaper things at that time, but when it came down to the more intimate things, I think the black blues singers gave us better descriptions even than the black writers did. Another thing especially in jazz music is repetition—repeating and repeating to get the point over—which I try to do in dialogue. I learned from music something that Hemingway also does and that is understatement. Certain musicians, like Lester Young, one of the greatest jazz saxophonists, could play around a note. For example, he didn't have to go through the old beat after beat of "Stardust." He could give you a feeling of "Stardust" by playing around the note. I tried to explain that in one interview when we did "The Sky Is Gray" for the film. In "The Sky Is Gray" the mother and her child must go to town to get the tooth pulled. They must sit in an all black waiting room. They can't have any food or drink or anything "uptown." They must go "back of town" in order to eat or drink. Now if I had wanted to hit the nail on the head, I could have put them in a white restaurant and had them thrown out, but by the fact that they have to go back of town, you know that they would not have been accepted uptown. So, I'm not saying, "Go in here and get thrown out," but instead I'm saying, "Go back of town to eat." This is what they would have had to do. The only whites they come in contact with are people who are kind to them—the old lady who gives them food at the very end, and others at the place where she can go in and pretend to buy an axe handle so the kid can warm himself. It's not hitting the nail on the head, but playing around it. I think this is much more effective.

You have a large collection of jazz albums and have commented before that you usually play music when you're writing. Do you still do that?

Oh, yes. Whether I'm playing jazz or classical music, or just the radio, I usually have music in the background, but soft, so it does not disturb me. I have to keep music. It relaxes me, and at the same time it gives me a sense of rhythm, of beat.

Do you think maybe it tells you the atmosphere or the kind of feeling you want?

I don't know that it sets a mood or anything like that. I think I have to sort of build myself to the mood before I begin to write. Yet at times, it can. It's possible that when I was writing *The Autobiography of Miss Jane Pittman*, because I played "Pictures at an Exhibition" just about everyday while I was writing it—two years I guess—maybe I needed that to get started. But sometimes I play music just for the background—but soft in the background. I don't play Beethoven's Fifth because that's too disturbing. I play some sort of soft music—violin or cello, or whatever—as sort of the background. It's just like you need water or coffee around the place, you know. You have some music in the background to keep you going that day, I guess.

How was music present in your world as you were growing up?

Well, of course, I came from a plantation. There was a church not very far from our house; I could hear the people singing all the time. I had to go to Sunday school and church as a child, and, of course, the people sang. I could never carry a tune myself, but the old ones did. And my mother sang, and my aunt. I didn't hear classical music or anything like that. I don't think the radio worked half the time, but there was always music, somebody doing something.

So far you've described the indirect importance music has had in your writing. Do you ever see it creeping in more directly, through musical language or musical references?

Oh, no. I don't think I ever use music really like that. In *Of Love and Dust*, Jim has a guitar. I think in "The Sky Is Gray," the young kid, James, thinks back on the old man who plays a guitar around the house. When I was a small child we did have a man like that who played the guitar around the place. But I don't know anything about music. I can't read music at all. I remember when I had to do the reading of the "Portrait of Lincoln" with the University of Southwestern Louisiana orchestra, I explained to the conductor, "I don't know one note of music, so whenever you want me to start reading, you must nod your head." We had a record of Carl Sandburg reading it so I could figure out the rhythm and speed, the way the thing should be read. But I couldn't follow the notes on paper. I don't know a thing about music.

What do you mean by a writer's "work" when you talk to students?

Well, I think if we're dealing with time, physical work is getting up and working at the desk. But

What Do I Read Next?

- Gaines's best-selling, critically acclaimed novel, *The Autobiography of Miss Jane Pittman* (1971), is in the form of the tape-recorded recollections of the fictional Jane Pittman, a 110-year-old woman who was born a slave but lived to see the coming of the Civil Rights movement of the 1950s and 1960s.

- *Uncle Tom's Children* (1938), by Richard Wright, is a collection of four novellas. Set in the American Deep South, it shows how post-slavery blacks resisted white oppression. In "Big Boy Leaves Home," two blacks accidentally kill a white man, and the black community desperately tries to arrange their escape. Unfortunately, one of the men is lynched by a white mob.

- *At the Hands of Persons Unknown: The Lynching of Black America* (2002), by Philip Dray, presents the history of lynching in the south as a systematic attempt by whites to maintain their power over blacks through a reign of terror. The book covers the period from Reconstruction and the 1875 Civil Rights Act to the mid-twentieth century.

- In Alex Haley's famous best-seller, *Roots* (1980), the author traces his ancestry back six generations to 1767, when a West African man boarded a slave ship bound for America. Haley's genealogical detective work makes for a riveting and moving story.

I would think that a writer never stops working as long as he is conscious; as long as he is awake, he is thinking about his work. And then he sits down four or five hours, six hours, whatever he does a day and does his work there. Work means having your antennae out, too, that you're tuned in. And as Hemingway once said—I have a lot of Hemingway quotes—a writer must have a built-in s— detector. He must know when someone is bulls—ting him. He must know fact from fiction. He must know when someone's pulling his leg; he must know when someone is touching him on the back, whether it's a good handshake, things like this. So the writer is always working. But maybe in work, I mean discipline and sitting down at that desk.

A writer is always observing people.

He is. Well, it's not observing people. He's being. People used to ask me, "Say, why do you go back to Louisiana from California?" And I'd say I'd go back to Louisiana just to be. I never did come back here with a microscope and say, put your hand under here; I want to see skin color and all that sort of thing. I never did just stare at people and say there's a man over there and he's five feet eight, nine inches tall. But when I'd come back, I'd come back just to be back, and then if I went to a cafe to eat, something would come into me. I don't have to look at the place and say this is a little thing I'm going to put down. But if I'm there, something will happen: the color of the oil cloth on the table—you know those checkered oil cloths?—whether blue and white or red and white or red and black, something would happen, and unconsciously I'd become aware of it. I'd become aware of the taste of the food. All this sort of thing because your antennae are out. You're not staring at things, but you're…

You're sort of absorbing it…

You're absorbing it, yes.

Do you ever get so involved with the fictional world that you're creating that you sometimes have difficulty telling the difference between that one and the one you're walking around in?

No, I don't. But when I was writing *Catherine Carmier*—and I think *Of Love and Dust*—I used to pray to God to turn it off sometime because I would be so involved that I could not rest. And I didn't care for anything else. And I would just say, "Listen, I'd rather be just a poor writer. If I have to be a good writer to go through this hell, please turn it off. I just can't take anymore of this stuff. I'd rather be just poor and ordinary, just one of the other guys, you know, but just turn it off." But I don't think I've ever reached the point where I was unaware of my surroundings. I've never been in the place that I was writing about.

Humor is very much a part of your writing. Do you feel that your vision is an essentially comic, optimistic one?

I don't really know that I'm very optimistic. I think in much black folklore and blues that even when things are at their worst there's often something humorous that comes through. Even with tough, hard men, whose lives are really rough, something funny at times can happen. I don't know that I'm pessimistic about life, but I don't know that I'm terribly optimistic either. I see lots of things as being humorous, even if it's in a ridiculous way. When people take advantage of people, or when people hurt other people, it's often just ridiculous and the humor comes through. My characters are not usually one hundred percent bitter, not hardened to the point that they cannot feel and give and change. Humor and joking are part of change. I don't know that it is a sign of optimism in my work. I don't go that far.

You've maintained that you wrote what you wanted to write about and that you wouldn't change your writing just to appeal to an audience or to sell your books. But you've also acknowledged making changes suggested by your editor in A Gathering of Old Men. *How do you see the relationship between writer and editor and what kind of relationships have you had with your editors?*

The most important relationship has been not with an editor but with my agent, Dorothea Oppenheimer. She would suggest things, and it was her opinion I appreciated more than anyone else's. I dealt primarily with her. Yet, at the same time, the editor did make these suggstions for *A Gathering*. He was right. I could understand how right he was. It was a matter of expediency. What I was trying to do originally was show how all these people lived before that moment, what they did with their lives before that moment that brought them all together. I had the guy sitting on his porch, or I had the guy sitting at the river fishing, or I had the guy doing something else before he arrives at Mathu's house. The editor said to have him come to Mathu's house while thinking back or have him speak with one of the other characters on the scene and then, in turn, tell what he was doing. That's what editors learn from television and movies. You always see the car arriving, especially on television. You don't know where he's coming from, but suddenly he arrives at a certain place like this. And through dialogue they explain where he had come from.

Now, when writing *The Autobiography of Miss Jane Pittman*, my editor, who was Bill Decker at Dial, told me from the beginning that the story should be told from the autobiographical point of view, and I couldn't understand what the hell he was talking about. He said to let Miss Jane tell the story. I was telling it from several characters just as I do in *A Gathering in Old Men*. The original title was *A Short Biography of Miss Jane Pittman.* Well, once it was "Sketches of a Plantation," then it was "A Short Biography of Miss Jane Pittman," when everyone else tells the story after she's dead. And he said that isn't working, but I couldn't understand what the hell he was talking about for a year. And then I realized, "Damn, it isn't working. It isn't going to work." That's what a good editor can do. A good agent, too, who reads carefully. Dorothea has suggested more than any editor. She was an editor before she became an agent. They can make damned good suggestions. Not always. Lot of times they make suggestions that you cannot accept. I remember that Bob Gottlieb made suggestions about *In My Father's House* that I could not accept at all. So I just said, "Well, no, I disagree with you." Bill made some good suggestions for *The Autobiography of Miss Jane Pittman,* just as Ed Doctorow made excellent suggestion for *Of Love and Dust.* He was my editor-in-chief at Dial at that particular time before he became a famous writer. For example, when he first saw *Of Love and Dust,* he said, "Ernie, I really like the first part of that novel, and I really like the last part of that novel, but the first part of that novel and the last part of that novel have nothing to do with each other." And he said you have to do one or the other with this novel, which I did. I sent it back to him in about three months, and he said it was a hundred per cent improved, and he said he wanted me to run it through the typewriter just one more time. Do whatever I want, just run it through one more time. I did and he published it.

In an article in The Southern Review *(October 1974), Jerry Bryant refers to a version in which Marcus and Louise escape.*

They escaped, but it was not working out. See, the first part was tragic. That's what Doctorow was saying: the first part was tragic, but the second part was humorous. Marcus was saying I'm getting out of this goddamned place. I'm going to show you guys how to do it. So he started bribing people and getting wine or whiskey or whatever at the grocery store. He knew they weren't going to kill him, so he went and got things on credit at the grocery store and he started selling it to the people in the quarters. They'd just take the bottle and turn it up, you know, for twenty-five cents or fifty cents, so he's accumulating money all the time. He was something like Snopes in "Spotted Horses." He was playing all kinds of tricks on people. He'd do anything since he knew that the guy would not kill him because he's supposed to work his way out of there. So he could do anything he wanted to do. After do-

ing all these things, after pulling all kinds of deals on all kinds of people, he escapes. And Doctorow says, "No, Ernie, no, no, no. We don't have any poetic justice here. This guy's a killer. He's going to kill her one day, and something has to work out here. If you want to make it a comic novel, make it a comic novel."

What Bryant says is that it wouldn't have been an acceptable ending to have the black man leave with the white woman at that time, implying that's why you changed it.

That was not Doctorow's criticism of it. He said I made it comic at the end. He said that the first part was tragic and the second part was comic. He didn't say he shouldn't escape with her. He said it does not follow that the first part of the book is tragic and you expect doom, you expect something to happen, something very terrible to happen, and then in the second part of the book he becomes a comic character and I'm having all kinds of fun with him. I told Doctorow, "Why the hell should he pay for it? The hell with it. Let the man get away." He was talking about balance. He was talking about form. He wasn't talking about the theme, the social thing. He wasn't worried about the ethics of it.

I didn't change it because of the social issue. I would never have changed it because of that. And that's one of the things I was saying a few minutes ago. Editors show me technique and how to do things, but don't ever tell me what to write. No, I did not change it because in the forties the black was not supposed to get away or anything like that.

You wouldn't change your writing to make people buy it.

No way! No way will I change, no! People have asked me quite often, who do you write for? I say I don't write for any particular group. But if there's a gun put to my head and someone says, "Okay, name somebody you write for," I'd say, I write for the black youth of the South. And if there are two groups, I'd say I write for the black and white youth of the South. Those are the people I would write for.

Number one, I would want the black youth to say, "Hey, I am somebody," and I'd want the white youth to say, "Hey, that is part of me out there, and I can only understand myself truly if I can understand my neighbor, if I can understand the person around me." That's the only way one can understand himself, if he can understand other things around him. You know Donne's "No man is an island" and "Don't ask for whom the bell tolls"—

> Of the fifteen voices joined to tell this story, only one is that of a black woman, Janey, and she is too hysterical to do anything but pray."

every little piece of things around us makes us a little bit whole. I mean we can go through the world being half people, and most of us do that most of our lives. But in order to understand more about ourselves and the world, we must understand what's around. So that's what I'd want: the white kids to understand what the black kid is, and the black kid to understand who he is.

Source: Marcia Gaudet and Carl Wooton, "An Interview with Ernest J. Gaines," in *New Orleans Review*, Vol. 14, No. 4, Winter 1987, pp. 62–70.

Mary Helen Washington

In the following essay, Washington gives a critical review of Gaines's novel, touching on the stereotypical modeling of the female characters.

Ernest J. Gaines's fifth novel, *A Gathering of Old Men*, is set in the black rural Louisiana parish where all his stories take place—in the cotton and cane fields northwest of Baton Rouge, near the bayous. It is the land where Gaines was born and where he spent the first fourteen years of his life. City people and Northerners may have a hard time understanding the codes of this place, for, in many ways, its inhabitants still live in the house slavery built. They work, usually as sharecroppers, on plantations; the "quarters," as they call the black housing area, look very much like a scene from slavery days—rows of rickety log cabins lined up on a flat, treeless plot of ground; nearby is the "big house," surrounded by magnolias, where the plantation owner lives. On the way to the little nightclub in town, one passes long, gray, lonely cane fields, almost as isolated as the little cemetery where Gaines says "many, many of my people are buried." These images, from a photo essay called "Home" which Gaines compiled between 1963 and 1969, show the bleakest existence, and yet one can see in them all the themes that motivate Gaines's fiction and from which he has created such powerful books as

Catherine Carmier (1964), *Of Love and Dust* (1967), *Bloodline* (1968), *In My Father's House* (1978), and the beautiful folk novel *The Autobiography of Miss Jane Pittman* (1971).

Change happens very slowly in this world; codes of behavior are rigidly observed; people live near one another for a lifetime and their kinship networks, like nothing else in their lives, are lasting and dependable. It's not an easy world for readers to enter. I imagine that many will share the impatience of the fast-talking city slicker named James in *Bloodline* who says of these backwoods people, "All they know is talk, talk, talk.... They do these little bitty things, and they feel like they've really done something. Well, back in these sticks, I guess there just isn't nothing big to do."

Yet these little bitty things James has dismissed—the living with violence, the patient refusal to give up one's dignity, the "bearing witness calmly against the predator"—are the very things which Adrienne Rich says have the power "to reconstitute the world." *A Gathering of Old Men* asks us to read the lives of black peasants as Rich reads women's lives: with attention to "the enormity of the simplest things."

When twelve old men from those Louisiana backwoods gather with shotguns to prevent a lynching, it is the most courageous and meaningful act they have ever performed. They have lived in continuous submission to the white power structure. Now in their 70s and 80s, they gather to confront the power that has humiliated and degraded them. When Beau Boutan, a vicious Cajun farmer, is found shot, the young white owner of the Marshall plantation, Candy Marshall, calls these aging black men to bring their guns and gather at the plantation before the whites demand "a nigger's blood." The story is told in a succession of voices, as each man explains the complex web of circumstances that drives him to take part in this ritual of resistance. The past weighs heavily on these men because each in his own way feels he has submitted to oppression. "We had all done the same thing sometime or another; we had all been our brother, sister, mama, daddy insulted once and didn't do a thing about it."

The most powerful moment in the novel occurs when the old men, each claiming to be the murderer almost as though he wants to assert that right, stand up to recite the wrong done to them, to acknowledge their complicity in a system of oppression and, in a sense, to reverse that history of themselves as failed men. Gable tells how they electrocuted his retarded 16-year-old son for allegedly raping a white woman: "Called us and told us we could have him at 'leven, 'cause they was go'n kill him at ten." Tucker tells how a white mob beat his brother Silas to the ground for defeating them in a contest between his mules and their tractor. Silas knew he was a nigger and was supposed to lose, and Tucker says he sold him out because he was afraid of the power of white men: "Out of fear of a little pain to my own body, I beat my own brother with a stalk of cane as much as the white folks did." Jacob Aguillard recalls: "It was me. . . . I remember what that crowd did to my sister." Another testifies: "I kilt him. . . . Me. What they did to my sister's little girl." A wall of old black men, each speaking his piece of history, a generation of black men living in the Jim Crow South, where the prerequisite for manhood was to break the law and where the price of one's dignity literally meant the willingness to offer one's life. Finally, these old men are prepared to stand against the white men's laws, to make history instead of lying passively beneath its flow.

I have often wondered how black people survived under Jim Crow in the years before the civil rights movement, when it seemed that they were constantly assaulted by laws, written and unwritten, which governed every aspect of their lives from how they were supposed to address a white person to where they could sit on a public bus. Richard Wright's "The Ethics of Living Jim Crow" suggests that many blacks internalized the submissiveness necessary to accommodate this system and stay alive. Black fiction writers have written about the Jim Crow South in two ways. They have written from the point of view of blacks who were trying to survive and who, in the process, created traditions that sustained and nurtured; or they have written, like Wright, of the power of whites not only to menace blacks but to define them.

Which viewpoint a writer selects is a critical esthetic and political decision. It is a tricky and complex issue, for blacks have always lived, as Du Bois pointed out, with that dubious gift of double consciousness, "this sense of always looking at one's self through the eyes of others." And in the South, where the brutality of whites was palpable, the question of viewpoint is all the more difficult. That artistic dilemma is posed in one of Alice Walker's stories of the South, "A Sudden Trip Home in the Spring." In it a young black artist is unable to paint the faces of black men until she resolves the question of who has the power to define:

The defeat that had frightened her in the faces of black men was the defeat of black forever defined by white. But that defeat was nowhere on her grandfather's face. He stood like a rock, outwardly calm, the grand patriarch of the Davis family. The family alone defined him, and he was not about to let them down.

Albert Murray, in *South to a Very Old Place*, also rejects white definitions of blacks:

When you heard them saying "boy" to somebody you always said mister to, you knew exactly what kind of old stuff they were trying to pull. They were trying to pretend that they were not afraid, making believe that they were not always a split second away from screaming for help. When they said Uncle or Auntie they were saying . . . you are that old now and more careful now so I don't have to be afraid any more. . . Their fears of your so-called niggerness became less hysterical not when they themselves grew up but when you grew older. . . . When some old chicken butt peckerwood says nigger this or nigger that naturally he wants to give the impression that he is being arrogant. But if you know anything at all about white folks his uneasiness will be obvious enough, no matter how trigger-bad he is reputed to be.

Gaines is most in touch with that black sensibility in *The Autobiography of Miss Jane Pittman* and in *Bloodline*. Jane Pittman's relationships to her husband, to her adopted son, Ned, and to the other people who live that hundred-year history with her are what establish her courage, her character and her identity. With his women characters Gaines seems freer to make those connections between character and community. But when Gaines considers the question of manhood (as he does in nearly all his stories), the arbiter of character is no longer the black community. In order to prove manhood, black men must stand up against white men, and the proof of their manhood is their ability to wrest respect from white men. All the passionate revelations in *A Gathering of Old Men* are made to the white sheriff, Mapes, and although the men are making their confessions to one another, the call and response is between the men and the sheriff.

What is even more disturbing than the white sheriff's dominant role is the subordination of women in this novel. The one woman who has a strong role is dismissed like a child. The white woman, Candy Marshall, the person responsible for the men assembling in the first place, is finally shown as just another threat to manhood. Women leading men is another form of slavery, so Candy must be eliminated. First she is warned by her black friend Mathu: "'I want you to go home,' he said. Not loud. Quiet. Soft. The way he used to talk to her when she was a little girl." That mild warning doesn't take because Candy is determined to retain her place of power in the men's world. In an act of public humiliation, she is carried off under her boyfriend's arm—at the sheriff's insistence and with the approval of all the black men—and is thrown, kicking and screaming, into her car. We are left at the end of this scene with a strange coalition: these elderly black men and a brutal white sheriff—bitter lifetime enemies—suddenly united in their antipathy for a strong woman.

Black women are just as effectively silenced. Of the fifteen voices joined to tell this story, only one is that of a black woman, Janey, and she is too hysterical to do anything but pray. No women are called to be a part of the resistance movement. The wives of the men involved play out the stereotype of the saboteur of the male quest for danger and glory. Failing to understand their men, they turn into distant and bitter shrews. Old Mat looks at his wife as he prepares to join his buddies and sees for the first time a stranger:

> I looked at that woman I had been living with all these years like I didn't even know who she was. My chest heaving, and me just looking at her like I didn't know who she was.... "All these years we been living together, woman, you still don't know what's the matter with me?"

Mat bitterly recounts the life they have lived under a system that has made him poor, cruel, angry and hopeless. But his anger and resentment are directed at her. Like the other old men, he leaves behind a confused, ignorant wife, cowed by this exhibition of manhood and unable to share in his political act.

These portraits of women leave me with a question I will not try to answer here. In exploring this vital issue of how black people can exert control over their history, why does Gaines so thoroughly deny the power of the women who contributed equally to that history? This disempowering of women compromises the novel's greatest strength—its recreation of the past through language. These communal voices constitute a kind of collective revision of history, giving proof in their own words of the existence of ordinary people whom the world noticed only briefly in the long-gone era of the civil rights movement. But in that revision, women are denied the right to suffer or to be heroic or even to claim the power of language.

Someone comes upon this strange scene of old men with shotguns and thinks how much like a Bruegel painting it seems—as weird as the paint-ing of Icarus falling out of the sky and disappearing into the sea while people who may have heard the splash continue with their everyday work. As W. H. Auden suggested in "Musée des Beaux Arts," suffering takes place while the rest of us are busy with our own lives—out having dinner or at a film festival. Ernest Gaines makes us witness the lives and suffering of people whose small acts of courage make up the history of the race. I only wish that *A Gathering of Old Men* acknowledged that half of those people were women.

Source: Mary Helen Washington, "The House That Slavery Built," in the *Nation*, Vol. 238, No. 1, January 1984, pp. 22–24.

Sources

Callahan, John F., "A Gathering of Old Men," in the *New Republic*, Vol. 189, December 26, 1983, pp. 38–39.

Forkner, Ben, "A Gathering of Old Men," in *America*, June 2, 1984, p. 425.

Price, Reynolds, "A Louisiana Pageant of Calamity," in *New York Times Book Review*, October 20, 1983, p. 15.

Review, in *People Weekly*, Vol. 20, November 14, 1983, pp. 24–25.

Tolnay, Stewart E., and E. M. Beck, *A Festival of Violence: An Analysis of Southern Lynchings, 1882–1930*, University of Illinois Press, 1992.

Washington, Mary Helen, "The House Slavery Built," in the *Nation*, January 14, 1984, pp. 22–24.

Further Reading

Babb, Valerie Melissa, *Ernest Gaines*, Twayne, 1991.
  This text is an analysis of Gaines's work in chronological order, with a chapter devoted to each novel. The emphasis is on Gaines's re-creation in writing of the oral storytelling intrinsic to rural Louisiana.

Estes, David C., *Critical Reflections on the Fiction of Ernest J. Gaines*, University of Georgia Press, 1994.
  This collection contains fourteen essays on all aspects of Gaines's work. On *A Gathering of Old Men*, Sandra G. Shannon writes about Gaines's "defense of the elderly black male," and Milton Rickels and Patricia Rickels discuss folk humor in the novel.

Gaudet, Marcia, and Carl Wooton, *Porch Talk with Ernest Gaines: Conversations on the Writer's Craft*, Louisiana State University Press, 1990.
  This work consists of interviews with Gaines conducted in 1986 and 1987, which explore his development as a writer and the process of transforming folk narrative and culture into literature.

Papa, Lee, "His Feet on Your Neck": The New Religion in the Works of Ernest J. Gaines," in *African American Review*, Vol. 27, No. 2, Summer 1993, pp. 187–93.
Gaines's novels focus on religion as a tool for self-definition, and he reinterprets Christianity from the African-American perspective. A number of characters, including Charlie Biggs from *A Gathering of Old Men*, interpret religion in personal terms and undergo an act of martyrdom that helps achieve a communal vision.

The Godfather

Mario Puzo
1969

As soon as it was published in 1969, Mario Puzo's novel *The Godfather* began setting sales records, becoming the fastest selling book up to its time. Its enormous popularity increased in 1972 when Francis Ford Coppola's movie version was released. The movie won several Academy Awards, including one for Coppola and Puzo's script adaptation of his novel. It is one of the highest-grossing movies of all time and is frequently cited by critics as one of the greatest American movies ever made. It has spawned two highly-respected sequels, both co-scripted by Puzo. The novel has consistently stayed in print and has sold over 21 million copies worldwide.

The story revolves around Vito Corleone, a leader of organized crime in the 1940s. He is a man who rules with quiet persuasion, asking those who wish favors from him for their loyalty and dealing mercilessly with those who cross him. When other criminals try to involve his organization in the drug trade, Corleone resists and the shield of power that he has built around his family is threatened. The aged crime lord must defend his family and pass control of his empire to one of his three sons.

This book helped define how the world views organized crime in America, framing the aspects of greed and violence that are inherent in the underworld with an emphasis on family, respect, and honor. The character of Vito Corleone, the Godfather, has been compared to Huckleberry Finn and Holden Caulfield as an archetype, a personality so true to the American experience that, though fic-

tional, he seems familiar to everyone. Far beyond being just another crime novel, *The Godfather* relates to all stories of immigrant families who are trying, over the course of generations, to fit into the mainstream of American life.

Author Biography

It is no coincidence that *The Godfather* turned out to be a bestseller: Mario Puzo, its author, planned from first to last that the book would be popular and make him money. Puzo was born October 15, 1920, to a family of Italian immigrants, and he spent his childhood in the Italian ghetto of New York called Hell's Kitchen. He was a young boy when he decided to be a writer, but he was discouraged in this by the family's impoverished circumstances. His mother aspired for him to work for the railroad, like his father and brother.

The tension between the life of a writer that Puzo wanted to lead and the traditional working class life that his family was steering him toward was broken by America's entry into World War II in 1941. During the war, stationed in Europe, he lived the life of freedom for a while, drinking and gambling and spending money freely on girls. While in the army, he married Erika Lina Broske. He returned to civilian life five years later and settled into a civil service job. He still wrote short stories and published them once in a while.

Puzo's first novel, *The Dark Arena*, was published in 1955, ten years after the war ended. It was a personal story, based on his experiences during the war. The novel gained him some critical acclaim—for example, Maxwell Geisher noted in the *Saturday Review* that "It is a very good novel indeed, and one reads it with the sense of discovery and pleasure that a new talent evokes." Puzo was disappointed to find that critical acclaim did not assure him economic independence: he only made $3,500 for that novel and $3,000 for his next book, *The Fortunate Pilgrim*, published in 1964.

Puzo was forty-five years old and owed more than $20,000 to friends and relatives when an editor from G. P. Putnam overheard him telling stories that he had heard throughout his life about the Mafia and offered him an advance of $5,000 for a book about the underworld. The book that Puzo wrote went on to sell more than 21 million copies. Although he did not become rich from *The Godfather*, he used his fame as a springboard to the kind of wealth of which he had always dreamed. His ex-

Mario Puzo

perience in cowriting the movies based on his novel led to a career as a screenwriter, with acclaimed scripts like *Superman* and *Superman II*, *Earthquake*, and *Christopher Columbus: The Discovery*.

His subsequent novels were, like *The Godfather*, designed to make the author rich. They included *Fools Die*, about professional gamblers (one of Puzo's strongest passions in life was high-stakes gambling) and *The Sicilian*, which was based on the true story of a notorious Italian bandit, incorporating several characters from *The Godfather* into its plot. All of Puzo's later books reached the bestseller lists, and all except the posthumously published *Omerta* have been adapted to film. He died of heart failure on July 2, 1999, at the age of 79.

Plot Summary

Book I

The Godfather opens in 1945, at the wedding of Connie Corleone, the only daughter of Vito Corleone, the head of the most powerful organized crime family in the United States. During the wedding, Corleone, respectfully referred to as the Don or Godfather, is obliged to meet with people who seek his help. As the novel explains, "by tradition no Sicilian can refuse a request on his daughter's wedding day." One man's daughter was raped, and he asks Don Corleone to punish the rapists; another man needs political support so that his daughter's fiancé will not be deported; another, the Don's actual godson, is a famous singer whose career will fail if he does not get the movie role that a Hollywood producer has refused to him.

The long wedding sequence is used to introduce the main characters. Don Corleone's oldest son, Sonny, is a hot-tempered ladies man; Fredo is a weak-willed drunkard; and his youngest son, Michael, has disappointed his father by staying out of the family business and joining the army. Michael is at the wedding with his girlfriend from college, Kay Adams, who does not know that the family is into organized crime until he tells her some chilling stories about other wedding guests. Other important characters include Tom Hagen, the Corleone family's adopted son, who serves the Godfather as a counselor in criminal activities, and Clemenza and Tessio, the captains in the Corleone army.

As soon as the wedding is over, Don Corleone takes his sons to visit his old friend and counselor, Genco Abbandando, who is dying in the hospital. That same night, Hagen is sent to California to make the movie producer give the required role to his godson, Johnny Fontane. While they are talking, the producer shows Hagen a beautiful race horse that he has bought. He says that he is sorry that he cannot cast Johnny in the movie. The next morning, the producer wakes to find the horse's severed head in his bed, and, realizing the ferocity and stealth of the Corleone crime family, he arranges to cast Johnny.

A meeting is arranged with Virgil Sollozzo, a drug dealer who wants the Corleone family to be partners with him. Don Corleone says that he will not be involved with drugs, but during the meeting Sonny shows interest.

Three months later, an assassination attempt is made on the Don's life. He survives, but while he is in the hospital, another attempt is made. Michael, who is visiting at the time, manages to scare off the assassins. A meeting of family officials determines that Sollozzo the drug dealer will stop at nothing to kill the Don. Michael, who has stayed out of the family business, is the only one who can get close enough to Sollozzo to kill him; he shoots him dead in a restaurant and goes into exile in Italy.

Book II

Book II follows Johnny Fontane's life in Hollywood. Taking the advice of the Don, he has left his second wife, who committed adultery, and has established a platonic relationship with his first wife and their two daughters. Tom Hagen comes to California to offer Johnny money to start his own production company.

Book III

Book III starts with Vito Corleone's childhood: as a boy named Vito Andolini in Corleone, Sicily, he was forced to flee to America when a local Mafia chief ordered his entire family killed over an insult. Later, in New York, Clemenza and Tessio taught Vito crime, and he showed his capacity for violence by killing a gangster who tried to rob him. His reputation rose as he did favors for the people in the neighborhood, asking only their friendship in return. His business grew as he imported liquor during Prohibition, helped elect politicians, and established gambling syndicates.

Book IV

The gang war that began when the Don was shot continues, with Sonny leading the Corleone family against the other families of New York. Detectives visit Kay Adams in New Hampshire to ask if she knows Michael's whereabouts. They tell Kay that Michael killed Sollozzo and the police officer that was with him, and they threaten to tell her father, a minister, that she and Michael stayed in hotels together. When they do tell Kay's father, the minister stands up for his daughter.

One day, Connie Corleone's husband, Carlo Rizzi, beats her up. When she calls the family house in Long Island, Sonny hears what happened, and he drives off toward their apartment in Manhattan in a rage. The family's enemies catch him in a trap and kill him in a hale of bullets.

Book V

After the death of Sonny, Don Corleone leaves his sick bed and returns to business. He arranges a summit with the heads of crime families around the country and negotiates an end to the gangland war. The Corleone family loses power and prestige, but the Don insists that the other families allow Michael to return to America in peace. A plan is devised to have another man who is already sentenced to death confess to the murders Michael committed.

Lucy Mancini, whose affair with Sonny began at the wedding of Connie and Carlo, has been sent to Las Vegas after his death. There, she meets Dr. Jules Segal, a brilliant surgeon. They start an affair, and he diagnoses a physical abnormality that prohibits her from having a satisfying sex life. He operates on her to fix the problem.

Book VI

In Sicily, Michael comes to appreciate the culture of his father's people. He falls in love with a local girl, Apollonia, courts her according to ancient Sicilian custom, and marries her. One day, when they are going on a trip, she decides to drive the car. Michael sees his bodyguard sneaking away seconds before the car explodes, killing his bride.

Book VII

Years after she last saw him, Kay Adams calls the Corleone house to find out that Michael has been back home for six months. They meet, renew their relationship, and marry.

In Las Vegas, Dr. Segal is introduced to Johnny Fontane and determines that his weak voice is not caused by years of smoking and drinking, but by warts on his larynx. He performs a very simple operation to remove them and Johnny's singing career is revived.

Michael goes to Las Vegas and offers to buy a casino from Moe Greene, for whom his brother Fredo has been working. He is rejected, and later Moe Greene is murdered. The Don, working in his garden one morning, suffers a massive heart attack and dies. Michael tells Tom Hagen that the head of a rival family will try to kill him, that the person who approaches him with a deal from his rivals will be a traitor. The next day, Tessio calls to arrange a peace meeting.

Book VIII

On the day that Michael stands as godfather at the baptism of Connie and Carlo's child, all of the family's enemies are murdered. These enemies include Tessio, the bodyguard from Sicily, rival mob bosses Tattaglia and Barzini, and Carlo Rizzi, who admits to having helped enemies trap Sonny. When Connie accuses Michael of being involved in Carlo's death, he lies to her and Kay.

Book IX

The Corleone family is restored to the position of most powerful crime family in America. Kay has converted to Catholicism. She leaves Michael and moves back to New Hampshire. Tom Hagen comes

out to tell her that Michael is willing to give her anything she wants to ensure their children's welfare. While there, he explains the pressures Michael lives with as the new Don, how it was his responsibility to kill Carlo and Tessio, as traitors. She ends up returning to him, burying her sorrows by going to daily mass and praying for Michael's soul.

Characters

Kay Adams

Kay is Michael Corleone's college sweetheart, a Protestant girl from New Hampshire whose upbringing is distinctly different from Michael's. At the wedding in the beginning of the novel, Michael tells her stories that only hint at the family business until, when pressed, he openly admits the atrocities committed by Luca Brasi in the family's service. When Michael is forced to leave the country, Kay remains faithful for a long time, expecting him to call, even as months pass. She keeps in touch with his mother for some time but lets the relationship cool. After a year, she calls Mrs. Corleone and finds out that Michael is back in America. When Kay goes to the Corleone house, she and Michael resume their affair and eventually marry. In the end, Kay knows that their relationship is based on lies, and she ends up praying for Michael's soul, the way that his mother did for his father's soul.

Vito Andolini

See Vito Corleone

Luca Brasi

Luca Brasi is the most vicious murderer in the underworld. He is entirely devoted to Don Corleone, although he is the one person in the world that the Godfather fears. When an attempt is made on Don Corleone's life, the members of the family fear that they would not be able to stop Luca from hunting down and killing those responsible. Brasi, however, has been ambushed and killed before the attack on the Don.

Peter Clemenza

Clemenza is one of the Corleone family's two *caporegimes* or captains. He is an old friend of Don Corleone, the person who first brought him into a life of crime in America, enlisting the young Vito Corleone to hide illegal guns and then, later, to help him with robberies. It is very seldom that Clemenza

Media Adaptations

- *The Godfather* was adapted as a film by Francis Ford Coppola in 1972. Starring Marlon Brando as the Godfather, Al Pacino as Michael, James Caan as Sonny, and Diane Keaton as Kay Adams, it is considered one of the greatest American films of all time. Mario Puzo co-wrote the Academy Award–winning script with Coppola. It is available on home video from Paramount.

- Many critics prefer the moral complexity of *The Godfather, Part II*, which was also written by Mario Puzo and Francis Ford Coppola and directed by Coppola. The major characters returned, with Robert De Niro playing young Vito Corleone in scenes from the novel that were left out of the first movie. Released in 1974, it is also available on home video from Paramount.

- None of the scenes from the novel is dramatized in the 1990 movie *The Godfather, Part III*. It picks up the story nearly twenty years after the close of the last installment, with Michael Corleone trying to get out of crime and make the family empire legitimate. The film stars Pacino, Keaton, Andy Garcia, Sofia Coppola, Joe Mantegna, and Eli Wallach. The script was co-written by Puzo and Francis Ford Coppola, with Francis Ford Coppola directing. It is available on home video from Paramount.

- All three Godfather films are available together in one deluxe DVD box set, with deleted scenes, full commentary by Coppola, sections of Puzo's script, interviews with key production people, and an option to watch the story in chronological order, starting in 1909 when young Vito Andolini leaves Sicily (which originally did not appear until the second movie). It is available from Paramount.

- An abridged audiocassette version of *The Godfather*, read by Joe Montagna, is available from B & B Audio, released in 2001.

is referred to without any mention that he has grown fat in his old age.

Apollonia Vitelli Corleone

While hiding out in Sicily, Michael falls in love with Appollonia and marries her. Within a few months, she is killed by a car bomb that was meant to kill Michael.

Connie Corleone

The Don's only daughter, his favorite child, tries to hide the fact that her husband beats her, worried that her father or brothers will have him killed. Throughout the novel, Connie does what she can to make her family accept Carlo, and when he is murdered she is devastated.

Costanzia Corleone

See Connie Corleone

Freddie Corleone

See Fredo Corleone

Fredo Corleone

Fredo is Don Corleone's middle son, the one with the weakest personality who is least influential in the family business. He is present when the Don is gunned down in the street, and suffers a nervous breakdown because of it. During the gang war that follows, Fredo is sent to Las Vegas to recover. Working in a casino brings out Fredo's true personality: he goes from being shy and awkward to being a suave ladies' man. Don Corleone disapproves of his constant sexual activity, and of the fact that he allows the casino owner to humiliate him in public, but Fredo's familiarity with Las Vegas's legalized gambling business makes him valuable to the family's plans to relocate in Nevada.

Michael Corleone

Michael is the focus of this novel, the character that undergoes the most severe change. In the beginning, he is distant from the family's organized crime business, having displeased his father, Vito Corleone, by going into the service during World War II. He is a distinguished war hero, but Don Corleone feels that he is wrong to fight on the behalf of strangers, and not for his family. Michael tells his girlfriend Kay of his family's past, but swears to her that he has nothing to do with the family business.

His attitude changes on the night he visits his father, who has been shot down in the street, and finds him alone and in need of protection. His father's enemies have bribed the police to leave Don Corleone unguarded, and it is only through Michael's help that he is not murdered. That night, a corrupt policeman breaks Michael's jaw, leaving him disfigured for years, mirroring the change that occurs in his heart. Soon Michael decides that the only way his father can be protected is if he himself kills the men threatening him.

After becoming a murderer, Michael goes to Italy to hide. In the land of his father, he comes to understand the old traditions in an entirely new way. He experiences some of the magic of the land when he is struck with love at first sight for a local girl whom he marries, but the country's violent history also becomes clear when she is killed in an attack meant for Michael.

After returning to America, Michael aspires to raise the Corleone empire out of organized crime and into legitimate businesses. He does this by planning, with the help of his father, the murders of the heads of the other crime families. The intelligence and strict morality that kept Michael out of organized crime in the beginning are applied to running the Corleone family the way that his father ran it.

Santino Corleone

Santino Corleone, called Sonny by everyone but his father, is the Godfather's firstborn child, and is generally expected to be the one to take over the family business. He is tall and muscular, intelligent, and ruthless enough to run the crime family, but he has a hot temper that takes control of him at times, making him dangerous. In a meeting about a new drug trade, for instance, Sonny blurts out his interest, leading the drug smugglers to attempt murdering Don Vito Corleone so that they can make a deal with Sonny. After a second attempt is made on the Don's life, Sonny impetuously orders murderous raids against members of rival families, driving the whole underworld deeper into a bloody war that has the public up in arms. In the end, Sonny dies because of his hot temper: he races out of the house without the protection of his bodyguards because he is infuriated with Carlo Rizzi, giving his enemies a chance to shoot him down when he is alone.

Sonny Corleone

See Santino Corleone

Don Vito Corleone

Vito Corleone is the novel's title character, the most powerful person in organized crime in America. He arrived in America at age twelve, orphaned after a local Mafia chief in Corleone, Italy had his entire family killed over an argument. Growing up in New York, Vito Corleone witnessed the workings of the local crime syndicate in the early decades of the twentieth century. At twenty he killed a gangster who threatened him, starting a career in crime that expanded with wise decision-making and a calm, quiet demeanor that never allowed for making decisions in haste or anger.

Although he is willing to use criminal means to achieve his goals, Don Corleone owes much of his power to the loyalty he has gained by doing favors for people over the course of many years. He is called by the honorary titles of Godfather and Don by those who respect and fear him. He is old fashioned and straight-laced about personal matters, disdainful of drugs and excessive alcohol consumption, and prudish about sex. The Godfather is seen by many in the novel as a sort of godly figure, one who has the power to punish the evil, reward the good, and who is willing to enact justice violently when conventional means are not reliable.

The novel establishes Don Corleone's method of operation in his meeting with an undertaker whose daughter has been raped: he will not agree to kill the rapists because, as he later explains to an assistant, "we're not murders"; also, he will not accept money from the undertaker, but only asks his promise for some favor in return sometime in the future. The rapists are later beaten brutally, giving the undertaker a feeling of justice that a supposedly legitimate society denied him.

Don Corleone's style of making people feel personally indebted to him becomes a key factor in the novel's plot: his enemies, realizing that much of the Corleone family's political influence comes from people's feelings about the Don himself, try to kill him in order to take over the Corleone family empire. When he is hospitalized after being shot, his sons are left to determine how he would handle the situation. The family business is in disarray until the Don is well enough to negotiate a peace settlement. When he retires and puts his son Michael in charge, his enemies feel that the Corleone empire will collapse without the charismatic and wise old man in charge.

Johnny Fontane

Johnny Fontane actually is Vito Corleone's godson, and so the Don has a special fondness for him. He is a successful singer at the start of the novel, with girls screaming and fainting when he opens his mouth to sing. When he comes to

Connie's wedding, Johnny is desperate. His voice is ruined, but he thinks he could have a good movie career if he could be cast in a new war movie. Don Corleone arranges for him to get the part, and he suggests that Johnny give up his show business lifestyle of drinking and womanizing. Johnny divorces his acrimonious second wife and establishes a good relationship with his children and his first wife. After the war movie is a success, making him a major movie star, the Corleone family invests in a production company that Johnny is to run, and the movies he produces turn out to be financially lucrative.

Later in the novel, Johnny becomes acquainted with Dr. Jules Segal, who is the house physician at the Las Vegas hotel where Fredo Corleone works. Hearing the raspy sound of Johnny's voice, Segal examines him and finds that the problem is relatively minor: he has warts on his vocal chords, which are easily removed. In addition to his film career, Johnny ends up having a successful singing career again.

Paulie Gatto

Paulie is a hood who is supposed to act as Don Corleone's driver. After finding out that Paulie called in sick on the day that assassins tried to kill the Don, Sonny finds out that Paulie has received suspicious phone calls, and so he has Clemenza kill him.

Tom Hagen

Soon after the start of the novel, Tom Hagen rises to be the Godfather's *Consigliori* or counselor. Hagen was raised by the Corleone family after Sonny Corleone found him wandering the streets as an orphan and took him home. Raised as one of Vito Corleone's sons (Michael even introduces him as "my brother"), he has been to law school and is a practicing lawyer, even though Don Corleone is his only client. Hagen's high position in the family business is so unusual for a non-Italian that members of the other crime families refer to the Corleones as "the Irish gang." When Sollozzo thinks that he has murdered Don Corleone, he has Hagen kidnapped, and explains that his deal makes sense, convincing Hagen to talk to Sonny about forgetting revenge and accepting the business proposition. Hagen feels self-conscious and doubts his ability to fill in for Genco Abbandando, the Godfather's former *Consigliori*, especially when Sonny is killed during a gangland war, but Don Corleone has complete faith in him. He is relieved of his position only when the family is planning to get out of organized crime and must separate Hagan from any illegal activities.

Lucy Mancini

Lucy starts out as Sonny's mistress and, over the course of the novel, blossoms into a smart businesswoman. Sonny Corleone meets Lucy Mancini when she is the maid of honor at his sister's wedding. At the wedding they start their affair, which continues throughout the gangland wars, with him visiting her while bodyguards are posted in the street outside the door. After his death, she feels that she will never be satisfied by another lover, but when Dr. Jules Segal sleeps with her, he realizes that she has a physical problem that can be fixed by relatively minor surgery. He operates on her, and they later marry.

Captain Mark McCluskey

After Michael foils an attempt to kill his father while he is in the hospital, Captain McCluskey shows up with a legion of police officers and threatens to put Michael in jail of he does not leave immediately. Michael insinuates that McCluskey works for his father's enemy, the Turk, and McCluskey is so insulted that he hits Michael, breaking his jaw. The Corleones soon find out that McCluskey does indeed work for the Turk, that he is hired to be his bodyguard, and that any attempt to kill the Turk would mean killing McCluskey. Killing a New York City Police Captain is an unthinkable crime, one that would cause problems throughout the underworld all over the country. Michael does kill them both, though, leaving some enemies to assume that he has acted out of a foolish need for vengeance against the man that disfigured him.

Albert Neri

When he takes charge of the family business, Michael brings in Albert Neri to be his bodyguard. Neri is unfamiliar to the traditional family loyalists, but he turns out to be a ruthless killer, like Luca Brasi.

Carlo Rizzi

Carlo comes from Nevada, and so he looks down at the old-world ethnics of the Corleone family. After marrying Connie, he is disappointed with the relatively small position the family provides for him. He takes his frustration out on Connie, beating her when she is pregnant and sleeping around with other women. After Sonny dies as he is coming to kill Carlo, his behavior becomes much better, and he is accepted into the family business, only to be murdered later for setting Sonny up.

Connie Rizzi

See Connie Corleone

Dr. Jules Segal

Dr. Segal is the house doctor at the Las Vegas hotel where Fredo Corleone and Lucy Mancini work. He is a brilliant surgeon who became an abortionist because he was discouraged by seeing the people he operated on returning to their destructive lifestyles. When he was run out of New York for being an abortionist, the Corleone family protected him and assigned him to the hotel position. In the novel, he diagnoses the problem with Johnny Fontane's vocal cords and with Lucy Mancini's sex organs, operating to cure them both. At Johnny's recommendation, he supervises the surgery to reconstruct Michael's broken face, making sure that the lead surgeons will not try to cause him harm.

Virgil Sollozzo

Sollozo is a heroin smuggler known as "the Turk." He asks for Don Corleone's help in setting up a major heroin operation in the United States. When the Don refuses to become involved in the drug trade, Sollozzo, thinking that Sonny might be interested if he were in charge of the family business, tries to have the Don executed. When two murder attempts fail, he arranges a meeting with Michael in order to negotiate a peace settlement. At that meeting, Michael kills Sollozzo.

Sal Tessio

Tessio is one of the Corleone family's two *caporegimes*, or captains. Tessio has a division of men in Brooklyn and is kept distant from the family in order to surprise the family's enemies. Of the two *caporegimes*, Tessio is often referred to as the smarter one. Michael takes particular note of Tessio's intelligence at the end of the book when, after Don Corleone's death, he makes a deal with the family's enemies to betray Michael.

Themes

Freedom

At a meeting with the heads of crime families from all over the nation, Don Corleone coins a phrase for the underworld that Puzo says will one day be as famous as the expression "Iron Curtain" that Winston Curchill used to describe the separation between communist and democratic countries.

The phrase, *cosa nostra*, means "our land," and the Don uses it to explain that he and his peers are free to live by their own rules, required to follow no laws. It occurs in the sentence, "We will manage our world for ourselves because it is our world, *cosa nostra*." In the same speech, he says, "We are all men who have refused to be fools, who have refused to be puppets dancing on a string pulled by the men on high."

It is a noble sentiment, and certainly one that gains more sympathy from the reader than would be gotten if Don Corleone said that he ran his criminal empire to make money. In this book, money is no object in itself, nor are the things that money can buy. The purpose for amassing wealth is the freedom that wealth brings. In the 1960s, particularly, when this book was published, freedom was a goal that seemed impossible. The government was seen as an obstacle to freedom since laws are written precisely to tell people to behave in certain ways. *The Godfather* takes the extreme view that the rulers of organized crime are and should be free of the rules that bind lesser persons.

God

Throughout this novel, there are indications that Don Vito Corleone is a supernatural force with powers to rival God. The first and most obvious hint of this is his nickname, Godfather, which combines the power of the Almighty with the benevolence of a patriarch. He uses his power like a god would, carefully concerned that his actions are just, that his power is not misused or abused. When Bonasera asks him to kill the men who raped his daughter, for instance, he asks the Godfather for the Old Testament sense of justice—an eye for an eye—which the Godfather is willing to give him, but only when Bonasera bows before him. Then, the Godfather gives a speech about why the justice he dispenses is more powerful and fair than that which is applied by the judicial system. He takes the god like position that justice is his to hand out or hold back, telling Bonasera, "consider this justice a gift from my wife."

The reach of the Corleone family is presented in terms that seem almost mystical. For example, in the real world, it is unlikely that one could enter a man's house and put the bleeding head of a horse into his bed without his noticing it, but Puzo presents the story of Jack Wolz, the movie producer, as if it is a sign that Don Corleone can have miracles performed whenever he should want to.

Topics for Further Study

- Conduct a mock trial of Michael Corleone for the shooting of Virgil Sollozzo and Captain Mark McCluskey. Have legal teams from each side present the best case for their point.

- Research the Corleone section of Sicily where Michael was sent into hiding. Report on how the government has dealt with the Mafia in the time since the novel took place.

- When this book was released, Italian Americans were upset because they felt it presented organized crime as a specifically Italian problem. Its defenders said that this closed community was based in historical truth. Write about one commonly held ethnic stereotype, research its base in reality, and judge whether you think it is realistic or not.

- In the book, Fredo Corleone is sent away to recover from a nervous breakdown while control of the family business passes from Vito to Sonny to Michael. Write a short story showing a day in Fredo's life if he had taken over.

- Write out the lyrics to a song that glorifies the gangster lifestyle. Explain how you think that, aside from the music, Don Corleone would respond to the ideas expressed in the lyrics.

In addition to being just and nearly omnipotent, Don Corleone has a strict moral code, which makes him turn down a lucrative drug deal. Tom Hagen even tries unsuccessfully to hide the fact that Sollozzo made money in prostitution, knowing that it will dissuade the Don from the current offer. Sexual infidelity, as practiced by his sons Sonny and Fredo, angers him. He does not obey the Ten Commandments of the Bible, but instead makes his own rules, with his own definition about whether he and his operatives are "murderers" or not.

While most of the people who come into contact with Don Corleone stand in awe of his godlike power, the one who is most awed by him is Genco Abbandando, his *Consigliori*. As his oldest friend, Genco should be the character most poised to see him as human: instead, he expects the Godfather to have power over death itself. "Godfather," Genco implores him, "stay here with me and help me meet death. Perhaps if He sees you near me, He will be frightened and leave me in peace."

Guilt and Innocence

Even though real-life criminals are responsible for injustice and suffering, readers tend to ignore the fact that the members of the Corleone family are guilty criminals. For one thing, Puzo sets up their opponents in all cases to be even worse persons, guilty in their own way and deserving of the fates that are brought down on their heads. For instance, Jack Wolz, the movie producer, shouts ethnic slurs and has an affair with a pubescent girl; Captain McCluskey actually is a crooked cop mixed up in the rackets, as the newspapers are ordered to portray him, and he also disfigures Michael by shattering his jaw; Fanucci, the first man Vito Corleone kills, is a weak man who pretends to be ferocious. In the moral universe established by the book, the Corleone's and their henchman seem almost obligated to use violence in enacting what can be interpreted as justice on their despicable victims. The actions taken by the idealized crime syndicate in the book are only taken against those who seem to deserve them.

The guilt of the Corleones's victims is often presented from the perspective of the criminals, as when Don Corleone muses on the relative innocence of those who enjoy the vice of gambling. But there are also times when Puzo's narrative helps readers see the ugly, repulsive aspects of those who are to suffer at the hands of the mob. He even has Tom Hagen explain to Kay why all of the people killed in the massive execution at the end of the book got what they deserved.

Family

Several times in the book, Puzo explains that the order of succession in the crime family is not necessarily hereditary. None of the laws of the organization requires that the person to rule the Corleone family after Vito would have to be Sonny, Fredo, or Michael. The use of the word "family" in the syndicate hierarchy is symbolic. At the same time, though, Puzo presents the Corleones as having the type of family structure that would ensure that the family business would stay with them.

At the beginning of the novel, there is a rift in the family. Fredo and Sonny work for their father, but Michael is trying to keep his distance. He does not approve of the family's involvement in crime, and his father does not approve of the fact that he enlisted to serve during the war. Their differences turn out to be slight, though, when danger arises. Michael runs to his father's side when he is in the hospital, and, when it is determined that there is no other way to protect his father, Michael volunteers to commit murder.

Subsequent to the murder, Michael is forced to spend time in the Corleone province of Sicily, the land where his father grew up. He comes to understand his father as a peer, and not just as an imposing authority figure. They have personality traits in common, such as cool heads and impeccable logic.

Critics have said that the true genius of the book is Puzo's way of melding the strong sense of family that pervades Italian families, and most immigrant families, to the structure of an organized crime unit. Everything becomes personal, an act of loyalty or betrayal, when crime partners are thought of as family. Family members become vulnerable when they are involved with crime.

Style

Antagonist

Throughout most of the book, there is no particular antagonist to create dramatic tension in the story. The Corleone family does have enemies who create danger for them, but the circumstances are all small and separate from one another, and so they are taken care of one at a time. The greatest danger in the beginning of the book comes from Virgil Sollozzo, the drug smuggler who tries to kill Don Corleone, but he is killed relatively early. After that, the danger to the family is indistinct. Puzo explains that members of the five families pose a serious threat, and they finally do kill Sonny, but they are given no clear identity.

It is not until the book is nearly two-thirds over that Puzo introduces the enemy, Don Emilio Barzini, at the conference of Dons. Barzini's support of Sollozzo and of the war against the Corleones is not made clear until late in the book. Their lives are fraught with danger, and that danger emanates from Barzini, but readers are not told who it is who has put Don Corleone's life in danger until the novel is nearly over.

Antihero

An antihero is a main character that lacks the qualities traditionally associated with heroism, but that frustrates the audience's or reader's judgement of him/her with elements of sympathy and mock heroism. Michael Corleone does have quite a few traditional heroic qualities: he is brave, he is loyal, he is willing to face death calmly. He is even referred to several times as a "war hero," and has been pictured in *Life* magazine because of his courage during combat. The novel reverses these aspects of heroism when Michael, the traditional hero, is turned into a murderer and a criminal while still being portrayed as admirable. Readers are expected to empathize with his decision to join the family business, realizing that Michael is putting the safety of his father and all those who work in his operation over the lives of outsiders, and over the security of a crimeless life.

According to traditional morality, a murderer could never be considered a hero. In the 1960s, however, films and literature began to focus on those outside of conventional moral judgement, to make audiences appreciate the stories of those who previous generations might have rejected. In 1966, for example, Truman Capote wrote *In Cold Blood*, giving the perspective of two amoral mass murders; Warren Beatty's 1967 film *Bonnie and Clyde* focused on a pair of desperate criminals; Sam Peckinpah's 1969 film *The Wild Bunch* followed a gang of violent outlaws as they made their last stand. It was not a time for heroes, but rather of tearing apart expectations of what a hero really is and reformulating them to fit the modern world. If a traditional hero could not be a murderer, then Puzo's portrayal of Michael serves to make audiences reexamine what they think of heroism.

Mythology

A mythology is a collection of myths that has been transferred verbally from one generation to the next. Most mythologies are well known in a culture before anyone writes them down. People usually think of such tales as having happened long ago: for instance, the myths that surround King Arthur and the Knights of the Round Table constitute a specific mythology. In the case of *The Godfather*, Mario Puzo set out to record the mythology of organized crime as he had heard it while growing up in New York. Many of the stories that he tells are *apocryphal*. That is, they probably are not true, but they sound so likely that people continue to tell them anyway.

For instance, the proposed custom that no Sicilian can refuse any request on the day of his daughter's wedding could not work in real life—what if someone asked the father of the bride for the deed to his house, or to do himself harm? Other stories in the book are the stuff of legend, such as the horse's head in the bed, the message of sending a fish in Luca Brasi's vest, and the massive extermination of the heads of all crime families in one day. These stories, in addition to many smaller tales that fill in the details of the Corleone saga, are based on stories that have been told, and Puzo weaves them all together into one compelling narrative. The irony is that his mythic organized crime family influenced the way that true criminals behaved. After the book and movie became popular, FBI wiretaps captured cases of real-life gangsters using phrases like "I'll make him an offer he can't refuse" or saying that somebody "sleeps with the fishes," phrases that Puzo had made up to imitate the gangsters.

Subplot

Readers of *The Godfather* who are familiar with the movie adaptations are often surprised about the book's long digressions into the lives of Lucy Mancini, Johnny Fontane, and Fontane's friend Nino Valenti. These stories, which take place in Nevada and California, are related to the Corleone family saga only because the characters have been in contact with the Corleones. Lucy moves to Las Vegas because Tom Hagen arranges it, but her medical condition and her affair with Dr. Jules Segal (who was also sent to Las Vegas by the Corleone family) have nothing to do with the main plot about Vito Corleone and Michael; Johnny Fontane's relationship with his ex-wife Ginny was suggested by the Godfather, but during their scenes together the Corleone family never comes up. Nino's closest connection to the main story is that his singing and film career is due to Johnny, who was encouraged by Don Corleone to help him. The Corleone saga would go on without any change if these subplots were left out of the novel.

And yet, the fact that they are there can be used to reveal facets of the main plot that might otherwise go unnoticed. When Johnny Fontane stabilizes his family life and ends up a better man for it, readers can see that Don Corleone's emphasis on sober family life really is a prescription for happiness. Nino, on the other hand, is like Sonny, a man who has all that he needs for greatness but ruins it because of his stubborn personality. Lucy in some way exemplifies the life that Michael hopes for

them all at the end of the novel. Moving to Nevada, Lucy leaves the world of crime behind her and finds true love to replace the dangerous affair that mystified her in New York. Readers might feel that these subplots are not worth the time they take from the main story, but they do add texture to the central plot line.

Historical Context

Organized Crime

Mario Puzo has said that he wrote *The Godfather* as a compendium of tales about criminals that he heard while growing up in Hell's Kitchen, an Italian section of New York City, along with information that he gleaned from research. Fans of the book often try to guess which real-life incidents served as Puzo's inspirations, but in fact much imagination has gone into transmuting history into fiction.

Like Vito Corleone, many of the most powerful figures in American organized crime at the middle of the twentieth century had made their fortunes during Prohibition, smuggling liquor into the country. In 1920, the production and consumption of alcohol was prohibited by the passage of the Eighteenth Amendment. There was still a great need for alcohol, and America had a prospering economy during the 1920s, and so it became a lucrative business to smuggle liquor in from Canada, Mexico, and Cuba. Small-time gangs rose during this period to national prominence. Pressure from the FBI to combat the rise of organized crime in the twenties only eliminated small operators—J. Edgar Hoover, the FBI's director, refused to acknowledge widespread syndicate activity until the late 1950s. Government pressure drove the small operators to seek protection under the umbrella of more powerful organizations. In 1933, Prohibition was repealed, in part because of the criminal activities that it caused and in part because the nation had entered an economic depression in the late 1920s and control of a popular substance seemed a silly and wasteful way to spend government resources. Like the fictional Corleone family, the crime organizations put the money they had made into other activities, most notably gambling, extortion, and political influence.

Control of organized crime passed through the ranks of different immigrant groups. In the early decades of the century, mobs were predominantly Irish. During Prohibition, Jewish and Italian immi-

Compare & Contrast

- **1940s:** American support for American involvement in World War II is overwhelmingly strong. The Godfather's anger that his son enlisted in the war is extremely unusual.

  1960s: American support for American involvement in The Vietnam War becomes weaker every day. More and more people sympathize with those who would like to keep their sons out of military service.

  Today: The United States has not drafted soldiers into military service since 1973.

- **1940s:** Women have a narrow, specific place in society. There are only a few professions, such as nurses and teachers, which are deemed appropriate for them.

  1960s: Women are in the midst of the struggle for liberation, so that social laws and prejudices will not limit their potential.

  Today: Women are accepted in most professions and activities, although there are still a few areas where disparity between the genders exists.

- **1940s:** Motion picture studio bosses have performers under strict contracts and can prohibit actors who are out of favor from working.

  1960s: Performers in motion pictures are free agents and can sign deals to work where they please.

  Today: Many top performers have formed their own production companies and in essence work for themselves.

- **1940s:** The American economy is one of the few in the world that was not wrecked by World War II, making this the land of prosperity.

  1960s: By the end of the 1960s, the U.S. economy is booming. Unemployment is at the lowest level it has been at since 1954, and the stock market has reached record highs.

  Today: The country has gone through a long period of prosperity in the 1990s but has cooled to modest levels.

- **1940s:** The government is concerned that communist agents are trying to subvert the American way of life.

  1960s: The government is concerned that agents of the Black Panthers and the Students for a Democratic Society are trying to subvert the American way of life.

  Today: The government is concerned that terrorists are trying to subvert the American way of life.

---

grants rose to control. After Prohibition, the crime organizations in the New York area were under the control of Italians, and these in turn organized a national syndicate, led by Charles "Lucky" Luciano. The organization of this syndicate was patterned after a centuries-old Sicilian paramilitary organization, the Mafia. Because the Italians were the most powerful group in the post-World War II period, when senate hearings on organized crime were televised, their group came to be associated with crime. This is a narrow impression that was cemented in the public imagination in the 1970s by the widespread popularity of *The Godfather* and its many imitators.

In 1931, in the midst of the Great Depression, the Nevada legislature passed a resolution allowing legal gambling in the state. After World War II in 1946, notorious gangster Benjamin "Bugsy" Siegel built the Flamingo Hotel with the financial backing of the East Coast syndicate. From this first casino came others, and the town grew into one of the nation's most popular vacation resorts in just a few short years. From its inception in the 1940s through the 1970s, Las Vegas was under the control of powerful crime organizations like the ones described in *The Godfather*.

While many of Puzo's details about organized crime are probably based on information readily available from research, there are specific incidents in the book that resemble events in crime history. The shooting of Don Corleone while he stands at a fruit stand is similar to the murder of Frank Scalise in 1957. The Godfather's political power, referred to so often in the book, mirrors the political control wielded by New York mobsters Thomas Lucchese and Frank Costello throughout the 1940s and 1950s. The story of Johnny Fontane being helped by Don Corleone and Luca Brasi to break his contract with bandleader Les Halley is based upon a common rumor that is probably not true, regarding Frank Sinatra's difficulty freeing himself from bandleader Tommy Dorsey when he was a young singer.

The Counterculture

In this novel, the Godfather is angry with his son, Michael, for having joined the Marine Corps during World War II. Puzo explains that arrangements were made for Michael to be exempt from military duty, along with mob operative Paulie Gatto and most of the other young men involved in the Corleone family operation. When the book was published in 1969, the country was enmeshed in the Vietnam conflict, a battle to keep the Russian-backed Communist government of North Vietnam from overcoming South Vietnam. It was a conflict that American soldiers had been involved in since 1961, regarding a political situation that had been unsettled since the 1940s.

To U.S. government strategists, it was imperative to stop the spread of communism in southeast Asia, and an American defeat would be too humiliating to accept. Therefore, the war escalated with each passing year. To many citizens, especially those on college campuses, American citizens were dying in order to win a pointless war in an unimportant, far-off country. The antiwar movement grew throughout the mid-1960s, with war protests covered almost daily in the media as celebrities and musicians spoke out against the military. Military-aged young men were encouraged to burn their draft registration cards and to sneak across the border into Canada, where the armed services could not get them.

Even though the youth of the country might have agreed with the Godfather on the subject of military service, there were also changes in the culture that would have shocked him. In the novel, he refuses to become involved in the drug trade, and in fact is shot for his resistance to it. In 1969, drug use ran rampant: marijuana was accepted as a casual recreation, and LSD was recommended by some as a consciousness-raising experience. As Harvard professor Timothy Leary advised in his 1965 book *The Psychedelic Reader*, "turn on, tune in, drop out." 1969 was also a high point for the sexual revolution. For the previous generation, sexual relations outside of marriage did happen, but they were socially frowned upon. In the 1960s, though, sexuality became more open. Women protested for equal rights, and homosexuals protested to show their resistance to persecution. The "straight-laced" values held by Don Corleone were giving way to radical new ways of thought throughout American society, while old-fashioned readers who bought *The Godfather* in 1969 could see the gentleman gangster of its title as a protector of traditional morality.

Critical Overview

Early reviews of the book acknowledged its potential for popular success while at the same time praising Puzo for his understanding of the Mafia culture. Pete Axthelm wrote in *Newsweek*,

> This is a big, turbulent, highly entertaining novel with ingredients that should assure its place on the best-seller lists: ample sex, a veritable orgy of bloodshed in many exotic forms, and several characters titillatingly reminiscent of real-life public figures.

In the *Nation*, Fred J. Cook called it a "brawling, irresistible tale" that "brings the reality [of Mafia life] home more vividly and realistically than the drier stuff of fact ever can." Cook went on to write that the book's "sexual scenes, plots and counterplots, murder and gore ... might have made it a work of cheap sensationalism, but *The Godfather* is deeply embedded in reality, and this sense of reality pervades the torrent of unending action."

As time passed, and the novel racked up record sales figures, reviewers began to de-emphasize Puzo's grasp of the nuances of the Mafia culture, especially when he publicly admitted that the book was based on no firsthand experience, that he had imagined the organized crime hierarchy and the attitudes taken by Vito Corleone and his family from research materials he had read. By 1972, when the motion picture version was released, the book was still selling briskly, with five million paperback copies and a million hardcovers sold (eventually, total sales of the book would reach the twenty-one million mark).

While Puzo's public comments made it difficult for other writers to cast him as a Mafia expert,

The Corleone family: Al Pacino (left) as Michael, Marlon Brando as Don Vito, James Caan as Sonny, and John Cazale as Fredo in the 1972 Academy Award–winning Part 1 of the Godfather *film trilogy*

they also made it difficult to approach *The Godfather* as a serious piece of literature. In an article titled "The Making of *The Godfather*," published in his 1972 collection *The Godfather Papers and Other Confessions*, Puzo lamented that he did not really write the novel as well as he could have:

> [*The Godfather*] got much better reviews than I expected. I wished like hell I'd written it better. I like the book. It has energy and I lucked out by creating a central character that was popularly accepted as genuinely mythic. But I wrote below my gifts in that book.

With the author himself admitting that his book is not a very fine accomplishment, it becomes difficult for reviewers to praise it. Many reviewers since the early seventies have quoted Puzo's regrets about the quality of *The Godfather*, and have gone on to examine it as a publishing phenomenon, speculating about what that says about American culture.

Like Puzo, most reviewers have pinned the source of the book's overwhelming popularity on the character of the Godfather himself, Vito Corleone. Barton Midwood examined this in his review in *Esquire*, in which he discussed an educated friend who could not put the book down specifi-

cally because, as he explained, "'this Godfather character is really fantastic.'" On his friend's recommendation, Midwood explained, he read the book himself: "As I had suspected, it is bad. . . . The prose has a moronic sound, and the whole affair is calculated to prey on the uglier prejudices and pathetic longings of an impotent public. The character of the Godfather is, however, as Wilson says, 'fantastic.'"

Other late reviewers, responding to the book after it had been out for a while and accepted by the public, showed interest in the fact that millions of presumably law-abiding citizens were drawn to the life story of an arch criminal. John C. Cawelti, questioning what the book's popularity says about American culture for the intellectual magazine *boundary 2*, examined Puzo's use of the metaphoric "family" to talk about social order. Cawelti's article granted that Puzo was skillful, and that he "brilliantly" developed the idea of family in his book. "[O]ne doesn't need much prescience to predict that this book will be a major turning point in the evolution of popular literature," Cawelti wrote in 1975, not even a decade after the book's publication, "perhaps comparable to the significance of Conan Doyle's Sherlock Holmes, certainly as important as Ian Fleming's James Bond." The longer the book has been around, the more likely reviewers have been to accept Puzo as a skilled artisan, just as the early reviewers did.

There has been, however, one more school of thought on the subject. None of Puzo's later novels reached either the popular success that *The Godfather* reached or the artistic success that reviewers often implied that he was capable of, leaving some later reviewers to conclude that Puzo was, in fact, an untalented writer who just happened to do one thing right once. This view was clearly explained by Allen Barra in a 2000 article for the online magazine *Salon*. Reviewing Puzo's last book, *Omerta*, which was published posthumously, Barra failed to recognize talent in any of the author's novels. "Somehow, a myth grew that he was a serious novelist who turned to writing commercial crap because his early books didn't sell," Barra wrote. He continues saying:

> This is classic self-delusion. Puzo's first two novels . . . weren't that good. In fact, they weren't as good as *The Godfather*, which itself would be unread today if people didn't go to it looking for a deeper relationship with the movie.

While Barra's comments may not be true, they do reflect the disappointment of the literary community that Mario Puzo never supported his reputation by writing anything else as powerful or engaging as *The Godfather*.

Criticism

David Kelly

Kelly is an instructor of creative writing and composition at Oakton Community College in Illinois. In the following essay, Kelly argues that, in spite of its popularity and technical achievements, irregularities in point of view make Puzo's novel weak.

Mario Puzo's 1969 crime epic *The Godfather* was hugely popular, shattering the sales records of its time. In addition to the number of books put into circulation, it created a trend in novels about organized crime, packing the paperback book racks at airports and drugstores with imitators, each using a copycat book design and using the word "father," "family," or "honor" in its title. But, beyond its popular success, it is not clear whether *The Godfather* succeeds as literature.

Of course, the two are not mutually exclusive—something can be popular and still be artistically worthwhile—but it is very seldom that a writer can achieve one without sacrificing the other. Books that attract millions of readers tend to have fans who see something of themselves in them. These fans are willing to see great merit even when it is not present, like parents who cannot concede that their perfectly nice children lack talent. On the other hand, artistic snobbery is real and powerful in building and destroying literary reputations: most artists starve, so the novels that do make money are automatically suspected of being hollow imitations of the real thing.

Making it even more difficult to judge the worth of Puzo's book is the fact that it was adapted to a movie that pleased everybody, critics as well as audiences. In the American Film Institute's list of top movies ever made, it comes in at number three, after *Citizen Kane* and *Casablanca*; it is number 121 in the list of all-time box-office grosses, and has been a consistent seller in video and DVD releases. As a result, literary critics have a tendency to think that the novel's continued success is less a result of its own merit, and rather a case of riding on the movie's coattails. One critic even guessed that because the movie's director Francis Ford Coppola co-wrote the screenplay with Puzo and the movie contained the book's best lines, the good parts of the book were actually Coppola's writing, even though the book was published and selling millions of copies before the two ever met. The book and the film of *The Godfather* will always be linked and the film will always be considered the greater artistic achievement. Coming in second in a field of two makes it difficult to judge Puzo's novel fairly.

The most accurate way to describe *The Godfather* artistically as a novel would be to say that it is quite good for a sensationalistic potboiler that was churned out to make money, and that it is quite weak as a serious document of the time it examines or the intricacies of human nature. Its virtues are many: its shortcomings are few, but they are serious enough to hold the book back from true greatness.

Puzo's finest achievement, the one that kept millions of readers turning each page, was his gift for giving each character more personality than just what the book's plot requires of them. His characters have depth: to use a publicist's phrase, they "jump off the page." The smaller, minor characters in any novel are bound to be stereotypes, but Puzo gives all, down to the least significant, some aspect that contradicts their stereotype, hinting at a full, breathing person passing through the story. Kay's father, for instance, only appears in the book for a few pages. He is a New England minister who is approached by the police about his daughter's involvement with organized crime and sexual relations with a suspected murderer. A less intelligent book would have made him act according to type, blowing up with anger or curling with hidden rage. Puzo has him behave with unexpected gentleness toward his daughter and firmness toward the police, giving readers a sharp little surprise without violating what little we know about this man. From the baker who is delighted with his little part of a Mafia wedding to Neri, the family-oriented hit man, the characters have a human touch that takes them beyond just being tools of the plot.

At the next level of characterization Puzo has the three Corleone boys. Independently, none is able to blossom beyond a flat characterization, but it is Puzo's luck or genius to have them all packaged together as a group. Sonny nearly reaches the depths of a vaudevillian comic character with his hot-blooded Mediterranean passions: swarthy, oversexed, and impetuous, he seems more like the sort of character that would be created by someone who had never met a real live Italian. Michael, of course, is the diametric opposite. He is never spontaneous or passionate: when after years he is reunited with the woman he loves, he suggests physical intimacy with, "We might as well go in the bedroom." Readers often wonder why Puzo took the time to create the third son, Fredo, who does little in the book but suffer a nervous breakdown and then turn into a womanizer who lets another gangster slap him around. His presence serves to mute the extremes of the other sons: rather than focusing on how, compared to each other, Michael and Sonny are almost unbelievably absolutes, readers focus on how the two sides contrast with the soft, amoral center.

The greatest creation of Mario Puzo's writing career is, without question, the character of Don Vito Corleone. He is all things to all people. He is a law-giver, an old-world moralist, a devout family man who loves his children and goes out of his way to help neighbors, asking only friendship in return; but, he is also a murderer and the criminal mastermind who controls everyone's lives to some unseen extent. Sentimentalists can love him as much as paranoids can fear him.

> **Puzo uses shortcuts that help him in the short term— tricks that the casual reader will not recognize but which, in the long run, damage the novel's literary worth."**

Over and above his memorable characters, Puzo also distinguishes himself with his superb sense of narrative structure, often underrated. *The Godfather* is not episodic, following just one crisis after another in the life of the Corleone family, but instead it follows a solid, direct line from Vito Corleone at his peak to the events that bring Michael into the family business to Michael's final triumph. This story is fed out slowly, though, so that readers do not even see it taking form at first. The main conflict, which is the gang war started by Sollozzo, does not show up until the long wedding has introduced the characters and the episode with Jack Woltz and the horse's head has established the family's omnipotence. Then, it is introduced subtly, as just another piece of crime business, with little indication that the meeting with Sollozzo will change the Corleone family forever. Puzo holds back Michael's importance to the plot even longer: before he ends up helping his father avoid assassins, a quarter of the way through the book, it would be difficult to guess that Michael would end up the story's main character. This pacing lets Puzo unleash powerful plot twists throughout the whole book that readers note, only after they have occurred, were inevitable all along.

Though the pacing is masterful and the characters are convincing representations, neither is achieved completely through skill. Puzo uses shortcuts that help him in the short term—tricks that the casual reader will not recognize but which, in the long run, damage the novel's literary worth.

For instance, he makes the Godfather a respectable, honorable, lovable character only by going to preposterous extremes to shade the world in which he lives. Not only does the book refuse to question whether running a crime syndicate might be wrong, it will not even admit that there could be cases where the Don's actions are anything less than angelic. The characters who oppose the Corleones suffer, but they deserve what they get, due to their moral weaknesses: this goes from the Tattaglias, who are involved in "bad" crimes such as drugs and prostitution instead of the Corleones's gambling, extortion, and influence peddling, to Johnny Fontane's first wife, who has not only violated the sanctity of marriage by luring him into divorce but is in addition a foul-mouthed tramp.

The Corleones's friends are shown to be just as innocent as their enemies are despicable. They include: Lucy Mancini, the concubine with a heart of gold; Jules Segal, an unerring and compassionate surgeon driven to abortions when he can not stand delivering terrible medical news to uncaring patients; and the widow Columbo, whom young Vito Corleone rescues from eviction. Puzo is able to make these characters contemptible or sympathetic, according to their place in the Don's universe, only by using verbal tricks—loaded language, such as when he describes Don Fanucci as "white, broad [and] smelly" just before Vito shoots him. Casual readers accept the idea that there is no moral complexity among the Corleones's friends and enemies. Attentive readers know that they are being sold an unlikely version of reality.

Technically, Puzo's greatest weakness is in his inability to hold a consistent point of view. The point of view changes every few pages: the action in a scene with Don Corleone and Tom Hagen might be from the Don's point of view, but then the narrative stays with Tom when he leaves and tracks his thoughts. This is acceptable, but it waters down the book's overall effect. Readers are not able to experience the action through any one character's eyes, so they cannot truly feel the effects of the action as they would with a unified narrative. With the point of view floating around like this, the emphasis is on the action and events, not the characters, whom readers come to know only superficially.

There is a way to stay in one character's point of view and convey another character's unspoken thoughts, by having the main character interpret what is going on in the other's head. Puzo does this frequently. For instance, when Kay phones Michael's mother, "Mrs. Corleone's voice came impatiently over the phone." Two paragraphs later, "Mrs. Corleone's voice came briskly over the phone." The narrative remains in Kay's point of view, but readers still know how Mrs. Corleone feels.

Puzo stretches this technique to its limits at times. For example, he has Johnny interpret Jules's thoughts: "Jules stood up. His usual cool was gone, Johnny Fontane noticed with satisfaction." Later in the scene, though, Puzo uses one character's looks to give background information that is in the minds of *two* characters: "Lucy and Jules looked at each other. From everything they had learned and knew about Johnny Fontane it seemed impossible that he would take a girl from a close friend like Nino." Johnny's thoughts are interpreted by Jules and Lucy simultaneously. Later that scene shifts to Johnny's point of view again. The information is conveyed, but Puzo sacrifices artistic consistency in order to let readers know what everyone thinks about everything.

It takes time to develop a consistent point of view, to introduce information into a novel in ways that could be experienced by just one character at a time. Mario Puzo apparently knew how to do this, but did not take the time. It also takes time and patience to face up to the fact that one's sympathetic characters can be acceptable to audiences in spite of their moral shortcomings, rather than simply ignoring the moral complexity of life. Puzo wrote *The Godfather* with the specific interest of creating a best seller and making money, and that he did: any variation on the formula might have hurt sales. But he also was quoted as saying that he wished he had written it better, and there is little doubt that he could have. The flaws in the novel are unnecessary, technical ones, but ones that keep it from greatness.

Source: David Kelly, Critical Essay on *The Godfather*, in *Novels for Students*, The Gale Group, 2003.

Fred L. Gardaphe

In the following essay, Gardaphe discusses the impact of The Godfather, *and considers what would happen in a case of reverse assimilation.*

The Godfather is Mario Puzo's third novel. His earlier novels represent his attempts to fulfill a dream of becoming an artist and escaping the ghetto world in which he was born. Like Fante, di Donato, and Mangione, Puzo's early encounter with such writers as Dostoevsky in his local library strengthened his belief in art and enabled him to "understand what was really happening to me and the people around me." It was not art, however, but war that finally enabled Puzo to escape his environment "without guilt." Out of his experiences in Europe during and after the Second World War he crafted his first novel, *The Dark Arena* (1955); ten years later he returned to his life experiences growing up in New York's Little Italy to create *The Fortunate Pilgrim* (1965). In *The Dark Arena*, the protagonist, Walter Mosca (in Italian, *mosca* means "fly"), returns home from serving with the American occupation army in Germany. Unable to take up where he left off before the war, Mosca returns to Germany as a civilian employee of the occupation government and resumes his life as a black marketeer. While the novel received some good reviews, Puzo was disappointed that it did not make much money. *The Fortunate Pilgrim* received similar notices and brought Puzo even less financial reward. Because of the poor sales of his earlier works, no publisher would advance him the money he needed to write a third novel. Twenty thousand dollars in debt, he began to look for a way out. "I was forty-five years old," he writes, "and tired of being an artist."

With the publication of *The Godfather* in 1969, Mario Puzo was immediately promoted to celebrity status. Not since the publication of Pietro di Donato's *Christ in Concrete* had an American author of Italian descent been thrust into the national spotlight on such a grand scale. The timing of *The Godfather*'s publication had much to do with its rapid climb to number one and its sixty-seven-week stay on the *New York Times* best-seller list. The novel came off the press in the middle of the ethnic revival period of the 1960s. It also followed nationally televised congressional hearings on organized crime and the publication of Peter Maas's nonfiction bestseller *The Valachi Papers*, in which mobster-turned-informer Joe Valachi describes his activities inside organized crime.

The Godfather has done more to create a national consciousness of the Italian American experience than any work of fiction or nonfiction published before or since. It certainly was the first novel that Italian Americans as a group reacted to, either positively or negatively, perhaps because it appeared at a time when Italian Americans were just beginning to emerge as an identifiable cultural and political entity. Even though this book is much more a work of fiction than any of the earlier, more autobiographical novels written by Italian Americans, it created an identity crisis for Italian Americans throughout the nation. Antidefamation groups denounced Puzo for creating a bad image of Italians in America; young Italian American boys formed "Godfather" clubs; and real mafiosi claimed that Puzo knew what he was writing about. For a while, Puzo wrote a number of essays on the subject of Italian America which appeared in major national magazines. These essays, while often

> **In other words, in this novel Puzo presents the question that in effect is the real Italian American dream: What if America assimilated to our ways?"**

undermining the image of Italians that he created in *The Godfather* and his later novel *The Sicilian*, are also quite critical of the Italian American's behavior in American society.

The effect of this one novel was tremendous. Since its publication, and especially since its film adaptations in the early 1970s, Italian American novelists have been writing in *The Godfather*'s shadow, and Puzo has become a recluse. Though sociologists and literary scholars may forever debate the value of Puzo's work, most would agree that he has left a permanent imprint on the American cultural scene through his representation of *Italianita* and his creation of a mythic filter through which Italian American culture would henceforth be read.

In "The Authority of the Signifier: Barthes and Puzo's *The Godfather*," Christian Messenger reads *The Godfather* through Roland Barthes's essay "Myth Today" for the purpose of determining the role that myth plays in the production of popular culture. Messenger points out that while the Corleone family "appeared to be a protofamily for our collapsing time," it also set up a false dichotomy between good murderers and bad murderers. Messenger reads Puzo's symbolizing as signifiers of a mythic language that result from artificially naturalizing history, a process that Barthes says is the function of myth. Messenger's reading of key scenes in the novel makes clear "the dialectal flow between naturalizing and historicizing" that Puzo's narrative obscures. *The Godfather* portrays the Mafia as a natural force in the Sicilian world from which Vito Corleone comes, a world he attempts to re-create in his new home in America. In this world the Don and his family are portrayed as the "good guys," and the American establishment with which they struggle—the institutions of law and business—are set up as the "bad guys." Messenger suggests that the key question asked by the novel is raised by Jack Woltz and Kay Adams: "What if everyone acted that way?" This question can guide us through a reading of the novel as an exercise in the portrayal of reverse assimilation. In other words, in this novel Puzo presents the question that in effect is the real Italian American dream: What if America assimilated to our ways? Before setting up this approach to reading *The Godfather*, let me first point to some of the aspects of the novel that can be connected to more traditional Western myths.

The Don's system of belief is based on the idea that each man has but one destiny. The Don's own destiny was determined when he killed Fanucci, the thug who extorted money from local merchants and demanded tribute from any criminal activity that took place in his neighborhood. When Fanucci demands a percentage of Vito's and his partners' crime, Vito decides to kill him. "It was from this experience came his oft repeated belief that every man has but one destiny. On that night he could have paid Fanucci the tribute and have become again a grocery clerk. . . . But destiny had decided that he was to become a Don and had brought Fanucci *to* him to set him on his destined path." Similarly, each of the Don's sons is seen as having his destiny determined by a single incident. Santino (Sonny), the oldest son, is destined to follow his father's ways, not only because of birth but, according to the Don, because he witnessed his father's shooting of Fanucci. Michael Corleone's destiny is revealed the night he shoots Sollozzo and the police captain. Fredo's position outside the inner workings of the family business is determined by his inability to defend his father during the assassination attempt.

Puzo borrows a figure from ancient mythology to describe the Don's children. Daughter Connie has a "Cupid-bow mouth." Sonny is described as having the face "of a gross Cupid." His large penis signifies his Dionysian behavior, which interferes with his ability to concentrate on the family business. Ruled by his emotions, Sonny is unable to become a good don. Fredo has "the same Cupid head of the family" and lacks "that animal force, so necessary for a leader of men." Predictably, Michael is the only child not described in terms of Cupid.

Throughout the novel the Don is characterized as a god or demigod who can negotiate affairs between humans and the supernatural. This is under-

scored by the hospital scene in which Genco Abbandando lies on his deathbed crying out, "Godfather, Godfather . . . save me from death. . . . Godfather, cure me, you have the power." The Don replies that he does not have such powers, but if he did, he should "be more merciful than God." Genco then appeals to the Don to stay with him as he faces death: "Perhaps if He sees you near me He will be frightened and leave me in peace. Or perhaps you can say a word, pull a few strings, eh?" When he is not being a god, Don Corleone is portrayed as a heroic figure who is able to struggle with the gods. Puzo characterizes Don Corleone as a rarity, a man of will, a man among "men who refused the dominion of other men. There was no force, no mortal man who could bend them to their will unless they wished it. They were men who guarded their free will with wiles and murder."

In the Don's speech to the heads of the other crime families after the murder of Sonny, he attempts to make peace through an appeal to the American Dream, but the whole speech is an example of *bella figura*, a public posturing designed to shield his true plans and to present the illusion that he is willing to assimilate to the American ways of doing illegal business:

> Let me say that we must always look to our interests. We are all men who have refused to be fools, who have refused to be puppets dancing on a string pulled by the men on high. We have been fortunate here in this country. Already most of our children have found a better life. Some of you have sons who are professors, scientists, musicians, and you are fortunate. Perhaps your grandchildren will become the new *pezzonovanti*. None of us here want to see our children follow in our footsteps, it's too hard a life.

The Don uses his power to make friends who will strengthen his position. His competitor, Sollozzo, is driven by the opportunity to make money through the high profits of drug manufacturing and distribution; however, he lacks a key ingredient for insuring the venture's success—the Don's friends in high places. This is the clash between the Old World sense of power bringing wealth and the New World's sense of wealth bringing power. Thus, when the Don pledges not to seek revenge for Santino's murder and to support drug trafficking, he does so because he sees that the only way to keep his family intact is to ensure Michael's safe return from Sicily. After this speech, the Don returns home and announces his semiretirement and his plans to stay home and work in his garden. But he can do this only because he knows that Michael will take over the business and enact the Corleone family's revenge.

What Do I Read Next?

- Puzo is often considered to have been a serious, artistic writer before he "went commercial" with the publication of *The Godfather*. Readers can judge this for themselves by reading his 1955 novel *The Dark Arena*, which was reissued by Ballantine Books in 1999.

- Among Puzo's other novels, *The Sicilian* comes closest in tone and subject matter to *The Godfather*. It opens when Michael Corleone is exiled in Italy. Before returning home, the Godfather asks him to find legendary bandit Salvatore Guiliano and bring him back to America. The book tells the story of Guiliano, who is based on an actual person. Published in 1984, it was reissued by Ballantine in 2001.

- One of the few academic studies of *The Godfather* is Christian K. Messenger's *Citing the Don: Mario Puzo and the Meanings of an American Popular Classic*. It was published by State University of New York Press in 2002.

- Giuseppe di Lampedusa's *The Leopard (Il gatto pardo)* is a hauntingly beautiful historical novel about Sicily. Lampedusa, himself a Sicilian prince, based his book on his great-grandfather and the turbulence that overcame Sicily as the aristocracy lost power. This book is essential reading for understanding the country and its people. It was published in 1958 and reprinted in 1998 by Pantheon Books.

- The same year that *The Godfather* was published, 1969, Peter Maas was on the best-seller lists with *The Valachi Papers*, the biography of Joseph Valachi, a true gangland boss whose life was similar to Don Corleone's. This book, now out of print, was published by Bantam Books.

- In 1999, Peter Maas wrote *Underboss: Sammy The Bull Gravano's Life in the Mafia*. This book, an "as-told-to" story by a crime operative that turned state's evidence, is full of details about how the underworld works today. It was published by HarperCollins.

- One of the most respected books in the overcrowded category of true stories about organized crime is Gay Talese's *Honor Thy Father*. Published by Ballantine in 1971 as part of the wave of interest in crime that *The Godfather* fostered, it is the true story of Joe Bonanno, one of the most notorious New York mob bosses.

Ironically, Michael, the son destined to take over the Don's power, is the one closest to total assimilation into American life. At the outset of the novel, Michael breaks the code of *omertà* by letting Kay Adams in on the history of his father's business. During his sister's wedding reception Michael tells stories about the more colorful wedding guests, like Luca Brasi. He explains to Kay what is going on at the meetings held inside his father's study and interprets the ambiguities she, an outsider, is unable to read. Later, on the night that his father is shot, Michael leaves Kay and returns to the family house, and "for the first time since it had all started he felt a furious anger rising in him, a cold hatred for his father's enemies." This fury drives Michael back into the family fold and leads him to avenge his father's shooting.

Up to this point, Michael has been as innocent as the women in the Corleone clan. He has been kept out of the family business and has had a hero's upbringing, the American equivalent of an aristocrat's education, with knightly training in the marines through which he achieves heroism during the war. His military service is part of his attempt to Americanize himself: It represents loyalty to a power that is not Sicilian and rebellion against his father's wishes, as the Don realizes: "He performs those miracles for strangers." Michael's murder of Sollozzo and the police captain takes place under the fated circumstances of an Orestes. His ancestral culture's code demands vengeance for his father's blood, and Michael acts accordingly.

After the murder, Michael flees to Sicily, that otherworldly ground of his being and his subconscious—a locus for so much of Western mythology. There he meets the characters who embody the new condition of his soul, which is physically manifest in his disfigured face. He learns the history of Sicilian culture and the role the Mafia has played in it through Dr. Taza: "He came to understand his father's character and his destiny . . . to understand men like Luca Brasi, the ruthless *caporegime* Clemenza, his mother's resignation and acceptance of her role. For in Sicily he saw what they would have been if they had chosen *not* to struggle against their fate." His bodyguards, like mythological dogs, defend him against the wolves (strangers outside the circles of family and friends) through their use of *lupara*, or "wolf guns." He meets Apollonia, his anima—the pure, good, noble, and beautiful, full of pietàs and innocence. This all takes place in the pastoral setting so thickly described by Puzo during the couple's first meeting and throughout their brief marriage. When Apollonia dies, the victim of a car bomb intended for Michael, it is because he is set on the course that kills the innocence and dirties the moral cleanliness inside himself. She dies in his place as the part of himself that his own actions kill. Her very name and physical appearance signify the *chiaroscuro* contrast, the Apollonian/Dionysian dichotomy that the new Michael has become. Their relationship is typical of the male/female social dichotomy in Sicilian culture in which the woman holds the good, the man shoulders the evil. As Don Corleone earlier reminded his godson Johnny Fontane, women "are not competent in this world, though certainly they will be saints in heaven while we men burn in hell."

While the typical successful hero in traditional myth returns from the otherworld strengthened and complete, Michael returns to America with nothing but a memory of the values represented by Apollonia. Instead of becoming a savior of American society as a fully realized human being, he returns and grows stronger as a monster; a hero in his family's society, he becomes a villain in American society. Unlike Orestes, he never receives the deus ex machina-like compassion of an intervening Athena to save him according to traditional myths. The education Michael receives during his exile in Sicily enables him to take command of his father's kingdom and ruthlessly rule it in the Old World manner.

While there is much in this novel that lends itself to interpretation through traditional myth analysis, Puzo also develops something that transcends the archetype approach. What Puzo has con-

tributed to Italian American culture is a myth of the assimilation of America into Italian culture. Vito Corleone's goal is to render powerless the forces that attempt to control him. And he does this by recreating the Old World in the midst of the New.

Many people read *The Godfather* as an allegory of a decadent America in the postwar period. But the novel can just as well be read as the struggle to protect a family and preserve it, no matter the cost, in a hostile environment. If the family is to be preserved, assimilation into American culture must be avoided, and this can be done only if the exact opposite happens; that is, if America assimilates into the culture of the Don and his family. Thus, the novel can be read as proposing the following question: What would happen if an Italian had the power to make America conform to his or her way of seeing/being in the world? In order for this to occur, the Italian would need to create an alternative world within the world, a world that competes with the American world, one that offers a viable alternative. It is inevitable that when these two worlds come into conflict with each other, the subsequent tension often erupts into violence.

The world that Don Vito Corleone replicates in America is built on the solid foundations of a centuries-old social order in which fate or destiny, more often than not through birth, determined the life an individual would lead. In the feudalistic system of Sicily and southern Italy, the peasant could not hope to aspire to a better life by challenging the forces that controlled his life. As a result, attention was focused on what could be controlled, the family unit. This is the reason so many Italians immigrated to America. The world into which they came had been built on the myth that through freedom, people can become whatever they want if only they work hard enough. This puritanical work ethic and the built-in reward system did not require the family to stick together, and often it led to the breakup of the nuclear family.

The Don's Old World notion of a work ethic requires that the family stick together, and any attempt by an individual to leave threatens the livelihood of the entire family. In fact, if a family is to survive with its Old World values intact, it must work against assimilation and strive to have its surrounding environment conform to the family's way of life. Thus, the central conflict of this novel is how to keep the family together for its own good in a land where people no longer depend on the family unit for survival. This conflict is introduced through the opening vignettes in the Don's office.

Amerigo Bonasera's family was harmed through the American youth who beat up his daughter, Johnny Fontane lives a mockery of a marriage to a Hollywood star, and to protect his family's honor the baker Nazorine must find a way for his helper, Enzo, a prisoner of war about to be deported, to marry his daughter. All three men have found success by adapting to the American way of life, but when the New World system fails them, when the nuclear family has been threatened or attacked, they return to the Old World through Don Corleone, just as villagers returned to the castle for protection from invasion during feudal times. In return for his assistance, Don Vito requires "that you, *you yourself* proclaim your friendship"; in other words, that you conform to his way of life. In this way Corleone not only perpetuates the Old World system but also further insulates and protects his own family. In many ways, Don Corleone is like the king of feudal times who offers protection to those whose problems he has helped to create. His consigliore, Tom Hagen, realizes this: "It was a pattern he was to see often, the Don helping those in misfortune whose misfortune he had partly created. Not perhaps out of cunning or planning but because of his variety of interests or perhaps because of the nature of the universe, the interlinking of good and evil, natural of itself." The Don, because he is the center of the world he has re-created in America, is like God who makes all things, good and evil, and is the force that is cursed as it is praised by those who live under his dominion. And so, Bonasera, Nazorine, Fontane, and most of the novel's other characters are monologic, all pieces in the puzzle Puzo produces, which reveals the power of Old World culture to maintain itself in a New World environment. Don Corleone is more concerned with maintaining *l'ordine della famiglia* and expanding its power than with increasing his profits; that is what he transfers to his son Michael, who has become Old World through his exile in Sicily. Michael achieves what Sonny and Fredo cannot because they lack the experience of life in the land of Mafia origins, an experience that would have balanced their beings. The Don does what he believes is necessary for men's families to thrive. He leads his godson, Johnny Fontane, back to taking care of his family and his friends through Nino. He will ensure through an act of Congress that Nazorine finds a good husband for his daughter. And his men will enact the vengeance that Amerigo Bonasera needs in order to return honor to himself and his family.

There are numerous examples of the Don's ability to make America and Americans assimilate to his ways. Tom Hagen, a German American orphan brought into the Don's home, is raised as one of his own, educated in the American system all the way through law school. Given this opportunity to become a successful American, Hagen opts instead to complete his assimilation into the Don's world. "'I would work for you like your sons,' Hagen said, meaning with complete loyalty, with complete acceptance of the Don's parental divinity." Later on, the Don remarks, "Even though you're not a Sicilian, I made you one." Yet, in spite of Hagen's near-native knowledge of Sicilian ways—he is the one able to read the Sicilian sign of the fish wrapped in Luca Brasi's bloodstained vest and is appointed acting consigliore on Genco's death—and because he is not of Sicilian blood, not "born to the ways of *omertà*," he is relegated to marginal status when Michael takes over. Tom breaks the code of *omertà* at the end of the novel when he explains to Kay why Michael had to kill Connie's husband, Carlo. It is as though Vito Corleone is a Midas whose very touch turns people into Sicilians. In spite of the power that the movie producer Jack Woltz has gained in the American system, he too must assimilate to the Don's world, he must give in to the Don's wish that his godson Johnny Fontane get the role that revives his film career and his loyalty to the family. It is Don Vito whose subtle machinations remind Johnny of how he neglected his responsibilities to help his boyhood friend and *paesano* Nino. The Don provides Johnny with the means to succeed, and ironically it also becomes the means by which Nino is destroyed.

The character who best illustrates this reverse assimilation hypothesis is Kay Adams. Kay, who can trace her ancestral lineage to the *Mayflower*, embodies all that is American, and her assimilation into the Corleone family is the strongest evidence of reverse assimilation. When Michael brings her to his sister's wedding, he does so to "show his own future wife to them, the washed-out rag of an American girl." He sits with her "at a table in the extreme corner of the garden to proclaim his chosen alienation from father and family." When the Corleones meet her they are unimpressed: "She was too thin, too fair, her face was too sharply intelligent for a woman, her manner too free for a maiden. Her name, too, was outlandish to their ears. . . . If she had told them that her family had settled in America two hundred years ago and her name was a common one, they would have shrugged." No matter how much he loves and trusts Kay, Michael

Marlon Brando as Don Vito Corleone in Part 1 of the film trilogy

realizes that she is an outsider when he sees her after his father has been gunned down. Michael does tell her enough about his father to give her the opportunity to back out of the relationship, but she does not. Even when she finds out from Michael's mother that what she had heard about Michael is true, she still holds on to the hope that she will see Michael again. Two years go by and Kay finds work teaching grade school, and she decides one day to call Mrs. Corleone. While talking to her, Kay finds out that Michael has been back in the country for six months. She becomes angry with Michael, his mother, and "all foreigners—Italians who didn't have the common courtesy to keep up a decent show of friendship even if a love affair was over," yet still accepts Mama Corleone's invitation to visit her at the Corleone home. During their reconciliation, Kay tells Michael he could have trusted her, that she would have "practiced the New England *omertà*. Yankees are pretty closemouthed too, you know." Kay accepts Michael's proposal for a Sicilian marriage, one in which she would be his wife but not "a partner in life," after he confides to her that the family will be legitimate within five years and after he provides her with a "final explanation" of his father's business philosophy.

The next we hear of Kay is when Michael is returning home from Las Vegas. We learn that they had been married in a quiet New England ceremony and that Michael was "surprised at how well Kay got along with his parents and the other people living on the mall." She is described as "a good, old-style Italian wife" who gets pregnant "right away." At the birth of her second child, Kay comes to understand that she is "on her way to becoming a Sicilian" after she realizes that the story Connie tells her about Carlo's fuss over the right baptismal gift must be transmitted to Michael. Kay leaves Michael when she realizes that he did have his own brother-in-law murdered. Then, against her own better judgment, she accepts Tom Hagen's explanation and returns to Michael and converts to Catholicism, something that does not please Michael, who wants "the children to be Protestant, it was more American." Nevertheless, she is converted to his world and accepts the role of the woman subservient to man. Ironically, the conversion takes place because of her interaction with Tom Hagen, who both breaks the code of *omertà* and treats her as an equal. The final scene of the novel finds Kay at Mass, praying, like Mama Corleone, for the "soul of Michael Corleone." And so, Don Con Corleone's bid to control his world has had its greatest impact. He has been able, through his son, to convert an American *Mayflower* Protestant princess into a proper Sicilian mother.

Through the marriage of Michael to Kay, Puzo represents the ideal, albeit mythical, synthesis of Italian and American cultures. No matter how much Michael expresses his desires to be legitimate and American on the surface, under his skin he is true to the Sicilian world of his father, and he recreates that world for the next generation. Thus, Puzo forges in fiction what is impossible to create in reality. The key to this novel's success lies in Puzo's ability to make readers envy and even fear the mystery and the power inside the *Italianità* that he represents through the Corleone family.

Source: Fred L. Gardaphe, "The Middle Mythic Mode: Godfathers as Heroes, Variations on a Figure," in *Italian Signs, American Streets: The Evolution of Italian American Narrative*, Duke University Press, 1996, pp. 86–118.

Thomas J. Ferraro

In the following essay, Ferraro discusses the "business of family" in The Godfather, *and the godfather figure as a cultural icon.*

In his 1969 blockbuster *The Godfather*, Mario Puzo presented an image of the Mafia that has become commonplace in American popular culture. Since that time, we have taken for granted that the Mafia operates as a consortium of illegitimate businesses, structured along family lines, with a familial patriarch or "godfather" as the chief executive officer of each syndicate. Puzo's version of the Mafia fuses into one icon the realms of family and economy, of Southern Italian ethnicity and big-time American capitalism, of blood and the marketplace. "Blood" refers to the violence of organized crime. "Blood" also refers to the familial clan and its extension through the symbolic system of the *compare*, or "co-godparenthood." In *The Godfather*, the representation of the Mafia fuses ethnic tribalism with the all-American pursuit of wealth and power. Since its publication, we have regarded this business of family in *The Godfather*, as a figment of Puzo's opportunistic imagination, which it remains in part. But the business of family in Puzo's Mafia is also a provocative revision of accepted notions of what ethnicity is and how it works—the new ethnic sociology in popular literary form.

During the late 1970s and early 1980s, there was a short outburst of scholarly interest in *The Godfather* and its myriad offspring. A consensus about the meaning of the popularity of this saga emerges from the books and essays of Fredric Jameson, Eric Hobsbawn, John Cawelti, and John Sutherland. The portrayal of the Corleone family collective allows post-Vietnam-era Americans to fantasize about the glory days of "closely knit traditional authority." The portrayal of the power and destructive greed of the Mafia chieftains allows them to vent their rage at "the managerial elite who hold the reins of corporate power and use it for their own benefit." The themes of family and business, in each instance, are disengaged from one another. As Jameson puts it, on the one hand, the ethnic family imagery satisfies "a Utopian longing" for collectivity, while, on the other hand, "the substitution of crime for big business" is the "ideological function" of the narrative. In such standard treatments, Puzo's narrative is regarded as a brilliant (or brilliantly lucky) instance of satisfying two disparate appetites with a single symbol. This perspective, formulated in the late 1970s, seems to have settled the issue of the popularity of the novel.

I want to reopen that issue. We need to return to *The Godfather* because we have too easily dismissed its representation of the Mafia as a two-part fantasy. Of course, *The Godfather* is not reliable as a roman à clef or a historical novel: Puzo's details are fuzzy, mixed up, and much exaggerated. "There was things he stretched," as Huck Finn would put

> **The seemingly feudal, deeply internalized ethos of family honor cements individuals together in American crime, structuring syndicates and giving them their aggrandizing momentum."**

it, and everyone knows it. But critics have been too ready to accept his major sociological premise— that family and business work in tandem—as pure mythology. I would argue that the importance of *The Godfather* lies not in its creation of a double mythology but in the way that it takes the fusion of kinship and capitalist enterprise seriously. Its cultural significance lies not in the simultaneous appeals of "family" and "business" imagery but rather in the appeal of an actual structural simultaneity, the business of family. If we fail to pause long enough to consider its surface narrative, we underestimate not only the strategies of the novel but the insights and intuitions of its huge audience as well.

Readers have underestimated the business of family because little in traditional theories of the family, ethnicity, and advanced capitalism has prepared them to recognize it. In both scholarly and popular treatments, ethnic culture and extended kinship are interpreted as barriers to successfully negotiating the mobility ladder, particularly its upper rungs. Southern Italian immigrants and their descendants have long been thought to exemplify the principle that the more clannish an ethnic group, the slower its assimilation and economic advancement. Herbert Gans's *Urban Villagers*, Virginia Yans-McLaughlin's *Family and Community*, Thomas Kessner's *Golden Door*, and Thomas Sowell's *Ethnic America* essentially update the social work perspectives of such writers as Phyllis H. Williams and Leonard Covello. In 1944, Covello wrote, "Any social consciousness of Italo-Americans within 'Little Italies' appertains primarily to sharing and adhering to the family tradition as the main motif of their philosophy of life. . . . The retention of this cultural 'basis' is essentially the source of their retarded adjustment."

But this long-standing tradition of identifying the Italian family structure as a dysfunctional survival runs aground when it comes to the Mafia.

Historians and sociologists attest to the difficulty of interpreting the Mafia in terms of a linear model of assimilation and upward mobility. All commentators recognize that the Mafia was not simply transported here: it arose from the polyethnic immigrant streets rather than passing from father to son; Prohibition was the major factor in shaping its growth. In *A Family Business*, sociologist Francis A. J. Ianni concedes these points, only to stress the family structure of the syndicates and the origin of this familialism in Southern Italy. The Lupullo crime organization "*feels* like a kinship-structured group; familialism founded it and is still its stock in trade. One senses immediately not only the strength of the bond, but the inability of members to see any morality or social order larger than their own." Ianni's research tempts him into abandoning the tradition of placing ethnic phenomena on a linear continuum running from Old World marginality to New World centrality. His research supports and his analysis anticipates, without quite articulating, the cutting edge of ethnic theory.

Scholars in a number of fields are working to change the way we think about ethnicity, ethnic groups, and ethnic culture. In identifying the social bases of ethnicity, theorists are shifting their emphasis from intergenerational transmission to arenas of conflict in complex societies. They argue that we need to examine ethnic cultures not as Old World survivals (whatever their roots) but as improvised strategies to deal with the unequal distribution of wealth, power, and status. In this light, ethnic groups include not only socially marginal peoples but any group that uses symbols of common descent and tradition to create or to maintain power. From a historian's perspective, European family structures and traditions do not necessarily dissolve in the face of capitalism but rather, as they have always done, evolve to meet its changing needs.

Anthropologist Abner Cohen conceives of ethnic groups as "interest groups" in which ethnic symbols function in lieu of more formal structures, such as the law. When he speaks of the symbolic apparatus of ethnicity, he refers to the emphasis on common history and tradition, endogamy and social boundary maintenance, religion and ritual, and everyday encoded behavior, including "accent, manner of speech, etiquette, style of joking, play" and so forth, that is, the rhetoric and codes of "blood." As Cohen explains, the symbolic apparatus of ethnicity incites genuine loyalty and emotion, the power and idiosyncrasy of which cannot be underestimated. But the apparatus also serves utilitarian purposes within society at large, including those of the economic marketplace. In many of our most familiar examples, the function of ethnic ritual is primarily defensive, to organize a group on the margins of society, but the uses of ethnicity can be quite aggressive as well. The Italian-American Mafia is a case in point. As Ianni and others have demonstrated, it is the ethos of ethnic solidarity that puts the organization into Italian-American organized crime.

In her discussion of *The Godfather*, Rose Basile Green comes the closest of any critic to unpacking what she calls the "socioeconomic ethnic image" of the Corleone crime syndicate. Unlike almost everyone else, Green takes seriously Puzo's portrayal of the syndicates—not as historical fact about actual gangsters but as a treatise (however romanticized) "dealing with the contemporary strategy of gaining and securing power." Yet Green's analysis splits into typical parallel paths: crime as a means for social mobility versus the family as a locus of traditional Southern Italian responsibility. Although Green identifies "a subtle line between personal interest and structural power," she, too, fails to make the strongest connection between the private family life ascribed to Don Corleone and the illegitimate enterprise he heads. When Green says that *The Godfather* explores "the contemporary strategy of gaining and securing power," she means the tactics of bribery, intimidation, the brokerage of votes, intergang warfare, and so forth that Don Corleone uses to conduct business outside the confines of his own organization. But the most noteworthy device for gaining and securing power in Puzo's depiction is internal to the Corleone syndicate: it is not a gun or payola, but, quite simply, that mystified entity, the "Southern Italian family."

In narrating *The Godfather*, Puzo adopts the familiar role of cultural interpreter, mediating between outside readers and a secret ethnic society. Puzo's agenda, implicit yet universally understood, is to explain why Sicilian Americans have made such good criminals. The answer, generally speaking, is their cult of family honor. The Corleones believe, with a kind of feudal fervor, in patriarchy, patronage, and protection. *The Godfather* is saturated with the imagery of paternity, family, and intimate friendship; with the rhetoric of respect, loyalty, and the code of silence; with references to

Sicilian blood and the machismo attributed to it; with the social events—weddings, christenings, funerals, meals, and so forth—that embody the culture of family honor. The business of crime is always interlaced with the responsibilities of family. In the film, for instance, Clemenza frets over a request from his wife Eve as he presides over the execution of Paulie Gatto: "Don't forget the cannoli!" Don Vito himself is a true believer in the mutual obligations of kinfolk. He seeks both to expand his wealth and power to protect his dependents and to make his protection available to more and more people. He recruits from within his family to keep the business "all in the family" for the family's sake. "It was at this time that the Don got the idea that he ran his world far better than his enemies ran the greater world which continually obstructed his path." At the same time, "not his best friends would have called Don Corleone a saint from heaven"; there is always "some self-interest" in his generosity. For everyone recognizes the wisdom of family honor, Corleone's Honor, given the special exigencies of operating in a big way in an outlawed underground economy.

In his analysis of the ethnic group as an interest group, Cohen stresses the growth potential wherever there is a sector of an economy that has not been organized formally:

> Even in the advanced liberal industrial societies there are some structural conditions under which an interest group cannot organize itself on formal lines. Its formal organization may be opposed by the state or by other groups within the state, or may be incompatible with some important principles in the society; or the interests it represents may be newly developed and not yet articulated in terms of a formal organization and accommodated with the formal structure of the society. Under these conditions the group will articulate its organization on informal lines, making use of the kinship, friendship, ritual, ceremonial, and other symbolic activities that are implicit in what is known as style of life.

The ethnic ethos means sticking together, respecting the authority of the group rather than that of outsiders, defending the group's turf, and abiding by tradition. The reasoning comes full circle, for tradition is equated with group solidarity. The family is the core element of the group and its most powerful symbol. Under appropriate conditions, the ethos of ethnicity is by no means anachronistic in late capitalism, no matter how rooted such values might be in the history of particular groups. Wherever ethnicity can facilitate enterprise, ethnicity as a system can be said to be one of the primary motors of capitalism, not its antithesis.

Focusing on the old moneyed elite of London, Cohen has argued that ethnicity functions among the privileged as well as among the impoverished, among "core" castes as well as among racial and national minorities. In another case study, historian Peter Dobkin Hall implicates family and tradition in the mercantile practices of Massachusetts elites in the eighteenth and nineteenth centuries. As both Cohen and Hall contend, a precondition for capitalized ethnicity is a legal vacuum. I would add to this a corollary based on the history of the Mafia: the desire to engage in enterprise, not simply in a vacuum (where law and formal arrangements are lacking) but in an economic zone outside the law and opposed to formal arrangements, makes some form of family and ethnic organization a necessity.

The seemingly feudal, deeply internalized ethos of family honor cements individuals together in American crime, structuring syndicates and giving them their aggrandizing momentum. Loyalty and devotion to group honor are the values according to which individuals are motivated, recruited, judged, and policed in the Mafia. These values are especially effective at binding criminals together and at making criminals out of those not otherwise drawn to the outlaw life. These values surfaced in the United States when Prohibition created an enormous unorganized sector of the national economy, legally proscribed but driven by immense appetites and the willingness of legal institutions to play along, especially for a price. Such values are also necessary to hold together the large-scale enterprises not structured or protected by law, which Prohibition created but which survived after it: rackets devoted to gambling, loan-sharking, prostitution, various forms of extortion, and eventually drugs. In legitimate business, a prized executive who sells himself and perhaps a secret or two to another company is written off as an unexpected operating loss. A *capo-regime* who becomes a stool pigeon can bring the whole system down. The ideologies of tradition and group solidarity, principally of the family, are ideal for rationalizing crime syndicates in both senses of the word "rationalize": ideal for organizing them because such ideologies are ideal for justifying their existence and their hold over their members.

The Godfather would warrant attention from scholars for the way it depicts an ethnic subculture that functions as an interest group even if, like Puzo's *Fortunate Pilgrim* (1964), it had disappeared into obscurity upon publication. But the novel has had a major impact on popular culture. The figure of "the godfather" outstrips all but the most ubiquitous cultural symbols, falling some-where between Huckleberry Finn and Superman, better known, perhaps, than Uncle Sam himself. By 1971, when the first film was released, there were over one million hardcover copies of the book in circulation—multiple copies in every library in every town in America—and at least ten million more paperbacks. Historically, the reading of the novel framed the film; not, as in academic criticism, the other way around. By the early 1980s, the book had become the best-selling novel in history, and it continues to sell steadily even outside the United States.

The most immediate spin-offs of the novel were the two films, versions of those films re-arranged for television, and the video format, in which the two films plus outtakes are combined as *The Godfather Epic*. By 1975, 260 more books on the Mafia theme had been released, principally of the hard-boiled variety. In 1984, Puzo himself tried again with his fictional account of Salvatore Giuliano, *The Sicilian*. Ethnicity in crime has figured in many major films, including *The Cotton Club* (co-scripted by Coppola, Puzo, and William Kennedy), *The Gang Who Couldn't Shoot Straight*, *Broadway Danny Rose*, *Heart of the Dragon*, *Scarface*, *Once upon a Time in America*, *Miller's Crossing*, and *Goodfellas*, Martin Scorsese's reply to Coppola. During the 1980s, the popularity of family-dynasty sagas, especially in their many ethnic varieties, can be traced in part to Puzo's model. Most telling has been the ceaseless production of *Godfather* clones, emphasizing the fusion of family and crime. Now a genre of its own, the proliferation includes (auto)biographical works such as Gay Talese's *Honor Thy Father*, Joseph Bonanno's *Man of Honor*, and Antoinette Giancana's *Mafia Princess*; novels such as Vincent Patrick's *Family Business* and Richard Condon's trilogy of the Prizzi family; and a legion of films and teleplays, including "Our Family Honor" (ABC's ill-fated attempt to combine Italian-American gangsters with Irish-American cops), *Married to the Mob* (which picks up on the feminist themes in Condon), the "Wiseguy" series (an affecting drama of homo-erotic underpinnings in the mob), *China Girl* (Abel Ferrara restages *Romeo and Juliet* between Italian and Chinese mobsters), and *The Freshman* (Brando parodies his portrayal of Vito Corleone). *The Godfather: Part III* was released on Christmas in 1990.

What are we to make of the lasting fascination with *The Godfather*? Since its appearance, scholars have recognized *The Godfather* as an artifact of the "new ethnicity." The timing of the novel and

its immediate offspring, from publication of the novel in 1969 to the television miniseries in the late 1970s, corresponds to an upturn in Americans embracing ethnic identity. This celebration included not only groups that were by and large still marginal—Native Americans, the descendants of Southern slaves, the newest comers from the Caribbean, the Hispanic Americas, and the Far East—but also the descendants of European immigrants, including the Italians, who were well on their way to middle-class security. Necessarily, the connections drawn between the increased salience of ethnicity and popularity of *The Godfather* have been premised on construing *The Godfather* as two-part fantasy in which family sanctuary and successful corporate enterprise are polar opposites. My reading of *The Godfather*, which emphasizes the complicity of family and business, calls for a re-examination of the role of the novel in the new ethnic self-consciousness. Both the popularity of *The Godfather* and the celebration of ethnicity are complex phenomena, reflecting myriad attitudes toward race, class, and gender as well as ethnicity, attitudes that often conflict with one another. By claiming that *The Godfather* articulates the business of family, I do not wish to mute these other voices but to point the way toward situating the voice of family-business within the larger cacophony of debate.

Scholars such as Jameson and Cawelti, who work within the frame of traditional *Godfather* interpretation, seek to locate within the novel an anticapitalist energy—not an overt critique so much as an impulse, the energy of a potential critique partially veiled and misdirected. Both critics argue that Puzo portrays the Mafia as the center of a capitalist conspiracy and, simultaneously and irreconcilably, as a refuge from the conspiracy of capitalism. Because Puzo's Mafia functions as "the mirror-image of big business," its brutality provides a focus for anticapitalist anxiety and an outlet for anticapitalist anger. Similarly, the equally powerful image of the family reflects, in Jameson's terms, a "Utopian longing" for escape from the prison house of capitalism. "The 'family' is a fantasy of tribal belongingness," echoes Cawelti, "that protects and supports the individual as opposed to the coldness and indifference of the modern business or government bureaucracy."

In the standard view, the putative double fantasy of *The Godfather* reflects the misdirected energies of the new ethnicity. The new ethnicity arises from frustration with capitalism yet mutes its resistance in clamor about the decline of the family and traditional values. My analysis of *The Godfather* suggests we might hesitate before we accept the majority opinion that the family in the novel embodies a refuge from capitalism. We need to question whether a case for the subversive nature of *The Godfather* can rest on the myth of the Italian-American family as a precapitalist collectivity, particularly when Puzo uses all his forces to undermine this false dichotomy. The representation of the Southern Italian family in *The Godfather* is not the kind of saccharine portrayal of innocent harmony, the haven in a heartless world, that scholars take as the benchmark of ethnic nostalgia. In *The Godfather*, capitalism is shown to accommodate, absorb, and indeed accentuate the structures of family and ethnicity. Americans respond to *The Godfather* because it presents the ethnic family not as a sacrosanct European institution reproduced on the margins of America, but as a fundamental American structure of power, successful and bloodied.

Scholars' desire to identify ethnic piety as a locus of anticapitalist energy has blinded them to the existence of an alliance between the new ethnicity and the procapitalist celebration of the family. This alliance is an insufficiently recognized strain within recent popular culture. At least until World War II, and perhaps into the 1970s, the dominant attitude was that the ethnic family in the United States was incompatible with capitalism, whether ethnicity was favored or not. The rabid Americanizers of the early decades attempted to strip immigrant workers of their familial and cultural loyalties. Many of the immigrants themselves feared that the price of upward mobility might be a loss of family solidarity, even as most relied on the family as a basis for group enterprise and mutual financial support. And intellectuals, who were partly or wholly skeptical of capitalism, based one strand of their critique on the damage that capitalism supposedly inflicted upon traditional family cultures. We hear less and less frequently from these nativist Americanizers and guardians of ethnic tradition, but the nostalgia among scholars remains pervasive nonetheless. The general public, however, increasingly has come to accept and indeed to welcome the idea of compatibility between ethnicity and capitalism. In the case of Italian Americans, for instance, public figures ranging from Lee Iacocca to Geraldine Ferraro and Mario Cuomo emphasize the role family values have played in their own success stories, occasionally stretching our imaginations. Similar rhetoric appears in the reemerging critique of the black family, in the widespread lauding of Asian- and

Caribbean-American merchants and their schoolchildren, and in the general appeal for a new American work ethic. In this light, *The Godfather* helped to introduce and continues to feed upon a strain of American rhetoric and expectation that has reached full salience in the last decade.

Perhaps no artifact of American culture, popular or serious, has made the case for the business of family with quite the force of *The Godfather*. At no time in United States history has ethnicity enjoyed the vogue that it first achieved in the years of *The Godfather*'s greatest popularity and, in large measure, now maintains. The convergence is no coincidence. While *The Godfather* does participate in the new ethnicity by celebrating the ethnic family, the Mafia achieves its romantic luster not because Puzo portrays the Italian-American family as a separate sphere lying outside of capitalism, but because the Italian-American family emerges as a potent structure within it. The ethnic family in *The Godfather* feeds off a market sensibility rather than undermines it. The Corleones can provide protection from the market only because they have mastered it. Indeed, Puzo reaches the height of romance in *The Godfather* by choosing the Mafia as a model for family enterprise, for illegal family enterprises are capable of growing and expanding to an extent that the structure and regulation of legitimate capitalism ultimately will not support.

If *The Godfather* does indeed harbor anticapitalist energies, as a thorough reading of the novel might suggest, then perhaps scholars have been looking for that energy in the wrong places. Jameson concludes:

> When indeed we reflect on an organized conspiracy against the public, one which reaches into every corner of our daily lives and our political structures to exercise a wanton and genocidal violence at the behest of distant decision-makers and in the name of an abstract conception of profit—surely it is not about the Mafia, but rather about American business itself that we are thinking, American capitalism in its most systematized and computerized, dehumanized, "multinational" and corporate form.

Jameson and the others may be correct in insisting that fascination with *The Godfather* is motivated, at a deeper level, by anti-capitalist anxiety. But the real scare *The Godfather* entertains, however much suppressed, is about capitalism, not in its "most systematized and computerized, dehumanized" form but rather in its more "intimate" varieties—ethnic, familial, personal. My reading of *The Godfather* suggests that if we wish to press charges against capitalism, we must press charges against family and ethnicity, too.

One strand of rhetoric in twentieth-century America, dating as far back as Howells's *Hazard of New Fortunes* and surveyed by *Christopher Lasch* in *Haven in a Heartless World* (1977), urges Americans to go home to escape the specter of capitalism. Professionals often complain about taking work home with them, mentally if not literally. How much more frightening, then, is the alternative Puzo represents: when some Americans go home to papa, they end up confronting the boss. Critics have been quick to interpret the brutality of the Mafia as a symbol for the violence to the individual inherent in capitalism, and to assume that the family represents an escape from that violence. Yet the melodrama of *The Godfather* implicates the family not only in the success of the Corleone empire but in its cycle of self-destructive violence as well. Michael reintegrates the family business only after burying a brother, murdering a brother-in-law, alienating a sister, and betraying his wife's trust. For Americans who experience family and economy as interwoven pressures (if not actual combined enterprises), the Mafia genre may allow them to focus their resentments, even if, inevitably, a Mafia analogy overstates them. For the cost of employing blood in the marketplace is finding "The Company" at home.

Puzo is often maligned for exploiting the stereotype of Italian-American criminality, which has long been used to discriminate against the general Italian-American population. But, in the final analysis, *The Godfather* does not so much rehash an old tale, whatever its strands of inheritance, as tell a new one. In *The Godfather*, Puzo refashions the gangster genre into a vehicle for overturning the traditional antithesis between ties of blood and the American marketplace. He thus transforms the stock character of the Italian-American outlaw into the representative super(business)man, and transforms the lingering image of immigrant huddled masses into the first family of American capitalism.

Source: Thomas J. Ferraro, "Blood in the Marketplace: The Business of Family in *The Godfather* Narratives," in *Ethnic Passages: Literary Immigrants in Twentieth-Century America*, University of Chicago Press, 1993, pp. 18–52.

Sources

Axthelm, Pete, "Happy Families," in *Newsweek*, March 10, 1969, pp. 69–70.

Barra, Allen, "The Schlockfather," in *Salon*, July 20, 2000, http://www.salon.com/books/feature/2000/07/20/puzo/index.html (last accessed May 1, 2002).

Cawelti, John C., "The New Mythology of Crime," in *Boundary 2*, Vol. 3, 1975, pp. 325–57.

Cook, Fred J., "Power of the Mafia," in the *Nation*, June 16, 1969, pp. 771–72.

Geismar, Maxwell, "Pit of Decay," in *Saturday Review*, February 26, 1955, p. 47.

Midwood, Barton, Review of *The Godfather*, in *Esquire*, February 1971, pp. 50–51.

Puzo, Mario, "The Making of *The Godfather*," in *The Godfather Papers and Other Confessions*, G. P. Putnam's Sons, 1972, p. 41.

Further Reading

Camon, Alessandro, "*The Godfather* and the Mythology of the Mafia," in *Francis Ford Coppola's "The Godfather Trilogy,"* edited by Nick Browne, Cambridge University Press, 2000.

> Although Camon is writing here about the films, the things he says about them apply equally to Puzo's novel, which has the same approach to its subject.

Capeci, Jerry, *The Complete Idiot's Guide to the Mafia*, Alpha Books, 2001.

> This book may have a frivolous title, but its author is an expert in the field of modern organized crime, having written a column on the subject for the *New York Post* for six years and producing one of the best compendia of crime information on the internet.

Lebo, Harlan, *The Godfather Legacy*, Fireside Press, 1997.

> This book is basically about the three films that came from Puzo's novel, but there is much about the author's life as background to how the films came to be made and how he wrote the scripts.

Puzo, Mario, "The Making of *The Godfather*," in *The Godfather Papers and Other Confessions*, G. P. Putnam's Sons, 1972. pp. 32–69.

> Puzo wrote this article so that he could quit answering interview questions about his experience in Hollywood. It is in-depth and full of background about his life and the writing of the novel.

Sterling, Claire, *Octopus: The Long Reach of the International Sicilian Mafia*, Simon & Schuster Trade, 1991.

> This is a comprehensive history of the connection between American and Italian organized crime, reaching back into the nineteenth century.

Lord Jim

Joseph Conrad
1900

Joseph Conrad's *Lord Jim*, first published in England in 1900, has long been acknowledged as a very difficult book for readers to understand, especially on the first read. However, those who have taken the time to understand the book acknowledge that the effort is worth it. *Lord Jim*, which Conrad began as a short sketch, grew into a novel that is widely recognized for its modernism—its tendency to buck the conventional narrative trends of its day. The most obvious technique that Conrad used was a shifting form of narration, in which the reader hears a tale first from one narrator, then another, and finally from several disparate accounts.

Like many Conrad novels, this book features autobiographical elements from Conrad's own naval past. The story concerns a young man named Jim, who undertakes the training to become a naval officer, but his certificate is revoked when he deserts his ship during a crisis, leaving eight hundred Moslem pilgrims to what he thinks is a certain death—although the pilgrims live to tell the tale of his cowardice. Jim continually runs from this past, eventually to Patusan, a remote island in the Far East. Here, Jim starts fresh, earning the respect of the natives, who call him Lord Jim and attribute his many successes to supernatural powers. Jim must face the fears from his old life, however, and his ability to finally do this leads to the novel's tragic and ambiguous ending. Conrad's tale is so complex and open to individual interpretation that many critics have noted that the book has no one meaning and that it is all based on a paradox.

Joseph Conrad

However, this ambiguity has captivated readers for over a hundred years, and since its publication, many have regarded the book as Conrad's best.

Author Biography

Conrad was born Teodor Józef Konrad Nalecz Korzeniowski on December 3, 1857, in the Polish Ukraine. He was an only child to his parents. His father, Apollo Nalecz, was mainly a poet and translator throughout his life. His mother, Ewa Bobrowska Korzeniowski, was a frail woman, who had come from a good family. Throughout his life, Conrad experienced loss, alienation, and rejection. This trend began with the loss of his parents during childhood. His father allegedly took part in anti-Russian activities and was sent into exile in northern Russia. Together the family endured exile in a harsh land of scarcity and illness, until Conrad's mother died of tuberculosis, sending his father into deep depression. Conrad was sent to his uncle's, and his father died four years later, a profound event in the young Conrad's life.

After receiving his education in Poland, Conrad took a trip through Europe and decided not to return to his homeland. Instead, in 1874, he moved to Marseilles, France, so that he could follow his dream of going to sea. He gained experience as a seaman, and in 1878, at the age of twenty-one, he saw England for the first time and began to sail on English vessels, where he also started to learn the English language; in 1886, Conrad became an English citizen. Conrad's experiences during his twenty years on the sea—during which time he rose through the ranks of the British Merchant Service—gave him the basis for many of his novels, starting with his first novel, *Almayer's Folly*, published in English in 1895. Conrad had started writing this novel while aboard a river steamer in the Congo. By the time the novel was published, Conrad was done with his life at sea, and he settled into the writing life. Conrad followed up his first novel with a number of other novels based on his maritime experiences, including *Heart of Darkness* (1899), one of Conrad's most famous works, and *Lord Jim* (1900), considered by many to be his greatest novel.

In any case, *Lord Jim* belongs to Conrad's early period as a writer, when Conrad was experimenting with modern narrative techniques, which most critics regard as the high point of his literary artistry. Following *Lord Jim*, Conrad wrote quickly and prolifically, publishing three more novels over the following five years: *Typhoon* (1902), *Nostromo* (1904), and *The Secret Agent* (1907).

At the outbreak of World War I, Conrad and his family barely escaped being imprisoned in Poland while on vacation. In England, Conrad was offered a knighthood by the British government, which he turned down. Conrad died of a heart attack on August 3, 1924, in Kent, England.

Plot Summary

Chapters 1–12

Lord Jim starts out with a capsule description of Jim—a tall, powerful man—by a third-person narrator, who gives both Jim's background and briefly mentions events that take place far in Jim's future. This jumping around in time is a common technique in the book. As a child, Jim is drawn to the sea and goes into training to be an officer, hoping to be a hero someday. His first attempts at heroism fail, and, in fact, the narrator starts to talk about a mysterious incident that happens to Jim on the *Patna* but does not explain exactly what happens. At this point, the story shifts to a first-person narration by Marlow, a man Jim meets at his yet un-explained trial. Marlow's language reveals that he is telling Jim's story to a group of people, and the reader is merely listening in. Eventually, the reader learns that Jim was one of the officers aboard the *Patna* who deserted the ship when they thought it was going to sink, leaving their eight hundred Moslem pilgrims to die. However, the ship is saved, and Jim stands trial for his dishonorable actions.

Chapters 13–21

The night before Jim's sentencing, Marlow offers him money to flee from punishment. Jim refuses to run, and faces his sentencing, which involves the revoking of his naval certificate. Marlow gives Jim a second chance by referring him to a job with Mr. Denver, the owner of a rice mill. However, when one of the *Patna* crew shows up and threatens to blackmail Jim for a full-time job, Jim leaves the position. He does this several more times, earning a reputation as a transient individual. When Jim throws a drunken navy officer off a verandah and into a river after the officer makes a remark about the *Patna*, Marlow realizes that Jim will never get over his guilt unless something is done. Marlow goes to see Mr. Stein, a merchant and butterfly collector, who says that Jim is a romantic and that a romantic cannot be cured, people can only tell them how to live. Marlow then describes the island of Patusan, introducing it to his audience and talking briefly about a visiting the island two years later, when he finds Jim is a changed man.

Chapters 22–27

At this point, Marlow jumps back to the time when he told Jim about Patusan. Although Jim is nervous at first, he warms to the idea of escape there, and Marlow helps him pack, giving him a silver ring that Stein received from Doramin, one of the island's leaders. Jim and Marlow say their emotional goodbyes, and Jim says that he never wants to come back. The narrative agains shifts and Marlow relates the details of his visit to Patusan two years later, when he goes to see Jim and to deliver a business message from Stein about setting up a proper trading post there. Marlow finds that the natives, especially the Bugis Malays, treat Jim with the utmost respect, revering him as "Tuan" Jim, or Lord Jim. Jim sits with Marlow and talks about his first experiences—how he was captured by Rajah Allang, one of the leaders on the island, and how he escaped and went to Doramin—showing him Stein's ring.

Jim learns of the three warring factions: Allang, who wants to have exclusive trading rights; Doramin, a native who opposes Allang and leads the Bugis Malays; and Sherif Ali, a half-Arab who believes in guerilla warfare and who watches over the area from a mountainous stockade, causing problems for the other two factions. Jim introduces Marlow to the monumentally fat leader, Doramin, and his son, Dain Waris. Jim recalls the past, telling Marlow of his great plan to bring peace to the island by dragging cannons up to the top of one mountain to blow up Sherif Ali's stockade, which is on the other mountaintop. The plan works, Dain and another native, Tamb' Itam, pledge themselves to Jim, and he is looked upon as someone with supernatural powers. From this point on, the villagers look to him for truth and justice in all matters.

Chapters 28–35

Following Jim's victory, Allang willingly submits, and the island is peaceful. Everybody assumes that Jim, like other white men, will leave some day, and Doramin hopes that when this day comes, his son, Dain, will rule in Jim's place. Marlow is unable to assure Doramin that Jim will go back home. Marlow talks about Jewel, the mulatto native whom Jim falls in love with and marries. Her stepfather, Cornelius, Jim's predecessor, does not like Jim. Jim tells Marlow about the night he got the inspiration for the attack on Sherif Ali's stockade and how Jewel supported him in everything, even rescuing him one night by waking him up so that he could defend himself against assassins. While Marlow is staying in Patusan, Jewel expresses her concern that Jim will leave her. When he is pressed, Marlow finally explains that Jim is not good enough for the outside world, but she does not believe it. In a distraught state, Marlow is accosted by Cornelius, who is distressed to learn from him that Jim does not plan on leaving. Marlow leaves Patusan the next morning.

Chapters 36–45

Marlow finishes his part of the story, and his confused audience does not know what to make of this incomplete ending. Two years later, one of the men in the audience gets a package from Marlow, containing the conclusion to the story and more information about Jim, which is spread out over many accounts, including a letter from Marlow, some frantic notes from Jim, a letter from Jim's father dated before Jim's ill-fated voyage on the *Patna*, a second letter from Marlow, which pieces together the story of Jim's death, and a final sheet of

Marlow's notes. Marlow writes about the so-called Gentleman Brown, a dirty pirate who plays the largest role in Jim's death and who considers Jim a coward for not fighting. The narrative jumps back to the previous year, when Marlow visits Stein, and Tamb' Itam is also confused over Jim's unwillingness to fight. Marlow talks to Jewel, who says she can never forgive Jim for leaving her.

The story shifts back to Brown, who has evaded capture by fleeing to Patusan, where he is stopping for supplies on his way to Madagascar. Jim is away from the fort and has left Dain Waris in charge. Both Dain and Jewel want to kill Brown and his men, but the Bugis Malays, afraid that Dain might die if he tries to kill the white men, want to wait for Jim to tell them what to do. When rumors of Brown's reinforcements circulate, Doramin sends Dain and his men downriver to head them off. A native from Allang's party, Kassim, arranges for Cornelius to meet Brown, to encourage an overthrow of Jim. Jim comes back, and Brown confronts him, guessing correctly that Jim, like him, has come to Patusan because he is running away from something. Jim's past haunts him once more, and he appeals to the Bugis to let Brown go, pledging his life against the lives of any Bugis who may be harmed by this decision. He also sends word to Dain not to fire on Brown. However, Cornelius betrays Jim, telling Brown where Dain's men are stationed and how to ambush them. Led by Cornelius, Brown's party kills Dain. Tamb' Itam catches Cornelius and kills him and then goes to talk to Jewel and Jim. Itam and Jewel urge Jim to flee or fight, but Jim feels compelled to adhere to his code of honor and goes to answer for Dain's death. Doramin shoots Jim, who dies with a proud look on his face. Although Jewel and Itam think Jim and his actions are a mystery, Marlow thinks he understands why Jim sacrificed himself and says that Jim took control of his destiny for the first time ever.

Characters

Sherif Ali

Sherif Ali is the corrupt head of one of the factions that opposes Jim and the Bugis Malays. After Jim has been with the Bugis for a while, Jewel alerts him to an attack by Ali's assassins. Jim kills one and sends the other three back to Ali as a message. Later, Jim sends a stronger message when he blows up Ali's mountaintop fort using Doramin's cannons.

Rajah Allang

Rajah Allang is the head of the faction that captures Jim when he first arrives at the island. Up until Jim arrives, Allang tries to maintain a monopoly on trade off the island by using force and intimidation. When Jim escapes Allang to Doramin, one of Allang's rivals, Allang chases him, but Doramin protects him. After Jim's successful destruction of Sherif Ali's fortress, Allang does not give him any more trouble and, in fact, becomes very docile around Jim, fearing Jim's charismatic power over the natives.

Blake

Blake is one of the two partners of Egström & Blake, a ship-chandler where Jim works for a while as a water-clerk. Blake is the more abusive of the two partners and insists on yelling at everybody who works at the ship-supplies store.

Brierly

Brierly is the accomplished naval judge at Jim's trial, who commits suicide by jumping into the sea—after realizing that he is a lot like Jim and could easily find himself in Jim's shoes one day.

Gentleman Brown

Gentleman Brown is an unscrupulous pirate who ambushes and kills Dain, setting off the chain of events that leads to Jim's death. Brown calls himself "Gentleman" because he comes from a good family. However, his piracy on the seas has earned him an evil reputation. In the process of fleeing from authorities, he stops in Patusan for supplies on the way to Madagascar. The natives stop him, and he realizes he is outnumbered. While the Bugis await Jim's return so they can receive his input on whether or not to kill Brown and his pirates, most people are anxious to kill them. When Brown meets the famous Lord Jim, he guesses luckily that Jim is hiding in Patusan from a shadowed past, just as he is. This knowledge helps to sway Jim to let Brown go. Once Brown is free, and with the help of Cornelius, he launches his attack on Dain. Interviewing Brown on his deathbed years later, Marlow tries to account for the circumstances of Jim's puzzlingly submissive death in order to understand Jim's enigmatic actions.

The Captain

The captain of the steamer *Patna* is Jim's commanding officer on the fateful voyage that leads to Jim's trial. Jim is not impressed by the New South Wales German captain when he sees him, since the man is coarse, tends to scream vulgarities at his crew, and is not too concerned with his appearance. When Jim, the captain, and the two crewman in the lifeboat are picked up by the *Avondale*, the captain repeats the lie that he and the two crewmen have fabricated about the *Patna*'s demise. This lie is exposed and useless when they reach shore and find out the ship did not sink. Although Jim stands trial for his actions, the captain disappears.

Cornelius

Cornelius is the person who used to hold Jim's job in Patusan and the one who betrays Jim. When Mr. Stein hires Jim to take Cornelius's place, Cornelius is jealous of Jim and immediately dislikes him. Cornelius is verbally abusive to his stepdaughter Jewel, and Jim offers to kill him, but Jewel says that Cornelius is miserable enough as it is. After Jewel and Jim are married, Cornelius seeks a payment in exchange for the loss of his stepdaughter, urging Marlow to persuade Jim to pay. When Cornelius finds out that Jim is not leaving, he searches for a way to get rid of him. He finds his chance in Brown, whom he helps to ambush Dain—an act that leads to Jim's sacrificial death.

Mr. Denver

Marlow gets Jim a job at Mr. Denver's rice mill, which goes well until somebody threatens to blackmail Jim using the *Patna* affair, and Jim quits. Mr. Denver, who does not understand why, writes an angry letter to Marlow.

Doramin

Doramin is the enormously fat chief of the Bugis Malays tribe, who kills Jim after Jim's actions lead to the death of Doramin's son, Dain. Doramin has befriended Stein in the past, and when Doramin gives Stein a silver ring denoting their friendship, Stein gives Doramin some cannons in exchange. When Jim escapes from Rajah Allang and comes to Doramin for help, he shows the chief Stein's ring, and Doramin takes him in. Using Doramin's cannons, Jim and the Bugis Malays are able to destroy the mountain fortress of Sherif Ali. In the process, Jim becomes great friends with Dain, Doramin's son. Although Doramin is the chief of the tribe, even he often waits for Lord Jim to give his opinion before making a decision, as when he

Media Adaptations

- *Lord Jim* was adapted as a black and white, silent film in 1925 by Paramount Pictures. The film was directed by Victor Fleming and featured Percy Marmont as Jim.

- *Lord Jim* was adapted as a film in 1965 by Columbia Pictures. The film was directed by Richard Brooks I and featured Peter O'Toole as Jim. It is available as a Columbia Classics video.

- *Lord Jim* was adapted as an abridged audio book by HarperCollins Publishers in 1999. It is narrated by Joss Ackland.

wants to kill Brown but waits for Jim's advice. Unfortunately, when Jim lets Brown go—offering his own life as compensation for any potential deaths—Brown ambushes and kills Dain. Jim presents himself before Doramin, who shoots Jim.

Egström

Egström is one of the two partners of Egström & Blake, a ship-chandler where Jim works for a while. Egström ignores the caustic behavior of his partner and tends to the actual management of the ship supplies store. He is very impressed with Jim's performance and does not understand why guilt over the *Patna* incident makes Jim leave.

The French Lieutenant

The French Lieutenant helps the *Patna*, after Jim jumps ship, by towing the crippled ship to land. The lieutenant stays on board the *Patna* for thirty hours. He is willing to let the damaged *Patna* sink if it starts to even though that means going down with it, if it starts to threaten his own ship. His biggest concern is that the Moslem pilgrims have no wine to drink with dinner.

Tamb' Itam

Tamb' Itam is Jim's friend and bodyguard. He does not understand why Jim chooses to die. When Jim and Dain lead the attack on Sherif Ali's fortress, Tamb' Itam is right behind them. Along with being Jim's bodyguard and confidant, Tamb' Itam serves as Jim's messenger. When Jim lets Brown go, he dispatches Tamb' Itam to tell Dain not to harm Brown as he passes. While still in Dain's camp, Tamb' Itam witnesses Brown's attack and Dain's death. Tamb' Itam realizes Cornelius has led Brown to the camp and kills Cornelius as a result. Tamb' Itam is the first to reach Jim with the news of Dain's death. He, like Jewel, does not understand why Jim will not either fight or flee Doramin, but he respects Jim enough to obey his wishes.

Jewel

Jewel is Jim's wife, who never forgives him after he willingly chooses to sacrifice his life. When Jim arrives in Patusan, he and Jewel, a mulatto native of the island, fall madly in love. She is worried about Jim leaving Patusan some day, even when both Jim and Marlow tell her that this is not an option, since the outside world does not want Jim. She is fiercely protective of Jim and warns him of assassins that try to kill him. She is also receptive to his ideas. However, when he says he is not going to fight or flee Doramin, who will surely try to kill him for Dain's death, Jewel accuses him of lying and abandoning her. Later, after Jim's death, Jewel speaks with Marlow at Stein's place and is still bitter and confused over her husband's choice to die.

Lord Jim

Lord Jim is the title character who redeems a life haunted by shame when he offers his life as payment for the life of his dead friend. Jim is an idealistic young man who dreams of being a hero and tries to achieve this dream by becoming a naval officer. His first attempts at glory are failures, yet he waits for his chance. When he deserts his ship, the *Patna*, leaving eight hundred Moslem pilgrims to what he thinks will be a horrible death, Jim feels he has betrayed himself. When the ship does not sink and the public trial of Jim reveals his actions, he loses his commission and can no longer serve as an officer. Through the help of Marlow, an older naval captain, Jim tries to reestablish himself by working in a job that Marlow gets for him. However, when somebody mentions the *Patna* incident, he leaves the job and goes to a different town. After doing this several times, his reputation becomes synonymous with the *Patna* incident. In an attempt to help him get away from all of this and start fresh, Marlow arranges for Jim to go to Patusan, a remote island in the Far East.

In Patusan, Jim finds a new life and a people who do not know of his past. Through a number of heroic deeds, including the overthrow of one of the two factions that war with the Bugis Malays—Jim's chosen tribe—Jim gains the respect of the Malays, who call him "Tuan," or "Lord," Jim and who believe he has supernatural powers. From this point on, they look to Jim to solve their disputes and tell them what to do. Jim marries Jewel, a mulatto woman who was born in Patusan, and his life is starting to fall into place, as Marlow sees when he visits Jim. However, at the arrival of a pirate who calls himself Gentleman Brown, the tide turns. When Jim's friend Dain is ambushed and killed by Brown on his way out of Patusan, Jim's wife and friends encourage him to fight or flee. However, Jim refuses to run again and presents himself to Dain's father, holding himself accountable for Dain's death. Jim seems happy as he dies, realizing that, for once, he has stayed true to his beliefs.

Marlow

Marlow is the person who serves as narrator for most of the tale. Marlow first speaks in the fifth chapter of the book, when the narration switches from third-person omniscient to first-person narration. Marlow, an old sea captain who features prominently in other Conrad tales, narrates the tale from this point for most of the book, presumably telling Jim's tale as an after-dinner story. When Marlow first meets Jim at the formal inquiry for the *Patna* incident, he is ready to dislike Jim, thinking that Jim is remorseless for his actions, as his cool demeanor seems to indicate. However, as Marlow gets to know the young man, he realizes that Jim is ashamed of his actions and tormented by guilt. The night before Jim is to be sentenced, Marlow offers Jim money and the chance to run away before his sentencing. Jim declines, not wishing to run. After Jim's commission is revoked, Marlow gives him a second chance by recommending him for a job. Marlow is glad to hear from Jim's employer that Jim is working out well, but he is distressed when he finds out shortly thereafter that Jim has left the job. When Marlow inquires into the particulars, he realizes that Jim left because somebody had brought up the *Patna* incident. This happens several more times, at which point Marlow seeks out the services of Mr. Stein, a merchant and butterfly collector.

With Stein's help, Marlow is able to send Jim to the remote island of Patusan, where Stein's friendship with one of the tribes, the Bugis

Malays, helps Jim to win favor early on. Marlow visits Jim two years later and is impressed to see how Jim has been transformed from a guilt-ridden young man into a confident leader. Everybody assumes that Jim, a white man, will not stay for long in Patusan, since most whites leave the island after awhile. Jim's wife, Jewel, thinks Jim will leave her and asks Marlow about why Jim cannot go back to the white world. Although Marlow tries to indicate that Jim is not wanted, she does not believe him. Marlow leaves the island shortly thereafter and never sees Jim again. At this point, Marlow ends his yet incomplete tale. However, for the next two years, Marlow seeks out information about Jim, including the events surrounding his death. He travels around the world interviewing witnesses, including the pirate Brown. At one point, he compiles all of these accounts, along with other items written by and to Jim, and sends them to one of his guests from the dinner party where he started telling the tale. Although Jim is the main protagonist in the tale, Marlow also undergoes changes as he tries to come to grips with why Jim acted the way he did on Patusan.

Mr. Stein

Mr. Stein is Marlow's friend, a merchant who offers Jim the chance to go to Patusan. Mr. Stein is a wealthy man, having made his fortune in business. However, he is a romantic and a naturalist and loves nothing more than collecting butterflies and beetles. He recounts to Marlow one day the story of when he found a particularly rare butterfly. He says that he felt at that point that his life was fulfilled and he could die. However, he lives for many years and is distraught over Jim's death, which he does not understand. When Marlow comes to see him after Jim's death, he finds Jewel and Tamb' Itam staying with Stein.

Dain Waris

Dain is Jim's friend and Doramin's only son, who is killed in an ambush by Brown. Dain is a strong warrior, who eagerly leads battles, as when he and Jim lead the attack on the fort of Sherif Ali. Dain and Jim become best friends, and Dain trusts Jim's opinion, even when he does not agree with him. Dain wants to kill Brown and his men but holds off when Jim instructs him to. As a result, he is at ease and not prepared for Brown's ambush, which takes his life.

Themes

Betrayal

The novel is saturated with the idea of betrayal and the consequences that result from it. The defining incident in the book, the *Patna* incident, is horrible in many people's eyes because of the betrayal involved. When Jim decides to jump into a lifeboat, leaving the passengers to what he thinks is a certain death, he betrays both his code as an officer and his personal code of heroism. When he first starts on his path to be an officer, he has visions of his "saving people from sinking ships, cutting away masts in a hurricane," and other heroic deeds. When he betrays that by abandoning the *Patna*'s passengers, the effect on his psyche is immediate, as he equates the physical jump from the ship with a fall from the heroism he so adored: "He had tumbled from a height he could never scale again." Jim is not the only one who either betrays or feels the effects of betrayal. At the end of the novel, Jim is betrayed by Cornelius, who, unbeknownst to him, dislikes him. Jim sends Cornelius as a messenger to the pirate, Brown, but Cornelius uses the opportunity to let Brown know that he "is acquainted with a backwater broad enough to take Brown's boat past Dain's camp." This information leads to an ambush of Dain, who dies in the process. Dain's death, in turn, leads to Jim presenting himself to Dain's father, holding himself accountable for his friend's death. When he does this, Jim's wife, Jewel, thinks he is betraying her: "'You are false!' she screamed out after Jim." Although Jim asks for her forgiveness, she is stung by what she sees as his betrayal of her, and she never forgives him for his death.

Heroism

Heroism is another major theme in the book. In addition to Jim's early heroic daydreams, Marlow also notes some "heroism" in Patusan's past, when the demand for pepper was such that men would "cut each other's throats without hesitation. . . . the bizarre obstinacy of that desire made them defy death in a thousand shapes. . . . it made them heroic." Of course, these are not the heroes of legend, or even of Jim's daydreams, who put their lives on the line for good deeds. For these men, the motivation is "mere greed," not altruism. However, Jim himself does exhibit the true kind of heroism that he aspires to do. After he has been staying with the Bugis Malays in Patusan for a while, he gets a vision one night of how he can conquer the other warring tribes and thus bring

Topics for Further Study

- Research what life was like as a sailor in the 1890s. What did it take to get this kind of job? Put yourself in the place of a sailor from this time period and write a mock letter home to a family member who is considering a life at sea. Provide this family member with details about the daily life of a sailor, including duties, types of food available, and any pastimes or recreational activities.

- In the story, the captain and Jim are taking Moslem pilgrims to the Holy Land. Research the history of such voyages from this time period. How does Conrad's account differ? How is it similar?

- Create a world map that indicates, in numbered order, all of the places that Jim has been in the world, using the text as your guide. Connect these destinations using one line. Now, research Conrad's own history on the seas, and plot these destinations on the same map. After you have drawn a line connecting these, compare Conrad's real-life journeys with those taken by Jim in the book.

- In the story, Jim befriends the Bugis Malays, who are long familiar with white faces, having been besieged by them when Patusan was regarded as a treasure trove for the pepper it held. Research actual colonization stories from around this time period, and discuss how the outside influence has affected the colonized area, the surrounding area, and the world in the past century.

peace to the island. Although "he had to drive it into reluctant minds," his idea finally takes hold, and Jim coordinates the massive effort of moving Doramin's heavy cannons up onto the mountaintop that faces Sherif Ali's "impregnable camp." After their successful attack on Ali, which destroys their rival's camp, Jim is made into a supernatural hero, and stories get around that he "had carried the guns up the hill on his back—two at a time." Jim becomes a superior being in the eyes of the natives, and he finally achieves the heroism that he craves.

Beliefs

Although many themes can be determined from Conrad's complex novel, the majority of them can be based on one larger theme that permeates the others: beliefs. What the characters believe is extremely important to understanding them. At the beginning, although young Jim dreams that he wants to be a hero, when he is put to the test on the *Patna*, his actions show that he believes first and foremost in his survival. Jim is not the only one. When Marlow talks to the French lieutenant whose ship rescues the *Patna* and tows it to shore, he notes that, even though he willingly stayed with the debilitated steamer, "all the time of towing we had two quartermasters stationed with axes by the hawsers, to cut us clear of our tow in case she . . . ." The man does not finish the sentence, but his meaning is clear: his ship's survival comes before the *Patna*'s.

In Patusan, after Jim has become a hero and a leader of the people, he meets Brown, a despicable sort, whom most of Jim's people advocate killing. However, Jim believes "that it would be best to let these whites and their followers go with their lives. It would be a small gift." Since Jim is a nice person, who believes in his heart that all people will be good if given a chance, he advocates letting Brown and his men go. ("It is evident that he didn't mistrust Brown.") Even though this move backfires on Jim, he is true to his beliefs in the end when he adheres to his romantic and idealized notion of honor by presenting himself before Dain's father and making himself accountable for Dain's death. At this point, unlike in the beginning, holding true to a code of ethics is more important to Jim than survival. "He hath taken it upon his own head," one of the members of the crowd around Dain's body says. For once, Jim chooses his destiny and dies knowing he has done the right thing by adhering to his beliefs.

Style

Narration

Narration is the most obvious technique that Conrad uses in *Lord Jim*. In the first line of the first chapter, the reader is introduced to the title character in the following way: "He was an inch, perhaps two, under six feet, powerfully built, and he

... made you think of a charging bull." For the first four chapters, narration continues in this way, in the third person, with an unseen, omniscient narrator, who introduces Jim and gives details about his background. Then, starting in the fifth chapter, Conrad introduces a first-person narrator, Marlow—a character from some of Conrad's earlier stories—who continues to tell Jim's story to the reader: "And it's easy enough to talk of Master Jim." Marlow talks of Jim for the remainder of the book, sometimes giving his own view of experiences he had with Jim. The first of these recollections describes how he met Jim at the inquiry into the *Patna* disaster: "My eyes met his for the first time at that inquiry." At other times, when Marlow is talking about parts of Jim's life when he was not present, Marlow gives the perspective of somebody else who was there: "I am sorry that I can't give you this part of the story, which of course I have mainly from Brown, in Brown's own words." These many accounts of the one story underscore the many ambiguities in the novel.

Bildungsroman

Lord Jim is a good example of a bildungsroman, a coming-of-age story in which a young protagonist must face painful challenges on his or her road to adulthood. Bildungsromans are educational novels that show how other young people have weathered the necessary initiation into adult society, with its mature values. In his case, Jim is plagued by his act of betrayal, when he forsook his duty and left the Moslem passengers to die on the *Patna* without trying to save them. This shameful episode haunts him wherever he goes and affects the course of his life; Jim ends up leaving several jobs where he is happy, when anything even close to the *Patna* incident is mentioned. When Jim's boss at Egström & Blake, a firm that sells provisions for ships, tells him, "This business ain't going to sink," even the unintentional reference to sinking is enough to speed Jim's departure. However, Jim eventually finds peace and happiness in Patusan, and when the past is mentioned again, he does not run from it. Instead, in the end, he faces up to his past, and when he is forced to be sacrificed out of honorable duty to his slain friend, he accepts his fate with "a proud and unflinching glance." As Marlow notes at the very end of the story, "Not in the wildest days of his boyish visions could he have seen the alluring shape of such an extraordinary success." Jim's mature, adult life is only "a short moment," much shorter than most protagonists who weather the storms of youth to become adults and who usually live to tell the tale themselves.

Modernism

Lord Jim is regarded by many as one of the best examples of literary modernism, a type of narrative writing that distinguished itself from most other late-nineteenth-century novels. Modern novels are often harder to read, requiring more work on the part of the author's audience. However, the payoff is also larger for the reader. Rather than use one narrator to tell his story straightforward, in chronological order—or at least in a simple order that is easily understandable to the reader—Conrad tries techniques that were relatively new at that time. As mentioned above, he employs more than one narrator. Also, Conrad keeps the reader in suspense by manipulating time in confusing ways. The author describes in chronological order the events that lead up to the *Patna* incident, but he only alludes to what is actually happening: "What had happened? The wheezy thump of the engines went on. Had the earth been checked in her course? They could not understand."

And neither can the reader, especially when at the start of the next chapter, Conrad has jumped ahead in time to the inquiry at which Jim is explaining his actions: "the official inquiry was being held in the police court of an Eastern port. He stood elevated in the witness-box." The reader knows that something bad has happened, and as the chapter goes on, suspects that the something is horrible: "They wanted facts. Facts! They demanded facts from him, as if facts could explain anything!" However, the horrible something is not revealed in full until many chapters later, when readers learn that Jim has deserted the Moslem passengers, but that against all odds the ship did not sink: "And still she floated!" In fact, where Jim and his crew failed, "two Malays had meantime remained holding to the wheel," thereby making Jim's embarrassment even deeper. Conrad uses this technique of delaying crucial background information many times in the novel. Using complex narrative techniques like multiple narrators and chronological ambiguity is a hallmark of the modern novel, which Conrad helped to develop through works like *Lord Jim*.

Historical Context

Conrad wrote his novel at the dawn of the twentieth century, when the world was rapidly changing

Compare
&
Contrast

- **1890s:** Horribly outnumbered, the British lose their battle with the Boers in South Africa's Cape Colony. However, since the Boers fail to place some of their men in strategically important places, they lose the opportunity to eradicate the British, who still have access to their naval base and supplies.

  Today: After decades of political instability brought on by strife between whites and blacks in South Africa, the region is enjoying an uneasy peace.

- **1890s:** The United States engages in a fierce jungle war in the Phillippines, which have been recently surrendered by Spain to America, although American citizens are divided in their support over the conflict.

  Today: The United States engages in a fierce desert war in the mountainous regions of Afghanistan. The majority of American citizens support this war, which resulted from terrorist attacks in the United States.

- **1890s:** Jewish French Captain Alfred Dreyfus is found guilty of betraying his country by spying for Germany; he is sentenced to life in prison on Devil's Island off French Guiana. Later that same decade, Dreyfus is formally pardoned by the French government in an attempt to end the allegations of anti-Semitism in the bitter controversy known as the Dreyfus Affair.

  Today: After the United States is attacked by Middle Eastern terrorists, many citizens of Middle Eastern descent are detained and interrogated by the American government over their possible connection with the terrorist groups. In several cases, these people are found innocent and released.

---

in many ways. One of the biggest changes was the massive and widespread colonization of islands and other remote lands by European countries and by the United States—in many cases to establish trade or military posts. These colonization efforts, which in many places had begun centuries earlier, came to a head in several conflicts and events at the end of the nineteenth century and beginning of the twentieth century.

In 1892, France, eager to gain more control over West Africa's interior, where it already had many holdings, launched a campaign against Dahomey—a country that provided much-needed access to the south coast of West Africa. The bitter conflict, in which the Dahomeyan army launched themselves at French forces several times, ended with a victory for France, although both sides suffered many losses.

In 1893, the United States, foreseeing the need for a military base in the Pacific Ocean near the rising power of Japan, annexed the Hawaiian islands—of which Pearl Harbor on the island of Oahu had already been ceded to the United States six years earlier. Although the United States came prepared to wage war if necessary, landing scores of marines who surrounded the Hawaiian capital, it was an easy annexation, as the islanders did not fight back. Queen Liliuokalani, who had been concerned about the increasing American influence, was deposed.

In 1894, England, wishing to strengthen the hold it maintained on South Africa, launched a war against the Matabele warriors who inhabited Matabeleland, modern-day Zimbabwe. Dr. Jameson, the administrator of Mashonaland, one of the neighboring English colonies, declared the war after Matabele warriors raided some Mashona natives working for the English. It was a very quick battle, as the English carried guns, whereas the Matabele warriors brandished spears.

In 1896, following the direction of an Italian government that sought the success of foreign conquest as a mask for troubles at home, General Baratieri and his army of sixteen thousand occupied northern Tigre. Ethiopa, angered by this affront, launched an army of one hundred thousand (many of whom carried Italian rifles) against the Baratieri, leaving almost half of the Italian force dead and sending a shockwave throughout Europe, which had been used to winning its battles.

In 1898, when Cuban rebels began to fight for their independence from Spain, a number of American newspapers created sensationalistic stories about the brutality that the Spanish were supposedly visiting upon the Cubans. The American public, and indeed Congress, spurred on by this hype, encouraged President McKinley to declare war on Spain, although McKinley was reluctant to do so at first. After the mysterious sinking of the USS *Maine* in a Havana harbor, which was sent to protect United States citizens resident in Cuba, war was inevitable. Within a couple of months, America had won. In the peace treaty drawn up later that year, Spain ceded Cuba, Puerto Rico, Guam, and the Phillippines to the United States for twenty million dollars.

Critical Overview

In the 1992 article *Lord Jim: After the Truth*, Ross C. Murfin notes that the book "was generally well received" on its first publication in 1900. Murfin says that reviewers were fond of "the novel's romance, the faraway feelings it evoked, and the original poetry of Conrad's language." However, they "decidedly did not like. . . . Conrad's way of telling his story, the odd narrative method that gives structure to the novel." The anonymous reviewer in the *New York Tribune* notes that even though the book "is a long narrative . . . it should be read, if possible, at a sitting. . . . because Mr. Conrad's mode of composition demands it." However, this reviewer was ultimately able to look past what could be an inconvenience and declared *Lord Jim* "a book of great originality, and it exerts a spell such as is rarely encountered in modern fiction." Another anonymous reviewer, for the *Spectator*, called the book "a strange narrative" and named it "Mr. Conrad's latest and greatest work."

Reviewers throughout the twentieth century had various reactions to the work, which was in retrospect identified as a modernist creation for its tendency to break the narrative conventions of the day. Although many early critics were confused by Conrad's ambiguous narrative structure, later critics, such as Paul B. Armstrong in the 1950s, note that Marlow "paradoxically feels at times that he knows less about Jim the more he acquires opinions about

Peter O'Toole as Lord Jim in the 1965 film version of the novel

him. Each interpretation seems 'true,' at least to some extent." Another critic from the 1950s, Albert J. Guerard, notes the ambiguity of the novel but talks about the "psycho-moral" implications, which have "no easy solution."

In 1979, Ian Watt, in *Conrad in the Nineteenth Century*, drew attention to the sources that Conrad used in his composition, following the progression of the novel from its first appearance as a small sketch. Watt believes that understanding this path is important "because it provides some initial clues both to the narrative form and the thematic development of the novel." In Daphna Erdinast-Vulcan's 1991 book, *Joseph Conrad and the Modern Temper*, the author notes that "A somewhat crude but useful distinction can be made between 'first generation' and 'second generation' critics of the novel." Erdinast-Vulcan identifies this first generation as focusing on creating "a stable ethical code by which Jim's story is to be judged," while she sees the second-generation critics regarding the novel as an unsolvable, "modernist expression." For her part, Erdinast-Vulcan sees the novel as an attempt to defeat the modern temper "by a regression to a mythical mode of discourse," using the term "'identifiction' to denote a literary text or genre on which a fictional character construes his or her identity." In other words, Conrad relies on traditional forms to tell Jim's story, which is romanticized to fit the genre.

Questions of Jim's authenticity and what, in fact, Conrad intended the novel to mean have plagued the book throughout its existence, although, as with the early critics, most modern critics acknowledge Conrad's literary artistry. The book has so captivated critical and public minds that in 2000, on the book's one hundredth anniversary, leading Conrad scholars were called together for a special publication, *Lord Jim: Centennial Essays.* As Allan H. Simmons, one of the editors of the book, notes in his essay, "'He Was Misleading': Frustrated Gestures in *Lord Jim*":

> Ultimately, the novel is based on a paradox that invites us to admire commitment to an ideal that can never be justified: the quest for an underlying moral truth that will somehow explain Jim implies the belief that such a truth exists; yet the belief itself is unsustainable.

Criticism

Ryan D. Poquette

Poquette holds a bachelor's degree in English and specializes in writing about literature. In the following essay, Poquette discusses the religious qualities of Conrad's novel, Lord Jim.

In his 1982 book, *Fiction and Repetition: Seven English Novels,* J. Hillis Miller echoes the same belief that many critics have held since the first publication of *Lord Jim* in 1900. Says Miller, the book "reveals itself to be a work which raises questions rather than answering them. The fact that it contains its own interpretations does not make it easier to understand." The enigmatic quality of Conrad's difficult book, found both in its complex narrative structure and in its capacity for yielding several conflicting interpretations, is inevitably part of any discussion about the work. Conrad was an acknowledged master at his art, and *Lord Jim* was written when the author was in the strongest, most experimental phase of his career, so the reader can surmise that this enigma was intentional. In fact, by examining *Lord Jim* in light of its religious references and themes, Jim's spiritual journey, and his ambiguous, messiah-like death, one realizes that Conrad is ultimately encouraging readers to examine their own beliefs.

A reader might be struck by the overwhelming number of religious references that Conrad includes. The book is positively saturated with religious words, which manifest themselves in a number of ways, from a number of people. When Jim is first introduced, the omniscient narrator says that Jim has "the patience of Job," a biblical character from the Old Testament whose faith was tried by God through a number of brutal trials. God is also mentioned directly many times in the novel. Even those who are not particularly devout, such as Chester, the slimy opportunist who tries to get Marlow to have Jim work for him on one of his colonial projects, invoke the name of God. This is true even when telling stories that are morally suspect: "the Lord God knows the right and the wrong of that story." Devils are also mentioned several times, such as when Conrad talks about the depths the lazy seamen will go to when trying to find easy work: "They . . . would have served the devil himself had he made it easy enough." Marlow says to his audience at one point, "I am willing to believe each of us has a guardian angel." Even descriptions of the coarse German captain of the *Patna* occasionally reference the divine: "The German lifted two heavy fists to heaven and shook them a little without a word."

These are but a handful of the religious references that are scattered throughout the book, underscoring the book's theme of beliefs. These references are particularly apparent during the descriptions of the ill-fated *Patna.* The steamer is carrying a large group of Moslem pilgrims, "Eight hundred men and women with faith and hopes," who "at the call of an idea . . . had left their forests, their clearings, the protection of their rulers." Indeed, through his language, Conrad depicts a war between good and evil, believers and non-believers. When he describes the lighthouse that the *Patna* passes, he notes that it was "planted by unbelievers on a treacherous shoal" and that it "seemed to wink at her its eye of flame, as in derision of her errand of faith." However, derision is not enough to stop the *Patna* and its devout passengers from reaching their destination, and Conrad gives an early indication that the ship is being protected by a higher power: "The nights descended on her like a benediction." The word *benediction* is a religious term used to denote a blessing. This is an odd way to describe a nightfall at sea, so it becomes one of the obvious cues that Conrad uses to underscore the religious tone of the story.

Later on, the reference is more direct. When Jim sees that the ship has beaten the odds and is still floating, he notes that the "sleeping pilgrims were destined to accomplish their whole pilgrimage" and remarks that it "was as if the Omnipotence whose mercy they confessed . . . had looked down to make a sign, 'Thou shalt not!' to the ocean."

The figure of Jim is juxtaposed next to this highly religious, almost miraculous incident. Jim has become a naval officer because he hopes to be a real hero someday, putting his life at risk for the benefit of somebody else. However, Jim is human, which means he is flawed. When the moment comes when he can prove his heroism, he panics, and, for whatever reason—Conrad makes it unclear in the end as to why Jim acts the way he does—deserts the ship, taking a symbolic fall from heroism to shame as he jumps into one of the lifeboats, leaving the eight hundred passengers in his care to go under on the partially sunken ship. Jim feels the effects of his actions right away: "There was no going back. It was as if I had jumped into a well—into an everlasting deep hole." The use of the word *everlasting* is particularly telling. In the Christian sense, Jim has "fallen" from grace, and fallen souls, if not redeemed, will be cast into an eternity of hell, another everlasting deep hole. From this point on in the story, Jim embarks on a spiritual journey, which Conrad paints in biblical terms at times. When Marlow is discussing the stormy night following Jim's trial and subsequent expulsion from officer service, Marlow uses some curious terms: "The downpour fell with the heavy uninterrupted rush of a sweeping flood, with a sound of unchecked overwhelming fury." For Marlow, these sounds call "to one's mind the images of collapsing bridges, of uprooted trees, or undermined mountains." This type of description evokes images of the flood that God calls forth in the Old Testament to wipe the earth clean of sinners.

Of course, the analogy is not a perfect one. Jim is not Noah, the one virtuous man whom God spared from the flood. Also in the Hebrew Bible, the Flood occurs long after the Genesis of Man, whereas in *Lord Jim*, Jim does not experience his genesis into his new life until he reaches Patusan, where "he left his earthly failings behind him." This reliance on certain biblical events in an unconventional order prevents the story from becoming a true allegory, a type of story in which many characters, settings, and events have a symbolic quality within the context of one greater theme. Jim is not Christ and attempting to label him as the Christian messiah while labeling the other aspects of the story as Christian symbols is a futile enterprise.

> Whether one views Jim as a redeemed human, a religious messiah, or a foolish romantic, in the end it is only relevant to the individual reader. The meaning of Jim's life, like the meaning of life in general, is ultimately beyond human explanation."

So if Jim is not Noah or Christ, who is he? At one point, after his near-death in the marshy Patusan creek, he becomes Adam, as Daphna Erdinast-Vulcan notes in her book *Joseph Conrad and the Modern Temper*: "He wakes up, covered with mud and 'alone of his kind' as Adam was when he was created." Just as Adam was pure and seems alien to modern, "fallen" humans, so does Jim appear to the natives of Patusan, although for different reasons: "He pelted straight on in his socks, beplastered with filth out of all semblance to a human being." This view of Jim as something other than a normal human is perpetuated as he begins to live among the Bugis Malays and leads the battle to destroy the camp of their rival, Sherif Ali. After this, the natives "called him Tuan Jim: as one might say—Lord Jim." The villagers create a legend around Jim, which, by the time Marlow visits him, "had gifted him with supernatural powers." The natives think that Jim has performed miracles, perhaps Christ-like to the reader, such as carrying heavy cannons "up the hill on his back—two at a time." In fact, the natives view Jim with "a strange mixture of familiarity and awe."

Once Conrad establishes the religious undertone of the book and then paints Jim as a religious messiah, he stays true to the fate of most messiahs and has Jim die at the ending of the book. However, even the way that Jim dies points to the religious theme. The last part of the book, which details the events that lead up to Jim's death, deviates from the rest of the narrative. For the majority of the book, Marlow narrates Jim's tale to a group of friends, based on what he has heard from Jim or experienced himself. But when Marlow ends his portion of the tale, Conrad finishes the story by using several, sometimes disparate accounts from

What Do I Read Next?

- Muhummad Asad's *The Road to Mecca* (2001) is a book about the author's journey through the Islamic world. The book discusses four different aspects about the journey: geographical, historical, linguistic, and spiritual.

- *Almayer's Folly*, Conrad's first novel, originally published in 1895, depicts a trader in the South Seas who becomes mired in the Malaysian environment through his business and his marriage and cannot leave to go back to Europe, as he wishes to. This book critiques the colonialism that was prevalent in Conrad's day.

- Conrad's *Heart of Darkness*, originally published in 1899, details Marlow's journey into the Congo to find a man who has gone mad and is hiding out in the jungle. The book inspired the famous movie *Apocalypse Now*, which set Conrad's story in Vietnam.

- Conrad's *Typhoon*, originally published in 1902, is a story about a man who spends his life at sea, writing monthly letters home to his uncaring wife. When he and his crew face a storm like no other, Conrad illustrates how different men react in crisis situations. The last part of the story is told by the letters that the captain and crew have written to their significant others.

- Conrad's *Under Western Eyes*, originally published in 1911, takes place in Russia, where a philosophy student gets caught up with a group of political refugees who plot a murder. His conscience causes him to confess to the police and then to tell his friends what he has done, even though he endangers his life by doing so.

- Conrad's *Victory: An Island Tale*, originally published in 1915, is a story about a man who lives in isolation in the South Pacific. He has a chance meeting with an English girl who is part of a touring orchestra group, rescues her from a man named Schomberg, and brings her back to his island home. Schomberg sends his henchmen to retrieve the English girl and kill the man.

- Thomas Hardy's *The Mayor of Casterbridge*, originally published in 1886, is a story about a man who achieves status, power, and esteem only to lose it all when events from his past come to light and when his greed and bad judgment get the better of him.

- Adam Hochschild's, *King Leopold's Ghost*, published in 1998, depicts the true story of a greedy Belgian king who committed horrific acts but who is largely unknown when compared with other brutal rulers like Hitler. During the time of European colonization, King Leopold II frantically scrambled to claim other countries as his own and won the modern-day Congo. His reign of terror killed several million indigenous people, while the remaining survivors were left to harvest rubber and mine ore.

---

various narrators. As Paul B. Armstrong notes in his article, "Monism and Pluralism in *Lord Jim*" for the *Centennial Review*: "considered as a group, the readings do not fit together. And because they are finally irreconcilable, they frustrate Marlow's attempt to develop a coherent, comprehensive view of Jim as much as they aid it." This narrative method evokes an image of the Bible, which was also written by several authors, who sometimes contradict each other in their telling of certain events. The events surrounding the death of Christ in the New Testament have been particularly scrutinized, since there is no one account that tells the events in chronological order, from beginning to end.

Conrad mimics this style, especially at the end, turning the events surrounding Jim's death into legend, as he paints Jim as a Christ-like figure. When he is faced with imminent death, as Christ was, Jim does not flinch from his destiny and instead chooses to conquer by submitting: "There was nothing to fight for. He was going to prove his power in another way and conquer the fatal destiny itself." As Ross C. Murfin notes in his book, *Lord Jim: After the Truth*, "Christ's 'new' law of self-sacrifice" is "at the heart of the Judeo-Christian faith." Like Christ, Jim ultimately dies for somebody else's sins. Christ died for the sins of all humanity, including his enemies', as Jim dies for the actions of Cornelius and Brown, the enemies who seal Jim's fate when they kill Dain and force Jim to make good on his promise to be accountable for the death. "I am come ready and unarmed," Jim says, when he presents himself to Dain's father, who immediately kills Jim. Says Erdinast-Vulcan of Jim, "He perishes, like a true biblical or mythical hero, by his own word."

In the end, many readers, like Marlow, walk away confused, feeling, as Marlow felt at one point, that Jim stands "at the heart of a vast enigma." It appears that Conrad has deliberately structured his story so that it negates a decisive interpretation. Even in this essay, where an abundance of religious references, Jim's spiritual journey, and the narrative method surrounding Jim's ambiguous death have been used as support to show Conrad's religious undertone, one cannot pin Conrad down to an overall guiding thematic structure—which is exactly how Conrad wanted it. Jim's life and death will hold different meanings for different readers, just as Marlow, Jewel, and Tamb' Itam all elicit widely different interpretations. Whether one views Jim as a redeemed human, a religious messiah, or a foolish romantic, in the end it is only relevant to the individual reader. The meaning of Jim's life, like the meaning of life in general, is ultimately beyond human explanation. The important thing is to be true to one's individual beliefs, religious or otherwise, as Jim is true to his beliefs in the end and so dies a fulfilled man—even if most of those left behind do not agree with or understand his actions.

Source: Ryan D. Poquette, Critical Essay on *Lord Jim*, in *Novels for Students*, The Gale Group, 2003.

Douglas Hewitt

In the following essay, Hewitt discusses Lord Jim *in contrast with* Heart of Darkness.

Lord Jim was begun immediately after Conrad had finished writing 'Youth' in the summer of 1898, dropped for a time, taken up again after he had written *Heart of Darkness*, and finished in the summer of 1900. 'My first thought', he says in the 'Author's Note' to the Collected Edition, 'was of a short story, concerned only with the pilgrim ship episode; nothing more'. But later he perceived that

the pilgrim ship episode was a good starting-point for a free and wandering tale; that it was an event, too,

> **The effect of muddlement which is so commonly found in *Lord Jim* comes, in short, from this—that Marlow is himself muddled."**

which could conceivably colour the whole 'sentiment of existence' in a simple and sensitive character.

Signs of this change in conception may be discerned, though not where we might expect to find them—in a thinness of material or an untidy linking of an illogical second part. Rather are they apparent in a certain muddlement throughout, an uncertainty of the final impression intended by Conrad.

In terms of plot there are undoubtedly two parts to the story: the defection of Jim and the disaster after he seems to have rehabilitated himself; certainly the second part has been added. But, as we have seen, and as I hope to show here in more detail, they are intimately connected. It is, indeed, difficult to imagine the first part alone as a satisfactory story—certainly as a story by Conrad; the account of a cowardly leap for safety alone could hardly be enough; it demands development.

The general lines of the story are given in miniature in the first chapter. Jim, having developed a romantic view of himself as one who will meet crises with calmness and determination, is not shaken in this faith by his failure to reach the cutter of his training ship when it puts out to effect a rescue. In the main crisis of the first part of the novel the failure is repeated under circumstances where he offends most unequivocally against 'the obscure body of men held together by a community of inglorious toil and by fidelity to a certain standard of conduct'. His crime is described in terms which are reminiscent of some passages of 'Heart of Darkness'—in terms of what, in that story, is called 'sordid farce'.

> It was part of the burlesque meanness pervading that particular disaster at sea that they did not come to blows. It was all threats, all a terribly effective feint, a sham from beginning to end. . . .

There is a flavour of shameless farce about all the weaknesses and crimes of which Conrad writes at this time; his mean characters are all horribly comic.

Jim's offence is one upon which the Court of Enquiry can have no mercy. But he insists on what, to many of the spectators, seems like trying to brazen it out. Brierly's question: 'Why eat all that dirt?' sums up the feeling of most of them. His hope, however, is that he can rehabilitate himself; as in his first failure in the training ship, he is still sure that at bottom he is ready for any emergency, that he has only been betrayed by circumstances. He will not accept his weakness and stay in a place where men know his story, and so he is driven farther and farther eastwards in the search for a refuge where he can start with a clean sheet and establish himself as a trustworthy man.

Finally, in the jungle settlement of Patusan, he rises to be 'Lord Jim', one whose authority and honour are never questioned and on whom all the natives are dependent. It seems that he has successfully isolated himself from his past, in a place where

> The stream of civilization, as if divided on a headland a hundred miles north of Patusan, branches east and south-west, leaving its plains and valleys, its old trees and its old mankind, neglected and isolated.

But, despite the fact that he has achieved 'the conquest of love, honour, men's confidence', his past comes in search of him. Gentleman Brown and his crew of cut-throats penetrate the 'wall of forests' which shuts Jim in his isolation. Physically the people of Patusan are more than a match for Brown, but mentally Jim is helpless before this man who combines with his ferocity 'a vehement scorn for mankind at large and for his victims in particular' and who 'would rob a man as if only to demonstrate his poor opinion of the creature'. Everything that Brown says recalls Jim's past weakness, undermines his certainty that he has put behind him a cowardice that was only momentary.

> He asked Jim whether he had nothing fishy in his life to remember that he was so damnedly hard upon a man trying to get out of a deadly hole by the first means that came to hand—and so on and so on. And there ran through the rough talk a vein of subtle reference to their common blood, an assumption of common experience; a sickening suggestion of common guilt, of secret knowledge that was like a bond of their minds and of their hearts.

Jim finds that 'his fate, revolted, was forcing his hand'. We remember the 'unforeseen partnership' with Kurtz which Marlow accepts in 'Heart of Darkness'; but here there is an explicit weakness in Jim to which the partner appeals, and he

confronts this appeal under circumstances which make his actions of vital importance for all the inhabitants of Patusan. He speaks no more than the truth when he says: 'I am responsible for every life in the land'. Unable to disown Brown, he brings disaster on the village, takes the death of the chief's son on his own head, and is killed as punishment.

In enlarging the simple story of the pilgrim ship episode, however, Conrad makes a more significant addition than the second half of the story; he introduces Marlow, who, although he does not appear as storyteller until the fifth chapter, is the person to whom we naturally look for commentary and judgment. Judgment we find in plenty—but, far from clarifying the moral issues, Marlow's reflections only succeed in making them more confused.

We remain at the end, I believe, uncertain as to what our verdict on Jim is meant to be. Many views are put before us. The elderly French lieutenant's is clear:

> But the honour—the honour, monsieur! . . . The honour . . . that is real—that is! And what life may be worth when . . . when the honour is gone—*ah ça ! par exemple*—I can offer no opinion.

This discourages Marlow; he feels that the lieutenant has 'pricked the bubble'. Yet at times he seems to see Jim as expiating his fault by taking on himself the punishment for the disaster to the village, finally re-establishing his honour. At other times a totally different verdict seems to be presented, as in the conclusion:

> But we can see him, an obscure conqueror of fame, tearing himself out of the arms of a jealous love at the sign, at the call of his exalted egoism. He goes away from a living woman to celebrate his pitiless wedding with a shadowy ideal of conduct.

We remain uncertain whether Jim's moment of panic is one which can be expiated or whether, in the judgment of Marlow the seaman, it has placed him for ever beyond the possibility of forgiveness, uncertain, indeed, whether he is to be blamed for hoping that his weakness can be forgotten or for being so morbidly conscious of it.

The reason for this uncertainty is clear; it is because Marlow, Conrad's mouthpiece, is himself bewildered. As in 'Heart of Darkness', which Conrad wrote while recasting the novel, Marlow plays a greater part than might at first be thought. We may reasonably wonder whether the feelings which brought 'Heart of Darkness' to birth may not be the chief cause why *Lord Jim* developed from a simple short story into a complex novel, for there are many resemblances between the relationship of Marlow and Kurtz and that of Marlow and Jim.

There is an 'unforeseen partnership' not only between Jim and Gentleman Brown but also between Jim and Marlow. 'Why I longed to go grubbing into the deplorable details . . . I can't explain' Marlow says, and wonders:

> Was it for my own sake that I wished to find some shadow of an excuse for that young fellow whom I had never seen before?

A relationship is quickly established between them. When Jim explains his hopes of regaining the respect that he has lost, Marlow says:

> . . . it was I . . . who a moment ago had been so sure of the power of words, and now was afraid to speak, in the same way one dares not move for fear of losing a slippery hold. . . . It was the fear of losing him that kept me silent, for it was borne upon me that should I let him slip away into the darkness I would never forgive myself.

Just as in 'Heart of Darkness' Marlow feels the power of nightmares which his previous experience and standards have not made him ready to understand, so here he is appealed to by Jim in ways for which he is not prepared.

> I was made to look at the convention that lurks in all truth [Marlow says] and on the essential sincerity of falsehood. He appealed to all sides at once—to the side turned perpetually to the light of day, and to that side of us which, like the other hemisphere of the moon, exists stealthily in perpetual darkness, with only a fearful ashy light falling at times on the edge. He swayed me. I own to it, I own up.

It is his own security for which Marlow fears; when he goes for information to one of Jim's fellow officers, it is because he hopes to learn of a redeeming motive for his offence.

> I see well enough now [he says of this incident] that I hoped for the impossible—for the laying of what is the most obstinate ghost of man's creation, of the uneasy doubt uprising like a mist, secret and gnawing like a worm, and more chilling than the certitude of death—the doubt of the sovereign power enthroned in a fixed standard of conduct.

It is obvious enough that Marlow is disturbed because Jim, a fellow English seaman, has not been true to the standards by which they all live.

> I was aggrieved against him [he says], as though he had cheated me—me!—of a splendid opportunity to keep up the illusion of my beginnings, as though he had robbed our common life of the last spark of its glamour.

But this alone is not sufficient to account for the disturbance of mind in which he is plunged. Jim has also raised doubts of the finality of the very standards themselves; he has suggested the possibility that there are hidden depths of feeling against which they are powerless. Marlow—and, as we shall see in a minute, Brierly—cannot cast Jim out as an offender and forget him, and this is not merely because he is a fellow Englishman, but because he seems to cast doubt on the values by which they could condemn him. Marlow speaks thus of the courage which Jim so signally fails to display:

> . . . an unthinking and blessed stiffness before the outward and inward terrors, before the might of nature, and the seductive corruption of men—backed by a faith invulnerable to the strength of facts, to the contagion of examples, to the solicitation of ideas. Hang ideas! They are tramps, vagabonds, knocking at the back-door of your mind, each taking a little of your substance, each carrying away some crumb of that belief in a few simple notions you must cling to if you want to live decently and would like to die easy.

Marlow would seem here to be at one with Winnie Verloc of *The Secret Agent* in her belief that life does not bear looking into very closely, and he continues with the direct implication that such courage is only possible for fools:

> This has nothing to do with Jim, directly; only he was outwardly so typical of that good, stupid kind we like to feel marching right and left of us in life, of the kind that is not disturbed by the vagaries of intelligence and the perversions of—of nerves, let us say.

He goes on to reminisce about 'that good, stupid kind' and about how moved he is when a boy whom he has taken to sea for his first voyage greets him after many years, now grown into one 'fit to live or die as the sea may decree', just as, in the voyage into the heart of darkness, the Marlow of that story clings for a moment to the manual of seamanship as the relief of something tangible in the midst of nightmare. The nostalgia for the normal, for the reliance on simple duties and uncomplicated virtues, is the same, and in both cases the relief can only be temporary.

The feeling of insecurity is deepened by the story of Brierly's suicide. That impeccable captain has felt the same apprehension as Marlow: '. . . the only thing that holds us together', he says, 'is just the name for that kind of decency. Such an affair destroys one's confidence'. We might feel the conclusion to be extreme, for in any group of men there will be some who will betray the faith reposed in them, but we know that, all the time he is enquiring into Jim's case, he is also sitting in judgment on himself and finding a verdict of 'unmitigated guilt'. Marlow speculates that, in his case too, it is the awakening of some idea:

... the matter was no doubt of the gravest import [he says] one of those trifles that awaken ideas—start into life some thought with which a man unused to such a companionship finds it impossible to live.

We are given no hint of what the 'idea' is, except that it is not a commonplace worry about drink, or money, or women, but the effect of what we are told about Brierly is to reinforce Marlow's own obliquely expressed conviction that the virtues of seamanship—all of which Brierly possesses in superabundant measure—are still vulnerable to 'ideas'—that they are not enough in themselves and can easily be imperilled.

For all those issues with which Brierly's virtues can deal, the judgment on Jim is certain, but, in Marlow's words, Jim's attempt to explain his deed gives the impression that

he was only speaking before me, in a dispute with an invisible personality, an antagonistic and inseparable partner of his existence—another possessor of his soul. These were issues beyond the competency of a court of enquiry.

The effect of muddlement which is so commonly found in *Lord Jim* comes, in short, from this—that Marlow is himself muddled. We look to him for a definite comment, explicit or implicit, on Jim's conduct and he is not able to give it. We are inevitably reminded of the bewilderment with which the Marlow of 'Heart of Darkness' faces Kurtz. By appealing to 'that side of us which, like the other hemisphere of the moon, exists stealthily in perpetual darkness' he confronts Marlow with 'issues beyond the competency of a court of enquiry' and thus shakes the standards by which he would normally be judged.

Here, as in the short story, the experience of Marlow goes far beyond that of the man whom he cannot disown. Kurtz is only a 'hollow man', Jim himself is, by comparison with Marlow, naïve, a romantic thinking in the terms of a boy's adventure story.

But the muddlement goes farther than this. I have so far begged the question by saying 'Marlow, Conrad's mouthpiece'. In fact the confusion seems to extend to Conrad's conception of the story, and this reveals itself in some of the rhetoric given to Marlow. A good deal of this is imprecise and some is little more than a vague and rather pretentious playing with abstractions. It is in these terms that he speaks of the approaching catastrophe:

Magna est veritas et ... Yes, when it gets a chance. There is a law, no doubt—and likewise a law regulates your luck in the throwing of dice. It is not Jus-

tice, the servant of men, but accident, hazard, Fortune—the ally of patient Time—that holds an even and scrupulous balance. ... Well, let's leave it to chance, whose ally is Time, that cannot be hurried, and whose enemy is Death, that will not wait.

There are many such passages, and they give the impression rather of a man who is ruminating to obscure the issue than of one thinking to clarify it. But they are not 'placed'—Conrad, that is, does not so present them that we see them as deliberate, part of the portrayal of a man who is bewildered. They come rather from his own uncertainty as to the effect at which he is aiming. There is, very clearly, a conflict in his own mind; he raises the issue of the sufficiency of the 'few simple notions you must cling to if you want to live decently', but he does not, throughout the book, face it consistently.

Lord Jim is, at bottom, concerned with the same preoccupations as 'Heart of Darkness' and other works of this period, but Conrad has chosen to treat them in such a way that he inevitably feels more directly concerned. As he says in the concluding words of the 'Author's Note': 'He was "one of us".' The uncertainty which remains even at the end of the book as to what judgment we should pass on Jim and the passages of imprecise rhetoric are, I believe, an indication that his feelings are too deeply and too personally involved for him to stand above the bewilderment in which he places Marlow. The fixed standards of the simple sailor are those which, above all others, Conrad finds it difficult to treat with detachment. He was too aware of the depths of treachery and cowardice of which men are capable not to cherish whatever seems to provide a defence against them, and at times we have the impression that, just as much as Marlow, he is himself fighting to retain a faith in the efficacy and total goodness of the 'few simple notions'.

Source: Douglas Hewitt, "Chapter III: *Lord Jim*," in *Conrad: A Reassessment*, Rowman and Littlefield, 1975, pp. 31–39.

Eban Bass

In the following essay, Bass discusses Conrad's difficulties with presenting speech, idiom, and dialect in his writing.

One does not have to read far in *Lord Jim* to observe Conrad's difficulties in making speech idiom read true. A Yankee deserter who is the crack marksman of Brown's derelict pirates, keeping his eye on a human target, says unconvincingly, "This there coon's health would never be a source of anxiety to his friends any more"; and later, when there are no further victims to shoot at, he pronounces the calm of Patusan to be "on-natural." The difficulty of rendering Jim's British idiom, however, Conrad seems to have turned into an asset rather than a liability. Jim is sometimes limited to a mere inept stutter, the mixture of pretense and modesty that is after all pretty much the base of his character. When Marlow proposes the Patusan venture to him, the young man speaks his gratitude in as embarrassingly stilted (and unauthentic) a manner as that of the Yankee deserter's phrases: "'Jove!' he gasped out. 'It is noble of you! . . . What a bally ass I've been,' he said very slow in an awed tone. . . . . 'You are a brick,' he cried next in a muffled voice. . . . 'I would be a brute now if I. . .'" The halting is more extreme here than elsewhere because Jim is deeply moved at being given a second chance in life, but hardly ever is he eloquent.

If his words sound unreal during times of strong emotion, so is Jim himself excessive as a romanticist. He does not speak so all the time, fortunately; in fact, he generally speaks rather little. Also informative are the verbal anomalies associated with Jim (these are sometimes auditory errors); they suggest an index to "the subtle unsoundness of the man" that so puzzles Marlow, who knows Jim best of all. Three incidents that come early in the novel show Jim as a victim of verbal confusion. Individually, they are errors that anyone might make, especially in the context of emotional tension in which they occur. Collectively, however, Jim's misunderstandings lead one to see them as symptomatic of a kind of inattention or failure on his part—almost, in a sense, as if language has come to mean something different to him from what it does to anyone else. Marlow's first encounter with Jim, on the steps of the courthouse where the *Patna* hearing is being conducted, is marked by a verbal-auditory error that dramatizes Jim's shame, as well as his belligerence, over his desertion from the ship. An acquaintance of Marlow's remarks of an ugly forlorn dog belonging to some Malay native, "Look at that wretched cur." Jim overhears the phrase and, already stinging from the shame of public disgrace, thinks this is a further insult directed toward him. Assuming Marlow to be his accuser, "He made a step forward and barred my way. We were alone; he glared at me with an air of stubborn resolution. I became aware I was being held up, so to speak, as if in a wood."

Marlow himself is highly articulate and persuasive, and once he wins Jim's confidence the troubled young man unburdens his problems to

> The disorder comes of a haphazard mixture of white and Malay culture. The half-caste shipmaster uses all the *cliches* of the 'white man's burden' and distorts them: the net effect, via language, is to show the failure of the white mission in the Far East."

him. Significantly, however, most of the incidents Jim recounts are couched in Marlow's words. One exception, however, is the second instance of Jim's verbal misunderstanding. It takes place when Jim goes below deck to investigate the bulkhead of the disabled *Patna* which may at any moment give way and flood the ship. Returning past some of the native passengers, Jim is stopped by one of them.

> "The beggar clung to me like a drowning man," he said, impressively. "Water, water! What water did he mean? What did he know? As calmly as I could I ordered him to let go. He was stopping me, time was pressing, other men began to stir; I wanted time—time to cut the boats adrift. . . . He would not keep quiet: he tried to shout; I had half throttled him before I made out what he wanted. He wanted some water—water to drink; they were on strict allowance, you know, and he had with him a young boy I had noticed several times. His child was sick—and thirsty. He had caught sight of me as I passed by, and was begging for a little water. That's all."

Needless to say, the potential panic of this scene is explanation enough for Jim's mistake, just as the misunderstanding of the epithet "cur" is not unusual, given the circumstances in which it occurs. Yet these two errors, told in the same order in Marlow's narrative as they are given here, prepare for Jim's fatal mistake of the *Patna*, which significantly is in part a verbal (or auditory) one.

Once the German captain and his deserting crew ineptly launch their life boat, Jim becomes more intensely aware than ever of the danger of panic among the native passengers. The ugly irony that rouses Jim from his inaction (really his refusal to help the deserters with their boat) is the collapse of the third engineer, apparently from a heart attack, on deck; Jim stumbles over the man's legs. Inasmuch as it is the "dead" man (he in fact stands once more, then collapses for good) who rouses Jim back to life, Jim in some respect assumes the engineer's identity. This must be the explanation for his erroneous response to the deserting officers' calls to their compatriot. "With the first hiss of rain, and the first gust of wind, they screamed, 'Jump, George! We'll catch you! Jump!' The ship began a slow plunge; the rain swept over her like a broken sea; my cap flew off my head; my breath was driven back into my throat. I heard as if I had been on the top of a tower another wild screech, 'Geo-o-o-orge! Oh, jump!' She was going down, down, head first under me . . ." Jim again is the narrator, rather than Marlow, but he breaks off for a moment with the strain, and Marlow remarks his vague gesture of sweeping away cobwebs with his hand, before Jim concludes his account: "I had jumped." His instant of cowardice can thus be viewed partially as a verbal error, but it is not so easily explained away as the "cur" and "water" mistakes. The less serious, more believable ones, however, lead up to the fatal, less justifiable error. Jim's rigid non-participation in the act of desertion, i.e. the actual lowering of the lifeboat, is not enough to relieve him of moral responsibility. The dead man stirs Jim back to life, and for a moment Jim assumes the dead man's identity and makes his cowardly escape in George's name.

One further auditory error by Jim occurs while he is in the lifeboat; it may be taken to be the nightmare effect of an ill conscience, and in a milder sense is comparable to the pink toads which the hospitalized crewman, in his D.T.'s, imagines to be under his bed. Jim's apprehension of the deserted pilgrims is less fantastic: while on board the lifeboat he imagines he hears shouts from the "sinking" *Patna*, even though the other deserting officers say they hear nothing—regardless of the firm conviction of all the deserters that the ship's passengers are indeed drowning. "I was relieved to learn that those shouts—did I tell you I had heard shouts? No? Well, I did. Shouts for help . . . blown along with the drizzle. Imagination I suppose. And yet I can hardly . . . How stupid . . . the others did not. I asked them afterwards. They all said No. No? And I was hearing them even then! I might have known—but I didn't think—I only listened. Very faint screams—day after day."

Jim's auditory errors are in keeping with his halting, boyish manner of speech. Marlow's comment on the young man's verbal mannerisms is in-formative: "He had confided so much in me that at times it seems as though he must come in presently and tell the story in his own words, in his careless yet feeling voice, with his offhand manner, a little puzzled, a little bothered, a little hurt, but now and then by a word or a phrase giving one of these glimpses of his very, own self that were never any good for purposes of orientation." Here we see the necessity of Marlow to "speak" for Jim: because Jim lacks a sense of verbal continuity and direction. More than once, Marlow notes Jim's lack of eloquence. Jim does not reveal, for example, what he said to Jewel once he did recover his voice after her heroic act of revealing the would-be assassins. "He did not tell me what it was he said when at last he recovered his voice. I don't suppose he could be very eloquent."

Marlow himself does not condemn this poverty of Jim's speech: "He was not eloquent, but there was a dignity in this constitutional reticence, there was a high seriousness in his stammerings." No doubt Conrad seriously tried to capture in Jim's heroic British slang the characteristic understatement that he admired in the national character of the man. That he largely failed in this attempt gives an interesting further dimension to the novel which Conrad must not have intended, but one which adds greatly to what Conrad in effect says about Jim's failure with language.

Jim is inarticulate when expressing gratitude, and his attempts are as painful for Marlow as they are for himself: "He couldn't think how he merited that I . . . He would be shot if he could see to what he owed . . . And it was Stein Stein the merchant, who . . . but of course it was me he had to . . . I cut him short. He was not articulate, and his gratitude caused me inexplicable pain." Jim's emotions are simply too extreme, whatever they happen to be, to admit verbal expression. Gratitude, humiliation, love, are among the feelings he is inept at conveying. "His lips pouted a little, trembling as though he had been on the point of bursting into tears. I perceived he was incapable of pronouncing a word from the excess of his humiliation. From disappointment too—who knows?"

When Jim leaves Patusan, Marlow puts him on board a ship whose captain employs a language symptomatic of the dilemma Jim will face. Though quite different from Jim's speech, the captain's is equally informative. The ship's master is a Westernized half-caste.

His flowing English seemed to be derived from a dictionary compiled by a lunatic. Had Mr. Stein desired him to "ascend," he would have "reverentially"—(I think he wanted to say respectfully—but devil only knows)—"reverentially made objects for the safety of properties." If disregarded, he would have presented "resignation to quit." Twelve months ago he had made his last voyage there, and though Mr. Cornelius "propitiated many offertories" to Mr. Roger Allang and the "principal populations," on conditions which made the trade "a snare and ashes in the mouth," yet his ship had been fired upon from the woods by "irresponsive parties" all the way clown the river; which causing his crew "from exposure to limb to remain silent in hidings," the brigantine was nearly stranded on a sandbank at the bar, where she "would have been perishable beyond the act of man."

This verbal hodgepodge is in keeping with the social and political disorder Jim encounters in Patusan—and out of which he temporarily brings order and meaning. The disorder comes of a haphazard mixture of white and Malay culture. The half-caste shipmaster uses all the *cliches* of the "white man's burden" and distorts them: the net effect, via language, is to show the failure of the white mission in the Far East. That is the final judgment of *Lord Jim*, expressed by the unnamed recipient of Jim's papers and of Marlow's final statement about Jim. Thus the language of the half-caste is a proper index to conditions in Patusan: an ugly amalgam of western enlightenment and eastern ignorance. As Marlow observes when trusting Jim to safe passage on board the half-caste's ship, "My heart was freed from that dull resentment which had existed side by side with interest in his fate. The absurd chatter of the half-caste had given more reality to the miserable dangers of his path than Stein's careful statements."

With his departure to Patusan, Jim supposedly escapes from the white man's world and his own failure in it, an index to which is his failure with its language. Yet his parting cry to Marlow from the ship of the half-caste reiterates the verbal anomaly of Jim's good name, his repute, and his vain hope of recovering his lost honor. "I saw him aft detached upon the light of the westering sun, raising his cap high above his head. I heard an indistinct shout, 'You—shall—hear—of—me.' Of me, or from me, I don't know which. I think it must have been *of* me." The ambiguity in this case may only be Marlow's failure to hear. But the mere fact that Jim still hopes to achieve heroism precedes another dimension the stature he achieves as a folk hero among the Malays of Patusan.

Jim cannot really shut himself off from the white man's world. At the time of his final departure from Marlow, who has once visited him in his

native kingdom, he says, "You shall never be troubled by a voice from there again." This bravado no man can live up to, and yet it is characteristic of Jim's error that he set up this sort of verbal responsibility for himself. Shortly after, Jim tempers it with a pathetic try at one more farewell to the white world. It is revealing for what it implies about the spirit of empire and the loyalty that spirit impressed on the men it sent to far nameless places. "'Will you be going home [to England] again soon?' asked Jim, just as I swung my leg over the gunwale. 'In a year or so if I live,' I said. The forefoot grated on the sand, the boat floated, the wet oars flashed and dipped once, twice. Jim, at the water's edge, raised his voice. 'Tell them . . .' he began. I signed to the men to cease rowing, and waited in wonder. Tell who? The half-submerged sun faced him; I could see its red gleam in his eyes that looked dumbly at me. . . . 'No—nothing,' he said, and with a slight wave of his hand motioned the boat away. I did not look again . . .'"

The language Jim uses in Patusan is his own, as well as that of the natives, but he has a fresh chance to speak authoritatively, in the words of idealized romance and heroism. Yet verbal error still dogs him: in one instance, there is a curious misunderstanding of the name he gives Cornelius's step-daughter, the woman he loves. Jim calls her "Jewel," but the shrewd practical world or rumor applies a literal, rather than Jim's figurative, meaning to the name. "Such a jewel—it was explained to me by the old fellow from whom I heard most of this amazing Jim-myth—a sort of scribe to the wretched little Rajah of the place;—such a jewel, he said, cocking his poor purblind eyes up at me (he was sitting on the cabin floor out of respect), is best preserved by being concealed about the person of a woman. Yet it is not every woman that would do. She must be young—he sighed deeply—and insensible to the seductions of love." Jim of course sees Jewel's own merits as precious; contrary to rumor, she guards no fabulous great emerald.

In teaching the girl to speak his own language, Jim educates her in his own private system of values which the outside world has had trouble understanding and which Jim was inept at expressing because of his own verbal limitations. "Her mother had taught her to read and write; she had learned a good bit of English from Jim, and she spoke it most amusingly, with his own clipping, boyish intonation." But in the end she does not really understand Jim's values, and she believes him to be a traitor for giving her his word, and then leaving her.

Jim's few verbal successes take place at Patusan, when he acts upon his own concept of chivalry, courage, and honor. The chivalry is vocal in Jim's attack on the unspeakable Cornelius for his mistreatment of Jewel.

> He let himself go—his nerves had been over-wrought for days—and called him many pretty names,— swindler, liar, sorry rascal: in fact, carried on in an extraordinary way. He admits he passed all bounds, that he was quite beside himself—defied all Patusan to scare him away—declared he would make them all dance to his own tune yet, and so on, in a menacing, boasting strain . . . He came to his senses, and ceasing suddenly, wondered greatly at himself. He watched for a while. Not a stir, not a sound. "Exactly as if the chap had died while I had been making all that noise," he said.

Jim's heroism is also successfully verbal on the occasion when he organizes one faction of the Patusan community against its own enemy. "Jim spent the day with the old *nakhoda*, preaching the necessity of vigorous action to the principal men of the Bugis community, who had been summoned for a big talk. He remembered with pleasure how very eloquent and persuasive he had been. 'I managed to put some backbone into them that time, and no mistake,' he said." In this event, as in the one in which he lashes out at Cornelius, Jim experiences deep satisfaction through his verbal success, and the action that results from it. But in neither case do we hear the actual words of these speeches, and it is characteristic of Conrad's uncertainty with Jim's speech idiom that he report only the manner and the effect.

The success of the white lord, in word and deed, is short-lived. Jim fails in the encounter with Brown and his fellow-pirate invaders of Patusan because of Brown's lucky verbal hits: what began as a debate across the river ends with Jim, who had all the initial advantage, mutely accepting Brown's accusations of dishonor. "When he asked Jim, with a sort of brusque despairing frankness, whether be himself—straight now—didn't understand that when 'it came to saving one's life in the dark, one didn't care who else went—three, thirty, three hundred people'—it was as if a demon had been whispering advice in his ear. 'I made him wince,' boasted Brown to me. 'He very soon left off coming the righteous over me. He just stood there with nothing to say, and looking as black as thunder— not at me—on the ground.'" Thus ends Jim's brief success as an orator and leader among the Malays. His old inarticulate gloom comes upon him again.

The inarticulate message Jim writes on the day of his disaster confirms the return of his old speechlessness. Addressed to no one in particular, it is his last attempt to make known the unspeakable within himself. "'An awful thing has happened,' he wrote before he flung the pen down for the first time; look at the ink blot resembling the head of an arrow under these words. After a while he had tried again, scrawling heavily, as if with a hand of lead, another line. 'I must now at once . . .' The pen had spluttered, and that time he gave it up. There's nothing more; he had seen a broad gulf that neither eye nor voice could span."

Unlike Jim, Conrad optimistically estimates his own success in mastering the English language.

> The truth of the matter is that my faculty to write in English is as natural as any other aptitude with which I might have been born. I have a strange and over-powering feeling that it had always been an inherent part of myself. English was for me neither a matter of choice nor adoption. The merest idea of choice had never entered my head. And as to adoption— well, yes, there was adoption; but it was I who was adopted by the genius of the language, which directly I came out of the stammering stage made me its own so completely that its very idioms I truly believe had a direct action on my temperament and fashioned my still plastic character.

Though Conrad achieved phenomenal success in a language he did not learn until he was twenty-one, his choice of a verbal dilemma as one aspect of Jim's failure as a man cannot be dissociated from Conrad's own sense of alienation in a foreign land. Before his recognition and success, the Polish-born novelist knew long, lonely years in England, and he spoke English with a heavy accent to the day of his death. In his short story "Amy Foster," he depicts a Carpathian immigrant shipwrecked on the English coast, a refugee who is assumed to be insane because the English farmers who take him in do not know his language. It is a curious irony that Conrad should have sought to depict a sense of verbal inadequacy in a young Englishman whose speech idiom Conrad himself had not perfectly mastered, just as it is ironic on another level that Jim understands so well the code of honor expressed in books and in the literary imagination (a linguistic repository) but that he should be so inept at speaking out his sense of honor in real life and acting upon it in a practical moment of crisis.

Source: Eban Bass, "The Verbal Failure of *Lord Jim*," in *College English*, Vol. 26, No. 6, 1965, pp. 438–44.

Sources

Armstrong, Paul B., "Monism and Pluralism in *Lord Jim*," in *Lord Jim: Authoritative Text, Backgrounds, Sources, Criticism*, edited by Thomas C. Moser, W. W. Norton & Company, 1996, pp. 470–71, originally published in *Centennial Review*, Vol. 27, No. 4, Fall 1983.

Erdinast-Vulcan, Daphna, "The Failure of Myth: *Lord Jim*," in *Lord Jim: Authoritative Text, Backgrounds, Sources, Criticism*, edited by Thomas C. Moser, W. W. Norton & Company, 1996, pp. 493–94, 496, 500, 504, originally published in *Joseph Conrad and the Modern Temper*, Oxford University Press, 1991.

Guerard, Albert J., "Lord Jim," in *Lord Jim: Authoritative Text, Backgrounds, Sources, Criticism*, edited by Thomas C. Moser, W. W. Norton & Company, 1996, p. 397, originally published in *Conrad the Novelist*, Harvard University Press, 1958.

Miller, J. Hillis, "*Lord Jim*: Repetition as Subversion of Organic Form," in *Lord Jim: Authoritative Text, Backgrounds, Sources, Criticism*, edited by Thomas C. Norton & Company, 1996, p. 453, originally published in *Fiction and Repetition: Seven English novels*, Harvard University Press, 1982.

Murfin, Ross C., *Lord Jim: After the Truth*, Twayne Publishers, 1992, pp. 23, 48.

Review of *Lord Jim*, in *Lord Jim: Authoritative Text, Backgrounds, Sources, Criticism*, edited by Thomas C. Moser, W. W. Norton & Company, 1996, pp. 393–94, originally published in *New York Tribune*, November 3, 1900, p. 10.

Review of *Lord Jim*, in *Lord Jim: Authoritative Text, Backgrounds, Sources, Criticism*, edited by Thomas C. Moser, W. W. Norton & Company, 1996, p. 396, originally published in *Spectator*, Vol. 85, November 24, 1900, p. 753.

Simmons, Allan H., "'He Was Misleading': Frustrated Gestures in *Lord Jim*," in *Lord Jim: Centennial Essays*, edited by Allan H. Simmons and J. H. Stape, Rodopi, 2000, p. 31–32.

Watt, Ian, "Composition and Sources," in *Lord Jim: Authoritative Text, Backgrounds, Sources, Criticism*, edited by Thomas C. Moser, W. W. Norton & Company, 1996, p. 424, originally published in *Conrad in the Nineteenth Century*, University of California Press, 1979.

Further Reading

Coundouriotis, Eleni, *Claiming History: Colonialism, Ethnography, and the Novel*, Columbia University Press, 1999.

    This book discusses the comparative arguments on how African writing and ethnography helped to shape colonial cultures, novel writing, and postcolonial ideology.

Secor, Robert, *Joseph Conrad and American Writers*, Greenwood Publishing Group, 1985.

    This book discusses the link between Conrad and the American writers he has influenced, including modern-day writers. It also includes a chapter on how film directors have portrayed Conrad's work. Throughout, the study records an extensive amount of bibliographic information for significant references.

Stape, J. H., ed., *The Cambridge Companion to Joseph Conrad*, Cambridge Companions to Literature series, Cambridge University Press, 1996.

    This comprehensive book on Joseph Conrad, including a biography about his life and essays about his major works, is a great general introduction to Conrad and his art. There is also a bibliography included that is a good source of additional readings on Conrad.

Watt, Ian P., *Essays on Conrad*, Cambridge University Press, 2000.

    Watt, a noted Conrad scholar, collects many of his previously unpublished essays that address Conrad's later work. Watt's insight into Conrad and his works has been influenced by Watt's own experience as a prisoner of war on the River Kwai.

The Plague

Albert Camus

1948

Albert Camus's novel *The Plague* is about an epidemic of bubonic plague that takes place in the Algerian port city of Oran. When the plague first arrives, the residents are slow to recognize the mortal danger they are in. Once they do become aware of it, they must decide what measures they will take to fight the deadly disease.

The Plague was first published in France in 1948, three years after the end of World War II. Early readers were quick to note that it was in part an allegory of the German occupation of France from 1940 to 1944, which cut France off from the outside world, just as in the novel the town of Oran must close its gates to isolate the plague. But the novel has more than one level of meaning. The plague may also be understood as the presence of moral evil or simply as a symbol of the nature of the human condition. Whatever the plague signifies, the various characters must face up to the situation and decide what their attitude to it will be. Should they accept their condition with a kind of religious resignation? Should they continue to seek their own personal happiness, ignoring what is going on around them? Should they deliberately exploit the situation in order to profit from it themselves? Or should they band together out of a sense of obligation to the community to do whatever is necessary to fight the plague? As the plague rages on, at its peak taking hundreds of victims every week, each of the major characters has his own unique approach to the situation.

Author Biography

Albert Camus was born on November 7, 1913, in Mondavi, Algeria. His French father, Lucien Auguste Camus, was killed less than a year later at the Battle of the Marne in France during World War I. Camus was then raised by his mother Catherine (who was of Spanish descent) in a working-class area of Algiers. He attended the lycée (secondary school) until graduation in 1930, after which he studied literature and philosophy at the University of Algiers.

In 1930, Camus had his first attack of tuberculosis, from which he suffered all his life. In 1933, as Hitler came to power in Germany, Camus joined an anti-Fascist organization in Algiers, and in the mid-1930s he became a member of the Communist Party, helping to organize the Marxist-based Workers' Theatre. But a year after his graduation with a degree in philosophy in 1936, he broke with the communists. Until the beginning of World War II in 1939, Camus was a journalist with a left-wing Algerian newspaper.

It was during the 1930s that Camus published his first books. *The Wrong Side and the Right Side* (1937) consisted of five short stories. *Nuptials* (1939) was a collection of four essays. Both volumes received only small circulation in Algeria.

In 1934, Camus married Simone Hié. The marriage broke up two years later. In 1940, he married Francine Faure.

From 1942 to 1945, Camus lived in Paris under the German occupation. He was a member of the French Resistance and edited an underground newspaper, *Combat*. He also published a novel, *The Stranger* (1942), a philosophical essay, *The Myth of Sisyphus* (1943), and two plays, *The Misunderstanding* (produced in 1944) and *Caligula* (produced in 1945). In 1944, Camus met Jean-Paul Sartre and associated with Sartre's group of existentialists, although he denied that he was an existentialist. After the war, Camus received a Resistance Medal from the French government for his wartime activities.

In 1948, Camus published *The Plague*, which was a great commercial success. He became a major literary and political figure in France. *The Rebel*, a philosophical work in which Camus elaborated on some of the issues presented in *The Plague*, followed in 1951. The hostile reception of the work by existentialists led to Camus's break with Sartre, which lasted until Camus's death.

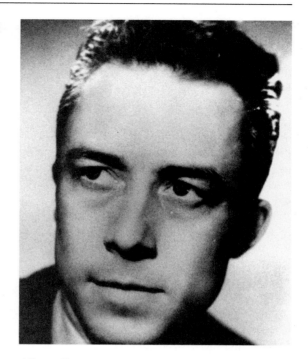

Albert Camus

Camus wrote little for several years following the attack on *The Rebel*. Then in 1956, he published *The Fall*, a short novel, followed by *Exile and the Kingdom* (1957), a collection of short stories. In 1957, Camus was awarded the Nobel Prize for literature.

In 1958, Camus's play, *The Possessed*, adapted from Dostoevsky's novel, was produced, and the following year he was appointed director of the new state-supported experimental theater.

Camus was working on a novel to be called *The First Man*, when he was killed in an automobile accident in France on January 4, 1960, at the age of forty-six.

Plot Summary

Part I

The narrator of *The Plague* announces that he is to relate the unusual events that happened during one year in the 1940s in the town of Oran, a large French port on the Algerian coast in North Africa.

The story begins in mid-April when Dr. Bernard Rieux discovers a dead rat in the building where he lives. Within a week, thousands of rats are emerging from their hiding places and dying in the street. A feeling of unease spreads over the town. Two weeks later, Michel, the concierge of Rieux's building is taken ill with a strange malady. The rats suddenly disappear, but Michel dies within two days.

Rieux is called by Joseph Grand, a former patient, to assist his neighbor, Cottard, who has tried to hang himself. The police call on Cottard, who sees them only with reluctance and who says he has no intention of trying to kill himself again.

The narrative is enriched by the observations of Jean Tarrou, who comments on life in Oran in his notebook.

More victims die. Castel, Rieux's older colleague, and Rieux agree that everything points to the disease being bubonic plague. But the townspeople are slow to realize what is happening; they do not believe in pestilence.

A health committee convenes to decide how to combat the plague. But the measures adopted are halfhearted, designed not to alarm the populace. Rats are to be exterminated, people are advised to practice extreme cleanliness, and all cases of fever (as the plague is officially described) are to be isolated in special wards at the hospital. The number of victims rises to thirty and forty a day. Rieux feels apprehensive and knows that the measures are inadequate. The regulations are tightened, and a serum is sent from Paris. But it will not be enough if the epidemic spreads. Finally, the French prefect sends a telegram instructing the authorities to proclaim a state of plague and quarantine the town.

Part II

The townspeople begin to understand the gravity of the situation. Many are cut off from loved ones in other cities. This includes Rieux, whose sick wife is in a sanatorium. Correspondence with the outside world is forbidden, and people in the town feel like prisoners and exiles, even though they are at home.

Rieux gets to know Grand and hears the story of his life. He also meets for the second time the journalist Rambert, who is in Oran to write a story about living conditions in the Arab quarter. But Rambert is now trapped in the city, while his wife is in Paris. He wishes to leave Oran at once and asks Rieux to help him, but Rieux says there is nothing he can do.

Rieux runs an auxiliary, five-hundred bed hospital for plague victims. He works long hours,

which strains his endurance. The first month of the plague ends gloomily, with the epidemic still on the rise. Father Paneloux, the Jesuit priest, preaches a dramatic sermon in the cathedral. He says that the townspeople have brought this calamity on themselves. Plague is a scourge sent by God as punishment for sin. Paneloux also says that the town should rejoice because the plague works for good by pointing to the path of righteousness. He urges them to pray.

Grand reveals to Rieux that he is writing a novel and that he ponders over every single word and phrase until it is perfect. He shows Rieux the opening sentence, which appears to be all he has written. Meanwhile, Rambert unsuccessfully pesters the authorities to allow him to leave.

The first hot weather of summer arrives, and plague deaths rise to nearly seven hundred a week. A new consignment of serum from Paris seems less effective than the first.

Tarrou visits Rieux and suggests a plan for volunteers to fight the plague. Rieux agrees to help him implement it. He warns Tarrou that his chances of surviving are only one in three. The next day Tarrou sets to work and organizes teams that work to improve sanitary conditions, accompany doctors on their house visits, and drive vehicles transporting sick people and dead bodies. Grand becomes general secretary and keeps statistics.

Meanwhile, Cottard introduces Rambert to Garcia, who can arrange to have Rambert smuggled out of the town. But after a number of frustrating experiences, Rambert tells Rieux that he wishes to become a volunteer until such time as he can leave the town.

Part III

In mid-August, the situation continues to worsen. People try to escape the town, but some are shot by armed sentries. Violence and looting break out on a small scale, and the authorities respond by declaring martial law and imposing a curfew. Funerals are conducted with more and more speed, no ceremony, and little concern for the feelings of the families of the deceased. The inhabitants passively endure their increasing feelings of exile and separation; despondent, they waste away emotionally as well as physically.

Part IV

In September and October, the town remains at the mercy of the plague. Rieux hears from the sanatorium that the condition of his wife is worsening. He also hardens his heart regarding the plague victims so that he can continue to do his work. Cottard, on the other hand, seems to flourish during the plague, because it gives him a sense of being connected to others, since everybody faces the same danger. Cottard and Tarrou attend a performance of Gluck's opera, *Orpheus and Eurydice*, but the actor portraying Orpheus collapses with plague symptoms during the performance.

Rambert finally has a chance to escape, but he decides to stay, saying that he would feel ashamed of himself if he left.

Towards the end of October, Castel's new anti-plague serum is tried for the first time, but it cannot save the life of Othon's young son, who suffers greatly, as Paneloux, Rieux, and Tarrou look on in horror.

Paneloux, who has joined the group of volunteers fighting the plague, gives a second sermon. He addresses the problem of an innocent child's suffering and says it is a test of a Christian's faith, since it requires him either to deny everything or believe everything. He urges the congregation not to give up the struggle but to do everything possible to fight the plague.

A few days after the sermon, Paneloux is taken ill. His symptoms do not conform to those of the plague, but the disease still proves fatal.

Tarrou and Rambert visit one of the isolation camps, where they meet Othon. When Othon's period of quarantine ends, he elects to stay in the camp as a volunteer because this will make him feel less separated from his dead son. Tarrou tells Rieux the story of his life, and the two men go swimming together in the sea. Grand catches the plague and instructs Rieux to burn all his papers. But Grand makes an unexpected recovery, and deaths from the plague start to decline.

Part V

By late January, the plague is in full retreat, and the townspeople begin to celebrate the imminent opening of the town gates. Othon, however, does not escape death from the disease. Cottard is distressed by the ending of the epidemic, from which he has profited by shady dealings. Two government employees approach him, and he flees. Despite the ending of the epidemic, Tarrou contracts the plague and dies after a heroic struggle. Rieux's wife also dies.

In February, the town gates open and people are reunited with their loved ones from other cities. Rambert is reunited with his wife. Rieux reveals

that he is the narrator of the chronicle and that he tried to present an objective view of the events.

Cottard goes mad and shoots at people from his home. He is arrested. Grand begins working on his book again. Rieux reflects on the epidemic and reaches the conclusion that there is more to admire than to despise in humans.

Characters

Asthma Patient

The asthma patient receives regular visits from Dr. Rieux. He is a seventy-five-year-old Spaniard with a rugged face, who comments on events in Oran that he hears about on the radio and in the newspapers.

Dr. Castel

Dr. Castel is one of Rieux's medical colleagues and is much older than Rieux. He realizes after the first few cases that the disease is bubonic plague and is aware of the seriousness of the situation. He labors hard to make an anti-plague serum, but as the epidemic continues, he shows increasing signs of wear and tear.

Cottard

Cottard lives in the same building as Grand. He does not appear to have a job, although he describes himself as "a traveling salesman in wines and spirits." Cottard is an eccentric figure, silent and secretive, who tries to hang himself in his room. Afterwards, he does not want to be interviewed by the police, since he has committed a crime in the past and fears arrest.

Cottard's personality changes after the outbreak of plague. Whereas he was aloof and mistrustful before, he now becomes agreeable and tries hard to make friends. He appears to relish the coming of the plague, and Tarrou thinks this is because he finds it easier to live with his own fears now that everyone else is in a state of fear, too. Cottard takes advantage of the crisis to make money by selling contraband cigarettes and inferior liquor.

When the epidemic ends, Cottard's moods fluctuate. Sometimes he is sociable, but at other times he shuts himself up in his room. Eventually, he loses his mental balance and shoots at random at people on the street. The police arrest him.

Garcia

Garcia is a man who knows the group of smugglers in Oran. He introduces Rambert to Raoul.

Gonzales

Gonzales is the smuggler who makes the arrangements for Rambert's escape.

Joseph Grand

Joseph Grand is a fifty-year-old clerk for the city government. He is tall and thin and always wears clothes a size too large for him. Poorly paid, he lives an austere life, but he is capable of deep affection. In his spare time, Grand polishes up his Latin, and he is also writing a book, but he is such a perfectionist that he continually rewrites the first sentence and can get no further. One of his problems in life is that he can rarely find the correct words to express what he means. Grand tells Rieux that he married while still in his teens, but overwork and poverty took their toll (Grand did not receive the career advancement that he had been promised), and his wife Jeanne left him. He tried but failed to write a letter to her, and he still grieves for his loss.

Grand is a neighbor of Cottard, and it is he who calls Rieux for help, when Cottard tries to commit suicide. When the plague takes a grip on the town, Grand joins the team of volunteers, acting as general secretary, recording all the statistics. Rieux regards him as "the true embodiment of the quiet courage that inspired the sanitary groups." Grand catches the plague himself and asks Rieux to burn his manuscript. But then he makes an unexpected recovery. At the end of the novel, Grand says he is much happier; he has written to Jeanne and made a fresh start on his book.

Louis

Louis is one of the sentries who takes part in the plan for Rambert to escape.

Marcel

Marcel, Louis's brother, is also a sentry who is part of the escape plan for Rambert.

M. Michel

M. Michel is the concierge of the building in which Rieux lives. An old man, he is the first victim of the plague.

Jacques Othon

Jacques Othon is M. Othon's young son. When he contracts the plague, he is the first to receive Dr.

Castel's anti-plague serum. But the serum is ineffective, and the boy dies after a long and painful struggle.

M. Othon

M. Othon is a magistrate in Oran. He is tall and thin and, as Tarrou observes in his journal, "his small, beady eyes, narrow nose, and hard, straight mouth make him look like a well-brought-up owl." Othon treats his wife and children unkindly, but after his son dies of the plague, his character softens. After he finishes his time at the isolation camp, where he is sent because his son is infected, he wants to return there, because this would make him feel closer to his lost son. But before Othon can do this, he contracts the plague and dies.

Father Paneloux

Father Paneloux is a learned, well-respected Jesuit priest. He is well known for having given a series of lectures in which he championed a pure form of Christian doctrine and chastised his audience about their laxity. During the first stage of the plague outbreak, Paneloux preaches a sermon at the cathedral. He has a powerful way of speaking, and he insists to the congregation that the plague is a scourge sent by God to those who have hardened their hearts against him. But Paneloux also claims that God is present to offer succor and hope. Later, Paneloux attends at the bedside of Othon's stricken son and prays that the boy may be spared. After the boy's death, Paneloux tells Rieux that although the death of an innocent child in a world ruled by a loving God cannot be rationally explained, it should nonetheless be accepted. Paneloux joins the team of volunteer workers and preaches another sermon saying that the death of the innocent child is a test of faith. Since God willed the child's death, so the Christian should will it, too. A few days after preaching this sermon, Paneloux is taken ill. He refuses to call for a doctor, trusting in God alone. He dies. Since his symptoms did not seem to resemble those of the plague, Rieux records his death as a "doubtful case."

The Prefect

The Prefect believes at first that the talk of plague is a false alarm, but on the advice of his medical association, he authorizes limited measures to combat it. When these do not work, he tries to avoid responsibility, saying he will ask the government for orders. After this, he does take responsibility for tightening up the regulations relating to the plague and issues the order to close the town.

Raymond Rambert

Raymond Rambert is a journalist who is visiting Oran to research a story on living conditions in the Arab quarter of the town. When the plague strikes, he finds himself trapped in a city with which he feels he has no connection. He misses his wife who is in Paris, and he uses all his ingenuity and resourcefulness to persuade the city bureaucracy to allow him to leave. When this fails, he contacts smugglers, who agree to help him to escape for a fee of ten thousand francs. But there is a hitch in the arrangements, and by the time another escape plan is arranged, Rambert has changed his mind. He decides to stay in the city and continue to help fight the plague, saying that he would feel ashamed of himself if he pursued a merely private happiness. He now feels that he belongs in Oran and that the plague is everyone's business, including his.

Raoul

Raoul is the man who agrees, for a fee of ten thousand francs, to arrange for Rambert to escape. He introduces Rambert to Gonzales.

Dr. Richard

Dr. Richard is chairman of the Oran Medical Association. He is slow to recommend any action to combat the plague, not wanting to arouse public alarm. He does not even want to admit that the disease is the plague, referring instead to a "special type of fever."

Dr. Bernard Rieux

Dr. Bernard Rieux is the narrator of the novel, although this is only revealed at the end. Tarrou describes him as about thirty-five-years-old, of moderate height, dark-skinned, with close-cropped black hair. At the beginning of the novel, Rieux's wife, who has been ill for a year, leaves for a sanatorium. It is Rieux who treats the first victim of plague and who first uses the word *plague* to describe the disease. He urges the authorities to take action to stop the spread of the epidemic. However, at first, along with everyone else, the danger the town faces seems unreal to him. He feels uneasy but does not realize the gravity of the situation. Within a short while, he grasps what is at stake and warns the authorities that unless steps are taken immediately, the epidemic could kill off half the town's population of two hundred thousand within a couple of months.

During the epidemic, Rieux heads an auxiliary hospital and works long hours treating the victims. He injects serum and lances the abscesses, but there is little more that he can do, and his duties weigh heavily upon him. He never gets home until late, and he has to distance himself from the natural pity that he feels for the victims; otherwise, he would not be able to go on. It is especially hard for him when he visits a victim in the person's home, because he knows that he must immediately call for an ambulance and have the person removed from the house. Often the relatives plead with him not to do this, since they know they may never see the person again.

Rieux works to combat the plague simply because he is a doctor and his job is to relieve human suffering. He does not do it for any grand, religious purpose, like Paneloux (Rieux does not believe in God), or as part of a high-minded moral code, like Tarrou. He is a practical man, doing what needs to be done without any fuss, even though he knows that the struggle against death is something that he can never win.

Mme. Rieux

Mme. Rieux is Dr. Rieux's mother, who comes to stay with him when his sick wife goes to the sanatorium. She is a serene woman who, after taking care of the housework, sits quietly in a chair. She says that at her age there is nothing much left to fear.

Jean Tarrou

Jean Tarrou arrived in Oran some weeks before the plague broke out, for unknown reasons. He is not there on business, since he appears to have private means. Tarrou is a good-natured man who smiles a lot. Before the plague came, he liked to associate with the Spanish dancers and musicians in the city. He also keeps a diary, full of his observations of life in Oran, which Rieux incorporates into the narrative.

It is Tarrou who first comes up with the idea of organizing teams of volunteers to fight the plague. He wants to do this before the authorities begin to conscript people, and he does not like the official plan to get prisoners to do the work. He takes action, prompted by his own code of morals; he feels that the plague is everybody's responsibility and that everyone should do his or her duty. What interests him, he tells Rieux, is how to become a saint, even though he does not believe in God.

Later in the novel, Tarrou tells Rieux, with whom he has become friends, the story of his life. His father, although a kind man in private, was also an aggressive prosecuting attorney who tried death penalty cases, arguing strongly for the death penalty to be imposed. As a young boy, Tarrou attended one day of a criminal proceeding in which a man was on trial for his life. However, the idea of capital punishment disgusted him. After he left home before the age of eighteen, his main interest in life was his opposition to the death penalty, which he regarded as state-sponsored murder.

When the plague epidemic is virtually over, Tarrou becomes one of its last victims, but he puts up a heroic struggle before dying.

Themes

Exile and Separation

The theme of exile and separation is embodied in two characters, Rieux and Rambert, both of whom are separated from the women they love. The theme is also present in the many other nameless citizens who are separated from loved ones in other towns or from those who happened to be out of town when the gates of Oran were closed. In another sense, the entire town feels in exile, since it is completely cut off from the outside world. Rieux, as the narrator, describes what exile meant to them all:

> [T]hat sensation of a void within which never left us, that irrational longing to hark back to the past or else to speed up the march of time, and those keen shafts of memory that stung like fire.

Some, like Rambert, are exiles in double measure since they are not only cut off from those they want to be with but they do not have the luxury of being in their own homes.

The feeling of exile produces many changes in attitudes and behaviors. At first, people indulge in fantasies, imagining the missing person's return, but then they start to feel like prisoners, drifting through life with nothing left but the past, since they do not know how long into the future their ordeal may last. And the past smacks only of regret, of things left undone. Living with the sense of abandonment, they find that they cannot communicate their private grief to their neighbors, and conversations tend to be superficial.

Rieux returns to the theme at the end of the novel, after the epidemic is over, when the depth of the feelings of exile and deprivation is clear from the overwhelming joy with which long parted lovers and family members greet each other.

For some citizens, exile was a feeling more difficult to pin down. They simply desired a reunion with something that could hardly be named but which seemed to them to be the most desirable thing on Earth. Some called it peace. Rieux numbers Tarrou among such people, although he found it only in death.

This understanding of exile suggests the deeper, metaphysical implications of the term. It relates to the loss of the belief that humans live in a rational universe in which they can fulfill their hopes and desires, find meaning, and be at home. As Camus put it in *The Myth of Sisyphus*, "In a universe that is suddenly deprived of illusions and of light, man feels a stranger. His is an irremediable exile."

Solidarity, Community, and Resistance

The ravages of the plague in Oran vividly convey the absurdist position that humans live in an indifferent, incomprehensible universe that has no rational meaning or order, and no transcendent God. The plague comes unannounced and may strike down anyone at any time. It is arbitrary and capricious, and it leaves humans in a state of fear and uncertainty, which ends only in death. In the face of this metaphysical reality, what must be the response of individuals? Should they resign themselves to it, accept it as inevitable, and seek what solace they can as individuals? Or should they join with others and fight back, even though they must live with the certainty that they cannot win? Camus's answer is clearly the latter. It is embodied in the characters of Rieux, Rambert, and Tarrou. Rieux's position is made clear in part II, in the conversation he has with Tarrou. Rieux argues that one would have to be a madman to give in to the plague. Rather than accepting the natural order of things— the presence of sickness and death—he fights against them. He is aware of the demands of the community; he does not live for himself alone. When Tarrou points out that "your victories will never be lasting," Rieux admits that he is involved in a "never ending defeat," but this does not stop him engaging in the struggle.

Rieux is also aware that working for the common good demands sacrifice; he cannot expect personal happiness. This is a lesson that Rambert learns. At first he insists that he does not belong in Oran, and his only thought is to get back to the woman he loves in Paris. He thinks only of his own personal happiness and the unfairness of the situation in which he has been placed. But gradually he comes to recognize his membership of the larger human community, which makes demands on him that he cannot ignore. His personal happiness becomes less important than his commitment to helping the community.

This is also the position occupied by Tarrou, who lives according to an ethical code that demands that he act in a way that benefits the whole community, even though, in this case, he risks his life by doing so. Later in the novel, when Tarrou tells Rieux the story of his life, he adds a new dimension to the term plague. He views it not just as a specific disease or simply as the presence of an impersonal evil external to humans. For Tarrou, plague is the destructive impulse within every person, the will and the capacity to do harm, and it is everyone's duty to be on guard against this tendency within themselves, lest they infect someone else with it. He describes his views to Rieux:

> What's natural is the microbe. All the rest—health, integrity, purity (if you like)—is a product of the human will, of a vigilance that must never falter. The good man, the man who infects hardly anyone, is the man who has the fewest lapses of attention.

Religion

In times of calamity, people often turn to religion, and Camus examines this response in the novel. In contrast to the humanist beliefs of Rieux, Rambert, and Tarrou, the religious perspective is given in the sermons of the stern Jesuit priest, Father Paneloux. While the other main characters believe there is no rational explanation for the outbreak of plague, Paneloux believes there is. In his first sermon, given during the first month of the plague, Paneloux describes the epidemic as the "flail of God," through which God separates the wheat from the chaff, the good from the evil. Paneloux is at pains to emphasize that God did not will the calamity: "He looked on the evil-doing in the town with compassion; only when there was no other remedy did He turn His face away, in order to force people to face the truth about their life" In Paneloux's view, even the terrible suffering caused by the plague works ultimately for good. The divine light can still be seen even in the most catastrophic events, and a Christian hope is granted to all.

Topics for Further Study

- What is the story told in the ancient Greek myth of Orpheus and Eurydice? What is the significance of the episode in which Tarrou and Rambert attend a performance of Gluck's opera, *Orpheus and Eurydice*?

- Research the history of Vichy France, from 1940 to 1944. What were the goals of the French leaders, such as Pierre Laval, who openly collaborated with the Germans? How did they justify their actions?

- Reread the first chapter of *The Plague*, in which Rieux describes the town of Oran and its people. Is Rieux really as objective a narrator as he claims to be? What are his main criticisms of Oran's citizens? How does the epidemic change their attitudes?

- Why does the narrator say, in Part II, that the "true embodiment of the quiet courage that inspired the sanitary groups" was not himself or Tarrou but Grand? In what sense is Grand a hero?

- Imagine a debate between a modern-day Father Paneloux and Dr. Rieux or Tarrou over the modern plague of AIDS. What might each man say and do in response to the epidemic?

Paneloux's argument is based on the theology of St. Augustine, on which he is an expert, and it is accepted as irrefutable by many of the townspeople, including the magistrate, Othon. But it does not satisfy Rieux. Camus carefully manipulates the plot to bring up the question of innocent suffering. Paneloux may argue that the plague is a punishment for sin, but how does he reconcile that doctrine with the death of a child? The child in question is Jacques Othon, and Paneloux, along with Rieux and Tarrou, witnesses his horrible death. Paneloux is moved with compassion for the child, and he takes up the question of innocent suffering in his second sermon. He argues that because a child's suffering is so horrible and cannot easily be explained, it forces people into a crucial test of faith: either we must believe everything or we must deny everything, and who, Paneloux asks, could bear to do the latter? We must yield to the divine will, he says; we cannot pick and choose and accept only what we can understand. But we must still seek to do what good lies in our power (as Paneloux himself does as one of the volunteers who fights the plague).

When Paneloux contracts the plague himself, he refuses to call a doctor. He dies according to his principles, trusting in the providence of God and not fighting against his fate. This is in contrast to Tarrou, who fights valiantly against death when his turn comes.

It is clear that Camus's sympathy in this contrast of ideas lies with Rieux and Tarrou, but he also treats Paneloux with respect.

Style

Point of View

Point of view refers to the method of narration, the character through whose consciousness the story is told. In *The Plague* this is Rieux. However, Rieux does not function as a first-person narrator. Rather he disguises himself, referring to himself in the third person and only at the end of the novel reveals who he is. The novel thus appears to be told by an unnamed narrator who gathers information from what he has personally seen and heard regarding the epidemic, as well as from the diary of another character, Tarrou, who makes observations about the events he witnesses.

The reason Rieux does not declare himself earlier is that he wants to give an objective account of the events in Oran. He deliberately adopts the tone of an impartial observer. Rieux is like a witness who exercises restraint when called to testify about a crime; he describes what the characters said and did, without speculating about their thoughts and feelings, although he does offer generalized assessments of the shifting mood of the town as a whole. Rieux refers to his story as a chronicle, and he sees himself as an historian, which justifies his decision to stick to the facts and avoid subjectivity. This also explains why the style of *The Plague* often gives the impression of distance and detachment. Only rarely is the reader drawn directly into the emotions of the characters or the drama of the scene.

Allegory

An allegory is a narrative with two distinct levels of meaning. The first is the literal level; the second signifies a related set of concepts and events. *The Plague* is in part an historical allegory, in which the plague signifies the German occupation of France from 1940 to 1944 during World War II.

There are many aspects of the narrative that make the allegory plain. The town Oran, which gets afflicted by pestilence and cut off from the outside world, is the equivalent of France. The citizens are slow to realize the magnitude of the danger because they do not believe in pestilence or that it could happen to them, just as the French were complacent at the beginning of the war. They could not imagine that the Germans, whom they had defeated only twenty years previously, could defeat them in a mere six weeks, as happened when France fell in June 1940.

The different attitudes of the characters reflect different attitudes in the French population during the occupation. Some were the equivalent of Paneloux and thought that France was to blame for the calamity that had befallen it. They believed that the only solution was to submit gracefully to an historical inevitability—the long-term dominance of Europe by Germany. Many people, however, became members of the French Resistance, and they are the allegorical equivalents of the voluntary sanitary teams in the novel, such as Tarrou, Rambert, and Grand, who fight back against the unspeakable evil (the Nazi occupiers).

Some French collaborated with the Germans. In the novel, they are represented by Cottard, who welcomes the plague and uses the economic deprivation that results from it to make a fortune buying and selling on the black market.

Other details in the novel can be read at the allegorical level. The plague that carries people off unexpectedly echoes the reality of the occupation, in which people could be snatched from their homes by the Gestapo and imprisoned or sent to work as slave labor in German-controlled territories or simply killed. The facts of daily life in the plague-stricken city resemble life in wartime France: the showing of reruns at the cinemas, the stockpiling of scarce goods, nighttime curfews and isolation camps (these paralleling the German internment camps). The scenes at the end of the novel, when Oran's gates are reopened, recall the jubilant scenes in Paris when the city was liberated in 1944.

In some places, Camus makes the allegory explicit, as when he refers to the plague in terms that describe an enemy in war: "the epidemic was in retreat all along the line; ... victory was won and the enemy was abandoning his positions."

Symbolism

Imagery of the sea is often used in Camus's works to suggest life, vigor, and freedom. In *The Plague*, a key description of Oran occurs early, when it is explained that the town is built in such a way that it "turns its back on the bay, with the result that it's impossible to see the sea, you always have to go to look for it." Symbolically, Oran turns its back on life. When the plague hits, the deprivation of this symbol of freedom becomes more pronounced, as the beaches are closed, as is the port. In summer, the inhabitants lose touch with the sea altogether: "for all its nearness, the sea was out of bounds; young limbs had no longer the run of its delights."

A significant episode occurs near the end of part IV, when Tarrou and Rieux sit on the terrace of a house, from which they can see far into the horizon. As he gazes seaward, Tarrou says with a sense of relief that it is good to be there. To set a seal on the friendship between the two men, they go for a swim together. This contact with the ocean is presented as a moment of renewal, harmony, and peace. It is one of the few lyrical episodes in the novel: "[T]hey saw the sea spread out before them, a gently heaving expanse of deep-piled velvet, supple and sleek as a creature of the wild."

Just before Rieux enters the water, he is possessed by a "strange happiness," a feeling that is shared by Tarrou. There is a peaceful image of Rieux lying motionless on his back gazing up at the stars and moon, and then when Tarrou joins him they swim side by side, "with the same zest, the same rhythm, isolated from the world, at last free of the town and of the plague."

Historical Context

Absurdism

The term *absurdism* is applied to plays and novels that express the idea that there is no inherent value or meaning in the human condition. Absurdist writers reject traditional beliefs and values, including religious or metaphysical systems that locate truth, purpose, and meaning in transcendental concepts such as God. For the absurdist, the universe is irrational and unintelligible; it cannot satisfy the human need for order or fulfil human hopes and aspirations. Human beings are essentially alone in an indifferent universe and must make their way through their bleak, insignificant existence in the best way that they can. As Eugene Ionesco, a prominent French writer of absurd drama (quoted by M. H. Abrams in *A Glossary of Literary Terms*) put it: "Cut off from his religious, metaphysical, and transcendental roots, man is lost; all his actions become senseless, absurd, useless."

According to Abrams, absurdism has its roots in the 1920s, in such works as Franz Kafka's *The Trial* and *The Metamorphosis*. But it is most often associated with French literature as it emerged from World War II, in the work of writers such as Camus and Jean-Paul Sartre. Camus's *The Stranger* (1942) was one of the first works that applied an absurdist view to a work of fiction. Samuel Beckett, an Irishman who lived in Paris and who often wrote in French and then translated his works into English, is often described as the most influential writer of absurdist literature. His most famous play is *Waiting for Godot* (1955).

France in World War II

After France capitulated to Germany in June 1940, Marshal Pétain, an eighty-four-year-old World War I hero, was installed as prime minister. The northern half of France, including the Channel and Atlantic ports, was placed under German occupation. French forces were demobilized and disarmed, and France was forced to pay all costs of the occupation. The Pétain government made its headquarters at Vichy, in unoccupied France, where it was granted a nominal independence. General Charles de Gaulle, who had been Undersecretary for War in the fallen French government, flew to England, where he enrolled a French Volunteer Force to cooperate with the British and continue the war.

The Pétain government pursued an active collaboration with the Germans, hoping to find a place for France in what it assumed would be a German-dominated Europe for the foreseeable future. Under the premiership of Pierre Laval, the Vichy government repressed the French underground movement, which was increasingly harassing the Germans by attacking their supply lines. In 1942, the Germans extended their occupation to include all of France, after which the Vichy government had little independent power and declining prestige.

Compare
&
Contrast

- **1940s:** World War II pits the major European powers against each other, with axis powers Germany and Italy, and later Japan, on one side and allied powers Britain, Russia and later the U.S. on the other. The entry of the United States into the war in 1941 tips the scales in favor of Britain and its allies.

  Today: The main European combatants of World War II are steadily moving toward more and more economic and political integration through the European Union. In January 2002, twelve European countries, including France and Germany, adopt a single currency, the Euro.

- **1940s:** Radio and newspapers are the media through which people get their information. Communication is via telephone, letters, and, in urgent cases, telegrams.

Today: Television has replaced the newspaper as the principle source of information for most people. The Internet is a rapidly growing resource for news and entertainment. Cheap telephone rates make worldwide communication easy, as does electronic mail and the facsimile (fax). Telegrams are a thing of the past.

- **1940s:** After the devastation of World War II, Europe starts to rebuild. The United States, fearing that an economically weak Europe will allow communism to make quick gains, provides large-scale financial assistance through the Marshall Plan.

Today: An increasingly unified Europe is a powerful economic competitor of the United States.

During the occupation, life in France was hard for French citizens. Communication from the occupied zone with family members who were on the other side of the demarcation zone was difficult. The Germans permitted only postcards containing the minimum of information to be sent (just as in *The Plague*, the townspeople can communicate with the outside world only through telegrams). There were many other restrictions, including curfews and food shortages. People waited in long lines for inadequate supplies. There was also a flourishing black market, which involved all levels of French society. As Milton Dank puts it in *The French Against the French*, "The large-scale black market was carefully organized by operators who made fantastic fortunes practically overnight at the expense of their starving compatriots."

Following the allied invasion of Normandy on June 6, 1944, the end of the war was in sight. French Resistance forces played a significant role in the battles that followed, sabotaging bridges and railways as the Germans were forced back. When Paris was liberated on August 25, 1944, Camus, who was the editor of the underground newspaper *Combat*, wrote the following:

Paris fired off all its bullets into the August night. In the immense stage set of stone and water, the barricades of freedom have once again been raised everywhere around that river whose waves are heavy with history. Once more, justice must be bought with men's blood.

Critical Overview

The Plague was an immediate success with the reading public, and the first edition of twenty-two thousand copies rapidly sold out. It was quickly reprinted, and in the four months between publication in June 1947 and September, more than one hundred thousand copies were sold. Reviews, including one by the existentialist philosopher Jean-Paul Sartre, were also positive, and the book established Camus's reputation as a major writer. *The Plague* was awarded the French Critics' Prize and was one of the reasons that Camus was awarded the Nobel Prize in literature in 1957.

The book proved to have more than ephemeral success. In 1980, it was still high on the list of best-

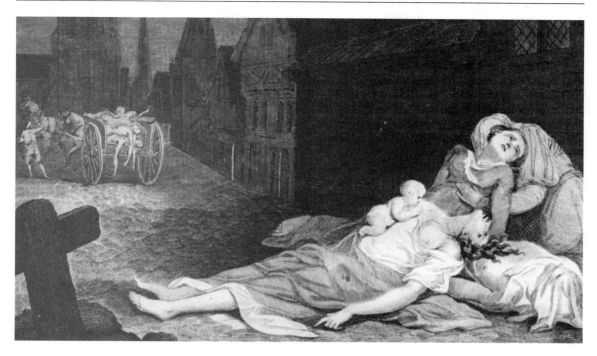

A 1665 artist's rendering of plague victims

sellers, having sold 3,700,000 copies. Translations had appeared in eleven languages.

Critical approaches to *The Plague* have varied. When it was first published, only two years after the end of World War II, much of the explication was based on the allegorical reading, in which Oran afflicted by plague represents France under the German occupation. But Camus was criticized by some, including Roland Barthes, for making the enemy a disease and so avoiding the moral question of whether people should take up arms against a violent oppressor. In a reply to Barthes, Camus rejected the criticism, saying that since terror has several faces, not just one, by not naming a particular terror he struck better at them all.

The Plague has also been read in the light of existentialism, even though this is a philosophy that Camus did not espouse, and from the point of view of absurdism—the belief that human life has no rational order or purpose. More recent critics have concentrated on the novel's narrative technique, its structure, and its language. There has also been work on how the novel fits in with the overall body of Camus's work. Germaine Brée, for example, following Camus's own statement that there was a line of progression in his works, argues that *The Plague*

appears as the first step in moving beyond the boundaries of the 'absurd,' or rather, perhaps, working within those boundaries to explore the power of human beings to make sense of their lot even in the most stringent circumstances.

Criticism

Bryan Aubrey

Aubrey holds a Ph.D. in English and has published many articles on twentieth-century literature. In this essay, Aubrey discusses the character of Tarrou in Camus's story, highlighting Tarrou's opposition to capital punishment and comparing this to Camus's arguments in his essay "Reflections on the Guillotine."

Of the main characters in *The Plague*, Tarrou is the only one who gives a long, first-person account of his life and the events that shaped his thinking. It is obvious that Camus attached great importance to Tarrou's story, which occurs toward the end of part IV, in his conversation with Rieux. Tarrou is a central character in *The Plague*, because it is he who organizes the volunteer sanitary teams, which he does because he believes it to be his moral duty. Tarrou's story of how his life had been shaped

"
The abolition of capital
punishment would be one major
step, he argues, in ending
worship of the State as an
embodiment of absolute values
and reaffirming respect for the
individual."

by his revulsion at the death penalty echoes Camus's own passionate opposition to capital punishment. Much of what Tarrou says about capital punishment can also be found in greater detail in Camus's essay, "Reflections on the Guillotine," which he wrote in 1956 and published the following year. Camus's essay, according to his biographer Olivier Todd, helped to create a climate that eventually led, several decades later in 1981, to the abolition of the death penalty by the French government. Today, the death penalty has been abolished by all member nations of the European Union but remains legal in the United States. Camus's views on the issue, both in *The Plague* and in his later essay, are a fierce contribution to one side of the debate.

In *The Plague*, Tarrou tells Rieux of his father, who was a prosecuting attorney. When Tarrou was seventeen, his father asked him to come to court to hear him speak in a death penalty case. What Tarrou remembered most about the trial was the frightened defendant. Tarrou did not doubt the man's guilt, but he was vividly impressed by the fact that the man was "a living human being" and that the whole purpose of the proceedings was to make arrangements to kill him. Instinctively, he took the side of the defendant.

Tarrou noticed also how his father's demeanor was different in court from his demeanor at home. Normally, he was a kindly man, but in his role as prosecutor he was fierce in his denunciation of the accused and in his call for the "supreme penalty," which Tarrou says should better be called "murder in its most despicable form."

From that point on, Tarrou took a horrified interest in everything to do with the death penalty, and he realized that often his father rose early in

order to witness the executions. It was Tarrou's horror at this that forced him to leave home and begin campaigning against the death penalty. He came to believe that the entire social order was based on the death penalty and that this "supreme penalty" was being applied even in the name of the political causes he supported. He fought against fascism in the Spanish Civil War (1936–1939) and admits that his side used the death penalty, but he was told that a few deaths were necessary for the creation of a new world in which murder would no longer happen. He reluctantly accepted this argument until in Hungary he witnessed an execution by firing squad. He tells Rieux that such an execution is far more grisly than the way it is usually imagined. The firing squad stands only a yard and a half from the condemned man, and the bullets blow a hole in his heart big enough to thrust a fist into. Since witnessing that execution, Tarrou has never been able to sleep well, and he has based his morality on the need to avoid becoming involved in anything that could lead directly or indirectly to the death penalty.

"Reflections on the Guillotine" expands on Tarrou's arguments and also sheds light on some of his more esoteric points. Just as Tarrou told a story about his own revulsion at the death penalty, so also Camus begins with a personal story, although it is not about himself but was told to him about his father. His father supported the death penalty, but on the only occasion when he attended an execution, he returned home and was apparently so disgusted and nauseated by what he had witnessed that he vomited. Camus uses this story to point out (as he had Tarrou do) how the death penalty is deliberately spoken of in euphemisms, such as "paying a debt to society," designed to conceal what really happens. Tarrou had said that all "our troubles spring from our failure to use plain, clean-cut language," and Camus takes up this point in his essay, arguing that if the truth were told, ordinary people would realize the horror of the act of severing a man's head from his body (the method of execution in France) and would no longer support it. According to Camus, society does not in fact believe what it proclaims about the death penalty setting an example for others, since, if it did, it would hold executions in public, show them on television, and publish eyewitness accounts and medical reports on what happens to a human body immediately after execution. (He quotes some accounts of actual executions that make for disturbing reading.)

Camus assembles more arguments against the death penalty, some of which will be easily recognized by those who are familiar with the contemporary debate over capital punishment in the United States. Camus claims, for example, that crime statistics show that the death penalty has no deterrent effect. Given this lack of correlation, Camus argues that the death penalty is merely an act of revenge, based on the primitive urge to retaliate, which, he says, is based on an emotion, not a principle. He also argues that the principle of equivalence (one death for another) does not operate either, for the punishment, since it is preceded by a period of confinement, is worse than the crime. For there to be equivalence, the state would have to

> punish a criminal who has warned his victim of the date at which he would inflict a horrible death on him and who, from that moment onward, had confined him at his mercy for months. Such a monster is not encountered in private life.

Camus also adopts the argument of the modern liberal, arguing that society is not entirely blameless for the crimes that individuals commit. He points to the link between crime and poor living conditions, and he also points out that many crimes are linked to the consumption of alcohol and that corporations make healthy profits from the sale of alcohol, some of which benefit members of parliament who have shares in those companies. In other words, the precise responsibility of the killer cannot be measured, since there are other factors involved.

This does not exhaust the arguments Camus marshals against the death penalty in his essay. He points to the possibility of error, which would involve the execution of the innocent, and to the arbitrary nature of the death sentence, since it can be influenced by irrelevant factors like the defendant's appearance and demeanor. He also claims that no one can ever know for certain that a man is so depraved that he will never be able to make amends for what he has done.

Finally, Camus turns to the question of the death penalty as carried out for political reasons. This is what had such a deep effect on Tarrou in *The Plague*, who appears to believe that taking part in politics of whatever sort makes him an accomplice to murder, since the death penalty is a weapon commonly used by those who wish to impose a particular ideology on others. Tarrou tells Rieux that, given his opposition to anything that results in state-sanctioned murder, he has no place in the world: "[O]nce I'd definitely refused to kill, I

doomed myself to an exile that can never end. I leave it to others to make history."

This argument must be understood in the context of the times. During the 1930s and 1940s, Nazism, Fascism, and Soviet totalitarianism were committing atrocities, including mass executions, and justifying them in terms of the new society they claimed they were building. In "Reflections on the Guillotine," written over a decade later, Camus's argument remains essentially the same. He was writing shortly after the Soviet Union crushed a revolt in Hungary, at a time when Spain was ruled by the fascist dictatorship of General Franco; when the Soviets sent political dissidents to slave labor camps; and Algerian nationalists fighting French rule were subject to execution. Memories of Nazism were also still fresh in people's minds. Against this background, Camus argues that the biggest practitioner of crimes against individuals is now the State and that it is the State that individuals must defend themselves against. The abolition of capital punishment would be one major step, he argues, in ending worship of the State as an embodiment of absolute values and reaffirming respect for the individual. It would be an acknowledgement that nothing authorizes the State to carry out a punishment of such severity and finality that it can never be reversed.

This aspect of Camus's argument (which is the same argument he gives to Tarrou in *The Plague*) belongs very much to its time and place. Since the demise of communism throughout the world in the late 1980s and 1990s, few people in the West today are prepared to see the solution to society's problems in terms of increasing the power of the state. But when Camus was writing, in the 1940s and 1950s, the defeat of totalitarian ideologies was not yet in sight, and his work was an attempt to grapple with real problems facing European societies. Curiously, it is in the United States, which historically has been the nation most wary of sacrificing individual freedom to the power of the state, that capital punishment has been retained and vigorously endorsed by politicians of all parties. But as far as Europe is concerned, Camus's dream, as he expressed it in "Reflections on the Guillotine," has come true: "in the unified Europe of the future the solemn abolition of the death penalty ought to be the first article of the European Code we all hope for." Today, no nation that still retains the death penalty can be admitted to the European Union.

Of course, whether abolition of the death penalty in Western Europe has in fact contributed, as Camus's character Tarrou desired, to the lessening of the "plague" in every human being—the tendency, under certain circumstances to do harm to another person—is another matter, less easily decided upon.

Source: Bryan Aubrey, Critical Essay on *The Plague*, in *Novels for Students*, The Gale Group, 2003.

David L. Kirp, Andrew Koehler and Jaime Rossi

In the following essay, Kirp, Koehler, and Rossi discuss The Plague *and Orwell's* 1984 *and how these works have helped shape the cultural landscape of the last half century.*

In the summer of 1948 an English translation of Albert Camus's *The Plague* was published, and George Orwell's *1984* appeared several months later. During the half-century since, those two books have helped to shape the cultural landscape. Books were weapons and the stakes survival in the politics-soaked late forties, when seemingly every event was viewed through the prism of democracy and its virulent enemies. At a loyalty board hearing conducted at the Brooklyn Navy Yard in 1949, a sheet-metal worker was questioned about what book clubs he subscribed to (shades of Kenneth Starr!). "The Book Find Club," he responded. "Does Dreiser contribute?" a board member queried. "Some of their writers adhere to the Communist Party line… They weave doctrine into a story." The worker responded in the manner of someone trying to evade the Thought Police. "I ain't that much of a genius. I read the words, not the weaving."

Literary niceties didn't matter overmuch in such a climate. Reviewers called *The Plague* a sermon and an allegory, and labeled *1984* a diatribe—characterizations delivered as praise, as if justifying the failure of the prose to do the usual work of fiction. So what if neither packed the punch of *Raintree County* or *The Naked and the Dead*, both of which, along with *The Young Lions* and *The Big Fisherman*, appeared on the 1948 bestseller list. Their messages matched the preoccupations of the time.

The Plague conjured in postwar readers' minds the insidious spread of Nazism and underlined the moral authority of resistance. For such a deadly serious book, it was a surprising commercial success, and most reviewers genuflected to its apparent profundity. "*The Plague* is one of the few genuinely important works of art to come out of Europe since the war's end," *Time* trumpeted. "It makes most recent American war novels seem tinny and thin by comparison."

1984 was published just as the Soviet Union was undergoing the fate of Orwell's Eurasia, transformed almost overnight from ally to archenemy. Orwell was renowned as an honest witness to injustice across generations and continents, and his novel was a smash hit—170,000 sold in the first year, another 190,000 of the Book of the Month Club edition. *Life* ran an illustrated, Classic Comics-style version of the novel. "Have you read this book?" a New York shoeshine boy asked English critic Isaac Deutscher. "You must read it, sir. Then you will know why we must drop the atom bomb on the Bolshies!" Writing in *The New York Times*, Mark Schorer was hardly less boosterish. "No other work of this generation has made us desire freedom more earnestly or loathe tyranny with such fulness."

The Zeitgeist shifts like a tectonic plate, and one generation's manifesto often becomes another generation's soporific. The Soviet Union that figures in *1984* ceased to merit its chief bogyman status years before its formal collapse, and the Nazism that informs *The Plague* has been no more than a political sideshow for generations. Still, these books shape our worldview. They keep selling; some 30,000 copies of *The Plague* and more than 100,000 copies of *1984* are sold each year in the United States. More than 10 million copies of *1984* have been sold, ranking it among the all-time U.S. bestsellers. In recent years each has been packaged as a movie, *1984* for a second time, and there is also a mock sequel, a conservative tract called *Orwell's Revenge*.

That *The Plague* features prominently in discussions about AIDS is understandable, since Camus's story centers on another plague. What's surprising, though, is that the message of the novel creeps into analyses of the Israeli-Palestinian conflict—where partisans on both sides have drawn comfort from the text—as well as Swiss money-laundering during World War II. Half a century after *1984*'s appearance, scarcely a week goes by without Big Brother, Newspeak or Thought Police turning up in public argument.

The morals of these morality plays turn out to be more capacious, the archetypes they represent more profound, than their creators could ever have anticipated. The imagery of *1984* and *The Plague* still produces the bile-in-the-throat feeling of utter panic that arises when we are pushed into confronting our absolute powerlessness. Dread nature rising up, the punishing Flood, the helpless individual who becomes the plaything of a malevolent fate: These are what our nightmares are made of.

Plagues and People

In 1948 memories of Nazi terror were vivid, and *The Plague* contains scenes that could have been lifted straight from those wartime memories: painful separations from loved ones, attempts to escape the war zone, the formation of isolation camps for the contaminated, the smell of dead and burning bodies. "There will be few readers," a *Herald Tribune* reviewer contended, "who will not see in it a parable of the condition of all mankind, especially during the recent war." *Time* relied on *The Plague* when analyzing the French Resistance: "To continue upholding one's human obligations when there seems the least possibility of fulfilling them is, if not heroism, the best that men can do."

Camus once described himself as committed to "everyday life with the most possible light thrown upon it." Long after the priest's sermons on faith and fatalism have faded from our memory of the book, what remains are those everyday life moments: the journalist's poignant decision to stay in a city where he has found himself by chance, rather than fleeing to his home and his fiancee; the death of the judge's child; the nightly performances of a play brought to town by a troupe of thespians entrapped by the plague, a ritual that ends only when one of the actors falls dead on the stage. Even in times that are truly unspeakable, Camus insists, we constantly construct the normal or else we go mad. "The task is to favor freedom against the fatalities that close in upon it."

The threat of a real plague had seemingly played itself out, medical science supposedly having triumphed over mass contagion, by the time the book appeared. Camus revives the image, and our sense of plague as threat now comes not from tales of medieval London but from his novel. The imagery has often been used to represent a fearsome intrusion, the uninvited guest at the garden party who smashes all the glasses. When a mad killer disrupts the "happy city" of Gainesville, Florida (the reference is to Oran), *The Plague* is summoned, as it is in the context of an outbreak of violence against the children of Bangor, terrorism in the Tokyo subways and arson in Laguna Beach. Even a baseball columnist drew inspiration from the novel: "Albert Camus, a heavy hitter in his own field, might have appreciated slumps as a symbol of random evil ... The malady speads, too. ... But the struggle goes on for a cure."

> "The imagery of *1984* and *The Plague* still produces the bile-in-the-throat feeling of utter panic that arises when we are pushed into confronting our absolute powerlessness."

The literal plague—the slow progression of a deadly, contagious disease and the various attempts to combat it—went undiscussed until the summer of 1981, when a brief story in *The New York Times* brought news of a disease that was killing gay men. With that first press reference to AIDS, *The Plague* became invested with new meaning.

Never mind Susan Sontag's plea, in *Illness as Metaphor*, that diseases be treated as signifying only themselves: Because AIDS especially menaced gay men, the epidemic became a breeding ground for metaphors that had less to do with the disease than the state of society. AIDS was God's judgment on homosexuals, fundamentalist Christian preachers thundered, even as medical science was bent to support this point of view. "If AIDS is the Plague of the Eighties," Michael Fumento insisted in *The National Review*, "then homosexuals are the rats."

On the other side of this great cultural divide, the fight against this disease and the social judgments barnacled to it became the moral equivalent of war. For Randy Shilts, whose *And the Band Played On* is the J'Accuse for AIDS, the preachments of *The Plague* turned into whips to flagellate the AIDS-phobic. But while Camus concludes optimistically that "in a time of pestilence ... there are more things to admire in men than to despise," the trajectory of AIDS has been less cheering.

Despite all the God-doubting and personal angst that news of the plague evokes among the residents of Camus's Oran, what was required to combat the epidemic was plain enough: universal reporting of infection, quarantine of the infected and the imposition of strict health measures on the healthy. Because the plague struck indiscriminately, maintaining the privacy of its victims was not a worry—indeed, respect for privacy would have meant more deaths.

What Do I Read Next?

- Camus's widely known first novel, *The Stranger* (1942), is about an alienated, aimless young Algerian man who gets caught up in bad company and ends up murdering an Arab. His subsequent imprisonment and trial reflect Camus's view of the absurd nature of life.

- *Vichy France* (revised edition, 2001), by Robert O. Paxton, is a classic study of France under the German occupation in World War II. Paxton shows how the Pétain government pursued a double agenda: an authoritarian and racist revolution at home and an attempt to persuade Hitler to accept this new France as a partner in German-dominated Europe.

- Alfred Cobban, in *A History of Modern France: 1871–1962* (1965), presents a readable overview of modern French history, including the tragic years of the German occupation and the Vichy government.

- *Plagues and People* (updated edition, 1998), by William H. McNeill, examines the enormous political, demographic, ecological, and psychological impact that infectious diseases have made on human history. Among the topics McNeill discusses are the medieval black death, the epidemic of smallpox in Mexico that followed the Spanish conquest, the bubonic plague in China, and the typhoid epidemic in Europe.

Dr. Rieux, the main character, is portrayed as brave because of his decisiveness, while the unheroic fret about panicking the populace by acting too quickly. Ironically, during the early years of the AIDS epidemic, the person whose behavior most resembled Rieux's was Lyndon LaRouche, who demanded universal testing and quarantine for those with H.I.V. Those positions made him a hero only to the AIDS-phobic, for reasons that illuminate the difference between these epidemics. AIDS was a condition that initially could be neither diagnosed nor treated. To be infected with the virus was so-cially devastating, so the call for universal testing spread panic. (When former Georgia governor and segregationist die-hard Lester Maddox was diagnosed with Kaposi's sarcoma, a form of cancer linked to AIDS, he was mortified; he'd much prefer to die from "straight cancer," he said.) While in Oran the plague ran its course in less than a year, AIDS could conceivably last forever.

"No one was prepared for AIDS," observed one of the first AIDS doctors. "It's like Albert Camus said in *The Plague*: 'Plagues and wars always afflict us but they always catch us by surprise.'" What resonates from the novel is how good people respond in terrible times—not by allowing themselves to be paralyzed or blaming the diseased for their affliction but by acting to contain the harm. "All who attend AIDS victims need to find the grace described in *The Plague*," wrote a journalist in the *Chicago Tribune* who went on to quote a 1986 statement from the American Medical Association. "Though unable to be saints, [health professionals should] refuse to bow down to pestilences and strive to their utmost to be healers."

That reading of *The Plague* sharpens the moral distinction. But the novel also invites the plague victim to contemplate the very different possibility that he has brought this condition upon himself, that the plague is our Flood. This understanding, which turns inward Fumento's diatribe about AIDS patients as rats, resonates with many gay men who live not only with a fatal disease but also with deeply internalized homophobia.

At the end of *The Plague*, Dr. Rieux reveals that he is not just a character in the story but also the narrator, returned to "bear witness in favor of those plague-stricken people, so that some memorial of the injustice and outrage done them might endure." In "When Plagues End," a *New York Times Magazine* essay, former New Republic editor Andrew Sullivan strikes a similar pose. In lieu of the dead rat in the hallway that is the harbinger of plague in Oran, Sullivan describes the suddenly darkened apartment of a stricken friend as signaling the advent of AIDS. He imagines he is seeing the end to this plague, marked by the development of new pharmaceutical regimes—hence the title of his article. But in this he is entirely premature. For AIDS, there is no happy ending, no Rieux on the train station platform, waiting for his wife and the chance to resume his ordinary life, only a disease that resists being domesticated by medical science and the persistent desire to find something, or someone, to blame. . . .

The Happy City

The imagery of *1984* may feel as tired and unimaginative today as the stale metaphors against which Orwell inveighs in "Politics and the English Language," but it is this very familiarity that explains why these symbols endure. The vision of *1984*, so startling half a century ago, has long since become ordinary, just as Freudian categories are taken-for-granted tools in our intellectual kitbag. Imagining a world without airbrushed history or a watchful eye, Big Brother or the computer databank is as hard as letting go of repression or sublimation. Fifty years on, *1984* lingers in the air. So too does *The Plague*, with its images of natural and insidious evil.

The idea that one might achieve utopia on earth, so tempting when these novels were published, has vanished except among the maddest of cults, a casualty of the many sins committed in the name of utopia. *1984* and *The Plague* urged against trusting the visionary, because we know that good times are never truly the best of times and worse times are likely lurking around the corner. Always there is the possibility of a clock waiting to strike thirteen or a plague that will "rouse up its rats again and send them forth to die in a happy city."

Source: David L. Kirp, Andrew Koehler, and Jaime Rossi, "Moral Rorschachs," in the *Nation*, Vol. 266, No. 16, May 4, 1998, pp. 32–36.

Steven G. Kellman

In the following essay, Kellman discusses the impact of The Plague *in the 1980s with the widespread emergence of AIDS.*

Even before his narrative begins, Albert Camus offers a cue on how to read *The Plague*. He positions a statement by Daniel Defoe as epigraph to the entire work. Any novelist writing about epidemics bears the legacy of *A Journal of the Plague Year*, the 1722 text in which Defoe recounts the collective story of one city, in his case London, under the impact of a plague, and uses a narrator so self-effacing that his only concession to personal identity is the placement of his initials, H.F., at the very end. Camus's *The Plague* insists that it is the "chronicle" of an "honest witness" to what occurred in Oran, Algeria, a physician named Bernard Rieux who is so loath to impose his personality on the story that he conceals his identity until the final pages. Rieux claims the modest role of "chronicler of the troubled, rebellious hearts of our townspeople under the impact of the plague."

> As in *The Plague*, a panicked populace responded in a variety of ways but without any cure. It is no longer possible to read *The Plague* with the innocence of Existentialist aesthetes."

The particular passage appropriated as epigraph to Camus's novel comes from another book by Defoe, from the preface to volume III of *Robinson Crusoe*. And, for the reader of *The Plague*, it immediately raises questions of representation: "It is as reasonable to represent one kind of imprisonment by another, as it is to represent anything that really exists by that which exists not." Coming even before we have met the first infected rat in Oran, the Defoe quotation is an invitation to allegory, a tip that the fiction that follows signifies more than the story of a town in Algeria in a year, "194_," deliberately kept indeterminate to encourage extrapolation. "I had plague already, long before I came to this town and encountered it here. Which is tantamount to saying I'm like everybody else," says a healthy Jean Tarrou, by which he suggests that the pestilence that is the focus of the story is not primarily a medical phenomenon; nor is it, like Camus's adversary, quarantined in one city during most of one year, from April 16 to the following February. "I know positively—yes, Rieux, I can say I know the world inside out, as you may see—that each of us has the plague within him; no one, no one on earth is free from it," declares Tarrou. Camus's novel invites its readers to recognize that they, too, are somehow infected, though the diagnosis seems more metaphysical than physical.

In 1941, a typhus outbreak near Oran resulted in more than 75,000 deaths. However, that epidemic was clearly a source not the subject for Camus's novel. *The Plague* is one of the most critically and commercially successful novels ever published in France. It has managed to sell more than four million copies throughout the world and to inspire an army of exegetes. For the generation that grew up in the 1950s and 1960s, it was, like *The Catcher in the Rye*, *Lord of the Flies*, and

Catch-22, a book that was devoured although and because it was not assigned in school. But its appeal has not been as an accurate case study in epidemiology. Particularly in North America, where Oran seems as remote as Oz, readers have accepted Camus's invitation to translate the text into allegory. *The Plague* offered a tonically despairing vision of an absurd cosmos in which human suffering is capricious and unintelligible. The lethal, excruciating disease strikes fictional Oran indiscriminately, and when it does recede it does so temporarily, oblivious to human efforts at prophylaxis. As in Camus's philosophical treatise *The Myth of Sisyphus*, the health workers of Oran combat each case from scratch without ever being convinced that their labors accomplish anything.

In a famous letter addressed to Roland Barthes in 1955, Camus attempted to narrow the terms of interpretation. He insisted that his 1947 novel be read not as a study in abstract evil but as a story whose manifest reference is to the situation of France under the Nazi occupation:

> *The Plague*, which I wanted to be read on a number of levels, nevertheless has as its obvious content the struggle of the European resistance movements against Nazism. The proof of this is that although the specific enemy is nowhere named, everyone in every European country recognized it. Let me add that a long extract from *The Plague* appeared during the Occupation, in a collection of underground texts, and that this fact alone would justify the transposition I made. In a sense, *The Plague* is more than a chronicle of the Resistance. But certainly it is nothing less. (Lyrical and Critical Essays . . .)

Long after the Liberation of France, readers, particularly those born after World War II, preferred to read *The Plague* as something more than a chronicle of the Resistance, as the embodiment of a more universal philosophical vision. The novel was, in fact, even more popular in the United States, which did not experience the Nazi Occupation, than in France, where Camus's aversion to torture and violence made him politically suspect by both the left and the right. The absence of an immediate historical context encouraged younger Americans to read *The Plague* as a philosophical novel. So, too, did our inexperience with plagues. "Oh, happy posterity," wrote Petrarch in the fourteenth century, when more than half the population of his native Florence perished in the bubonic plague, the Black Death, "who will not experience such abysmal woe and will look upon our testimony as a fable."

Before 1980, *The Plague* was facilely read as a fable. Polio had been vanquished, and the smallpox virus survived only in a few laboratories. Aside

from periodic visitations of influenza, usually more of a nuisance than a killer, epidemics, before the outbreak of cholera in Peru in 1991, had been as common in this hemisphere as flocks of auks. Those of us who first read *The Plague* during the era of the Salk and Sabin vaccines were hard put to imagine a distant world not yet domesticated by biotechnology, in which a lere bacillus could terrorize an entire city. We read *The Plague* not as the story of a plague, an atavistic nemesis that seemed unlikely to menace our own modern metropolises. The story was a pretext, an occasion for ethical speculation, in short an allegory without coordinates in space and time.

However, though published long before the first case of AIDS was diagnosed and thirty-five years before the acronym was even coined, *The Plague* assumed a new urgency during the 1980s, as it became apparent that epidemics were not obsolete occurrences or quaint events confined to distant regions. Not long after a 1981 article in *The New England Journal of Medicine* reported seven inexplicable cases of severe infection, AIDS became a global pandemic. In the United States alone, more than 160,000 have died from the disease, and another 80,000 have been diagnosed with the deadly disorder. Close to 2 million Americans have been infected with the Human Immunodeficiency Virus, believed to be the precondition for AIDS. At first, AIDS seemed to target homosexual men, Haitians, and intravenous drug users, but, like Camus's plague, it was soon striking capriciously, without any regard to the social status of its hundreds of thousands of helpless, hapless victims. As in *The Plague*, a panicked populace responded in a variety of ways but without any cure. It is no longer possible to read *The Plague* with the innocence of Existentialist aesthetes. Joseph Dewey suggests that, for a contemporary novelist in quest of a paradigmatic AIDS narrative, it is not profitable to read *The Plague* at all—"Camus's use of contagion as an undeniable occasion of mortality that tests whether those quarantined in the Algerian port can find significance in life within an infected geography seems too metaphoric, a luxury when compared to what AIDS victims must confront: the indignities of a slow and grinding premature death."

Laurel Brodsley, however, does not dismiss *The Plague*. She takes it seriously enough to try to demonstrate how Defoe provides a model for it and two other twentieth-century plague books: Paul Monette's *Borrowed Time*, and Randy Shilts's *And the Band Played On*, both of them AIDS narratives.

Yet it would be more accurate to say that Camus mediates between Shilts and Defoe—and even between Shilts and the contemporary pestilence whose first five years he recounts. Published in 1987, *And the Band Played On: Politics, People, and the AIDS Epidemic* is a detailed report on the onset and spread of AIDS and of the spectrum of reactions to it. What, to a student of Camus, is remarkable about Shilts's book—which, selected for the Book of the Month Club, was a bestseller in both hardcover and paperback—is how much it has in common with *The Plague*. Not only does Shilts document the same pattern of initial denial followed by acknowledgment, recrimination, terror, and occasional stoical heroism that Rieux recounts during the Oran ordeal. But it is clear that Shilts has read Camus and has adopted much of the style and structure of *The Plague* to tell his story of an actual plague. Where Camus appropriates Defoe for the epigraph to his novel, Shilts mines Camus's *The Plague* for epigraphs to four of his book's nine sections: Parts IV, V, VI, and VII. In Part II, describing baffling new developments among homosexual patients, Shilts echoes Camus's absurdist *Myth of Sisyphus* when he states: "The fight against venereal diseases was proving a Sisyphean task." That same Greek myth, for whom Camus is the modern bard, is alluded to two other times by Shilts—flippantly, in reference to AIDS victim Gary Walsh's "Sisyphean task" of renovating his Castro District apartment and, more portentously, in reference to the "Sisyphean struggle" against AIDS directed by Donald Francis, a leading retrovirologist at the Centers for Disease Control. . . .

Early in *The Plague* its still anonymous narrator attempts to establish his credibility by assuming the humble role of historian. He insists on his distaste for rhetorical flamboyance and literary contrivance, assuring the reader that: "His business is only to say: 'This is what happened,' when it actually did happen, that it closely affected the life of a whole populace, and that there are thousands of eyewitnesses who can appraise in their hearts the truth of what he writes." Rather than his own eccentric fabrication, what follows, he assures us, is an impartial account adhering scrupulously to reliable sources. "The present narrator," says the present narrator, in an attempt at objective detachment even from himself, "has three kinds of data: first, what he saw himself; secondly, the accounts of other eyewitnesses (thanks to the part he played, he was enabled to learn their personal impressions from all those figuring in this chronicle); and, lastly, documents that subsequently came into his hands." . . . .

Camus is of course writing fiction, and his artful prose aspires to the spare eloquence of the solitary sentence that Joseph Grand is forever honing into an economy of eloquence. Shilts's massive book overwhelms his reader with the numbing evidence of actuality. Footnotes would have been an impertinence to *The Plague*, but they are essential to Shilts's claim on the reader's belief. Nevertheless, not every reader has honored that claim. Douglas Crimp reacted harshly to Shilts's deployment of conventional novelistic technique, and James Miller, who contends that "Shilts has artfully mated *Hard Times* with *Oliver Twist* to produce a symphonic opus of public oppression and private suffering", is enraged over the book's Dickensian caricatures and emotional excesses. "I suspect that Shilts is making lots and lots of money out of his *success de scandale*," rails Miller, "by feeding his straight and some of his gay readers exactly what they want: large dollops of guilt." Readers often turn pages because they want to find solutions. *And the Band Played On* is, like *The Plague*, a whodunit, a book designed to arouse and shape our curiosity about causes. What are the origins of catastrophe? Judith Williamson in fact faults *And the Band Played On* for exploiting the conventions of detective fiction so effectively that it demonizes Gaetan Dugas, Patient Zero, as the primal culprit in the global drama: "While Shilts's book is rationally geared to blame the entire governmental system for failing to fund research, educate the public and treat those infected, he nevertheless cannot entirely resist the wish for a source of contamination to be found, and then blamed."

Whatever the sources of misfortune, Camus leaves us with his plague in temporary remission, but, in Shilts's final pages, AIDS is merely gaining momentum. Neither disease is near a cure. Yet both epidemics and both books leave us enlightened about the limitations of human understanding but the need to act on what we know. William Styron spoke for many American admirers when he praised Camus for his tonic recognition of a bleak cosmos: "Camus was a great cleanser of my intellect, ridding me of countless sluggish ideas and, through some of the most unsettling pessimism I had ever encountered, causing me to be aroused anew by life's enigmatic promise." Stronger on enigma than promise, Shilts has nevertheless created a book designed to arouse.

Source: Steven G. Kellman, "From Oran to San Francisco: Shilts Appropriates Camus," in *College Literature*, Vol. 24, No. 1, February 1997, pp. 202–12.

Sources

Abrams, M. H., *A Glossary of Literary Terms*, 4th ed., Holt, Rinehart and Winston, 1981, p. 1.

Camus, Albert, *The Plague*, translated by Stuart Gilbert, Alfred A. Knopf, 1971.

———, "Reflections on the Guillotine," in *Resistance, Rebellion, and Death*, Alfred A. Knopf, 1961, pp. 173–234.

Dank, Milton, *The French against the French: Collaboration and Resistance*, J. B. Lippincott Company, 1974.

Ellison, David R., *Understanding Albert Camus*, University of South Carolina Press, 1990.

Kellman, Steven G., ed., *Approaches to Teaching Camus's "The Plague,"* Modern Language Association of America, 1985.

Further Reading

Amoia, Alba, *Albert Camus*, Continuum, 1989.
Amoia's book is a lucid introduction to Camus's work. Amoia sees *The Plague* as a depiction of man's struggle against solitude and death, and he emphasizes Rieux's respect for the individuality of each human's personality—a quality he consistently finds in Camus's life and work.

Bloom, Harold, ed., *Albert Camus*, Modern Critical Views series, Chelsea House, 1988.

This text is a collection of essays on all aspects of Camus's work, notable for Bloom's negative assessment of *The Plague* and for the essay on the same work by Patrick McCarthy.

Brée, Germaine, *Camus: A Collection of Critical Essays*, Prentice-Hall, 1962.

This collection of essays was published not long after Camus's death and shows the way contemporary critics interpreted his work. Gaëton Picon in "Notes on *The Plague*," faults the novel for failing to create unity between the two levels on which it operates, the realistic and the symbolic or allegorical.

Luppé, Robert de, *Albert Camus*, translated by John Cumming and J. Hargreaves, Funk & Wagnalls, 1966.

Luppé traces the development of Camus's ideas, which he identifies as dualism (life and death, love and hatred) and the attempt to maintain equilibrium between contrary and exclusive terms.

Merton, Thomas, *Albert Camus's "The Plague": Introduction and Commentary*, Seabury Press, 1968.

This brief introduction to the novel is by a leading religious thinker and former Roman Catholic monk. Merton is particularly lucid in analyzing Camus's attitude to Christianity, and he also compares Camus's thought to that of a modern Catholic thinker, Teilhard de Chardin.

Todd, Olivier, *Albert Camus: A Life*, Alfred A. Knopf, 1997.

This thorough biography presents Camus's life and times but avoids detailed exposition of the works.

That Was Then, This Is Now

Susan Eloise Hinton, known to her multitudes of readers as "S. E. Hinton," a trick that she and her early publisher used to mask her gender, is credited with revolutionizing the young adult book industry with the 1967 publication of her coming-of-age book, *The Outsiders*, which she published when she was only seventeen years old. Her second effort, 1971's *That Was Then, This Is Now*, also dealt with the realistic themes of youth violence and tragedy that had characterized her first work, and some critics considered this sophomore effort even better than the first. Both books, and in fact most of Hinton's books, are based on events that she witnessed as a teenager in Tulsa, Oklahoma. *That Was Then, This Is Now* tells the tale of Bryon Douglas, a sixteen-year-old greaser who finds himself growing up and growing apart from his foster brother, Mark, whom he adores. As Mark refuses to accept responsibility for his actions and gets involved with selling drugs, Bryon must face the hardest decision of his life—whether to turn Mark in. With its graphic depictions of gang life, the hippie lifestyle, and the potentially crippling effects of drugs, *That Was Then, This Is Now* offered a snapshot of the turbulent and transitional times in which it was written and has stood the test of time, becoming a favorite with teens, adults, and educators.

S. E. Hinton
1971

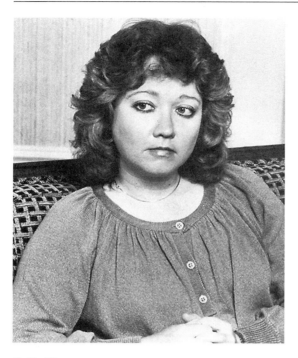

S. E. Hinton

Author Biography

Susan Eloise Hinton, known to her readers as S. E. Hinton, was born in Tulsa, Oklahoma, in 1950, a setting that has influenced the majority of her young adult novels. In fact, Hinton is commonly credited as the person who revolutionized the tone of young adult fiction, by using gritty, realistic settings such as the Tulsa-like background of her hugely successful debut novel, *The Outsider*. Published in 1967, when Hinton was seventeen and a student at Tulsa's Will Rogers High School, the book also set the standard for future young adult novels, by addressing hard issues that teens faced, such as gang violence. The novel was published under her initials, because the publisher feared that their audience, mainly young men, would not accept a female author, especially since most of her narrators are male. Even though Hinton's gender was eventually revealed, she has used her initials for all of her published books thus far.

Hinton's second young adult novel, *That Was Then, This Is Now*, featured the same type of setting and themes that made *The Outsiders* such a success. However, since *That Was Then, This Is Now* was published four years later, in 1971, it also addressed current issues, such as drug use, and ex-

amined the hippie lifestyle. Both *The Outsiders* and *That Was Then, This Is Now* were made into film adaptations, and the former was directed by *Godfather* director, Francis Ford Coppola. Hinton was actively involved with both adaptations, which featured such future stars as Emilio Estevez, Matt Dillon, Patrick Swayze, Rob Lowe, and Tom Cruise. Two other Hinton novels, *Rumble Fish*, published in 1975, and *Tex*, published in 1979, were also adapted as films. Coppola also directed *Rumble Fish*, which he filmed in black and white to emphasize one character's color blindness. Hinton's most recent works include two children's books, *Big David, Little David* and *The Puppy Sister*, both published in 1995. Hinton continues to live and work in Tulsa, Oklahoma.

Plot Summary

Chapter One

That Was Then, This Is Now begins when the narrator, Bryon Douglas, and his foster brother, Mark, both teenagers, go to one of their favorite hangouts, Charlie's Bar, a rough pool hall where they often try to hustle people for money. Later, they find their hippie friend, a kid with the nickname M&M, who tells them that his sister, Cathy, is home from private school. They hang out for a while, but M&M gets bored and leaves. Mark and Bryon follow, just in time to stop some gang members from beating up M&M. Mark, Bryon, and M&M start walking home, and Mark suggests they beat up somebody else. M&M yells at them for their hypocrisy, and Bryon reflects on what M&M has said.

Chapter Two

The next day, Mark and Bryon go to the hospital to see Bryon's mother, who has just had an operation and who says they should visit a beaten-up kid across the hall. Bryon goes downstairs to the hospital's snack bar, where he meets Cathy, M&M's sister who is back in town, and asks her out. Bryon talks with the severely beaten-up boy, Mike Chambers, who tells Bryon that he got beaten up after he saved a young black woman from being harassed by his own gang members. Mike drove the woman home, and when he dropped her off, she told her friends to kill him. Mike tells Bryon that he does not hold it against the woman, and Bryon sees some merit in his point of view, although Mark does not.

Chapter Three

Bryon looks for a job but does not have any luck, even with Charlie, who tells him that he needs to change his ways before anybody will hire him. Charlie lets Bryon borrow his car, however, and Bryon asks Cathy to the school dance. At the dance, Bryon and Cathy are the center of attention, since nobody recognizes her. Mark gets knocked unconscious with a bottle, after he tries to stop somebody from attacking Ponyboy Curtis, one of his friends. Bryon realizes that his ex-girlfriend, Angela Shepard, set up the attack on Curtis and vows to get revenge on Angela.

Chapter Four

The next morning, Bryon returns Charlie's car and finds out that Charlie has received his draft notice to fight in Vietnam. Bryon and Mark reminisce about their gang childhood together and how life has changed since then. Bryon simply says, "that was then, this is now." At school the next day, Bryon is very reflective and feels separate from everybody else. The next week, the school principal catches Mark driving his car. The principal does not press charges because Mark explains that he needed to borrow the car so that he could get to his weekly parole appointments, which, ironically, are for Mark's past history of stealing cars. Bryon notes that Mark can get away with anything.

Chapter Five

Bryon and Mark go hustling one night, and Charlie tells them that the army is not going to draft him, because of his police record. Bryon and Mark hustle two rough Texans, who ambush them after the bar closes, holding them at gunpoint in the alley. Charlie comes to their rescue but gets killed in the process. The police give Charlie's car to Mark and Bryon. Unlike Mark, Bryon feels guilty about Charlie's death and begins to spend more time with Cathy, who understands him.

Chapter Six

The Texans are caught, and Mark and Bryon testify at the trial. Bryon's mom is in the hospital for a month, and Bryon decides to take Charlie's advice and clean up his appearance and his attitude so that he can get a job and help pay bills. Cathy tells Bryon she thinks M&M is doing drugs. One night, Bryon, Mark, Cathy, and M&M go cruising down the Ribbon—a popular, two-mile-long strip of restaurants, drive-ins, and supermarkets—and M&M takes off with some friends, saying he's never coming back.

Chapter Seven

M&M does not come home the next day, and Bryon and Cathy spend every night for a week driving down the Ribbon looking for him. Bryon gets a job at a supermarket and starts to bring in some money. Mark also brings in money, which Bryon assumes is from gambling. Bryon and Mark go out cruising together one night and pick up Angela. Mark gets her drunk until she passes out and then cuts her long hair off, getting back at her for setting up the fight at the dance. At home, a drunk Bryon cries about all of the bad stuff that happens to people, and he wishes M&M were okay. Mark says he knows where he is, and he will take Bryon there.

Chapter Eight

The next day after work, Mark directs Bryon to a house in a rundown part of town. The people in the house know Mark and call him "Cat." Mark asks about "Baby Freak," M&M's hippie name, but he's not there. Bryon goes to Terry Jones's place that night for a party. While he's waiting on the porch for the others to show up, Angela's brothers and two other guys attack him, beating him badly for cutting Angela's hair. When Bryon wakes up, Mark is there. Bryon asks him not to get even with the Shepards, saying he's sick of all of the getting even and wants to drop it.

Chapter Nine

On the way home from the hospital the next morning, Mark is frustrated that Bryon will not let him get even with the Shepards. Cathy comes to visit Bryon at home, and Bryon tells her he loves her and says he has a lead on where M&M might be staying. That week, Bryon makes a visit to Charlie's grave, thanking him for saving his life. Two nights later, Bryon and Cathy go to the hippie house, where they find M&M huddled in the corner of a room, crashing from a massive LSD-induced hallucination. Cathy calls her father, who meets them at the hospital.

Chapter Ten

The doctor tells them that M&M will never be the same, although Bryon tries to reassure her that M&M will get better. At home, Bryan is lost in thought, reflecting about how much his life has changed. Desperate for a cigarette, he looks in Mark's secret stash, where he finds a canister of drugs. In a flash of insight, he connects Mark's selling drugs with M&M's condition and calls the police to turn Mark in. Mark comes home and tries to defend his actions, but Bryon realizes clearly, for the first time, that Mark has no sense of right or wrong. The police take Mark away, while he keeps asking Bryon why he's doing this.

Chapter Eleven

Bryon wakes up the next morning, unsure that he was justified in turning in Mark. Bryon finds he no longer loves Cathy and pushes her away. He testifies against Mark, whose blatant, unrepentant confession gets him five years in the state reformatory. Bryon devotes himself to work, where he gets promoted from sack boy to clerk. At the end of the summer, Bryon visits Mark, who looks hardened and dangerous from his brief time in the reformatory. Bryon tries to apologize, but Mark tells him he hates him and never wants to see him again. When Bryon refers to their past good times, Mark throws Bryon's words back at him, saying, "that was then, this is now." Mark is sent to the state prison; Bryon notes that he has lost the ability to care. He constantly replays the last year's events in his head, trying to figure out if things could have turned out differently. He is unsure of anything and mourns his lost youth, wishing that he could go back to simpler times, when he used to have all of the answers.

Characters

Baby Freak
See M&M

Bryon's Mother
See Mrs. Douglas

Cathy Carlson

Cathy Carlson is Bryon's girlfriend; it is out of his love for her and concern for her brother M&M that Bryon decides to turn Mark in for dealing drugs. Cathy is a shy, innocent teenager, who comes back from private school when she runs out of money. Unlike Bryon's ex-girlfriend, Angela, Cathy does not get jealous and is a good influence on Bryon. This influence puts her at odds with Mark, who feels he and Bryon are starting to grow apart. This becomes more noticeable after Charlie dies saving Bryon and Mark and Cathy understands Bryon's feelings of guilt, whereas Mark does not. Cathy worries that her brother, M&M, whom she loves very much, is smoking marijuana and, since he is so trusting, may end up taking LSD as well.

She says that M&M is not happy because he gets so much harassment at home over his hair, and so M&M has started hanging around other places. Cathy is distraught when M&M runs away, and she and Bryon drive up and down the Ribbon every night for a week, looking for her brother.

After Bryon gets beaten up by the Shepards, Cathy comes to see him at home, where he lets her know he has got a lead on M&M's whereabouts. When Bryon gets better, Cathy goes with him to the hippie house where M&M has been staying. She is horrified when she sees the effects the LSD has had on her brother but still finds the strength to call her father and drive M&M to the hospital. Cathy is distraught when the doctor tells them that M&M may never be the same but is comforted by the love and affection that Bryon shows to her throughout this ordeal. This makes it all the more difficult for Cathy the next day, when she goes to see Bryon, after hearing that Bryon turned Mark in to the police for dealing drugs. Bryon is no longer in love with her, and she can tell. They never speak again, and she starts dating Ponyboy Curtis, although M&M says that she liked Bryon the most.

Mr. Jim Carlson

Jim Carlson is Cathy's dad, whose constant criticisms of his son, M&M, help to drive M&M out of the house and into using drugs. Bryon first meets Mr. Carlson when he picks up Cathy for their date, and he can see how he antagonizes M&M over the length of his hair and because he is flunking math and gym. When M&M leaves home, Mr. Carlson thinks that it is a phase and that he will be back, but as Cathy projects, he does not. Mr. Carlson likes Bryon, especially after Bryon helps find M&M and gets him to the hospital. Mr. Carlson is a wreck when he sees the effects that the drugs have had on his son and is concerned that the news will devastate his wife.

M&M Carlson

M&M Carlson, Cathy's thirteen-year-old brother and one of Bryon's friends, has a bad experience with LSD, which motivates Bryon to turn in Mark for dealing drugs. Even M&M's family call him by this nickname, which he earned for his addiction to the candy of the same name. M&M is the consummate hippie. He wears his hair long, wears an old, loose-fitting army jacket everywhere he goes, and has a metal peace symbol on a rawhide cord around his neck. He is extremely trusting, and even tough characters like Charlie think he is nice, if a little weird. He is thankful that Bryon and Mark save him from getting thoroughly beaten by Curly Shepard but is frustrated at Mark's hypocritical suggestion that they beat somebody else up that same night. M&M tips off Bryon that his sister is home, which helps Bryon figure out who Cathy is when he first meets her.

M&M is not happy at home, mainly because his father constantly criticizes him about his long hair and his bad grades in math and gym. As a result, he starts hanging around more often with other hippies, who introduce him to marijuana. After M&M gets fed up at home and runs away, he moves into a hippie house, where he earns the name "Baby Freak," since he is several years younger than everybody else in the house. It is here that he experiments with LSD, a much more potent drug. When Bryon first goes to the house with Mark, M&M is not there, but somebody else says that he is "flying" and that he is going to "crash." Later, when Bryon takes Cathy to the house, they find him huddled in the corner of a room, in the aftermath of a massive LSD-induced hallucination, in which spiders have been eating him and colors have been talking to him. When Bryon runs into M&M at the end of the story, he tells Bryon the long-term effects of his LSD trip—he may have flashbacks, he might not be able to have normal children, and his grades are not good anymore, since he cannot remember much. Also, M&M does not want kids, which is different from before his acid trip, when he used to say he wanted a large family. M&M also tells Bryon that Cathy is dating Ponyboy Curtis but that he knows that Cathy liked Bryon the best. This news, however, does not affect the emotionally detached Bryon.

Mrs. Carlson

Mrs. Carlson is Cathy's mother, who worries that her husband is giving their son, M&M, too much grief about his long hair. When M&M is at the hospital getting treated for his LSD hallucinations, her husband worries how she will take the news.

Cat

See Mark

Mike Chambers

Mike Chambers is the beaten-up teenager in the hospital, whose story and viewpoint help to inspire Bryon not to hate others and to stop the endless cycle of violence. Mike belongs to a gang from a different neighborhood, and one night some of his gang members start picking on a young black

Media Adaptations

- *That Was Then, This Is Now* was adapted as a film in 1985, directed by Christopher Cain, written by Emilio Estevez, and starring Craig Sheffer as Bryon, Estevez as Mark, Kim Delaney as Cathy, and Morgan Freeman as Charlie. Hinton assisted with the production of the film, which is available on video from Paramount Home Video.

woman. Mike sticks up for her and then gives her a ride home, but she still tells her friends to kill Mike, and they beat him very badly. Mike tells Bryon and Mark that he does not hold it against the woman.

Charlie

Charlie is a twenty-two-year-old bar owner, who dies while saving Bryon and Mark from two Texans whom they have hustled. Charlie is the older brother of one of Bryon's ex-girlfriends, and he sometimes gives Bryon and Mark Cokes on credit at his bar. His tough reputation ensures that Bryon and Mark always pay him back. It is this same reputation that has earned him respect from both the police and Charlie's tough customers. Charlie tries to warn Bryon and Mark that they should be careful whom they hustle, but they do not listen. Charlie receives his draft notice for the army, to go fight in Vietnam, but in the end, they do not take him because he has a police record. He gets this joyous news shortly before he dies. The police are impressed with Charlie's heroic act in saving Bryon and Mark and give the two boys Charlie's car. Later in the story, Bryon takes a trip to Charlie's grave, where he thanks his dead friend for saving his life and letting him use his car.

Ponyboy Curtis

Ponyboy Curtis is one of Mark's friends, although Bryon holds a grudge against him because Curtis had the good sense to stay away from Angela Shepard. Actually, as Bryon learns, Curtis, a quiet and shy teenager, had no idea that Angela was interested in him, although he does know that Bryon is mad at him for something. At the school dance, Mark introduces Curtis to Cathy, and Bryon is wary, although he soon realizes that Cathy is not interested in leaving him for Curtis, as Angela did. Bryon finds new respect for Curtis at the dance, after he lets Bryon know that Mark has been hurt. Although Cathy makes jokes to Bryon about Curtis asking her out—when she wants Bryon to—at the end of the story, Curtis and Cathy do start dating, when Bryon pushes her away.

Dirty Dave

The man who calls himself Dirty Dave is one of two Texans who attempt to beat up Bryon and Mark after they hustle him and his friend at pool. Both Texans are sentenced to life in prison after they kill Charlie, for which Bryon and Mark testify against them.

Bryon Douglas

Bryon Douglas is the narrator of the story, in which he tells how he and his foster brother, Mark, grew apart and how he made the decision to turn Mark in for dealing drugs. When they are kids, Bryon and Mark are inseparable troublemakers and love each other like brothers. When they are sixteen, however, they start to grow apart, as Bryon begins to become his own person, while Mark wants to cling to their mutual past. Still, Bryon and Mark care about each other. For his part, Bryon shows it by taking care of Mark after he gets cracked on the head with a bottle in a fight and by taking a beating for Mark by falsely claiming the blame for cutting off the hair of Bryon's ex-girlfriend, Angela. Bryon undergoes a major transformation in the story, which begins when he and Mark talk to Mike Chambers and Mike's story of getting beaten up and not wanting revenge resonates with Bryon. Bryon's feelings of moral responsibility increase when he feels guilty over the fact that Charlie lost his life while saving them. Bryon's emotional journey includes falling in love with Cathy, who is the first girl he actually cares about.

When Bryon's mother ends up in the hospital for a month, he decides to clean up his act and get a job. When M&M runs away from home, Bryon helps Cathy find him and helps her take him to the hospital after he has a bad LSD hallucination. When he finds the drugs that Mark has been selling and connects them with M&M's condition, he decides once and for all that Mark does not know

right from wrong and turns him in to the police. Although he is not sure he made the right choice, Bryon testifies against Mark. From this point on, Bryon becomes emotionally detached and pushes Cathy away. He does not see Mark again until a few months later, when he tries to apologize. However, Mark tells him he hates him and never wants to see him again. At the end of the story, not even the news that Mark has been sent to prison affects Bryon, who has lost the ability to care. He constantly replays the last year in his head, trying to figure out what would have happened if he had done something differently. He yearns for his youth, when he had all the answers.

Mrs. Douglas

Bryon's mother, Mrs. Douglas, is known for her tendency to try to help stray animals and people, as she does when she adopts Mark after his parents kill each other. Bryon's mother is in the hospital for much of the story, for reasons that are never made known, other than she has had surgery. She encourages Bryon and Mark to talk to Mike Chambers, a boy in the hospital who was beaten by several black men after he tried to help a young black woman. She lets Bryon and Mark live their own lives, trusting that when they stay out late or get into trouble, they are smart enough not to get caught. When Mark starts bringing in a lot of money from his drug sales, she starts to wonder where it is coming from but, like Bryon, does not ask Mark. After Bryon has turned Mark in, she tells Bryon that she does not hate him and that he should not hate himself. She is also optimistic that Mark will learn his lesson and come home, whereas Bryon knows that is not possible.

Terry Jones

Terry Jones is one of Mark and Bryon's friends, who factors into the major beatings of both Mark and Bryon. When Mark and Terry are at the school dance, Terry provides the beer bottle that Curtis's attacker later uses on Mark's head. Likewise, when Bryon gets beaten up by the Shepards, it is while he is waiting at Terry's house for everybody to show up for Terry's party.

Mark

Mark is Bryon's foster brother, whom Bryon turns over to the police when he finds Mark dealing drugs. Mark, whose last name is never mentioned, comes to live with Bryon and his mother after Mark's parents kill each other in a drunken fight over the illegitimacy of Mark's birth. When they are kids, Mark and Bryon hang around in the same gang, break the same laws, and love each other like brothers in the process, which is still apparent at sixteen. Mark gets Bryon a new shirt for Bryon's first date with Cathy, refuses to leave Bryon's side when the two Texans they have hustled ambush them, and takes care of Bryon after Bryon is beaten by the Shepards. However, while Mark desperately tries to cling to the gang personality, Bryon begins to embrace his own adult identity, and the divide between them grows. Whereas Bryon feels guilty over the fact that Charlie lost his life while saving them, Mark does not show any remorse, one of the examples that makes Bryon realize Mark has no concept of right and wrong.

Mark does not understand when Bryon begins hanging out with Cathy instead of causing trouble with him, and he dislikes Cathy as a result. Mark is also frustrated when Bryon will not let him continue the cycle of violence by getting even with the Shepards, especially since it was Mark who cut off Angela's hair. When money is tight, Bryon goes out and gets a job at a supermarket, but Mark's police record prevents him from doing the same. Since he wants to help bring money into the household, too, Mark starts selling drugs to hippies, who call him "Cat." He does not feel that this is wrong, since he does not take any himself and since he does not push it on people. Because Mark is active in the drug world, he knows where M&M is staying and shows Bryon. When Mark hears Mike Chambers's story, he says he would never be able to forgive somebody who hurt him that badly, a promise he makes good on after Bryon gets him put away for drug dealing, and he tells Bryon he never wants to see him again. In the end, Mark refuses to clean up his act and gets sent to the state prison.

Second Texan

After Bryon and Mark hustle him at pool, the unnamed Texan holds the boys at gunpoint in an alley, while his friend, Dirty Dave, prepares to beat them with brass knuckles. Both Texans are sentenced to life in prison after they kill Charlie, for which Bryon and Mark testify against them.

Angela Shepard

Angela Shepard is Bryon's ex-girlfriend, who broke up with him in favor of Ponyboy Curtis, although she tried to win him back when Curtis did not realize she existed. Angela is stunningly beautiful, but Bryon notes that it is wasted beauty, since Angela has a tough-as-nails personality and is not

very nice. At the school dance, Angela gets one of her friends to attack Curtis, but Mark steps in, getting cracked in the head with a bottle. When Bryon realizes that Angela set up the fight, he vows to get even with her. Shortly after Bryon and Mark are ambushed by the two Texans, Angela gets married to one of her brother's friends, thinking she is pregnant with this man's child.

Later that year, after M&M disappears, Bryon and Mark run into Angela on the Ribbon. She is extremely drunk and goes for a ride with Mark and Bryon when Mark says he will get her more alcohol. For one of the first times in her life, Angela breaks down and cries on Bryon's shoulder, telling him she is miserable in her marriage and that he is the only one for her. When Angela passes out, Mark cuts off all of her prized long hair. The next morning, Angela tells her brothers, Tim and Curly, that Bryon did it, prompting them to beat Bryon up, even though Angela saves her pride in public by telling everybody else that she had decided to cut it off. At the end of the story, after Bryon has turned in Mark, Angela runs into him and tells Bryon that it was a low thing to do.

Curly Shepard

Curly Shepard is one of the older brothers of Angela Shepard, Bryon's ex-girlfriend. He helps beat up Bryon after Mark cuts off Angela's hair. Curly belongs to the Shepard Gang, led by his older brother, Tim. While Bryon considers Tim a real hood, he thinks Curly just plays the part, even though he has spent time in prison.

Tim Shepard

Tim Shepard is one of the older brothers of Angela Shepard, Bryon's ex-girlfriend. He helps beat up Bryon after Mark cuts off Angela's hair.

Themes

Coming of Age

That Was Then, This Is Now is the story of Bryon Douglas's coming of age during his adolescence. When the story starts, Bryon is concerned only about himself and Mark. Early in the story, however, he meets Cathy, M&M's sister, and falls in love with her. As they begin dating more, Bryon notes, "I had quit thinking only about myself." And when M&M runs away and Bryon comforts a crying Cathy, he realizes that "it was the first time I'd ever felt bad for anyone except Mark." Bryon also

Topics for Further Study

- The Vietnam War influenced the lives of many young American men who were called upon to fight in a war in which many did not believe. Research the political and social climate in America during this time period and write a journal entry from the point of view of a young man who has just been drafted.

- Hinton was a teenager when she published her first young adult novel, which she hoped would resonate with other teens who had similar experiences. Write a one-page synopsis for a young adult novel based on observations you have made about your high school or other teenage experiences.

- Although the majority of reviewers credit Hinton with creating realistic tales, some maintain that teen life in the 1960s, even in gangs, was not as bad as the author's depictions. Research gangs and gang life during the 1960s and discuss how the actual history of the time period compares to Hinton's depictions.

- In the story, the narrator, Bryon, turns in his foster brother to the police and, as a result, loses the ability to care about anyone. Study current psychological research that addresses instances in which people experience loss of emotions. Using your research to support your claims, give a diagnosis of what you think happened to Bryon.

- Study the current methods that the government and public service organizations are using to fight drug distribution and use. How have these methods been effective? How have they failed? Propose your own idea for how to fight the war on drugs.

makes the transition from feeling that he can do whatever he wants to and get away with it to somebody who makes sacrifices and who understands that his actions have consequences. For example, in the beginning of the story, Bryon notes that he really needed a job, but that nobody would hire him. Charlie gives him a tip, saying that he should really look inside himself and he would see "the reason why you haven't gotten a job before now." Later, after Charlie is dead and Bryon is starting to change his views, he realizes what Charlie was talking about and asks himself, "Who's going to hire a mouthy kid who acts like he already knows it all?" Bryon sucks up his pride and gets a "haircut, clean clothes, and a really big change in attitude." Unfortunately, Bryon is aware of his transformation, and also is aware that "I was changing and [Mark] wasn't."

Violence

Bryon's and Mark's lives are saturated with violence, and they jump at the chance to save M&M from getting beaten up by Curly Shepard and his gang: "Me and Mark looked at each other, and Mark flashed me a grin. We both liked fights." M&M, however, does not like fights and criticizes Bryon and Mark when Mark notices a black guy and suggests they "jump him." Says M&M, "You just rescued me from some guys who were going to beat me up because I'm different from them, and now you're going to beat up someone because he's different from you." Although M&M's words have little effect on Mark, Bryon starts to think about what he's said and realizes that in the past he has not liked it when he "was the one getting mugged."

Bryon's uncertainty towards violence as a solution increases when he talks to Mike Chambers, a young gang member who got beaten up by a young black woman's friends after he tried to help her. Although most gang members Mike's age would find a way to get even, Mike does not hold it against the woman. Bryon can see Mike's point "about not hating the people who beat him up," but Mark does not.

Although they have been accustomed to violence since they were kids, it takes on a darker tone when Mark gets in a fight and gets cracked "across the side of the head" with a beer bottle and has to be taken in an ambulance to the hospital to get stitched up. When Mark realizes that Angela set up the fight, he finds an opportunity later to get her drunk and cut off her hair. Because Angela's brothers think Bryon has done it, they continue the cycle of violence and beat Bryon badly. He ends up with a "black eye . . . stitches in my lip," and "smashed ribs." After Bryon gets beaten, Mark wants to "go look up the Shepards," but Bryon stops him. "I don't want to keep this up, this getting-even jazz. . . . so if you're planning any get-even mugging, forget it." Bryon thinks back to Mike Chambers and realizes that, just as Mike did not hate his attackers, "I didn't hate the Shepards either."

Gang Life

While Bryon comes of age and embraces his adult identity, Mark desperately tries to cling to the gang life that they enjoyed as kids. Says Mark, "It was great, we were a bunch of people makin' up one big person, like we totaled up to somethin' when we were together," and that "it's kinda sad, really, when you get to where you don't need a gang." Although Bryon tries to get Mark to see that it is good "when you know your own personality so you don't need the one the gang makes for you," Mark is unsure and still yearns for the past, when "we were like brothers, not just you and me, but all of us together. We woulda died for each other then." Although the gang is not as close as they used to be, the violence inherent in their surroundings still prompts occasional displays of support. For example, when somebody tries to attack Pony-boy Curtis with a bottle, Mark puts himself at risk by stepping in between them, saying, "Hey, come on, man, fight fair," for which he earns a crack on the head with the bottle. And as mentioned above, when Bryon gets beaten up by the Shepards, Mark immediately wants to go and get even with them. This idea of protecting one's gang members extends to friends who are not technically part of the gang. When Bryon and Mark are about to be beaten by the two Texans whom they have just hustled, Charlie saves them, threatening the men with "a sawed-off shotgun." Even when the men shoot at Bryon, Mark, and him, Charlie "slammed both of us to the ground," a heroic act that saves Bryon and Mark and kills Charlie in the process.

Responsibility

Along with Bryon's other transformations in his emotional journey, he comes in touch with his sense of moral responsibility. When he was younger, Bryon "wasn't above taking a pack of cigarettes from a drugstore, but that was about it." Bryon is willing to steal small things but cuts himself off at a certain point. Furthermore, as he notes, "I still felt that stealing was wrong." Mark, on the other hand, "was really bad about stealing things" when he was a "kid." And, as Bryon notes, "Mark couldn't see anything wrong with stealing stuff." When Charlie dies trying to save Bryon and Mark, after he has already warned them about hustling, Bryon's seed of moral responsibility blossoms, and

he feels really bad for the first time in his life. "I couldn't get it out of my mind, Charlie's warning us about hustling." As he tells Mark, "Charlie is dead! He was all set for life, he wasn't gonna get drafted, he had his business . . . and then we blew it for him." Mark, however, refuses to believe they are responsible, saying, "he knew those cowboys had a gun, he knew what kind of a chance he was taking."

At the end of the story, when Bryon finds the drugs Mark has been selling, he realizes that "Mark had absolutely no concept of what was right and what was wrong; he didn't obey any laws, because he couldn't see that there were any." Bryon thinks about Cathy, M&M, and the pain her family is going through, and he feels that it is his responsibility to turn Mark in: "M&M was in the hospital, and maybe he was messed up for life—and Mark was selling the stuff that made him that way."

Alcohol and Drugs

Like violence, the community that Bryon and Mark live in is rife with alcohol and drugs, both of which are shown to lead to bad consequences. Mark's attacker uses one of the beer bottles from the "six six-packs" that Terry Jones sneaks into the school dance, to hurt Mark. Likewise, Mark uses alcohol to make Angela pass out so that he can cut off her hair. M&M's marijuana smoking leads him to try stronger "stuff" like LSD, which has many long-term effects, including the possibility of having "messed up" kids. This is devastating to M&M, who originally wanted "a large family."

Style

Narration

The story is told in the first person viewpoint, from the perspective of Bryon Douglas, which is consistent with Hinton's other teenage novels. By doing this, Hinton imbues her book with a deep sense of emotion. In the beginning, Bryon notes that "Mark was my best buddy and I loved him like a brother." In the end, Bryon is emotionally dead and says, "I don't even care about Mark. The guy who was my best friend doesn't exist any longer, and I don't want to think about the person who has taken his place." Along the way, Bryon leads the reader through all of the ill-fated steps that led to this transformation. Had Hinton used a third-person narrator to tell Bryon's story instead of letting Bryon tell it, the feeling for the character would not be as personal, and the shocking ending, where Bryon turns Mark in for dealing drugs, would not have as much impact.

Foreshadowing

While the ending has impact, the careful reader can pick up on a number of Bryon's statements that foreshadow Mark's drug dealing and his resulting feelings for Bryon when he is put away. The first of these happens after Bryon and Mark visit Mike Chambers in the hospital. Although Bryon sees how Mike could forgive his attackers, Mark says that he could never forgive anybody who hurt him that badly. In an offhand comment to the reader, Bryon responds to Mark's comment by saying that, at the time, he did not think much of Mark's statement, "later I would—I still do. I think about it and think about it until I think I'm going to go crazy." Although most readers have not been given enough information to realize that Bryon is talking about Mark's eventual hatred for him, readers are still left to wonder what happens in the future to make Bryon think so hard about this statement.

Mark's eventual career as a drug dealer is also foreshadowed. Later, when Bryon is trying to get a job, Mark tells him, "I'm goin' to start bringin' in some money," and "I ain't gonna sponge forever." Mark does not say how he is going to bring in money, but to Bryon, that is not as odd as why Mark said it. Up until this point, Bryon notes, Mark had "never said anything about being dependent on us." Still, Bryon does not question him on it. Neither Bryon nor his mother question Mark when he starts "bringing in money ... more than he ever had before." Bryon tells the reader that at the time he had assumed that Mark was winning the money by playing poker, but Bryon also goes on at length about the issue in this passage, which signals the reader that the reality was different from what Bryon had thought at the time. Bryon draws attention to Mark's income again later on, saying that Mark was "spending more and more time away from home" and that even Bryon's mom, who normally does not pry into Mark or Bryon's business, is "bugged about where he was getting the money." Although Bryon "still figured he was doing some serious poker playing," the way that Bryon sets this up leads the reader to believe that it is something more than that, a setup that pays off when Bryon finds the drugs and realizes "Mark was a pusher. That was where he was getting his money."

Irony

Irony is the unique awareness that is produced when someone says something and means another, or when somebody does something, and the result is opposite of what was expected. In *That Was Then, This Is Now*, the irony is the latter: situational irony. In this case, Hinton employs the irony for tragic purposes. Out of his love for Cathy and concern for M&M, Bryon sacrifices Mark by turning him into the authorities. However, in a cruelly ironic twist, this act causes him to lose his love for Cathy: when she stops by the next day, he is cold to her, knowing that he is "hurting her," but not caring. Bryon notices the change in himself even as he is saying the hurtful things, and he wonders "impersonally why I didn't love her any more. But it didn't seem to matter." He also realizes that to him, M&M is "just some brother of hers in the hospital ... not my friend, not somebody I too cared about." In fact, Bryon realizes, "I don't seem to care about anything any more. It's like I am worn out with caring about people." Although Bryon makes this realization calmly, it is devastating for the reader, who can still care and who feels the effects of Hinton's tragically ironic tale.

Historical Context

Vietnam and the Antiwar Movement

The 1960s and early 1970s were turbulent times, and the war in Vietnam did not help abate this tension. The conflict in Vietnam had actually begun in 1946, shortly after World War II ended. WWII had left many areas in Southeast Asia unstable, and over the next two decades, the United States quietly provided support to South Vietnam and those allied with the country, which was fighting against Ho Chi Minh's Communist forces in North Vietnam. The United States, so fearful of the spread of Communism that it viewed the loss of Vietnam as the start of a "domino" effect in Southeast Asia, escalated its involvement in the area. In 1964, President Johnson asked Congress for support, after one United States destroyer—performing a covert operation—was attacked by North Vietnamese forces off the coast of North Vietnam and another was allegedly attacked. (Later, it was shown that the second destroyer had not been attacked.) Johnson, who assured Congress that the destroyers were on routine, overt missions, convinced Congress to pass the Tonkin Gulf Resolution, which effectively gave Johnson unlimited

Compare & Contrast

- **1960s–1970s:** The United States significantly escalates its military involvement in Vietnam, prompting the government to "draft" its young men to fight and igniting the antiwar movement. Many young Americans enroll in college—the only legal way to avoid being drafted—stage protests, burn their draft cards, and even flee to other countries to avoid having to fight in the war.

    Today: After an unexpected attack on the Pentagon in Washington and the World Trade Center in New York City, the United States engages in a full-scale, international war on terrorism. The American public rallies to support this decision, and the military experiences a surge in its ranks as patriotic young men and women enlist to help wage the war.

- **1960s–1970s:** Many hippies and other members of the counterculture movement—who are often in their twenties or younger—experiment with "recreational" drugs to expand their minds and rebel against the establishment. For some people, these drug experiments backfire and cause permanent brain damage or other side effects that limit the person's ability to function in society.

    Today: America's public service organizations help to fight the war on drugs through influential advertisements that depict drugs as a barrier to success. These ads are aimed mainly at young children and teenagers, the primary target of many drug pushers.

- **1960s–1970s:** The peace symbol, tie-dyed shirts, and other wild developments in fashion become symbols for hippies, who use their unconventional clothes as one of many ways to express their desire to rebel against the establishment.

    Today: Many teens who want to appear trendy wear "retro" clothes and jewelry from the 1960s and 1970s, although they do not necessarily follow the hippie way of life. In addition, these clothes are often produced by large corporations, which are part of the establishment that the hippies were rebelling against.

---

power to escalate the Vietnam conflict. At this point, most Americans were unaware of these happenings.

By 1965, when fifty thousand new United States ground troops were added to the twenty-three thousand already stationed in Vietnam—posing as military "advisors"—the American public was more educated—much to the government's dismay. As James S. Olsen and Randy Roberts noted in their 1996 book, *Where the Domino Fell: America and Vietnam, 1945–1995*, "The decision to Americanize and militarize the conflict in Vietnam jump-started the antiwar movement in the United States." Olsen and Roberts note that in 1965 alone, "more than thirty other antiwar organizations sprouted," joining the existing groups. Much of the resentment came from the numbers of American troops required to feed the war machine. As J. M.

Roberts notes in his *Twentieth Century: The History of the World, 1901 to 2000*, "In 1968 there were over half a million American servicemen in Vietnam."

In order to meet these numbers, the United States government relied on the Selective Service System to "draft" young American men into the war. In *That Was Then, This Is Now*, Bryon notes the affect that draft notices had on many Americans, when he returns Charlie's car to him after the dance and tries to talk to him: "He didn't seem too interested, but he was having his own troubles. He'd got his draft notice." Although Charlie is ultimately saved from being drafted because of his police record, many others were not and showed their protest against the war by burning their draft notices, staging public demonstrations, or fleeing the country, usually to Canada. By the time the United

States government admitted defeat and began to withdraw its forces in 1973, the war had claimed the lives of fifty-eight thousand American men.

Hippies and Drugs

During the war, as the casualties rose, those involved in the antiwar, counterculture movement reacted in different ways, some violent, some not. One of the most enduring images from the era is that of the "hippie," derived from the word, "hip," meaning somebody who is trendy. Unlike some of the more militant antiwar groups, hippies believed in freedom, peace, and love, a philosophy that was often expressed through nature imagery such as the flower. In fact, a famous example of this "flower power," as David Steigerwald cited in his *The Sixties and the End of Modern America*, was during the hippies' march on the Pentagon in 1967: "Protesters sang to the troops, called for them to 'join us!,' and stuck flowers in gun barrels." However, while Steigerwald notes that hippies staged their protests using these and other nonviolent methods, such as creating a line of people by "locking arms and sitting down," he also notes that their opponents did not always reciprocate. The same Pentagon demonstration is a good example: "The marshalls . . . . made a serious assault, dragging protesters out of their lines and beating them with billy clubs." In *That Was Then, This Is Now*, Bryon, a "greaser" who loves to pick fights, notes his own reaction when he and Mark jump their first hippie: "I hadn't realized those guys refuse to fight back, and what happened to the one we got hold of, it made me sick. . . . after that we left them alone."

In addition to their nonviolent demeanor, hippies, like M&M in the story, were also characterized by their long hair and deliberately shabby clothes, in an attempt to embrace their freedom and rebel against the establishment. One of the other major ways in which hippies achieved these goals was through the use of recreational drugs. As Terry H. Anderson noted in his *The Movement and the Sixties*, "freaks," another name for hippies, commonly used dope—marijuana and hallucinogens like LSD—to "expand sensory perception and 'blow the mind.'" However, as Anderson notes, experienced hippies stayed away from drugs that led to a "bad trip." In Hinton's story, M&M earns the nickname "Baby Freak" because he is so much younger than the other hippies. Also, when M&M takes some LSD, the pusher who gives it to him tells Bryon and Cathy that he is "on a bad trip." Like M&M, whose brain is permanently damaged from the LSD, historian Martin Gilbert noted that the "'drug cul-

ture,'" which gained influence in the early 1960s, poisoned "the minds of millions of people."

The Civil Rights Movement and Racial Tension

In the 1960s, the Civil Rights movement was in full swing. Civil rights leaders like the Reverend Martin Luther King, Jr. and Malcolm X inspired African Americans to protest the discrimination and segregation they had experienced in the United States. In some cases, as with the hippies, blacks staged peaceful demonstrations. However, in the late 1960s, amid growing tensions between whites and blacks, racially motivated riots broke out in major cities such as Los Angeles, New York, Chicago, and Detroit.

Critical Overview

That Was Then, This Is Now belongs to a class of books known as young adult novels. However, in 1971 when the book was published, this field was completely different. In fact, Hinton herself helped to inaugurate the new tone of the field with her immensely successful young adult novel *The Outsiders* (1967), which was published when Hinton was a teenager herself. As she noted in *Speaking for Ourselves*, the lack of books for young adults in the 1960s was disconcerting: "If you were through with the horse books and not ready for adult books there wasn't much to read except *Mary Jane Goes to the Prom*, and I couldn't stand to read that stuff." Hinton thought that other teenagers, like herself, might want to read about books that dealt with real issues.

This was especially true, since some teenagers had for years been reading controversial adult books like *Catcher in the Rye* (1951), a fact that in turn helped to invoke the ire of self-imposed censors. Unfortunately, Hinton's tendency to discuss realistic themes in her young adult novels has also landed books like *That Was Then, This Is Now*—with its overt violence and drug references—on censored book lists.

Fortunately, the book has fared better in the reviews. Published four years after *The Outsiders*, *That Was Then, This Is Now* was a relief for Hinton, who had suffered from a huge case of writer's block since she had published her first novel. As Jay Daly noted in *Presenting S. E. Hinton*, "the cycle was broken at last upon the insistence of her boyfriend (and husband-to-be), David Inhofe," who

Emilio Estevez as Mark Jennings in the 1985 film version of the novel

was a student with her at the University of Tulsa. Reviewers were delighted at the new book, having waited eagerly for another Hinton book for five years. An overwhelming majority of reviewers noted the similarities to the *The Outsiders*, such as Michael Cart of *New York Times Book Review*, who called both books "powerful, realistic stories about being young and poor." Others remarked on the graphic themes of the book, such as Sheryl B. Andrews, who called it "a disturbing book" that "will speak directly to a large number of teenagers" and that "does have a place in the understanding of today's cultural problems." On a similar note, *Times Literary Supplement* called the book both "violent and tender," "a punch from the shoulder which leaves the reader considerably shaken."

However, not everybody adored the book, and as Hinton has published more books, some critics have gotten more vocal. In his 1986 essay, "Tough Puppies," *The Nation*'s Michael Malone criticized the idea many popular and critical reviewers have that Hinton's books are realistic. Citing the unrealistically brutal violence and neglect, Malone said that "it is difficult, if not horrifying, to think that millions of 12-year-olds.... find any more in them than the most remote connections." Malone concluded that "despite their modern, colloquial tone," Hinton's novels are "fairy tale adventures."

The next year, Daly also questioned the validity of early criticism, but for different reasons. Daly considered *That Was Then, This Is Now* "more disciplined" and "well-crafted" than *The Outsiders* but said that it "was not necessarily better." However, as Daly noted, he believed that many other critics had the "tendency to enshrine *That Was Then, This Is Now* without looking too deeply," which Daly surmised was "a belated climbing-on-the-bandwagon of *The Outsiders*." Daly also thought some reviewers, like Andrews, mentioned above, "seemed to dislike the book but could not quite bring herself to say why," so instead she retreated "to the safe haven of the sociologist-critic position."

In the end, the attempts to ban Hinton's books or the questionable criticism about *That Was Then, This Is Now* have not made much difference. Hinton and her books—whose timeless themes resonate with people from different generations—have continued to find success with popular audiences.

Criticism

Ryan D. Poquette
Poquette holds a bachelor's degree in English and specializes in writing about literature. In the

> However, in the adult world, as Bryon's story illustrates, consequences must be acknowledged and dealt with. Charlie's death and the emotional change it inspires in Bryon cannot be undone; the broken relationship between Bryon and Mark cannot be repaired."

following essay, Poquette examines Hinton's use of Charlie's death as the main catalyst for Bryon's emotional growth in That Was Then, This Is Now.

That Was Then, This Is Now is one of Hinton's—and young adult fiction's—classic coming-of-age stories. Hinton stages her story amidst the gritty street background that characterized many of her young adult books, and employed the same realistic themes that helped to change the tone of young adult fiction in general. As Hinton discussed in *Speaking for Ourselves*, when she was a teenager, "there wasn't much to read except *Mary Jane Goes to the Prom*, and I couldn't stand to read that stuff." Instead, Hinton's teenagers face adult situations, make adult decisions, and deal with adult consequences. In *That Was Then, This Is Now*, the teenager is Bryon Douglas, who makes the transformation from a carefree kid to a mature, responsible, but emotionally devastated adult. Although many factors influence Bryon's transformation, it is the symbolic death of Charlie that provides the ultimate catalyst.

In the beginning of the story, Bryon is a street kid, whose rough lifestyle is established with the first line of the book: "Mark and me went down to the bar/pool hall about two or three blocks from where we lived with the sole intention of making some money." Throughout the rest of the first chapter, Bryon tells the reader the other ways he lives his life besides hustling pool, such as how he treats girls, "telling them I loved them and junk, when I didn't. I had a rep as a lady-killer—a hustler." Bryon also demonstrates his tendency to fight with other kids, when he and Mark gladly

come to M&M's rescue, after M&M gets jumped by Curly Shepard and his gang. "Me and Mark looked at each other, and Mark flashed me a grin. We both liked fights. We ran out and jumped on them." Most important, Bryon is tied to his foster brother, another street kid: "Mark was my best buddy and I loved him like a brother." At this point, Bryon is starting to have some minor doubts about his lifestyle, such as when he takes M&M's cue and starts to realize that fights are not all that great: "I didn't feel quite as good as I had before. I was thinking about what M&M had said about beating up people because they were different." However, Bryon is only starting to have these feelings, and even after he remembers his own bad experiences with being mugged, he still notes, "I liked fights."

At the end of the story, however, Bryon has changed. He has turned in his "brother," Mark, to the authorities for drug dealing and is very confused about why he does this. "Why had I turned on Mark? What had I done to him?" Bryon quickly finds that his actions have a profound effect on his emotional state. When Cathy comes to visit, he is distant, cold, and deliberately hurtful to her. As he notes, "I wondered impersonally why I didn't love her any more. But it didn't seem to matter." Furthermore, Bryon is no longer living the carefree lifestyle he had, picking fights and causing other types of trouble. Instead, he follows a mature, responsible life routine. "I went to school and went to work and went home and studied." He performs this routine without thought and gets "straight A's" and a promotion, "from sack boy to clerk. I didn't come to work hung over and I didn't give the manager any lip."

So what causes this huge transformation? Although many factors contribute to Bryon's change, it is the death of his friend Charlie that sets the change in motion. In fact, Charlie's death is strategically placed within the novel, almost exactly halfway through the narrative, dividing the book into two equal parts, the period in Bryon's life before Charlie's death and the period after Charlie's death. This is not an accident on Hinton's part. As Jay Daly said in his book, *Presenting S. E. Hinton*, "*That Was Then, This Is Now* is, in nearly everyone's view, a much more disciplined novel than *The Outsiders*." Daly notes that Hinton used this discipline "to fashion a well-crafted book." Looking at the book with this fact in mind, it is easy to see that Hinton deliberately places Charlie's death at the center of the book, providing a clear pivotal point for Bryon's emotional journey.

Even before his death, Charlie is an important person in Bryon's life, since he is the only adult-like influence that Bryon has; Bryon and Mark live in a world that is relatively free from adults. The *Nation* reviewer, Michael Malone, noted this trend in Hinton's books: "Rather than ask her characters to cope with adults, wryly or otherwise, Hinton either removes them or removes their authority." These two situations are definitely true in *That Was Then, This Is Now*. Mark loses his parents at an early age: "His parents had killed each other in a drunken fight when he was nine years old and he saw it all." Following this tragic event, young Mark knows, "I can go live with Bryon and his old lady." However, for much of the story, Bryon's "old lady" is not around either, since she's in the hospital with an unnamed illness.

Even when Bryon's mother is around, however, her style of parenting is very hands-off. She is a compassionate person who is known for her tendency to take in strays, but she does not exhibit much concern for her sons' actions, even when they are hurt. As Bryon notes, "That was a good thing about Mom—she'd cry over a dog with a piece of glass in his paw but remained unhysterical when we came home clobbered." Malone also noted this "remarkable lack of maternal responsibility or even curiosity." Bryon's mother is not around when Bryon and Mark make their biggest decisions, and she is unaware of the types of activities that they pursue in general. Bryon says that this is normal: "Parents never know what all their kids do. Not in the old days, not now, not tomorrow. It's a law." In fact, at the end of the story, after Bryon has made his life-changing choice to turn in Mark to the police for his drug dealing, Bryon notes that it is at this point that "Mom woke up. She didn't know what was going on. She could only stand helpless in the kitchen doorway." This line underscores the lack of parental involvement and authority in the story.

In this world that is relatively isolated from adults, the only true parental figure, somebody who has a real influence over Bryon, is Charlie, the twenty-two-year-old bar owner. Although Charlie is only six years older than Bryon, he is the one who gives Bryon fatherly advice, encouraging Bryon to look inside himself for answers, such as when Bryon asks him for a job and he turns him down: "You just think about it, and I think you'll come up with the reason why you haven't got a job before now." Charlie also gives Bryon other reasons for not giving him a job, such as Charlie's concern for Bryon's safety: "Besides, Bryon, it gets rough in here late at night . . . you'd better just take my word for it that you'd be better off someplace else." For this last reason, it makes sense that Charlie is the one who makes the ultimate sacrifice—his life—when he saves Mark and Bryon from the two Texans. When Bryon and Mark start to come out of the alley, Charlie scolds them, as a parent might, saying, "I hope you two learned something from this." However, when one of the Texans uses this distraction as an opportunity to dive for his gun, Charlie's first instinct is to protect Bryon and Mark. He drops his shotgun and, as Bryon notes, "slammed both of us to the ground."

Charlie's death symbolizes the death of Bryon's own childhood; without Charlie, Bryon's only adult-like influence, Bryon must start to think on his own. Charlie's death is also the first time that Bryon has had to face a major consequence from his actions. Bryon thinks to himself: "I couldn't get it out of my mind, Charlie's warning us about hustling." Mark, who has always related to him before, does not understand Bryon's guilt over Charlie's death: "We didn't blow nothing, Bryon. Things just happen, that's all there is to it." Bryon looks elsewhere for solace, to Cathy. "I could talk to her about anything, talk to her better than I could anyone, even Mark." As a result, Bryon gets put in the middle of a battle between Mark and Cathy. Mark wants Bryon to be the same carefree kid he's always been, causing trouble with Mark and never thinking about the consequences. Cathy, on the other hand, understands Bryon's impulse to be a mature adult, even telling him at one point that she thinks he would "be a good influence" on her brother, M&M, who she suspects is starting to use drugs.

Bryon feels this struggle between Mark and Cathy, between childhood and maturity. Bryon and Mark talk about this one night when Bryon is drunk, and Bryon asks Mark why bad things happen to people. Mark warns Bryon: "You start wonderin' why, and you get old. Lately, I felt like you were leavin' me, man." Bryon *is* getting old. He is starting to see, as with Charlie's death, that his actions have consequences, and this knowledge of responsibility influences his reactions to other events. For example, he feels bad that they picked up his ex-girlfriend, Angela, and cut off her hair in a vengeful act, something that in his old life, he might not have had a problem with: "Poor Angel—we shoulda left her alone, Mark. That was a mean thing to do, cut off her hair like that." This same mature awareness of responsibility for one's actions influences Bryon's decision to turn Mark in when he finds Mark's drugs and, in a flash of insight, realizes that "M&M was in the hospital, and maybe he was messed up for life—and Mark was selling the stuff that made him that way." Bryon further realizes that "Mark had absolutely no concept of what was right and what was wrong" and feels he has no choice but to turn him in. Bryon's mother, in one of her few "motherly" statements, tells him at the end of the book that "what you did was for his own good." Nevertheless, this act renders Bryon emotionally dead at sixteen, wondering if things could have turned out differently. As Michael Cart noted:

> The phrase 'if only' is perhaps the most bittersweet in the language, and Miss Hinton uses it skillfully to underline her theme: growth can be a dangerous process. As Bryon moves toward maturity he faces the dangers of the emotional vacuum that waits to be filled after loss of innocence.

This cataclysmic ending underscores, more than anything else, that Bryon is now an adult who must face the consequences of his actions. Says Sheryl B. Andrews, "Bryon's final commitment to himself and to his future is harshly and realistically underlined in an ending that offers no pat promises." This harsh ending has prompted questions from Hinton's teenage readers. In his article, "On Tulsa's Mean Streets," *Newsweek*'s Gene Lyons noted of Hinton's fan mail, "Sometimes correspondents are moved to ask things like ... 'Can't you write another book and get Bryon and Mark back together?'" However, in the adult world, as Bryon's story illustrates, consequences must be acknowledged and dealt with. Charlie's death and the emotional change it inspires in Bryon cannot be undone; the broken relationship between Bryon and Mark cannot be repaired.

Source: Ryan D. Poquette, Critical Essay on *That Was Then, This Is Now*, in *Novels for Students*, The Gale Group, 2003.

Erik France

France is a librarian, college counselor, and teacher at University Liggett School and teaches writing at Macomb Community College near Detroit, Michigan. In the following essay, France compares Hinton's novel with Larry McMurtry's The Last Picture Show *as a coming-of-age novel.*

S. E. Hinton's *That Was Then, This Is Now* is a coming of age novel set during the Vietnam War around the late 1960s. It takes place in an unnamed city very much like Tulsa, Oklahoma, that shares significant characteristics with Larry McMurtry's *The Last Picture Show*, set in the vicinity of the fictional Thalia, Texas, during the Korean War in the early 1950s. Following the lives and trials of teenagers as they progress through cycles of hope and loss, both novels provide details of setting, and strong plots, that give readers sympathetic access to character in times of crisis. Both have been made into movies, and both leave a profound sense of sadness about the human condition.

The settings to *That Was Then, This Is Now* and *The Last Picture Show* are clearly laid out as places where teenagers have a difficult time finding something wholesome to do. In both cases, driving around aimlessly, playing pool, drinking, and looking for trouble are common forms of entertainment. Lack of money plays a large role in both, too, and the main male teenage characters have to spend a considerable amount of their time scrounging, scamming, or working petty jobs to earn enough for dates and living expenses. Even transportation requires cooperation and careful planning, with Mark and Bryon having to borrow their friend Charlie's car from time to time in *That Was Then, This Is Now* and Sonny and Duane having to share use of their friend Sam the Lion's pickup truck, often having to negotiate and alternate dating times because of this limitation, in *The Last Picture Show*. Mark and Bryon have a somewhat larger playing field because they live in a moderate sized city, whereas Sonny and Duane live in the much smaller Thalia in West Texas, a windswept little town that is surrounded by oil fields and vast empty spaces. Also, Mark and Bryon, at the time of Hinton's novel, live in a period nearly twenty years after the setting for McMurtry's, and they are exposed to drugs and hippie culture, including marijuana, pills, and LSD; alcohol, though, is common to both settings and easily available to resourceful teenagers, despite legal statutes aimed at limiting access to it. The drugs in *That Was Then, This Is Now* are a more serious matter in terms of what happens to characters. This is particularly evident in the overdose, hospitalization, and clear psychological damage of Cathy Carlson's thirteen-year-old brother M&M (known to his hippie friends as Baby Freak), and in Bryon calling the police and turning in Mark, his brotherly best friend, for pushing pills. Finally, sexual mores and situations are more frankly discussed in McMurtry's novel, partly because Sonny and Duane are seniors and then high school graduates during the course of the plot, whereas Mark and Bryon are sophomore or juniors (it is not specified); and partly because drugs provide the major plot rationale that substitutes for sex in Hinton's novel.

Supporting male characters play pivotal roles in both *That Was Then, This Is Now* and *The Last Picture Show*. Most important are Charlie and M&M in the former and Sam the Lion and Billy in the latter. They are very special people. Charlie, only twenty-two, runs a bar and pool hall and serves as a mentor and protector for Bryon and Mark. Sam the Lion is much older and runs a pool hall and owns other properties in Thalia; he also takes care of Billy, a retarded orphan, and Sonny, his friend, and to a lesser extent, Duane, whose father is an alcoholic. Like Charlie, Sam is well-respected, has a rough background himself, and does his best to guide the young men who look up to him. Coincidentally, or in a possible homage to McMurtry, Hinton has Bryon, the narrator of *That Was Then, This Is Now*, repeatedly describe Mark as having the qualities of a lion, referring to his "lion-like grin," and to him acting "like a teased lion who's had enough," like "a stray lion;" once he outright calls him "Mark the lion." Aside from this, there is a more direct parallel in that the demise of Charlie and Sam the Lion represent major turning points in each book, accelerating changes in Hinton's Bryon and Mark and in McMurtry's Sonny and Billy respectively. Charlie, armed with a sawed off shotgun, is killed while trying to drive off two Texans who are threatening, at gunpoint, to beat up Bryon and Mark for having hustled them at pool. In *The Last Picture Show*, Sam the Lion dies suddenly of natural causes only days after giving Sonny and Duane extra money and his blessings for a trip they take to Mexico in the pickup truck; they learn of his death almost immediately upon their return. As Sonny observes, nothing is the same once Sam dies. Sonny receives Sam's pool hall and charge of Billy from Sam the Lion's will, while in *That Was Then, This is Now*, Bryon and Mark are given Charlie's car by the local authorities where they live. Soon after the deaths of these strong male role models, respective female characters complicate and destabilize Bryon's, Mark's, Sonny's, and Duane's lives further, leading eventually to complete breaks in all of their relationships.

Though there are more than two important female characters in both *That Was Then, This Is Now* and *The Last Picture Show*, two are crucial catalysts for change: Cathy in the former and Jacy in the latter. Duane and Sonny literally come to blows over Jacy, with Duane crashing a beer bottle over Sonny's head. In Hinton's novel, Mark has a beer bottle smashed over his head, too, in a fight set up by one of Bryon's past girlfriends (Angela), but it is when Bryon falls in love with Cathy that Mark

> In both novels, the principal characters experience the death of friends; they come to know love only to lose it; and they lose each other in the process."

truly starts losing Bryon's friendship and their shared feeling of brotherhood. Jacy is beautiful, flirtatious, and, the only child of oil-rich parents. She becomes a femme fatale (a seductive and disastrous girlfriend) for both Duane and Sonny. She breaks up with Duane, who eventually goes off to work as a "roughneck" in the oil fields hoping to win her back, only to learn of her dating Sonny in his absence. It is when he returns and confronts Sonny about this that they have their climactic street brawl. Sonny subsequently marries her, only to have her arrange their elopement's almost immediate annulment, to his utter confusion and devastation. Sonny joins the Army and climbs on a bus, heading for military service during the Korean War. With Jacy gone, Duane first makes a sort of sad peace with Sonny (for they are veterans of the same love and war with Jacy), letting him drive the car he bought with oil field wages while he is away. Cathy is very different from Jacy, but the end result is just as disastrous for all involved. Cathy comes from a large lower middle class family, one that is concerned and loving toward their children. Bryon is the first person she seriously dates, and they fall in love mutually. Younger than Jacy, Cathy is more mature for her age and has set her heart on college and a stable life. She comes to think of Mark as a bad influence on Bryon, and Mark, therefore, comes to resent her and feels hurt as her influence gains power over Bryon. Tension builds between the two, and both Bryon and Mark begin to feel a gulf developing between them. Bryon begins to change, to care about Cathy and her little brother M&M. When Mark tries to hold on to what they had, Bryon feels remorse and guilt. Unlike Jacy, Cathy is no femme fatale. Instead, she vocalizes her strong opinions about right and wrong and renders bluntly honest observations that quickly annoy Mark and eventually annoy Bryon as well.

A street gang like the one in the novel

With Cathy profoundly affecting the relationship between Bryon and Mark in *That Was Then, This Is Now* and Jacy doing the same to Sonny and Duane in *The Last Picture Show*, both novels head in the same parallel direction, ending in breakups in the relationships all of these friends. The strong male role models Charlie and Sam the Lion have already died; now the more gentle and pitiful characters M&M (Baby Freak) and Billy suffer respective disasters that propel Sonny (in *The Last Picture Show*) and Bryon (In *That Was Then, This Is Now*) to desperate, almost forlorn acts. In the McMurtry novel, Sonny has already lost Sam the Lion to death, Jacy has left him, and Duane departed left for military service, when a seemingly cruel universe takes Billy from him, too: for the retarded Billy is run over by a truck driver while sweeping the street. His last act is to go back to try to seek amends with the 40-year-old wife of his former football coach whom he (Sonny) had abandoned for Jacy. In the Hinton novel, the tragedy is propelled by the principal characters remaining after Charlie's death. M&M has run away from home (he is still only thirteen) to join a hippie house and gotten tangled up in drugs. Mark knows the place well, for he sells drugs to some of the hippies there and he has a presumably sexual relationship with at least one of the young women who stays there. Knowing that Cathy and Bryon are upset and trying to find M&M, Mark takes Bryon to the house. Though M&M is out at the time, Bryon realizes Mark's familiarity with the hippies, which disturbs him, for he is troubled by the illegality of their activities. Crisis comes when Bryon later brings Cathy to the house where they discover M&M (Baby Freak) on a "bad trip" muttering about spiders and talking colors. They rush him to the hospital, but his mind is disturbed and, by the end of the book, his life seems to be shattered. Immediately upon return from the hospital, Bryon discovers a stash of drugs under Mark's bed, realizes that Mark is a drug pusher, and calls the police to turn him in. This irrevocable act ends everything: Mark, who had loved him like a brother, is thrown into prison and now hates him, and Bryon in turn, who had so loved Cathy, now hates her.

In conclusion, *That Was Then, This Is Now* and *The Last Picture Show* are coming of age novels that start the principal male characters off in strong friendships that would seem to last forever but that undergo profound and ultimately disastrous changes. The settings are somewhat different in time and place (Oklahoma in the late 1960s, Texas in the early 1950s), but they tell essentially the same story about the human condition, particularly at the age of reaching adulthood. They are, in this sense, rites of passage. Indeed, they are tales of emotional, psychological, and physical change from a time when these young men felt that everything was sure, easy, and permanent, in many ways a frolic, into a time as adults when it would seem the world is much crueler and they are suddenly and unexpectedly alone, or virtually so. The principal characters all experience great trauma by the end. In both novels, the principal characters experience the death of friends; they come to know love only to lose it; and they lose each other in the process. The survivors are left to try to recreate themselves in the adult world, but they will remember their losses and be left with a profound sadness, as will the reader of both novels. The reader is left to wonder how the haunted adult lives of Bryon in *That Was Then, This Is Now* and Sonny in *The Last Picture Show* will turn out, for Hinton and McMurtry inspire us to care about their lives, and ours.

Source: Erik France, Critical Essay on *That Was Then, This Is Now*, in *Novels for Students*, The Gale Group, 2003.

Michael Malone

In the following excerpt, Malone discusses the unrealistic language used by teenagers in Hinton's books.

In *That Was Then, This is Now* "golden dangerous Mark," the narrator's best buddy, also discovers that he is mistaken about his parentage—his real father turns out to be another rodeo cowboy. Bryon tells us about it like this: "Mark had lived at my house ever since I was ten and he was nine and his parents shot each other in a drunken argument." Later we learn the argument was over Mark's parentage; the shots were fatal, and the child, hiding under the porch, heard it all. As Mark recalls: "And then they start yelling and I hear this sound like a couple of firecrackers. And I think, well, I can go live with Bryon and his old lady. . . I didn't like livin' at home." The desire to leave home is a sentiment with which most teen-agers can empathize, but few are given so graphic an opportunity to do so. Nor do the majority, I hope, respond to family indifference like Dallas Winston of The Outsiders, who "lied, cheated, stole, rolled drunks, jumped small kids," even if they occasionally feel the same way about their parents: "What do they matter? Shoot, my old man don't give a hang whether I'm in jail or dead in a car wreck or drunk in the gutter. That don't bother me none."

What is clear from the recurrent themes of Hinton's novels, like the discovery of mysterious parentage, is that despite their modern, colloquial tone, they are fairy tale adventures (Luke Skywalker's father is really Darth Vader), and their rumbles as exotic as jousts in Ivanhoe or pirate wars in Treasure Island. What is curious is that grownups insist on the books' veracity. Hinton announces, "The real boy like Dallas Winston [the role Matt Dillon plays in *The Outsiders*] was shot and killed by the police for having stolen a car." Tim Hunter, director of the film *Tex*, says he was drawn to Hinton's work because of the way she weaves social problems "into the fabric of a realistic story."

In fact, the fabric is mythic. There are no verisimilar settings. Presumably the books take place near Tulsa, Oklahoma (the films do), but place names are never mentioned, and were it not for occasional references to rodeos, one would have little notion of the Western ambiance so evident in the movie versions. Characters live in "the neighborhood"; sometimes they go to "the city" or to "the country." The city is bacchanalian: "There

> **The heightened language of her young narrators intensifies the glamour and sentiment of their stories, but it will not strike readers as everyday school-locker lingo."**

were lots of people and noise and lights and you could feel energy coming off things, even buildings". (*Rumble Fish*). The country is pastoral: "The clouds were pink and meadowlarks were singing" (*The Outsiders*). Temporal location is equally vague, *The Outsiders* published in 1967, might as easily have been written ten years earlier, in the fifties of its real progenitor, James Dean movies, true, some parenthetical hippies are up to some druggy no-good in *That Was Then, This Is Now* (1971), but the Motorcycle Boy in *Rumble Fish* (1975) might have ridden right off the screen of *The Wild One*. Far from strikingly realistic in literary form, these novels are romances, mythologizing the tragic beauty of violent youth, as the flashy surrealism of Francis Ford Coppola's *Rumble Fish*, with its film noir symbolism and spooky soundtrack, all too reverently attests.

Moreover, while praised for its "lean Hemingway style" and natural dialogue, Hinton's prose can be as fervid, mawkish and ornate as any nineteenth-century romance, although this is less true in the later books, especially *Tex*. The heightened language of her young narrators intensifies the glamour and sentiment of their stories, but it will not strike readers as everyday school-locker lingo. Ponyboy, 14, and Bryon, 16, fling adjectives and archaic phrases ("Hence his name," "heaven forbid") around like Barbara Cartland. Bryon notes that his friend Mark's "strangely sinister innocence was gone." Ponyboy describes his brother, Sodapop, as having "a finely drawn, sensitive face that somehow manages to be reckless and thoughtful at the same time," as well as "lively, dancing, recklessly lauging eyes." Ponyboy is also given to quoting from memory long snatches of Robert Frost's "Nothing Gold Can Stay," and to using words like "merrily," "gallant" and "elfish." Of course, Bryon and Ponyboy point out to us that

What Do I Read Next?

- Eve Bunting's *Someone Is Hiding on Alcatraz Island* (1984) features the story of Danny, a San Francisco boy who saves an old woman from a mugger's attack. Unfortunately, in the process, Danny offends the Outlaws, a gang at his high school. He tries to escape to Alcatraz Island, but the gang follows, and Danny, with the help of a park ranger, must survive on the grounds of the old prison. The book was published in reprint edition in 1994 by Berkley Publishing Group.

- *The Chocolate War* had a very controversial reception when it was first published in 1974. Robert Cormier's popular and ground-breaking novel features the story of Jerry Renault, a freshman at a Catholic high school, who does the unthinkable when he inspires a movement in refusing to sell chocolates for the school fundraiser, even though his actions eventually provoke the retaliation of the Vigils, the school gang. The book was published in a reprint edition in 1986 by Random House.

- Hinton's *The Outsiders* (1967), the unexpected smash success that paved the way for grittier young adult novels, including *That Was Then, This Is Now*, details the struggle between two gangs, the poor greasers and the rich Socs (short for socials). In Hinton's book, the greasers were the ones who normally got attacked by the Socs, which flipped the standard model of violence on its head. The book was published in a reprint edition by Prentice Hall in 1997.

- Hinton's *The Puppy Sister* (1995) is technically a children's book, but, like her young adult novels, Hinton's book has been enjoyed by people of all ages. The story is pure fantasy and features the tale of a young puppy who does not realize that she is a dog. She decides that she can become a human, and, through sheer will she does, a transformation that involves the whole family. The book was published in a reprint edition by Bantam Books in 1997.

- Hinton's third novel, *Rumble Fish* (1972), continues to explore the life of street teens, in this case, Rusty-James, who fights with his fists and has always been bailed out by his older brother when his own fists were not enough. Rusty-James's life is torn apart through a cataclysmic series of events, and for once his brother is not around to save him. The book was published in a reprint edition by Laurel Leaf in 1989.

- Hinton's *Taming the Star Runner* (1988) deviated from her normal style by using a third-person narrator to tell the story of troubled fifteen-year-old Travis Harris, who is sent to his uncle's Oklahoma ranch as an alternative to juvenile hall. Although Harris is reluctant to adapt to his rural surroundings at first, he eventually develops a relationship with Casey Kincaid, a horse trainer—who is in the process of training the stallion, the Star Runner—and publishes a book about his life. The book was published in a reprint edition by Laurel Leaf in 1989.

- Hinton's books often concern the story of gangs or gang members in young America, particularly in the 1960s and 1970s. *Gangs in America III*, edited by C. Ronald Huff and published by Sage Publications in 2001, is a popular anthology that collects the most up-to-date information about contemporary gangs and the current law enforcement efforts used to prevent and control gang violence and crime. Through a series of essays, the contributors thoroughly examine how and why young people join gangs, the effects gangs have on communities, and the newest potential solutions.

- Paul Zindel's *The Pigman* (1968) tells the story of John and Lorraine, high school students who pass the time by playing phone pranks on people. Through one of these pranks, they meet "The Pigman," a sad widower named Mr. Pignati, who changes their lives forever and gets them to see that their actions have consequences. The book was published in a reprint edition by Bantam Starfire in 1983.

although they seem to spend all their time hanging out with the gang, they are both honor students: "I make good grades and have a high IQ." But even Rusty-James of *Rumble Fish*, stuck in "dumb classes" and, by his own admission, no student ("Math ain't never been my strong point"), waxes poetical: "I wouldn't have her to hold anymore, soft but strong in my arms." Sententious moralizing coats the pages: "That was what he wanted. For somebody to tell him 'No'. . . If his old man had just belted him—just once, he might still be alive." "You start wondering why, and you get old." "We see the same sunset."

The lyricism, the lack of novelistic detail, the static iconography of Hinton's books keep the clutter of creation from interfering with the sources of their obviously persistent appeal—their rapid action (mostly violent) unfettered by the demands of a plot, their intense emotions (mostly heavy) and their clear-cut moral maps. Hinton's fictional universe is as black-and-white as an old cowboy film. *The Outsiders* is the ur-text. In it there are Socs (Socials) and there are greasers; unlike that of the warring Hatfields and McCoys, Montagues and Capulets, Jets and Sharks, this eternal enmity is neither familial nor racial, but financial. Socs are rich, greasers are poor; Socs are "the in crowd," greasers are "the outsiders." Socs always wear madras and English Leather and drive Mustangs or Corvairs. They always "jump greasers and wreck houses and throw beerblasts for kicks." That's pretty much all we get to know about Socs; they're just the enemy. A Soc girl, Cherry Valance, makes a brief appearance to point out to Ponyboy, "We have troubles you never even heard of," but those troubles are not explored; instead she schematizes neatly: "You greasers have a different set of values. You're more emotional. We're sophisticated—cool to the point of not feeling anything." Given this fundamental difference (and despite the fact that they see the same sunset), Cherry is obliged to warn Ponyboy: "If I see you in the hall . . . and don't say hi, well, it's not personal. . . . We couldn't let our parents see us with you all."

Our heroes, greasers, are also initially defined by their appearance and their style of antisocial behavior: "We steal things and drive old souped-up cars and hold up gas stations once in a while . . . just like we leave our shirt-tails out and wear leather jackets." But popular culture has taught us to interpret this style with sympathy, if not rabid infatuation. The narrators pay continual, indeed obsessive, attention to their own and their friends' appearance. We hear constantly about "strange golden eyes," "light-brown, almost-red hair," faces like "some Greek god come to earth." They are always asking and reassuring each other about their good looks, particularly the beauty of their hair.

Funky costume and flamboyant hairstyle have long been the outward signs of inward romantic rebellion—from Shelley's flowing locks and open collars through Ginsberg's sandals to Elvis's sideburns—and Ponyboy's identifying himself through his hair oil ("I am a greaser") announces his place in a tradition that goes back to Bronte's crush on Heathcliff, and associates him with such suffering gods as James Dean. It's significant that many of the young men who played in Coppola's 1982 film of *The Outsiders* were to become adolescent idols within the next few years: Dillon, Rob Lowe, Tom Cruise, Emilio Estevez, Patrick Swayze. A leather jacket, bloody knuckles and a sensitive soul is an irresistible combination. Pain and sadness help too.

There is no sweeter sorrow than the self-pity of our teens, no pain more rhapsodized than our adolescent anguish; adults simply lose the will to sustain such Sturm und Drang. Like the protagonists of all Bildungsromans, Hinton's leather-jacketed young Werthers are lyrical on the subject of their psychic aches and pains. Tough as nails on the street, yeah, hey—but alone in the dark, they're as naked and afraid in a world they never made as any Herman Hesse hero. Confused, lonely, slighted, they share with, they feel for, their readers that most profound pubescent emotion: "I don't belong." In the classic apprenticeship novel, the youngster—Tonio Kroger, Stephen Dedalus, Paul Morel, Eugene Gant—experiences and reflects on this sense of alienation and so grows to understand the particular difference that is his self. When, in *The Outsiders*, Ponyboy tells us, "I cried passionately, "It ain't fair that we have all the rough breaks,'" his *cri de coeur*, like the novel's title, suggests the tribal rather than personal thrust of Hinton's use of the theme, as well as its simplistic economic nature. ("You can't win because they've got all the breaks.") In Hinton's books, selfhood is subsumed in the tribal gang. "It was great, we were a bunch of people making up one big person" (*That Was Then This Is Now*) "Why did the Socs hate us so much? We left them alone." "It wasn't fair for the Socs to have everything. We were as good as they were" (*The Outsiders*) So magically does the gang incorporate its members tha in the opening of *The Outsiders* it miraculously appears out of the night to save Ponyboy from the motiveless malignity of a carful of Socs: "All the noise I had heard was the gang coming to rescue me." "Somehow the gang sensed what had happened."

The gang is the family: "We're almost as close as brothers." And in contrast to "a snarling, distrustful, bickering pack like the Socs," greaser gangs are unfailingly loyal and free of rivalry. Maybe they have "too much energy, too much feeling, with no way to blow it off" except through marauding violence, but with one another they are as gentle as maidens on a Victorian valentine, innocently sleeping with their arms around each other, choking with tenderness for one another's pain. Johnny in *The Outsiders* is the most vulnerable, most pathetically hurt gang member (the Sal Mineo part in *Rebel Without a Cause*; for his film of *The Outsiders*, Coppola even found in Ralph Macchio an actor who looks just like Mineo). Ponyboy's solicitude for him is shared by even the toughest of the greasers. He is "a little dark puppy that has been kicked too many times and is lost in a crowd of strangers... His father was always beating him up, and his mother ignored him... If it hadn't been for the gang, Johnny would never have known what love and affection are." Like Mineo's Plato, Johnnycake is clearly pegged for tearful sacrifice. And sure enough—having accidentally stabbed a Soc to death and then redeemed himself by saving some children from a burning church—he dies from burns and a broken back after a series of heart-rending hospital-bed scenes. As might be expected in fiction for adolescents, the blood brother bond supersedes all other emotional commitments. *That Was Then, This Is Now* opens, "Mark and me went down to the bar"; and Bryon's love for Mark, like the love of Beowulf or Roland for their companions, runs like a lyric refrain through the novel.

These characters do sometimes have girl-friends, but their erotic relationships come nowhere near the power of male camaraderie. Hinton reports she almost didn't agree to sell *Tex* to Walt Disney Productions because she "thought they'd really sugar it up, take out all the sex, drugs and violence," but there is actually far less sex in her books than in the films made from them. Her instinct, conscious or not, that young readers could take endless physical violence and heartbreak but would be embarrassed by physical passion is quite sound. On the page of *Rumble Fish*, Rusty-James tells us of his visit to Patty, "I just sat there holding her and sometimes kissed the top of her head"; on the screen this becomes a torrid tumble on a couch. Rusty-James's description, "there were some girls [at the lake] and we built a fire and went swim-

ming," becomes on screen an orgiastic montage of naked bodies. Similarly, unlike the films, the books are as free of profanity as *Heidi*. We are told people "talk awful dirty," but the only curses we hear are almost comically mild: "Glory!" "Shoot!" "Oh blast it!" Indeed, gang members warn the younger ones to avoid "bad habits" like cursing. They may smoke cigarettes, integral to the image, but they don't much care for booze and are leery of drugs. As well they might be. M&M, *That Was Then, This is Now*'s counterpart to the doomed Johnnycake, takes LSD, goes psychotic, is hospitalized (the doctor announces solemnly, "He may have lost his mind forever") and is told that his chromosomes are so messed up that he must forget his dream of a large family.

In *Rebel Without a Cause*, James Dean is trying to cope with a new society, with a new girl, with his parents, with adult authority. He copes in part by means of wry humor, a detachment that is missing in Hinton's books and in the films made from them. Rather than ask her characters to cope with adults, wryly or otherwise, hinton either removes them or removes their authority. The Oedipal struggle is displaced to older siblings. Ponyboy's parents are dead; he lives with and is supported by his big brother, Darry, a football star who gave up college to keep the family together. Ponyboy fears and idolizes him. Tex's mother is dead (after a fight with his father, she walked off in the snow to go dancing, caught pneumonia and quickly succumbed), and his father forgets for months at a time to return home or to send money. Tex lives with and is supported by his older brother, Mace, a basketball star, who he fears and admires. Rusty-James's mother ran away; his father, once a lawyer, is a hopeless drunk on welfare who wanders in and out of the house mumbling, "What strange lives you two lead," to Rusty-James and his idolized older brother, the Motorcycle Boy (about whom Hinton seems to feel much as Lady Caroline Lamb felt about Byron: "Mad, bad and dangerous to know"). Like Dallas Winston, the Motorcycle Boy is shot to death by the police, leaving the hero to inherit his romantic mantle—even to the extent of going color-blind. Bryon has no father but does have a mother, depicted as a model of saintly virtue. She behaves, however, with a remarkable lack of maternal responsibility or even curiosity. Not only do Bryon and Mark sometimes not "come home for weeks" without being reprimanded but their being beaten black and blue elicits little concern. Mom notices ten stitches in Mark's head: "How did that happen?" "And Mark answered, 'Fight,' and the subject was dropped. That was a good thing about Mom—she'd cry over a dog with a piece of glass in his paw but remained unhysterical when we came home clobbered. . . . Parents never know what all their kids do. . . . It's a law." The laws of Hinton's books are the laws of the cowboy movies, the laws of romance.

Source: Michael Malone, "*That Was Then, This Is Now,*" in the *Nation*, Vol. 242, March 8, 1986, pp. 276–79.

Sources

Anderson, Terry H., "Hippies and Drugs," in *The 1960s*, edited by William Dudley, Greenhaven Press, Inc., 2000, pp. 200–01, originally published in *The Movement and the Sixties*, Oxford University Press, 1995, pp. 259–60.

Andrews, Sheryl B., Review of *That Was Then, This Is Now*, in *Horn Book Magazine*, Vol. XLVII, No. 4, August 1971, pp. 388–89.

Cart, Michael, Review of *That Was Then, This Is Now*, in *New York Times Book Review*, August 8, 1971, p. 8.

Daly, Jay, *Presenting S. E. Hinton*, Twayne Publishers, 1987, pp. 41–43, 46–47.

Gilbert, Martin, *A History of the Twentieth Century*, Vol. 3, *1952–1999*, Perennial, 2000, p. 307.

Hinton, S. E., "S. E. Hinton," in *Speaking for Ourselves: Autobiographical Sketches by Notable Authors of Books for Young Adults*, edited by Donald R. Gallo, 1990, p. 95.

——, *That Was Then, This Is Now*, Laurel Leaf Books, 1985.

Lyons, Gene, "On Tulsa's Mean Streets," in *Newsweek*, Vol. 100, No. 15, October 11, 1982, pp. 105–06.

Malone, Michael, "Tough Puppies," in *Nation*, Vol. 242, No. 9, March 8, 1986, pp. 276–78, 290.

McMurtry, Larry, *The Last Picture Show*, Dial Press, 1966.

Olson, James S., and Randy Roberts, "Johnson's Escalation and the Antiwar Movement," in *The 1960s*, edited by William Dudley, Greenhaven Press, Inc., 2000, pp. 110–11, originally published in *Where the Domino Fell: America and Vietnam, 1945–1995*, St. Martin's Press, 1996.

Review of *That Was Then, This Is Now*, in *Times Literary Supplement*, No. 3634, October 22, 1971, p. 1318.

Roberts, J. M., *Twentieth Century: The History of the World, 1901 to 2000*, Penguin Books, 1999, p. 673.

Steigerwald, David, "The Antiwar Movement," in *The Sixties and the End of Modern America*, St. Martin's Press, 1995, originally published in *The 1960s*, edited by William Dudley, Greenhaven Press, Inc., 2000, pp. 138–39.

Further Reading

Baum, Dan, *Smoke and Mirrors: The War on Drugs and the Politics of Failure*, Little, Brown & Company, 1997.

This retrospective look at the United States' war on drugs deviates from other books in this genre, which tend to use anecdotes to depict the government as deliberate participants in the spread of drugs. Instead, Baum, a journalist, provides balanced criticism about why the war on drugs has failed, using facts to back up his assertions.

Burkett, B. G., *Stolen Valor: How the Vietnam Generation Was Robbed of Its Heroes and Its History*, Verity Press, 1998.

Burkett, a Vietnam veteran and reporter, was featured on the newsmagazine show *20/20* for this unflinching look at the ways in which Vietnam veterans have been misunderstood, in part due to the actions of some who have tarnished the image of this generation. Exhaustively researched, the book helps to set the record straight about a very painful time in American history.

Marshall, Joseph E., and Lonnie Wheeler, *Street Soldier: One Man's Struggle to Save a Generation, One Life at a Time*, VisionLines Publishing, 2000.

About the time Hinton was writing *The Outsiders*, Marshall was starting his career teaching in a poor section of San Francisco, where young people often faced the issues Hinton wrote about. Two decades later, with the introduction of guns and drugs like crack into the schools, the situation worsened, and Marshall took action. This book details the inspiring story of how he started the Omega Boys Club and began to reach a group of troubled black teens from the ghetto, helping many of them get on track and go to college.

Miller, Timothy, *The Hippies and American Values*, University of Tennessee Press, 1991.

Miller's information-packed book goes a long way towards setting the record straight about the main beliefs that hippies and the counterculture maintained and demonstrates the massive impact that hippies have had on American culture since the 1960s. The book features a bibliography of well-known and obscure underground newspapers, trivia facts, such as when the first Earth Day took place, and pictures of rock groups and posters.

The Turn of the Screw

Henry James

1898

Henry James's *The Turn of the Screw* has inspired a divided critical debate, the likes of which the literary world has rarely seen. When the short novel was first published in 1898, it was published in three different versions, as a serial in *Collier's Weekly* and in book form with another tale, in both American and English editions. James later revised the story and published it in 1908 in the twelfth volume of the New York Edition of *The Novels and Tales of Henry James*. It is the 1908 version that the author preferred and to which most modern critics refer. However, no matter what version readers encounter, they may find themselves falling into one of two camps supported by critics to this day. Either the story is an excellent example of the type of ghost story that was popular at the end of the nineteenth century or it is a psychoanalytic study of the hallucinations of a madwoman.

As a ghost story, then the tale details the classic struggle between good and evil and dealings with the supernatural. If one takes it as a psychoanalytic study, then the story emphasizes sexual repression and the sources of insanity. In either case, *The Turn of the Screw* has delighted readers for more than a century and continues to serve as one of the many examples of James's literary artistry, among such other notable works as *The American*, *The Ambassadors*, and *The Portrait of a Lady*.

Author Biography

James was born on April 15, 1843, on the edge of Greenwich Village in New York City. Born into a wealthy family, James was exposed to a traveling lifestyle. Less than a year after James was born, his parents took him and his brother, William, to London. A little over a year later, they visited Paris and then returned to New York, where they stayed for a decade.

As a child, James was not interested in school, and his education came periodically at day schools or from in-home tutors. People constantly surrounded James; his house was filled with an assortment of family, governesses, friends, and other visitors. Among the more distinguished visitors were writers Ralph Waldo Emerson and William Makepeace Thackeray. In 1856, James and his family moved to Europe, where he eventually fell in love with Paris and the French language. In 1858, the family returned to America, to Newport, Rhode Island. The stay was not long, and the family moved back to Europe again in 1859. However, a year later they once again moved back to America, this time to indulge brother William's desire to study art in a Newport studio.

In 1861, the Civil War broke out in America, and two of James's brothers left to fight. James, however, had injured himself severely—although scholars do not know how exactly—and could not fight. Instead, he attended Harvard Law School for one year, apparently so that he could get access to Harvard's library, literary social scene, and literature lectures. For the five years after Harvard, James stayed with his parents at home, which at this point was Boston, since his parents had followed him to Harvard. During this time, James, who had long harbored ideas of a writing career, began to produce his own literature.

His early writings consisted of short stories, reviews of other books, and critical notes. In 1869, James traveled to England, where his family's connections put him in touch with such notable British thinkers as Charles Darwin, George Eliot, and John Ruskin. He toured much of the rest of Europe, favoring Italy most. In fact, he started writing his first novel, *Roderick Hudson* (1876) in Florence.

James was such a prolific writer—important in the development of the modern novel—that critics have divided his literary career into three phases, based on the level of development in his craft. At the end of the middle phase, in the 1890s, James decided to experiment in a number of ways. One

Henry James

of these experiments, *The Turn of the Screw*, published in 1898, is a ghost story that has kept critics guessing as to the story's interpretation and James's original intent for more than a century.

During James's final phase, known as the "major phase," he produced the novels that most critics—and James himself—consider the novelist's best works. These include *The Wings of the Dove* (1902), *The Ambassadors* (1903), and *The Golden Bowl* (1904). Although James was born in America, England was his adopted home for much of his life, and in 1915 he became a British citizen. James died of edema on February 28, 1916, in London.

Plot Summary

A Terrible Tale

The Turn of the Screw begins on Christmas Eve during the 1890s, in an old house, where a group of men and women friends are gathered around a fireside telling ghost stories. When the book starts, somebody has just finished telling a particularly gruesome tale involving a ghost and a child. Later in the evening, a man named Douglas comments on this tale, saying that he agrees that since the tale involves a child, it magnifies the horrific effect, which he refers to as "another turn of the screw." He proposes to top this tale with a ghost story involving two children, but when pressed to do so, he says that he must read the tale from the account of the person who has experienced it and that the account is in a book in his home in the city.

Over the next couple of days, while the group is waiting for the book to arrive, Douglas gives a short prologue to the tale. In this preview, he reveals that the story involves a young governess in the mid-1800s, who has been hired by a young man to take care of his niece and nephew. The one condition that the governess must adhere to is that she can never trouble the man about anything involving the children. Some of the other major characters are introduced, including Mrs. Grose, the housekeeper who is currently watching over the house and children; Miles, the ten-year-old nephew, who was sent away to school after the death of the previous governess; and Flora, the eight-year-old niece. When the group presses Douglas for more details, such as how the previous governess died, he is very guarded, preferring to let them make their own interpretations as he reads the account verbatim—which he does when the book arrives.

The Governess's First Days at the Estate

From this point on in the book, Douglas and the guests disappear, and the reader hears only the firsthand account of what the governess has written about her experiences at Bly, the country estate. When the governess arrives at Bly in the spring, she is a little nervous, since this is the first time that she has had so much responsibility. The governess wonders why Mrs. Grose seems to hide her eagerness to see the governess. The governess is delighted when she meets charming Flora. Her first night at Bly, the governess hears noises but does not think anything of them. When she goes to pick up Miles two days later, she is apprehensive, since she has received a note from his school saying that he is being sent home and can never return. When the governess presses Mrs. Grose as to whether Miles is a bad boy, the housekeeper is cryptic, as she is about the details surrounding the death of the previous governess. The governess meets Miles and cannot understand why anyone would dismiss such a charming boy.

Summer

Several weeks later, the governess sees a strange man while she is walking in the garden one evening. The man disappears, and the governess assumes he is a trespasser. The next Sunday, as the governess and Mrs. Grose are preparing to go to church, she finds the same man staring at her through a window. She runs outside to confront him, but he is gone. When she describes the man to Mrs. Grose, the housekeeper says that the governess has described Peter Quint, their employer's deceased valet, who was not a very nice person when he was alive. The governess feels that Quint has come for Miles and charges herself with the moral task of trying to save the two children's souls from being corrupted. Shortly thereafter, while the governess and Flora are in the garden, the governess sees a woman, whom she later guesses is Miss Jessel, the former, deceased governess. Although the governess swears Flora has seen her, too, the little girl shows no sign that she has.

The governess presses the housekeeper for more information about the two apparitions and discovers that the two were lovers when they were alive, and that Quint had questionable dealings with Miles while Miss Jessel had suspicious dealings with Flora. Several days pass, and still the children do not betray that they have seen any ghosts. One night, the governess sees Quint again, upon the stairs. She stands her ground, unafraid, and he disappears. That night, the governess finds Flora peering out of her window, but when the governess confronts her, Flora denies seeing anybody. One night, as she is doing her now routine sweep of the staircase, the governess sees Miss Jessel looking very sad, but she disappears after an instant. Shortly thereafter, the governess catches Miles out of his bed and wandering on the lawn, presumably to speak with the ghosts, although the children still deny any wrongdoing. The governess takes up the matter with Mrs. Grose, who encourages her to contact their employer. However, the governess is reluctant to break her vow not to disturb him.

Autumn

Summer passes into autumn, and although the governess searches for the ghosts around every corner, they are not apparent for many weeks. One Sunday, while they are walking to church, Miles asks the governess if he can be sent away to school and threatens to complain to his uncle if she does not let him. The governess is so stricken by this that she walks back to the house, intending to leave it for good. When she sees Miss Jessel sitting at her desk in her classroom, she resolves to stay. She also decides to write to their employer about the suspected behavior of his niece and nephew. Before she writes the letter, she goes to talk to Miles, trying to find out his experiences at school before he was sent home. When she pries too deeply, she suddenly feels a blast of cold air and the candle goes out, although Miles tells her that he blew it out.

The next day, Miles is very happy and offers to play piano for her. The governess is delighted at the music, until she realizes that Flora is not around. Miles feigns innocence over Flora's whereabouts, so the governess seeks the aid of Mrs. Grose. Before the two women leave to search, the governess places the letter to her employer on the table for one of the servants to mail. The governess and Mrs. Grose go to the lake, where they find the boat missing. After walking around the lake, the governess finds Flora and, for the first time, asks her bluntly where Miss Jessel is. The ghost appears to the governess; however, Mrs. Grose sees nothing and sides with Flora, who also says that she sees nothing and never has. Furthermore, she asks to be taken away from Bly, away from the governess.

Sickness and Death

The next morning, the governess finds out from Mrs. Grose that Flora was struck with a fever during the night and that she is terrified of seeing the governess. However, Mrs. Grose does say that the governess was justified in her suspicions of Flora, because the child has started to use evil language. The governess encourages Mrs. Grose to take Flora to her uncle's house for safety and also so that she can try to gain Miles's allegiance in his sister's absence. Before she leaves, Mrs. Grose says that the governess's letter never got sent and that it has mysteriously disappeared.

When the governess is alone with Miles after dinner, she asks him if he stole her letter. Before he can respond, she feels the presence of Quint and shields Miles from seeing the ghost. Miles admits that he stole the letter so that he could read it. When she presses him to talk about his experiences at school, he says only that he said bad things to others. The governess holds him tightly to keep him from the window, and he asks her if it is "she." She tells him no, it is "the coward horror," and the boy finally names Quint. When Miles looks to see the ghost, Quint is gone. Miles screams and falls into the governess's arms, dead, his heart having stopped.

Characters

Douglas

Douglas is the person who reads the governess's tale to the narrator and the assembled guests at the Christmas party. In the introduction to the governess's tale, Douglas offers to tell a terrible tale that heightens the terror effect by "two turns" of the screw, since it tells about ghostly interactions with two children. Douglas is very cryptic about his relationship to the governess, saying only that she was ten years older than he was and that she was his sister's governess, which is when she told him her tale. Once Douglas starts telling the tale, it is told entirely from the governess's point of view, from the account that she wrote down for Douglas.

Flora

Flora is the eight-year-old girl who the governess thinks is being tempted by the ghost of Miss Jessel, her former governess. When the governess arrives at Bly to take care of Flora and Miles, she is overwhelmed by Flora's charm; Flora is a model student in the classroom. When the governess sees Miss Jessel while alone with Flora in the garden, she believes that Flora saw the ghost, too. However, the girl sweetly denies that anything is amiss when the governess tries to question her in vague terms about what is happening. Even when the governess catches her peering out of the window in the room they share, Flora denies anything is wrong.

One afternoon, the governess realizes that she does not know where Flora's whereabouts. She and the housekeeper, Mrs. Grose, go looking for the little girl by the lake, where they see she has taken the boat. They walk around the lake, and the governess confronts her, asking where Miss Jessel is. At this moment, the ghost of Miss Jessel appears to the governess, but the little girl, no longer charming, tells the governess that she does not see the ghost and never has. She tells Mrs. Grose that she wants to be taken away from Bly, away from the governess. That night, Flora gets ill with a fever. The next morning, Mrs. Grose tells the governess that Flora has been using evil language. The governess has Mrs. Grose take Flora away from Bly to her uncle's home.

The Governess

The governess tries to save Miles and Flora from Peter Quint and Miss Jessel, two ghosts she claims she has seen. In the introduction to the tale, Douglas, who says that he was friends with the

Media Adaptations

- *The Turn of the Screw* was adapted as a television movie and shown by the National Broadcasting Company (NBC) in 1959. The production was directed by John Frankenheimer and starred Ingrid Bergman as the governess, Isobel Elsom as Mrs. Grose, Paul Stevens I as Peter Quint, and Laurinda Barrett as Miss Jessel.

- *The Turn of the Screw* was adapted as a television movie and shown by the American Broadcasting Company (ABC) in 1974. Directed by Dan Curtis, the production stars Lynn Redgrave as the governess, Megs Jenkins as Mrs. Grose, James Laurenson as Peter Quint, and Kathryn Leigh Scott as Miss Jessel and features an ending that differs dramatically from James's original text. The movie is available on video from Artisan Entertainment.

- *The Turn of the Screw* was adapted into an opera with a prologue and two acts in 1954, by the famed English composer, Benjamin Britten. The opera was filmed in Czechoslovakia in 1982 by Pgd/Philips. Directed by Petr Weigl, the film features Czech actors lip-synching the musical parts, which are sung by others, including Helen Donath as the governess, Ava June as Mrs. Grose, Robert Tear as Peter Quint, and Heather Harper as Miss Jessel. Filmed in naturalistic settings, as opposed to a stage set, the opera is not widely available but is worth the effort of looking for it.

- *The Turn of the Screw* was adapted as a cable television movie in 1990, co-produced by Shelley Duvall. Directed by Graeme Clifford, the movie features Amy Irving as the governess. It is available on video from Warner Home Video.

- *The Turn of the Screw* was adapted as a film in 1992. Directed by Rusty Lemorande, the film features Patsy Kensit as the governess. It is available on video from Artisan Entertainment.

- *The Turn of the Screw* was adapted as a *Masterpiece Theatre* movie in 1999 by Anchor Bay Entertainment. Directed by Ben Bolt II, the film features Jodhi May as the governess, Pam Ferris as Mrs. Grose, Jason Salkey as Peter Quint, Caroline Pegg as Miss Jessel, and Colin Firth as the governess's employer—whose appearance deviates from James's original tale.

- *The Turn of the Screw* and *Daisy Miller*, two of James's short novels, were adapted to an abridged audiocassette by Dercum Press Audio in 1987.

- *The Turn of the Screw* was adapted as an audiocassette and audio compact disc in 1995 by Naxos Audio Books. Both abridged versions are read by Emma Fielding and Dermot Kerrigan.

- *The Turn of the Screw and Other Short Works* was adapted as an audiocassette by Blackstone Audio Books in 1994, read by Pat Bottino.

---

governess before her death, gives her background. The governess is a young woman during the events of her tale, and she has been given the task of taking care of Miles and Flora. The children's uncle has hired her on the condition that she never bothers him with matters involving the children. When she arrives at Bly, the governess is nervous, having never had this much responsibility. She is instantly taken with Flora and dismisses sounds that she hears her first night there. After receiving a note from Miles's headmaster that says he is being expelled, she is nervous about meeting the boy but finds him to be charming. It is not long after she arrives that the governess starts to see ghosts—first a man, then a woman. With Mrs. Grose's help, the governess identifies these ghosts as Peter Quint, the former valet, and Miss Jessel, the governess's predecessor. Feeling that the children's souls are in grave danger, the governess sets herself the task of protecting them from the ghosts and stands up to the apparitions on several occasions.

Meanwhile, the governess keeps an eye on the children and attempts to get them to confess that they have seen the ghosts, too, approaching the subject in vague terms. When the children are unresponsive, she becomes more insistent, watching them at all hours and questioning them when she finds them out of their beds at night. She writes a letter to her employer to let him know of the suspicious activities at Bly, but Miles steals it. When she confronts Flora at last, naming Miss Jessel, Flora denies seeing the ghost and becomes sick. The governess has Mrs. Grose take Flora to her uncle's. When the governess confronts Miles about his association with Quint one night, she sees the ghost at the window. She presses the boy, who finally names the valet. When the boy turns to look at the ghost, it is gone, and the boy shrieks, falling into the governess's arms, dead.

Mrs. Grose

Mrs. Grose is the housekeeper at Bly, who gives the governess information about the identities and lives of Miss Jessel and Peter Quint. When the governess first arrives at Bly, Mrs. Grose seems to be overjoyed at her appearance, although she hides this emotion, which the governess finds odd. After the death of Miss Jessel, and prior to the arrival of the governess, Mrs. Grose—who is of a lower class than the governess—has been taking care of Flora, while Miles was sent away to school. Mrs. Grose cannot read, which the governess realizes when she hands Mrs. Grose a letter. When the governess sees the second appearance of Quint, she confesses the sighting to Mrs. Grose, who identifies the ghost.

From this point on, Mrs. Grose is the governess's confidant in the ghostly matter, although Mrs. Grose rarely gives information to the governess unless pressed to do so. Even then, she gives many vague responses, which sometimes cause the governess to come to her own conclusions. When Flora is found missing, Mrs. Grose and the governess go to look for her. When they find her by the lake, Mrs. Grose does not see the ghost of Miss Jessel, although the governess does. Because she cannot see the ghost and because the governess tries to browbeat Flora into saying that the child has seen Miss Jessel, Mrs. Grose starts to think that the governess is seeing things. However, that night after Flora has a fever and starts to use bad language, Mrs. Grose is inclined to side with the governess once again, and she agrees to take Flora to her uncle's.

Miss Jessel

Miss Jessel is one of two ghosts who the governess claims is trying to corrupt Miles and Flora. The governess is the only one who claims directly to have seen the ghost of Miss Jessel, which appears to her several times throughout the story. The first time Miss Jessel appears, the governess recognizes her, having already spoken about ghosts with Mrs. Grose after seeing the apparition of Peter Quint. Through Mrs. Grose, the governess also finds out that Miss Jessel, the former governess, was having an affair with Quint, who was much lower in class, and that Quint treated Miss Jessel horribly. When the governess and Mrs. Grose find Flora has stolen away to the lake, the governess sees the ghost of Miss Jessel once again. However, Mrs. Grose does not see the ghost, and Flora claims not to either, even when the governess presses her to confess her meetings with the ghost. After Flora becomes ill and is sent to her uncle's, the governess does not see Miss Jessel again.

Miles

Miles is the ten-year-old boy whom the governess thinks is being tempted by the ghost of Peter Quint, her employer's former valet. Shortly after her arrival at Bly, the governess receives a letter that says Miles is being sent home from school and that he can never return. When Miles arrives at Bly, however, the governess thinks the headmaster must be mistaken, because Miles is a charming boy. Miles is a model student in the governess's classroom and sweetly denies that anything is amiss when the governess tries to question him in vague terms about what is going on. Even when the governess catches Miles wandering around the lawn at midnight, he denies that there is anything wrong other than that he is causing some mischief. When the governess questions him about his activities at school, he is curiously silent; although at one point, Miles asks the governess if he can go away to school again.

One night in his room, the governess asks the boy once again about his experiences at school, and a gust of cold wind comes out of nowhere, blowing out the candle. Miles says he has blown it out, but the governess is unsure. The next morning, Miles is conspicuously happy, and he coaxes the governess into listening to him play the piano. When she realizes that Flora is missing, she thinks that Miles has set her up. The governess goes to search for Flora, leaving a letter to her employer—apprising him of the suspicious activities at Bly—on the table. Miles steals the letter, an act that he

Topics for Further Study

- In *The Turn of the Screw*, Miles dies at the end, presumably from fright. Research the known causes of heart failure in young children and discuss whether or not you think that it was realistic to have Miles die in this way. Use examples from the novel and your research to support your claims.

- The governess in the story believes that the ghosts, although they look like humans, are sinister beings who are trying to steal the children's souls. Research the views regarding ghosts during the nineteenth century in both life and literature and discuss how the governess's beliefs either adhere to or deviate from depictions in other nineteenth-century ghost stories.

- The governess is drawn to her employer, a gentleman who has a higher rank than she, and she makes much of the illicit affair between the previous governess, Miss Jessel, and Peter Quint, a man of much lower class. Research the various class titles that existed in England in the mid-1800s, from royalty to the peasantry. Using your research, organize the titles in hierarchical order on a chart, giving a one-paragraph description of each title.

- In the story, the governess assumes that the ghosts of Miss Jessel and Peter Quint are evil, and hers is the only point of view given. Put yourself in either Jessel's or Quint's place, and give a short plot summary that narrates the events from the ghost's point of view. You may choose to make your ghost evil, good, sympathetic, or any other type, provided you are able to use the story's events to back up your assertions.

later admits to the governess. During the same conversation, Miles tells the governess that he got kicked out of school for using bad language. When the governess sees Quint's ghost at the window, she presses the boy to say his name. He says, "Pe-

ter Quint—you devil!" and then looks for the ghost, but he is gone. Miles screams and falls into the governess's arms, dead.

The Narrator

The narrator is the unnamed person who speaks in the introduction to the governess's tale and who tells the reader that he is reading the exact tale that was read to him, from an exact copy of the manuscript. The narrator disappears after Douglas starts reading the governess's account of her experiences.

Peter Quint

Peter Quint is one of two ghosts who the governess claims is trying to corrupt Miles and Flora. The governess is the only one who claims directly to have seen the ghost of Quint, which appears to her several times throughout the story. The first time he appears, the governess mistakes him for an intruder. After his second appearance, the governess's description to the housekeeper marks him as Quint. The housekeeper tells her that Quint was the former valet and was a vile man when he was alive. He had an affair with Miss Jessel, the previous governess, even though he was a servant and she belonged to a higher class. According to Mrs. Grose, Quint had suspicious relations with Miles while still living.

The Uncle

Miles's and Flora's uncle is the unseen employer, who, at the beginning of her employment, makes it clear to the governess that she is not to bother him about the children. The uncle never appears in the story and is only referred to by others.

Themes

Ghosts

Any discussion of *The Turn of the Screw* would be incomplete without addressing all of the major themes that various critics have identified in this ambiguous tale. The first and most apparent theme is that of ghosts. When the governess first arrives at Bly, she hears some traditionally ghost-like activity, the faint "cry of a child," and the sound of "a light footstep" outside her door. She pays no attention to these sounds, but a short while later, upon the second sighting of a man who she thinks is an intruder, she chases the man. However, as the governess notes, when she comes around the corner where the man was standing, "my visitor had vanished." When the governess sees Miss Jessel the first time, she notes the "identity of the apparition," using a word that is commonly associated with ghosts. The governess uses the word again when she sees Quint on the stairs, but it is curious to note that Quint appears "as human and hideous as a real interview," as opposed to appearing faint or ethereal, like many other traditional ghosts.

Good versus Evil

Even though the ghosts appear as human, the governess makes it very clear that they are evil and that hers is a fight of good against evil. When she is first talking with Mrs. Grose about Quint, she identifies the ghost as "a horror." Later, when she has learned the identities of the ghosts, she describes them, even in their earthly life, as "fiends." The governess decides to pit herself against the evil ghosts, noting to herself that "the children, in especial, I should thus fence about and absolutely save." Although, at one point, after she learns more about the children's relationship with Miss Jessel and Peter Quint during their lives, she thinks, "I don't save or shield them! It's far worse than I dreamed—they're lost!" However, the governess does not give up the fight, and at the end of the book, as Mrs. Grose is leaving with Flora to go to the child's uncle's house in the city, the governess notes her plan for Miles: "If he confesses, he's saved." When the governess gets Miles alone that night, and she does finally force him to say Quint's name, Miles asks, *Where*?" looking for the ghost. At this point, the governess thinks she has won the battle versus evil, and says: "What does he matter now, my own? . . . *I have you* . . . but he has lost you for ever!" However, after Miles shrieks and falls into the governess's arms, she realizes that, though she believes she has banished the ghost, Miles has died in the process.

Insanity

Could the governess be hallucinating? Besides actual ghosts, this is the other popular theme to which many critics point. There is evidence in the novel that perhaps the governess is seeing things. First and foremost, there is the fact that nobody except for the governess has ever plainly stated that they have seen ghosts. The one time that the governess thinks she will be vindicated, when the ghost of Miss Jessel appears before her and Mrs. Grose, the governess realizes she has a "thrill of joy at having brought on a proof." However, the housekeeper does not see the ghost: "What a dreadful

turn, to be sure, Miss! Where on earth do you see anything?"

The governess herself hints at the possibility of madness at other points in the narrative. When she is describing the state that she is in after the first ghost sightings, when she is watching in "stifled suspense" for more ghostly occurrences, she notes that if this state had "continued too long," it could "have turned to something like madness." The governess faces a much longer dry spell, in which she sees no ghosts, during several weeks at the end of the summer and early autumn. Although she does not describe herself in "stifled suspense," she does say that one would think that the lack of ghosts would "have done something toward soothing my nerves," but it does not. If one uses this and other examples of the governess's nervous condition, the ghosts can be explained as hallucinations.

Style

Setting

Bly, a "country home, an old family place" in the country, is a classic setting for a ghost story. When the governess first arrives, she is impressed by the "greatness that made it a different affair from my own scant home." When she receives her first tour of the place by Mrs. Grose, the governess notes the "empty chambers and dull corridors . . . crooked staircases," and a "square tower that made me dizzy." All of these descriptions fit the profile of the classic spooky old house. So does the fact that the house features large, sweeping grounds, which include a lake and several pathways, both of which are imbued with the same feeling as the garden, the "lonely place" in which the governess first sees the ghost of Peter Quint.

Narration

Although the main body of the story has been written down by the governess, it is unclear as to when she recorded her story, since she notes in the story that she has "not seen Bly since the day I left it" and gives some hypothetical observations that might appear to her "older and more informed eyes" if she were to see it again. For his part, Douglas merely says that when she was his sister's governess, "It was long ago, and this episode was long before." Nevertheless, the governess has written the story down and sent Douglas "the pages in question before she died." As noted in the introduction, Douglas then reads the pages to the narrator and other assembled guests. Later, before Douglas's death, the narrator notes that Douglas "committed to me the manuscript," which the narrator is now telling to the reader. Because the story is from an exact transcript, the story can be assumed to be exactly as the governess wrote it down.

Because it is told in the first person narrative mode, the reader is called upon to trust that what the governess is saying is true. However, the governess has all of the traits of a classic unreliable narrator, meaning that it is unclear as to whether the reader can trust her or not. For starters, there is the question of how much time elapsed between Miles's death and her recording of the tale, as mentioned above. In addition, because the governess sees things that others do not and poses the idea that her sanity is in danger, the reader has cause to believe that perhaps the governess's viewpoint is not accurate. In fact, at one point, she admits to herself—and the readers—that she is attempting to "retrace today the strange steps of my obsession." The fact that her fight between good and evil became an "obsession" may have clouded her ability to tell the tale accurately.

Allegory

The good versus evil theme follows a specific narrative technique, known as allegory. An allegory is a second level of meaning in the story, which affects every part of it. In this case, the allegory becomes one of God versus the Devil, with the governess representing God-like or divine qualities, while the ghosts, and sometimes the children, represent Devil-like or evil qualities. The governess invokes the name of God on many occasions. When she has first seen her main opponent, the ghost of Peter Quint, she remarks to Mrs. Grose: "God help me if I know *what* he is!" A few lines down from this comment, Mrs. Grose says, "It's time we should be at church." Church is a traditional symbol of God, and indeed the governess looks to her church for strength when she feels she is starting to lose the battle for Miles's soul. She is on her way to church with the boy and thinks "of the almost spiritual help of the hassock on which I might bend my knees."

She also notes of Miles that "I seemed literally to be running a race with some confusion to which he was about to reduce me." At times, the governess describes Miles with demon-like adjectives, saying that it was his "wickedness" that got him kicked out of school. For the ghosts, the allegorical meaning is also clear. The governess uses terms of evil to describe them throughout the story,

but at the end, when Quint makes his final appearance to her, she notes "his white face of damnation." She also remarks that, when she pulls Miles close to her to protect him, "It was like fighting with a demon for a human soul," a clear reference to the classical fight between God and Satan for human souls. Finally, when the governess finally presses Miles to name who "he" is, Miles says, "Peter Quint—you Devil!"

Historical Context

The Growth of Towns

The governess's employer, the uncle of Miles and Flora, is conspicuously absent from the story, always in the city, at his house on Harley Street. In Europe in the mid-nineteenth century, this was not uncommon. In 1800, London had approximately nine hundred thousand inhabitants. By 1900, just after James wrote *The Turn of the Screw*, the population had expanded to 4.7 million. For some, city life meant poverty, as the towns were segregated by class, with the poorer inhabitants living in slums. The more wealthy residents, like the governess's employer, lived in more fashionable districts. As the governess notes, "He had for his town residence a big house filled with the spoils of travel and the trophies of the chase." However, like other wealthy landowners who were able to maintain a second residence, "it was to his country home" that the governess is sent.

Sickness and Medicine

The nineteenth century saw many advances in the science of medicine—including a greater understanding of physiology and the use of vaccines and other preventative methods. However, since these methods were not always used universally and since medicine had not yet evolved into a standard, regulated practice, the effectiveness of medical attention was largely due to the individual knowledge and skill of the practitioner. People could not hope for a cure if they were to get sick. As a result, people attempted to reduce their susceptibility to even minor illnesses, which could develop into larger and more problematic ones. Between 1830 and 1850, people in Europe were especially cautious, as there was an epidemic of cholera in both London and Paris. In the book, the governess chastises Miles when she finds him walking outside at midnight, telling him that he has "caught your death in the night air!" Likewise,

Compare & Contrast

- **1850s:** Cholera rages through London and Paris, taking many lives and putting many people on guard against illness.

  1890s: Because of better public hygiene, industrial towns have started to reduce the transmission of cholera and other contagious diseases. On a similar note, vaccines and x-rays come into use.

  Today: As modern medicine creates antibiotics and other medicines to combat disease, bacteria evolve, prompting the creation of newer medications.

- **1850s:** With rare exception, middle-class women are expected to fulfill their traditional role of bearing and raising children. For those who are unmarried, serving as a governess in somebody else's home, helping to raise other people's children, is an acceptable option.

  1890s: Women work more and devote less of their lives to bearing and rearing children, and their expectation of life increases.

  Today: Women have many options for both work and family. Some choose not to have children at all, whereas others remain at home, rearing their children and tending the home. Others pursue challenging careers in the same fields as men, and many balance both a career and a family.

- **1850s:** As a result of industrialization, cities increasingly become the center of business, and many English gentlemen keep city residences so they can better handle their affairs, leaving the hired help to watch the country estates.

  1890s: In both England and America, the rapid spread of industrialization has widened the gap between the haves and the have-nots. The privately wealthy live in sumptuous estates, whereas many poor are forced to live in tight-packed slums in cities.

  Today: Technology is a necessary part of many people's lives. Those who own and invest in these technologies become the new rich, whereas the poor continue to get poorer.

---

when the governess and Mrs. Grose realize that Flora has gone outside without telling them, Mrs. Grose is shocked: "Without a hat?" Wearing a hat to cover one's head, where much of the body's heat is lost, was one common preventative method to avoid getting sick.

The Governess

The idea of employing a live-in lady to teach children—especially girls—dates back to the Middle Ages, but became more popular near the end of the eighteenth century when the middle classes in England grew in wealth and size. However, the romanticized English governess familiar to readers of nineteenth-century novels like Charlotte Brontë's *Jane Eyre* (1847), Anne Brontë's *Agnes Grey* (1847), and many of James's novels has helped to instill the idea that governesses were common installments in every wealthy home during this time

period. In reality, only a small percentage of women who worked served as governesses. For those who did employ a governess, the woman was intended to help the mother—or the widower, if the mother were not alive—with the intellectual and moral raising of the children. Like the governess in the story, who is "young, untried," and who is "taking service for the first time in the schoolroom," most governesses did not have any special training.

Critical Overview

James's *The Turn of the Screw* is considered one of literature's greatest ghost stories. Since its publication in 1898, it has been popular with both critics and the public. For the critics, the debate has always been sharply divided. When it was first published, the issue was whether the tale was artisti-

*Tenor Peter Pears (right) as Quint in a 1954
English Opera Group production of the novel*

cally sound or a morally objectionable story. Many
critics, like an *Outlook* reviewer, note both: "it is
on a higher plane both of conception and art. The
story itself is distinctly repulsive." Likewise, a
Bookman reviewer notes: "We have never read a
more sickening, a more gratuitously melancholy
tale. It has all Mr. James's cleverness, even his
grace." And a review in the *Independent* says that,
"while it exhibits Mr. James's genius in a powerful light," the book "affects the reader with a disgust that is not to be expressed."

Those who found negative things to say about
the book were often commenting on the subject
matter, the damnation of children, which was a
taboo and relatively unexplored theme at the time.
A reviewer for the *Independent* expresses this feeling best, noting that Miles and Flora are "at the tod-
dling period of life, when they are but helpless
babes," and that through their participation in reading the story, readers assist "in an outrage upon the
holiest and sweetest fountain of human innocence"
and help to corrupt "the pure and trusting nature of
children." Some early reviewers did purely enjoy
the tale as a good ghost story, and recognized
James's efforts to improve his medium. A reviewer
for the *Critic* states that the story is "an imaginative masterpiece," and William Lyon Phelps, the

stenographer to whom James dictated the story,
calls it "the most powerful, the most nerve-shat-
tering ghost story I have ever read," providing for
"all those who are interested in the moral welfare
of boys and girls an appeal simply terrific in its intensity."

For the next few decades, most critics continued to view the story as a ghost story, whether or
not they agreed with the moral quality of the tale.
However, in 1934, with the publication of Edmund
Wilson's "The Ambiguity of Henry James," the debate was sharply divided again, this time into those
who read the tale as the frantic ravings of a repressed woman and those who still believed it to
be a ghost story. Wilson's assertion that "the young
governess who tells the story is a neurotic case of
sex repression, and the ghosts are not real ghosts
at all but merely the governess's hallucinations,"
provided the fuel for the former viewpoint. Since
then, the critical debate has been almost comical,
as various people have come along and stated, with
absolute certainty, that one viewpoint was true and
the other was false. In 1948, Robert Heilman says,
"It is probably safe to say that the Freudian interpretation of the story ... no longer enjoys wide critical acceptance."

In 1957, Charles G. Hoffman notes that "the
Freudian interpretation of *The Turn of the Screw*
can never be denied since ... the governess is psy-
chopathic." In the same decade, Leon Edel shifted
the focus somewhat, saying that the novel "has become the subject of a long and rather tiresome controversy arising from a discussion of circumstantial
evidence in the narrative." Edel further notes that
most critics fail "to examine the technique of the
storytelling, which would have made much of the
dispute unnecessary." Edel focused on the method
of narration to illustrate that the governess is an
unreliable narrator and concluded that it is the governess "who subjects the children to a psychological harassment that in the end leads to Flora's
hysteria and Miles's death." In other words, another
vote for a Freudian reading.

However, the traditional ghost story view did
not dry up, and, as David Kirby notes in the foreword of Peter G. Beidler's 1989 book, *Ghosts,
Demons, and Henry James: The Turn of the Screw
at the Turn of the Century*, "the battle has been so
even over the years that it looked as though neither
side would prevail unless new evidence were gathered." In fact, Kirby claims that "Beidler has settled the issue conclusively; he is the new master of
Bly and its occupants." Beidler, after reading

through about two thousand ghost stories from James's era, uses his research to demonstrate that "the evil-ghost reading" is more likely. However, as Robert L. Gale notes in his entry on James for *The Dictionary of Literary Biography*, "the critical battle is still raging, and it is likely to do so indefinitely, since James seems consciously to have salted his text with veins leading in different directions."

Criticism

Ryan D. Poquette

Poquette holds a bachelor's degree in English and specializes in writing about literature. In the following essay, Poquette discusses how the absent employer sets off a chain reaction that triggers the governess's hallucinations in James's novel.

It is very difficult to make an argument about most aspects of *The Turn of the Screw* without first announcing whether one belongs to the group that views the tale as a ghost story or to the group that feels the governess's ghosts are really hallucinations. This essay will take the latter view as a starting point and discuss the reasons behind the governess's hallucinations. It is her master's curiously absent status, coupled with the governess's unrequited love for him, that drives the young woman to her hallucinations.

When the governess applies for the job at Bly, her employer tells her that there is one binding condition that no other woman has been able to meet: "she should never trouble him—but never, never: neither appeal nor complain nor write about anything." Instead, the governess is to be totally in charge and should "meet all the questions herself . . . take the whole thing over and let him alone." The governess is unsure at first, especially because she knows the position will entail "really great loneliness."

If she had her way, on the other hand, she would be governess in the house of the master himself, on whom both Douglas and the governess imply she has a crush. As Douglas notes in his introduction to the tale, when the governess first meets the master, she notes that he is "a gentleman, a bachelor in the prime of life, such a figure as had never risen, save in a dream or an old novel, before a fluttered, anxious girl out of a Hampshire vicarage." The governess is drawn to him on their first meeting and gives other clues throughout the

> The governess *is* cruel, and likely mad. She has been cruel to the children with her psychological torture, driving one into hysteria and one into the grave, and she is certainly displaying the signs of one who is mentally unbalanced."

story that she is pining for a romantic relationship, preferably with him. This feeling is compounded, first of all, by the fact that Bly is her first assignment: "She was young, untried, nervous."

As Leon Edel notes in his article, "The Point of View": "she has ample reason to be nervous about the duties and responsibilities conferred upon her . . . a young girl taking her first job." Even though she is nervous at the thought of the job at Bly, she is also eager to impress her new master, as she notes when she takes her walks alone in the garden: "I was giving pleasure—if he ever thought of it!—to the person to whose pressure I had responded." The governess thinks that she has made her employer happy since she is the only one who has been able to adhere to his guideline of no contact. She starts to congratulate herself immensely: "What I was doing was what he had earnestly hoped . . . and that I *could*, after all, do it proved even a greater joy than I expected." In fact, the governess starts to fancy herself "a remarkable young woman and took comfort in the faith that this would more publicly appear." In other words, she is hoping that her great deed will attract the master's attention.

It is telling that, in this frame of mind, she starts to have a romantic daydream, "a charming story suddenly to meet someone." Who is this someone? The governess's further description identifies this "someone" as a person who "would stand before me and smile and approve. I didn't ask more than that—I only asked that he should *know*." The governess is having a romantic daydream, imagining that her master will appear so that she can see his approval "in his handsome face." As Harold C. Goddard notes in *Nineteenth-Century Fiction*, the

What Do I Read Next?

- Although James was American-born, he was an Englishman by preference, and many of his stories, including *The Turn of the Screw*, take place in England. For other ghost stories that take place in England, a good introduction is *The Oxford Book of English Ghost Stories*, edited by Michael Cox and R. A. Gilbert and published by Oxford University Press (1989). This massive anthology includes forty-two stories, written between 1829 and 1968, from such literary greats as Walter Scott, Bram Stoker, Rudyard Kipling, and Edith Wharton.

- One of the most enduring English stories involving ghosts is Charles Dickens's holiday favorite, *A Christmas Carol*, first published in 1843, concerning the famous three ghosts—The Ghost of Christmas Past, The Ghost of Christmas Present, and The Ghost of Christmas Future, along with the ghost of Ebenezer Scrooge's friend, Jacob Marley. Together, the three ghosts warm the frigid heart of Scrooge, who realizes the error of his miserly ways. A current version of the short novel was printed in 1999 and is available from Bantam Classics.

- *Voices of Madness, 1683–1796*, edited by Allan Ingram, collects four texts written in Britain in the late seventeenth and eighteenth centuries. All four authors—one woman, three men—were regarded as insane, and their narratives tell of their experiences, including their treatment by others. The book was published by Sutton Publishing in 1997.

- *The Legend of Sleepy Hollow* (1819), Washington Irving's classic tale of American horror, features a timid teacher, Ichabod Crane, who encounters The Headless Horseman, a spooky ghost in the backwoods of rural New York. The story is available in a 1999 edition from Penguin USA.

- Like *The Turn of the Screw*, which was written a year later, James's *What Maisie Knew* (1897) fell into the part of his career when he was experimenting with new writing techniques. In the case of the latter novel, James also creates a sense of ambiguity. In this case, the confusion comes from the thoughts of Maisie Farange, an adolescent girl who witnesses her parents getting divorced and remarrying, and slowly comes to understand the greater moral issues involved in all of these relationships. The book is available in a 1998 edition from Oxford University Press.

- One of the undisputed masters of the supernatural was Edgar Allan Poe, whose chilling tales have delighted readers for ages. In *Edgar Allan Poe: Complete Tales & Poems* (2001), one can see why. Along with the perennial favorite stories, such as "The Tell-Tale Heart," "The Fall of the House of Usher," and "The Pit and the Pendulum," the collection includes little-known works like "The Angel of the Odd," as well as Poe's famous poem "The Raven."

- Through extensive interviews, research, and documentary photos, Leslie Rule's *Coast to Coast Ghosts: True Stories of Hauntings across America*, details some of the nation's spookiest locations. Written in a conversational style, Rule's book was published by Andrews McMeel Publishing in 2001.

---

absence of the master is having a very real effect on the governess's psyche. Says Goddard, when "a young woman, falls in love and circumstances forbid the normal growth and confession of the passion, the emotion, dammed up, overflows in a psychical experience, a daydream."

However, the daydream that appears before the woman on the tower is not the one she expects—"the man who met my eyes was not the person I had precipitately supposed." Her conscious mind is asking for the appearance of the master so that she can show him how good she is being and perhaps be rewarded. But it is the deeper, subconscious mind, freshly affected from all of her thoughts about how she wants to prove herself to the master, that precipitates the "ghostly" vision. In her mind, the governess is creating a challenge for herself, something that is greater than merely following the master's orders and something that will perhaps yield a greater reward, once the master sees how she has been victorious.

The governess does not realize this, of course, and attributes the vision to the dead ghost of Peter Quint, once she has spoken with Mrs. Grose and gotten this idea in her head. However, Mrs. Grose has already planted other ideas in the governess's head, prior even to the time when the governess sees her first hallucination. Shortly after the governess arrives, she inquires after her predecessor, and Mrs. Grose tells her that "She was also young and pretty—almost as young and pretty, Miss, even as you." The governess notes that "He seems to like us young and pretty!" and it is here that Mrs. Grose slips and mentions a mysterious "he," which the governess notes but then forgets. More important, however, is her subconscious mind, which is recording that fact and adding it to the other strange things it has noticed at Bly—the cryptic death of her predecessor, the sounds she hears at night, the fact that Miles's headmaster has dismissed him. Although she does not think about these things consciously at first, all of these first impressions, coupled with her desire to appear a hero to her employer, help her subconscious to create a suitable challenge.

Once the governess's vision has gotten out of hand and she has whipped everyone into a frenzy, Mrs. Grose suggests contacting their master, an idea that would undercut everything that the governess is trying to accomplish at Bly. She thinks about her master's reaction: "his derision, his amusement, his contempt for the break-down of my resignation at being left alone and for the fine machinery I had set in motion to attract his attention to my slighted charms." The fact that she mentions her "slighted charms" confirms that the governess's intentions with the master are more than professional. In fact, she is so protective of her vision, and of her reputation with her master, that she threatens Mrs. Grose not to send for the master behind her back: "I would leave, on the spot, both him and you."

It is not her love for the master alone that creates the governess's hallucinations. The young woman's tendency for nervousness has already been noted. But she herself indicates that she might be drawn toward something more, under certain circumstances. At one point, while waiting in "stifled suspense" to see the ghosts again, she remarks that if this tense state were to continue for too long, it could turn "to something like madness." Is the governess mad, or does she just have an overactive imagination brought on by unreleased passion? The second case has already been addressed, but the story gives indication that the first may be true. When the children start prying into the governess's background, she notes that they try to dig out the "many particulars of the eccentric nature of my father." Depending upon the meaning James attaches to the word "eccentric," the governess could be saying that her father was insane. Goddard is much more certain of the father's condition. He says that she is "the daughter of a country parson, who, from his daughter's one allusion to him in her story, is of a psychically unbalanced nature; he may, indeed, even have been insane."

If this is the case, then the romantic daydreams about her master may have tapped into some genetic madness that she inherited from her father. In any case, as the story goes on, the governess does start to appear a little crazy. She imagines that the children—under the influence of the ghosts—are plotting against her: "It was not . . . my mere infernal imagination . . . they were aware of my predicament." The governess believes that her tactful but vague allusions to the ghosts of Quint and Miss Jessel are being deliberately ignored by the children: "so much avoidance could not have been so successfully effected without a great deal of tacit arrangement." In all reality, the children are probably confused as to what the governess is referring, or if they do understand her, they may think her mad, too.

Regardless of what the children think, they suffer as a result of the governess's delusions. She watches them constantly, and on certain occasions, seems ready to give in to a mad rage, as when she thinks Flora is keeping something from her: "At that moment, in the state of my nerves, I absolutely believed she lied." The governess lets the reader know that "if I closed my eyes it was before the dazzle of the three or four possible ways in which I might take this up." In other words, the governess is seeing three or four ways that she can deal with Flora, either to punish her for lying or to beat an answer out of her. The hint of violence is soon made real, when she almost succumbs to one of the visions, which "tempted me with such singular intensity that, to withstand it, I must have gripped my little girl with a spasm that, wonderfully, she submitted to without a cry or a sign of fright." The governess's mental state is rapidly deteriorating, and she can barely constrain herself from doing something harmful to the children. Edel notes that the governess is reading "sinister meanings into everything around her" and suggests that it is the governess's "psychological harassment that in the end leads to Flora's hysteria and Miles's death."

If even one other person were able to verify a ghost sighting, then perhaps this statement could be refuted. The governess gets her chance near the end of the novel, when she sees the ghost of Miss Jessel while she is standing with Mrs. Grose and Flora. The governess is happy that somebody else will be able to testify as to the ghosts' existence: "She was there, and I was justified; she was there, and I was neither cruel nor mad." Unfortunately, Mrs. Grose sees nothing, and as this essay has shown, the governess *is* cruel and likely mad. She has been cruel to the children with her psychological torture, driving one into hysteria and one into the grave, and she is certainly displaying the signs of one who is mentally deranged. Perhaps when the ghost of Peter Quint disappears at the end of the story, her subconscious mind has declared herself a winner and so banished that particular illusion. She certainly claims triumph for herself, with her exclamations to Miles—"*I* have you . . . but he has lost you for ever!" However, given her nervous state, she could easily succumb to another hallucination at her next job—if, of course, there is a handsome young gentleman who inspires her subconscious mind to create another challenge.

Source: Ryan D. Poquette, Critical Essay on *The Turn of the Screw*, in *Novels for Students*, The Gale Group, 2003.

Dennis Chase

In the following essay, Chase discusses the idea of innocence in The Turn of the Screw.

Few critical theories about literary works have engendered as much controversy as Edmund Wilson's thesis in "The Ambiguity of Henry James" (1934) that in *The Turn of the Screw* "the ghosts are not real ghosts but hallucinations of the governess," who "is a neurotic case of sex repression" (*Homage . . .*). Wilson never abandoned his Freudian hypothesis, in spite of sharp rebuke from many Jamesian scholars. Dorothea Krook, for example, speaks of "his misguided Freudianism" and accuses him of "arriving at conclusions which are no longer even perverse but merely fatuous." And Krishna Vaid contends that he "makes a travesty

of the text" and has even "violated . . . the larger context more flagrantly and more persistently than any adherent of his theory." Wilson's interpretation is like the proverbial horse that has "been much beaten but never yet . . . to death," and more than one critic would like to see it given a "decent burial" (Krook . . .). But the Freudians are still active. A Freudian reading alone, however, which shows that Miles is as much a sexually precocious young man as he is a ten-year-old boy, results in ambiguity. This ambiguity can be resolved only if the innocence of the two innocents, Miles and the governess, is recognized. Both are inexperienced characters who blunder at one another throughout the novel, especially in chapter 17.

The theory that the governess is sexually repressed is well founded: she is the daughter of a country clergyman, suggesting limited informal contact with the opposite sex; she is infatuated with her handsome employer, whom she never sees after their single interview; and she states, immediately before her first sighting of Peter Quint, that "it would be as charming as a charming story suddenly to meet some one"—a man, presumably. The Freudian innuendoes, whether intentionally or subliminally inserted, are evident: the figure of Peter Quint on the tower (a phallic symbol), the lake (the female sex organ) in front of Miss Jessel, and the piece of wood that Flora intently maneuvers into the hole of another piece of wood (*Hommage . . .*). And as Robert Liddell observes, even the words *turn* and *screw* in the title of the work are suggestive.

Many factors contribute to the governess's anxious state of mind, especially the letter dismissing Miles, the presence of Miss Jessel and the children, and the governess's mixed feelings toward the handsome man who employed her and thus gave her the responsibilities of Bly. After a conversation with Miles (chapter 14), during which he insists that "a fellow . . . [cannot] be with a lady *always*," the governess feels that she must learn why the boy has been dismissed from school and, furthermore, must inform his uncle, even if that means her employer must come to Bly. As she collapses on the staircase (chapter 15), the governess becomes aware of the presence of Miss Jessel and calls her predecessor a "terrible miserable woman"; but when she talks with Mrs. Grose afterward (chapter 16), she asserts that Miss Jessel told her that "she suffers the torments . . . of the lost. Of the damned" and therefore has come to take Flora "to share them." When the governess and Mrs. Grose speak of the letter from school, the governess blames the children's uncle for all that has happened because he left the two in the care of Miss Jessel and Peter Quint. Because Miles is "so clever and beautiful and perfect," the governess believes that he must have been dismissed "for wickedness." Resolving to write to her employer that night but unable to start the letter, she goes to Miles's doorway. She explains that "under [her] endless obsession," she listened "a minute" at Miles's door for "some betrayal of his not being at rest." He, too, has been listening for and hoping to see someone—specifically, the governess—as is suggested by his cordial and seemingly prepared invitation for her to enter, in a voice that conjures up images of "gaiety in the gloom", "gaiety" because of his happiness at hearing just whom he wanted to hear—and see. When she asks him what he was thinking of as he lay awake, Miles says, "What in the world, my dear, but *you*?" He adds, "Well, I think also, you know, of this queer business of ours." As she "mark[s] the coolness of his firm little hand," she asks what he means. Miles replies, "Why the way you bring me up. And all the rest!" The governess has to hold her breath "fairly . . . a minute" as she continues her questioning: "What do you mean by all the rest?" He smiles "up at [her] from his pillow": "Oh you know, you know!" She can "say nothing for a minute . . ."

The governess's youthfulness and inexperience are important to note, and the suggestion is that the age difference between her and Miles is no greater than that between her and Douglas. The governess may well be one of James's "thwarted Anglo-Saxon spinster[s]" (*Homage* . . .), but she is also sexually excited by the innuendoes of this exchange, as is Miles. The young boy whose hand she holds is sexually aroused by this attractive young woman. Undoubtedly influenced by Peter Quint and by his uncle, Miles is part boy, part man. He has the sexual urge, but not the confidence which comes with maturity. He can only try to express himself through his enigmatic responses. Despite the governess's momentary inability to answer Miles, she does reveal her thoughts: "I felt as I held his hand and our eyes continued to meet that my silence had all the air of admitting his charge and that nothing in the whole world of reality was perhaps at that moment so fabulous as our actual relation."

At once—compulsively or inadvertently—she returns to a topic that can only add to the excitement of each. She tells Miles that he can return to school, although it must be "another, a better" school. As she reminds him that he has never told

> These innuendoes are fully explicable only if they are viewed as the products of the innocence and resulting confusion of two characters—Miles and the governess—whose real complexity has thus far eluded both the Freudians and the non-Freudians."

her anything about the school or his companions there, her imagination creates an image that is, at least temporarily, emotionally acceptable to her: "His clear listening face, framed in its smooth whiteness, made him for the minute as appealing as some wistful patient in a children's hospital; and I would have given, as the resemblance came to me, all I possessed on earth really to be the nurse or the sister of charity who might have helped to cure him." As he smiles and calls "for guidance," something about him "set . . . [her] heart aching, with such a pang as it had never yet known." As she prattles on about his not telling her about the school, her "absolute conviction of his secret precocity [or his sexual precocity?] . . . made him . . . appear as accessible as an older person." Her confusion in the situation reveals itself as she speaks of that precocity as "whatever I might call the poison of an influence that I dared but halfphrase." The entire exchange must be read as the ambiguity of innocence and innocents. How, for example, can her next remark, "I thought you wanted to go on as you are," be interpreted? At one level it can refer to his remaining in the country (she responds to his desire to "get away" by asking if he is "tired of Bly"), where he is constantly her close companion. Or this can be seen as a reference to his virginity.

The basic problem of *The Turn of the Screw* is the narrative point of view. To distance the story, James employed the time-worn device of the old manuscript to authenticate the events at Bly. But the mind of the governess is the filter through which those events must come. The memories are hers, but does she record what actually happened

at Bly or what she imagined, what she unconsciously wished for? Therein, of course, lies the
crux of the debate between the Freudian and non-
Freudian readings of *The Turn of the Screw*.

The memory of the governess suggests that in
this sequence Miles is as excited—or as confused?—as she. In response to her question about
going on as he is, "he just faintly coloured." Admitting that he "likes Bly," he insists, "Oh *you*
know what a boy wants!" To her immediate inquiry
as to whether or not he would like to return to his
uncle, Miles blurts out the sexually explosive line,
"Ah you can't get off with that." She unhesitatingly
replies, "My dear, I don't want to get off!" But she
then is the one "who changed colour."

The emphasis on the word *you* and the exclamations "Oh" and "Ah" suggest that she remembers the incident as emotional and containing an
urgent, if oblique, attempt at communication with
the precocious boy. The expression "get off" illustrates the sexual quality of the governess's memories. Today that phrase can mean "to have an
orgasm," as in the line from a contemporary novel:
"All he wants to do is get in, get off and get out as
fast as possible" (King . . .). It can also mean to
"become . . . intimate with" (Freeman . . .), "to become friendly with, or deliberately attract, a member of the opposite sex" (Cowie and Mackin . . .),
and "to have sexual intercourse with" (Delbridge
. . .). Although the last usage occurs more frequently
in modern Australian English, it is also found in
English Renaissance Literature. In John Fletcher's
The Wild-Goose Chase, produced in 1621, Belleur,
thinking about his planned seduction of Rosalura,
says, "I am resolved to go on; / But how I shall get
off again. . . ." Once "on," that is, he will not want
to "get off" anymore than the governess in her sexual fantasy wants to "get off" Miles. In this reading of the term, the only difference between
Belleur's and the governess's fantasies is one of
position. Belleur's words carry the "innuendo of
sexually dismounting from the woman after copu-
lation" (Henke . . .); the governess's observation ("I
don't want to get off!") would indicate that she
imagines herself in the superincumbent position. It
is important to note that James was quite familiar
with Fletcher. Some time after James's admission
to London's select Reform Club in 1878, he observed, "Since my election, I have done nothing but
sit there and read Jowett's Plato and Beaumont and
Fletcher" (Edel . . .). This evidence, along with the
fact that "get in" implies sexual intercourse in
Thomas Dekker's 1630 play *The Honest Whore,
Part II*, that "go" and "off" are used separately to

suggest various aspects of intercourse elsewhere in
Renaissance drama (Henke . . .), and that "to get
with" has meant "to beget," or "to impregnate," at
least since the time of Christ, gives credence to a
sexual reading of this interchange between Miles
and the governess—and others as well, most notably that in which Miles comments on her ability
to "bring . . . [him] up." James is clearly a master
of sexual innuendo.

The governess's mention that Miles "lay beautifully staring" at her during the conversation adds
to the suggestiveness of the scene, as does his further remark that "I don't want to go back. . . . I want
a new field." That remark moves the governess to
action. Speaking again of his "unimpeachable gaiety" and troubled by the idea that if he left, he
would probably reappear "at the end of three
months with all this bravado and still more dishonour," the governess asserts that she could not
stand such an event:

> . . . and it made me let myself go. I threw myself upon
> him and in the tenderness of my pity I embraced him.
> "Dear little Miles, dear little Miles—!"
>
> My face was close to his, and he let me kiss him.

But here occurs another twist of the ambiguity, for Miles accepts the kiss, "simply taking it
with indulgent good humour," saying "Well, old
lady?" That remark might well have encouraged
her to make the next move; it is adult, something
Quint or his uncle might say. But Miles cannot
maintain an adult pose, especially when the governess asks, "Is there nothing—nothing at all that
you want to tell me?" He turns from her, looking
round only to remind her that he had earlier told
her "to let me alone."

The woman in the governess is persistent; she
does not want to "lose" her "man." Urged on by
his "faint quaver of consenting consciousness," she
drops to her knees at his bedside to "seize once
more the chance of possessing him"—his soul possibly, his body certainly. When she says to him, "if
you *knew* how I want to help you," she is subtly
offering herself to him; she even acknowledges to
herself that she has "gone too far" to retreat. At this
moment an inexplicable, "extraordinary blast" of
air shakes the room "as if . . . the casement had
crashed in," causing the boy, in an orgasmic frenzy,
to utter "a loud high shriek which . . . might have
seemed . . . a note either of jubilation or of terror."
Though Miles is not physically capable of an orgasm, the adult in him experiences it symbolically,
and because of the nature and novelty of the experience, he is elated and terrified. Appropriately, the

candle (a phallic symbol) that the governess takes with her to Miles's room is extinguished. The boy-man's sexual desire has been symbolically satisfied and the heat from the flame of the candle has been dispelled by the "chill" from the "gust of frozen air." Of course, Miles's fire has been extinguished, not by cold air, but by the governess. And Miles, once again more the man than the boy, reveals that he has done his part to facilitate matters; his extinguishing the candle not only darkens the room for the secret tryst but also symbolizes his active role as lover.

James mentions the candle seven times in this short chapter, the repetition reinforcing its symbolic importance. That it generates heat, is phallic-shaped, and is usually found in the governess's hand makes it an ideal symbol for conveying her sexual desires. Early in the chapter when Miles, lying in bed, asks her what she is "up to," the governess is standing over him with candle in hand; she is "up to" a number of things. And when the candle is not in her hand, it is "designedly, a short way off"—always within reach, to be sure.

Whether James intentionally included the Freudian imagery in the novel is a moot point, but recognition of its existence is not tantamount to calling "a great writer 'a repressed governess'" (Liddell . . .). Edward Davidson advises not to fall victim to "the obvious human failing to confuse life and literature—to assume, in other words, that what a man wrote he inevitably was in his own person. If a writer dealt with . . . eroticism, he was of necessity . . . erotic." The sexual innuendoes in no way undercut James, but rather add to the richness of his characterizations. These innuendoes are fully explicable only if they are viewed as the products of the innocence and resulting confusion of two characters—Miles and the governess—whose real complexity has thus far eluded both the Freudians and the non-Freudians.

Source: Dennis Chase, "Ambiguity of Innocence: *Turn of the Screw*," in *Extrapolation*, Vol. 27, No. 3, 1986, pp. 137, 198–202.

Millicent Bell

In the following essay, Bell discusses the thematic use of the principle of uncertainty in The Turn of the Screw.

The preoccupation of a generation of critics with the reality status of the ghosts in Henry James's *The Turn of the Screw* has always seemed to me misplaced. One may grant that the spectral appearances to which the governess in the tale tes-

> **It is not the ghost of the two dead household servants that the governess seeks to validate, but something more undenotable, an evil in the children and in the world which the ghosts can be said simply to represent."**

tifies cannot be proven to be supernaturally actual or her illusion, that we are in a condition of uncertainty over the question and that the story merits the title of "fantastic" which Todorov gives it. But is this not a minor source of our interest? The reader's epistemological quandary, his inability to be positive about how to "take" the phenomena reported by the narrator is, of course, rooted in his inability to verify or refute her first-person account; we cannot escape the enclosure of her mind, and all efforts to find internal clues of veracity or distortion in what she tells us are baffled by its essential mode. The confidence she has inspired in her fictional editor, Douglas, does not really help, either, for he, too, is a possibly compromised and implicated speaker over whose shoulder the first-person narrator of the frame-story looks at us without either reassurance or skepticism. But her report perplexes the reader in other ways too; the principle of uncertainty operates more fundamentally in leaving us in doubt about her way of reading experience generally, her evaluation of herself and others, her identification of motive and meaning in their behavior and her own, her moral vision. One may say that the presence or absence of the Miss Jessel and Peter Quint at Bly is crucial in such a judgment; if they are to be believed in, she is justified in her view of the children and her sense of her own duty, and if not, she is a victim of delusion. But, in fact, this is not so. Though the story gains its special *frisson* from its fantastic element, one can conceive an equally powerful Jamesian mystery that might be based entirely on the moral uncertainty alone. One has only to think of another work, *The Sacred Fount*—to see that James could have composed a fiction whose indeterminacy is rooted in our unease concerning the narrator's deductions and judgments about others, his purely visual perceptions being never in doubt.

Todorov has himself noticed that in some of James's ghost stories the quality of the fantastic is threatened by the possibility of allegory. In "The Private Life," the double who sits at his desk writing while another self occupies himself with mundanity may or may not be a supernatural presence, but he is so much more obviously a symbolic figure in a fable of the artist's nature that the hesitation of the fantastic is almost eliminated. He finds *The Turn of the Screw*, on the other hand, James's most realized example of the fantastic, one that maintains its uncertainty throughout the text and keeps it to the forefront. But I would argue that it, too, is a fable. And I would support this view by means of another insight of Todorov which he does not apply closely to *The Turn of the Screw*—that many of James's fictions concern themselves with the act of perception turned towards an absence, that they are quest stories in which the pursuit of some phantasmal object without presence except to the perceiver threatens the ambivalence of the fantastic, makes meaningless the question, "Does the ghost exist?" Precisely this happens, I think, in *Turn of the Screw*. The story, I would urge further, represents a search for an absence that is not restrictedly "ghostly." It is not the ghost of the two dead household servants that the governess seeks to validate, but something more undenotable, an evil in the children and in the world which the ghosts can be said simply to represent. This absence can never be converted to presence; precisely for that reason all reader curiosity about the children's relation with the dead or proofs of their corruption must be frustrated.

James would seem to have deprecated any attempt—such as this one—to take his tale very seriously, tending to reply to questions about its meaning with the evasive declaration (to H. G. Wells in 1898) that "the thing is essentially a potboiler." He could still refer to it in the preface to his revision in the New York Edition as "a piece of ingenuity pure and simple, or cold artistic calculation, an amusette to catch those not easily caught." But what trap is laid for the over-clever may, after all, be precisely illustrated by the way puzzlement over the ghostliness of the ghosts has leld so many astray. His other remarks in this same preface are worth examining, and suggest that by calling his work one of pure ingenuity he may have meant that he had dispensed with any claim to the realistic. What he has written, after all, he tells us, was something in the mode of romance, "a perfect example of the imagination unassisted . . . unassociated, a fairy-tale pure and simple . . . an annexed but independent world."

But if the ghosts in *The Turn of the Screw* belong to the realm of romantic dream rather than to literal reality this does not mean that they are the dreams of a sick young woman who has hallucinated. Their irreality functions mythically, to create a profound perception about the structures of human experience. Leon Edel, perhaps taking a hint from the preface, has noted the connection with the two fairy-tales James particularly mentions. Like Cinderella, the governess is the youngest child who ventures alone into the world dreaming of a meeting with Prince Charming. And Bluebeard's last wife, Fatima, is given the keys to the treasures and told not to enter a forbidden room. But her curiosity overcomes her and she finds the bloody corpse of her predecessors as, indeed, the governess, longing for her absent master, comes upon *her* dead predecessor. What such archetypal narratives may mean as representations of human desire and fear should concern us even in James's transforming context. He saw his governess's visions, the putative evil spirits, the demons of fairy-tale, as having a symbolic function: "They would be agents, in fact; there would be laid on them the dire duty of causing the situation to reek with the air of Evil." By their capacity for, as it is said in the story, "everything," by the material absence of that capitalized absolute, they would suggest a general vision which he was sure the reader could make present sufficiently out of his own memories.

But Romance is essentially Manichean. It sees the world in terms of opposed purities, allowing only for ideal virtue and undiluted viciousness, for heroes and heroines, villains and villainesses diametrically opposed, for evil and good in so complete a state that no experience we recall can fully express them. The condition of romance depends upon absence (as realism does upon presence) not because romantic narratives do not contain details but because the details are never *enough*; no amount of them will ever fill the void of the absolute, supply enough wicked deeds to justify the Wicked King's title, describe the Good Prince so that his goodness is fully accounted for. Implicit in the diametrics of the romance is the mythos of the Christian tradition which, while according responsibility for creation to one sacred being yet suggests that God's contest with Satan splits the universe into domains of equal power, inexhaustible sources of the divine and the demonic.

In *The Turn of the Screw* this version of life is the governess's private one; she is the writer of romance, the absolutist of the Manichean interpretation of the Christian tradition. In a way, therefore, our interest in her must, after all, be psychological—not in the sense of Edmund Wilson and his followers so that we may discover the cause of her hallucinations in erotic tensions but so that we may find the story's subject in her theory of experience. James's chosen technical method, the first-person narrative unillumined by exterior comment, focuses us upon her mind and its schemes of judgment. James had remarked of the host story generally—in another preface in the New York Edition—that "the moving accident, the rare conjunction, whatever it be, doesn't make the story,—in the sense that the story is our excitement, our amusement, our thrill and our suspense; the human emotion and the human condition, the clustering human conditions we expect presented, only make it."

James seems to have realized only as he wrote that the story's subject was the governess's mind. He had begun with a different focus, the idea of the effect on the children of *their* sight of the apparitions, as his notebook germ, the story told him by the Archbishop of Canterbury, shows. In this notation there is no hint of the narrator James would create; the archbishop had related that he had been told about the haunted children by "a lady who had no art of relation, and no clearness." This original focus on the children's perceptions is preserved in the prologue of the story when Douglas speaks of the interest his tale will offer: "I agree—in regard to Griffin's ghost, or whatever it was—that its appearing first to the little boy, at so tender an age, adds a particular touch... But if the child gives the effect another turn of the screw, what do you say to *two* children—?" But, in fact, the screw of childish perception of horror is never really turned at all in the story we subsequently receive. We never witness as dramatized mental events the appearance of Quint and Miss Jessel to Flora and Miles; indeed, this gap in the presentation is so marked that there are grounds for supposing that the children never see them at all, even though the governess thinks otherwise. Instead, characteristically, James has given us still another of his studies of a consciousness intellectually and emotionally mature and refined enough to provide drama and theme. It may not be accidental that James chose to include *The Turn of the Screw* not with some of his other ghost-stories but in the volume of the New York Edition that contains, *The Aspern Papers*, in which the narrator's self-presentation is the subject we are called upon to grasp and evaluate.

That the governess's mind was the story's subject Virginia Woolf perceived in 1918 when she remarked in the course of reviewing a book about the supernatural that the ghosts "have neither the substance nor the independent existence of ghosts. The governess is not so much frightened of them as of the sudden extension of her field of perception, which in this case widens to reveal to her the presence all about her of an unmentionable evil. The appearance of the figures is an illustration, not in itself specially alarming, of a state of mind which is profoundly mysterious and terrifying." As Woolf points out, the appearance of the figures, the onset of the "state of mind" which is suddenly opened up to the unknown in itself, is preceded "not by the storms and howlings of the old romances, but by an absolute hush and lapse of nature which we feel to represent the ominous trance of her own mind." One remembers, at Woolf's reminder, the wonderful sentence in the story—"The rooks stopped cawing in the golden sky, and the friendly evening hour lost for the unspeakable minute all its voice," which precedes the first appearance of Quint. The world of nature and the self, "golden" and "friendly" as Bly appears, is about to reveal itself as deceptive and corrupt.

Deceptive and corrupt, however, to a particular way of seeing. "Seeing" is more than a matter of the eyes and the truthful record of what they register. The governess's "seeing"—moral and metaphysical—is what we are made, by the devices of the story, to ponder, to question. James remarks in his preface that the record the governess keeps is "crystalline," but he adds, "by which I don't of course mean her explanation of them, a different matter." If she is an "unreliable narrator" it is on the grounds of judgment. If the governess sees always with an imagination that shifts alternately from a view of Bly as paradise unfallen to a view of it as permeated with corruption, it is because her mind is like one of those designs which allow us to see a flock of white birds crossing a black sky from left to right or a flock of black birds crossing a white sky from right to left—but never both flocks at once. It is an imagination incapable of perceiving ambiguity, only capable of admitting one view and excluding the other. It cannot reconcile and combine, can only exchange the view for its exclusive opposite.

Maybe this accounts for the fact that the characters' configuration in the story the governess tells consists of doubled pairs representing alternate versions of the same reality with the exception of Mrs. Grose, whose simple, whose admirable "grossness" makes such a division impossible. The governess sees herself duplicated twice, in opposite ways, in the person of Miss Jessel and little Flora. She sees the master, whose masculine actuality is represented in her imagination as a figure either of infinite grace or infinite corruption as both little Miles and Quint.

For who is Quint in this drama of the self's revelation to itself? He is, of course, a version or inversion of the owner of Bly, the God-like fine gentleman who has sent the governess upon her mission there with the injunction never to appeal to him—and who has caused her to fall in love with him. The governess has already admitted to Mrs. Grose that she was "carried away in London," and the housekeeper says, "Well, Miss, you're not the first—and you won't be the last." The master's sexual magnetism has exercised itself—for good or evil—before, and is, in fact, soon confused with Quint's in the conversation that ensues when the governess inquires about her predecessor. That predecessor, moreover, is also a projection from within the governess—this time, of her own capacity for sexual subjection. "She was young and pretty—almost as young and almost as pretty, Miss, even as you," says Mrs. Grose. "He seems to like us young and pretty," says the governess, to which the answer of Mrs. Grose is, "Oh, he *did*. . . I mean that's *his* way—the master's." Her seeming to correct herself in this curious fashion suggests to the governess that the housekeeper is speaking of someone else. Indeed, she may be, for Quint, who is the master's "man," also "liked [them] young and pretty," it is soon made clear to us. On the other hand, the housekeeper may not really be referring to anyone but the master. It is only the governess who must divide the master from a double who has his capacity for vice, or from that role in relation to women which arouses her resentment.

It is after this conversation that the objectified image of the master as an object of hatred rather than love appears just when she has been half-expecting to meet the gentleman from Harley Street. She thinks—with one side of her mind, one might say—that he will suddenly appear, smiling and approving of her handling of the problem presented by the letter from Miles' school—the letter that suggests to her that the perfect little boy has committed some unmentionable wickedness. She has, of course, decided to do nothing—unwilling to establish the nature of the child's offense or to clear him of fault, as she could do by writing the school an inquiry. She thus retains her capacity for alternate visions of Miles who, as I have said, is also a representative of the master. And now the master's double appears in his place, an apparition whose description at first is only that he wears no hat—and so is *not* a gentleman—but otherwise might be the master or the master in ungentlemanly aspect, for he wears his "better's" clothes and "looks like an actor," that is, an impersonation of someone else.

Quint is her intuition, then, of the evil in the fine gentleman, the benevolent masculine authority who has commanded and possessed her erotic fancy, or a version of the master as her suspicion and resentment conceive him now, at a moment of trouble when he cannot be appealed to. Miss Jessel, as I have already stated, is herself. The predecessor is seen later in postures that the governess even recognizes as her own. When she is about to write a letter to the master she is confronted by sight of this figure at her own desk, occupied in writing "like some housemaid writing to her sweetheart." The governess has collapsed at the foot of the steps in the lonely house after her return from her conversation with Miles outside the church—a conversation in which he tells her definitely that he must leave. She realizes that it is exactly there, identically bowed, that she has seen "the spectre of the most horrible of women." Her own emotions, at this moment, are those of guilt and shame—she has deserved Miles's reproach that he is kept from school and "his own sort" by her possessive surveillance. And, perhaps, in the figure of despair, the haggard and terrible Miss Jessel, she sees the self within her which could deserve to be cast off by the master. But she cannot see herself as, in a mingled human way, both of these at the same time.

Her attachment to Miles is, by this same division of mind, also a representation of her attachment to the master. The ten-year-old boy is a "little gentleman," an exquisite, tiny representation of male glamor, dressed, like Quint, if not in the master's clothes, at least by the master's tailor. If he is an unfallen child, an avatar of the good master, he is also Quint from whom he acquired the wickedness of adult masculinity. He has become a nephew also of Quint who as a sort of surrogate uncle, ruled the household in the master's stead, making "too free" with the maids and with "everyone," as Mrs. Grose remembers. To the governess, Miles is beguilingly graceful and gallant; he calls her "my dear," he makes love to her with his flattery of her as a "jolly perfect lady," and in the scene after

Flora's departure when they dine together alone, the governess herself thinks of them as a pair of newlyweds, too shy to speak before the waiter. Indeed, she has been utterly "carried away," just as Mrs. Grose predicted when she said, "You will be carried away by the little gentleman," words that echo the statement that the governess had already been carried away in Harley Street. Critics have observed that the governess fastens her sexual passion, frustrated of its object in the master, upon the child, but it should be noted that Miles has enacted for his own part the master's seduction. And as its sequel, he will abandon her, by his resolution to go back to school. This is such an abandonment as she knows, the poor governess, she might expect from the master—who would also want to go back to his "own sort," his own class. Miss Jessel, one takes it, was used and abandoned if not by the master *in proprie persona* then by his alternate, Quint.

Flora, of course, completes the symmetry of the three couples—the governess and the master, Miss Jessel and Quint, and the two children, and though there is no sexual relation between the children to make for exact duplication, she, too, stands in a slighter way for the governess. In her original beauty and innocence she is an absolute of the governess's own goodness more perfect because presexual, unfallen. She, too, would be abandoned by Miles who wants to leave for his "own sort," this time the world of masculinity from which she is divided, as a girl, as absolutely as the governess is divided from the master's and Miles' world by both class and sex. In the end, her beauty becomes suddenly ugly, hard, like Miss Jessell's, when she seems "an old, old woman" to the governess who has, herself, by this time, lost her own innocence forever.

I have elaborated the pattern of duplicates in the story to emphasize its structure of mirroring and reversal. One can seem to say almost the same thing as I have been doing by identifying all these paired figures, or a least Miss Jessel and Quint, as hallucinatory projections of the governess's repressions. But this is to literalize the poetic design of James's fable, and to diminish its thematic strength. That design and import is rather, as I have said, the vision of a world divided, bifurcated, just as the paired figures are, into absolutes of good and evil. If such perfection of beauty, goodness, grace as represented by the children exists in the world, then the opposite of these qualities is implied by them. The governess's own nature is an exhibition of a love that is hate, trust that is fear, solicitude that is destructiveness. I believe that James wishes to sug-

gest a criticism of this view of human nature and the world at large. In this moral fable the governess's tragic fall from the role she imagines for herself—savior and protector, agency of absolute goodness—brings her to that opposite condition which is conjured also by her imagination, that of destroyer. In her demand that the children admit that they have known and seen the ghosts, she is demanding their admission of their own absolute evil which must simultaneously exist as an alternative to the absolute good she has seen in them. She will not believe in Miles's attempt to convince her that he can be ordinarily bad. Believing in his absolute goodness she insists upon his capacity for some inconceivable demonstration of damnation.

A close reading of the entire story will show how its ambiguity, so often referred to, is really a kind of binary permutation in which alternatives maintain their exclusiveness. The governess's narrative language reinforces at every point the effect of a viewpoint in which assertions can be read backwards, so to speak, to mean their opposites. Such effects can be summarized in the governess's own phrase when she starts her tale: "I remember the whole beginning as a succession of flights and drops, a little see-saw of the right throbs and the wrong." The see-saw rhythm is immediately initiated. She had, she tells us, somehow dreaded her arrival at Bly, but was, instead, delighted by its beauty—the "bright" flowers, the "golden" sky—and she is received "as if I had been the mistress," a fulfillment, seemingly, of her dream of marriage to the master. On this first evening she meets the beautiful, perfectly named Flora, and goes to bed in a grand room. But there is a "drop" in Mrs. Grose's eagerness to see her, an excessive eagerness that implies another reading of appearances. And appearances are just what the governess will not ever trust, since all things may be replaced by their opposites.

Even when she seems to assert that things are wholly what they seem, doubt invades her sentences and makes them mean another thing entirely:

> But it was a comfort that there could be no uneasiness in a connection with anything as beatific as the radiant image of my little girl, the vision of whose angelic beauty had probably more than anything to do with the restlessness that, before morning, made me several times rise and wander about the room to take in the whole picture and prospect, to watch from my open window the faint summer dawn, to look at such stretches if the rest of the house as I could catch, and to listen, while in the falling dusk the first birds began to twitter, for the possible recurrence of a

sound or two less natural and not without but within, that I had fancied I heard.

There could be no uneasiness—yet uneasiness is precisely what the image of Flora, described in Edenic terms,—provokes in her. And, not surprisingly, she soon hears, she believes, "the cry of a child" sometime during the night. These "fancies" were thrown off, she adds immediately, yet she contradicts their identification as fancies by promptly going on to say that: "in the light, or the gloom, I should rather say, of other and subsequent matters" these impressions would return. Examining her feelings the next morning, she produces a statement which, denying, seems to assert a ground for fear: "What I felt the next day was, I suppose, nothing that could be fairly called a reaction from the cheer of my arrival; it was at the most only a slight oppression produced by a fuller measure of the scale, as I walked round them, gazed up at them, took them in, of my new circumstances." As little Flora conducts her from one part of the house to another she rocks from one attitude to another: "I had the view of a castle of romance inhabited by a rosy sprite, such a place as would somehow, for diversion of the young idea, take all colour out of story-books and fairy-tales. Wasn't it just a story-book over which I had fallen a-doze and a-dream? No ; it was a big ugly antique but convenient house, embodying a few features of a building still older, half-displaced and half-utilized, in which I had the fancy of our being almost as lost as a handful of passengers in a great drifting ship."

And so the first little chapter ends, and the next begins with a "this" whose referent is, presumably, this second view of Bly which is said to have come home to her when she went to meet "the little gentleman" and during the evening was "deeply disconcerted" by the letter which arrives from Miles's school. She does not read it to Mrs. Grose but she admits that it says only that he cannot be kept on, which immediately means to her "that he's an injury to others." She asks Mrs. Grose if she has ever known the boy to be bad—to which the housekeeper, who does not think in absolutes, as I have said, eagerly assents, while vigorously rejecting the terms the governess employs—"contaminate," "corrupt"—in reference to him. As I have already noted however, the governess will never really be convinced, even by Miles himself, that he is capable of venial fault, only, as he is angelic, of demonic wickedness, like Satan himself for whom there could have been no half-way halting-place between Heaven and the Hell to which he fell. So, she continues to invoke by denial a wicked Miles.

After meeting him, she is ready to pronounce it "monstrous" she says, that "such a child as had now been revealed to me should be under an interdict." And her sentences still continue their curious game: "It would have been impossible to carry a bad name with a greater sweetness of innocence."

It becomes structurally necessary, as the story advances, that this see-saw play be kept up, that the choice between the alternatives be put off as long as possible. So the governess never does the obvious things that might resolve the problem of choice. She does nothing about the letter from the school—she does not show it to Mrs. Grose, and we are ourselves prevented from judging the nature of its contents. She does not write to the boy's uncle about it; she does not write to the school authorities to inquire of them the exact cause for his dismissal; she does not question Miles himself. Yet the perfect trust on which this attitude seems to be based is ready to yield to its opposite. The gentleness of the children is called "a trap that put her off her guard," the peacefulness of the succeeding days, "the hush in which something gathers or crouches."

When she has her first vision of the man on the tower, she does not make general inquiry about a possible intruder—but only after the figure's second appearance sneaks to Mrs. Grose about the being she describes as "a horror," or "like nobody," as though he could not be identified in ordinary human terms. Miles, meanwhile, continues to astound her by his perfect goodness, which she scrutinizes for evidences of its opposite: "If he had been wicked he would have 'caught' it, and I should have caught it by the rebound—I should have found the trace, should have felt the wound and the dishonour. I could reconstitute nothing at all, and he was therefore an angel." Without warrant, it would seem, then, she "knows" that there has been something between Miles and the dead valet, and that the spectre is trying to continue relations—and her suspicion is confirmed by Mrs. Grose's revelation, to her "sickness of disgust," that, alive, Quint had been "too free." So Miles is corrupt after all! She begins to watch the children with an attentiveness of suspicion that she calls a "service admirable and difficult," a devoted guardianship, but her own words betray her: "I began to watch them in a stifled suspense, a disguised tension, that might well, had it continued too long, have turned into something like madness." And what "saved" her from this madness, the madness of being unable to move from the pole of trust to the pole of condemnation? Why, "proofs" of the children's infernal natures, the first of these being the appearance of Miss Jessel and Flora's appearance of pretending that she has not seen this female figure of "quite as unmistakable horror and evil." But she will not confirm or dismiss her hypothesis by questioning the child herself.

The alternatives are, as always, absolutes. If the child meets the dead governess willingly, isn't it, asks Mrs. Grose, "just proof of her blest innocence?" But the governess counters, "If it isn't a proof of what you say, it's a proof of—God knows what ! For the woman is a horror of horrors." At this point, the governess announces, "It's far worse than I dreamed. They're lost." So, the governess has moved from her vision of perfect goodness to its opposite. But now it is her own worth and validity that she describes in the self-contradictory language that suggests negation even as it affirms, as in the following which pretends to exonerate Flora: "To gaze into the depths of the child's eyes and to pronounce their loveliness a trick of premature cunning was to be guilty of a cynicism in preference to which I naturally preferred to abjure my judgment." In the presence of the children, however, the see-saw is again in motion, and "everything fell to the ground but their incapacity and their beauty" until, as it swings back to the negative side she feels "obliged to re-investigate the certitude" of Flora's "inconceivable communion."

By questioning Mrs. Grose she ascertains, to her satisfaction, that Miles had known about the relation between Quint and Miss Jessel and had concealed this knowledge and been corrupted by it. It is no use for Mrs. Grose to cry, "If he was so bad then as that comes to, how is he such an angel now?" Everything the governess now thinks she learns about the relations of the children and the dead pair suits "exactly the particular deadly view [she is] in the very act of forbidding [herself] to entertain." She resolves to wait for the evidence of Miles's damnation. Even as she waits, however, the effect of her pupils' appearance gives a "brush of the sponge" to her convictions and she begins "to struggle against [her] new lights." Their charm, as it maintains itself, seems "a beguilement still effective even under the shadow of a possibility that it was studied." Their graceful responsiveness to her succeeds "as if [she] never appeared . . . literally to catch them at a purpose in it." "If" the children "practised upon [her], it was surely with the minimum of grossness."

It is then she has her third encounter with Quint and finds that Flora, at the window, denies that she has seen or looked for anyone but the governess herself—who reflects, "I absolutely believed she lied." And she sees Miss Jessel on the stairs before, on another night, the little girl is again at the window, and the governess declares with conviction, "She was face to face with the apparition we had met at the lake and could now communicate with it as she had not then been able to do." She herself sees only little Miles in the garden, but is convinced that he is gazing up at the tower above her head, the tower at the top of which, standing in the same spot, she had herself seen the valet's ghost. So, the governess concludes and concludes, and her images betray her self-knowledge or her suspicion of absolute evil in herself when she describes how Mrs. Grose listened to her "disclosures" her theories. It was, she says, "as had I wished to mix a witch's broth and propose it with assurance, she would have held out a large clean saucepan."

Miles's explanation is the very center of the story, the nub of the problem I have been describing as the governess's absolutist obsession. He tells her that he simply wanted to bring down a little her conception of his unnatural goodness, to make her think him "for a change—*bad* !" He had been very naughty; he had sat up without undressing until midnight, and then he had gone out and nearly caught cold. "When I'm bad I *am* bad!" he says, in triumph. And she is nearly persuaded to see-saw once again thinking of "all the reserves of goodness that, for his joke, he had been able to draw upon." But the returns to her conviction that the children are engaged in a continuous deception and that "the four . . . perpetually meet." She tells Mrs. Grose: "Their more than earthly beauty, their absolutely unnatural goodness. It's a game. It's a policy and a fraud!" Miles's plea for a normal human allowance of good and bad commingled has failed.

Yet more and more her language betrays that she, who has dreamed the role of savior, has become by her own converting vision, demonic. "It was not, I am sure today, then, my mere infernal imagination," she declares, or, after she sees Miss Jessel at her desk, "she was there, so I was justified, she was there, so I was neither cruel nor mad." Against the weak denial of the syntax the powerful epithets, "infernal," "cruel," "mad" thrust themselves. The children continue affectionate, and she says, "Adorable they must in truth have been, I now feel, since I didn't in these days hate them!—and we are made to suspect that hate them she did and does. Miles's reasonable plea for school and his liberty arouses her determination to prevent it, it would seem, for *now* she will write the master and inform him of the expulsion from the old school. Again, when Mrs. Grose asks the nature of the child's offense, she—and we—are denied, and the governess answers in terms, once more, of the evil-goodness alternatives: "For wickedness. For what else—when he's so clever and beautiful and perfect?" Only abstract wickedness can be the counter-truth of such an appearance of completest goodness. She is driven now, beyond her former discretion, to even ask him what had happened and to receive for answer only his shriek as she appeals to him, drops on her knees, to "seize once more the chance of possessing him," and he blows out the candle—or Quint does. The admission, the proof absolute, still evades her while she reflects, "Say that, by the dark prodigy I knew the imagination of all evil *had* been opened to him; all the justice within me ached for the proof that it could ever have flowered into act."

And so the children continue *either* divine or infernal, as the governess's use of the words betrays. She calls their contrivance to keep her from simultaneously observing them (Miles plays the piano for her while Flora goes off to the lake), "the most divine little way to keep me quiet." "Divine?" echoes Mrs. Grose, and the governess rather giddily responds, "Infernal then!" The governess is now ready to speak out, to say, "Miss Jessel," to Flora, and point to the opposite bank of the lake with triumph and even "gratitude" that the apparition is there and the moment of proof has arrived, but the child sees nothing and says to Mrs. Grose, who sees nothing also, "Take me away from *her*!"

There is nothing more to be hoped for from Flora, and she must be taken away by Mrs. Grose, who gives the governess what "justifies" her when she reports the "horrors"—again undenotable—that she has heard from the child. She is, consequently, alone with Miles, still to extract a confession from him. She is assailed by a "perverse horror" of her own efforts; "for what did it consist of but the obtrusion of the idea of grossness and guilt on a small helpless creature who had been for me a revelation of the possibilities of beautiful intercourse?" But the illumination passes. She asks him if he stole her letter and Quint's "white face of damnation" appears at the window once more just as the boy admits that he has taken it. And then she asks him what he had done at school and gets only his vague reply that he "said things ... to those I liked." It sounds altogether so meagre a criminality that the governess swings, for the last time, away from her conviction of his depravity and feels "the appalling alarm of his being perhaps innocent.

It was for an instant confounding and bottomless, for if he were innocent what then on earth was I?" It is *her* innocence, finally, that may be its opposite, that is, damnation. And this, in fact, is what she must find confirmed at the very last. Pointing to the wraith she sees at the window, clasping the terrified child, to her breast, she hears him cry out, "Peter Quint—you devil!" She has triumphed; it is "a tribute to her devotion ;" he has named the "hideous author of our woe," almost identified, in the Miltonic phrase, with the Devil himself. *Or* she has been herself named the devil of the story, she who has believed in the absolute beauty of childish innocence, in the master's unimpugnable grace, in her own holy motives—for Miles, who sees nothing that she sees, is dead.

Source: Millicent Bell, "*Turn of the Screw* and the *recherche de l'absolu*," in *Delta*, Vol. 15, November 1982, pp. 33–48.

Sources

Beidler, Peter G., *Ghosts, Demons, and Henry James*, University of Missouri Press, 1989, p. 237.

Edel, Leon, "The Point of View," in *The Turn of the Screw: An Authoritative Text, Backgrounds and Sources, Essays in Criticism*, edited by Robert Kimbrough, W. W. Norton & Company, 1966, pp. 228, 233, originally published in *The Psychological Novel: 1900–1950*, 1955, pp. 56–68.

Gale, Robert L., "Henry James," in *Dictionary of Literary Biography*, Vol. 12: *Realists and Naturalists*, edited by Donald Pizer, Gale Research, 1982, pp. 297–326.

Goddard, Harold C., "A Pre-Freudian Reading of *The Turn of the Screw*," in *The Turn of the Screw: An Authoritative Text, Backgrounds and Sources, Essays in Criticism*, edited by Robert Kimbrough, W. W. Norton & Company, 1966, pp. 186–87, originally published in *Nineteenth-Century Fiction*, Vol. XII, June 1957, pp. 1–36.

Heilman, Robert, "*The Turn of the Screw* as Poem," in *The Turn of the Screw: An Authoritative Text, Backgrounds and Sources, Essays in Criticism*, edited by Robert Kimbrough, W. W. Norton & Company, 1966, p. 215, originally published in *University of Kansas City Review*, Summer 1948, pp. 277–89.

Hoffman, Charles G., *The Short Novels of Henry James*, Bookman Associates, 1957, p. 71.

Kirby, David, "Foreword," in *Ghosts, Demons, and Henry James*, University of Missouri Press, 1989, p. ix.

"Most Hopelessly Evil Story," in *The Turn of the Screw: An Authoritative Text, Backgrounds and Sources, Essays in Criticism*, edited by Robert Kimbrough, W. W. Norton & Company, 1966, p. 175, originally published in *Independent*, January 5, 1899, p. 73.

"Mr. James's New Book," in *The Turn of the Screw: An Authoritative Text, Backgrounds and Sources, Essays in Criticism*, edited by Robert Kimbrough, W. W. Norton & Company, 1966, pp. 172–73, originally published in *Bookman*, Vol. LX, November 1898, p. 54.

Phelps, William Lyon, "The 'Iron Scot' Stenographer," in "Henry James," in *The Turn of the Screw: An Authoritative Text, Backgrounds and Sources, Essays in Criticism*, edited by Robert Kimbrough, W. W. Norton & Company, 1966, p. 178, originally published in *Yale Review*, Vol. V, July 1916, p. 794.

"The Recent Work of Henry James," in *The Turn of the Screw: An Authoritative Text, Backgrounds and Sources, Essays in Criticism*, edited by Robert Kimbrough, W. W. Norton & Company, 1966, p. 174, originally published in the *Critic*, Vol. XXXIII, December 1898, pp. 523–24.

"The Story * * * Is Distinctly Repulsive," in *The Turn of the Screw: An Authoritative Text, Backgrounds and Sources, Essays in Criticism*, edited by Robert Kimbrough, W. W. Norton & Company, 1966, pp. 171–72, originally published in *Outlook*, Vol. LX, October 29, 1898, p. 537.

Wilson, Edmund, "The Ambiguity of Henry James," in *The Question of Henry James: A Collection of Critical Essays*, edited by F. W. Dupee, Allan Wingate, 1947, p. 172, originally published in *Hound & Horn*, Vol. VII, April–May 1934, p. 385.

Further Reading

Griffin, Susan M., ed., *Henry James Goes to the Movies*, University Press of Kentucky, 2001.

In this diverse collection of essays, Griffin assembles fifteen of the world's most noted Jamesian scholars. The various writers discuss why James has become so popular to a wide variety of filmmakers, as well as the impact that James has had on film and the impact that film has had on James. The book also contains a complete filmography and a bibliography of work on James and film.

Lewis, R. W. B., *The Jameses: A Family Narrative*, Farrar, Straus & Giroux, 1991.

This unique group biography offers portraits of Henry James's highly intellectual family, starting with the novelist's grandfather, William, in 1789 Ireland and ending with the death of the author in 1916. Through his shrewd business dealings, James's grandfather William made one of America's largest fortunes in the nineteenth century, which helped to shape the lives of the younger members.

McGurl, Mark, *The Novel Art: Elevations of American Fiction after Henry James*, Princeton University Press, 2001.

At one point, there was no such thing as an art novel in America—and then Henry James came along. In his book, McGurl discusses how James's novels influenced the change in thinking that led to the widespread development of the modern art novel and then traces the development of modern conception after James.

Pippin, Robert B., *Henry James and Modern Moral Life*, Cambridge University Press, 2000.

In this critical study of James's major fictions, Pippin argues that the author was motivated by his morals and that this theory of moral understanding permeated his stories. Written in an accessible, nontechnical style, Pippin offers new interpretations of many of James's fictions, including *The Turn of the Screw*.

Pool, Daniel, *What Jane Austen Ate and Charles Dickens Knew: From Fox Hunting to Whist—The Facts of Daily Life in Nineteenth-Century England*, Touchstone Books, 1994.

This highly informative reader's companion is perfect for those who wish to learn more about the language, culture, and customs of nineteenth-century England. As such, it serves as an indispensable guide to the fiction of James, Austen, Dickens, and other authors of the era whose stories are set in England.

Glossary of Literary Terms

A

Abstract: As an adjective applied to writing or literary works, abstract refers to words or phrases that name things not knowable through the five senses.

Aestheticism: A literary and artistic movement of the nineteenth century. Followers of the movement believed that art should not be mixed with social, political, or moral teaching. The statement "art for art's sake" is a good summary of aestheticism. The movement had its roots in France, but it gained widespread importance in England in the last half of the nineteenth century, where it helped change the Victorian practice of including moral lessons in literature.

Allegory: A narrative technique in which characters representing things or abstract ideas are used to convey a message or teach a lesson. Allegory is typically used to teach moral, ethical, or religious lessons but is sometimes used for satiric or political purposes.

Allusion: A reference to a familiar literary or historical person or event, used to make an idea more easily understood.

Analogy: A comparison of two things made to explain something unfamiliar through its similarities to something familiar, or to prove one point based on the acceptedness of another. Similes and metaphors are types of analogies.

Antagonist: The major character in a narrative or drama who works against the hero or protagonist.

Anthropomorphism: The presentation of animals or objects in human shape or with human characteristics. The term is derived from the Greek word for "human form."

Antihero: A central character in a work of literature who lacks traditional heroic qualities such as courage, physical prowess, and fortitude. Antiheroes typically distrust conventional values and are unable to commit themselves to any ideals. They generally feel helpless in a world over which they have no control. Antiheroes usually accept, and often celebrate, their positions as social outcasts.

Apprenticeship Novel: See *Bildungsroman*

Archetype: The word archetype is commonly used to describe an original pattern or model from which all other things of the same kind are made. This term was introduced to literary criticism from the psychology of Carl Jung. It expresses Jung's theory that behind every person's "unconscious," or repressed memories of the past, lies the "collective unconscious" of the human race: memories of the countless typical experiences of our ancestors. These memories are said to prompt illogical associations that trigger powerful emotions in the reader. Often, the emotional process is primitive, even primordial. Archetypes are the literary images that grow out of the "collective unconscious." They appear in literature as incidents and plots that repeat basic patterns of life. They may also appear as stereotyped characters.

Avant-garde: French term meaning "vanguard." It is used in literary criticism to describe new writing that rejects traditional approaches to literature in favor of innovations in style or content.

B

Beat Movement: A period featuring a group of American poets and novelists of the 1950s and 1960s—including Jack Kerouac, Allen Ginsberg, Gregory Corso, William S. Burroughs, and Lawrence Ferlinghetti—who rejected established social and literary values. Using such techniques as stream of consciousness writing and jazz-influenced free verse and focusing on unusual or abnormal states of mind—generated by religious ecstasy or the use of drugs—the Beat writers aimed to create works that were unconventional in both form and subject matter.

Bildungsroman: A German word meaning "novel of development." The *bildungsroman* is a study of the maturation of a youthful character, typically brought about through a series of social or sexual encounters that lead to self-awareness. *Bildungsroman* is used interchangeably with *erziehungsroman,* a novel of initiation and education. When a *bildungsroman* is concerned with the development of an artist (as in James Joyce's *A Portrait of the Artist as a Young Man*), it is often termed a *kunstlerroman.* Also known as Apprenticeship Novel, Coming of Age Novel, *Erziehungsroman,* or *Kunstlerroman.*

Black Aesthetic Movement: A period of artistic and literary development among African Americans in the 1960s and early 1970s. This was the first major African-American artistic movement since the Harlem Renaissance and was closely paralleled by the civil rights and black power movements. The black aesthetic writers attempted to produce works of art that would be meaningful to the black masses. Key figures in black aesthetics included one of its founders, poet and playwright Amiri Baraka, formerly known as LeRoi Jones; poet and essayist Haki R. Madhubuti, formerly Don L. Lee; poet and playwright Sonia Sanchez; and dramatist Ed Bullins. Also known as Black Arts Movement.

Black Humor: Writing that places grotesque elements side by side with humorous ones in an attempt to shock the reader, forcing him or her to laugh at the horrifying reality of a disordered world. Also known as Black Comedy.

Burlesque: Any literary work that uses exaggeration to make its subject appear ridiculous, either by treating a trivial subject with profound seriousness or by treating a dignified subject frivolously. The word "burlesque" may also be used as an adjective, as in "burlesque show," to mean "striptease act."

C

Character: Broadly speaking, a person in a literary work. The actions of characters are what constitute the plot of a story, novel, or poem. There are numerous types of characters, ranging from simple, stereotypical figures to intricate, multifaceted ones. In the techniques of anthropomorphism and personification, animals—and even places or things—can assume aspects of character. "Characterization" is the process by which an author creates vivid, believable characters in a work of art. This may be done in a variety of ways, including (1) direct description of the character by the narrator; (2) the direct presentation of the speech, thoughts, or actions of the character; and (3) the responses of other characters to the character. The term "character" also refers to a form originated by the ancient Greek writer Theophrastus that later became popular in the seventeenth and eighteenth centuries. It is a short essay or sketch of a person who prominently displays a specific attribute or quality, such as miserliness or ambition.

Climax: The turning point in a narrative, the moment when the conflict is at its most intense. Typically, the structure of stories, novels, and plays is one of rising action, in which tension builds to the climax, followed by falling action, in which tension lessens as the story moves to its conclusion.

Colloquialism: A word, phrase, or form of pronunciation that is acceptable in casual conversation but not in formal, written communication. It is considered more acceptable than slang.

Coming of Age Novel: See *Bildungsroman*

Concrete: Concrete is the opposite of abstract, and refers to a thing that actually exists or a description that allows the reader to experience an object or concept with the senses.

Connotation: The impression that a word gives beyond its defined meaning. Connotations may be universally understood or may be significant only to a certain group.

Convention: Any widely accepted literary device, style, or form.

D

Denotation: The definition of a word, apart from the impressions or feelings it creates (connotations) in the reader.

Denouement: A French word meaning "the un-knotting." In literary criticism, it denotes the resolution of conflict in fiction or drama. The *denouement* follows the climax and provides an outcome to the primary plot situation as well as an explanation of secondary plot complications. The *denouement* often involves a character's recognition of his or her state of mind or moral condition. Also known as Falling Action.

Description: Descriptive writing is intended to allow a reader to picture the scene or setting in which the action of a story takes place. The form this description takes often evokes an intended emotional response—a dark, spooky graveyard will evoke fear, and a peaceful, sunny meadow will evoke calmness.

Dialogue: In its widest sense, dialogue is simply conversation between people in a literary work; in its most restricted sense, it refers specifically to the speech of characters in a drama. As a specific literary genre, a "dialogue" is a composition in which characters debate an issue or idea.

Diction: The selection and arrangement of words in a literary work. Either or both may vary depending on the desired effect. There are four general types of diction: "formal," used in scholarly or lofty writing; "informal," used in relaxed but educated conversation; "colloquial," used in everyday speech; and "slang," containing newly coined words and other terms not accepted in formal usage.

Didactic: A term used to describe works of literature that aim to teach some moral, religious, political, or practical lesson. Although didactic elements are often found in artistically pleasing works, the term "didactic" usually refers to literature in which the message is more important than the form. The term may also be used to criticize a work that the critic finds "overly didactic," that is, heavy-handed in its delivery of a lesson.

Doppelganger: A literary technique by which a character is duplicated (usually in the form of an alter ego, though sometimes as a ghostly counterpart) or divided into two distinct, usually opposite personalities. The use of this character device is widespread in nineteenth- and twentieth-century literature, and indicates a growing awareness among authors that the "self" is really a composite of many "selves." Also known as The Double.

Double Entendre: A corruption of a French phrase meaning "double meaning." The term is used to indicate a word or phrase that is deliberately ambiguous, especially when one of the meanings is risqué or improper.

Dramatic Irony: Occurs when the audience of a play or the reader of a work of literature knows something that a character in the work itself does not know. The irony is in the contrast between the intended meaning of the statements or actions of a character and the additional information understood by the audience.

Dystopia: An imaginary place in a work of fiction where the characters lead dehumanized, fearful lives.

E

Edwardian: Describes cultural conventions identified with the period of the reign of Edward VII of England (1901-1910). Writers of the Edwardian Age typically displayed a strong reaction against the propriety and conservatism of the Victorian Age. Their work often exhibits distrust of authority in religion, politics, and art and expresses strong doubts about the soundness of conventional values.

Empathy: A sense of shared experience, including emotional and physical feelings, with someone or something other than oneself. Empathy is often used to describe the response of a reader to a literary character.

Enlightenment, The: An eighteenth-century philosophical movement. It began in France but had a wide impact throughout Europe and America. Thinkers of the Enlightenment valued reason and believed that both the individual and society could achieve a state of perfection. Corresponding to this essentially humanist vision was a resistance to religious authority.

Epigram: A saying that makes the speaker's point quickly and concisely. Often used to preface a novel.

Epilogue: A concluding statement or section of a literary work. In dramas, particularly those of the seventeenth and eighteenth centuries, the epilogue is a closing speech, often in verse, delivered by an actor at the end of a play and spoken directly to the audience.

Epiphany: A sudden revelation of truth inspired by a seemingly trivial incident.

Episode: An incident that forms part of a story and is significantly related to it. Episodes may be either self-contained narratives or events that depend on a larger context for their sense and importance.

Epistolary Novel: A novel in the form of letters. The form was particularly popular in the eighteenth century.

Epithet: A word or phrase, often disparaging or abusive, that expresses a character trait of someone or something.

Existentialism: A predominantly twentieth-century philosophy concerned with the nature and perception of human existence. There are two major strains of existentialist thought: atheistic and Christian. Followers of atheistic existentialism believe that the individual is alone in a godless universe and that the basic human condition is one of suffering and loneliness. Nevertheless, because there are no fixed values, individuals can create their own characters—indeed, they can shape themselves—through the exercise of free will. The atheistic strain culminates in and is popularly associated with the works of Jean-Paul Sartre. The Christian existentialists, on the other hand, believe that only in God may people find freedom from life's anguish. The two strains hold certain beliefs in common: that existence cannot be fully understood or described through empirical effort; that anguish is a universal element of life; that individuals must bear responsibility for their actions; and that there is no common standard of behavior or perception for religious and ethical matters.

Expatriates: See *Expatriatism*

Expatriatism: The practice of leaving one's country to live for an extended period in another country.

Exposition: Writing intended to explain the nature of an idea, thing, or theme. Expository writing is often combined with description, narration, or argument. In dramatic writing, the exposition is the introductory material which presents the characters, setting, and tone of the play.

Expressionism: An indistinct literary term, originally used to describe an early twentieth-century school of German painting. The term applies to almost any mode of unconventional, highly subjective writing that distorts reality in some way.

F

Fable: A prose or verse narrative intended to convey a moral. Animals or inanimate objects with human characteristics often serve as characters in fables.

Falling Action: See *Denouement*

Fantasy: A literary form related to mythology and folklore. Fantasy literature is typically set in non-existent realms and features supernatural beings.

Farce: A type of comedy characterized by broad humor, outlandish incidents, and often vulgar subject matter.

Femme fatale: A French phrase with the literal translation "fatal woman." A *femme fatale* is a sensuous, alluring woman who often leads men into danger or trouble.

Fiction: Any story that is the product of imagination rather than a documentation of fact. Characters and events in such narratives may be based in real life but their ultimate form and configuration is a creation of the author.

Figurative Language: A technique in writing in which the author temporarily interrupts the order, construction, or meaning of the writing for a particular effect. This interruption takes the form of one or more figures of speech such as hyperbole, irony, or simile. Figurative language is the opposite of literal language, in which every word is truthful, accurate, and free of exaggeration or embellishment.

Figures of Speech: Writing that differs from customary conventions for construction, meaning, order, or significance for the purpose of a special meaning or effect. There are two major types of figures of speech: rhetorical figures, which do not make changes in the meaning of the words, and tropes, which do.

Fin de siecle: A French term meaning "end of the century." The term is used to denote the last decade of the nineteenth century, a transition period when writers and other artists abandoned old conventions and looked for new techniques and objectives.

First Person: See *Point of View*

Flashback: A device used in literature to present action that occurred before the beginning of the story. Flashbacks are often introduced as the dreams or recollections of one or more characters.

Foil: A character in a work of literature whose physical or psychological qualities contrast strongly with, and therefore highlight, the corresponding qualities of another character.

Folklore: Traditions and myths preserved in a culture or group of people. Typically, these are passed on by word of mouth in various forms—such as legends, songs, and proverbs—or preserved in customs and ceremonies. This term was first used by W. J. Thoms in 1846.

Folktale: A story originating in oral tradition. Folktales fall into a variety of categories, including legends, ghost stories, fairy tales, fables, and anecdotes based on historical figures and events.

Foreshadowing: A device used in literature to create expectation or to set up an explanation of later developments.

Form: The pattern or construction of a work which identifies its genre and distinguishes it from other genres.

G

Genre: A category of literary work. In critical theory, genre may refer to both the content of a given work—tragedy, comedy, pastoral—and to its form, such as poetry, novel, or drama.

Gilded Age: A period in American history during the 1870s characterized by political corruption and materialism. A number of important novels of social and political criticism were written during this time.

Gothicism: In literary criticism, works characterized by a taste for the medieval or morbidly attractive. A gothic novel prominently features elements of horror, the supernatural, gloom, and violence: clanking chains, terror, charnel houses, ghosts, medieval castles, and mysteriously slamming doors. The term "gothic novel" is also applied to novels that lack elements of the traditional Gothic setting but that create a similar atmosphere of terror or dread.

Grotesque: In literary criticism, the subject matter of a work or a style of expression characterized by exaggeration, deformity, freakishness, and disorder. The grotesque often includes an element of comic absurdity.

H

Harlem Renaissance: The Harlem Renaissance of the 1920s is generally considered the first significant movement of black writers and artists in the United States. During this period, new and established black writers published more fiction and poetry than ever before, the first influential black literary journals were established, and black authors and artists received their first widespread recognition and serious critical appraisal. Among the major writers associated with this period are Claude McKay, Jean Toomer, Countee Cullen, Langston Hughes, Arna Bontemps, Nella Larsen, and Zora Neale Hurston. Also known as Negro Renaissance and New Negro Movement.

Hero/Heroine: The principal sympathetic character (male or female) in a literary work. Heroes and heroines typically exhibit admirable traits: idealism, courage, and integrity, for example.

Holocaust Literature: Literature influenced by or written about the Holocaust of World War II. Such literature includes true stories of survival in concentration camps, escape, and life after the war, as well as fictional works and poetry.

Humanism: A philosophy that places faith in the dignity of humankind and rejects the medieval perception of the individual as a weak, fallen creature. "Humanists" typically believe in the perfectibility of human nature and view reason and education as the means to that end.

Hyperbole: In literary criticism, deliberate exaggeration used to achieve an effect.

I

Idiom: A word construction or verbal expression closely associated with a given language.

Image: A concrete representation of an object or sensory experience. Typically, such a representation helps evoke the feelings associated with the object or experience itself. Images are either "literal" or "figurative." Literal images are especially concrete and involve little or no extension of the obvious meaning of the words used to express them. Figurative images do not follow the literal meaning of the words exactly. Images in literature are usually visual, but the term "image" can also refer to the representation of any sensory experience.

Imagery: The array of images in a literary work. Also, figurative language.

In medias res: A Latin term meaning "in the middle of things." It refers to the technique of beginning a story at its midpoint and then using various flashback devices to reveal previous action.

Interior Monologue: A narrative technique in which characters' thoughts are revealed in a way that appears to be uncontrolled by the author. The interior monologue typically aims to reveal the inner self of a character. It portrays emotional experiences as they occur at both a conscious and unconscious level. Images are often used to represent sensations or emotions.

Irony: In literary criticism, the effect of language in which the intended meaning is the opposite of what is stated.

J

Jargon: Language that is used or understood only by a select group of people. Jargon may refer to terminology used in a certain profession, such as computer jargon, or it may refer to any non-sensical language that is not understood by most people.

L

Leitmotiv: See *Motif*

Literal Language: An author uses literal language when he or she writes without exaggerating or embellishing the subject matter and without any tools of figurative language.

Lost Generation: A term first used by Gertrude Stein to describe the post-World War I generation of American writers: men and women haunted by a sense of betrayal and emptiness brought about by the destructiveness of the war.

M

Mannerism: Exaggerated, artificial adherence to a literary manner or style. Also, a popular style of the visual arts of late sixteenth-century Europe that was marked by elongation of the human form and by intentional spatial distortion. Literary works that are self-consciously high-toned and artistic are often said to be "mannered."

Metaphor: A figure of speech that expresses an idea through the image of another object. Metaphors suggest the essence of the first object by identifying it with certain qualities of the second object.

Modernism: Modern literary practices. Also, the principles of a literary school that lasted from roughly the beginning of the twentieth century until the end of World War II. Modernism is defined by its rejection of the literary conventions of the nineteenth century and by its opposition to conventional morality, taste, traditions, and economic values.

Mood: The prevailing emotions of a work or of the author in his or her creation of the work. The mood of a work is not always what might be expected based on its subject matter.

Motif: A theme, character type, image, metaphor, or other verbal element that recurs throughout a single work of literature or occurs in a number of different works over a period of time. Also known as *Motiv* or *Leitmotiv*.

Myth: An anonymous tale emerging from the traditional beliefs of a culture or social unit. Myths use supernatural explanations for natural phenomena. They may also explain cosmic issues like creation and death. Collections of myths, known as mythologies, are common to all cultures and nations, but the best-known myths belong to the Norse, Roman, and Greek mythologies.

N

Narration: The telling of a series of events, real or invented. A narration may be either a simple narrative, in which the events are recounted chronologically, or a narrative with a plot, in which the account is given in a style reflecting the author's artistic concept of the story. Narration is sometimes used as a synonym for "storyline."

Narrative: A verse or prose accounting of an event or sequence of events, real or invented. The term is also used as an adjective in the sense "method of narration." For example, in literary criticism, the expression "narrative technique" usually refers to the way the author structures and presents his or her story.

Narrator: The teller of a story. The narrator may be the author or a character in the story through whom the author speaks.

Naturalism: A literary movement of the late nineteenth and early twentieth centuries. The movement's major theorist, French novelist Emile Zola, envisioned a type of fiction that would examine human life with the objectivity of scientific inquiry. The Naturalists typically viewed human beings as either the products of "biological determinism," ruled by hereditary instincts and engaged in an endless struggle for survival, or as the products of "socioeconomic determinism," ruled by social and economic forces beyond their control. In their works, the Naturalists generally ignored the highest levels of society and focused on degradation: poverty, alcoholism, prostitution, insanity, and disease.

Noble Savage: The idea that primitive man is noble and good but becomes evil and corrupted as he becomes civilized. The concept of the noble savage originated in the Renaissance period but is more closely identified with such later writers as

Jean-Jacques Rousseau and Aphra Behn. See also Primitivism.

Novel of Ideas: A novel in which the examination of intellectual issues and concepts takes precedence over characterization or a traditional storyline.

Novel of Manners: A novel that examines the customs and mores of a cultural group.

Novel: A long fictional narrative written in prose, which developed from the novella and other early forms of narrative. A novel is usually organized under a plot or theme with a focus on character development and action.

Novella: An Italian term meaning "story." This term has been especially used to describe fourteenth-century Italian tales, but it also refers to modern short novels.

O

Objective Correlative: An outward set of objects, a situation, or a chain of events corresponding to an inward experience and evoking this experience in the reader. The term frequently appears in modern criticism in discussions of authors' intended effects on the emotional responses of readers.

Objectivity: A quality in writing characterized by the absence of the author's opinion or feeling about the subject matter. Objectivity is an important factor in criticism.

Oedipus Complex: A son's amorous obsession with his mother. The phrase is derived from the story of the ancient Theban hero Oedipus, who unknowingly killed his father and married his mother.

Omniscience: See *Point of View*

Onomatopoeia: The use of words whose sounds express or suggest their meaning. In its simplest sense, onomatopoeia may be represented by words that mimic the sounds they denote such as "hiss" or "meow." At a more subtle level, the pattern and rhythm of sounds and rhymes of a line or poem may be onomatopoeic.

Oxymoron: A phrase combining two contradictory terms. Oxymorons may be intentional or unintentional.

P

Parable: A story intended to teach a moral lesson or answer an ethical question.

Paradox: A statement that appears illogical or contradictory at first, but may actually point to an underlying truth.

Parallelism: A method of comparison of two ideas in which each is developed in the same grammatical structure.

Parody: In literary criticism, this term refers to an imitation of a serious literary work or the signature style of a particular author in a ridiculous manner. A typical parody adopts the style of the original and applies it to an inappropriate subject for humorous effect. Parody is a form of satire and could be considered the literary equivalent of a caricature or cartoon.

Pastoral: A term derived from the Latin word "pastor," meaning shepherd. A pastoral is a literary composition on a rural theme. The conventions of the pastoral were originated by the third-century Greek poet Theocritus, who wrote about the experiences, love affairs, and pastimes of Sicilian shepherds. In a pastoral, characters and language of a courtly nature are often placed in a simple setting. The term pastoral is also used to classify dramas, elegies, and lyrics that exhibit the use of country settings and shepherd characters.

Pen Name: See *Pseudonym*

Persona: A Latin term meaning "mask." *Personae* are the characters in a fictional work of literature. The *persona* generally functions as a mask through which the author tells a story in a voice other than his or her own. A *persona* is usually either a character in a story who acts as a narrator or an "implied author," a voice created by the author to act as the narrator for himself or herself.

Personification: A figure of speech that gives human qualities to abstract ideas, animals, and inanimate objects. Also known as *Prosopopoeia*.

Picaresque Novel: Episodic fiction depicting the adventures of a roguish central character ("picaro" is Spanish for "rogue"). The picaresque hero is commonly a low-born but clever individual who wanders into and out of various affairs of love, danger, and farcical intrigue. These involvements may take place at all social levels and typically present a humorous and wide-ranging satire of a given society.

Plagiarism: Claiming another person's written material as one's own. Plagiarism can take the form of direct, word-for-word copying or the theft of the substance or idea of the work.

Plot: In literary criticism, this term refers to the pattern of events in a narrative or drama. In its simplest sense, the plot guides the author in composing the work and helps the reader follow the work. Typically, plots exhibit causality and unity and have a beginning, a middle, and an end. Sometimes, however, a plot may consist of a series of disconnected events, in which case it is known as an "episodic plot."

Poetic Justice: An outcome in a literary work, not necessarily a poem, in which the good are rewarded and the evil are punished, especially in ways that particularly fit their virtues or crimes.

Poetic License: Distortions of fact and literary convention made by a writer—not always a poet—for the sake of the effect gained. Poetic license is closely related to the concept of "artistic freedom."

Poetics: This term has two closely related meanings. It denotes (1) an aesthetic theory in literary criticism about the essence of poetry or (2) rules prescribing the proper methods, content, style, or diction of poetry. The term poetics may also refer to theories about literature in general, not just poetry.

Point of View: The narrative perspective from which a literary work is presented to the reader. There are four traditional points of view. The "third person omniscient" gives the reader a "godlike" perspective, unrestricted by time or place, from which to see actions and look into the minds of characters. This allows the author to comment openly on characters and events in the work. The "third person" point of view presents the events of the story from outside of any single character's perception, much like the omniscient point of view, but the reader must understand the action as it takes place and without any special insight into characters' minds or motivations. The "first person" or "personal" point of view relates events as they are perceived by a single character. The main character "tells" the story and may offer opinions about the action and characters which differ from those of the author. Much less common than omniscient, third person, and first person is the "second person" point of view, wherein the author tells the story as if it is happening to the reader.

Polemic: A work in which the author takes a stand on a controversial subject, such as abortion or religion. Such works are often extremely argumentative or provocative.

Pornography: Writing intended to provoke feelings of lust in the reader. Such works are often condemned by critics and teachers, but those which can be shown to have literary value are viewed less harshly.

Post-Aesthetic Movement: An artistic response made by African Americans to the black aesthetic movement of the 1960s and early '70s. Writers since that time have adopted a somewhat different tone in their work, with less emphasis placed on the disparity between black and white in the United States. In the words of post-aesthetic authors such as Toni Morrison, John Edgar Wideman, and Kristin Hunter, African Americans are portrayed as looking inward for answers to their own questions, rather than always looking to the outside world.

Postmodernism: Writing from the 1960s forward characterized by experimentation and continuing to apply some of the fundamentals of modernism, which included existentialism and alienation. Postmodernists have gone a step further in the rejection of tradition begun with the modernists by also rejecting traditional forms, preferring the anti-novel over the novel and the antihero over the hero.

Primitivism: The belief that primitive peoples were nobler and less flawed than civilized peoples because they had not been subjected to the tainting influence of society. See also Noble Savage.

Prologue: An introductory section of a literary work. It often contains information establishing the situation of the characters or presents information about the setting, time period, or action. In drama, the prologue is spoken by a chorus or by one of the principal characters.

Prose: A literary medium that attempts to mirror the language of everyday speech. It is distinguished from poetry by its use of unmetered, unrhymed language consisting of logically related sentences. Prose is usually grouped into paragraphs that form a cohesive whole such as an essay or a novel.

Prosopopoeia: See *Personification*

Protagonist: The central character of a story who serves as a focus for its themes and incidents and as the principal rationale for its development. The protagonist is sometimes referred to in discussions of modern literature as the hero or antihero.

Protest Fiction: Protest fiction has as its primary purpose the protesting of some social injustice, such as racism or discrimination.

Proverb: A brief, sage saying that expresses a truth about life in a striking manner.

Pseudonym: A name assumed by a writer, most often intended to prevent his or her identification as the author of a work. Two or more authors may work together under one pseudonym, or an author may use a different name for each genre he or she publishes in. Some publishing companies maintain "house pseudonyms," under which any number of authors may write installations in a series. Some authors also choose a pseudonym over their real names the way an actor may use a stage name.

Pun: A play on words that have similar sounds but different meanings.

R

Realism: A nineteenth-century European literary movement that sought to portray familiar characters, situations, and settings in a realistic manner. This was done primarily by using an objective narrative point of view and through the buildup of accurate detail. The standard for success of any realistic work depends on how faithfully it transfers common experience into fictional forms. The realistic method may be altered or extended, as in stream of consciousness writing, to record highly subjective experience.

Repartee: Conversation featuring snappy retorts and witticisms.

Resolution: The portion of a story following the climax, in which the conflict is resolved. See also *Denouement.*

Rhetoric: In literary criticism, this term denotes the art of ethical persuasion. In its strictest sense, rhetoric adheres to various principles developed since classical times for arranging facts and ideas in a clear, persuasive, appealing manner. The term is also used to refer to effective prose in general and theories of or methods for composing effective prose.

Rhetorical Question: A question intended to provoke thought, but not an expressed answer, in the reader. It is most commonly used in oratory and other persuasive genres.

Rising Action: The part of a drama where the plot becomes increasingly complicated. Rising action leads up to the climax, or turning point, of a drama.

Roman a clef: A French phrase meaning "novel with a key." It refers to a narrative in which real persons are portrayed under fictitious names.

Romance: A broad term, usually denoting a narrative with exotic, exaggerated, often idealized characters, scenes, and themes.

Romanticism: This term has two widely accepted meanings. In historical criticism, it refers to a European intellectual and artistic movement of the late eighteenth and early nineteenth centuries that sought greater freedom of personal expression than that allowed by the strict rules of literary form and logic of the eighteenth-century neoclassicists. The Romantics preferred emotional and imaginative ex-

pression to rational analysis. They considered the individual to be at the center of all experience and so placed him or her at the center of their art. The Romantics believed that the creative imagination reveals nobler truths—unique feelings and attitudes—than those that could be discovered by logic or by scientific examination. Both the natural world and the state of childhood were important sources for revelations of "eternal truths." "Romanticism" is also used as a general term to refer to a type of sensibility found in all periods of literary history and usually considered to be in opposition to the principles of classicism. In this sense, Romanticism signifies any work or philosophy in which the exotic or dreamlike figure strongly, or that is devoted to individualistic expression, self-analysis, or a pursuit of a higher realm of knowledge than can be discovered by human reason.

Romantics: See *Romanticism*

S

Satire: A work that uses ridicule, humor, and wit to criticize and provoke change in human nature and institutions. There are two major types of satire: "formal" or "direct" satire speaks directly to the reader or to a character in the work; "indirect" satire relies upon the ridiculous behavior of its characters to make its point. Formal satire is further divided into two manners: the "Horatian," which ridicules gently, and the "Juvenalian," which derides its subjects harshly and bitterly.

Science Fiction: A type of narrative about or based upon real or imagined scientific theories and technology. Science fiction is often peopled with alien creatures and set on other planets or in different dimensions.

Second Person: See *Point of View*

Setting: The time, place, and culture in which the action of a narrative takes place. The elements of setting may include geographic location, characters' physical and mental environments, prevailing cultural attitudes, or the historical time in which the action takes place.

Simile: A comparison, usually using "like" or "as", of two essentially dissimilar things, as in "coffee as cold as ice" or "He sounded like a broken record."

Slang: A type of informal verbal communication that is generally unacceptable for formal writing. Slang words and phrases are often colorful exaggerations used to emphasize the speaker's point; they may also be shortened versions of an often-used word or phrase.

Slave Narrative: Autobiographical accounts of American slave life as told by escaped slaves. These works first appeared during the abolition movement of the 1830s through the 1850s.

Socialist Realism: The Socialist Realism school of literary theory was proposed by Maxim Gorky and established as a dogma by the first Soviet Congress of Writers. It demanded adherence to a communist worldview in works of literature. Its doctrines required an objective viewpoint comprehensible to the working classes and themes of social struggle featuring strong proletarian heroes. Also known as Social Realism.

Stereotype: A stereotype was originally the name for a duplication made during the printing process; this led to its modern definition as a person or thing that is (or is assumed to be) the same as all others of its type.

Stream of Consciousness: A narrative technique for rendering the inward experience of a character. This technique is designed to give the impression of an ever-changing series of thoughts, emotions, images, and memories in the spontaneous and seemingly illogical order that they occur in life.

Structure: The form taken by a piece of literature. The structure may be made obvious for ease of understanding, as in nonfiction works, or may be obscured for artistic purposes, as in some poetry or seemingly "unstructured" prose.

***Sturm und Drang*:** A German term meaning "storm and stress." It refers to a German literary movement of the 1770s and 1780s that reacted against the order and rationalism of the enlightenment, focusing instead on the intense experience of extraordinary individuals.

Style: A writer's distinctive manner of arranging words to suit his or her ideas and purpose in writing. The unique imprint of the author's personality upon his or her writing, style is the product of an author's way of arranging ideas and his or her use of diction, different sentence structures, rhythm, figures of speech, rhetorical principles, and other elements of composition.

Subjectivity: Writing that expresses the author's personal feelings about his subject, and which may or may not include factual information about the subject.

Subplot: A secondary story in a narrative. A subplot may serve as a motivating or complicating force for the main plot of the work, or it may provide emphasis for, or relief from, the main plot.

Surrealism: A term introduced to criticism by Guillaume Apollinaire and later adopted by Andre Breton. It refers to a French literary and artistic movement founded in the 1920s. The Surrealists sought to express unconscious thoughts and feelings in their works. The best-known technique used for achieving this aim was automatic writing—transcriptions of spontaneous outpourings from the unconscious. The Surrealists proposed to unify the contrary levels of conscious and unconscious, dream and reality, objectivity and subjectivity into a new level of "super-realism."

Suspense: A literary device in which the author maintains the audience's attention through the buildup of events, the outcome of which will soon be revealed.

Symbol: Something that suggests or stands for something else without losing its original identity. In literature, symbols combine their literal meaning with the suggestion of an abstract concept. Literary symbols are of two types: those that carry complex associations of meaning no matter what their contexts, and those that derive their suggestive meaning from their functions in specific literary works.

Symbolism: This term has two widely accepted meanings. In historical criticism, it denotes an early modernist literary movement initiated in France during the nineteenth century that reacted against the prevailing standards of realism. Writers in this movement aimed to evoke, indirectly and symbolically, an order of being beyond the material world of the five senses. Poetic expression of personal emotion figured strongly in the movement, typically by means of a private set of symbols uniquely identifiable with the individual poet. The principal aim of the Symbolists was to express in words the highly complex feelings that grew out of everyday contact with the world. In a broader sense, the term "symbolism" refers to the use of one object to represent another.

T

Tall Tale: A humorous tale told in a straightforward, credible tone but relating absolutely impossible events or feats of the characters. Such tales were commonly told of frontier adventures during the settlement of the west in the United States.

Theme: The main point of a work of literature. The term is used interchangeably with thesis.

Thesis: A thesis is both an essay and the point argued in the essay. Thesis novels and thesis plays share the quality of containing a thesis which is supported through the action of the story.

Third Person: See *Point of View*

Tone: The author's attitude toward his or her audience may be deduced from the tone of the work. A formal tone may create distance or convey politeness, while an informal tone may encourage a friendly, intimate, or intrusive feeling in the reader. The author's attitude toward his or her subject matter may also be deduced from the tone of the words he or she uses in discussing it.

Transcendentalism: An American philosophical and religious movement, based in New England from around 1835 until the Civil War. Transcendentalism was a form of American romanticism that had its roots abroad in the works of Thomas Carlyle, Samuel Coleridge, and Johann Wolfgang von Goethe. The Transcendentalists stressed the importance of intuition and subjective experience in communication with God. They rejected religious dogma and texts in favor of mysticism and scientific naturalism. They pursued truths that lie beyond the "colorless" realms perceived by reason and the senses and were active social reformers in public education, women's rights, and the abolition of slavery.

U

Urban Realism: A branch of realist writing that attempts to accurately reflect the often harsh facts of modern urban existence.

Utopia: A fictional perfect place, such as "paradise" or "heaven."

V

Verisimilitude: Literally, the appearance of truth. In literary criticism, the term refers to aspects of a work of literature that seem true to the reader.

Victorian: Refers broadly to the reign of Queen Victoria of England (1837-1901) and to anything with qualities typical of that era. For example, the qualities of smug narrowmindedness, bourgeois materialism, faith in social progress, and priggish morality are often considered Victorian. This stereotype is contradicted by such dramatic intellectual developments as the theories of Charles Darwin, Karl Marx, and Sigmund Freud (which stirred strong debates in England) and the critical attitudes of serious Victorian writers like Charles Dickens and George Eliot. In literature, the Victorian Period was the great age of the English novel, and the latter part of the era saw the rise of movements such as decadence and symbolism. Also known as Victorian Age and Victorian Period.

W

Weltanschauung: A German term referring to a person's worldview or philosophy.

Weltschmerz: A German term meaning "world pain." It describes a sense of anguish about the nature of existence, usually associated with a melancholy, pessimistic attitude.

Z

Zeitgeist: A German term meaning "spirit of the time." It refers to the moral and intellectual trends of a given era.

Cumulative Author/Title Index

Cumulative
Nationality/Ethnicity Index

Subject/Theme Index

D

Damnation
The Turn of the Screw: 267, 269–270
Dance
The Day of the Locust: 18, 20
That Was Then, This Is Now: 225, 231, 233
Death
The Day of the Locust: 2–4, 9, 11, 17, 19, 21
The End of the Affair: 24, 26–31
Fathers and Sons: 78, 82–85, 95–96
A Gathering of Old Men: 120, 122, 127–128, 130, 134–138
The Godfather: 152–153, 158–159, 162, 168, 170–171
Lord Jim: 179, 181–182, 185–187, 189–193
The Plague: 203–205, 208–210, 214–215
That Was Then, This Is Now: 225, 230–231, 236–240
The Turn of the Screw: 248–249, 253–254, 256
Deceit
Evelina: 57–60, 65
Devil
The Turn of the Screw: 264, 268, 270
Dialogue
Evelina: 65–66
A Gathering of Old Men: 138–139, 141–142, 144
Disease
Fathers and Sons: 78, 85–86
The Plague: 202, 204–205, 208–211, 213, 216–221
The Turn of the Screw: 249, 254–255
The Divine
The End of the Affair: 29
Drama
Evelina: 53, 69, 74
Fathers and Sons: 91, 100
Dreams and Visions
The Day of the Locust: 15–21
The Fountainhead: 111–112
The Turn of the Screw: 263–264, 266–269

E

Emotional and Physical Disconnection
The Day of the Locust: 8
Emotions
The Day of the Locust: 8, 11
The End of the Affair: 29–30, 32, 34–36
Evelina: 45, 56, 64, 71

Fathers and Sons: 84, 99
The Fountainhead: 118
A Gathering of Old Men: 129
The Godfather: 168, 174
Lord Jim: 181, 197–198
The Plague: 204, 210, 215, 221
That Was Then, This Is Now: 231, 236, 238, 240, 243–244
The Turn of the Screw: 258, 261–262, 265–266
Error
Lord Jim: 197–200
Eternity
Fathers and Sons: 94–96
That Was Then, This Is Now: 232, 235
Europe
The End of the Affair: 24, 30–31
Evelina: 42, 44–46, 50, 52–54, 70–73
Fathers and Sons: 75, 78, 85–88
The Fountainhead: 104, 109–110, 119
The Godfather: 152–153, 159, 166–171
Lord Jim: 179, 188–189
The Plague: 202, 210–215, 219–220
The Turn of the Screw: 254–255
Evil
The End of the Affair: 29
Evelina: 57, 69–71, 74
Lord Jim: 188
The Plague: 202, 209–210
The Turn of the Screw: 246, 249, 253–254, 257, 263–270
Execution
The Plague: 214–215
Exile
The Plague: 204, 208
Exile and Separation
The Plague: 208
Exploitation
The Day of the Locust: 17, 20–21

F

Failure and Impotence
The Day of the Locust: 9
Family
The Godfather: 158
Family Life
Fathers and Sons: 91, 94
The Godfather: 160, 171, 173–174, 177
Farm and Rural Life
Fathers and Sons: 76–78, 82, 86
A Gathering of Old Men: 120–122, 127, 131
Fate and Chance
The Day of the Locust: 3–4, 11
Fathers and Sons: 93–94, 96

A Gathering of Old Men: 139, 141, 143, 145
The Godfather: 168–170
Lord Jim: 181–182, 186–187, 189–194, 196
The Plague: 205, 208, 210, 213, 216–218
That Was Then, This Is Now: 225, 230–231
The Turn of the Screw: 263–264, 270
Fear and Terror
The Fountainhead: 113–114, 116–117
Lord Jim: 195–196
The Turn of the Screw: 264–265, 267–270
Film
The Day of the Locust: 1–4, 7–12, 15
A Gathering of Old Men: 138–140, 142, 144
The Godfather: 150, 152, 157–160, 161–162, 164
That Was Then, This Is Now: 241, 243–245
Folklore
The Turn of the Screw: 264, 267
Forgiveness
Lord Jim: 182, 185
Freedom
The Godfather: 157
French Revolution
Evelina: 52–53

G

Gang Life
That Was Then, This Is Now: 231
The Generation Gap
Fathers and Sons: 82
Ghost
A Gathering of Old Men: 135–136
The Turn of the Screw: 246–249, 252–260, 263–267, 269–270
Ghosts
The Turn of the Screw: 252
God
The End of the Affair: 24, 26–27, 29, 32–40
A Gathering of Old Men: 135, 137
The Godfather: 157, 168, 171
Lord Jim: 190–191
The Plague: 204, 208–211
The Turn of the Screw: 254
Good Versus Evil
The Turn of the Screw: 253
Goodness
The Turn of the Screw: 264, 267–270
Great Depression
The Day of the Locust: 10–11

Subject/Theme Index